Sarada Ramakrishna Vivekananda
Associations
SRV Associations (Hawaii Center)

# ATMIC TESTAMENT ON YOGA
## VOLUME 2, PADAS 3 & 4

BEING THE RECORD OF A TEN-YEAR, IN-DEPTH
STUDY OF PATANJALI'S RAJA YOGA SYSTEM
BY WESTERN STUDENTS AND PRACTITIONERS

*Babaji Bob Kindler*

2025  Babaji Bob Kindler
All rights reserved.
Published by SRV Associations

No part of this book may be reproduced in any manner without written permission of the author or publisher except for quotations embodied in articles or reviews. For further information write to:

SRV Associations
P.O. Box 1364
Honoka'a, Hawaii  96727
srvinfo@srv.org   www.srv.org


The publication of this book was made possible by donations from friends and students of the SRV Associations.

Printed in the United States of America

ISBN  978-1-891893-38-4


**Acknowledgements:**

Cover art — Subhavrata Chandra; proofreading by Mahesh Madhav & Annapurna Sarada

Our thanks to Mahesh Madhav, and Lokelani Kindler, for their kind donations towards helping to publish this book.

# Table of Contents

List of Charts. . . . . . . . . . . . . . . . . . . . . . . . . . . . . . . . . . . . . viii

Introduction . . . . . . . . . . . . . . . . . . . . . . . . . . . . . . . . . . . . . . . x

Sutras of the 3rd Pada . . . . . . . . . . . . . . . . . . . . . . . . . . . . 2
    Index of Lesson Highlights:
        Sutras on Dharana, Dhyana & Samadhi . . . . . . . . . . . . . . . . . . . . 15
        Samadhi, Samyama, & Dissolving Samskaras . . . . . . . . . . . . . . . . . 41

Sutras of the 4th Pada. . . . . . . . . . . . . . . . . . . . . . . . . . . 432
    Index of Lesson Highlights:
        Past Lives . . . . . . . . . . . . . . . . . . . . . . . . . . . . . . . . . . . . . . . . 428
        The Three Gunas. . . . . . . . . . . . . . . . . . . . . . . . . . . . . . . . . . . 456
        Kaivalya & Atman. . . . . . . . . . . . . . . . . . . . . . . . . . . . . . . . . . 506

Raja Yoga Sutras in English (repeat from Volume 1) . . . 549

Yoga Sanskrit Glossary. . . . . . . . . . . . . . . . . . . . . . . . . . . 559

# List of Illustrations/Charts

India's Sanatana Dharma . . . . . . . . . . . . . . . . . . . . . . . . . . . . . . . XII
The Eight Limbs of Patanjali's Yoga (repeat from Volume 1) . . . 1
The Two Forms & Eight Types of Meditation . . . . . . . . . . 27
The Process of Samprajnata to Asamprajnata . . . . . . . . . 61
Controlling the Chitta-Vrittis in Yoga . . . . . . . . . . . . . . . . . 71
The Ocean of Awareness and its Yogic Waves . . . . . . . . . . 81
Patanjali's & Shankara's Yoga of the Mind . . . . . . . . . . . . 92
Controlling the Five Senses in Yoga . . . . . . . . . . . . . . . . . . 95
Yogic Correlations/Connections in Meditation Practice . . 269
The Twelve Levels of Vairagya, Dispassion . . . . . . . . . . . 348
The Five States of the Mind-Field in Yoga . . . . . . . . . . . 383
Some Obstacles and Solutions in Spiritual Life . . . . . . . . 394
The Six Esoteric Yogic Gateways . . . . . . . . . . . . . . . . . . . 501

# Dedication

To Lex Hixon – known by such honorable names as

Ramakrishnadas Baul,
Sheikh Nur Al-Jerahi,
Jikai –

who loved aspirants of all religions and denominations, and who encouraged us to freely enter into serious explorations of all of the world's sacred traditions from the safe and secure ground of our own select path and Ideal.

May Peace and Bliss be upon him, eternally.

# Introduction to Volume 2

The second volume of this work on Patanjala (Yoga), containing sections (padas) 3 and 4 in its sweep, picks up where some 75 truth-seeking spiritual aspirants (mostly Westerners) left off. The date was approximately December 3rd, of 2010, which by then had seen and covered 56 lessons to that date after the entire course had begun, in 2005.

My estimation of this group effort, which lasted some ten years in total, is that there is hardly anything quite like this type of collective study, particularly in an age where few beings value, or even know much about spiritual life and its aims and ends. After personally writing a dozen or so books on spiritual subjects over the years of my life, including the recent philosophically expansive work entitled *Footfalls of the Indian Rishis*, this new book in two volumes, offered here, to me, is among the best of them all.

This is because it is a "hands on" literary work, for one, based upon consistent participation and perseverance. Further, it gives us a historical record in these contemporary, spiritually benighted times of the introduction of a timeless yet mostly forgotten pathway to Truth into minds and countries that have been formed and raised in materialism for centuries, even millennia. As Lex Hixon, the founder of SRV Associations, once said — and I paraphrase: "These are the types of books that are needed the most today, since they show us living, striving souls who are caught in the midst of doing daily practice, all the while encountering the many obstacles of both earthly and spiritual life, and working them out with accomplished teachers of this day and time."

Another important facet of this endeavor, speaking of group efforts, is the bringing together of three great commentators— the composer of the Yoga Sutras himself, Patanjali; the Father of Vedanta, Vedavyasa, and the current World-teacher, Swami Vivekananda. This provides not just "some light shed on Yoga," but three, intense and expansive wide-angle floodlights leveled directly at the individual, collective, and cosmic mind-fields of the present age (Mahayuga). For, in an age such as the present one (kali yuga), it is not only hidden truths that need to be revealed and recalled via such benign exposure, but untold and unseen shadows — entire series of subterranean caverns of human ignorance — that need the sunlight of Wisdom duly shone upon them in order to reveal their total lack of any real substance. For, as the Avadhuta Gita declares: *"Ignorance is unreal; therefore, how can it cause you any real doubt?"* What to speak of devas, devis, auras, and ancestors, the belabored, embodied human being needs to know that what flusters and impedes him/her in life here on earth, in relativity, has no basis for existence at all, and therefore no reason for occupying the human mind whatsoever — especially since, as the Indian darshanas all conclude, *Sarvam Khalvidam Brahman*, "All this is Brahman."

With the nondual and universal perspective just stated, the reader may look to the following page for a glimpse at how high-minded and far-reaching Indian dharma is. Yoga, though key to both presence and practice, is one among many of Mother India's salient systems of authentic religion and comprehensive philosophy — as the chart on the next page reveals. This is followed by a repeat of the Eight Limbs of Yoga chart utilized in Volume 1, at the outset of this course of study.

Transported on towards the Light of Consciousness, then, we pick up the remaining two sections of Patanjali's Raja Yoga, with an abundance of additional teachings. Volume 1, with its first two padas, has already taken us through crucial and essential declarations and instructions of the Ashtanga system, including kleshas and antarayas, yamas and niyamas, Kriya Yoga, ways of mastering the restless and slothful mind, lower and higher samadhis, the import of mantra and Ishvara, and a minimal mention of the very few instances of posture and breathing exercises that appear in the Raja Yoga system. It is now for the sedulous seeker to search for and find the additional treasures of Yoga, lying in the sutras like precious gems awaiting discovery — all so that the soul who is unaware of its innate perfection, can fit them into life and mind in order to afford dharmic life, divine life, and Transcendental Existence — all three.

# India's Sanatana Dharma

*"The Eternal Religion of the Rishis has been in existence from time out of mind. The Sanatana Dharma contains all forms of worship — worship of God with form and worship of the Impersonal Deity as well. It contains all paths — the path of knowledge, the path of devotion, and so on. Other forms of religion, the modern cults, will remain for a few days only, and then disappear. The Sanatana Dharma declared by the Rishis will alone endure."* — Sri Ramakrishna

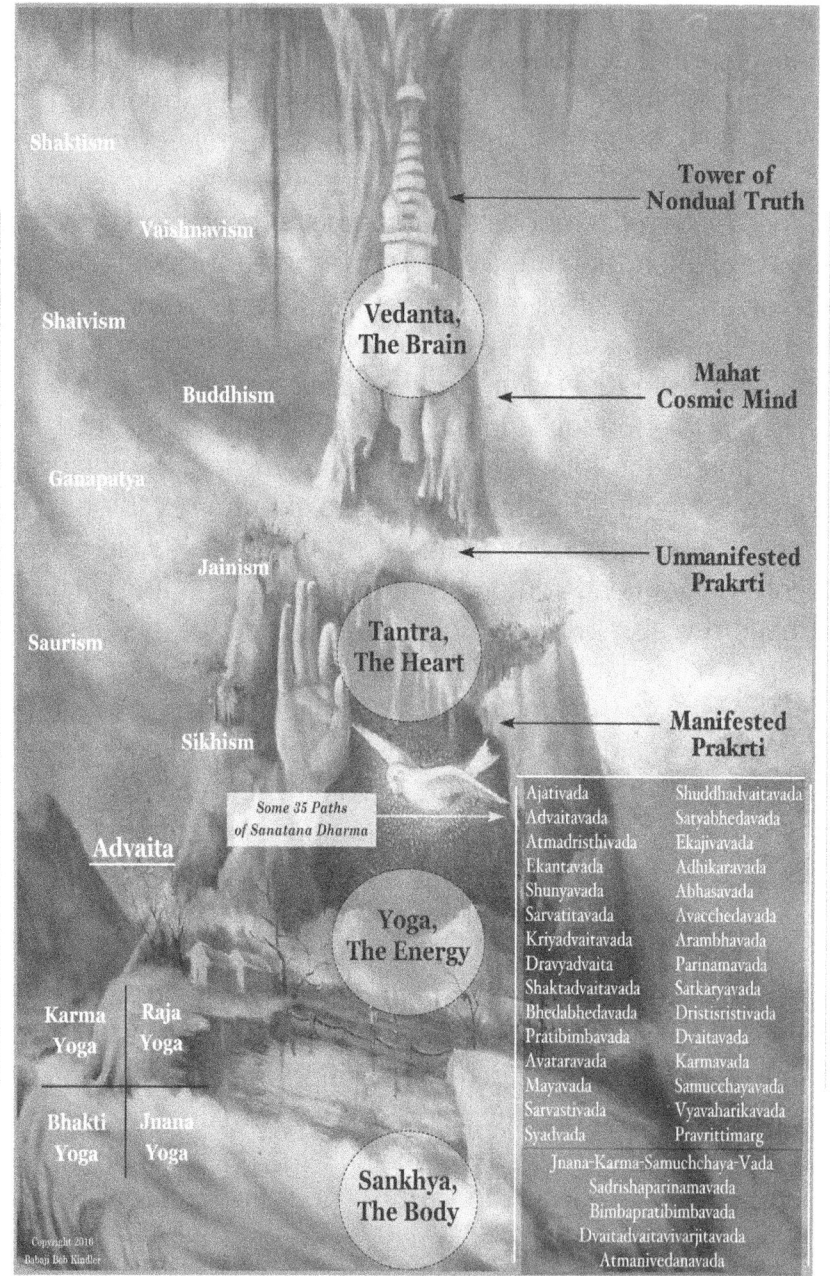

*"This great immortal frame of Indian Philosophy operates efficiently on four great powerhouses: Sankhya, its Body; Yoga, its divine Energy; Tantra, its loving Heart; and Vedanta, its universal Mind."*

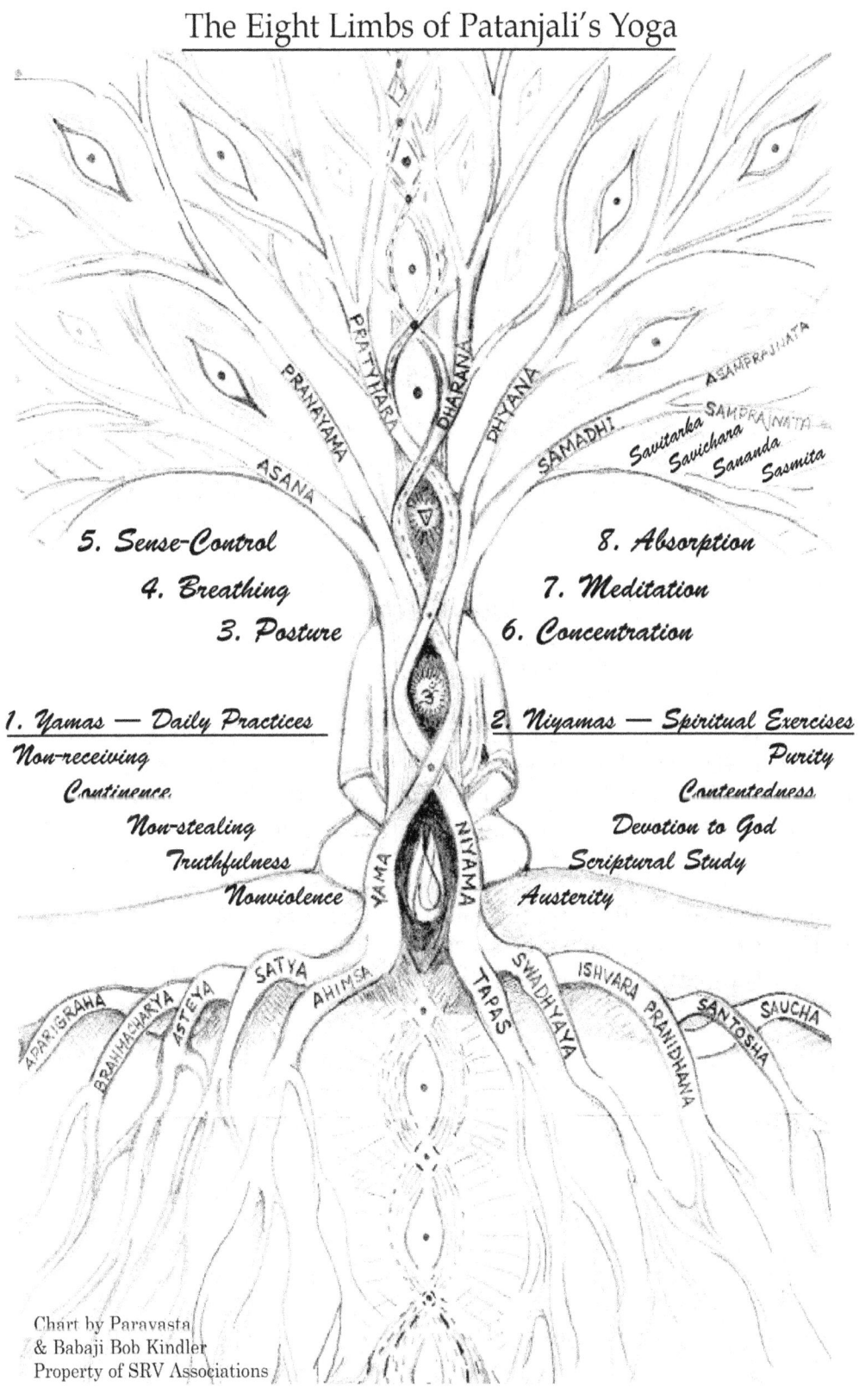

**Raja Yoga Email Classes, Volume II**
For: SRV disciples, devotees, and students of Yoga

Originally offered by Babaji Bob Kindler and the SRV Associations
through the mediums of email and "snail mail."

Invocation:
*yogena chittasya padena vaccham
malam sharirasya cha vaidyakena
yo'pakarot tam pravaram muninam
patanjalim pranjalir anato'smi*

"He who removed the impurities of mind (by teaching Yoga), of speech (by exposition of grammar), and of body (by composing works on the science of medicine), unto that great sage of sages, Patanjali, we bow down with reverent salutations."

# Pada Three
### Lesson Fifty-nine, 3/29/11
#### Pada III, Sutra 1 & 2

As we enter into the third chapter of the Yoga Sutras, the important rungs of the ladder of Yoga assigned as dharana, dhyana, and samadhi are being encountered for our collective and individual study. In this lesson we will take up the first two of these limbs, leaving the subject of samadhi for lesson 60. All students are encouraged to revisit the early chapters (padas) already studied so as to enforce all new knowledge taken in from this ongoing process of Jnana Yoga. There is the first chapter, called *Samadhi pada;* the second chapter, called *Sadhana Pada;* the third chapter, now under study, called *Vibhuti Pada;* and soon to come we will study the fourth chapter, called *Kaivalya Pada.* To begin this lesson, we look into the responses from the previous lesson by students of the Raja Yoga list, to see what concerns and insights are surfacing in the course of this profound spiritual exercise.

### Questions and Answers for Lesson 59
S.C. from Hawaii writes:
QUESTION: "What is best: the 'I am' perspective of the Self, or the Emptiness view?"
ANSWER: This is an important question. For the best results, an aspirant should learn to hold a many-sided and all-inclusive perspective. This is necessary in order to move past all mental blocks and intellectual conundrums. Philosophy is for developing greater understanding, not for debate and argumentation. Acceptance of other views and respect for those who hold them are

important. But for moving on in one's own spiritual trajectory, the Great Ones, like Lord Buddha, have always emphasized the "I-am" as the consummate way. The Dhammapada makes this clear. The "I am not" way is excellent for the preceding stages of practice, however. Synthesis is best, and holding more than one view is possible, even preferable. Holding no views, depending how that expression gets interpreted, runs the danger of courting worldliness on one side, or nihilism on the other.

Having one view as your own, and holding other dharmic views as supports, is best — like a wheel with one felly but many spokes, as the Vedic Rishis said. As the Great Master, Sri Ramakrishna put it, simply: *"The cows all mix in the field in the daytime, but when the farmer brings them home at night and places them in the barn, they each get their own stall."* You can well figure, I think, the meaning of this saying in the present context.

QUESTION #2: "What does 'Practicing the Presence of God' mean? I have never heard of this."

ANSWER: "Practicing the Presence of God" is a well-known saying in spiritual circles, even among modern Westerners who value and court higher Awareness. But it demands a path and a teacher. Lord Vasishtha states that being without these two while seeking Truth is like *"trying to grow crops only at night."* Despite what some deluded individuals say, practice is not to be considered overrated. The pseudo-advaitists have it all wrong when they opine that one need not do anything because one is already the Self. *"One is not the Self until one realizes the Self"* is a better proceeding point. To work hard (sadhana) proves the fact of nonduality to the mind, which previous to that dawning is still ensconced in relativity (maya). That is why most of us are "here" — to realize our true nature even under the harshest, most trying of circumstances. Seeing through illusion will free us for all time, beyond time.

So, spiritual aspirants practice the presence of God, which to differing schools and their adherents means things like observing one's inner Nature, developing Witness Consciousness, becoming aware of the Atman, and the like. It is a good phrase in that it leaves the method to each individual while accenting the existence of the actual Essence Itself. May all move into this superlative practice, each in their own way and to their own capacity.

Suprema from Pennsylvania writes:
QUESTION: "I came upon a great word in relation to sutra #55! From the book *Jivan Mukti Viveka,* Vasishtha is quoted on page #312 as saying: *'The inward cool — antahsitalata — tranquility, of the one who sees this world as only the combination of the three modes (gunas) and which is not-self, is called concentration.'* Oh, to remain unconnected to the phenomenal world! Swami Vidyaranya continues the explanation that this 'coolness' is the result/form of the effacement of latent impressions, or 'quenching of thirst' necessary for the next gift of dissolution of the mind. Would you comment?"

RESPONSE: Though I am not that fond of the translation of the English here, nor the wordage used, the point by Lord Vasishtha is well taken. Further, the point of Yoga is not to be "unconnected," (how is that possible?) but to connect, then transcend. All the while that these two movements are being attained, all things of a relative nature merely return to their sources and origins — whether that be in the body, senses, mind, intellect, or ego...or the Word, in deeper respects. The result of this spiritual undertaking is equanimity, the "inward cool" spoken of here (trying to bring the sloka into current and popular verbiage makes it suffer, methinks). Lord Vasishtha was a great one for recommending the course of uncovering origins, called *utpatti,* wherein — similar to both Sankhya and Yoga — one observes outer phenomena, meditates upon it in increments (the tattvas), and thereby traces it back inside to stations such as the mind, the intelligence, and the Word. What else but a pervasive feeling of "inner cool" could come from such a journey? In Yoga, the solution for fear is the study of nature and phenomena with the detached and honed mind. When one sees all within the self/Self, brooding and doubt fly away forever.

K.D. from Hawaii writes:
QUESTION: "Last night I re-read the Chapter 7 elucidation very slowly and carefully, trying to digest all the wisdom contained within. I am still at the Yama/Niyama stage of course, with the goal of purifying thought, word, and deed, as well as gaining contentment and peace of mind. I am practicing pranayama, but the goal of control of prana seems overwhelming and in the distant future. Control of the prana would mean I could heal long distance and slow down my heart-rate to almost nothing. It would mean I would gain powers which I would have to be very conscious not to use, correct? There must be a mid-stage control of prana that opens the door to samadhi and enlightenment and that does not require complete mastery, right?"
ANSWER: Stages of growth are noticed along the path, no doubt, even those which have to do with the gaining of power via mastery over the prana. It is a precarious stage in itself, to be sure, and one that many aspirants fall in. I mean, you can well imagine! The sleeping individual, having ignorance of all that is great and grand, suddenly comes to find that the mere breathing process is replete with power, and then begins to see that power, *prana,* flowing in everything. Previous to that awakening life had been drab, restricted, devoid of any real vitality. Worse still, all of human construct and convention had been fabricated around those very limitations. As Swamiji has said, the ordinary man works through the physical nervous system only, while the yogi gets work done through the expanded nervous system and its prana.

And all of this involves the early to mid-stages of mastery. Complete mastery has to do specifically with Consciousness, not energy (and certainly not with mere matter). Many, those caught in what the Great Master called *"the tricks of prana,"* do not realize this. As Vedanta states, *Consciousness as Consciousness,* and *Brahman as Consciousness* — quintessential axioms like these escape inspection by those meekly flying low under the radar of higher Awareness. They do not detect it. As the *Svetasvataropanisad* says, which is also the newest meditation chant that SRV students are presently memorizing:

*Te dhyanayoganugata apashyan*
*devatmashaktim svagunairnigudham*
*yah karanani nikhilani tani*
*kalatma yuktanya-adhitisthat yekah*

"Practicing the Yoga of Meditation, those rishis saw the indwelling Self and its divine energy, which though veiled by its own gunic obstructions, was nevertheless one with Ultimate Reality, and which previously had been imperceptible due to the limitations of their own intellects."

This sloka is very fine, demonstrating, as its does, how Reality is always present (though we have to "practice" that Presence) but remains undetectable, even inconceivable to most, due to mental impurities. Remove those and, as the Upanisads state, *"It shines through naturally of Its own true nature."*

QUESTION #2: "In the meantime, my karma is becoming instant, and that I am grateful for. Every angry thought brings pain, every emotional reaction brings quick repercussions, every flippant comment stabs me in the back, every failure to forgive creates unhappiness. Also, I am perceiving my sciatica disability as a wake up call. It is much better as a result, and I am moving normally now and can go back to work this week. I am also contemplating release of all desires and thereby having momentary experiences of relief when I attain that state, however brief. I am now ready for Chapter 8 — well, in a way I am ready, but knowing that it will bring me to the actual study of the aphorisms, I will go back and re-read the first 7 chapters for continued clarity. I do have a question about predestination. I resist that concept because I want to believe that I can influence the future by conscious choices made in the present. Are we born with the script of our life in relative existence already written? Even attempts to create desired futures? Ah, it is the 'd' word, desire. If my grandson is very sick and destined to die young, then there is nothing to be done? But then maybe I am predestined to try, and also predestined to either fail or succeed?"

ANSWER: In previous lessons the principle of predestination has been taken up. Please search for and read those. But as for your specific questions here, when you speak of influencing the future by conscious choices, that is karma and will at work, not predestination. It is true that, in a series of lifetimes with their attending karmas, the transmigrating soul has fixed a regimen of seed-causes in the mind which will then naturally get figured as effects into all events to come. We can see, then, that even so-called predestination is really only karma in action, in fructification. If we speak of the Divine Will, and Its patent decisions, even then we need not cower about helplessly in the face of our own ill-considered acts and decisions of the past, for as Holy Mother has told us, *"What the Mother of the Universe has written in the book of destiny, She can also erase."* That power which comprehension of the laws of karma invests us with enables us to go beyond destiny, even predestination, since that was/is all our own doing anyway. *"What you sow you must reap,"* as the saying goes. But for the Vedantist, the Yogini, what the spiritual aspirant after freedom must say is, "What you sow you can unsow," so that you do not have to reap what you do not want. Sadhana, spiritual self-effort, accomplishes the neutralization of past karmas. And for what has already fructified, which we must face up to (i.e., this lifetime, this body), remaining focused on Reality will handle that for us by what Shankara calls *"....closeness to Brahman,"* So, do your sadhana, practice the presence, and try to live in a nondual state. All will even out. Follow the dictates of your chosen path and the advice of your precious guru; never quit or give up.

QUESTION #3: "Swamiji writes *'Take this book: as a book it does not exist outside, what exists outside is unknown and unknowable...The real universe is the occasion of the reaction of the mind...These vrittis are our universe.'* Is he saying that it is impossible to have an objective experience of reality? Or is he saying that the book does not actually exist in physical form. I understand and accept that thought projection and this person I imagine myself to be do not exist. It is all smoke in the wind. However I do believe that there is a world of matter and that if I cease to be and all sentient beings vanish from the face of the earth, the physical universe will remain. I do not understand how everything that exists is mere thought projection. I understand the 24 cosmic principles and that the most subtle forms are the cause of grosser forms. I suppose these kind of ideas and concepts can only be understood through direct experience beyond all ideas and concepts, correct? In direct experience the mind is gone, or at least the vrittis have dissolved (into cosmic mind?) and the lake is crystal clear. Then Reality can be perceived. Is the book part of that Reality?"

ANSWER: Swamiji is not saying that it is impossible to have an objective experience of this world and its objects, he is saying that it is not possible to know the object as it seems due to its lack of real substance (which is why mere experiences are not enough, and are thus overrated). Why? Because it only exists as a formulation of the mind viewed through the five senses. Science has already proven that the object is really a mass of swirling particles, all changing at an exceedingly rapid rate of speed (vibration/vrittis) which renders it incomprehensible — as if nonexistent. In short, a billionth of a second's existence is no existence at all. Get a life, particle! As Dalai Lama has said, there is the appearance tree (its wooden form); there is the real tree (its existence as a mass of particles); and then there is the Buddha Nature Tree, which is the indestructible and eternal essence of the tree — what the Vedic seer would call as an everlasting member of the Omkara Loka (The Word). That is the only place where one can truly meet the tree or book as it is. On all other levels you will only meet the appearance tree/book projected by the power of the mind — individual, collective, and cosmic. Even its solidity, so convincing to us as reality, is just a property of the mind. This is why most beings have the experience of it all being a vast and passing dream, and why cogent philosophies have spoken of all this as being so.

The solution? Wake up and see everything as it really is, which will mean questioning, doubting, even denying what you experience with the senses entirely. The book, the tree, all objects, they are a part of Reality, as you have surmised. It is just that they cease to appear when the mind ceases functioning

— like in deep sleep, nondual meditation, and samadhi. Even at death most beings go into a state of unknowing where worlds and objects disappear. Sentiency is the key to this conundrum, called pure Awareness. As the Svetasvataropanisad states, *"Matter is perishable, but God is imperishable. The only Reality, God, rules over perishable matter and individual souls. By meditating upon that Reality there comes union, and a cessation to all illusion in the end."* And not content to leave it in the realm of faith and theism, Svetasvatara states further: *"The conscious subject and the unconscious object, the master and the dependent — both are unborn. That force (Shakti/Divine Mother) who brings about their relationship is also unborn. When all three of these are realized as Brahman, the self becomes infinite, universal, and free from the sense of agency."*

One can well see why Shankara defined Maya, this stultifying realm of appearances, as neither real, nor unreal, neither real and unreal, nor a combination of both! What is insentient cannot exist on its own, as there is no reality separate from Brahman. A second thing would render Reality relative! All has proceeded from the medium of the mind, the matrix of "creation," and without that no external worlds or objects would be possible. Contrary to popular opinion, Consciousness does not visit planets and bodies after they have formed over eons on their own steam. Prana, and the other forces and energies that construct and move elements for cohesion and gestation, have to have an origin as well. That origin is in the mind via the Atman. *"From whence has this life force proceeded?"* asks the Prasnopanisad. *"From the Atman, via an act of will of the mind."* But let us not fall into the error of immature philosophers who deem all that the mind produces to be empty, with no substance whatsoever. As the peace chant declares, rightly so: *"From the Infinite the finite has come, and since it came from There, it too is infinite."* One cannot extract essence from an object and its experience just like one cannot get nutrition from a meal of cotton candy. But one can enjoy the sweetness if one realizes that it is as ephemeral as a fleeting taste on the tongue.

QUESTION #4: "I do not know anyone who calls in evil spirits. That, to me, is what I always thought of as occult. Now I have a different idea of the occult. There is a woman I know who can commune with the spirit world and peer into the future, and I have had 4 sessions with her in the past 30 years. I did not think of her as occult before, but I assume you would classify her 'oracle' work as occult and recommend avoiding sessions with her, right?"

ANSWER: If mediums and psychics — beings of that ilk — are authentic, then there is little harm in seeing them occasionally. However, a spiritual seeker ought to know that their art is one which operates on a very base level, spiritually speaking, and thus any answers which may come from it will also be basic — to be taken with a grain of salt. Moreover, deeper answers (to deeper questions) will arise from one's own inner contemplation as soon as the mind is able to master concentration and sit formally, making mediums and the like nothing short of unnecessary for spiritual aspirants.

And what I write above is the up side of the subject! The downside is that one is receiving information from a person who either has no purificatory practice going on, or whose practice is focused in on the level of physic prana only, devoid of crucial connections both anterior to and preceding that level. Fragments of knowledge, at best, may come, but will be missing the innate connections which make up a Sankhya teaching, a Yogic insight, or a Vedantic realization. One may also stumble upon some real charlatans, and risk receiving knowledge that is not only mixed and questionable, but outright impure, being mingled in with some of the "unholy" spirits with which said medium or clairvoyant has been communing with. In my own experience I have had to intervene and actually help disassociate a few of my students from these types of influences using the mantra and the Divine Form as interceders on their behalf. Hauntings and possessions of the mind by unclean influences are not "spooky," as in the movies, but may grab the mind's attentions and, at least, keep it worrying and distracted while, at worst, can turn it towards habitual nervousness and fragmentation. Types of mental illness begin here.

Akshaya-Bhakti from New England writes:
COMMENTS: "The first thing that attracted my attention in Lesson 58 was your poignant statement, dear teacher, 'Whenever I have come to an impasse, I have stopped and asked, then affirmed, that I love God,' This is so indicative of your life, and is most comforting. Sometimes I feel that I take Sri Ramakrishna's/Holy Mother's grace and love for granted. My emotions echo so well the first line of *Om Hring Ritang* (written by Swami Vivekananda himself, on Jai Ma Music, Puja Hymns): *'You are to be adored. You are Truth unchanging. You are the Lord of the three gunas. In my weakness, I have neglected, O Remover of Delusion, to worship you earnestly and unceasingly; therefore, I claim refuge in Thee, O Friend of all Beings.'* Then, the hymn goes on to say that by chanting His Name we can be awakened from our delusion. How beautiful!
QUESTION: "I often use the term 'Master' to refer to Sri Ramakrishna, but in the Gospel he is quoted as saying he did not wish to be called by that term (as I understand, because he did not have an ego). Therefore, I sometimes feel uncertain about using it. Could you please comment?"
ANSWER: Even Holy Mother called Him Master at times. What else can one say? The thing is that He Himself could not rightly do so. He also did not vibrate well with the titles "father" and "guru." Yes, His lack of any egoism is partly responsible for this. But whatever the case, and now well over a century after His passing, millions of beings are calling Him "Master," and "The Great Master." What to speak of centuries past, Swami Saradananda, a direct disciple, titled his book *Sri Ramakrishna, The Great Master.* I think there is no harm in it, then, wouldn't you say?
QUESTION #2: "I appreciate the chart of 'The Four Sensitivities.' It is especially uplifting to contemplate the Soul's radiance. I have always found your lists/charts so helpful in organizing and highlighting the teachings. Before we move on to the next chapter, could you please explain the last part of Sutra 28:

*'...by the practice of the different parts of Yoga, the impurities being destroyed, knowledge becomes effulgent up to discrimination.'* With deepest appreciation as always for any comments and elucidations."

ANSWER: That is, when initial practices (earlier limbs) in Yoga are accomplished, the impurities then being removed by these, one beholds the natural radiance of wisdom finally free of the veils of ignorance and follows that light to the Self — the original Mind (Mahat, Word, Purusha). From there a vision of the Atman is possible, and the actual merging into Brahman (Nirvikalpa Samadhi). Thus, discrimination, *viveka,* in all its stages and at every juncture of the spiritual path, is not just a Vedantic tool, but appears and is fixed in all the darshanas of India, each with its own take and emphasis on it.

D.H. from Pennsylvania writes:
QUESTION: "It has only been in the past couple of days that I've been able to understand something of the unreality of the mayic world in a way that is something other than merely academic. I have, all my life, been unconsciously believing that 1) I can ultimately and finally find fulfillment in the mayic world and, 2) that the mayic world can ultimately and finally harm me. In point of fact, seeing who and what I truly am as Atman, it can do neither, and ideas that it can are totally false. This insight has stripped away many of the projections that I was casting outward upon the mirror of life, projections involving fantasies of fulfillment or harm so that the world, more clearly than ever before, emerges in my perception as Brahman. Yet, I find myself wanting to take another, deeper step, so that I not only see the world as Brahman, but also respond to it, moment by moment, as an act of service to the Brahmic reality. I want to not only see life as holy, but I also want to engage it in an appropriately holy manner. The 'how' of how to do this eludes me, though. In the 'old days,' when I was a Krishna devotee with Iskcon, it was clear: one gathered flowers for the Deity in the temple room, or one washed the guru's dishes, and so forth. The connection of activity to Deity was, in other words, clear, leaving me with a constant and vivid sense of service to Ishvara. In the situation I'm in now, however, the matter is not so clear. In fact, it's not clear at all how actions like washing my clothes or filling out forms for government agencies can be service. In the manner of a karma yogin, I can be unconcerned about outcomes, and that is helpful, yet what I'm aiming at is still missing, and that is the sanctification of my day to day, indeed, moment to moment movement through the world. Even if I cannot directly turn all of my activities into service, how can I at least sanctify my way?"

ANSWER: Judging by what you have expressed here, I would say that it is time for you to do this "sanctification" in a more integrated way, in a way more comprehensive than guru seva alone — say, through what Gaudapada calls the "Nontouch Yoga." This is described as the *"activeless act of nonseparation of the Ultimate Truth and the relative truth."* That is, after deeper realizations begin to dawn due to yogic practices, the yogi continues to do all that he did previously, knowing fully that all is Brahman. As Gaudapada would say,

*"There is Absolute Consciousness."* It is *Kevala Asti* — It is Consciousness alone. This is not a matter of dispute between Shankarites and Ramanujans. It is not even a matter of Indian philosophy alone. It actually is where the investigation originates, where it exists — Exists. As Lex Hixon, SRV's founder, used to say, there are a vast number of different kinds of people from different walks of life and differing perspectives who verify this Absolute Truth together experientially all of the time, and they do this without relying on Iskcon, Christianity, Hinduism, or anything. They rely, knowingly or not, on the nature of the Reality Itself, and the fact that they all *are* that Reality — that all and everything is that Reality.

There are two preeminent things which Gaudapada would add to his presentation of the disarming simplicity of pure Awareness. First, that It contains no "other" (is one without a second), and therefore has no opposite, no competition. Second, that It has three modes of expression. These he calls the three modes of relative awareness. Do not imagine that "twoness "or duality enters in here. Envision instead the mudra of perfection (sported by Lord Buddha, for instance) which shows three fingers connected to the thumb, all curved into a connected circle. These demonstrate and symbolize the objective, the subjective, and the integrated (waking, dreaming, and deep sleep states), plus Turiya, which is Absolute Consciousness symbolized by the empty circle. All of these supposedly different principles are contained in one gesture. To boot, the little finger flies independent. like the svara of AUM.

Along with the symbology and the philosophy, the main point is the nonseparation of the one Consciousness, even in and during the apparent separation of its manifold expressions. People can sense this uniqueness of Awareness without all the intellectual verbiage, but when sophistication comes to the practicing aspirant, an appropriate, if not ingenious, way of expressing it all comes to the fore, and delusion is suddenly struck down for all time. Then, as Gaudapada's disciple, Shankara, states: *"After observing the external and the internal, and rendering them into one indivisible state, meditate upon that State, pass your time contentedly, and be free."* May it ever be so.

QUESTION #2: "In repeated listening to your sets of talks, *Axioms of Advaita*, I have noted with considerable interest how Shankara created an Advaitic version of the eight steps of Patanjali's yoga — for example, where the meditative ekasana is dealt with as a matter of being stabilized in Brahman. This is beautiful, especially since I have been working with the asana I use in meditation which has been insufficient and has been disturbing my ability to concentrate. I am writing to ask if you have you correlated, in any of your writings, the steps of Patanjali's yoga with Shankara's teaching on the same? Perhaps in a back issue of Nectar? Secondly, could you fill me in on the teaching about rolling the eyes down the bridge of the nose when concentrating in the Heart? I am also studying the nuances of the meditative ekasana, to pull the quality of this way up. Discomfort in my body and sloppy technique have been limiting how long I can sit and how well I can focus. Generally, though, all is going well, and I remain grateful, as always, to have found my way to you and to SRV."

ANSWER: I note with satisfaction that you picked up on Shankara's interpretation and expansion of Patanjali's Yoga, which always interested me as well. And yes, I have written on and about it in issue #10 of *Nectar of Nondual Truth*, page 13, an article called *Advaita Yoga — Patanjala as Revealed by Shankara*. Please secure a copy of that from SRV offices and study it, or find it online.

It has always been my contention that focusing on the tip of the nose was not only odd, and odd looking, but a misinterpretation of the real intent of concentration in meditation. Of course, if the occult power of the subtle sense of smell is desired, the hatha yogi may focus on the nose, I suppose. But gazing down the tip of the nose towards the heart, or focusing the attention on the heart chakra, is the purpose in Raja Yoga, and in meditation per say, which is also what Krishna speaks of in the Gita, i.e., *"Fixing the attention in the heart, and the prana between the eyebrows, set your asana, neither too low nor too high, upon which to practice meditation, and then close all the gates of the body while uttering the monosyllable, AUM."* The attention is to be placed on the heart chakra, as we see Swami Vivekananda doing in his classic meditation picture pose.

Sanatanand from Hawaii writes:
COMMENTS: "As I continue with the study of these illumined writings and your insightful explanations and clarifications, I am feeling eternally blessed for this great gift. So much gratitude and appreciation I offer to you and this great tradition. In this reading, the *Four Beneficial Attitudes* are discussed. They seem so simple that it might be easy to dismiss them as something lacking great significance, yet after considering their impact I find that they are indeed profound. And in the context of the *Seven Methods for Attaining Mastery of Consciousness*, they are what stand out as the practice that speaks to me most. While all the rest have their merits, I find that these qualities develop in a daily and continuous way, an awareness that can really be transformative. As you point out in Vyasa's elucidation of these, one can see how to apply them as the situation arises. When one sees another who is happy, friendliness is a value that helps one see and share the divinity in that person. Seeing one who suffers, rather than ignoring them or failing to acknowledge their condition, one can offer empathy. The gladness that one would offer to a virtuous person might create a bond to inspire oneself to follow that example and rise to a higher level. And finally, rather than expressing judgment to one who is unrighteous, one can simply allow it to pass, without impugning anything malignant about them and allowing them to find their own way. I find that this kind of practice can really help in building an awareness that is less than periodic, as meditation can be, and of great value in rising to a higher awareness that is present always."
RESPONSE: I am very glad to hear of this appreciation for the Four Beneficial Attitudes, which is a very simple way of practicing sadhana in everyday life. There are other practices, deeper and more profound, which could and should be undertaken, and the Four Attitudes have their own subtle shades of difficulty, to be sure. But people are always talking about a better world. Well, here is a

way of achieving that which is not merely through social service, or via hoping and wishing, but which is active and conscious with spirituality at its base. It is wisdom (Jnana Yoga) acting through devotion (Bhakti Yoga) to achieve selfless action (Karma Yoga), and thus it is a comprehensive form of meditation (Raja Yoga). When there are simple yet powerful practices like this peppering the darshanas of Vedanta and Yoga, what excuse does the human being have for not practicing?

S.B. from Los Angeles writes:
QUESTION: "In the discussion on prana in Chapter 3, it is mentioned that, *'The whole universe is composed of two materials, one of which they call Akasa. It is the omnipresent, all penetrating existence. Everything that has form, everything that is the result of compounds, is evolved out of this Akasa.'* Is this 'Akasa' the same as or related to the 'Akashic Record' which I have heard referred to many times, and which is, according to Wikipedia, 'a Sanskrit phrase used to describe a compendium of mystical knowledge encoded in a non-physical plane of existence?' These records are described as containing all knowledge of human experience, and the history of the cosmos. They are metaphorically described as a vast internal library. Thank you for your time and great knowledge."
ANSWER: Similar to words like karma, guru, and avatar, the Sanskrit word, akasha, has also undergone some serious misinterpretation and mistreatment from the secularly-minded materialistic West. However, the definitions you cite here are not far off the mark, are just incomplete, as all short descriptions of something that is beyond ordinary comprehension are bound to be.

Suffice to say here, in this short description of mine, that akasha is space, but that in Hindu cosmology based upon ancient Vedic insight and realization, space has some five levels to it. It is not just ether, as in one of the five elements. It is not only outer space either, which is only the external crust of the manifold, all-pervasive akasha. In fact, the study and knowledge of akasha will illumine the human mind by both informing it of esoteric wisdom and its hiding places, and by making connections to the realms within, what Jesus called *"The kingdom of Heaven within"* and *"My Father's mansion which holdeth many chambers."*

Why the arm moves, why the eye sees, why the ears hear, no one in the conventional, sense-bound, intellectually-oriented world has ever been able to sufficiently explain. Is it due to the energy from food? But *"Man does not live by bread alone."* We must come to admit that there is prana, and then there is Consciousness. When the Westerner speaks of time, space, and causation, he means linear time, physical space, and cause and effect restricted to planetary movement and physical bodies. But when the eastern seer speaks of these three, prana, akasha, and Cosmic Mind must be brought forward and accounted for.

And on the level of akasha, there is a space of objects (bhutakasha), a space of energy (pranakasha), a space of mind/thought (chittakasha), a space of wisdom (jnanakasha), and a space of Spirit (chidakasha). Among other important connections, these five explain where the transmigrating soul has gone after its so-called death. The five akashas listed above can be correlated to the realms of the human beings, the ancestors, the celestials, the luminaries, and Atman, respectively. Thus, a man does not die, nor does he go nowhere, into nothingness (though if he be ignorant he may go unconscious). He goes inward, where else? — based upon the level of akasha that he is headed for and accustomed to. For example, millions of souls are moving in and out of the realm of the ancestors (pranakasha) all of the time. Humans and their ancestors are exchanging places all the while. Does it not explain why whole nations and entire races are worshiping the ancestors? Such worship is not without due reciprocation. Where consciousness desires to go, there it will venture.

As for the akashic record, the idea here is that all vibrations must leave an impression. Just as powerful thoughts, positive and negative, leave an impression in the mind (samskara), so too will acts, deeds, and events leave "dents" in the akashas — great ones leave big dents, and small ones, little dents. Most "psychics" are only able to read the physical akasha, called history, and maybe see a little into the pranakasha where the "departed" have gone. A Swami Vivekananda, as we know, or a Buddha, can see and commune with luminaries long gone from the physical fabric of this world. More can be said, but this little may suffice to generate interest. Read *Yoga Vasishtha* for more.

Nischayatma from Portland writes:
QUESTION: "In contemplating the teaching of pratyahara, I have been focusing on the fourfold mind. It seems that assigning one's level of consciousness will naturally change the quality of one's consciousness. My understanding of manas is that it is the level of the mind where duality and doubt come into play. I have been shifting my focus from manas to ahamkara, and even trying to experience the buddhi. It is hard to know, but all I can say is that the more I go inward with the fourfold mind, the more light I feel. I have actually experienced a shift in my reality, or at least how I am experiencing reality. Is this a kind of pratyahara? And here is a question: Doesn't one's consciousness need to be at the level of the buddhi to experience dharana? Can one experience it at the level of ahamkara? Can one overlay the fourfold mind with these levels of Yoga (i.e., pratyahara, dharana, and dhyana)? Is Samadhi at the level of Mahat or beyond? Can you expand on the fourfold mind, because I want to understand its qualities better in order to transcend it."
ANSWER: When we take apart any of the aspects of life and practice, whether it be the fourfold mind, the ingredients of the body, molecular structures, or even the various types of samadhi which Patanjali is teaching, we must remember that we are doing so only to provide a more complete analysis in order to benefit our understanding — or in other words, that these areas we are studying are not airtight compartments, and that they not only are essentially integrated, but overlap one another and interpenetrate each other as well.

With this in mind we can complete all of our exercises without meddling with the natural unity and integrity of any given system — such as singling out an atom and finding that it contains great power, then piercing it and using said power for destruction (later to find radiation raining down on our heads). The same can be said for the mind and its powers and aspects. Viewing them as an integrated whole first, then inspecting them to find out what is causing us to keep from seeing their innate unity, is acceptable, sometimes necessary. But when we do this, we should find the keynote which will not only benefit ourselves, but also will aid us in helping others, in bettering society, in raising children properly, and in conducting earthly matters with intelligence.

And all of this, rightly seen, correctly implemented, *is* concentration. Pratyahara, then, is only the natural disposition of the mind which values peace and contentment. It is less of a labor, even a practice, and more of a state of satisfied mental attention. That state is uniform, eurythmic — grateful and graceful, not contrary or averse. When the mind easily refrains from contact with the objects of the senses because it knows them to be insufficient for higher insight and realization, then dharana, even and uninterrupted concentration of mind, is already waxing full, offering its own rich array of benefits and rewards. Formal meditation under the auspices of this concentrated mind is devoid of obstacles, the likes of which novices and intermediates complain about constantly. What is wrong there? Can't they feel the Presence, peaceful and blissful, residing within? Why do they allow the fragmented mind to cheat them by *"bartering away the true gold of original Awareness at the center of their being for the cheap baubles and glass marbles of illusory existence?"*

So, rather than "overlay" the fourfold mind over the limbs of Yoga, strive to perceive the limbs as natural concomitants of mind, as indigenous to the lands of Awareness Itself. We should know then, or come to know, that in true Yoga practice we are not trying to chastise the mind, nor train it in some method that is alien to its nature and character. Our precious attention, granted to us by this selfsame mind, has fallen; that is all. It is now coming to rest upon undesirable, unhealthy, even unclean things — much like *"a fly which lights on sweets one moment and filth the next."* This ignobility of the originally regal mind ought to be corrected as soon as possible, for not only will the superlative benefits of higher Mind be forfeited, but the countless ills and diseases of the fragmented mind will soon collect, leaving little room for peace and contentment, what to speak of yogic realization. As Ramprasad sings, *"Oh Mind, what a petty Potentate you have become! Natural Sovereign of all the inner realms you created, you once upon a time listened to the counselors of higher wisdom who reside internally and eternally in your vast kingdom. But now you take the advice of mere courtiers, servants, and slaves, such as the rascal ego, the many fleeting thought-forms, and the five senses. You have become like a real black bee buzzing around false flowers woven into an immense tapestry."*

With encouragement from devotional wisdom seers, we press on to gain back some important ground which never should have been lost in the first place. And for that end we study, in perfect and synchronistic timing, the sutras pertinent to the final three limbs of Yoga.

### Pada III, Sutra 1

*deshah bandhah chittasya dharana* (*deshah,* area, locale; *bandhah,* restriction; *chittasya,* thoughts of the mind; *dharana,* concentration).

*"Concentration (the sixth limb of yoga) consists of directing the mind's thoughts to one area, locale, or ideal."*

In the all-important arena of concentration, the seers advise beginners to focus on a physical object such as a candle flame or a stone obelisk. Swami Vivekananda notes that such as these are called *pratikas* or *pratimas* in India. The mind is truly an unstable fellow, and the least outer stimuli will cause variation in it, including undue vibration. The greater problem here is that once the mind gets called out, away from its center (Mahat, Ishvara, or Atman, depending on the quality of consciousness), it tends to stay out, and soon forgets the safety, peace, bliss, and respite which is held eternally within. In other words, the natural state for the human mind, until it gets enlightened fully, is not manas, but more like Mahat. Attaching to, obsessing with, and fretting over objects is really beneath its station. With this higher perspective comprehended, we can possibly gain a glimpse of both how low mankind has fallen, and how frustrating this fall and its lack of correction is to the luminaries.

And correcting this downward plunge of the mind in maya is what the great souls are all about. This problem of the deviation of souls from peacefulness was on the mind of Lord Buddha when he tailor-made the Four Noble Truths some six centuries before the birth of Jesus. It became the Nazarene's main preoccupation too some 500 years later, when he witnessed the ignorant state of mind of both the common people and the intellectuals and religionists of his time. Some five or six centuries after that, Gaudapada and his lineage, attended by the great spiritual phenomenon, Adishankaracharya, bent all efforts and spent all energies towards alleviating the heavy and despondent minds of the people by trying to get them to consider nonduality and its superlative benefits. Another six or seven hundred years after Shankara, Lord Chaitanya came to sing, dance, and teach among the devotees, shedding the luster of Divine Love everywhere so as to lift the worldly mind up out of sloth and torpor. And it was certainly the case after another five hundred years had passed when Sri Ramakrishna was born on earth to help others snap the chains of this world and attain to samadhi.

Samadhi is the eighth and final limb of Patanjali's system. It is facilitated or brought into possibility by the sixth and seventh limbs of Yoga, which are represented here by the two sutras under inspection. This new chapter we are embarking on is called *Vibhuti Pada.* We ought to note that the vibhutis, or powers, which are brought into our possession by yogic practices are none other than concentration and meditation. The seers are not speaking of the occult powers here, or of any of the ordinary abilities of the mind at all. It is neither earthly genius nor the nominal knowledge of the worldly-wise which occupies our thoughts and aspirations here, but rare qualities seldom attained in this far-flung akasha (Bhutaskasha). Such is the value that great souls like Patanjali and Vedavyasa place on concentration and meditation, that they are given the highest rung-of-the-ladder status. Other practices, previously prescribed, have led up to the due consideration and careful evaluation of these twin powers, and there should be no falling off, or back, at this juncture for the sincere and resolved aspirant. It is only left to plunge in, armed with all that has been gleaned before, and reach the goal of human existence — Samadhi. There will be time enough for bliss and selfless works afterwards, for neither of these will ripen or exist, uninterrupted, without samadhi.

In our tradition there is a meditation called *Tailadharadhyan,* which refers to an unbroken flow of the mind's awareness towards the receptacle of Brahman. Literally, the phrase means the flow of oil from one container to another. This is the ideal, especially for the advanced practitioner, or the one who, having heard the teachings on Yoga and studied the sutras, is ready to put forth the most intense and persevering effort towards concentration and meditation. As Swami Vivekananda has stated in this regard, *"The powers of the mind should be concentrated and turned back upon itself to penetrate its innermost secrets."*

What are the *powers of the mind?* Concentration, meditation, and samadhi, leading to samyama. What are *its innermost secrets?* That all worlds, all things, all knowledge, exist within it, and that peace and realization are present for the taking when it realizes its identity with Brahman. And this is precisely why the mind should *"turn its powers back upon itself."* By inspection of the mind by the concentrated mind, the source of its powers can be traced. When this occurs, the realized yogi or yogini can switch off all powers at the source, entering into that state of formlessness which matches Atman/Brahman exactly. As the Japanese roshi said upon finding out this secret: "Supplies!" Surprisingly, then, the innermost secret of secrets that the mind has to reveal to us is that of "No-mind." Creation, creativity, projection, production, form, nature, energy, time, birth, heaven, earth, evolution, growth, enjoyment, manipulation, success, inspiration, antipathy, sankalpa, vikalpa, and all outward and inward moving things; and all the mass of reactions which proceed from these such as destruction, boredom, withdrawal, disease, decay, death, hell, failure, depression, rage, war, the problem of survival, and endless cycles — enough of these! The great ones wanted out of such contrasting sets of opposites, this melange of maya, and so they removed themselves from them and all that they infer by learning to switch off the multifarious machine of the mind once and for all (called *Kaivalya* in Yoga). As Swami Aseshananda used to say, humorously, *"No mind, no matter; no matter....never mind!"* In other words, if one knows the innermost secret of mind, called no-mind, and knows, too, that Consciousness precedes the mind as vehicle, then no matter (physical or situational) will ever congeal — thus no forms, names, objects, and worlds. And if there is no matter, well, as the disinterested say, "Never mind." The entire affair requires no attention, is of no significance. The only significance then is, as Swami Vivekananda has written in his marvelous poem, Song of the Sannyasin: *"The Self is all in all, and none else exists, and 'Thou Art That.'"*

**Pada III, Sutra 2**
*tatra pratyaya ekatanata dhyanam* (*tatra,* within that space; *pratyaya,* effort at focus; *ekatanata,* constant single-mindedness; *dhyanam,* meditation).

"*Within that blissful space of focused thoughts occurs the single-minded state of meditation.*"

Continuing on in the vein of the writings above, we perceive the concept of one-pointed mind, endear ourselves to it naturally, and then begin to practice holding the mind in that singular mode for longer and longer periods of time. This process will manifest differently for various practitioners, but the important and pivotal stage of concentration has been gained, so all that is left to do is to sit regularly — to "do" nothing. There is not even any more "emptying of the mind," just as there is no more need to empty and fill the lungs. Why remain at lower stages of practice when attainment has already taken place? Does a high school graduate go back to grade school? Now! The superlative moment of meditation is upon you. Sink yourself deep into that moment and take in the silence of Peace, *Shanti* — "*a Peace which passeth all understanding.*" There is nothing left to do. All deeds will do themselves; all work will work itself; all thought will resolve itself; the world will take care of itself. It always has. As Tibetan Buddha dharma has it:

•*Good deeds and misdeeds naturally meet with rewards and remedies, so the one-pointed mind remains undisturbed.*

•*Work is the realm of phenomena, and all phenomena are simultaneously empty and luminous, so the one-pointed mind meditates spontaneously in the manner of nondoing and noneffort.*

•*The nascent universe is thought itself, objects are mind made manifest, and all misconceptions and errant thoughts are liberated in formless Awareness, so the one-pointed mind meditates in the shining realm of its own illumination, which can never be disturbed, touched, or conceived.*

Study, practice, and meditate aspiring yogis and yoginis. Samadhi is yet to come — in the sutras, and in your Self.

## Lesson Sixty, 4/20/11
### Pada III, Sutra 3

The time for Raja Yoga studies is at hand again, though I doubt that there is a time, or will ever come a time, that such contemplations will ever become untimely. And in that regard I am sending a huge "mahalo" to all of the students who have been writing in of late to express their growth in the spirit, their challenges and obstacles, and thus their questions. This study continues to expand, and our list continues to grow, including as it does the disciples, the general devotees, elements of the public sector, the prison population students, and even the teens and youth who are becoming influenced by these healthy forms of spirituality that are Vedanta and true religion. This study, with your participation, will soon form a book, proving that Westerners are more than mere readers, but practitioners as well, and also that modern mediums like web and email can be used for positive and beneficial ends, spiritually speaking, rather than for just business, advertisement, constant negativity, and so much mundanity — and even banality.

Let us begin lesson 60 in the traditional manner, with questions rising from both the past lesson, and lessons previous, which new members of the list are bringing up. Yoga (intrinsic oneness) is the subject, study (jnana yoga) is the medium, and practice (sadhana) is the qualifier.

**Questions and Answers for Lesson 60**
S.C. from Hawaii writes:
QUESTION #1: "I have read my present lesson over and over and feel confused and delighted by the words. I'm totally confused by the four types of Pralaya in two categories. What are they? How does this relate to meditation? What is Pralaya?"
ANSWER: Pralaya, a Sanskrit word, means dissolution, but not in the sense of either western science or westernized religion wherein all comes from nothing (a nothingness, or "dust") and goes back to nothing (a void, or ashes). In the more enlightened view, "nothing does not exist," which means that all comes from the unmanifest, plays awhile in the manifest mode, and returns to the unmanifest without anything ever really happening or changing. This all occurs (as phenomena) via the dynamic power (shakti) lying inherent within Reality (Brahman) through the projecting power of Mind at cosmic (God's Mind), collective (All beings, such as gods, goddesses, celestials, ancestors, humans, animals, etc), and individual (personal ego) levels of consciousness (*sarvam khalvidam brahman, All is Consciousness).*

It all must be going somewhere, correct? Incorrect. Maya, relativity, phenomena of the mind, has no particular direction, is a form of mass collective mental dreaming with consciousness (unbeknownst to most) at its hub. There is no aim in maya, no higher purpose. Higher purpose, if one were wont to search for one, is the Reality which is always and already transcendent of maya. Thus, falling into maya in ignorance, into form in time and space, is the initial mistake, the primal error, the "original sin" as far as illumined souls are concerned. To conclude, whether one inhabits form (namarupa) or remains in a formless state (pralaya), the awareness of conscious intelligence *(pratibha-chaitanya)* must be retained; otherwise there is hell to pay....and heaven(s).

As far as the two categories of pralaya are concerned, they have been inferred already by the explanations above. That is, the passage of inestimable cycles of time (yugas), in addition to what is the basis for a myriad of incarnations in terms of classes of living beings (jati), is the first category of pralaya. It has to do with the passage of time and the occupation of spatial regions (which are not "created," to repeat an important point, but which are projected by Mind at its three levels). The other category of pralaya is what is called *Mahapralaya,* which brings an end to cycles of time and all levels of worlds, realms, and lokas. Mind rests *(avritta-buddhi)*. In what? That is the prime question, is it not? Metaphysically speaking, then, Mahapralaya is equivalent to Natural Formlessness, to Primal Awareness, to Pure Consciousness. It is the "Great Dissolution." Everything previously manifest recedes back to its essential nature. It is nidra-samadhi.

QUESTION #2: "I'm learning all this, but it is still in my head. It seems I have two lives: one in my head/my studies, attempting to understand everything; and the other is my life of living with people where I revert to the self/habit of a personality. I have my feet in two worlds, and it's jarring and confusing. I prefer the first world, but fall back into the second. Any comment?"

ANSWER: As Sri Ramakrishna has commented about seekers in general, they are something like a tadpole that one day climbs out on shore, sheds its tail, and develops frog's legs. It can then live in two elements, land and water. The meaning is obvious. Those who are seeking truth must learn to acclimatize to Its "breathless air of heights," and at the same time adjust to living in the world with this new and fresh perspective and view. It is much like moving out of the city and taking up residence on a hill overlooking that same city. One still visits there to conduct business (activity), but prefers the peaceful climes and even vibrations of the hilltop home — Siva, the "Home of Peace."

So the answer is, just as you have learned to respect and revere all religions, you must do the same with Reality and relativity; for they are not different from one another; not in essence. We must adjust so as to realize that "All is Brahman." Otherwise, we are still carrying a subtle form of duality within us, in our minds, and this will, now or in the future, confuse us rather than clarify all issues.

QUESTION #3: "I still don't understand involution & evolutes, please help?"

ANSWER: When we say involution in Vedanta, we mean the transmigrating soul's inner journey away from material nature and towards the nonmaterial or spiritual Essence. Since we have come out of somewhere, externalized or manifested ourselves, and find ourselves vulnerable and dissatisfied out here in relativity for the most part, we at one point in time, via yearning, want to reverse the trend and merge into our true nature.

And as to evolutes, specifically, like we studied in our Sankhya retreat at South Point, they are the 24 Cosmic Principles (tattvas)— from unmanifest nature all the way down to the element of earth. All of them, and association with them, has defined our "journey" outwards from the Source (Brahman). So, if we want to journey back to the Source, our true Nature, Atman, we have to follow them inward, and remember what they are, that they are insentient, while "I," the Soul, am the Sentient Principle. "I Am."

Suprema from Pennsylvania writes:
QUESTION: "This mind wants to be free and it is fettered. This is where mind gets stuck again and again. It gets mixed up in 'no mind,' 'Consciousness' using the mind as a vehicle and the 'predecessor' to Consciousness as 'That' again coming back to 'no mind.' There is a niggling notion that Realization is

'identification' with this 'no mind' state. When mind comes to know 'Thou art That,' is 'That' a Consciousness or void of Consciousness? Is Freedom, 'no thing' and how would one stay away from nihilism if this were the case? Words here are difficult. There is no way to describe the burst to knowing that You are One with All Things, never alone. The wording is coming off as ignorance, which in most ways surely is true. No more can there be carried, for any period of time, the past romance once held with spiritual concepts, yet the mind cries for that comfort those concepts allowed. There is little comfort found in what this mind conceives as The Absolute, prior to Consciousness. This mind keeps demanding an either/or perception and is unable to break out of it. How to be content in the arms of Mother, and in the knowing that the arms are, ultimately, illusion?"

ANSWER: Contentment, *uparati,* is the opposite of *avirati,* discontent. It is a very subtle quality, and most difficult to attain, especially in an unbroken mode. More specifically, and as an aid to practice (as opposed to just complaint), the problem of avirati springs from a lingering perception of the objects in one's life, and the desire to have concourse with them. In other words, one still considers them, and the world in which they appear, as real. People cannot get rid of this misconception that what appears to the senses and mind is actual. They have seen, heard, tasted, touched, and smelled the objects for so long, for so many lifetimes, that all of it has impressed itself on their minds as *samskaras.* Then, since objects cannot be possessed, in any way, shape or form, cannot even be known (since they are nothing but vibrating particles congealed by the projecting power of the mind which does not yet know its own power and processes), discontent sets in.

So, it is good that you have brought the mind's romance with unreal objects to a close; now cause the mind's dalliance with the thought of objects being real to experience a similar fate. How to do that? Detachment *(vairagyam)* alone is often not sufficient, not unless one has uncommon powers. Acknowledgement of what Is, is sometimes the missing factor. Spend time, and thought (i.e., study, contemplation and meditation), on affirming what Is. Of the two great Yogas — Mahayoga (everything is), and Abhavayoga (everything is not) — both of them extremely powerful in overcoming all that ails the soul, Mahayoga is supreme. In the end, everyone declares "I Am." No one ends up concluding "I am not." To quote my guru, the illumined Swami Aseshananda, *"You may go on and on denying everything, saying "not this, not this," but no one can deny the existence of the One who is doing the denying"*...certainly not in the end.

The arms of Mother, "illusion?!" How is that? Make fast friends with Reality; make Her your Eternal Companion. Peace of mind will commence from the moment that you do.

K.D. from Hawaii writes:
QUESTION: "I have a question on evolution. Aparinama is defined as *'progressive manifestation by unreal superimposition.'* I understand that superim-

position means placing something unreal over something real and covering it up. I am having some trouble understanding the whole concept here about evolution. I would appreciate some clarification."

ANSWER: Along with what has already been written in my previous answers to questions above, I can add that whenever a form appears, whether that form be a celestial one, a human one, a planet, or an object, then we should figure that maya is in operation, or that nature is in its manifest phase, not its unmanifest mode. That is termed *Parinama (evolution by real modification),* which we must look at with some suspicion. That is, we know that Reality, Brahman, is free of change or transformation. Since our true nature, Atman, is That, It, too, is immutable. Then we are to look at the objects, like worlds, bodies, sense objects, and so forth. At first inspection it seems sure that they change (parinama). At second glance, we see that they change both constantly and with incredible speed (vibrating particles). At third glance, we surmise that they must not exist at all, since they have no abiding substance and also depart our perception in deep sleep, death, nondual meditation, and samadhi. If these conclusions are correct, then where does that leave the theory of evolution? In short, the seeker of Truth sees that all is unchanging. Even that which seems to change, really only does so in appearance, not in actuality.

So, *"progressive manifestation by unreal superimposition"* means that there seems to be a constant progression of manifestation and expression flowing towards, around, and past us, but that we should come to know that all of it and its various motion is all nonactual. The phrase, *evolution by real modification* fails to relate that since all change is nonactual, there is no evolution going on in reality, or, since all is Brahman, i.e., changeless, all modifications and transformations are mere appearances. The Advaitists explain this by the analogy of "gold and gold ornaments." Are they different? The essence is gold, so the only difference is in the form, called "ring." The form, ring, has now been superimposed over the essence, gold. But no change has really taken place, except by way of appearance. The gold did not change as the ring seemingly modified it. What is more, thousands of rings can be formed, and that still does not affect "gold." Further, all ornaments can be melted back down to their essential component, gold. Thus, all forms are soluble in Brahman. And when forms do appear before the senses, taking on the property of solidity, we are to know that these formulations are only an assumption — in short, that Reality has the power to take on form.

To conclude, and in line with Aparinama, the fantasmagoria of phenomena is best seen and understood from the standpoint of the Atman being stationary — that the real "You" is motionless and actionless. Meditate in this mode and attain formlessness. Drink in the Peace there.

QUESTION #2: "Purusha is another name for the Atman, right? When Purusha becomes very identified with mind and intellect, the ego becomes involved. What is a developed ego as opposed to an undeveloped ego? Can the developed ego more easily detach from objects and sensations?"

ANSWER: Sri Ramakrishna has told us that there is the unripe ego (apakvahamkara), and then there is the ripe ego (pakvahamkara). Briefly described, the former is the type of ego which has not surrendered itself to God (Divine Reality/Truth), and the ripe ego is one that is a devotee of the Lord — however the individual perceives That, with form or beyond form, or both. Basically, the unripe ego is a danger to itself and to others, even if the individual is "nice" and seemingly balanced. It cannot be trusted. Therefore, the spiritual aspirant has to choose friends and companions carefully — beware, and be aware. For instance, to choose a wife or husband that is worldly will definitely stifle one's spiritual life. Have you seen them all, going about their mundane habitual existences? as Vivekananda says, their *"gray little studies of lives."* Shudders! They are like fish in a net, unawares of being caught. At least acknowledge being caught so that the struggle to get free can begin.

And yes, the detached ego, or ripe ego, finds it quite easy to remove itself from undue contact with objects. In fact, it is preferable to do so. Freedom from attachments is its own type of bliss, and very attracting.

Atman, Purusha, and ahamkara are three shades of self/Self. One would not think that the Self could be divided, but what is impossible for maya to accomplish? As consciousness becomes more and more refined via spiritual practices, reaching higher and loftier regions of Awareness, I think of these divisions as subtle strata of the Self. Just as there is a distinction noticed between unripe and ripe ego due to certain refinements, so too does the ripe ego encounter more transparent shades of itself over time and with practice, until, as Shankara writes, *"the hailstone of my mind has fallen into the formless and bliss-filled ocean of Consciousness...."*

Akshaya-Bhakti from New England writes:
COMMENTS: "When we began our Raja studies, I wasn't sure if japa/mantra practice would fit in. Then we discussed how Patanjali favored such practice, and later, that there were sutras that included concentration on 'OM' and reflection upon Ishvara. But I don't think the term japa itself has been used, especially in conjunction with any of the 8 limbs."
QUESTION: "Now it has occurred to me that performing japa/mantra is, in fact, one way to practice Dharana. Would that be all that is needed if it is done in Knowledge? Could you please comment?"
ANSWER: It is true that mantra is a key to concentration, and if it were not for the outright bliss that we see practitioners of japa going through, we might think that concentration was the main purpose for it. Both Ishvara and mantra are used, as terms, in the Yoga sutras, sometimes by other names or references. Yoga's relationship with the Bhakti path is not estranged, but it is also not exceedingly warm. "Jnana and Dhyana" are more to its liking, being that they do not brook any foolery and take one, in excellent shape and thoroughly qualified, to the source of Love straightaway. Though more difficult, nothing excels the combination of jnana and dhyana for speedy recovery from the trammels of ignorance.
QUESTION #2: "In your commentary on Sutra III:1, there is mention of the

Tailadharadhyan Meditation. Could you explain more about how to practice this 'unbroken flow of the mind's awareness towards the receptacle of Brahman.'"

ANSWER: One way is through visualization, wherein one envisions that the mind's awareness is a flow of intelligent attention, and that Brahman is the receptacle. As the Upanisad states, *"....like an arrow, one sharpens the mind by thoughts of Reality alone, and then takes up the bow of the nondual teachings and aims at the mark.....the Eternal Brahman."* Long and constant practice, with one-pointedness free of distraction, will net a substantial result, like an experience, rare and unique, which will remain with one throughout one's lifetime. This is the beginning of an era of deep meditation, and signals the end of the intermediate phase, and the beginning of adeptship.

QUESTION #3: "In *Spiritual Quest: Questions and Answers,* by Swami Tapasyananda, he is asked how to use our dream state to 'progress our learning.' Unlike just analyzing our dreams, the answer relates how he 'abstracts himself from the waking consciousness and views it as a memory.' Then through 'proper spiritual discipline upon waking, a split takes place in consciousness and the subject pole of consciousness is able to stand apart and remain unaffected by all the fluctuations of the object pole of consciousness.' Could you explain more about how can we use that brief time between sleeping and waking to practice the 'nonseparation of the One Consciousness,' as well as the 'presence of God' as discussed in Lesson 59?"

ANSWER: Not having read that book, I cannot comment extensively on the remarks made by the swami. "Practicing the presence" in the waking state, however, is accomplished by both acutely focused meditation daily, and performing all work as worship. This combination of action and inaction trains the mind thoroughly, purifying it of its dross, and rendering it flexible and open to spiritual suggestion.

The best way to use the sleep state for spiritual advancement is by reciting the mantra just before falling asleep, and attempting to carry it, along with the visualization of one's Ishtam, into the sleep state. Both dreams and the deep sleep stated may become more lucid in this fashion. Spiritual vision in dream, as well as the hearing of the primal sound, AUM, are the results for adamant practitioners.

Sanatanand from Hawaii writes:
QUESTION: "It is wonderful and illuminating to continue sailing this course with the inspiration of an astute preceptor, and with fellow travelers to share and converse with. The current sutras gave me some opportunity for rumination, but some questions came up as well. Perhaps more to the point, there is a desire for clarification. There is the statement that there are sense-perceptions related to focus on the various parts, e.g. 'if the mind becomes concentrated on the tip of the nose, one begins to smell wonderful perfumes. If it becomes concentrated at the root of the tongue, one begins to hear sounds; if on the tip of the tongue, one begins to taste wonderful flavors,' etc. Swamiji seems to indi-

cate that after a few days this can occur. So is this an example for his penchant for understatement regarding the time and effort to achieve these effects, and further, I am wondering what the value is here anyway? I assume that this is, at best, something that is associated with the rising of consciousness, and not an end in itself, since Sri Ramakrishna himself strongly advised against the acquisition of siddhis."

ANSWER: I believe that in the beginning and intermediate stages of practice, many of these inner phenomena simply appear and get experienced. This does not mean that the practitioner, if he or she be of a noble character, would get at all distracted by them. They would only pass, and the yogi or yogini would have the good sense to let them do so and only move on towards what is obviously the goal, or higher goals, of yogic practice. In other words, it is only the foolish, the curious, the indeterminate, the mystery-mongerers, or the easily distracted, who would halt their forward progress in such an unadvised fashion, to dabble with these *"crow droppings beside the road to Realization."*

QUESTION #2: "The next thing that has come to mind in the broader pursuit, and parenthetically it has arisen in some of the discussions, is regarding the nature of paradox in pursuing this spiritual life. One example that came up yesterday in class was the idea that the use of scripture in meditation is a valuable tool. When the mind is filled with trivial thoughts it would be markedly better to at least examine ideas of wisdom instead. Then it was mentioned that an emptiness of mind was to be avoided. Yet ultimately, Nirvikalpa Samadhi, the highest level of Samadhi, consists (if it can be said to consist) of a completely empty mind, free from all thought. A further example of this is when you mentioned that Sri Ramakrishna examined a photo of himself, not knowing that he was the subject of the photo, and proclaimed that this picture would be revered and worshiped by millions of people. So, to me, the paradox seems to be that here what could be seen as enormous ego is yet absolutely free of ego, both at the same time. Perhaps better examples could be offered, but I have come to see that often the deepest paradoxes contain within them the greatest kernels of Truth. I wonder if you could expand on this and offer some insight as to why this might be the case."

ANSWER: The very fact of a Reality which contains relativity within it, like a snake full of poison that still lives, is a major paradox. The mind that tries to figure out this paradox is, itself, also a paradox. From paradox to paradox we go, so long as maya is in operation. Only in Nirvikalpa does this paradox end, along with all others. It is "no mind," and that is the key to nonparadox.

But we should not imagine that "no mind" means emptiness in the usual or common sense of the term, or even in the pseudo-spiritual way the term is used nowadays. Emptiness there (in nondual samadhi) means the absence of objects, worlds, thoughts, and separate beings. Consciousness still exists, for it *is* Existence. What That is, none can say, for mouth, tongue, prana, mind, and the intelligence that allows one to forge thoughts and turn them into words, is silenced there. All is Bliss; all is Peace. Put another way, is unstinted Freedom empty, simply because it cannot be spoken of?

Kanyakali from Hawaii writes:
COMMENTS: "I'm finding that 'turning the mind's powers back on itself' is a very effective practice for me. In my efforts to realize the Self as Brahman, I've concluded that I can finally give up my life-long search for my True Self because I already am It. I recently realized that I've been searching as though I've been trying to find an object outside of myself, despite the fact that I've heard otherwise countless times! However, now when I sit and meditate on Brahman, my tricky mind still wants to turn Brahman into an object and call out instead, "I'm It!" So this separation between me and Brahman continues, and I'm attempting to root out that separation once and for all. But it's so hard to keep my mind from going outward, creating more and more things. So now I am using my mind to turn it back on itself and contemplate where the mind originates, and the unity of the Self with Brahman. If I can keep my mind occupied long enough by either focusing on my Ishtam, or by calling up the teachings, then I experience moments of just simply Being. I gather that this is what Existence/Consciousness is, which is what Brahman is. And I have never felt closer to my True Self! Because I am That, and none else exists! The crux for me right now is how to maintain this without the mind creeping back in and wanting to objectify the experience. My mind is definitely resisting the formless, but steeping myself in the nondual teachings is beginning to wear down its resistance! I am ever so grateful for your excellent explanations of these sutras!!"
RESPONSE: This is great inner work, the kind that needs to be done after studies are over and the mind has contemplated well the teachings. Coming full circle like this will bring an end to other circles, the kind of which, as described here in your comments, keep the mind guessing and always in states of confusion. So, *svasti vaha paraya tamasah parastat:* "Godspeed to you in crossing over to the farthest shore, beyond all darkness."

S.B. from Los Angeles writes:
QUESTION: "I have been pondering and re-reading chapter four with deep contemplation because in all that we are learning I have been really taking to and embracing the idea of non-dualism at the deepest core of everything, e.g., I am not awake nor asleep, alive nor dead, happy nor sad, et cetera — I just AM. Therefore, when I read in chapter four the analogy of various electrical currents (tempered by thoughts and breath, or the lack thereof) that run or can run through our body, and how the spine terminates at the top (brain) in a bulb of water much like the corporeal body itself births from a womb of water, I am struck by the thought that it seems that absolutely nothing exists except the mind (the Greater Mind) and our minds are like tiny fractals of this Greater Mind, and our bodies are like tiny fractals of our fractal mind's creation. The Mandelbrot set of self similarity comes to mind as to how this might look visually, and leads to my question. Is creation and the chance to create the perpetual reason for all existence, wherein, within that paradigm, the higher mind using the idea of striving toward creating patterned order within our breath (pranaya-

ma) and body patterns (raising kundalini energy) to control and will 'motion' is in order to ultimately lead the body back into the mind and become liberated from the body? If yes, then isn't this creational process much like a giant expanding that ultimately leads back to retracting almost as if the universe itself is inhaling and exhaling with each separation (birth of a person) and ultimate return of that person from that false sense of feeling like separated fragments (via death or better, yet, via finding the path to higher consciousness while still 'in body and/or via achievement of samadhi?"

ANSWER: I cannot follow well the intent of some of your (long) sentences here, but if I understand the main point, it concerns creation in the midst of a Reality that does not change (aparinama). Kindly look back on some of the answers I have given earlier on this subject to others in this lesson, for more clues.

It is interesting that the word Brahman infers expansion by its root, "Brh," which leads us to conclude that It is both static and dynamic, still but active, all-pervading yet expansive. So, not one or the other, but both, is the answer. We must also include the answer "neither," as well. It all depends upon what vantage-point the Self occupies when It looks to perceive Its Essence. If It sees from the matrix of maya, then Brahman will seem a safe and peaceful refuge of blissful transcendence, free of movement. On the other hand, if It gazes from "On High," it may delight in entering into the host of realms and lokas which consist of Its very own light-filled Intelligence.

The sutras for this lesson carry us on into explication of the highest limbs of Yoga after having studied well the crucial intermediary rungs of pratyahara and dharana. Let us see what Patanjali has to offer next, along with our great commentators:

**Pada III, Sutra 3**
*tad evarthamatranirbhasan svarupashunyam iva samadhih* (*tad*, that; *eva*, the same; *artha*, place or object; *matra*, alone/single; *nirbhasam*, radiates; *svarupa*, essence; *shunyam*, empty; *iva*, as it were; *samadhi*, absorption).

*"When all places and objects become empty or equal, as it were, and deep meditation only on the essence occurs, radiating forth meaning, then the mind gets absorbed in samadhi."*

Sutra three of this third pada, our only sutra for this lesson, brooks the hard to define subject of meditation. It is hard to define, and to teach (what to speak of attain), because it is so personal, so inward. The teaching which I have put forth on meditation through SRV Associations, given that the subject is not "taught" by teachers in general, is the one on the Two Forms and Eight Types of meditation. For a complete view of this, and for study, practice, and memorization, please see the chart I have placed on page 27.

Broadly speaking, there are two types of meditation: the one on form, and the formless meditation. Generally, the one on form involves a devotee's *Ishtam,* called a "Chosen Ideal," signifying an all-important decision reached by guru and disciple at the time of initiation. At that auspicious moment in time

# Two Forms & Eight Types of Meditation
## Deification & Transcendence of Forms, Concepts, & Objects

**S A G U N A**     **B R A H M A N**

*Create Realm*

**P R O J E C T I O N**

### Pratika-pratimadhyana — Meditation on Objects
*"By meditation upon those objects which are most agreeable, the yogi's mind attains blissful equipoise."* Lord Patanjali

### Sukshmadhyana — Meditation on Subtle Truths
*"To come to know the methods for removing desire, and how best to worship the acharya, the seer studies those scriptures which treat Atmic Reality and point the way to Self-cognition."* Lord Vasishtha

### Vyakti-upasanadhyana — Meditation on God with Form
*"For many it is best to think of God as possessed of qualities and having a form. This way their minds will become easily concentrated."* Swami Sivananda

### Lila-dhyana — Meditation on the Avatar's Divine Play
*"Lila as God, Lila as the deities, Lila as man, Lila as the universe; take delight in the Naralila."* Sri Ramakrishna

---
**Meditation with Form (Saguna Brahman)**
**Meditation beyond Form (Nirguna Brahman)**

---

**N I R G U N A**     **B R A H M A N**

*Acreate Realm*

**D I S S O L U T I O N**

### Tailadharadhyana — Meditation on One-pointedness
*"The powers of the mind should be concentrated and turned back upon itself to penetrate the innermost secrets."* Swami Vivekananda

### Svarupadhyana — Meditation on the Inner Self
*"The Self is master of the self; who else can the master be? With the finite self subdued, one obtains the sublime refuge most difficult to achieve."* Lord Buddha

### Brahmakaravrittidhyana — Meditation on Brahman
*"Remain quiet, indifferent to the body, and by that one thought of Brahman, become one with Brahman."* Sri Shankara

### Layachintayadhyana — Meditation to Achieve Immersion
   a) Bhuta-layachintayadhyan – of the physical
   b) Antahkarana-layachintayadhyan – of the mental
   c) Omkara-layachintayadhyan – of the initial cause
*"When the mind is completely absorbed in the Supreme Being — Brahman, the world of appearances vanishes."* Sri Shankara

---

*"The practice of meditation will lead your mind to such one-pointedness that you will not want to give it up. But don't just seek God; see God! Does God exist only when eyes are closed, and cease to exist when they are open? Simply quiet the mind and practice."* Sri Sarada Devi

the disciple selects a preferred Form which represents his heart's utter love and surrender. A mantra for that deity is then transmitted. Patanjali refers to this Great Soul in the sutras, calling Him/Her a specially qualified and advanced being who is overseer of the many worlds and their occupants. The Ishtam can be a member of the Trinity, a God or Goddess, an Avatar, or an especially illumined soul. Meditation on this transcendent Form then ensues, and the devotee gets shaped inwardly by the influence of this powerful being. As the Upanisads state, succinctly: *"By meditating on the Lord, one gets the qualities of the Lord."* Thus, meditation with form is crucial for the spiritual development of mankind.

On the chart featured in this lesson (page 27), we can see listed four different methods which fall under this category, classified under the heading of Saguna Brahman, God with attributes. First there is meditation on an ordinary object, not ordinary in the sense of being mundane or common, but only in terms of something practical, and that can inspire higher thought, even inspiration. That is called a *pratika* or a *pratima* in Sanskrit. Since the Hindus are well-versed, over expansive cycles of time, in worshiping images via the mode of deifying the world and its contents, the aspirant is in good hands when taking up a practice of this kind. Please notice the quote by the Father of Yoga under this heading on the chart, for one can see the support and encouragement for such a practice coming through him.

The second type of meditation under the God with Form category is called *Sukshma-dhyan.* It is meditation, or contemplation, on the wisdom contained in scripture. As Lord Vasishtha declares, studying Atma-jnan scriptures that treat nondual Reality is a way of purification and leads "omward" to extraordinary spiritual advancement. The Yoga of Jnana is based upon this principle, but so is Raja Yoga. After all, we are studying the sutras as they appear in scriptural form. Karma Yoga proceeds via study as well, despite its accent on works, and Bhakti Yoga has its own set of scriptures, like the *Bhakti Sutras* of Narada. Point well taken, I hope.

Next comes *Vyakti-upasanadhyan,* which not only includes focus upon the Chosen Ideal mentioned earlier, but extends outward to embrace all divine forms, even forms in nature. Of course, the pratika form of meditation discussed above can count its articles as being from nature as well. Herein, sunsets, seascapes, starscapes, and such, are valuable for this superlative art, as long as they are taken up and perceived in their essence (see sutra 3 and its transliteration) to afford a true meaning, rather than one involved with appearances alone. This, in part, is why Patanjali encourages meditation on the *alambanas* early on, so that the qualified soul can see through surface beauty in nature and receive the profound impact of what nature is really communicating to us. For example, space, with its millions of stars, planets, galaxies, etc., is really speaking to the eternal and boundless nature within us, called Paramakasha. The ocean, with its constant formulation of waves, and their equally consistent disappearance, is relating that the many souls who make their appearance on the surface of existence really only merge again into their essence, thus, no birth or death, or origination. The sun, shining without break, symbolizes the endless emanation of wisdom which is ever-illuminating, thus the Soul's self-effulgent nature. And the myriad raindrops falling into the verdant earth's many bodies of water signifies the merging of souls into the ocean of Consciousness after their play in form is over, thus reincarnation free of bondage, or jivanmukti.

And speaking of playful sport, the fourth type of meditation with form is that of *Lila-dhyan*. The aspirant, disciple, or devotee is encouraged to take up any divine personality and the scenes of His or Her life and engage in a deep introspection of them. Like the Christians do with Jesus and His life, from the manger up until the crucifixion, and the Hindu's do with the lives of Ramchandra and Krishna, and even the Buddhists do with the exemplary life of Sakyamuni Buddha and its highlights, just so should the seeker of deeper states of Awareness place the ardent and one-pointed mind upon God sporting as man. This is the sweetest kind of meditation overall.

The rest of the chart on page 27 is taken up with meditation in the Nirguna mode, or God without attributes. Getting a willful grasp in the mind is first needed, of the kind that Patanjali mentions when he gives out the teaching on the Five States of Mind of A Yogi. As Vivekananda has interpreted it in our class text, the scattered mind must be brought into a mode of "gathering." When the state of "gathered" is accomplished, then "focusing" can begin. And finally, fully focused is attained. This specific gradation of stages applies to *Tailadharadhyan* very well, since all the mind's thoughts must be not only controlled, but concentrated en masse, in force. The practice of intense coalescing of the mind's power, day by day, can result in some profound insights and realizations. Practicing the transmission of one's consciousness force towards the ultimate goal of Brahman, as if pouring honey from one beaker into another, prepares the mind for deeper states of meditation in the formless vein.

This is where the appearance of the Self, called Atman, plays its excellent role in meditation. *Svarupadhyan* is meditation upon one's own inner essence, svarupa. For many, this is the apex of meditation, and nothing further needs to be gained. The spiritual phenomena of Oneness of Atman and Brahman, or Jivatman and Paramatman, occurs naturally after this. By the quote posted on the chart under this heading we can see that even the Buddha was not against using terminology such as "self" to explain the presence of Essence in mankind. Even the small self, the anatman, will necessarily have to merge in its big brother component, the Great Self, at some time or other. In Svarupadhyan, then, the Atman leaves off of its temporary association with the five sheaths, the koshas of Vedanta, and takes up its true nature, free of assumed modifications.

One further thing may be said of Svarupadhyan, and that is what it makes possible in terms of *Brahmakaravrittidhyan*. The still embodied soul, with Atman realized, can now spend time meditating directly on Brahman in rapt formlessness, an actionless act which was hardly possible before the Great Self was realized. Only glimpses were experienced previously, and these while still in the play of mock separation, seemingly real. Now, as Shankara avers, the undivided ocean of Consciousness is available for fathoming, where no barriers are present or possible.

One other form of formless meditation should be added to our list in accord with this sutra and its chart. It is rather an overall conglomeration of all levels of meditation that the soul passed through on its way to purely nondual meditation. It is valuable for return, too, for some souls who attain immersion may decide to forgo absorption and return to the world of individual play for various divine reasons. In this wise they will require some training in the art of *Layachintayadhyan* and its three phases. Laya, as we have learned earlier in this lesson, means dissolution. Thus, all the projections which form the realm of the bhutas, which reside in the antahkarana, and which spring from Omkara, must be dissolved, again and again, from top to bottom, inside out, and forwards and backwards, in order that this most refined of meditational tools be mastered. The perfect Soul then drives enlightenment deeper into every level, aspect and principle of life, from the grossly physical all the way to the purely spiritual. With this accomplished, a yogi or yogini can live anywhere in total immersion, and even partake of complete absorption continually, in a fully conscious way.

The import of this sutra is only superceded by what is to come, namely, the sutras on samyama. Much on seeded samadhi has already been treated earlier, in some of the sutras of Volume 1. Before we undertake samyama, some additional study here, along with more remarks and questions, will be helpful for all. Please enter into the spirit of this lesson and respond before the deadline for our next lesson, and may the Mother of the Universe and all Her precious spiritually illumined children help you in this noble and uplifting process — and in deepening your actual meditations, replete with all these tools and facets of authentic Yoga.

## Lesson Sixty-one, 5/13/11
### Pada III, Sutra 4

Dear Raja Yoga students.

I am writing to you from the San Francisco ashram, where lesson #61 is being prepared for you. The questions below include some submissions from students new to the list, even starting back as early as lesson #1. At its present location, it concentrates on a single sutra — the one concerning samadhi and samyama. Since 2011 ushers in a phase of Upanisadic study in SRV, I have also included excerpts from the "minor" Upanisads at the end of this lesson. Yoga and Vedanta are in perfect accord, and share teachings between them as if they were one darshana. Please absorb all this valuable information and render it fit for contemplation in the yogic mindset as per our penchant for Truth and all that supports and leads inwards to It.

## Questions and Answers for Lesson 61
D.H. from Pennsylvania writes:
QUESTION: "Here are my questions for the May deadline. Many of my reflections are mixed in with the questions, since checking on the veracity of some of my own ideas is a part of the questioning process for me. Would you please correlate the different levels of samprajnata samadhi with the koshas and alambanas to which they correspond? To query along these lines further, I wonder if the savitarka and nirvitarka samadhis might relate primarily to manas (and manomayakosha), the jnanendriyas, and the bhutas, thus making them samadhis wherein the equanimity of turiya is brought to bear on the dual world? Might the savichara and nirvichara samadhis relate to the vijnanamayakosha, (and maybe, in regard to alambanas, the tanmatras)? Could the sananda and sasmita samadhis relate to the two aspects of the anandamayakosha, (that is, ananda as it pertains to the causal sheath, and asmita/ahamkara)? And if I am correct about this, to what alambana(s) would these last two samadhis relate? I am thinking that these correlations could give me further insight into the nature of these samadhis."
ANSWER: One may engage in such speculation between the darshanas, like between Yoga and Vedanta, but it would be better to actually practice gaining them and thus reveal such connections naturally, and at the auspicious time. But generally speaking, the Turiya experience is gotten beyond all five of the koshas. One could also state that the "Sananda" (with bliss) samadhi of Yoga could nicely correlate with the Anandamayakosha of Vedanta. And yes, the savitarka/nirvitarka levels of seeded samadhi could have a connection with the vijnanamayakosha.
QUESTION #2: "In the five different akashas, what are the five kinds of particles? Searching through the SRV literature, I seem unable to find them."
ANSWER: In the bhutakasha, the particle is matter. In the pranakasha, the particle is of life-force. In the chittakasha, the particle is of thought-force. In the jnanakasha the particle is of living intelligence. And in the Chidakasha, surprise!.....there is no particle. All is one homogenous mass of pure, conscious Awareness.
QUESTION #3: "Lately, before meditation, I have been sitting with the picture of Sri Ramakrishna and allowing interactions to rise. Sometimes this gets very powerful and it can also be quite helpful. Yesterday morning, the image was of Sri Ramakrishna standing on the porch of his room, gazing out at the Ganges. It was spring and, in the wind, purple flower petals blew across the porch. I was there with him as this occurred, and it sometimes seemed he pointed things out to me, or it seemed as if he was simply talking or standing with me. A deep sense of bliss arose with all this. So then I set my timer and shut my eyes for meditation per se. I visualized Sri Ramakrishna in my heart as I always do. Before long, the klishta-vrittis started throwing out their distracting trains of thought; almost immediately, though the image of me standing with the Master by the Ganges came, and that image wiped the distracting thoughts right out! In the sense of peace and calm that I felt, they melted away like dewdrops

with the rising sun. After that I returned to my central image of the Master in my heart. This happened over and over. So my question is, should I continue with this approach to meditation? I ask because, while this approach is extremely effective in wiping away klishta-vrittis, my meditative focus, at the same time, is not strictly one-pointed. It is instead divided between the image of the Master in my heart and whatever devotional image is arising that morning. I am, in other words, not sure this division in attention is yogically sound and I wonder if it might lead to problems further down the road."

ANSWER: No, no problem can come from this type of visualization, especially since it is being very effective for you at this time. The practitioner is to make use of what transpires in any given phase of meditation practice, and these phases will come and go, each with their set time of expression and time for completion. This upasana-dhyan, or visualization meditation, is a part of spiritual unfolding, which leads up to and prepares the mind for nondual experiences yet to come, and also sets the ground for returning to form after formlessness has been plumbed. As the Great Master has said, *"No matter how high a bird may fly, it must at some time come to rest on a branch."* So establish meditation on God with form first. This is both exceedingly sweet and extremely practical. In my view, Advaita is incomplete without the experience of God with form.

Jagadaya from Portland writes:
QUESTION: "Does Atman differ from Purusha? I recognize I am mixing two different darshanas, I think."
ANSWER: It is difficult to answer by dint of the scriptures, mainly because it is hard to assign historical or chronological time periods to Gita, Upanisads, and others. The word, "Purusha," was of common usage in the Sankhya period, and we know that was quite ancient. It was also used by Sri Krishna in the Gita, but the word "Atman" is also there.

But whatever the case may be, Purusha in Sankhya carries the connotation of an individual soul, whereas Atman in Vedanta smacks of the transcendent and nondual Soul wherein It is one with Brahman so long as the five koshas are pierced. So, depending from what perspective one perceives at any given vantage-point in consciousness, both terms can be utilized for relative or absolute Selves or Souls. After all, we have the word "ahamkara" in relation to the ego self, so it is not correct to assign either Purusha or Atman to that level of self. In this relation, I have used ahamkara for the ego self, Purusha for the true individual Self, and Atman for the universal Self. There is also a Cosmic Self, or Ishvara. Thus, and unlike some Buddhist schools, we need not be afraid or wary of the term "self," so long as we can define the level and meaning adequately. In short, the terms Buddha Nature and Tathagatagarbha (also Lord Buddha's mention of Prajnaparam) in Buddhism are directly in correlation to Vedanta's Atman or Brahman, and the term anatman or nonself in Buddhism corresponds nicely with our term, ahamkara, or ego self. So, it is perfectly true that there is no individual self — at least not when the mind is transcended (for the ego is a part of the mental complex). But if one correlates Self with Absolute Consciousness, well, who would be so careless, so callous, as to take that away and leave some heartless void in its place?

QUESTION #2: "For those of us Westerners who were raised believing that God is in everything, and to not hold 'false idols,' working toward a relationship with Ishvara can seem like a step backwards. Yet, in meditation, especially in the ashram shrine, I feel intense devotion toward the Deities, allowing me to "embrace the cosmic personality" which I understand will allow me, in time, to immerse in the Formless. I can also feel that cosmic devotion and the beginnings of union, occasionally in nature, and when in connection with the Divine in others. At those times I instinctively thank God. But then I wonder: should I be thinking of this as Holy Mother? I believe my question is: how do I put my mind at ease with all this. As I write this I realize at least some of the answer is to stop my questioning mind and get beyond the senses to what is truly Real. Now, days later, as I prepare for puja, I have reread Annapurna's lovely introduction to the Puja Manual. She addresses this very issue and I realize some of my quandary has more to do with offering puja and not feeling 100% qualified and able to feel at one with the Deities through their pictures. I will continue to pray, practice and work on this. I love your phase 'OMward' and try to take that to heart."

ANSWER: This process you describe is a very healthy one, and one that many beings have had to pass through to gain right understanding of all the levels of worship and wisdom conjoined. But back to your first sentence, I do not believe that seeing God in everything is what most Westerners are taught, and certainly not what occurs here in the West. Seeing God in everything is only possible after having had samadhi, and very few people in the West, even in the world, have had that, despite what they say in their money-making brochures.

There is, no doubt, a rather green and naive form of seeing God in everything that persists here in the West, based mostly on a sort of sentimental glamour-oriented relationship with nature as God. But as the seers tell us, God/Reality cannot be found in form — can never be objectified or formed by anything in nature. This is what Sri Ramakrishna called a "green coconut oneness," which means that when the coconut is still unripe, it is all one solid mass. It is only when it ripens that it breaks into five separate layers — outer husk, inner husk, shell, meat, and liquid. And there is a thing rattling around in it too when one shakes it. It does not adhere with the other five layers. This analogy means that the Atman, the true Self of mankind, is not a part of nature, of the five sheaths of matter, energy, mind, intellect, and ego. It is independent, always and ever. And this occurs to the mind of man only after it "ripens" into higher understanding. Otherwise he thinks that the body is the soul, and the soul is the body, and never discriminates for higher wisdom. Such a person walks about saying glibly that he sees God in everything, but he is really only seeing objects, personages, heavens, earths, and hells, etc. If he was really seeing Divine Reality he would demonstrate the signs of a knower of Brahman or a lover of God, with samadhis and tears of bliss flowing profusely over his person and countenance. For, how often do we see a soul like this, in such a condition?

And so, that lofty station of seeing God everywhere is not to be passed out like penny candy. It is earned by long, deep, and subtle inner work, which fructifies only after many lifetimes. It is not something that hacks and charlatans can claim for themselves, as everyone intuitively knows better and sees right through them.

Kanyakali from Hawaii writes:
QUESTION: "I have a question about vyakti-upasanadhyana (meditation on God with form). Is it ever inadvisable to meditate directly upon a Goddess as powerful as Mother Kali? And if so, why?"
ANSWER: When the time is right, She Herself, the Chaitanyarupa Devi, the Brahma Sanatani Devi, will draw the mind of Her acolyte to Her, unerringly. One need not force the issue, and would not want to anyway if he/she knew what was in store for the mind if it actually perceived this singular and awesome Presence.

And so, the acharyas, the preceptors, tell us that meditating directly on Kali is like looking at the sun. That light is too bright for physical eyes. In the same way, the Light of the Goddess is too dazzling for the mind in meditation. One is therefore advised to look upon the moon (The luminaries of Kali Ma, like Sri Ramakrishna) for a time, to get it used to the light overall. Then, by degrees, and when the time comes naturally, the Light of Kali can be perceived more fully, by degrees. Or, we can put it this way: if it took a comprehensively adept spiritual being like Sri Ramakrishna some twelve years of intense practice to gain a vision of Mother Kali, then maybe we should take a page from His book and example and proceed at a speed and level which is suitable with our ability to practice and realize.

C.S. from Canada writes:
QUESTION: "First thank you so much for holding this class. I feel blessed to have a teacher who understands the subject at a deep (or is it high?) level. The questions that come to mind for me are: I understood Purusha to be the eternal soul and Prakriti to be the animating aspect, but this does not seem to correspond to your description of Purusha as sentient and Prakriti as insentient. I also must have misunderstood Prakriti as a descriptor for the Divine Mother. Can you clarify this?"
ANSWER: You are not incorrect in either of your deductions here. Neither am I. It all depends upon which direction one is looking. That is, from the ultimate angle, that of nonduality, Purusha is the substratum for existence. Prakriti is insentient, and unable to move anything without Purusha. Perhaps that is why some "improvements" on the early Sankhya view were needed and warranted by both Vedanta and Tantra. The provision of acknowledgement of the principle of Shakti was this gift. Brahman, or Purusha if you will, by Itself, is not interested in playing with forms, being fully content within Itself, and nondual.

Its shakti element therefore does all the playing, all the sporting, all the manifesting of names, forms, worlds, and objects.

The Static Brahman and the Dynamic Shakti are therefore the full package with which to realize the nature of Consciousness. If it is only left to the principles of Purusha and Prakriti, and without some definitive explanations to go with, the whole matter becomes perhaps too simplistic, unsatisfying. This medium that lies between facilitates the relationship; both the Upanisads and the Gita say so. In the Gita, there are really four principles in play: Brahman, the Reality; Ishvara, the sacrificer; Atman, the soul; and Prakriti, nature. (Adhyatma, Adhidaivata; Adhiyajna, and Adhibhuta). The latter two are mediums or go-betweens for the former couple. That is, Ishvara (or Ishvari) and nature facilitate the relationship necessary for expression and relative existence in form. This makes further sense when one comes to know that it is Ishvara that manipulates (controls) nature, not mankind. Thus, Ishvara/Ishvari in the scriptures are consonate with the principle of Shakti, the Moving Force, but without these connections, these bits of essential knowledge, life becomes instead, a moving farce.

As for Prakriti as a designator for Divine Mother, yes, it is true in part. The tendency to relegate Mother to nature only, however, or to position womankind in the category of nature only shows up glaringly as a grave defect in Hindu scriptures, responsible — in both monastic and lay traditions — for the downfall of women in general. This aside for now in lieu of the point of your question, since Mother manages insentient nature, and lends it its animating power (prana, etc.), it is then easy to label Her as nature. But we must remember that She is more: She is the Mother of the Universe, and by the word "universe" here, we mean more than just the physical worlds and planets in space. All the inner worlds, fashioned from Her maya, are also under Her jurisdiction. Therefore, anyone who wants, needs, desires, or has to take form must go through Her for it. That is, from free souls to bound souls, all must propitiate Her for the use of the body. The final boon of liberation — that, too, is granted by Her.

QUESTION: #2 "I was very interested to read about vrittis constantly rising and being modified in the manas/buddhi. Have I recently experienced this consciously? I got, at a deeper level, how the negative, judging thoughts, voiced or not, create detrimental effects internally and externally. Consequently I have been able to desist much more easily from forming those thoughts (quite a relief I find). This seems to correspond with the assertion that the internal world creates the external world. As well, the knower of this seems different from the thinker of the thoughts. Can you help me understand this clearly? (I appreciate the Vedanta description of the mind – like the moon that shines by borrowed light, bereft of any inherent self-effulgence of its own)."

ANSWER: The teaching of late in SRV around this subject has been to help the aspirant draw a distinction between the brain and the mind. The thinker is more in the brain, which could also be called the ordinary mind, while the observer or witness is more present in the clarified, clear, and pure mind. Since the mundane mind and its conventional and quotidian thoughts is taken up with matter and what science says about it, the body and senses and how the medical profession sees them, and the brain and how psychology measures it, no attention is lent towards higher mind, what to speak of spirituality. What is being titled "Wholistic Health" nowadays does not even leave the door open for the intellect and its exercise and expression. In this limited atmosphere the talk and accent is all on quantum measurements and neuro-peptides, medicines and laser surgeries, habits, memories, and complexes, all of which fall into the category of matter or, in spiritual philosophy, in the realm of Maya.

    The sun which steals the light away from the hypnotizing moons of matter and Maya is the Atman, defined as Pure Consciousness, or Timeless Deathless Awareness in Vedanta. Though Unmanifest, it forms the foundation for all that spills into form. The hub, matrix, or medium called the mind/ego mechanism (antahkarana), with its inherent intelligence and ability for thoughts (chitta), plays the main role in bringing all into manifestation. And that sometimes dubious gift of mental expression is indeed presented by it, while Pure Consciousness remains unchanged, refusing to break into vibrations and forms. As has been sung and written about the Atman, "Nature finds it impossible to form It." But the mind — at cosmic, collective, and individual levels — plays with those powers, called "projection" in this philosophy, rather than "creation" in western Theology. Simply put, creation is not a possibility, since everything exists eternally. The appearance and disappearance of multitudinous forms over interminable cycles all occurs on the roiling surface of a boundless ocean of Awareness which Itself is both raptly still and immaculately transformationless at Its core, in Its depths, by Its very nature.

    The process of involution of the mind is what proves such esoteric information to the striving individual. Dissolving the body into the senses, the senses into the subtle senses, those into the prana, the prana into the mind, the mind into the intellect, the intellect into the ego or small self, and the small self into the "Great Self," or Atman, is the classic inward journey of those who have become weary of secular explanations for matters smacking of human awareness and hidden wonders. It is left up to the individual, then, to pursue such inward practices under the guidance of an illumined preceptor, and reach what the luminaries of spiritual life call *"the goal of human existence"* in this lifetime. As the Upanisads state, *"Godspeed to you in crossing over to the farthest shore, beyond all darkness."*

QUESTION #3: "I also read with interest and amusement your description of Ahamkara. No wonder Ramakrishna said one needs to train the ego to be a servant of the Divine – it's not going anywhere. Self-surrender and worship of Ishvara are required to ripen the ego. Is this referring to Bhakti yoga? I look forward to your response. With Love and Great Respect."

ANSWER: Yes, what does not really exist has no place to go. The ego is a most subtle projection, the location of which is most difficult to find. Meditators search with deep scrutiny and fail to oust it from its hiding place. But the Great Master, as you say here, has found out a unique way to deal with ahamkara, that being to ripen it by turning it into a devotee of the Lord. For those not inclined so much towards bhakti, a devotee of the Lord can just as easily be a lover of Truth. In either case, the ego will fall into abeyance and obedience, the result being a ready compliance with all that had previously mediated against spiritual progress.

S.C. from Hawaii writes:
QUESTION: "I've never heard of the Prasthanatrayam, Would you tell us about this?"
ANSWER: That is a Sanskrit term which designates the "three landmarks in scriptural history." This means that the rishis bestowed the highest reverence and authority upon The Upanisads, The Brahma Sutras, and the Bhagavad Gita amongst all the many great scriptures contained within the various orthodox and unorthodox Indian darshanas. In these three, one will find the nondual lines, the permeating thread of pure spirituality which, when discovered and meditated upon, makes complete sense out of all religious quandaries and philosophical conundrums.
QUESTION #2: "What is Satyagraha? It isn't in any of your teachings that I have seen, but I saw it and wondered."
ANSWER: It is a term made popular in more current times by Mahatma Gandhi. It is really the giving of Truth in all situations, and the maintaining of its tenets at all times.
QUESTION #3: "Would you say more about how the Vijnanamayakosha and Anandamayakosha and their close connection can be a focus away from Atman?"
ANSWER: The sheath of intellect and of ego are rife with many powers and possibilities. That is not hard to fathom when one looks at the play of intelligence and the many selves occupying the worlds of name and form. Of the many distractions, then, many of them being very common, even banal, these two head the list of distractions, which can lead one off the spiritual path and onto paths of gathering knowledge for knowledge's sake, and sporting in the realms of pleasure with no real purpose. When placed together, all knowledge becomes a personal possession, and all acts the auspice of personal agency. The line of demarcation between Spirit and matter becomes enlarged at this juncture, and swells to obscure both the real purpose of human embodiment, and the true nature of the embodied being. If these sheaths are purified, however, a great impetus can come from them, especially if the threefold threat of ownership, agency, and sense of separation are avoided. A singular focus on Pure Awareness keeps all this in perspective.
QUESTION #4: "Help me understand the difference between enjoying the 10 objects of the senses and conscious awareness of what the senses bring — like being aware of a sound in meditation?"
ANSWER: Having studied in the Vedanta for a while, you probably know that the Vedantists are into giving the ego and senses only what is their basic due, for such restrained acts will both maintain the spiritual path evenly and lead to

the awakening of higher centers of awareness. Renunciation is at the root of this spiritual tendency, which, when developed and matured, is a type of bliss all its own.

Along the mounting of this precipitous and unpopular way, however, the rudimentary steps of taking into account the body's functions, the sense-experiences, and the feelings and emotions of the outer heart are not completely counted out, especially for the householders who have their own specific set of considerations around family and society. But overall, it is all a matter of honing and implementing discriminating wisdom (viveka), just as one does for the mind and intellect when the time comes. Nevertheless, what the senses bring is rather finite and generally not that helpful compared to what knowledge of, say, the inner senses, bring. In India, the mind has often been considered the main sense, since all the five senses are connected to and, in the case of a discriminating person, directed by it.

But whatever the case may be, for any given aspirant at any given time, the awareness of one's overall consciousness — what is looking on, or observing, or witnessing — is the cutting edge in spiritual, even intellectual, growth. So, to note and widen the line of distinction between the seer and the seen becomes a valued attempt of the novice and adept, and is a favorite preoccupation of the wise. As Patanjali and Vedavyasa put it, the yogi loves to give away more than to receive, and therefore hastens to lighten his or her load in life rather than to burden down. But again, the householder has a different set of considerations, and as long as his or her lifestyle is based in dharma, possessions and accumulations may not harm. As Sri Ramakrishna has said, with practicality in mind, *"The monk does not save for the morrow, but the mother bird has to store up for the sake of her offspring."* Thus, it is up to the individual to take account of the present station in life and act accordingly, while at the same time leaving the door open for changes that both resist against stagnation and complacency, and also improve one's stature and position along the spiritual path.

QUESTION #5: "From Sutra 10: Let's say that my feet are cold. If I attempt to warm them to avoid the experience of cold, am I being ignorant of my true nature as Purusha? When meditating, sitting through the pain, discriminating, rather than being cruel or suffering hell, could this tend to weaken the sensations and calm the mind?"

ANSWER: There is always the option to rise above the body's pains in meditation. One can push the envelope a bit and find both relief and strength by doing so. For the yogi, this is not cruelty or carelessness, but command. But for the novice and the beginner, some caution in this area may be exercised, for both the body and the mind are not ready for such austerities. Again, each individual can determine the extent of what he or she can handle at any given stage, and must also take into account that within these shifting stages there is both progress and regress occurring day by day, month by month, in turns. However, if one does not attempt to push through such pains and discomforts, then little inner strength will ever get developed — the kind of inner strength which will come in handy in everyday life when we face off with such challenges as life-threatening illnesses, difficult societal and monetary situations, or even a common cold. As Swami Vivekananda has said, *"Spiritual life is not for the weak-minded."*

Sanatanand from Hawaii writes:
QUESTION: "As we delve ever more deeply into the nature and practice of meditation, I am reminded of a quote from Alice in Wonderland: 'It gets curiouser and curiouser.' There seem to be so many variations or, perhaps better said, pathways, into a deep meditative state. It is mentioned that concentrating on the example of a great being or deity is one way to still and deepen the practice. Or, one can seize upon the inspired dream state. And still, there is the centered, luminous state of the heart to guide one. I guess I am wondering, since my practice consists of focusing on the heart, when might one want to employ these other ways, if at all? I guess what I surmise from these sutras is that the method is really not the important thing, but rather whatever process is most available to each to take them to that interior state whereby each can access the deeper spirit within. I would appreciate any comments and elucidations."
ANSWER: Proper method at the right time is invaluable for spiritual progress. The "right time," however, is really what is at question. Generally, if you have come to a path and taken a preceptor for that pathway, it is a good bet that you have received the method which is best for you at this time. For, the "right time" refers to a lifetime rather than to a set of years, or even decades. People do not come to spirituality in small increments of time, but are working on coming to it over lifetimes. This is called the "long view," and to us here in the West, and in present times, the long view has come to mean just what our short and rather weak memories can conjure up for us. Awakening to spiritual life means, among other things, that divine *smriti* also awakens. Smriti is memory, but not just of recent events in a single life span, but of all that occurred to one previously in a series of lifetimes, and which has formed their prarabdha karma — those effects that have formulated our present life and its conditions.

A teaching presently being given in SRV is that of the real meaning and dynamic of reincarnation. That is, most beings — those who even consider it — think of it as the manifestation of an ego-personality, over and over again. But that is neither accurate nor reliable. Reincarnation is what you see when you look into the mirror of your mind, and also what you see when you look at your own face and eyes in a mirror. That is, your karma is upon you here and now; that is prarabdha. Your sanchita karma stored up from past thoughts and actions has come forward in the "now." There is no need to try to ferret out "who" you were in a past lifetime, for that was then, and is now a mere dream, a projection. What you really are overall is in your prarabdha, and if you do not like what you see then you must take steps to change it. Even if you like what you see, you should always strive to improve it, for "looks can be deceiving." Basically, no one, not even the guru, knows you as well as you do — not unless you are one of those who are always trying to run away from the Self *(svaru-*

*payathanbhava)* rather than towards the Self *(svarupapratistha)*.

So, come to know and use the signs along the path, just as an expert tracker might. Your present features, habits, preferences, aversions, tendencies, mind-set, and such, are barometers with which to gauge and measure both past lifetime residuals and present and future conditions of mind. With those in hand one may not only receive a well-considered sadhana and method from the preceptor, but then and also learn to apply and benefit by it so as to neutralize all karma and annul the residue of all lifetimes excepting for the one that really counts — the present one. For it is in this present lifetime that, if we awaken in the "Insomnia of Yoga," we can readily and willingly trade in the tired and tawdry old set of plodding and pedantic lives for that which the seers and Avatars have called Eternal Life, or Divine Life. As the Upanisads say, *"May it be so."*

K.D. from Hawaii writes:
QUESTION: "I have also been contemplating the nature of sadhana as a means of dissolving past karma rather than a means of achieving self-realization. In the book, The Avadhut, you mention that goal-oriented and process-oriented sadhana are less than ideal. I had thought that sadhana is a means of quieting the mind in order to achieve a single focus, and ultimately to merge with the Divine. Much to contemplate. I suppose there are questions embedded in these comments."
ANSWER: Sadhana has that benefit of quieting the mind, and making it sure of itself in the struggle for perfection. Along the spiritual way it is also effective in removing poisons, destroying karmas, and availing the soul of other inner wonders of that ilk, depending on what form of sadhana one is engaging in. It is all meant to lead to one-pointedness, however, which in the yogic way is necessary for real meditation and samadhi. In other words, sadhana is an all-round panacea for what ails us here in relativity. Through it, relativity itself will transform into nothing other than Reality. Short of natural enlightenment — and precious few of us can claim that — sadhana is the cutting edge practice, the definitive shaping tool, beating methods such as conventional religion, secular education, and various types of therapies hands down for true transformation of mind and character.

When I make the point regarding goal-oriented sadhana in the book, *The Avadhut and His Twenty-Four Teachers in Nature,* it is to be taken at face value. That is, sadhana that is engaged in willingly, via traditional means, accompanied by aid from the revealed scriptures, and well-informed by the spiritual preceptor, will never be goal-oriented; such dangers will simply not be present. In other words, follow the Eight-fold path of right orientation, right perspective, right livelihood, etc., for the best results. Then, karmas will be neutralized almost as a matter of course, and samskaras removed without necessarily laboring or being acutely aware of them. As my teacher used to tell us, *"If we all knew who we really are, there would be little use for sadhana."* Well, in a better world, perhaps. In the meantime, goals or not, there is one supreme way of successfully working through these unseen obstacles which are the causes for all the impediments that manifest in our lives daily. Other methods are, as we have seen over and over again, either worthless, or helpful for the short-term duration only. And as I have said above, we need to develop the long view to gain any higher view of what is happening to us against our own higher will.

A.K. from New Delhi writes:
QUESTION: "I have read lesson 3 and have the following questions. 1: Cosmic mind, or Mahat — I do not understand it. Is it the mind of God, but God means the Self? 2: Also, I do not understand the teachings on vibration."
ANSWER: These are a real good combination, these two questions you have posed. As to the first, yes, Cosmic Mind, called *Mahat* in Sanskrit, particularly in the language of Sankhya Yoga, is what we can refer to as "God's Mind." There is the mind of mankind in the *vyasti* mode, meaning individual; then there is the mind of mankind in the collective mode, called *samasti*. But God's Mind rests in the "cosmic" mode *(vyapi),* meaning very balanced, called *"sattvic"* in Sanskrit. All of the projections from that all-powerful Mind are sweet and beneficial. Anthropomorphically we equate it to Lord Brahma, a supreme Master at fashioning the worlds of name and form in time and space out of Mind — or mental vibration, if you will.

And that broaches your second question: when the mind is vibrating, like in the waking state, all manner of manifestation is under way. When it ceases to vibrate, as in deep sleep or samadhi, these vibrations are quelled, and "nothing" is present. One does not even remember their present life, body, family, and ego, in deep sleep. Sri Krishna refers to this latter state as the "unmanifested" in the Bhagavad Gita. One could also equate it to AUM, the "Primal Vibration." They call It the "Unstruck Sound," which indicates its most subtle nature. The lack of any gross vibration, thus physical manifestation, even thought forms, is that very atmosphere. This is why, to help aspirants and seekers to understand the presence of formless Consciousness, which is present even when thoughts and objects are absent, spiritual preceptors have them meditating upon AUM, and attempting to dissolve all thought vibrations into It.

The sound of AUM appears in the inward-turning consciousness of the practitioner, and is to be followed to its Source over years of self-effort until consciousness gets established in It. Thus, AUM is the "Word" of God, synonymous with all manifestation held in abeyance, yet in potential at a swift moment's notice. So, Peace and AUM......

## Pada III, Sutra 4
*trayam ekatra samyama* (*trayam*, the three; *ekatra*, as one; *samyama*, the final three limbs integrated).
*"The final three limbs, integrated together as one, are known as samyama."*
In the previous lesson I lent some time and space to an explanation of the subject of meditation, the seventh limb of Yoga. Therein I gave out some

teachings on the eight forms of meditation, divided into two modes — with form and beyond form. Part of the reason for providing this is the way in which the first five sutras of this pada are set up, which does not afford dhyan much of a sole mention or scrutiny. It is as if when the meditator concentrates properly, that *is* meditation, and the result of it is samyama. In other words, when rightly accomplished and performed, there is hardly any distinction in the last three limbs of Yoga. This is why a concentrated mind, when it has developed the uninterrupted type of dharana (concentration), is already merged in the seeded (samprajnata) levels of samadhi, as if effortlessly. Some practitioners, holding samadhi as a far distant goal (which is not a bad practice or perspective to hold for a time), are often surprised when they find out after the fact that samadhi has been upon them and with them for some years without their knowledge and identification of it. Whatever the case may be, in the broad spectrum of diverse practitioners and their various perspectives, meditation as a topic all its own is very beneficial nonetheless. Therefore, and drawing from our most revered scriptures, the Upanisads, I place below several selections on meditation. These are esoteric slokas, being from the 98 "minor" Upanisads that we do not hear or see much of — which will help inform us and further fuel our own practice:

From the Darshana Upanisad — *"I (Dattatreya) will now tell you about meditation, which destroys all sorrow. Meditation should be done on Maheshvara, the Lord of all the Worlds, who is the excellent and effective medicine for all the vexing problems rising out of and attending the birth process, who Himself constitutes the main discipline and the fundamental basis of the world, and who is called Para Brahma, the Supreme Brahman. That is the masculine presence upwards and the feminine power reaching down into the worlds, and is therefore the very form of all realms and lokas. Called Virupaksha, It is the Ideal of all the yogis who say, "I am That."*

*So, always endeavor to perform meditation on That Divine Presence, the personification of Satchidananda, Who is the indivisible and all-pervasive Soul Itself in person, and the One responsible for granting liberation. For the great embodied soul who practices such, known as the Purusha, the incomparable science of Vedanta will automatically appear in the mind naturally. There is no doubt about this."*

From the Maha-Narayana Upanisad — *"In the citadel of the body there is a small, sinless, and pure lotus of the heart which is the residence of the Supreme. Deeper within the interior of this lotus there is a sorrowless Ether. That is to be meditated upon continually. That Ether is the atmosphere of the Divine Person, and into that One everything is dissolved at the time of rapt nondual contemplation. One should meditate on this Supreme Being — The Limitless, The Unchanging, The All-knowing — always and ever dwelling in one's own heart. The wise meditator focuses within the subtle Ether of the heart, comparable to an inverted lotus bud. It is to be envisioned as being a finger's length below the Adam's apple and above the navel. That space is the abode of all the universes in space and time. In It everything is supported."*

From the Muktida Upanisad — "*Sri Ram told Hanuman, 'By repeatedly practicing meditation upon Brahman without ego, Samprajnata Samadhi is attained. When all mental modifications die away in that Light of the Spirit devoid of all that is not Brahman, Asamprajnata, loved by the yogins, is perceived. The wise know that the mind is bound by impressions. They also know that when the mind is released from them, liberation is at hand. So put the mind's impressions out like a lamp. Peace and bliss will be the result.*

*What is the method for liberation? The destruction of impressions, the cultivating of knowledge, and the dissolution of the mind, when practiced together, will yield fruit. If these three are not practiced together there will be no success, even after hundreds of years, like the taking and reciting of many mantras instead of one. The many impressions of life in relativity cannot be dissolved without long-standing practice. One must also avoid accumulating more of them via the search for pleasure. Instead, nourishing the mind with Vedanta, keeping contact with holy persons, giving up the gathering of mental impressions, and quelling the pulsations of the prana are enjoined upon the seeker of Truth. Those who try to destroy the mind via force, or with vacant, mindless sitting, are like a man who searches for a lost lamp in the soot of a dark basement.*

*So, by concentration shall you raise the inherent knowledge in you, and from that will dhyana, the means for deep meditation, get imparted and instilled. Therefore, dissolve all thought in reverse order of appearance and perceive only what remains — Pure Consciousness.'*"

From the Sandilya Upanisad — "*Sandilya questioned Atharvan about the limbs of Yoga. About dharana, dhyana, and samadhi, Atharvan said: 'Dharana, concentration, is of three kinds: fixing the mind on the Atman; bringing the external akasha into the akasha of the heart; and contemplating the five murtis, or sacred forms, residing in the five elements of earth, water, fire, air, and ether.*

"*Dhyana is of two kinds: Saguna, with qualities; and Nirguna, without qualities. Saguna is meditation on a form. Nirguna is meditation on the reality of the Self.*

"*Samadhi is the union of the Jivatman, the individual self, with the Paramatman, the Supreme Self. It is free of the distinction between the knower, the known, and knowledge. It is of the nature of extreme Bliss and pure Consciousness.'*"

From the Saubhagya-Lakshmi Upanisad — "*That day, Narayana, the Supreme Lord, told the gods with regard to their request to know meditation: 'Like salt in water, melted and fused, so the mind and the self are blended in oneness. Breath dwindles and mind dissolves, and homogenous Bliss is discovered. Through the fusion of the higher and lower selves, free from all imaginings, rid of the light of the waking state and freed from the mind that dreams, and free as well from all pain, totally devoid of all reflection, such is concentration, meditation, and samadhi conjoined.*

"*Through ceaseless concentrated insight, where the thought of the body is naught, that immovable Self is realized. Then, wheresoever that lucidly aware mind wanders, it is There, only There, in that primeval Abode. It is There, only There, in the Supreme Brahman, and abides There like everywhere else.'"*

Study well, in the sacred art of *Svadhyaya*,

## Lesson Sixty-two, 6/16/11
### Pada III, Sutra 5 & 6

We are presently abiding in between the two dharma visits of Spring and Summer, with the Summer retreat on the American River fast approaching. Further, and of interest to all who take Raja Yoga seriously, we are about to give a retreat here in Hawaii on the Eight-Limbed Yoga (June 23rd through 25th), focusing on its practice, and using some 14 charts created specifically for that darshana.

As far as our location in the sutras, we have recently broached the third pada (of four, total) and are presently taking in Patanjali's astute declarations regarding the uppermost limbs of Yoga, accompanied by Vedavyasa's ongoing commentary, as well as Swami Vivekananda's Raja Yoga text. Wonderfully, people — including youth and teens — are always joining the course, so you should be seeing questions from other quarters in the lessons which follow.

The few questions that have come in are listed first, just below, ushering us into the atmosphere of spiritual practice and leading "omwards" into the sutras themselves.

**Questions and Answers for Lesson 62**
D.H. from Pennsylvania writes:
QUESTION: "Here is a question on ajativada, or non-origination. To date, I have been understanding this to mean that existence is without beginning, in the causal sense. I've been thinking, in other words, that the term refers to the idea that we can never find a first cause for anything because anything caused will itself have been caused (and so on, back and back), and thus, existence, while in fact existing, nevertheless has no beginning, or no origin. Now I am questioning if this is what ajativada means. I've been thinking that ajativada might instead refer to the beginninglessness of Atman-Brahman (rather than the beginninglessness of the phenomenal world composed of the twenty-four principles); and I have been thinking that aparinama (the doctrine that ajativada so often gets paired with), perhaps puts the phenomenal world into a perspective acceptable to Advaita by denying and illustrating its unreality, or by at least illustrating that it is not real in the way we think it is and, ultimately, that it is only Atman-Brahman too. How close am I to understanding these doctrines? And where (if anywhere) does my first idea fit — namely, the idea that existence is non-originated in the sense of having no first cause?"
ANSWER: All of what you say here is rightly put, and rightly understood. And there is more. Ajativada, or nonorigination (no birth, no death; no creation, no

destruction) refers to both the Soul and Nature; all is unborn. This is the conclusion of the Upanisads, and of Sri Krishna in the Bhagavad Gita. Thus, all is Brahman. The only distinction to make, for that discriminating seeker wanting to avoid mental delusion forever, is that the Soul is Sentient while Nature is not. To put it in the pre-Vedantic (before the upanisadic era) language of the rishis, Brahman/Atman is the Unchanging Reality, while Mind (Antakarana/Nature) is the changing Reality.

Another helpful siddhanta (philosophical conclusion) to draw is that Nature has come out of the Antahkarana, or Great Mind (Mahat) via its projecting power. For, if one moves to perform the necessary negation at one phase of its understanding and, either out of ignorance, oversight, or aversion, excludes the world from the picture, then the world becomes not just "unreal" (which in Vedantic language means changing), but completely illusory. This will not do, for the Soul/souls have a relationship with Nature which is important to mental development — even if such be only a type of Lila, or sporting (sporting is different than dreaming, by the way).

And here is where aparinama enters into the picture. There is no transformation, i.e., change is not possible in Brahman; It is Immutable, perfect as It is. And so, the change one sees, or any transformation that one witnesses, is 1) occurring only in nature (mind + maya + the projecting power), and 2) is all apparent only. This is the double downwards-spiraling helix of maya, which as Sri Krishna says, is very difficult to pierce through. Stroke one of maya is this constant flux and change. Stroke two is that all change is nonactual, apparent only. Due to this dual deluding power (avarana/vikshepa) of maya, beings get stultified.

But maya has more confusion to visit on the mind. There is a third stroke, and it occurs to those beings who, unwilling to give up and give in to stultification, press on and try to find answers. For these adamantine souls, maya comes to be considered as being unreal itself (big mistake), and all and sundry is then thrown away in the rush for complete renunciation of the world, of name and form.

But how can this be? Maya, as defined by the knowers of Brahman (they have seen through maya because they have arrived and now dwell in Brahman), is neither real, nor unreal, nor a combination of both. As Vivekananda has put it in this day and age, maya is a "statement of fact." Only in Nirvikalpa (Asamprajnata) does maya disappear, does name and form cease to insinuate itself. And even here it does not go away completely, for does not the law of ajativada which we just affirmed state that there is no creation and no destruction? Perhaps it is that the conjuring up of something out of nothing makes that assumed something impossible to destroy.

The defense for this triple stroke of maya on the heads of aspiring beings is consciously making the connection (now a reconnection in this day and age) between mind and nature; that is, that all of form, i.e., nature, has come out of the Great Mind, or out of the Word, if one prefers. What is meant by this is that, being spiritually informed, one can no longer live in a world divorced from nature, the self, all selves, and The Self. A fragmented existence is no existence at all. Nature is just my Self in an objectified and insentient state, brought to that condition by the fabricating power of my mind, of all minds, of the Great Mind. As the scientist, James Jeans, said towards the end of the previous century, and I paraphrase: "We studied nature for a long time, and to us it looked like a machine. But now, under deeper study, it begins to look more like a thought." Yes, a thought. And a thought must have its origin in a mind.

So, in an active and inward sadhana or spiritual discipline/practice, the soul must go beyond the material cause (food/body) and find the efficient cause (nature). Then it must go beyond the efficient cause (after making the necessary connection via meditation) and find the primordial cause (prana). After this, the next step is to uncover and explore the subtle cause, or mind. Along this inward trajectory all salient connections are to be made. If they are not, and only a cursory or an intellectual inspection is made, the real purpose of the inward journey gets frustrated. The result is atheism or nihilism, or science and its immature/premature conclusions — even fundamentalist religion which is not much more than a set of limitations and fallacies today. And beyond the subtle cause is the cosmic cause (maya and its laws), and then the remote cause (the Word), and finally the Causeless Cause — Brahman.

To summarize, maya's greatest trick is to convince beings that it does not exist. But unlike the Christian devil in this regard, just hanging out waiting to get you, maya in Vedanta and Tantra is indicated to be insentient. In short, there is no process outside oneself, and other than the doings of one's own mind, that can hamper or waylay you. Recognition of this, pratyabijna, is the thing needed. You created the dream, or illusion, and you are to awaken from it. The guru can slap you awake, but if you only want to fall back asleep, what can be done? You are the devil, then. God or maya does not need to send an external agent to torture the soul who is already expert at doing that to itself. So: *"Renounce the poison of renunciation; renounce the poison of non-renunciation. You are the nectar of Knowledge, homogenous Existence, like the Sky."*

Akshaya Bhakti from New England writes:
COMMENTS: "My mind has been returning again and again to the image of the peaceful hilltop residence above the city presented in Lesson 60. I love how it exemplifies what it is like to live in the world with the 'fresh perspective' of Truth. But especially, I have found it to be very helpful as a symbol of transcendence. Watching my 95 year-old mother deteriorate from the standpoint of attachment culled over our 63 devoted years together (in this lifetime alone!) is extremely painful. But when I am able to gain even a momentarily wide perspective from my 'residence' on the hill — that of the nature of earthly life for all creatures — I am immensely comforted. Now I just need to give up my 'home' in the city and only visit there when I want to, not being held a prisoner there by the reactions of my mind filled with its memories and fears."
QUESTION: "Could you please explain what it means to bring the external akasha inside? Although we have often been enjoined to envision the whole

body of our Ishtam, and there is even the practice where one 'builds' this image from the feet up. I find myself drawn so much to Sri Ramakrishna's compassionate face that I continually find this other difficult to do."

ANSWER: Sri Ramakrishna is that inner akasha, and It is already present in us. We only need to become more and more aware of it. The akasha (as we can see by the example of physical planets in space), can take on forms. Similarly, the subtle space within us can take forms, all at the behest of our own sweet will. The whole thing is, however, whether our will is truly sweet with wisdom or synthetically sweet with naive worldliness.

So speaking in terms of "bringing it" comes from the standpoint of practice, a necessary boon for all who are still working on mastering the mind and realizing the Atman. Yoga is all about practice. One may as well not bring nondualism into the picture there, except as the backdrop. Otherwise, one places nose to the grindstone and "works the plan," as Vivekananda has told us. The Atman may not need purification, but the mind — the source of re-embodiment — certainly does.

Throughout, we ought to remember Lord Vasishtha's teaching on the five akashas; that there is not only one akasha, that of physical space (that is the mistake of science), but several more subtler ones stacked atop one another, inward flowing, with specific types of diminishing particles all their own. These, clearly, form the "kingdom of heaven" within us. We must map them out, at least if we are to be knowers of Reality in all Its facets. Peace and Om.

QUESTION #2: "In Lesson 61, I appreciate all the quotations on meditation. In the one from the Sandilya Upanishad it says: 'Fixing the mind on the Atman, bringing the external akasha into the akasha of the heart.....' Could you please comment? I am trying to see Samyama in the light of actual practice. In Dharana, I have chosen my Ishta for the object of concentration as facilitated through japa and mantra. Then as my concentration on this 'object' lasts longer and longer, it will become Dhyana, until it becomes perfect and unbroken when it will then become Samadhi."

ANSWER: "Bringing the external akasha into the heart" refers to rendering all that is outside into the internal, and then transforming the internal into the eternal. External, internal, and eternal — it is a great triputi to meditate upon. As Shankara put it, *"Brahman is an indeterminable mass of pure, conscious Awareness. Thus, taking what is outside, and what is inside, render them both into one indivisible State. Then meditate upon the State, be content, and be free."*

QUESTION #3: "Since Samadhi apparently doesn't happen all at once, how do these various stages come about?"

ANSWER: Usually, and as we have been seeing in the Yoga sutras, it all begins with wisdom samadhi in its two forms — with outer thought (savitarka) and with inner thought (savichara). This leads to samadhis of bliss, called sananda. Then comes sasmita, where the final sense of separate I-ness is released and the I-am takes its place. All of these are "seeded" samadhis. "Seedless" samadhi comes about in increments following these, depending on the aspirant. This is a basic description.

To match up Yoga's description of the samadhis with our Vedanta teachings, Savitarka samadhi takes place on the levels of the annamayakosha and pranamayakosha. Savichara samadhi takes place on the level of the manamayakosha. Sananda samadhi takes place on the level of the buddhi, or vijnanamayakosha. Sasmita samadhi takes place on the level of the anandamayakosha. Thus, these samadhis are spread out across the three bodies called gross (stula), subtle (sukshma), and causal (karana). Seedless samadhi, Asamprajnata, transcends the five sheaths and the triple body.

QUESTION #4: "In my sadhana I want to incorporate as much as I can of our Raja Yoga teachings, but still find it hard to synthesize it all. By the time one has reached these last 3 steps of Yoga, is one still having to direct one's mind, or will it continue to 'go forward' (as the guru advises us) on its own? It seems by this point that the contemplation stage will have been fulfilled and one will be maintaining the same 'object,' such as the Ishta, even though it will become more and more subtle."

ANSWER: Sri Ramakrishna tells the story of the sailor who puts out to sea, and just several miles offshore is hit by a great storm. He strikes the sails and bails water for his very life, exerting strenuously. But soon the clouds part, the moon comes out, and the winds blow favorably. He then trims his sails, puts the rudder on automatic pilot, and sits back with his pipe to enjoy a smoke while gazing at the stars. The entire gist of the story goes to describe how spiritual life is all effort in the beginning, and that one has to "bail water" to stay alive. But after the teachings are learned and meditation has been performed, all becoming second nature, as it were, the aspirant can "go forward" as you say here, without trouble, most naturally.

QUESTION #5: "Would this be like experiencing the stages of the Word and akin to fulfilling the last 3/4ths of the mantra, the first being given by the guru at the time of initiation?"

ANSWER: The mantra plays a tremendous role in early spiritual striving, acting as both protection and inspiration while the sadhaka fulfills all the preliminary requirements. It then transforms into ambrosial nectar, bubbling up spontaneously in the atmosphere of natural practice as ongoing insight and realization. So, yes, I think you can make this correlation.

S.C. from Hawaii writes:
QUESTION: "I am grateful for the lessons I've learned in this class about meditation not being a ritual, but coming naturally as part of life. Worship has always confused me, but now I'm seeing it as gratitude. Thank you. What is yaksha? Prag-bara?"

ANSWER: When the Westerner — either uninformed about the nature of true worship (deification, not idol-worship), or tired of old, tired ritual — comes to appreciate it, even through the auspice of another tradition, it is a great moment. Thank you for undertaking the effort to gain such realization. As for Prag-bara, the term infers a dam, or a damming up of a flow. Thus, *kaivalya prag-bara* would suggest a damming up of the river of return to earthly life in the physical world. This is a good thing. Conversely, *samsara prag-bara* would refer to a dam that restricts souls from transcending the physical worlds, thus keeping them in the downward flow of impure prana that returns to the embodied state. This, except for in the case of the realized souls, is not usually a good thing.

The word *yaksha* refers to a being of semi-divine status. Such a being has some divine powers, and is usually nonviolent. But the reason it is not fully divine has to do with its attachment to wealth. Some of the wealthy persons of this world were probably drawn from the realm of the yakshas, just as many others have come from the loka of the ancestors.

C.S. from Canada writes:
QUESTION: "I think I have a pretty good understanding of the information covered in the chapter, First Steps, and your elucidations helped, of course. One thing I wonder: Swamiji writes about exercise and diet, saying we have to keep the body fit and take care of what we eat and drink. Then, in his writing, and in yours, if I understand it correctly, he says don't pay any attention to these things. Just say before meditation, 'I have a strong mind and a strong body, and that is all.' Is this correct? I can't remember exactly where I read it, but in another of his writings I recall he did encourage physical fitness, but only as a means to keep the body fit so that physical problems did not distract one from one's spiritual work. Can you comment please?"
COMMENTS: Swamiji placed some emphasis on physical health, since he knew that a weak body was a hindrance to the austerities one needs to undertake in order to follow the spiritual path. He and Rakhal (Sw. Brahmananda) used to wrestle in school. And seeing the weakness of the Hindu person, he wanted them all to engage in some sort of exercise, and better eating habits. But you are right, and it is correct, that all of this is for the sake of spirituality, not for the sake of health in and of itself. For we have seen, and are seeing even today, that people may become healthy human beings but ever fail to realize their divine nature. This problem is noticed glaringly in the definition of "Wholistic Health" that "experts" put forth today, wherein not a mention of spiritual practice is noted or included. There is not even much of mental health mentioned, particularly by the supreme method of purification.

Yet the fact remains that all diseases and illnesses come from the mind, not from nature. Since nature came from the mind, then so does all that nature manifests and expresses. This is why Lord Vasishtha has said that reincarnation is the first and main disease. He follows, that only discriminating wisdom will help a soul waylay the onslaught of disease in the embodied condition. This is why the yogis live long if they wish, and are not plagued much by suffering and illness. If in their mind there is a disease-resisting samskara, then so too, in their brain and body there will be a gene that resists contracting disease. They have mastered the mind, while others have not. How can the body, which proceeded from the mind's projecting power, be plagued with disease if the mind that projected it is pure? Thus, in the West, we need to look into the mind first, and into its unwise and ongoing dalliance with karma and reincarnation to find the ultimate solutions for questions which, otherwise, have none.

Sutras III:5 and III:6 are now taken up for study, both dealing with the superlative subject of Samyama.

**Pada III, Sutra 5**
*tajjayat prajnalokah* (*tad,* that; *jayat,* victory; *prajna,* living intelligence; *lokah,* appears).

*"By gaining victory over that, living intelligence appears within the adept yogi."*

We have heard in the Vedic slokas that mankind is led from lower truth to higher truth. This is true of aparavidya, and it is also true of Paravidya. That is, just as one must proceed to gain knowledge, then wisdom, so too should wisdom be exquisitely refined into direct spiritual experience. This is the *"sublime sweetness of sublimation."* As Sri Ramakrishna said, *"The more you boil sugar-cane juice, the more refined it becomes. First it is sugarcane juice, then molasses, then sugar, and finally it becomes sugar candy."* This analogy applies well with regard to the refined tool of Samyama. Another commentary, from my anthology of Sri Ramakrishna Stories *(An Extensive Anthology of Sri Ramakrishna's Stories)*, explains this:

*"At the outset, the awakening devotee of the Lord is like 'sugarcane,' which has to be squeezed energetically to acquire the sweet juice of aspiration while shedding the sheaths of gross attachment and desire for the world. Then, a thickening naturally occurs, and the 'cane juice' of intensified aspiration transmutes into the 'molasses' of substantial attainment of spiritual qualities. Later, when these qualities have multiplied and have become established in the inner being of the devotee, the 'sugar' of Self-realization is formed, and spiritual transformation has successfully taken place. This is an extremely auspicious moment in the evolution of the embodied being, often occurring over many lifetimes, and it signals the breaking apart of the mind's limiting concepts and complexes. To quote Swami Vivekananda's description of this process:*

*'Always discriminate that your body, your house, these jivas, and the world are all absolutely unreal like a dream. Always think that this body is only an inert instrument. And the self-contained Purusha within is your real nature. The adjunct of mind is His first and subtle covering. Then, there is this body which is His gross, outer covering. The indivisible, changeless, self-effulgent Purusha is lying hidden under these delusive veils, therefore your real nature is unknown to you. The direction of the mind which always runs after the senses has to be turned within. The mind has to be killed. The body is but gross — it dies and dissolves into the five elements. But the bundle of mental impressions, which is the mind, does not die soon. It remains for some time in seed-form and then sprouts and grows like the form of a tree — it takes on another physical body and goes the round of birth and death until Self-knowledge arises.'"*

The present sutra's meanings are all wound up in teachings such as these. The need for refining one's knowledge, the press towards gaining the seeded samadhis, and the ability to burn the seeds of the mind that are causing resistance to gaining the "seedless state," are all of great import to the ensuing stages of Yoga. But there are obstacles to this great attainment.

If we look back at earlier sutras, which the onset of more students joining this ongoing study is facilitating for us, we see that the first five limbs of Yoga have all been refined in order to procure this yogic tool called Samyama. In Pada II:5, Vedavyasa gives the suggestion of what stands in the way to yogic attainment of the highest kind, mainly avidya, and the commentators of Yoga were not long in expanding on this suggestion.

Basically, the klesha of avidya, ignorance of our true nature, has a fourfold strata. In a rather Vedic turn of teaching, we find that these four cross-sections of avidya consist of 1) beings fooling themselves into thinking that what is transitory is really eternal; 2) beings always moving deceptively to replace what is pure and perfect with what is impure; 3) beings constantly seeking that which is the cause of suffering, thinking it to be the cause of happiness; 4) beings persistently taking the unreal for the real, the physical world for the spiritual Atman. This is the meaning of the sutra which reads, *antiya ashuchi duhkha anatmasu nitya shuchi sukha atman khyatih avidya.* Given that this is the nature of our ignorance, plainly put, it is easy to understand why we need a refinement process for the mind, and why the seers prescribe sadhana for the earnest seeker striving to get rid of suffering and attain samadhi. Others, less aware, remain clueless as to the tendencies of the misguided mind in maya. As Panchashikha says, *"Rejoicing at the growth of his own presumed entity-hood, a man thinks gleefully of his body and senses, believing them to be himself. And when they diminish and wane, he grieves, thinking that he diminishes and wanes. Every person who thinks and broods in this wise is unenlightened as to his true nature."*

In this most worthy of efforts towards refinement, Samyama is king, since it combines the three already practiced and refined yogic elements of concentration, meditation, and samadhi. And how does this rarefied combining, this sagacious integration take place? By avasthas, or stages.

**Pada III, Sutra 6**
*tasya bhumishu viniyogah* (*tasya,* this; *bhumishu,* via levels; *viniyogah,* application).

*"The application of this should proceed via succeeding levels."*

The artform of teaching by way of avasthas, or stages, is one that is rare and seldom seen in the one-size-fits-all religious climate of the world of today. The yogi or yogini who learns the art of samyama can then act as a guide for others, no matter what level each individual is operating on. Each soul is brought to the next stage of its spiritual evolution adeptly through its far-seeing structure.

The acquisition of samyama, however, is a very elevated attainment. There is scarcely any higher. This is why, to ensure that complete mastery of it is gained, the aspirant who climbs the eight-limbed tree of Yoga must undergo intense scrutiny over a succession of levels. Samadhi alone will not suffice. This is more than self-inquiry, called atma vichara by the seers, which was undertaken by the soul seeking graduation from lower knowledge to higher wisdom. It is an examination of the most exquisite kind, performed by an adept master to ascertain whether the loftiest states of God-Consciousness have been secured. The criterion for such as this will be taken up in the forthcoming sutras, in lesson #63.

## Lesson Sixty-three, 8/8/11
### Pada III, Sutra 7 & 8

With the memorable summer retreat in Forest Hill along the American River now a part of the auspicious SRV past, we turn to our ongoing study of the Raja Yoga system. Recent lessons have been taken up with the consummate limbs and levels of Yoga concerning concentration, meditation, and samadhi — which we have seen are nearly impossible to separate from one another. A person who can concentrate the mind, even in secular matters, has satisfied the prerequisite criteria for early attempts at that most unique level of focus called spiritual concentration. From there the force of gathering consciousness will kick in, bringing with it both the desire and the ability to experience higher states of mind in meditation. This, in turn, will usher in the possibility for "seedless" samadhi, that long lost companion of the mind that has been pushed to the back of human awareness due to preoccupation with matters of momentary concern, superficial design, and worldliness. This lesson and its sutras bring in the subject of seedless samadhi, called Asamprajnata Samadhi, and sport a chart on the process leading up to it.

With the advent of contemplation on the recent sutras, questions have arisen in the mind of seekers, and been sent in for consideration and clarification. These begin this lesson below, to ready the mind for further study in this most important area of human endeavor.

**Questions and Answers for Lesson 63**
K.D. from Hawaii writes:
QUESTION: "I have a question about why Yama is the name for the basic moral principles of Patanjali's 8 limbs. I guess this is because one begins the process which results in death of the ego and the false sense of self?"
ANSWER: I have also thought in the past that the assignment of the word "yama" to the initial observances of Yoga has something to do with the death of the small self and its limiting habits. It is a natural thought to entertain. For a more basic definition of the word, however, we can look at its inference along the lines of restraint. To restrain the outgoing senses in an initial way, thereby doing away with weakness and bad habits, is the idea, which is a kind of death all its own — the death of the mind's penchant for brooding, falling out of awareness, and for entertaining vrittis (vibrations) of a negative and unproduc-

tive nature. So, yama is restraint in the early stages, for no one would be a yogi or a yogini without this ability to pull back, to resist, to deny the ego, mind, and senses what is not ultimately good for them, or not for their highest good in the end. It is in this vein that Sri Krishna tells Arjuna in the Gita that *"What is sweet in the beginning but sour in the end is undesirable (pleasure, etc.), and what is sour in the beginning but sweet in the end (sadhana, self-effort) is preferable."* May the devotees all recognize this distinction and begin to refine the mind with the help of positive restraints such as found among the yamas and niyamas.

S.C. from Hawaii writes:
QUESTION: "What does Kriyamani mean"?
ANSWER: Several definitions are to found to this profound term. In the area of karma, though, it is that type of cause and effect which springs up spontaneously, as if from nowhere, and spoils the seeker's otherwise gradual but uninterrupted rise to higher limbs of attainment in Yoga. Ramprasad, the poet/saint of Bengal, refers to it in one of his wisdom songs to Mother Kali when he sings: *"The little white beetles of desire are appearing on the walls and woodwork of the house of my mind, and I know not where they come from."* The phrase, "as if from nowhere," refers to a kind of karma which does not seem to have any cause, unlike prarabdha, the presently operative karma, which is obviously the effect of past karma, called sanchita.

But kriyamani does have a cause. It is its own cause. That is, as a type, it is fueled by actions of the same nature from past lifetimes. In other words, worry and fear-based thinking is a habit unto itself, and creates an environment in the mind which produces a tendency of mind conducive to that mindset only, and which habitually conjures up and casts forth random effects spontaneously. In this day and time it has been referred to as "putting out fires," the result of which takes the seeker away from cancelling out prarabdha karma which should be dispensed with, first and foremost. Thus, kriyamani karma is directly responsible for waylaying the seeker from matters pertinent to and necessary for the fulfillment of life's main purposes. The old tired mantra, "I will get to that later," or "It will all happen in its own sweet time," is the utterance of those stymied by kriyamani's flummoxing presence. Ending this tendency of the mind will therefore be required in order for the aspirant to live a life of uninterrupted commitment to realization and its requisites.

QUESTION #2: "In the realm of ancestors, don't those beings reincarnate, and so no longer dwell there?"
ANSWER: Just as limited human consciousness (transmigrating souls) moves from one level of awareness to another, like from waking to dreaming, so too do human beings and their ancestors exchange places from life to life, all without going anywhere. They are locked into such cycles for many lifetimes, and in a predestined way. Only the force of awakening to higher awareness, and the acquisition of a spiritual practice that helps one to transcend such cycles, are effective in removing the transmigrating soul's penchant for rebirth in such

realms. It is all "third chakra" specific, as Kundalini Yoga would explain. This means the manipura chakra correlative with the center at the level of the stomach. Reincarnating beings, in the form of prana carried mind-stuff, are passing in and out of this center at the time of birth and death. Physically speaking, eating, digestion, conception, pregnancy, and desire for progeny, gravitate and transpire in this area. Humans and ancestors all hold this level as a collective consciousness, and hold on to it as well. This is seen by certain cultures, nay, even whole countries, whose denizens worship the ancestors specifically, even to the exclusion of all other levels of existence (i.e., celestials, gods/goddesses, seers/sages, and the Trinity), which are at once higher and deeper levels.

The phrase above, "prana carried mind-stuff," is worthy of further examination as well. The esoteric systems of India and Tibet describe the twin inward movements of exiting and entering the body by citing the soul's creation of a pranic bubble, in this case the third chakra called manipura, into which the unresolved contents of the mind are emptied at the time of the body's demise. This is an unseen projection, and on a different level of existence than the physical, extending out of the chakra or spiritual center there. This pranic bubble containing the transmigrating soul, or mind/ego complex, then attends upon the realm of the ancestors (roughly equivalent with heaven in the Christian tradition, only divided into lower, middling, and higher heavens) for a time, and then searches for hosts, or parents, when its unresolved karmas from previous existences bring it earthward again.

Needless to say, illumined souls do not undergo this process, with its contrasting feelings of pleasure and pain, formulation and dissolution, and exit from the higher chakras correlative with the levels of awareness at the heart, throat, third eye, and crown (anahata, vishuddha, ajna, and sahasrara) chakras. These beings, meditating all their lives upon transcendent verities such as deities, illumined souls, the Trinity, or the Light of Consciousness (the Formless Brahman), go to the realms which correlate with subtler forms and truths. Thus, beings caught up in the maya of conventional thinking, intellectualism, and moral and ethical codes devoid of higher wisdom tend towards life in relativity, thus reincarnation. For the luminary, reincarnation is a relative law only, and they know the real Soul, Atman, to be motionless and eternally stable — "all-pervasive' is a good term in English.

Therefore, reincarnation "happens" to those whose minds play into the illusion (dream) of transmigration, and whose actions and thinking process gravitate to the realm of time, space, and causation, foregoing the higher wisdom of the eternal Soul as the witness of all phenomena in maya.

QUESTION #3: "Would you say more about how one can resist desires rather than repressing them, and more about how that relates to transcending time?"

ANSWER: Basically, and what it relates, is that to attempt to satisfy, satiate, or repress desire is both futile and dangerous, at least until a life of dharma and its valuable precepts are undertaken, understood, and practiced. The wheel of misguided existence, conventional existence, and moral existence continue to rotate until higher understanding dawns. And this dawning involves getting oneself off of the wheel of ordinary life by means of committing to spiritual vows and precepts which make the soul healthy once again, removing the confusion and delusion which worldly life generates continually, even life to life. Vows and precepts are also transcended, once learned, and the cutting edge of spiritual practice is resorted to. The difference between salvation and liberation begins here, thus the possibility for enlightenment.

In brief, desire has two modes: one that binds, and another that leads towards dispassion. The passion in desire is therefore not negative only, but can and should be utilized for engendering energy for higher aspirations. Rooting out desire is generally not recommended by the wise, then, at least not for souls who have, as yet, not developed real strength in them. A gradual transcendence is better. And as for the transcendence of time, that is left for an ability that matures much later in spiritual life than that of removing desire. Called kalatita, it is more associated with the recognition of the illusoriness of time in keeping with seeing it as a cosmic law in all its phases.

Akshaya Bhakti from New England writes:
COMMENTS: "'Sri Ramakrishna is the inner akasha, and It is already present in us....' I felt a surge of joy in hearing this reply to my question, because it reaffirmed that all manner of spiritual fulfillment can be found in Him. I am growing in my understanding that He must ultimately be experienced on successively subtle levels (going beyond His physical form all the way to the eternal Atman). This awareness was deepened by the correlation of the 5 koshas to the levels of samadhi."
QUESTION: "He has told us that He would be available in his subtle body for 300 years after his passing from the physical body. Could you please discuss this and how it might fit into the discussion of samadhi?"
ANSWER: For those who attain samadhi, at least in its deepest or nondual form (asamprajnata), all akashas are already transcended. An illumined soul could "come down" to akashic levels, no doubt, but the formless essence that resides so completely in Avatars like Sri Ramakrishna would be fully present beyond their forms, and totally accessible there.

But for those who are waiting, as it were, for the vision of Ramakrishna in form, in meditation, or by His grace, are necessarily abiding in the relative atmospheres, or akashas, and are working out karmas that are only like personally constructed veils in the way of such visions or qualities. No doubt, as well, that the Great Master, like Jesus and Buddha, will be available even after a 300 year period for those sincere souls who have deep connections with Him. It is more that those who really need Him will benefit from meditation upon Him, and devotion to Him, even though great luminaries like Vivekananda and others sought Him out as well. From the loftiest to the most sinful, all will take refuge in this incomparable being, and any akasha that they temporarily inhabit will vibrate with a singular transformative power capable of turning transgression into truth.
COMMENTS 2: "In another part of the reply it is explained that 'one may as

well not bring non-dualism into the picture there except as the backdrop, otherwise one places nose to the grindstone and works the plan.' If I understand this correctly, this means that it is easier to achieve liberation by recognizing Ishvara (as opposed to non-dualism) as we had discussed in one of the beginning lessons. But I am not sure what Swami Vivekananda means by 'work the plan.' Honestly, regarding elucidation of the states of samadhi, I don't think that Lesson 16, Sutra 15 can be much expanded upon, since the various stages are so beautifully detailed there. But although I know I still need to exert much more effort in preparation for experiencing samadhi on the intellectual level, I am greedy to hear as much as I can about this awesome, yet natural state. Under savitarka for example, that lesson states that 'this concentration on the material principles is not on the objective world with its external forms, but relates to vrittis to be controlled which exist in the sentient personality, to be mastered within the mind.' I was excited to come across this category of samadhi as I was reading the English version of the *Lila Prasanga,* where Sri Ramakrishna's experience of the cranes against the dark cloud is denoted as savitarka."

QUESTION #3: "Could you please discuss this samadhi that He had at such a young age and also give some examples of these lower levels of samadhi in ordinary devotees, since you once previously mentioned that some beings may have experienced samadhi without even realizing it?"

ANSWER: First of all, the statement of "work the plan" by Swamiji refers to a regimen of action to be done in this world around awakening others to divine Reality, not only ourselves. But as they say on the airlines nowadays, "Kindly put your own oxygen mask on first before helping others." So we must be especially sure that ignorance has died in us before attempting to help on levels of awareness that are beyond acts of altruism and the like. Once this is accomplished via guru, path, and practice, all over a long and dedicated time free of betrayal of such boons, then we can effectively work the plan. Service of God in mankind is the mainstay here, at whatever level each individual is presently operating on, or failing to operate on, as the case may be.

    As to your second query, and the desire to know more, the actual experience of the various levels of samadhi, as outlined marvelously by Lord Patanjali, is enjoined on every seeker. Even advaitans such as Shankara advise the "practice of samadhi" until the nondual experience dawns. Sri Ramakrishna's version of this advice comes in the story of the man who sees a bowl of wax fruit across the room and gets hungry at the sight. Crossing the room to secure a piece of fruit, he finds that they are mere wax representations of the real articles. However, they do inspire him to go to the store to procure the actual items. In like manner the seeker after higher limbs of Yoga — especially those ones who have studied and installed the yamas and niyamas, mastered their posture, and controlled the prana via pure food, mantra, and breathing exercises — is to assume the station of samadhi in order to attract it to the mind, or the mind to it. This is because samadhi is the natural state of one's (original) mind, whereas every state that occurs prior to it has involved some kind of fall into shades of mental conditioning, i.e., sankalpa/vikalpa (dream-based existence), brooding on sense objects (fear-based existence), or the study of relative truths only (secular-based existence).

As far as a description of Sri Ramakrishna's samadhi of the cranes is concerned, to understand it is to comprehend that the consciousness of the man/boy was in a refined state, not that anything in nature was directly responsible. Anything, even the brushing of one's teeth, as they say, is grounds for samadhi. It all depends on the condition of one's consciousness. This is where the metaphor of contemplating a lotus comes from. It is not the lotus that inspires samadhi, nor its contemplation; those are objects, acts, and experiences. Samadhi is not a result of any of these. People have been attributing samadhi to experiences, and vice versa, ever since philosophical systems were presented by the seers in earliest times in India. This overlooks the fact that the mind is in samadhi (or not) to begin with, and as a result, every little thing and every object around one is seen in samadhi's incomparable light. In other words, samadhi is not something that happens to the seeker, nor anything that the seeker strives to make happen. It is the natural state of one's intrinsic Awareness entered into when all obstructions are finally done away with — including the barrier of experience seeking. This is why Patanjali, when listing the four main obstacles to Yoga, includes the seeking of bliss as the subtlest of all of them. It is also why Sananda samadhi must be transcended in order for the mind to move from the seeded samadhis to the singular Unseeded Samadhi — Asamprajnata.

Having emphasized this, we can look at the samadhi that "comes" to ordinary people unasked. Unlike natural samadhi, sometimes called *sahaja,* this inkling of higher experience is not without cause. The cause is a change in the gunas resulting in a sattvic condition of mind, combined with a sudden lapse in the manifesting power of mental samskaras and an equally sudden but temporary absence of the force of cycles of karmas from past lives (sanchita). Left in such a state, the great Light dawns in the mind, and people are amazed. It is like the great, complex clock with many gears in Kolkata that Sri Ramakrishna mentioned, that lines up once a year for one day only and allows the fortunate onlookers who are present to see right through the entire mechanism. The problem with such samadhis is that they pass. They cannot be held, due to the return of gunas, samskaras, and karmas, and all that comes with them. As is often mentioned, the phone rings, the boss fires you, and the old mindset returns again, fraught with brooding. Thus, the samadhi vanishes, "poof!"

C.S. from Canada writes:
QUESTION: "This lesson about Prana has had me consider everything from the perspective of prana and akasa. Is it correct that emotion is akasa and the ability to feel emotion is prana? Or is feeling also akasa. Is there only one level of prana, and lower and higher levels of akasa?"
ANSWER: Feeling and emotion do not define prana and akasha, simply because prana and akasha are insentient. They do not "shine by their own

light," as the Upanisadic mantra says, but depend on other principles for their existence, flow, and appearance.

As far as their forms and enumerations go, prana is one, but appears in five forms. Akasha, too, has five forms or main levels: one that supports physical beings, one that supports heaven (celestials/ancestors), one that supports the mind, one that supports intelligence, and one that is purely spiritual. These are named Bhutakasha, Pranakasha, Manakasha/Chittakasha, Jnanakasha, and Chidakasha, respectively. Each is made of a subtler and subtler particle, so that there is no need or real sense to accounting for the physical particle (atom) alone and leaving out particles made of life force, thought, intelligence, etc. If this oversight is committed, the result is materialism, and a society or world of beings who have lost connection to the many internal worlds within them. Just as there are a host of unseen micro-organisms on the physical level, so too are there hosts of beings in worlds and lokas much too fine to measure with mere nanometer technology. The world of quantum physics will apply only on the physical level, then, while the real sense and meaning, and the true workings of the "grander scheme of things" will be perceived and known through the auspice and impetus of inner life.

For instance, when Jesus saw his future disciples living along the river and fishing for their survival, he told them that they had wives, children, boats, nets, a river, and fish to catch, but that they were missing one thing: an inner life. Having learned this, they became fishers of men, and became qualified to awaken others to the hazy presence of worldliness, from the thraldom of maya. Such awakening is what contemporary people are missing as well, and a start can be made by looking into the ancient wisdom and taking note of the observations and realizations noted there. The five akashas and the fivefold prana are keys to this deeper awakening, as they are not accounted for in any of our knowledge systems — which is precisely why the West has to go to the East for real Wisdom, rather than mechanical technological knowledge. The main gaps in western thinking impinge upon mankind's lack of clarity around the phenomena of birth and death, and the beginningless and endless nature of existence — Reincarnation and Eternity. The third main axiom, called the nontransformational nature of Consciousness, must also be listed, but it will take some time for this to be seen and accepted, partly because these two lynch-pins of prana and akasha, once they are known, are seen to flow and change constantly. This movement will flummox the mind of the observer and cause premature conclusions, such as life force is God, space is God, time is God, etc. In other words, the changeless nature of Reality and the immutable Essence of Consciousness will, once again, get overlooked in the awe that is caused by the discovery of "new" things. Only practices such as meditation, once undertaken and adhered to for some time, will ground the soul, alternating its perspective from the shifting sands of maya to the bedrock of Spirit until the stable and all-pervasive Being is perceived.

A final word about prana is that it is a most chameleon-like principle. Starting out as the gross energy in food, and the moving power in body and nature, it transforms at deeper levels of man's existence into the power which causes the senses to function, the force that carries thoughts (upwards or downwards, as the case may be), and the superlative dynamism of shakti itself. At a most refined level it can hardly be recognized as anything other or separate from Kundalini. Thus, it is Divine Mother's own power of intelligence, flowing from on high and on down into the regions of solidity, liquidity, radiance, homogeneity, and all-pervasiveness (earth, water, fire, air, and ether). But at the level where most beings encounter it, most of them unconscious of the fact and of its existence, it is just energy from food. But *"Man does not live by bread alone."*

Sutras III:7 and III:8 are now taken up for study.

**Pada III, Sutra 7**
*trayam antar angam purvebhyah* (*trayam,* these three; *antar,* internal; *angam,* limbs; *purvebhyah,* prior).

*"The three limbs (of concentration, meditation, and samadhi) are more subtle than all those previous."*

When the earlier or preceding limbs of yama, niyama, asana, pranayam, and pratyahara, have been well mastered, to a degree that is as thorough as the aspirant can attain, the upper limbs of Yoga become accessible to the avid practitioner. This is the practice stage par excellence. All these prior stages and their practices were underpinnings, preparing the aspiring yogi for spiritual heights yet to come.

Spiritual life is one of subtlest, or as Swami Vivekananda states in his commentary on an earlier sutra, the meditations at this level are of gross, grosser, grossest, and fine, finer, finest. So are the samadhis which attend them. And as the next sutra states, the subtle nature of this lofty level is nothing compared to that of the singular seedless samadhi the adept is leading up to.

The commentators all agree that having the seeded level of samadhis only — savichara, savitarka, sasmita, and sananda — leaves a risk of, as Vivekananda puts it, *"getting more bodies."* Only asamprajnata removes the mind's samskaras, leaving only samskaras of samadhi in its superlative wake. It is no wonder, then, and easy to see, how pure the minds of great beings are filled with Light when they return to earth under the auspice of awakening others. Since the fuel of karma is only combustible here on earth, these souls must have had a pure mind before they left their previous body. Thus, there exist ever-perfect souls (nitya-siddhas) like Vivekananda, past masters, newly awakened masters, still striving advanced yogis, those in the state of early awakening, those caught in cycles of reincarnation amongst the endless sea of ancestors and human beings, those bound into cycles in outright ignorance, and those lost in worlds of seemingly endless suffering.

And through them all exists the eternal perfection which never changes or alters its essential nature. As Lord Buddha put it, and much more simply, there are those who have fully awakened to Buddha nature, and those who have not yet awakened.

**Pada III, Sutra 8**
*tad api bahir angam nirbijasya* (*tad,* these; *api,* comparatively; *bahir,* external; *angam,* limbs; *nirbijasya,* seedless samadhi).

*"Yet, even these three lack subtlety compared to seedless samadhi."*

In the preceding samadhis, those of a seeded nature, the world still persists, along with all the powers that bring it into being. But similar to deep sleep where all form, all thought, all sense of separation, ceases, the seedless samadhi, also called Nirbija, sweeps away all thoughts of the universe and the accompanying powers that help the mind project it. Other powerful words pertinent to Yoga and Vedanta attend upon this nondual atmosphere, like Nirvasana (freedom from desires), Nirvikalpa (the end of time and its phases and activities). and Mahanidra (the great sleep). Overall, it is indescribable, and so must be entered into after satisfying all the demands and qualification that a yogi undertakes along the great path inwards towards Enlightenment. "Along the great path inwards" is what the chart on the facing page is all about, which will aid us all in seeing and noting facets of samprajnata and Asamprajnata, alike.

# Lesson Sixty-four, 9/20/11
## Pada III, Sutra 9 & 10

Greetings to the entire Raja Yoga list from Nepal, where myself and eight SRV students are presently spending two weeks or more near the "Great Snow Mountains" hallowed by the footfalls of many divinities. This is a fine place from which to present the teachings of Patanjali, the systematizer of the rare and honorable Yoga, which only introduces itself to the sincere seeker after hundreds of well-lived lives. Therefore we can consider ourselves most fortunate, and the dawning of this lifetime particularly auspicious wherein we have both interest in Yoga's timeless tenets, and the will to engage in its ongoing practice leading to enlightenment.

The questions which some of you have sent in reflect these two ingredients: a well-directed life, and a dharmic existence. And we shall take them up prior to the contemplation of two powerful sutras of the third pada presently under study.

**Questions and Answers for Lesson 64**
K.D. from Hawaii writes:
COMMENTS: "I enjoyed yesterday's class and feel gratitude for continuing access to this most intriguing body of knowledge, and your expertise and deep understanding and dedication to imparting this knowledge to bring about purity of the mind, body, and spirit."
QUESTION: "In Lesson 16, in the section on Sasmita samadhi, you discuss the I-sense, the ego sense. I assume this is the fully matured ego which has become transparent, since it only functions to give the soul a vehicle in which to navigate the world of relativity. Is that right? Then the ego, ahamkara, dissolves

# The Process of Samprajnata to Asamprajnata Samadhi

*"In the mind's move towards unification it must meditate on the alambanas, the 24 states of matter, until it reaches the seedless samadhi."* Lord Patanjali

## Savitarka Samadhi

- Concentration on the gross Alambanas, including Virat and the 16 Visheshas →
  * On the nature and order of their origins
  * On their appearances in time and mind
  * On their positive and negative attributes
  * On their effects on the psyche and emotions
  * On the relationship between names, words, sounds, meanings, and objects
- Objects, the sense of perception, and the mind become more unified
- The hidden nature of the alambanas get revealed

> **The Sixteen Visheshas — Final Products of Nature**
> 5 cognitive senses
> (hearing, seeing, touching, tasting, smelling)
> 5 active senses
> (speaking, acting, moving, procreating, excreting)
> 5 gross elements (ether, air, fire, water, earth)
> 4-fold mind (ego, intellect, thoughts, mind)

## Savichara Samadhi

- Concentration on subtle Alambanas — 6 Avisheshas →
  * On the nature and order of their origins
  * On their appearances in time and mind, etc.
- The mind becomes concentration itself
- Expansion of the chitta awakens wisdom
- The nature of the object/principle is known
- Ego begins to be brought under control

> **The Six Avisheshas**
> The Five Tanmatras — Intermediate Links
> 1. Audibility
> 2. Visibility
> 3. Tangibility
> 4. Flavor
> 5. Odor
> Ahamkara — Individual Sense of I-ness
>
> *"Tanmatras are primal matter, the subtle elements out of which the gross elements are formed. They remain in an undifferentiated state before the quintuplication process takes place at the time of creation."*

## Sananda Samadhi

- Meditation upon subtle ahamkara and individual buddhi →
- The bliss of Sananda must be seen by the:
  * nature of its origin, appearance in time and mind, attributes
  * effects on the psyche and emotions, etc.
- The fount of personal joy is located and encountered
- Ego and senses are fully mastered; rajas and tamas are subdued
- Occult powers come as temptations; the true yogi resists them
- The sense of a separate I begins to reveal its limitations

> **Subtle Ahamkara**
> **Individual Buddhi**
>
> *"Having gained that which is considered the greatest gain, and wherein he is not shaken even by the heaviest affliction, let this bliss which is the disconnection from exposure to all pain be known by the name of Yoga."*
> Sri Krishna

## Sasmita Samadhi

- Meditation on Linga-matra — The Cosmic Mind →
- Ahamkara dissolves into mahat, the first evolute of prakrti
- Mahat/Buddhi perceives the presence of prakrti in itself
- Viveka-khyati reveals the separate nature of Buddhi and Purusha
- Mahat disregards all evolutes and reflects only Purusha
- Mahat fully dissolves into the Unmanifested — A-linga →
- Asmita is transcended and Kaivalya, the final break between spirit and matter, occurs
- Dharma-megha samadhi, the raincloud of virtues and the knowledge of all things, transpires
- Chiti-shakti emerges fully, revealing pure Existence, free of all conditions, evolutes, and processes

> **Linga-matra**
> Mahat — Universal Buddhi
>
> **A-linga**
> Prakrti — Unmanifested Nature

## Asamprajnata Samadhi

- Abides/meditates on the awareness of cessation — Mahanidra →
- Paravairagya has dawned  • In control of or void of all vrttis
- Contains only samskaras of samadhi  • Is Self dwelling in Self

> **Mahanidra — The Great Sleep**
> • Nir-bija, free of seeds of creation
> • Niralambana, needing no supports
> • Abhava, unconditioned existence

into Mahat, which meets Purusha here and only here. Since Mahat is the first evolute of prakriti, this is where prakriti meets purusha. This is hard for me to understand. Are you saying that the only time that the soul and nature, as the Cosmic Mind, meet, is in Sasmita Samadhi? Is the individual soul, the Atman, always completely separate from all aspects of nature? Surely it is unaffected by nature, but is it also completely separate? In Sasmita samadhi, does the individual I-sense experience the Mahat and the light reflected on the Buddhi for the first and only time? I know that is what you wrote, but I am asking for elaboration, since it is hard for me to actually formulate my question. I hope you get a sense of what I am asking."

ANSWER: There is no doubt that the entire sweep of the twenty-four cosmic principles provides a sort of meeting ground for Consciousness and Nature, Purusha and Prakriti. The main thing to keep in mind is that only Purusha is sentient, while nature is not (remember that in the "mind-only" schools of philosophy, nature comes out of the mental complex, not from a creator God). This is the reason for the division in Sankhya — for all divisions of this kind in Indian darshanas — so that the Soul can separate itself out (kaivalya) and see Itself, undistracted by objects and undiluted by various admixtures of all types. To a soul that has accomplished this essential extraction, and has seen and realized its own Sentiency, all of manifestation becomes a fit meeting place for Awareness and its evolutes. But to a soul that has not, the wisdom samadhis would represent the first time that any type of clear perception of this rare variety occurred. There may be glimpses early on over the long course of gradual awakening (krama mukti), but these do not have the compelling weight and liberating impetus — the maya penetrating force — that the wisdom samadhis confer on the mind, as they (these glimpses) only pass and are forgotten amidst a plethora of other experiences which take precedence in the everyday life of the human being.

Another point to keep in mind is that, ultimately, samadhi is not an experience. There is no separation or any sense of difference between Soul and Matter at the nondual level, where thought of the experiences and the Experiencer are absent. The nondual thread in the Indian darshanas makes sense out of all qualified and dualistic states and philosophies, and is their common and unbroken ground as well.

QUESTION #2: "My other question has to do with ego being the source of the tanmatras. What is this ego which can be the source of the subtle elements? It must be even more subtle, then. Is the individual sense of a separate self somehow so subtle that it is the source, ultimately, of the five gross elements, since the gross emanates out of the subtle?"

ANSWER: Ego, ahamkara, has it place and plays its role in the manifestation process, from the descent of tattvas on down to the formulation of the events of everyday life. It is not, as Westerners think of it, only the source of pompousness or degradation, pride or humility. These are just modes. As the fundamental sense of individual self, the separate "I-maker," ahamkara assists (via its mutual powers of projection) in both the trickle down process of subtle thoughtforms into gross worlds and objects, and the enjoyment of all that Cosmic Mind produces. Ahamkara also maintains the line of demarcation between God and mankind, Spirit and nature, creature and Creator until such a time when its limiting powers are seen through, penetrated, ripened, and discarded in lieu of higher experiences of a purely spiritual nature. Often, when it is ripe, it even adds impetus to this penetration, aiding the soul in realizing the Soul.

At the level you are speaking of, that of tanmatras and the elements, ahamkara acts as the synthesizer, the efficient coagulator of subtle and gross levels of existence, and rather like a glue or cement as well. Consciousness, of course, is the main integrator of all things, all experiences, but in Its absence (most beings are not aware of their own Consciousness on many levels) what else but the ego is going to act that part and facilitate that function? Thus, as one looks around the world with the fresh eyes of new awakening, one cannot help but notice the pervasive and insinuating (quite often malodorous) presence of the ego. It colors everything that worldly and conventional people do and say, and awakened persons welcome any encounter that is gained which is free of it. That is why the devotees seek out the holy company of guru, dharma, and sangha.

QUESTION #3: "You say that the yogi comes to experience the limiting nature of bliss and moves onto Sasmita samadhi where Mahat and Buddhi await. You wrote 'It is here that the agent of apprehension who oversees elements and objects, operates the subtle essences and is the perceiver of bliss that is enjoyed, is encountered.' Who is this 'agent of apprehension?' Can you elaborate on this sentence?"

ANSWER: It is the subtle or ripened ego. The immature ego is the separate I-maker and despoiler, but the ripened ego is the coordinator of experiences which involve the meeting of humankind with his/her own true nature. Thus, it plays its part in the confrontation of the small self with the Great Self. It also introduces the devotee to his or her Chosen Ideal, Ishvara/Ishvari, and with that encounter participates in its own slow death. Soon there will be nothing but a semblance of ego left in the mind, as is instanced so well by Sri Ramakrishna's life and samadhis in this day and age.

QUESTION #4: "I have comments and questions concerning my meditation on the alambanas. I was listening to this CD of primordial sounds and became very meditative with it. I experienced each sound emanating from the infinite ocean of consciousness, the unified field of Brahman. I was meditating on ether to reconcile it as a gross element. I felt like I was having an experience of the emanation of AUM as the first and most subtle vibration. I felt that I finally understood the meaning and significance of AUM as embodying the complete cycle of creation, preservation, and dissolution that sets the stage for the differentiation of all the other elements as a way for consciousness to experience itself. Sound, as the most subtle element, would come first since what is subtle creates what is gross. But then I thought it could not have been sound since there were no ears to hear it, and sound is not sound unless it is heard, sent to the brain which relays it to the mind which recognizes it and gives it significance. It was just a vibration. Am I on the right track? Is ether the first element to appear on the scene? How is ether substantially different from consciousness, since it is all-pervasive and limitless? Was my interpretation of AUM anywhere in the ballpark? I understand that there are entire upanishads written on AUM and that means it is a complex phenomenon. Can you simplify this complexity and explain the essence of the emergence of AUM, or explain if it is infinite like Brahman?"

ANSWER: In the conception, construction, maintenance, and dissolution process, it is AUM which acts as the hub, the matrix, for manifestation. Your comments on ether are also key in the process, especially where human beings and their level of existence are concerned. But ether and its connection does not depend solely on ears and hearing for its existence, and not even for its perception. One hears the Unstruck Sound long before the rest of "creation" gets expressed. The Tantracists say, *"No one sounds this primal vibration. It sounds Itself. It goes on vibrating eternally under its own inherent power and nature."* Therefore we see how God's Word is so crucial -- both for existence and for a fuller comprehension -- for the aspiring devotee.

As for ether being the first element on the scene, that is an understatement. Of course, if by "the scene" we mean the physical universe, this is true, but if we include in our scope the subtle universes, the "kingdoms of heaven within," then we might want to perceive ether's own subtler component, called all-pervasiveness. In this way it has much in common with Brahman or Pure Consciousness, the only shortcoming there being one of Sentiency.

FINAL COMMENTS: "I also had this real experience during this meditation of a Tibetan Buddhist monk appearing to me and beckoning me to follow the compassionate path. I communicated that I was too messed up and carrying too much sadness to go along. He then pulled open his robe and showed the immense suffering he had experienced in his life with the cruel invasion of China, the murder and torture of his people. He then closed his robe and indicated that I could follow. Interestingly enough, the next day I found a book entitled *The Tibetan Book on Living and Dying,* by Sogyal Rinpoche on my shelf, and found out that my friend had recently put it there. Well, I am almost finished reading it and it has been very helpful in realizing the "logic of compassion" and applying it to my life. I understand how Buddhism is Vedanta, though I was not really interested in the parts which explained the Buddhist cosmology/metaphysics in complex systems with new words that I have no interest in learning.....because Vedanta is complex enough."

RESPONSE: This is a very wonderful and beneficial experience, with many of the trappings (of a Buddhist monk) of spiritual evolution built into it. The call to service is also of great import. Expansion of capacity, forbearance, and the building of character — the real spirituality in this world — are also contained herein. I would indeed follow.

D.H. from Pennsylvania writes:
COMMENTS: "Your new book on reclaiming Kundalini is turning out to be

helpful to me beyond anything I could have expected. The extremely clear instructions on conscious eating, first of all, are serving well to resolve my lifelong difficulties with food. I wonder, at a deep level, what mukhyaprana really is, though. Is it something that is in food generally, which then passes out of our system unclaimed when we do not have the proper attitude toward food? I ask because I am truly amazed at the state of energized calm and balance that I can create in myself through blessing the food and eating consciously in a suitable environment, but above all, by simply remembering that food is a form of God arising through nature, or as I put it to myself, 'Annam is Brahman.' I remember this not only before meals, but also through them, and even for a little while after eating, and I can truly feel myself claiming something in food that I otherwise missed all this time. Obsessive eating, which has been a lingering problem for me in the area of self-control, is fading thanks to all of this.

"In regard to meditation (the practice of creating the meditative ekasana in my mind before I sit down, also described in your new book), and maintaining that through meditation if I see that it's fading, my posture now continues to come from the inside of me. This is wondrous. I see now that I was trying to impose asana on myself from the outside, and that was a mistake; it needs to come from the inside, with the body following and assuming its position almost as a shadow of what's in the mind. This makes meditation so much more comfortable and so much easier.

QUESTION: "In Raja Yoga lesson #52, there was the assignment of writing in to you about our favorite yama or niyama. My favorite yama, hands down, without a doubt, is svadhyaya. I do not have direct association with the holy and with devotees, and despite recent efforts on my part to secure that on a continuing basis, it's looking as if this situation will continue for awhile. But through svadhyaya I have the association of avataras and sages for hours every day. I know that this is not the same as personally having their association, but the strengthening effect is undeniable. Apart from this, I am able to continually recharge the batteries of my sadhana with utsaha through study; and then there is also the progressive unfolding and integration of my understanding. For me at least, vision has to be whole for faith to be whole, and the niyama of svadhyaya allows that to move forward daily. I can say very truly that, without svadhyaya, I would not have been able to continue on the spiritual path through all these years I have been alone — alone in the sense of isolated from holy association. Svadhyaya is the staff I lean upon as I walk my daily spiritual life; without it, I would have no spiritual life."

RESPONSE: All that is said here is like music to a teacher's ears, from the reclamation of the meaning of food and its energy for spiritual life, to the import of the study of the revealed scriptures. I would venture to say that if western aspirants could understand and apply just this much, then true spirituality would emerge and rejoin them as a matter of course in due time. Then, with perseverance, all would unfold and manifest — that being a Divine Life lived in the dharma for purposes of individual enlightenment and the highest good of all souls, at all levels of consciousness.

Akshaya Bhakti from New England writes:
COMMENTS: "Even though I know we should not indulge in evaluation of our spiritual status, it is still encouraging to hear that 'a person who can concentrate the mind, even in secular matters, has satisfied the prerequisite criteria.' The reply to my questions about the later stages of samadhi was so enlightening, especially to know the difference between natural, inner samadhi and its preliminary stages which may be influenced by outer sources, and to hear how this should be practiced until the ultimate state comes along. I am very eager to review and synthesize all the Raja teachings at the upcoming retreat at Hidden Lake!"

QUESTION: "I liked hearing about the 'pranic bubble' and would like to know more about how that connects to the concept of the 'cosmic egg' or Hiranyagarbha. Is that referring to the same thing, or is the first on an individual level which succeeds the latter? It brings back the wonder of how the One becomes the many, and our discussions on the juncture of the seer and the seen."

ANSWER: The pranic bubble, as we call it, is a facilitator for the rebirth of the as yet unrealized soul and its return to the realms of gross name and form. Really, it can be discarded as of no further use after enlightenment has dawned, for if there are no contents (of the mind) then there need not be any container.

Put another way, a higher form of prana, leading up to Shakti power itself, becomes the facilitator, and takes refined consciousness to deeper levels of awareness for experiences that fully transcend the gross worlds of name and form. Anthropomorphically, this refined carrier is exemplified by the presence and form of Garuda, the great dragon bird, that carries Vishnu on many flights (of wisdom) to various inner realms. The swift speed of this primal mount far outstrips the slower movements of the gross or ethereal prana, which itself is much faster than the speed of light here on earth. The Tantracists call this "manojavittvam," the speed of the mind and its thought. People of this technologically advanced but spiritually benighted age would be well served to take stock of this subtle energy that transports the mind in microseconds to higher states of awareness, and brings it back to a perception of grosser things as well. Sound familiar? It is samadhi with its ebb, flow, and recession. Controlling the mind is all about this too, is it not, as well as controlling the prana?

So forget the loony cartoony dragon birds of Hollywood and get ahold of the real Garuda. Then, instead of fantasy flights (sankalpa/vikalpa), you will experience the lightning fast rise and fall of spiritual moods too numerous and blissful to count. Enough of dangerous fuel-driven forays into physical skies, and the thin air of open spaces. Try Inward Ascension and swiftly reach the goal of human existence.

QUESTION #2: "I find it most helpful to think of the elements as states of existence as mentioned in the answer to C.S., but could you please elucidate, dear teacher, what it means for air to be "homogeneity?"

ANSWER: In the way that I am using it here, homogeneity is the mode of being everywhere, like water or air, while not permeating objects -- like an island resisting an ocean or a mountain dividing the overall body of air. All-pervasiveness is the word I have chosen for something that interpenetrates everything, like ether with planets. It is not only around them, but it shoots through and through them as well. And so, by analogy, we see that air represents mind/intellect, while ether represents Atman. As referring to the tanmatras, which you infer here, airs' subtler component is the idea of homogeneity in the mind of God. That is where air came from, starting out as a word/thought and finally, after a substantial trickle-down process, congealing on the physical level as the element we call air.

Lord Buddha gave us another way to think of the five elements. They are the five types of desires of living beings. This perspective gives even more validity to the "mind-only schools" way of thinking, which propose to us that the universe is not created out of nothing (nothing doesn't exist!), but comes forth via the thought processes of masses of beings existing in various lokas at cosmic, collective, and individual mental levels. Thus, earth has five forms (akashas) and so do the other four elements. Water at a subtler level is the flow of prana. Fire at a subtler level is the light of intelligence, etc.

Further, what brought them forth practically and cosmologically is different from but intrinsically linked to why they came forth, which is also linked to who brought them forth. The "why" is desire, and the "who" is the mind/ego complexes of tamasic, rajasic, and sattvic beings. Over the course of this great Cosmic Projection, "who" got the desire to ask "why" (or "why not"), and projected the "what" some "where" "when" it willed it. Thus the Five "W's" came into being. Unfortunately, the "who" has been discarded in these times for the other four "double U's" (two selves instead of one), and people are thus unaware of the Self (Who) and fixated with why, what, where, and when — i.e., cause and effect, matter/objects, space, and time, respectively.

In short, and with regards to desire, kama, mankind wanted a solid place to "lay his head" (big mistake) so he projected earth (with the help of mind, maya, and nature — and a little invisible help of shakti power); he desired to drink, to enjoy, to generate and quench, so he projected water; he yearned for radiance to light up the solid and subtle worlds so he projected fire; he longed to move freely, to be warm and cool, to fill and empty, so he projected air; and finally he desired to transmute between worlds of his own design, and choosing so, he projected the ethers — all from the abundant power inherent in his own mind on three joint levels. Desire, then, is a powerful thing, and must be watched with care...is it not?

QUESTION #3: "In the *Gospel of Sri Ramakrishna,* on p. 141, He is telling Keshab about the different natures of men, and He says that *'Some have an excess of sattva....'* I am wondering how can sattva be too much. Am I correct in thinking it has to do with becoming so attracted to it that we settle for it, instead of moving beyond it to complete enlightenment? Deepest gratitude."

ANSWER: Yes, it is as you say, but includes at least one other perspective. The more enlightened beings, once having graduated and mastered the guna of sattva, use it for both rising above the vagaries and vicissitudes of the world, and returning from excursions into samadhi as well. Theirs is less of an attachment and more of a facility. The Great Master had some of these types of rare beings among His fold, and they were both householders and monks as well — Bhavanath, Baburam, and others. They are so sattvic that their houses are sometimes empty of furniture, wide open, ever peaceful, and with cobwebs collecting in the corners of the roof. It was with reference to beings such as these that Sri Ramakrishna said, *"These sattvic beings spend much of the time sitting on their beds behind mosquito nets. Ordinary people think them to be sleeping, but they are really sitting up, repeating the mantra, and meditating upon God into the wee hours of the night."*

**Pada III, Sutra 9**
*vyutthana nirodha sanskarayorabhibhava-pradurbhavau nirodhakshannachittanvayo nirodhaparinamah* (*vyutthana,* emerging; *nirodhah,* neutralizing; *samskara,* mental impression; *abhibhava,* expiring; *pradurbhavau,* projection; *nirodhah,* neutralizing; *ksana,* spontaneous; *chitta,* mind's thoughts; *anvayah,* relation; *nirodhah-parinama,* attainment of cessation).

*"Where there is the practice of neutralization of the emerging mental thoughts in relation to their expiration, the mastery of cessation occurs in spontaneous fashion."*

The utterance or inscription, "mastery of cessation," is a spiritual statement, to be sure, and rarely mentioned or contemplated. It is truly an esoteric turn of phrase. What to speak of ordinary beings, or those under the press of tamas, even creative beings miss entirely the efficacy of stopping the thought process and seeing what lies in the vast and silent recesses of the otherwise vibrating and vacillating mind. The impulse or desire to actually stop the endless trains of thought running constantly through the mind never occurs to most beings, then, and so they miss out on all that lies beyond the "kingdoms of heaven" — namely, formless Reality.

And, under the influence of the incessantly flowing mind, peace of mind also begins to escape them as well, which is certainly one of the greater calamities that befalls mankind. All of the unfortunate thoughts and their repercussive actions that man is guilty of spring from this parched atmosphere stripped of inner peace. Thus, in the Tantric Shakti scriptures, the Divine Mother, Sri Durga, when She gets tired of warring with the demonic and egoistic forces and factions surrounding Her on all sides, simply utters the bijam, *Hum* — *"Cease and be still,"* and the battlefield of relativity suddenly falls silent. A few of the verses describing this are sublime indeed:

*O Mother Durga, You nourish all beings, neutralize negative forces and shower abundance upon the Gods! You delight Shankara, but are a terrible sight to the demonic forces who oppose Thee. Rejoicing in ferocious battle, You dance across the universe, humbling pride and vanquishing evil. Your Presence transforms the poison of countless transgressions, for You were born of the healing waters of eternal life. Victory to Thee, O destroyer of demons, beloved of Shiva and daughter of the eternal snow mountains. Victory unto Thee!*

*Arrayed across the battlefield of relative existence appear the demon hoards of Chanda and Munda, the arrogant devils who defeated the Gods in Battle! Undaunted by these, You directed the invincible armies of Mother Kali and Her infantries of terrible power to crush them. Amidst herds of thundering elephants, howling jackals, and screaming women warriors of striking appearance, You strode boldly into the fray and severed the heads of the two powerful demons! Victory to Thee, O destroyer of demons, beloved of Shiva and daughter of the eternal snow mountains. Victory unto Thee!*

*Hundreds of negative forces are annihilated in accordance with Thy special powers, O Universal Mother. Even Raktabija, the demon capable of reproducing himself many fold from drops of his own blood spilled in battle, was destroyed when You manifested Mother Kali, who drank every drop of his blood with Her prodigious tongue! Trident, Thunderbolt, arrow, sword and spear — these and many other weapons are utilized by Thee with supreme mastery. When the battle ends, You stand triumphant amidst the carnage while Your spirit hosts reduce flesh and blood bodies to nothingness. Victory to Thee, O destroyer of demons, beloved of Shiva and daughter of the eternal snow mountains. Victory unto Thee!*

*My mind still reels with awe remembering the spectacle of Your terrible majesty as You stride across the field of battle with inspiring self-assurance! Surrounded by hosts of glorious Demigods sporting an infinite array of shining weapons, the battlefield reverberates with cries of conflagration, while a spiritual intensity experienced only at times of great sacrifice, permeates the atmosphere. Your devoted armies of dedicated servants spring into action, armed with the invincible weapon of Immortality. Victory to Thee, O destroyer of demons, beloved of Shiva and daughter of the eternal snow mountains. Victory unto Thee!*

*The complete annihilation of countless armed warriors strewn across the battlefield of relativity now fades in transformation. The appearance of many courageous women-warriors of scintillating beauty transfigures earth into a heavenly paradise! Among them You reside easily and naturally, O Mother, full of inherent Bliss. Who is this awesome feminine presence, more beautiful than the rarest flower in full bloom on an intoxicating spring morning? Victory to Thee, O destroyer of demons, beloved of Shiva and daughter of the eternal snow mountains. Victory unto Thee!*

Therefore, the phrase "mastery of cessation" joins the company of some very few but very precious expressions in our English language that convey a sense of authentic spirituality usually indescribable by other means. And imagine, too, the Yoga of cessation (nirodha) wherein no effort towards calming or quiescence is necessary, or even possible. We have come upon both these declarations in the Yoga sutras of Patanjali. Coming to know of them alone is "worth the ride," as they say. Now it falls upon the seeker and aspirant to approach these levels of consciousness, comprehend their import and efficacy, and possess and install them eternally within the mental complex, using them for the highest good of all living beings and the transcendence of all ills, problems, obstacles, diseases, complacencies, despoilers, distractions, and relative goals.

**Pada III, Sutra 10**
*tasya prashantavahita samskarat (tasya,* that; *prashanta,* quiescent; *vahita,* flow; *samskara,* mental impression).

> *"That quiescence of mind and its natural flow itself forms a samskara."*

The good news of Yoga is not fully expressed yet, even given the wonderful statements encountered in the last few sutras. And here we find that the law of like attracts like is not necessarily a negative principle, but has very positive overtones — at least for those who take the time to put forth the effort to gain the *"Pearl of Great Price."* That is, just as there is a flow of thought, both depressing and creative, which is most difficult to alleviate, we find too that there is a state of mind beyond these insinuations — what Patanjali is calling *"prashantavahita,"* a quiescent flow of mind.

Better still, if one were to cultivate it for long periods of time in the mode of practice (sadhana), it too, just like negative thoughts, would create an impression on or in the mind. This is why Patanjali has informed us early on in the sutras about the teaching of klishta and aklishta vrittis. With the ordinary mind going from negative to positive thoughts and back again, constantly, a samskara of duality based in pleasure and pain forms. No peace visits the mind, then, and certainly no "flow of quiescent thoughts." For another look at the conflicting vrittis of the mind, the chart opposite (page 71) forms a good study.

So, we see now how positive samskaras are a big part of the picture, and why, as well, there are souls born here on earth in states of happiness, contentment, peace, bliss, and higher realization. This explains the (higher) reason behind the many lifetimes proposal, and defuncts the one lifetime scenario as the impossibility that it is (unless one is a videhamukta). It also explains the relative law of karma to us, and assists us in using it for a higher purpose leading to moksha or mukti.

"What are we waiting for?," as the opportunists say. Knowing this fact will cause the wise seeker after Truth and Divine Life to rush to the sanctuary of silence, cessation, meditation, or certainly, at least, a one-pointed mind-set that is both extremely practical and deflective of all the negative modes that the mind in maya is capable of.

The principle of samskara is a potential art to be learned, and even if taken on the level of theory or intellectual study, is most edifying. On another level it is an absolute boon to the one who can imbibe and utilize it as a way of reading life, circumstances, and the minds of human beings and their tendencies. Take, for instance, those who go in for the difficult task of child-rearing. Knowing that the mind of their infant, though as yet undeveloped, is actually not a clean slate at all, but is instead full of many contrasting impressions, like fallow seeds, which, when watered by the influences of upbringing, society, peer pressure, and fructifying karmas from previous births, will shape and form

# Controlling the Chitta-vrttis in Yoga

*"Yogash chitta-vrtti-nirodhah — quelling and mastering the vibrations of the mind — is conducive to attaining Yoga, union with Reality."*
— Lord Patanjali

## Klishta Vrttis
### Pain-bearing thought vibrations

- are caused by the kleshas ───────── Avidya, Ignorance
  Asmita, Egotism
- are causes of the kleshas ───────── Raga, Attachment
  Dvesha, Aversion
  Abhinivesha, Clinging to Life
- become the field for karma (karmashaya)
  (Due to the vrttis, kleshas arise and the field of karma gets further seeded.)

- produce samskaras which create more vrttis (perpetuating the wheel of samsara.)

## Aklishta Vrttis
### Non pain-bearing thought vibrations

Pleasure and pain, virtue and vice, attract and repel, creating vasanas

Craving for vrttis causes acceptance or rejection of life-experiences

- do not give rise to the kleshas

The fruits of karma are sought via false proof caused by the buddhi's misinformation from mind & senses

- mirror klishta vrttis but are unaffected
  (Directed towards objects they are klishta. Directed inwards they become blissful.)

Fostering aklishta vrttis resists ignorance, desire, and karma

Rajas and tamas get reduced

- control klishta vrttis ───────── The buddhi is rendered sattvic

- do not liberate but foster discernment ───── Abhyasa, desire to practice, initiates

- strengthen with spiritual practice ───── Khyati, discernment, develops

- help mature the samskaras ───── Agama and anumana, scriptural authority and inference, increase

- produce excellent qualities ───── Path is gained, guru is consulted

- get transcended via Paravairagya ───── Vairagya, detachment, burgeons

Prajna-prasada, clear wisdom, dawns

*"Dissolve the gunas of rajas and tamas by taking recourse to sattva. Then, rise up above sattva by developing pure sattva and abide there."* — Sri Krishna

the mind and actions of the personality, gives the concerned father and mother of that newly embodied soul a very definite advantage in the area of parenting.

And when the soul, if he or she is most fortunate (is yearning for Truth), begins to seek for a path and a teacher to lift them out of the many sufferings of worldly existence, the guru versed in the art of samskara reading can both lead the aspiring soul towards his or her higher potential, and remove obstacles which are bound to rise up in any aspirant's inward journey. Thus, knowledge in this crucial and forgotten area is a time-saving device, and therefore a suffering alleviating tool as well.

As the joke in spiritual circles goes, "Samskaras (some scars) are deeper than others." That is, there are some effects from unseen causes which will have to see the light of day somehow, and this is not always a good thing. Better then to never have formed the mental scar in the first place. This knowledge of the presence of samskaras in the mind which are not even acknowledged by western science, psychology, society, politics, or even religion — not, at least, within the framework of reincarnation and previous lifetimes — will go a long way towards eliminating those impediments that continually rise up, unchallenged, in everyday life.

What is more, it is important that people know that when these unwanted effects from previous thoughts (sanchita karma) and actions (the thought is father to the deed) do insinuate themselves on human life and mind, that they should be immediately and unreservedly exposed to and dispensed with in the atmosphere of Holy Company (guru, dharma, sangha, and sadhana) so that they will not rise up again in the future (as agami karma). Here, it is of further import to know that conventional modes of attempted relief and correction (such as physical exercise, diet, hearsay and advice from friends and family, therapy, and ethical and moralistic practices born of fundamentalist religious approaches) will not destroy a samskara. They may clear the surface of the mental field of trials and troubles, but the cause of them does not get burnt at the very roots. Only sadhana can accomplish that. Otherwise, these despoilers will only crop up again somewhere down the road of life — and probably, and characteristically, at the worst possible time.

In this lesson we have taken two most powerful and edifying sutras from the storehouse of Patanjali's wisdom on the yogic pathway, which are also several of my personal favorites. The Truth is being revealed, even in written form. Now it is up to us as sincere devotees to transform words into wisdom, preaching into practice, effort into ecstasy, and philosophy into Freedom. God speed to all of us in crossing over to the farthest shore beyond all darkness.

## Lesson Sixty-five, 11/05/11
### Pada III, Sutra 11 & 12

We are presently in the depths of concentrated study of Patanjali's Yoga darshana. My intention is that all students involved in this become practitioners of Yoga, for then will we, as a culture, or a cross section of a culture at least, bring Yoga out of books, temples, and especially away from hatha yoga studios where it is being dumbed-down, its deeper tenets, forgotten. If we are true to this aim, living yogis and yoginis will walk the earth again, even amongst the householders. It is an ideal worth waiting for, and working towards.

Let us take a look at the problems and experiences of the modern day aspirants, then, and scan them for solutions which will afford walking the spiritual path in earnest, and with wisdom.

**Questions and Answers for Lesson 65**
K.D. from Hawaii writes:
QUESTION: "I have been reading and re-reading (at least 5 times) chapters 16 and 17, and have comments and questions. In meditating on the alambanas, I have been experiencing the merging of the elements and their evolutes. I envision fire as earth in molten lava, water flooding out fires, fire turning water into steam, into vapor which becomes part of air. I see air fanning and feeding flames, as well as snuffing them out. Ether remains the mystery, but seems to be the space that holds all of it together and is unaffected by any of it as the insentient principle closest to the sentient Brahman. All the evolutes remain distinct and separate, and seem arbitrary. Why should feeling, tangibility, be an evolute of air rather than earth or water? Why should locomotion, seeing, sight, be an attribute of fire rather than water which flows continually? I accept it the way it is, but wonder where the inspiration came from. I understand that it is Sankhya yoga from Lord Kapila but just curious as to how he made these deductions. It really does not matter. The important thing is that I am finally making essential connections. Before I did not know how the 24 cosmic principles tied into the whole metaphysical system of Yoga/Vedanta. Now it is clear that it is a road map to find the way to authentic spiritual experiences — the Samadhis."
ANSWER: Whereas I think I know what you are describing here, the way you have put it needs adjusting. The elements themselves are the evolutes, and the meditator is to merge them into their sources. The five gross elements have come out of the tanmatras. With this explained, then, as you say, what really matters is making these connections, from outer to inner, and beyond. A start must be made, as they say, and Sankhya offers us that. What is more, thousands upon thousands of souls have gained access to Brahman again by following such adroit and conclusive pathways like Sankhya, Vedanta, and Yoga. We have only to follow and to see, to knock and have it be opened unto us.

And there are reasons, most subtle, why it has all been set up as it is. Deeper meditation will show us these. For instance, air, tangibility, is in our lungs even before we can touch water and earth. Prana is foremost, and breathing/air is most primal. Once we have this, we can then swim and walk. Further, fire/light/sun helps us to see the water we are about to swim in, or drink. Where would the power of locomotion be without light?

This road map, as you have fittingly called it, is a boon of profound proportions, a way to explore and realize all the building blocks of our universe — not just the atomic particle universe which only leads to emptiness, but the lokas lying within consciousness, to be discovered by our own Awareness — an Awareness that formulated them in the first place.

QUESTION #2: "I have questions about ego and meditation on ego. Vedavyasa remarks that 'the unqualified ego' is experienced in Sasmita Samadhi. I am often aware of how my delusional ego is trying to take some kind of artificial credit for anything and everything that I do, think, and feel. It often seems rather pathetic, and I am looking forward to the day when it drops away like a dead leaf off of a tree. I would like a clearer understanding of how the ego progresses from the delusional ego to the unqualified ego of Sasmita Samadhi. It is interesting, and I am gratified to know that this sense of I-ness does not disappear and should not be expected to disappear before the final and highest Asamprajnata Samadhi. I was under the misconception that somehow we were supposed to dissolve our individual sense of self ASAP. Can you expound more on the steps involved in letting go of the little delusional ego to reach that state of sattvic I-ness which is the *'composite of spirit and matter'* experienced in Sasmita Samadhi?"

ANSWER: First of all, the delusional ego, or facade ego, does not "progress"; rather, it dissolves. It was not real to begin with — no substance, no longevity. Its disappearance is caused by the soul seeing its true self, and here is where any sequence of events, or transformation, occurs, if it can be allowed for.

Other than a station for consciousness (ahamkara), or a facade (illusory ego), a case can be made for the Purusha being the true individual self. Sankhya Yoga philosophy allows for many individual selves, in a real sense and not a feigned or prideful sense. Whether Kapila himself intended this (for it was not accepted by later darshanas), the fact remains that when a soul awakens to his spiritual nature, a sense of self, albeit ripe, still persists for a time. What to speak of "for a time," that real individual self is a solid foundation from which the advanced aspirant makes a jump into formlessness (egolessness), and it is also waiting for him when he returns to "normal" consciousness. We saw this in the case of Sri Ramakrishna Paramahamsa time and time again, in these more recent times.

It might be said then, to further the illustration, that with enough of these jumps to the formless state made by the ardent practitioner, the subtle structure of the real individual self begins to thin, like a membrane when it has been breached too many times, and soon nothing remains other than the Transcendent Self, or Atman. So as not to upset some Buddhist schools and their philosophies, we can affirm here that the Real Self indicated is identical with Buddha Nature, what the Lord called Prajna-Param. And, the illusory self which obscures inner sight of the Tathagatagarbha is the base ego, the nonself.

Suffice to say, then, that there is the illusory self, unfigurable, like maya, which is here and not here — here when consciousness occupies (dreams) its imaginary station, and gone when that station is abandoned for greater substance. That greater substance is Ahamkara as a cosmic platform, which means not only the individual dreamer, but the collective, and even the Cosmic ego — the tamas, rajas, and sattva of the ego. Seeing beyond that, a real individual soul, Purusha, as I have described it above, is reached. That real ego is like a vehicle, unimpeded by the limitations of lower selves, and willing and able to move between levels of consciousness, or lokas, usually in order to assist in the Divine Mother's work in the Three Worlds and Seven Spheres. For Atman, one with Brahman, and divested of the Five Sheaths, does not move; does not need to. It is all-pervasive, and one would be reticent to title it Soul, Self, or anything else other than Pure Consciousness, or Timeless, Deathless Awareness. So here is a proposed sequence for you, in answer to your query.

QUESTION #3: "In Savichara Samadhi you write that 'As the immediate cause of tanmatras, ego begins to be brought under control.' In Sananda Samadhi, 'The ego has been reached, but Buddhi and Mahat are yet to come.' In Sasmita Samadhi, 'Ahamkara dissolves into Mahat. It is here and nowhere else that purusha and prakriti meet, but it is the buddhi that receives the reflection of prakriti, not purusha, which remains unaffected. Mahat is turned inwards, away from ego, looking at Purusha. While it is turned outward, it produces ego, which in turn produces mind, senses and objects.' My questions are these: Who/what is this great cosmic ego that causes mind, senses and objects from subtle to gross? Whose ego is this? Is this the ego of Mahat? Since Mahat is defined as the nonself, since it is limited by the sattvic guna, does it have an ego? Ahamkara dissolves into Mahat, so in that merging does it disappear? Was Mahat the first to differentiate from Brahman? I would appreciate your elucidation on these matters since this is where my mind goes in meditation."

ANSWER: In the Yoga sutras, and Vedavyasa's commentary on them, we find that avidya is the first of the five klesha, impediments to Yoga. This avidya is defined as being 8-fold. This ignorance consists of the soul thinking of itself as 1) Unmanifested nature; 2) Mahat; 3) Ahamkara; 4-8) and the five subtle elements (tanmatras). One can see, here, that the ego is a part of this ignorance, maybe at the root of it, and thus, in answer to your question, this Mahat does have an ego. What is its nature, or whose is it? It is God's ego, but since Brahman can have no form, and no ignorance, this set of very elevated principles belong to Ishvara. Just as you, the Atman, sport an ego with which to take form with, so too, must Ishvara, in order to appear in form, sport an ego. Meditating upon this cosmic ego of Ishvara is a powerful practice, and it purifies the mind of the practitioner like no other. This Archetypical Soul or the "Godhead" as it is sometimes called, is the Divine Personality. It consists of the combined essence of millions of luminaries, described by poet-saints as "koti surya" — the brilliance of a million suns.

But like all forms, this Grand Form is not its projections (Subtle Elements), nor is it Its Ego, Mind, or Its infinite inner playground (Unmanifested Prakriti). As the awakening soul sees the Truth, it too drops, piece by piece, station by station, its association with elements, mind, ego, and nature. For the soul is Atman, nothing material or of form. Just so, the Divine Being is not its forms, stations, or projections. They are all the nonself. But whereas they are insentient in and of themselves, they have the capacity for a great power of investment by Ishvara, just as the mind and intellect of human beings contains great force.

QUESTION #4: "I thought I understood that Purusha or Soul was the same as the Atman. From this reading it does not seem correct, since only in Asamprajnata Samadhi does a yogi/yogini experience that formless, timeless Divine reality. Could you please define Purusha as distinct from Atman?"

ANSWER: Please see my answer to Question #2 on the previous page of this lesson.

QUESTION #5: "Mahat is the universal Buddhi as Brahman is the universal Atman, right?"

ANSWER: Yes. A portion of this massive cosmic Intelligence breaks into many sparks, as it were, and is found in the various souls that inhabit the many worlds in time and space.

QUESTION #6: "I understand that true renunciation, and therefore true freedom from egoic impulses, depends on 'giving up all that smacks of ownership, agency, and separation.' This confuses me, but I resolve that confusion by telling myself that identification with things owned, actions performed, and existence as a totally separate entity, is the thing to be avoided. Or, it may be more accurate to say that misidentification with ownership, actions or doership, and separation, is the obstacle. I have property, vehicles, flutes, and many other items that I claim as mine. I am always doing things, but know that I am not the doer — or at least I am much more than just a person doing things, achieving goals, and acting separate, vulnerable, and alone. It seems impossible to give up all that 'smacks' of ownership, agency, and separation. How does one do it, since we all own stuff and have lots of actions and accomplishments to our credit?"

ANSWER: Each does it according to their inner capacity for it. The worldly beings do not do it at all, since they have not awakened from the somnolent slumber of matter and maya. *"They do not think of God even by accident,"* as the Great Master quipped. In sincere aspirants, however, is where the birth of aversion to the ego begins. Rubbing shoulders with people, society, and relatives, brings home the presence of the rascal ego, initially, and from there one notices it throughout life in the form of humanity's misguided claim on everything it says, does, thinks, and intuits — from work, to objects, to knowledge, and right on up to the spector of the spiritual ego.

In spiritual circles is where the ego stands out the most, for its cover is stripped from it while it tries to stand among the knowers and lovers of God, but it cannot bear such exposure. Posers, pretenders, betrayers, doom-sayers, bullies, spooks, thieves in the night — these are just a small host of character types who start into the spiritual path, then back out, unthinkingly and unceremoniously. When guileless and pure souls see this pathetic sideshow, with all its pomp, sensationalism, emotionalism, and attention getting — the "drama queen" syndrome — they espy exactly what is at the root of all suffering, and what needs to be promptly renounced as well.

Meanwhile, among the illumined souls, is seen the ripening of the ego rather than its rotting. Great deeds are done, great works accomplished, great words spoken — all capable of inflating the ego — but in the spiritually sincere soul it never happens. Peace reigns supreme. All comes from Mother, returns to Mother, and no residual effects from the ego ever mar this picture of perfection. The ego has been effectively dealt with in such beings as these, and the triple bondage of ownership, agency, and separation from God is foiled before it can set in.

QUESTION #7: "I wonder, as well, about the role of emotions in these systems. They are never mentioned except briefly when described as part of a duality like pleasure and pain, and joy and sorrow – part of the impermanent nature of relative existence. Are emotions just another aspect of the mind-stuff? For myself, they are much more of an obstacle than mere thoughts, which can be more easily discarded. Sometimes emotions appear suddenly, then thought follows; and sometimes there seems to be first thought, followed by emotions. Is the 'bliss that knows no opposite,' a supreme emotion, a refined purified feeling that accompanies the purified, 'unqualified' ego?"

ANSWER: Emotion in the mature mind is devotion. Love of God is where the heart and its feelings move to in the case of the devotees of God. But the unrefined mind and ego complex gravitates towards sentimentalism and, falling lower still, soon is wallowing in a sweep of base emotions unbefitting of the noble soul. This is really a form of selfishness, and its influence pulls all and everything, and everyone, around it, down into sorrow and bitterness. Therefore, spending time in spiritual practices such as worship, meditation, and selfless service keeps the mind from plunging towards this abyss, and develops character that uplifts the thoughts — charges up the chitta. We must remember Sri Ramakrishna's cautionary saying that, *"The ordinary mind's natural tendency is to go downward, like rainwater that seeks the lowest place to settle, while the aspiring mind and it's thoughts are more like the hot air balloon, which only rises higher and higher."*

A.M. from Portland writes:
QUESTION: "Things are 'moving' in my life. I was offered and accepted a job yesterday. Not my Life Mission work, but work. And I read this passage from the Bhagavad-Gita yesterday before my interview. The whole section spoke to me, but this passage really stood out. I know it speaks more about 'duty in spirit,' but it still seemed appropriate for worldly work: *'Do your duty, always; but without attachment. That is how a man reaches the ultimate Truth; by working without anxiety about results. In fact, Janaka and many others reached enlightenment, simply because they did their duty in spirit. Your motive in working should be to set others, by your example, on the path of duty.'* Can you comment further?"

ANSWER: What is brought up here is specifically about work in the Spirit, not "worldly" work. Worldly work disappears and does not persist anymore for the one who gets into this spirit of Karma Yoga, for he fast learns about the dissolving of karmic repercussions through this secret of selfless works. It is a wonder why more beings do not learn this, and go forward along this winsome way. But the attraction for worldliness only breeds more worldliness. It is the *"chronic disease of this age,"* as Sri Ramakrishna has said.

It may be added that the word "duty" here, like the word "worldly," ought to be carefully defined. For just as worldly work will disappear when the laws of Karma Yoga kick in, so too will duty cease to be mundane and heavy when dharma is discovered and implemented. As Vivekananda has said, *"Duty is the scorching midday sun that is burning the very vitals of humanity."* But when dharma, and higher modes of dharma (like jnana and bhakti) are studied and applied to life in the world, the need for and attraction to duty, both, will get transcended. This move towards spiritual elevations is for the Truth-seeker, not for those who still have great attachment for the world and the superficial and mutable things it offers. Until a higher calling is heard — like on a "Life Mission" level — duty will retain its import as a mode of example to teach others how to "go from lower truth to higher truth," as we say.

And along those exact lines, you will find by exploring deeper in the Gita that Sri Krishna eventually advises the transcendence of dharma as well. Thus, there is adharma, life and work in ignorance of spiritual laws; then there is dharma, life and work that is in accord and harmony with knowledge of the purpose of life; and then there is svadharma, one's highest destiny — which is towards using life and work for the attainment of Enlightenment.

One could also make a point that, as Sri Krishna says further, the abidance in "Loka Sangraha" — doing everything for the highest good of all beings — is next in line, for as long as the body persists for the enlightened soul, he/she is to use it for service of others, on all levels. To act in such a way that causes people to see beyond the paltry things of this world is real compassion. In this regard, removing suffering really is not possible here, nor would one strive to remove the very thing that helps beings move inward towards realization. The world, the body, and suffering — these all go and belong together.

Whatever takes the mind away from such distractions, then, is best, and work as worship, or labor as love, is precisely that for the luminary. And since happiness, contentment, and peace are missing in this world, and love is *"a mere word here"* as Holy Mother has said, all of these qualities and others are to be sought after and realized at the level of consciousness where they exist, not where they do not exist. Problems are of the world. Solutions are of the mind that created the problems. But transcendence and its absolute Peace are of the Spirit. When consciousness dwells in its own element, or, as Shankara has said, *"dotes on its own object"* (Atman), there the mind becomes free — that is, realizes its inherent Freedom, beyond even the thought of bondage.

Work, duty, dharma, and true service of God in mankind, then, are intrinsically intertwined. The wise ones know them all, and their distinctions, and know, as well, how to lead aspiring souls from one to the other, in inward ascension style, towards "The Goal Supreme."

As for those who do not aspire, except for those most indolent and resistant of souls, their time for sleeping in ignorance is fast coming to an end. A brilliant and all-penetrating Light naming Itself "Sri Ramakrishna" has come to earth in this time, this Kali Yuga. When such a blazing radiance floods the dark fields of the unawakened mind, all beings, even those lying under thick covers, will have to awaken. As they do they will feel the natural need to escape the bonds of this world, and help others do the same. If there is any real facility for work here on earth, it is this. Or, as Swami Vivekananda has put it, the only purpose for work is to help in the development of knowledge. When spiritual strength and inner muscles of this kind are developed, the soul will leave the *"gymnasium of this world"* and take up residence in its true nature forever, never to dream again in maya.

Kanyakali from Hawaii writes:
QUESTION: "I like the phrase 'awareness of cessation' very much. It so aptly describes the point at which the mind's thoughts cease, and what remains is pure awareness. Keeping this idea at the forefront as I enter meditation has helped me avoid falling into the void once I finally enter the silence. Although I'm drawing a great deal of sustenance from the peace that wells up from this still place, I see the potential pitfall of slipping into a sort of passive state of bliss. You have advised us instead to remain alert and watchful so that we don't miss what happens next. My question is, what is supposed to happen next? I find myself in need of further instruction around this specific stage of meditation. Although it has probably been explained before in the sutras and the commentaries, I'm still searching for clarity."
ANSWER: What happens next is nothing. What else would the "awareness of cessation" be? In brief, there is no more movement. Rather, from this uniquely still position, the seer sees all, knows all, and merges into Brahman. Only, you do not want to miss the merging, i.e., being aware of immersion, aware of Awareness. Put another way, this is the last act/movement that transmigrating consciousness will make. Simultaneously, the soul will become aware that no movement ever really took place, that all was always still and peaceful. Now, just rest in that *"Peace that Passeth all Understanding,"* and be free. Remain in the depths of that Sea of Awareness, the "Sorrowless Ocean of Light." It took so long to breach its surface, and you know what lies upon the surface. So now you know that Consciousness is Brahman and Shakti combined — the Eternal Static State, and the Dynamic Power, "ever one, appearing as two." Move between these two, gracefully, once you have learned the ability to avoid splitting them further into sets of dualities (dvandva mohena) and hosts of varieties (vaichitra) better not meddled with except by past Masters.

## Pada III, Sutra 11
*sarvarthataikagratayoh kshayodayau chittasya samadhiparinamah* (*sarvarthata,* multiplicity; *ekagrata,* single-pointedness; *kshaya,* dissolved; *udaya,* aspiring; *chittasya,* of the mind field; *samadhi-parinamah,* transformed into samadhi).

*"When single-pointed aspiration unifies the mind-field so that the tendency towards multiplicity is overcome, then mind itself transforms into samadhi."*

A close study of the human mind in meditation will reveal its tendency towards multiplicity, followed by its urge to act on all these variegations. The key word here is "meditation," the seventh limb of Yoga. It is the witness in human form. Revealingly, thinking is not equal to the task of this objective inner inspection, which is precisely why thinkers and seers represent two vastly different levels of human soul.

In this day and age, and in this modern mechanized culture, thinkers are the ones who are routing societies and living beings further and deeper into maya, while seers who meditate are the ones we eventually turn to in order to free us from the same. Thinking, as an alternative to brooding, or to witlessness, is more than acceptable. But the thought process stripped of its objectivity and its discrimination leads to all manner of ill-considered acts, thus karma. Living under the hard press of karma, in turn, develops samskaras (mental impressions) that not only force the soul to act carelessly in this present lifetime, but follow the soul into succeeding lifetimes as well, playing havoc there. This is only one negative repercussion. The other, and more lamentable, is that samadhi will not get experienced.

Concentration, meditation, and samadhi, leading to the ability for samyama, is the height of the tree of Yoga, combining its three best limbs at the top. Far from the early days of initial practice, when the aspirant had to combine three of the best niyamas together (kriya yoga), there is no hope, or struggle, or premature expectation. Only a grand view from the heights of realization!

About the impractical aspirant, Sri Ramakrishna has given the story of the man who, with his right foot set on the lowest branch of a tree, has his eyes already fixed upon the cluster of fruit on the tip-top most branch. Impatience is in him, and desire for attainment, of "fruits." How different is the mindset of the aspirant who occupies even the middle limbs of the tree of Yoga, who is still mastering the hard task of pratyahara, of training the mind away from sense objects. For him there is no thought of ultimate fruit in his mind, only securing basic control of his mental organ; that, alone, would make him exceedingly happy.

"When single-pointed focus unifies the mindfield, what inner calm attends it; what unreserved inspiration pervades it; what unalloyed bliss permeates it. The mind, now a boundless ocean unto itself, its thoughts coalesced and amassed into the very form of Awareness Itself, can do nothing other than to merge ecstatically, like a massive whirlpool which the ecstatic liquid essence of a thousand waterfalls is merging into, receiving all of Consciousness into Itself. This is the actual rapturous implication of what the line of words in sutra 3:11 are relating, when beyond practice and philosophy, the soul merges with Brahman. It is Yoga, and it has many expressions — as the chart opposite reveals.

# The Ocean of Awareness & Its Yogic Waves
## Universal Pathways to Enlightenment

"Sitting up on the snow peaks of the Himalayas, I repeat from the Upanisads: *'He has neither disease, nor decay, nor death, for, verily, he has obtained a body full of the fire of Yoga.'"* ——————— *Swami Vivekananda*

"The truth is this: he who is really anxious to cross the ocean of this world will somehow break his bonds. No one can entangle him."

*Sri Sarada Devi,
The Holy Mother*

### The Four Main Yogas
*Jnana Yoga, Bhakti Yoga
Raja Yoga, & Karma Yoga*

"This is the new religion of this age, the synthesis of Yoga, Knowledge, Devotion, and Work, the propagation of Knowledge and Devotion down to the very lowest, without distinction of age or sex...."

*Swami Vivekananda*

### Yogas of the Bhagavad Gita

Ananya-yoga
Abhyasa-yoga
Sankhya-yoga
Sanyasa-yoga
Vibhuti-yoga
Jnana Vijnana-yoga
Purushottama-yoga
Akshara Brahma-yoga
Rajavidya Rajaguhya-yoga
Jnana-karma Sanyasa-yoga
Shraddhatraya Vibhaga-yoga
Vishvarupa Darshana-yoga
Gunatraya Vibhaga-yoga
Kshetra Kshetrajna-yoga
Daivasura Sampad-yoga
Moksha Sanyasa-yoga

## Some Traditional Yogas

Advaita-yoga
Antar-yoga
Buddhi-yoga
Charya-yoga
Laya-yoga
Mantra-yoga
Prema-bhakti-yoga
Kriya-yoga
Vasana-yoga
Chaturdasya-yoga
Siva-yoga
Lakshya-yoga
Dhyana-yoga
Brahma-yoga
Siddhi-yoga
Ashtanga-yoga

"According to Patanjali, there are erratic thought waves, called vrittis, in the human mind, which must be pacified. Further, there are mighty waves of Yoga in the Ocean of pure, Conscious Awareness, and they must be utilized for this task." — *Babaji Bob Kindler*

**Pada III, Sutra 12**
*tatah punah shantoditau tulyapratyayau chittasyaikagrataparinamah* (*tasya*, thus; *punah*, repeated; *shanta-uditau*, quiescent rising and falling; *tulya-pratyayau*, similarities; *chittasya*, thoughts of the mind field, *ekagrata-parinamah*, transformed to one-pointed).

"*Thus, as the thoughts of the mind-field rise and fall repeatedly in similar fashion, the transformation of one-pointedness prevails.*"

Like the full cycle of a human breath, or the expansion and contraction of the planet earth in space, or the constant swelling of the ocean waves in their eternal cycles — but all on the spiritual level — such is the harmonious ebb and flow of spiritualized thought in the mind that is now entertaining the transcendent station of samadhi. The realized soul seeks to rest at the central core of this superlative expansion and contraction process, there to observe all that rises and falls from the eternal Word, AUM, and all that scintillates off of the boundless breast of the Ocean of Light, Paramjyoti. From the conscious climes of Yoga to the inner territories of Kundalini Yoga, the poet-saint, Ramprasad, sings ecstatically —

> *Her Face beaming with awesome splendor, the bright black Goddess*
> *rocks blissfully on the red lotus of my secret heart.*
> *The wind of inward awareness swings Her gently, night and day.*
> *This dynamic Mother is none other than the vast peace of Ultimate Reality.*
> *She manifests as luminous channels of energy*
> *extending throughout the precious human body.*
> *Her dark blue Feet of Mystery have crimson soles*
> *that flash brilliantly as She dances.*
> *One glance at Her transcendent Beauty*
> *dissolves egocentric passions and delusions.*
> *The person who attains the vision of Mother's mystic Lotus Swing*
> *leaves Her Lap and develops to maturity.*
> *Again and again, this poet chants in ecstasy:*
> *"Watch Mother Kali swing! Let Her swing!"*

## Lesson Sixty-six, 12/19/11
### Pada III, Sutra 13 & 14

In our continuing study of the profound Raja Yoga Sutras, we find ourselves deep into the third pada, contemplating all that Patanjali, Vedavyasa, and Vivekananda have to say about them. We are taking them sutra by sutra, one or two per lesson, in order to glean as much from them as possible — and hopefully finding ample room in our lives, both earthly and spiritual, to apply them accordingly. These lessons are coming to our growing list of Yoga students about one every three weeks to a month, my teaching schedule providing. This affords the practitioner time to consider the contents and implement the results into what we call our "inner life." Since most beings in this day and time are devoid of an inner life, those who actually possess one are fortunate indeed.

At present, we are blissfully (but not without some occasional consternation) encountering sutras on the art of meditation, pertinent to the three upper limbs of Yoga, which provide the seeker of esoteric wisdom with answers and teachings that are rare, thus welcome in the stretch of time allotted to things spiritual in our lives on earth. Of course, questions indicative of considerable depth themselves come forth as the aspirant delves into the tenets and principles of classic Yoga, especially in correlation with actual practice and self-discipline. Some of these queries follow, below:

**Questions and Answers for Lesson 66**
S.C. from Hawaii writes:
QUESTION: "Would you say more about the purification of location? It's confusing to me."
ANSWER: With the reference being to the three purifications — act, location/atmosphere, and mind — the purification of location has to do with creating a space, probably in one's home, where matters specific to spirituality alone can go forth, unmixed and uninterrupted by affairs of an external nature — mainly any activities, but importantly, insinuations of worldliness. Worldliness is the chronic disease of this current age, causing beings to engage in secular and mundane activities and undertakings devoid of connection to their Source, Atman, as we call it in Vedanta. By creating a sacred space within reach, one can attend there and put into motion all the practices associated with spirituality. Worship, study, and meditation are practiced there, either alone or in the company of others of like mind. One must keep the space sacrosanct, especially at first, so that peace of mind can occur more easily. Later, the living presence will attend there, evidenced by the intense holy atmosphere that is present, palpably, at sacred places of worship one attends elsewhere. But bringing it all home is a further step in this, particularly for the householder of this day and time.
QUESTION #2: "One sees Prakriti and Prakrti. Do the different spellings make a difference?"
ANSWER: No. They are the same word, meaning the same thing. It is probably best, however, to maintain consistency.
QUESTION #3: "What does it mean that 'There are many conscious Purushas?'"
ANSWER: The reference is to the perspective of the Sankhya Yoga of Kapila. In those ancient times it was opined by many that each soul was distinct, a separate reality on its own. The idea of one Soul had not yet come into "vogue." Personally, I like the idea of entertaining both perspectives at once, sort of like many clouds occupying one sky. That is, from the standpoint of the clouds, each has its own existence, no matter how fleeting it may be or seem to be, while from the standpoint of the sky, all are contained within its expanse. Since

everything Is, and is Eternal, does one cancel the other out? Perhaps, better, that each one confirms the other — sort of like form and formlessness.

QUESTION #4: "So, there is the distinction of yamas being vows of devotion, and niyamas being restraints & practices."

ANSWER: Thus are the yamas and niyamas conveniently divided for the benefit of greater understanding (and practice) of the aspirant. For instance, ahimsa is first a vow one takes in order to establish a precedent for thought, act, and deed. Later, after this firm avowal, one can put it into practice by way of the other yamas, and the various niyamas as well. If one would hold a vow not to inflict violence by thought, then the practice of svadhyaya, scriptural study, will not be violated. If one takes a vow of nonviolence around the word, what one speaks, then the tenet of purity is not in danger. If one takes a vow of ahimsa with regard to deed, then the principle of celibacy and moderation are not harmed. There are dozens of connections like these which apply in crossover fashion to the yamas and niyamas.

K.D. from Hawaii writes:

QUESTION: "Can you please explain the difference between liberation and freedom?"

ANSWER: There is none, really, except where a deeper application is applied by those who are keeping watch over nonduality. That is, the word liberation implies more directly that one was once bound, whereas the word freedom states its nature and does not so explicitly declare otherwise. Liberation and bondage are often taken together, but we scarcely hear the word "nonfreedom." This may be why Swami Vivekananda loved the word freedom best in the English language.

QUESTION #2: "I am wondering about my inability to detach from worldly concerns. For instance, it is very difficult for me to detach from the health concerns I have about my grandchildren and the hideous food that they eat. I know there is life after death, and the worst case scenario is only the eternal soul's continuing journey in ignorance, but that does not help at times as I get wrapped up in negative emotions of worry, fear, and anger. Is there a remedy for this?"

ANSWER: The remedy, at least immediately, is to give up worry, fear, and brooding. These three will accomplish nothing, and do no good to anybody. So that is the first step. Sometimes one will find that when the negative tendencies are removed from one's own mind, that the problem simply either changes, becomes less important, or goes away entirely. This is to say that people will do what they want to do, based upon past karmas and samskaras, and will not change for the better until they themselves are ready to do so.

If one does venture to educate friends and family in what one considers to be more refined ways of dharmic living, one should know this fact, and also be prepared to be disappointed and disillusioned — a lesson that applies to oneself more than to others. In other words, the appearance of how attached one is may be the entire point of the exercise overall.

QUESTION #3: "I have some confusion understanding the relationship between the realm of relativity as being totally unreal, even though it is infused with the power of the truth that 'Existence Is.' I had resolved that dilemma in the past by realizing that the world of name, form, time, space, and causation is unreal in the sense that it is impermanent and therefore always changing. Now even that change is unreal, being Parinama. The saying that the dream is unreal but the dreamer is real and only needs to wake up applies here, but we are ultimately real only as Atman, right? Even Ishvara and AUM disappear in Asamprajnata Samadhi, so does that mean that these highest principles are not real as well?"

ANSWER: Holding two views, though difficult, is often very beneficial, and it can be done, but more effectively only at a more advanced stage of mental and philosophical refinement. Such is the case with the combined contrast and coalescence of relativity and Reality by the mind of the spiritual seeker. Both are eternal; that fact alone helps immensely towards the comprehension of all that is either difficult or impossible of comprehension (Maya and Brahman).

To summate in brief, and to form a siddhanta (philosophical conclusion), one is eternal and eternally changeful, while the other is Eternal and Changeless. And as far as the dreamer and the dream go, the same conclusion can be applied. That is to say (videlicet), what dreams of the past do we now remember, what to speak of hours, days, weeks, months, years, and decades of our recent past. Then there are our unremembered past lives. Are they not all dreamlike? You, alone, remain the same. And if you want to remember yourself (Self) as you truly are, you will simply wake up and do so one day, one moment. Here, it is falling back to sleep that is the problem.

QUESTION #4: "I understand that the act of perception is inaccurate. Even the dense element of lead is mostly empty space, and yet we cannot perceive it. Visible light is only a very narrow slice of the electromagnetic spectrum, and we cannot observe it, so our perception is limited indeed. Yet how does that correlate with "Existence Is?"

ANSWER: A little secret here: Perception, itself, is the source, whether it be false or true, limited or unlimited, real or dreamlike. That is the fact of "Everything Is." Nonperception is a misnomer. Even the general state of deep sleep is remembered after we wake up, inferred after the fact. Reality is cognized by every modification of the mind, say the Upanisads. There is verily nothing that is not real, and all that is not real — that, too, is traceable to Reality. That is why Sri Krishna states in the Gita, beautifully, that *"The unreal never is; the Real never ceases to be. The truth about both of these has been known by the seers."* So now, become a seer and realize the truth of both relativity and Reality — based upon the only distinction that applies and is helpful — that one is eternal and eternally changeful, while the other is Eternal and Changeless.

QUESTION #5: "I have another question to add to my last. It is in a similar vein, and has to do with what is real and what is unreal. In lesson 24, when discussing the way that illumined souls stay in Brahman consciousness while forbearing the effects of relativity, you wrote: 'In short, resistance to Maya is futile (since it is neither real or unreal or a combination of both) but denial of

Brahman is impossible, unthinkable.' If Maya is neither real or unreal, then what is it? Apparently real? If it were only apparently real, then that would mean it is unreal. I appreciated how you wrote that resistance is futile, and that illumined souls learn to 'float' above the apparent world."

ANSWER: *"Resist not evil"* is a more contemporary saying that applies to Maya. Also, *"Get thee behind me."* Shallow thinkers occupying the moral surface of great teachings like these, opine that Christ was speaking about a real evil, or an incarnate devil. This is religious superstition. Tantric seers who have observed Maya over time from a safe distance — like watching a fog bank from a mountaintop — have told us that maya is not only eternal (eternally changing too), but also insentient. There is no devil out to get you, not unless you have set your own mind upon yourself. Maya is inscrutable, unknowable. As a principle it is but a simulacrum. To try to know a mirage in the desert as a reality will only lead us astray, or insane. So we content ourselves in knowing that it is just a mirage.

Some hints are possible, however. The Tantras say that *"Maya is she who covers our eyes with one hand and leads us on with the other."* Also, Sri Ramakrishna used the analogy of the mango skin. It covers and protects the fruit until it is ripe, but no one eats it afterwards. They discard it and take the flesh of the fruit alone.

So, yes, apparently real, but not ultimately real — that much can be said. It persists up and until formless samadhi is attained. It may return, as well, if the realized soul deigns to return to its realm. Well, we take refuge in Mahamaya at that point, and even prior, yes? Only She can guide us through that flexuous and impermeable maze, the illusory labyrinth of legerdemain that is Maya.

Avinashi (earlier D.H. prior to SRV initiation) from Pennsylvania writes:
QUESTION: "This question relates to the blessing and offering of food. I need to get food from food banks occasionally (I just recently needed to), and when it comes to food banks, one gets what one gets. I eat pure food as much as financially possible, but when the money sometimes runs out, I have to eat what's given. Some of what's given is not pure food; it is not food that one would usually offer to a deity or to the Master, so I feel a little bit in a dilemma about it. I can bless it, but can I offer it, in front of the picture of the Master, to the Master? As you can see, there are probably several questions within this question. I want to actually offer my food to the Master before I eat it, as Holy Mother did: how do I do that? Do I use the usual blessing prayer (Om Brahmarpanam Brahmahavir...) when I bring the food, nicely arranged on a plate, before the picture of the Master? Or is there another prayer I would properly use to actually offer the food? And when it comes to actually offering food to the Master, can I offer the impure food, or only bless it? I remember the Master ate food from the Kali temple, which was not pure vegetarian. And I think, too, of something I read in one of Swami Shivananda's books that I memorized: 'Never condemn or speak ill of any kind of food, since food is the first

gateway to Brahman; wherever one sits before food daily, say, 'Annam is Brahman.' I think of wandering sannyasins, as well; they ate whatever ended up in their bowls, and they must have surely blessed their food and probably offered it too. So please resolve these conundrums for me, and will you also please give me whatever prayer I need to actually offer my food to Sri Ramakrishna, (if I need a special prayer for that)?"

ANSWER: I am very glad to find that some western people are thinking in these terms, since the natural sanctity around food has been either missing or horribly compromised in this culture, and now the world in general. I say "natural sanctity" because, as Swami Brahmananda's quote above infers, all food is to be considered sacred. The food that beggars or pariahs eat may not be fit for others, but it is right for them at the time, and whatever condition it is in must be accepted as a part of daily circumstances and karma.

But this brings in the other element in your set of questions, that the holiness of food can be added to, and whatever impurities have crept in can be greatly done away with by a conscious act of offering of the mind. Bringing one's thoughts, i.e. concentration, to bear upon food is what is needed for this act to consummate. It is much like concentrating on anything. If the act is done half-heartedly, then the result is inferior. Think of the act of cutting vegetables, or performing surgery, or conceiving children — should they be done with half of one's attention? Of course not, or dire effects will occur. Yet people today do most of what they do in a state of partial concentration, if that. Even "multitasking," unless done masterfully, is a violation of the laws of concentration. Full concentration on any given thing is both wise and fulfilling, and wonderful. And in Yoga, it is penultimate to Samadhi.

In the actual offering of food to the deity, one who is trained in the puja for it has all manner of mantras, mudras, and slokas to offer. That type of thing is done for the deity and the onlookers as well. When offering at home, on one's own, clean hands/body, tidy place of preparation, pure mind, the best foods one has access to — all of these play a big part in sanctifying food. One's thoughts, before and at the time of offering, are important too, and let us not forget that to take the food and use its energy for spiritual practice is the most important of all. For, what does the deity need with your food? He or She is either beyond the need for food, or living in a loka where it abounds in its purest and best forms!

Thus, the real secret, the real consummation, is utilizing food that has been purified and permeated by one's concentration and devotion in order to raise Kundalini Shakti inwards to the Source. This is also what the deity wants of you; not so much your worship, but your wakeup. As Sri Ramakrishna used to say, *"I came here to dance, sing, eat, and make merry with the devotees of the Lord. It was my only desire, to be the king of the devotees."* But how could He do that if people were unable to join Him with a clear mind and conscience, or if they considered themselves unclean or not equal to the task, or the pure presence of the Paramahamsa?

Let us remember, then, that "The Lord, Our God" is not squeamish, is not under the restrictions of cast or society, is never waylaid or put off by rules around food and activities, and is never under the press of shame, aversion, or a holier than thou attitude. He/She will sit and eat with you what you have, whatever you offer in a heartfelt manner — whether He is here in a form on earth with you, or in a state of formless form residing in your own heart and mind. As Sri Krishna has told us, He who was Ramakrishna in an earlier form: *"I accept whatever they offer Me, a leaf, a flower, some bread, since it is the humble offering of their own heart."*

QUESTION #2: "On the insides of some of your CD inserts it is written that you will eventually offer a set of talks, (or maybe it's a book), describing the special characteristics of the Sri Ramakrishna incarnation. Will you write some on that now? What are the most central, salient characteristics? I would be so interested to hear the answer to this question!"

ANSWER: In my experience in this lifetime, and after meditating for over forty years in uninterrupted style on the Great Master, with no other God before me, and with all the many blessings from my initiatory guru and other teachers that contributed — and not disregarding that there are a score of secondary characteristics He possesses as well — I think it is safe to say that the main characteristics of Sri Ramakrishna Paramahamsa incarnation are three:

    First, He is the Kali Avatar, which means that an incarnation of the Universal Mother has finally descended, simultaneously epitomizing and emanating the Supreme Feminine Divine in a way that has not occurred here on earth previously. This fact is emphasized by the appearance of Sri Sarada Devi with Him, who is His equal in feminine form, and who is not only a consort like Radha and Sita were, but who is the Goddess Herself, manifesting in Her chosen form.

    Secondly, there is the fact of His full and complete incarnation, contrasted to the partial emanations of the past, and instanced by the frame of time, or yuga, that He has come in, the Kali Yuga, where darkness in the form of spiritual ignorance is as if natural to the beings living on earth, and those transmigrating souls inhabiting the realms of the ancestors and celestials — what to speak of the lowly, the fallen, the weak, and impoverished — always the Avatar's special point of compassion.

    Thirdly, there is the warm and welcome principle of Universality. It was far past time for someone of great merit and realization to both exemplify and pronounce it as the winning way for all beings in this day and time, particularly in connection with Advaita, Nonduality. On one hand, there has been enough religious narrowness, bigotry, and limiting sectarianism here on earth to last a Mahayuga of lifetimes, what to speak of all the violence and atrocities that man has committed in the name of religion. The simple but direct principle of Universality, well, that should never have been forgotten, should always be held sacrosanct by living beings. And on the other hand, it is not just an escape or solution to all these particular problems of the world, but is a source of eternal bliss and wisdom itself.... *"where rolled the stream of knowledge, truth, and the bliss that follows both,"* as Vivekananda has written.

Much more could be said on this level, about this subject, obviously, but in the context of Patanjali's Yoga which is our present study here, suffice to say that with such a soul as Sri Ramakrishna as our example, we will never fail the goal of Yoga. And even if we do, individually, He will see us (His devotees) through to that blissful end. This is because, and simply put, that there has been no one on historical record who has both had access to and deeply and repeatedly experienced so many different kinds of samadhis, many more than are listed in Patanjali's sutras. This fact alone endears Him to us, the practitioners, what to speak of the hosts of beings I have just mentioned above.

QUESTION #3: "What does the mantra 'hring' mean? If it does not 'mean' anything, still it must connect with factors like chakras or whatever. And the title of Swamiji's beautiful vesper hymn 'Om Hring Ritang' of course employs this mantra. What does it mean and what does it connect to?"

ANSWER: Like all bijas, the meaning is to be found out in the cave of the heart, when uncovering just who the Tripura Sundari — the Triple Goddess — is. One third of Her is given at the time of mantra-diksha through the mantra. The other two thirds are discovered during the ongoing process of the devotee's japa and meditation. But as a basic understanding, Hring or Hrim, is a bija of transformational power on the spiritual level. Like the great bija AUM is directly correlative with Brahman, the great bija Hring is intrinsically connected to Divine Mother. So, transcendent equipoise and dynamic power, one could hardly ask for a more effective combination in a mantra. Now all that is left is to repeat them without ceasing, and let them do their inner work on us.

QUESTION #4: "Lately the problems of life have subsided, leaving me free for totally undisturbed sadhana, and it is going well! Better than well. I can only thank you a thousand, ten-thousand times for all you have given me. I am using all of it. I do not have to struggle to get to the meditation cushion anymore; in fact, it is one of my favorite places to be. My evening arati quickly changed its form. However, it turned into just a second meditation session. I don't think there's anything wrong with that, and I can say so surely that doing two sessions a day deepens my practice compared to just one! It is as if I am in meditation all day long, all the time. It gets so intense that sometimes all I can do is surrender — the mind is floundering like a swimmer in a heavy sea and I just have to let it be overcome by the waves of meditation. This is what it feels like. But a question comes up as well. Lately, I have been frequently finding myself very happy. This is probably due to the strength and consistency of my spiritual practice at present. But this happiness raises questions, and what I conceive to be potential problems. So the question is: is it okay to be happy if everyone around me is sad? Is it possible that happiness in this situation could be inappropriate, or even lacking in empathy? I suspect it could at least be misinterpreted. So how does one handle one's happiness in situations like this? Should one hide it, or what?"

ANSWER: As for your gratitude, it sounds sweet, indeed, but mainly because one like myself loves to hear a spiritual success story, especially in this world where there are so many struggles ending in failure. All of us fail, and people follow this pattern for years, even lifetimes, but when the real formula is found, taken to, and implemented with success, that signals a very special time of life(s). Do enjoy it; do be happy about it; but more, cherish it and protect it in this world. As Jesus said, *"Does a man light a candle and then hide it under a bushel?"* He meant that we are to let our light shine. I suppose that when such light manifests, one only has to know when to shine it and when to take it inward, like Sri Ramakrishna at the Panahati Festival. For, the world will misunderstand it, and trouble can ensue in that atmosphere.

As I have reminded you, and others, and in the vein of flexibility, when worship turns to meditation, when action turns to inaction, when periods of work turn to phases of study, etc., one should merely go with the flow. This is the benefit of spiritual life as it moves forward. Who would think of stopping a river? As long as it is flowing towards Kaivalya, and not towards Samsara, then we are to follow it where it leads.

And this is the real meaning of "follow your heart," not the whimsical new age version which has one frittering away time, day by day, under the false pretense of "living in the present."

Only, keep up the studies. In a nutshell, it is this: that bhakti and dhyanam are excellent. However, they both require Karma Yoga to be complete, to come full circle. In other words, they can fall short unless they are tested in the fires of motiveless action and selfless service. But Karma Yoga itself is worthless, even dangerous, if it is not subjected to Jnanam. Thus, it is Jnanam that justifies the other three...at least for the one who is seeking consummate Yoga, Integral Yoga. Both the world, and the world of spiritual aspirants, bears this fact out so clearly in this day and age.

QUESTION #5: "You often say that "To see God, one must see as God sees." How does God see?"

ANSWER: I think that was Meister Ekhart's expression, and a good one. What is meant, at least by the Vedantist or nondualist, is twofold: one, that God sees through a single eye; and two, that what the people of this world take to be God and His Will is a surface understanding only. They attribute judgements, decrees, acts, and the granting of boons to That which is beyond all these. As the Gita would put it, all action takes place in Nature, not in the Soul/God.

The expression, "God acts through human beings," then, is to be analyzed closely, with a strong handle on nondual philosophy. If one reflects deeply enough, and meditates on and with the single eye of Truth for a time, one will see that most of what gets attributed to this Divine Power is really coming from the mind. True, God's Mind, called Mahat in Sankhya, is a part of this. But somewhere along the arc of divine descent the line gets blurred, and the collective and individual mind fall victim to what is called false superimposition in Vedanta — a very misleading tendency. Seers call this mental projection as well, and as it gets utilized, as with any power, various distortions accompany the process.

But these distortions do not exist in the atmosphere of God-Consciousness. Timeless, Deathless Awareness is unassailably clear. It disencumbers the soul from that which weighs it down. Sight, there, is omniscience; sound is all-pervasiveness; touch is ecstacy, taste is the highest wisdom, and fragrance is the mind's samadhi. Thus, God's "seeing" is vastly different from what embodied beings think it to be.

Suprema from Pennsylvania writes:
COMMENTS: "Hope I didn't wait too long to comment. The metaphor you used to explain the Reality or 'discovery' of Atman was so powerful for me that it is being used daily as a meditation in itself. I imagine, because I have not yet made the 'ultimate connection' and still use the crutch of concept, that 'self' is thinning — the sheaths of tissue or membrane of separation, as You put it, thinning to nothing and thus revealing the Self in All. I can break down the elements, keep going 'back' to 'who' I was before the separations began, before 'I' was born. An exercise only? Maybe. One day I long to 'breach.' Come dissolution."
RESPONSE: With thoughts and reflections such as these, deep experiences of the Self are bound to attend the soul. This is the subject and objective of Patanjali's Yoga. Breaching like whales, out of the dense water and into the thin air of heights, may we free ourselves of the gravity of relative existence in rapt meditation and have that samadhi which is the essence of our Existence.

Akshaya Bhakti from New England writes:
QUESTION: "How blessed I felt to be able to attend the Raja Yoga retreat in Oregon, even more so because I didn't expect to! Despite this gift of reinforcement to my Raja study and the intensive lessons we have already received, I still long to learn more about Pratyahara, knowing that without perfecting it I will not be able to approach Samyama (or the 3 highest integrated steps of Patanjali's Yoga). I was particularly intrigued by the chart presented at the retreat which compared the steps of Patanjali's Yoga to that of Shankara's interpretation, because the intermediary steps added by Shankara sound like they might cast light on Pratyahara, seeing as they come between it and the stage of Asana. I am wondering if there is a text still available which is devoted to Shankara's version of Raja Yoga so that I can explore this further? Even if I were able to obtain such a copy, I would still very much appreciate a brief explanation of Shankara's version including these additional steps: Tyaga/renunciation, Mauna/silence, Desha/space of consciousness, and Kala/Brahman as Witness, Nirodha/restraint of Maya by Brahman, and how to understand Pratyahara as 'seeing the Atman in all.' Further, some thoughts on Asana at the mental level would be good."
ANSWER: For the answer to two of your questions/requests here, I refer you to Shankara's scripture titled, *Aparokshanubhuti,* and my article on the subject of Shankara's commentary on Patanjali's Yoga in issue #10 (page 13) of Nectar of Nondual Truth. There is plenty to contemplate in both these sources. And since this book is titled *Atmic Testimony on Yoga,* being a statement of how Vedanta looks at Yoga, I place that selfsame chart you mention here on the fol-

# Patanjali's and Shankara's Yoga of the Mind

| Patanjali's 8-Limbed Yoga | Shankara's Advaita Yoga in 15 Parts |
|---|---|

*"The controlling of the mind should be the first duty of the practitioner of Yoga and Concentration."*

| Patanjali's 8-Limbed Yoga | Shankara's Advaita Yoga in 15 Parts |
|---|---|
| I  Yamas | Yamas — Seeing all as Brahman |
| II  Niyamas | Niyamas — Control of the Mind |
| *"External renunciation is achieved by giving up gross things; internal by giving up the ego."* | Tyaga — Renunciation |
| *"Control of the speech is the first door to Yoga."* | Mauna — Silence |
| *"Think of soul in the soul, not in the body or mind."* | Desha — Space of Consciousness |
| *"There is One who is the witness of all states."* | Kala — Brahman as Witness |
| III  Asana | Asana — Posture of Meditation |
| *"Give up the idea of the Self in the sheaths and recognize yourself as Brahman."* | Nirodha — Restraint of Maya by Brahman |
| *"That one who is free in the body, he is free without a body also."* | Deha-samatva — Equipoise of the Body |
| *"Settled knowledge — understanding the difference between the seer and the seen — is perfect seeing."* | Drdhata-drshya — Firmness of Vision |
| IV  Pranayama | Pranayama — Mental States as Brahman |
| V  Pratyahara | Pratyahara — Seeing Atman in All |
| VI  Dharana | Dharana |
| VII  Dhyana | Dhyana |
| VIII  Samadhi | Samadhi |

*"Attain samadhi by controlling the senses, and remain always in peace. By attaining samadhi, destroy the darkness that arises from ignorance by the practice of seeing oneness always and everywhere. These are the main doorways to Yoga. Then control speech and mind, give up all expectations and all desires, and seek solitude."*     Adishankaracharya

lowing page (92) so that all of us engaged in this study can apply compare the points:

As for mental asana, it is one of my favorite topics, being as it is an innovative technique peculiar to advanced Yogic practice, and coming as it does at a place in time where people are so body-oriented and mentally and spiritually lazy that the very word, "Yoga," is being taken for or replaced in everyday vocabulary by what is really only hatha.

A good reminder, and remedy to this gross oversight and insult to the noble system of Raja Yoga, is the assumption of mental asanas by the serious practitioner, one in particular — Nondualism. Establishing oneself in powerful mental asanas the likes of "I am one with Brahman," or "This Self is Brahman," or "This Self is Pure Awareness," or "That Thou Art," real and true transcendence is bound to come in authentic fashion in due time. When a tornado lifts a tree out of the ground, roots and all, of what use is its physical position anymore? Similarly, when samadhi dawns on the mind, springing from a supreme mental asana, held firmly and with great resolve, the assuming of various bodily postures seems, as Shankara has stated, *"like the twisting and turning of a dried up old tree in the wind."* The least that can be said is that the discipline of mental asana is for advanced seekers of Truth, and of God.

QUESTION #2: "One thought I had to enhance Pratyahara was to recite the prayer about turning the external into the internal, since this step seems to be a pivotal point between the two. Could you please give that prayer, dear teacher, with some of your own annotations on it?"

ANSWER: Here is that chant you call to our attention. It is one I have asked the students of SRV to memorize, and use in their daily meditations:

*Om drishyam pratitam pravila payan san*
*sanmatram ananda ghanam vibhavayam*
*samahitas san bahir antaram va*
*kalam nayetah sati karma bandhe*
*Om Shanti, Shanti Shantih*

*Brahman is an indeterminable mass of pure, conscious Awareness,*
*boundless, infinite, and eternal.*
*Therefore, taking what is internal, and what is external,*
*render them into one indivisible state.*
*Then meditate upon that state, pass your time contentedly, and be free.*

Beautiful in its poetic lines, as well as its nondual message, this exquisite sloka from the Vivekachudamani of Shankara places everything into perspective. Spiritual aspirants, at least until they have attained the necessary and penultimate boon of peace of mind, spend far too much time entertaining their own type of brooding. That is, the worldly brood about family, money, occupation, and death. But the spiritual aspirant broods about whether he/she has the right path or teacher or not, why he is not making progress along his chosen path, why he is not doing the practice given by the guru in daily fashion, whether or not the mantra given is the right one for him, or why enlightenment has not come — things of this nature.

In this sloka, the Truth is stated at the outset, then the problem of duality is cited, and then the solution proclaimed. It is brilliant! Finally, the conclusion is that once the Truth is known, one has only to be content with It, and then one is free. If this seems to be untrue due to the mind's cycles (gunas), then one has only to meditate on the nature of oneness wherever twoness appears. Also get constant corroboration from the preceptor.

This is a brief and simple explanation for this sloka. And where it applies to the practice of pratyahara is in its ability to take over the mind entirely when it is deeply contemplated. Pratyahara is the ability to take one's thoughts off of relativity and its pleasures, problems, and distractions. These all go away in contemplation of a sloka such as this, so we should spend more time in such meditative pastimes.

QUESTION #4: "Finally, in the chart pertaining to Raja Yoga entitled, 'Stages of Dissolution of the Mind in Yoga,' there are '4 Aids' to practice that are listed under the '7 Methods of Achieving the Dissolution of the Mind'. Could you please list these aids? They seem like they might be a good interim practice."

ANSWER: On that chart, there is what is called the "Seven Methods for Mastery." Then there are the "Seven Levels of Attainment." Please specify which you are interested in knowing about, and resubmit your question [Reader can please look in Volume 1 of this work, page 310, to view this chart].

## Pada III, Sutra 13

*etena bhootendriyeshu dharmalakshanavastha parinama vyakhyatah* (*etana,* due to these; *bhuta,* senses, object, elements; *indriyasau,* senses connected to mind; *dharma,* form; *lakshana,* condition of time; *avastha,* stage; *parinamah* transformation; *vyakhyatah,* description).

*"The ongoing transformation of form, time, and various stages are thus understood in relation to objects, elements, and the mind and senses."*

To understand our universe is key to understanding ourselves — and our Self/Atman. These three — nature, self, and Self (prakriti, ahamkara, and Atman) — are so constituted as to lead the soul, presently posited in the world of name and form in time and space, back to its naturally transcendent condition. But if this attempt at comprehension is engaged in with senses connected to a mind which looks only outwards, the main purpose for life on earth is stymied. The chart on the facing page reminds us of the connections between Patanjali's mention here of *"objects, elements, and the mind and senses."* Referring to the quote at the top of this chart (page 95), then tracing the several five-fold sets of tattvas from the bottom up to the mind via the prana, a good idea of the practice of inward ascension by the Self-seeking soul is revealed.

Therefore, it is a contemplative life and mind given over to meditation that allows such an inward journey. Even to call these changes that are taking place all around us "transformations," and call the happenings of our lives "transitions," is to rub up against an otherwise impermeable truth that cannot be avoided for long. When such transformations and transitions are studied under

# Controlling the Five Senses in Yoga

*"By meditating upon the elements, the senses, and mind, the hidden truth about objects gets revealed. Meditation upon the subtle elements and the sense of I-ness expands thought, awakens wisdom, and tames the ego. Then, meditation upon the true individual along with its intelligence delimits the ego and exposes the fount of Joy within oneself. The Purusha then transcends the very idea of selfhood and meditates on the awareness of cessation. Thus do the samadhis of knowledge, bliss, and I-ness lead to Formlessness.     Patanjala Yoga*

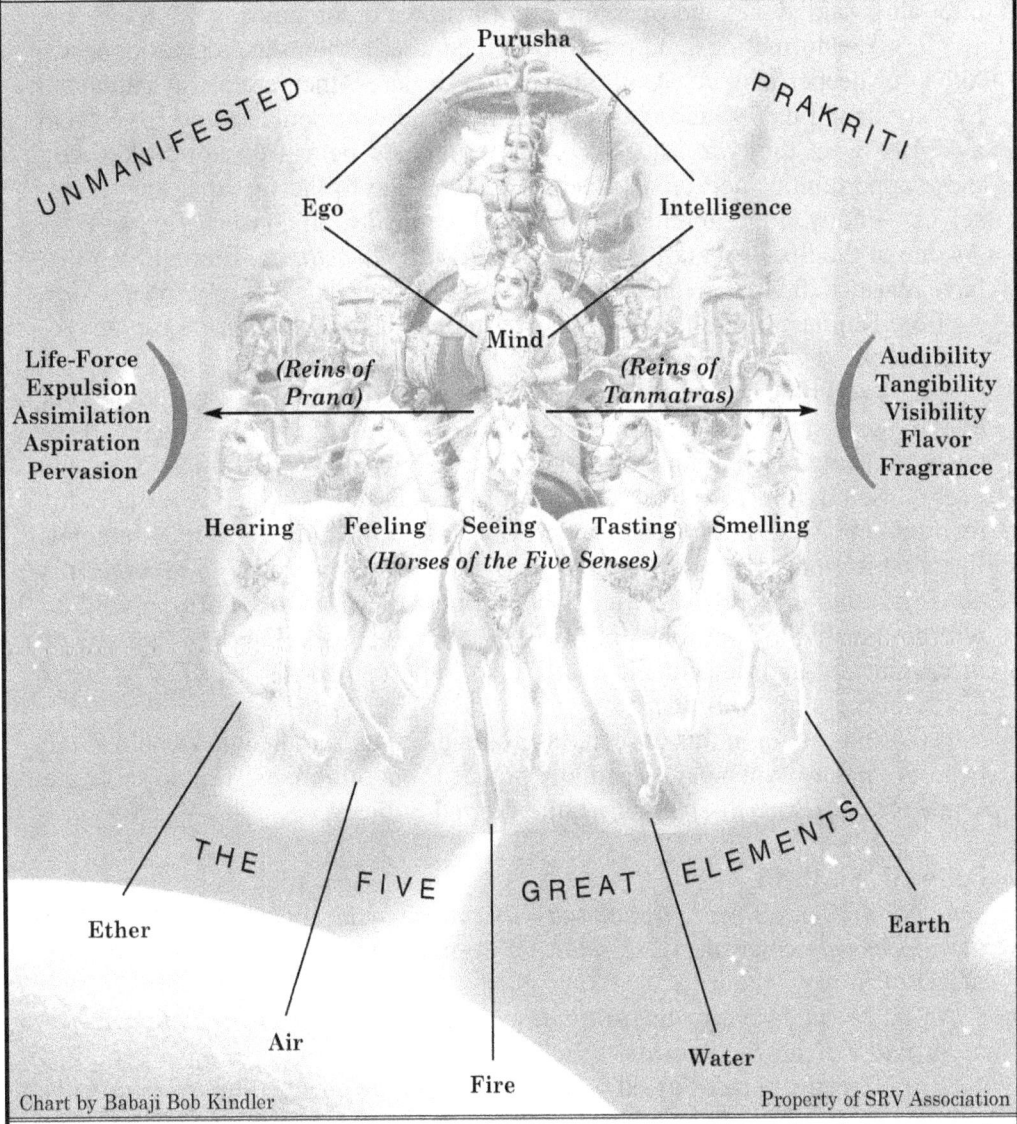

UNMANIFESTED     PRAKRITI

Purusha
Ego — Intelligence
Mind

Life-Force / Expulsion / Assimilation / Aspiration / Pervasion
(Reins of Prana)     (Reins of Tanmatras)
Audibility / Tangibility / Visibility / Flavor / Fragrance

Hearing   Feeling   Seeing   Tasting   Smelling
(Horses of the Five Senses)

THE FIVE GREAT ELEMENTS

Ether    Air    Fire    Water    Earth

Chart by Babaji Bob Kindler                             Property of SRV Association

*"Meditating with intense focus upon the principles of existence, the seeker de-fragments the mind and unifies himself with nature. Unification, here, is not one of identity, but one of connection. That is, oneness with nature would mean his Soul is one with birth, decay, and death, and this is not the case. The Soul is eternal Existence. Thus, realizing that all of nature has come out of his mental process via the power of projection, the yogi takes stock of the evolutes of nature, from gross to subtle, contemplates them, and masters them. In this way he separates the true Self from the apparent self, and from nature.     Babaji Bob Kindler*

the microscope of the contemplative mind and attitude, a view of the principle of mental projection soon comes to visit man's awareness. The phenomena that are going on in the physical universe then get cast away, and scrutiny of what is apparent, or nonactual, ensues. It is that inspection, accomplished under the mantle of a haunting suspicion that a ruse is being perpetrated on the soul, that leads to real progress, thus Freedom. Until that part of the journey is undertaken, man only goes round and round in cycles of time in his own mind which, after all is said, done, and over, are all of his own doing anyway.

Transformations and transitions, then, are in themselves great opportunities for deeper insight. As the next sutra declares, they are always attended by "constant flux" which, to an inwardly observant soul, should give them away for what they are, illusory. Why embodied beings do not strike upon these opportunities and unveil such insights is due to the fact that they themselves — body, mind, intellect, and ego — are always in constant flux as well. As one of the Six Proofs of Purusha, called *Nitya-avasthana*, Eternal Stability, have revealed, it takes an unmoving witness to cognize an ever moving exterior. As Lord Kapila has put it, in very ancient times, *"Universal motion can be recognized only by that which is eternally stationary."*

To put this in personalized terms, the embodied soul, always on the run, ever moving, seldom ever stopping except to sleep, and fully believing in all the changes taking place around him, can never see what is called by the seers his ever-conscious and cohesive substratum *(Kutasthanitya)*, which is actually his own pristine Awareness, free of overlays and modifications. He may be intelligent concerning matters of the world, but his real Intelligence *(Sat-buddhi)* is either missing or sorely lacking. Until he remedies this discomfiting void he will not be able to find freedom *(Moksha)*, nor even develop the inner arts of discrimination and detachment that are so important to his detached Witness Consciousness *(Sakshi-bhutam)*.

And caught in this unseen, inscrutable conundrum he will remain at the behest of nature, when nature actually proceeds out of him, existing to serve the sentient Soul *(Prakriti-samavaya)*, the Eternal Subject.

## Pada III, Sutra 14

*shantoditavyapadeshyadharmanupati dharmi* (*shanta,* abiding; *udita,* arising; *avyapadeshya,* constant flux; *dharma,* form; *anupati,* proceeding; *dharmi,* object of form).

*"The underlying and all-abiding state is acted upon by the appearance of form and objects in constant flux."*

Here, the phrase "acted upon" does not mean changed in any way. It is one of the Great Axioms and endearing wonders of the truth of Vedanta, that despite the ongoing cycles of time in space based upon cause and effect, the Transcendent Brahman never alters. Brahman is, as Sri Ramakrishna has attested to, *"The only 'thing' that has always gone untouched and uncorrupted by the mind and tongue of man."* Knowing this unalterable Reality immediately uncovers the ruse of false superimposition in the mind. But if jumping to this highest station of Awareness is not possible, then the soul inspects nature, the self (ego), and the true Self, to establish inner connections, which are likened to a trail of bread crumbs leading within. This process opens to what Jesus termed the "Kingdom of heaven within."

How all of this applies to daily life also becomes obvious once one begins to entertain the thinking of the ancient (and modern) rishis. Terms like *"dwelling like a maidservant in a foreign man's home," "living like a ghost or a ghoul," "moving about like an automaton," "not of myself do I do," "those who know that action is inaction, and inaction, action, they truly know,"* and other ways of expression apply here. The monastic way of viewing it is that all phenomena are illusory, but few can accept and imbibe such a radical and ultimate conclusion. Most default to the zone of *"real as long as it appears, unreal when it disappears from my view."* And this is an acceptable position to hold as long as one has not been able to completely dissolve the mind in nondual meditation.

Until then, name, form, worlds, time, space, objects, nature, the body, celestial bodies, et al, will occupy life and mind and influence the "mind-stuff," the chitta, causing it to "take form" as Patanjali points out. For the seer, this is not a problem, despite what sufferings may arise. But for the ignorant soul, this benighted perspective is deluding, thus poisonous, as it obscures the truth of his very being — that he is an infinite, sentient Soul, not a finite body/mind mechanism.

## Lesson Sixty-seven, 1/21/12
### Pada III, Sutra 15 & 16

It is the new year of 2012, and we start it off with a fresh zest for Yoga and its lofty accomplishments, positioned in the middle of the third pada of the sutras as we are. Dozens of lessons have been taken in via this course by those who desire to delve deep into the teachings of Mother India. Among them, Patanjala holds a very high place, both in philosophical esteem and in the devotional life of Truth-seekers. The lifestyle prescribed is a superior one, with aspects of renunciation and close attention to conscious everyday life equally mixed in.

Questions from members of "the list" are arranged below, indicating the level of interest in this subject and the difficulty of mastery as well. Sutras on concentration and samyama conclude the lesson, revealing to what heights we have already ascended to in our long-lived study. May this effort benefit all beings, purifying the mind on both individual and collective levels.

**Questions and Answers for Lesson 67**
Ramakrishnadas from New England writes:
QUESTION: "Here is a practical question regarding sutra, III:14. What tools are most necessary to reach the all-abiding state? Japa seems to work away at

the illusion of permanence. If one's japa has not yet blossomed into full Meditation, are there other areas where sadhana can help open the omniscient eye? What Yogas work best at this stage of the understanding of Brahman? Does the practice of the yamas and niyamas have any tricks to actually fulfill them to perfection? Any suggestions?"

ANSWER: Not tricks, per se, but modes of gradual fructification. The yamas and niyamas are, as I have often said, not commandments, but rather guides along the spiritual path, and ways of intensifying sadhana and its results. *"Thou shalt not kill,"* for instance, transforms into the realization that "Thou cannot kill" under the influence of ahimsa The Atman is deathless, since it was never born. Via the practice of asteya, *"Do unto others as ye would have them do unto you"* turns into the realization that "you" and "others" are not two separate souls at all, but always one; therefore helping one is helping all.

Thus, these yamas and niyamas, rightly seen and thoroughly practiced, are the tools that take one towards the all-abiding state. That state itself is not something to be "reached," however, but an eternal state of awareness already at hand. As Holy Mother has told us, sadhana and japa, etc., will not bring one enlightenment, but they will purify the mind so that it will reveal the Light of Consciousness. One suddenly finds oneself there, in a breathtaking moment, and all such things as effort and practice are seen as if useless beside That.

For comprehensive seekers, however, those who have acuity and are persevering, some "hints" are given by the luminaries at that level of effortless practice. A reading of nondual scriptures like Yoga Vasishtha will reveal some of these. Scour these great works for teachings that the seers left behind for us. Many of them did not systematize the whole matter like Patanjali did so carefully for us here, but that less orthodox mode has its benefits as well.

QUESTION #2: "I am now practicing meditation on the heart chakra as you have directed, and find it difficult to maintain concentration there, as I have not had the seat of my meditation there in the past. There was great success early, but now there is difficulty. Any hints?"

ANSWER: Difficulty is not a bad sign; not at all. A yogi welcomes such challenges, which will only give impetus to the forthcoming realization when he pierces through to the light of the next level. Suffice to say that there is an entire set of lokas in the heart chakra, enough to keep any devotee busy for countless eternal seconds. Open up your mode of meditation and have the mind's thoughts course along the nadis that lead to the heart and inwards. I did not say to shut down the third eye center, but only to direct it towards the anahata. As Sri Krishna says in the Gita, *"Keep the energy focused in the head, and the attention set in the heart."* In this way the inner seeker beholds all that occurs within him, and remains aware at as many levels of awareness as he can manage. Above all, breathe the light of aspiration and intelligence into your sessions. Then each one will be loftier.

Avinashi from Pennsylvania writes:
QUESTION: "I am not sure, but does 'Thakur' mean 'Master'? Sometimes I get

the feeling it was something like a first name, though I know that formally, it wasn't. Was this form of address only respectful, or was it also affectionate? And is it appropriate to address the Master as 'Thakur?' I feel less distant from him when I think of him by this term of address."

ANSWER: Thakur means "Lord." In "His" case, this is a spiritual term, and not one of worldly address. It is both reverential and affectionate. When one understands this, it is no wonder that intense devotion visits the heart.

QUESTION #2: "Experientially and philosophically, what is the difference between the bliss of the causal body and the bliss of Absolute Brahman? I would guess that the bliss of the causal body is a reflection of the bliss of Absolute Brahman, So where, then, is the difference? Is it just a matter of intensity, or is there some kind of difference in the character of the bliss?"

ANSWER: You have stated it. There is a difference in the nature of the bliss. While the bliss felt at the causal level is sweet, it emanates from the refined and sattvic ego at the level of the Anandamayakosha. It is the Sananda Samadhi that Patanjali teaches us about. That samadhi proceeds directly to the Sasmita variety, which means "with sense of self." No matter how overwhelming it becomes, in and out, and how endearing it is to the adept, it is limited. How to describe it has been a concern on the mind of the seers for ages. As I have understood it, there is a place of exit, or advance, or elevation, wherein the soul in love with the bliss of the unmanifested, of a sudden, turns in an entirely different direction and espies a much fuller Light. It realizes that the entirety of bliss it is experiencing cannot be held in the ego/soul, no matter how refined that vehicle has become. It must *"let go its hold,"* and such an ingenious and brilliant inner advance is exactly the type of subtle movement that allows for the merging of the self into the Great Self, of going beyond samprajnata into Asamprajnata.

Another way it can be seen, which is one of my own favorite ways of expressing it, is that all beings, even the gods, are facing away from the Light of Brahman. They may know that it exists, can even feel it, but cannot turn towards it — as if such a turn would mean the extinction of their very forms. The Trinity, too, Brahma, Vishnu, and Siva, stand at the apex of all the worlds with the Light of Brahman at Their backs. Like Light shining through a many-colored crystal dome, as the poet Shelley expresses it, this emanation of Consciousness gleams through Them, flows out of their pores, and then turns into the many worlds and lights all of them up, simultaneously. Only, these three unique Divinities can, and will, occasionally turn towards that Light (signaled by a realized soul entering samadhi on earth), and when They do they provide entrance into Brahman for those realized souls who are leaving the worlds of name and form forever, to merge into the Formless Reality completely.

All of that subtle difference that is occurring has to do with both the causal realm and what lies beyond it. For the embodied soul, the human being, deep sleep and matured spirituality, respectively, are the symbols for both. Thus is the import of allying study of the three matras of the Word, Aum, with the waking, dreaming, and deep sleep states of mankind, and thereby mastering them and proceeding towards Turiya, "the Fourth." Vedavyasa, in his commentaries on the Yoga sutras, brings Turiya into the mix, with many correlative teachings. Thus, and through the many darshanas of the most excellent seers, we see the connection between samadhi, nirvana, moksha, mukti, kaivalya, turiya, and other fine spiritually indicative terms.

QUESTION #3: "At 58 years of age, the personality I've formed in this incarnation is not going to be radically altered. It is what it is for the most part, and it seems to me that attempting to shape it into some ideal pattern at this late stage would only involve me in endless, mostly futile, struggles, struggles that would only detract from any fruitful and further development of yogic skills or progress, So, while I exert myself to strictly adhere to the yamas and niyamas since they 1) increase the power to concentrate by reducing conflict with others and, 2) set into place the most essential foundations for yogic practice, I also intend to just stop worrying about this personality and its rough edges. My becoming a saint, in other words, will be entirely an accident if it happens at all. This personality is what is, and will be what it will be till it ends, and that's my attitude now. What do you think? Is this attitude yogically healthy?"

ANSWER: It is certainly more healthy than brooding, which is the greatest waste of time in an aspirant's life. But there is also a practicality in it, as it simultaneously deflates that selfsame ego personality and sets it up for surrender. Besides, concentrating on practice is the real point of yoga, at least until spiritual life kicks in and flows, or reveals subtler problems to tackle. I also think that there is the inflated ego (unripe), the deflated ego (ripe), and the divine personality. In other words, it is not that the ego needs be a problem and impediment. It can just as easily be a doorway. To turn it into one is usually a matter, as you have inferred here, of hardly noticing it until it takes one by surprise. In other words, the divine visits the human being through mature ego. One cannot rid oneself completely of the ego anyway, not as long as one sports a human mind and body. So, "good luck" to you in the advent of accidental sainthood!

QUESTION #4: "How do I surrender the fruits of my meditation and japa? Perhaps there is some prayer or chant that would help me do this? I see the necessity for surrendering the fruits of meditation and japa, but when I get to the edge of actually doing it, I simply sit there, confused. More generally, how do I surrender the fruits of austerities? The translated lyrics in one of your songs run this way: *'It is by austerity offered to thee that the mind comes under control.'* But as is the case with meditation and japa, I am at a loss when it comes to how to surrender the fruits of austerities."

ANSWER: I would advise that along with avoiding the problem of the personality, you also not worry about this either. What I mean is that what one offers to God should be pure and considerable in one's estimation. Let's wait to surrender things of such magnitude until they have accrued and are worthy. In the meantime, surrendering the heart's love will be more than enough to get the Mother's attentions.

QUESTION #5: "There are two sets of terms in your teachings describing the sequence of hearing, reflecting, and realizing that I am getting confused. I think maybe that's because they're from different darshanas. The terms are shravana, manana and nididhyasana; and shruti, yukti, and anubhava. I've grouped these terms in the way I think is proper, but I'm not sure I have it right. I understand what these terms mean individually, but I just can't correctly associate the terms with each other or associate them with the proper darshanas. There is a second part to this question: would you elaborate upon the meaning of the term 'sakshatkara,' which, as I understand, is the mostly unmentioned fourth step in the process of hearing, reflecting, and realizing? In one of your CD discourses you describe sakshatkara as the process of integrating what we've realized into our lives. At the same time, as suggested by other statements of yours, it seems there may be more to it than just this integration."

ANSWER: Sakshatkara is divine realization of Absolute Reality in action. You are right that it is seen and known as the natural result of shravana (to hear the Truth), manana (to contemplate the truth in the mind), and nididhyasana (to realize the Truth). This assumes, then, that there must be stages of experience between realizing the Truth and experiencing It. That stage, or series of stages, is known by the name, "sakshatkara." It is seldom spoken of, probably because it is a moot point once the Truth is realized, that being because such realization is already impossible to put into words, and courses into areas unknown to most spiritual seekers, even adepts. I must, then, leave it in the realm of the inexplicable.

As for the first part of your question, there are a host of teachings I have gathered which all to point out why the scriptures of Mother India have lasted so long, and why they are Sanatana — Eternal. The two systems you have so clearly and rightly gleaned in your studies are two of those. In one, the designation is of *The Three Proofs of Truth*. In the other, it is called "The Three Potent Practices." They are really the same, but the titles set them off as being both principles and practices — a comparison that I like very much, and which is intended by the seers.

S.C. from Hawaii writes:
QUESTION: "What are the 6 treasures of the Godhead, of which Vijnana is one?"
ANSWER: Sri (Unlimited Abundance); Bala (Magnificent Glory); Aishvarya (Irresistible Strength); Vijnana (Penetrating Wisdom); Tyaga (Natural Renunciation); and Tejas (Awesome Splendor).
QUESTION #2: "What happened to Ma Sarada when Ramakrishna's devotees became monks in the math? Nothing is mentioned about her in the Gospel after Ramakrishna passed."
ANSWER: After the passing of the Great Master (into Nirvikalpa Samadhi, not death), there was a period where She returned to Kamarpukur, and Joyrambati, the village of Her birth, She knew obscurity for some time, living in Kamarpukur in great privation. Then She emerged as the Mother of the Ramakrishna Order after the Math grounds were purchased, when She moved

to Kolkata to take up this supreme position and its duties. Hundreds were initiated by Her, and some came to the West to initiate many of us. For that whole story one can read *The Gospel of Holy Mother,* or Swami Nikhilananda's book, *Holy Mother,* or four or five others that are now available. For those who are attending our forthcoming pilgrimage to Kolkata in December, we will see many of the places associated with her birth and times, all very sacred.

QUESTION #3: "I still don't understand the evolutes. Does it mean products or modifications?"

ANSWER: Both. They are products of subtler evolutes that precede them, and they are modifications in the sense that they alter outwardly as they work their way from their source on down the chain of cause and effect. Practicing the dissolution of this mental stream of thought, one goes in reverse order and posits the gross back into the subtle, and then into the causal. Thus, earth is withdrawn back into the sense of smell, the sense of smell back into odor (tanmatra), that back into the pranas, the pranas back into mind, then to intelligence, ego, and formless matter. Now, looking outward again, one sees that each of these was an evolute of its predecessor. Cause and effect (karma) on the spiritual level (not just in physics) is seen in this way, and one comes to know the building blocks of all the worlds, not just the physical one.

Sanatanand from Hawaii writes:

QUESTION: "God is in everything. We are used to thinking of God as good. And yet in the Hindu tradition, God can be seen as evil as well. I am interested in incorporating a Higher understanding in my day-to-day life. I wish to have my perceptions shift so that these higher understandings are not mere intellectual ideas, but sensible thoughts and feelings as I go about in the world. Is there a way to see/feel/perceive God in every person, circumstance I meet?"

ANSWER: Naive people think God to be good. Conventional forms of Hinduism and Buddhism propose that God can also wear a mask of evil. Vedanta declares God is neither, but is Transcendent. This introduces the formless aspect of Reality.

To have perspectives shift towards higher understanding one must familiarize oneself, both through study and meditation, with the Formless aspect of God. Only then can one see God in everything. For, as long as form is there, so too will all manner of imperfections be present. How will it be possible to see the ever-perfect Reality in forms that are fraught with imperfections — everything from disease and death, to sin and transgression, etc.

As far as one's thoughts and intelligence are concerned, these are to be refined by sadhana until that internal perfection that is Brahman begins to shine through everyone and everything one sees and experiences, Such inner vision somehow rises above and beyond the otherwise onerous presence of human foibles and the drawbacks and calamities of (otherwise beautiful) nature.

The beneficial side of seeing the negative mask of God (gods, demons, wrathful deities, trials and tribulations, etc.) is that it allows one the opportunity to rise above them all. That chance is not provided for in a world where all is imagined to be bright and cheery. As Vivekananda said, *"A good world is a contradiction in terms, like saying hot ice...."* Everything is an admixture here, with good prevailing at times, and negativity at other times. Vice and sin are chased out of the picture by pious reformers who see things only on the surface level, but they only *"take new seats"* after a time. Coming to know of this game of constant change (maya), the illumined souls, and those desiring illumination, practice what Tantra calls *"transmuting poison into Nectar."* Lord Siva is the special deity of this spiritual artform. Yoga also recommends it. When it is mastered, even to a small degree, the difficult happenings of life are placed on a new footing, and that fresh perspective which people are seeking along all the wrong pathways suddenly becomes accessible, and preferable. It all takes some time to attain, but is well worth it in the end. One could say that life in the world is really made for and well suited for such attainments, whereas pleasures and occult powers run in the opposite direction, making one weak and vulnerable to maya and her seductions. The superior soul takes the path of austerity, the Jnana Marga, and avoids the path of enjoyment, the Bhoga Marga. As Sri Krishna puts it in the Bhagavad Gita: *"What is sweet in the beginning and sour at the end is to be avoided, but what is sour in the beginning and sweet in the end, the Yogi takes to that."*

Suprema from Pennsylvania writes:
COMMENTS: "Dear Father: Sutra III-14 and your commentary has been bobbing in my mind for weeks now. I keep going to the concept of 'As If' living, not of my own making, but one a dear friend named Floyd Henderson has taught in his writing. I hope the intent is in line with the thought formation of how we live in this world, 'balancing' Absolute Reality overlaid on relativity. It is a style of living, 'but without a person's attachments, delusions, and emotional intoxication.' As if' living involves meeting responsibilities and providing for the body understood as just a group of elements (Ramakrishna's 'bag of bones') while knowing full well that 'this world' is nothing more than an imagining in a limited perception until Realization.' 'It is a lifestyle during which (You) can witness feelings rise and fall without any emotional intoxication, reacting, over-reacting, or setting off a chain of reactions' — a lifestyle free of the misery generated by fears and desires.' This all really makes perfect sense to me!"
RESPONSE: Relativity is overlaid (vivarta) over Absolute Reality, form upon formlessness upon Formlessness. Once this world is realized as nothing other than Brahman with qualities, the false superimposition disappears. Absolute Reality needs no "balancing." The mind, once balanced (sattva), can begin to both see this and live in It — Brahman. As both the Gita and Upanisads declare, *"A seeker of Truth who realizes Brahman, lives in Brahman, no matter what be his mode of living."* The work that such a soul engages in is free of binding repercussion, for the hand that acts and the mind that thinks does so in awareness of Brahman. And this ability for witnessing everything from the transcendental mode plays a part in such purity of perspective.

K.D. from Hawaii writes:
COMMENTS: "These lessons are so full of important insights and clarifications that at times Raja Yoga seems more like an overview course than an in-depth study. I could spend weeks studying and contemplating just Aparigraha for instance. It was quite an eye-opener for me to read your elucidation of this Yama, because I had first reacted to it at the beginning of the study of Raja Yoga with argument that I now view as a form of cynicism. I thought it was rather archaic. What could possibly be wrong with giving and receiving? Now I can clearly see that I am caught in a spider web of giving and receiving, and it is invaluably helpful to have this insight in order to extract myself from this bondage as well as to avoid creating more sticky webs in the future. Something you said at the recent Wood Valley retreat has already loosened the bonds. You mentioned something about being the spider who created the web rather than the poor bug caught hopelessly in its tangle. I can now crawl freely from one end of my cage to another. You had written that it is the intention behind, the motivation for the giving and receiving that actually causes the bondage. Hence my question –
QUESTION #1: "Illumined souls and even advanced spiritual aspirants can give and receive without creating negative karma. Is this because of their supreme detachment from such objects or energies? Is it possible for aspirants such as myself to avoid creating negative karma by carefully examining my motivation for giving and receiving, and being as certain as I can of its purity?"
ANSWER: Of course such conscious and careful contemplation can help. For the illumined souls, however, it is more than just detachment from objects and situations. The mind has become adept at Niskama Karma, and by carefully following its laws and dictates, they skillfully maneuver their way through the field of karma which other beings are constantly stumbling over. And so, it is less of a matter of leaving off creating negative karma, and more a matter of observing spiritual laws that will never lead them astray. They do not betray or transgress these laws, whereas others, if they are even aware of them yet, are continually breaking them and reaping the just rewards.
COMMENTS #2: "The discussion of the obstacles to spiritual progress was a review and a reminder to strengthen my discipline in regards to meditation and study. I am guilty of styana, usually a form of procrastination. My days are so full, and there are always excuses to postpone study and meditation. However, I am almost always contemplating the spiritual truths that are becoming more and more familiar to me as I hear about them on multiple occasions and apply them to my life. I view the world with different eyes than I did a year and a half ago when I went to my first SRV retreat. I evaluate everything in terms of its reality or unreality. Reality is that which does not change, which leaves the whole phenomenal world as insubstantial yet still real enough to me even temporarily. I am becoming more quickly conscious of gross egoic impulses and more honestly reflective of a life previously driven by desires and varying degrees of ignorance. I am often 'trying' to attain ekagra – one-pointed consciousness as an essential to direct spiritual experience. Your comment that

'Transcendence of the earth and its sufferings is a matter of necessity rather than aversion' adds a clarity and urgency to awaken from the dream that perpetuates this suffering. I recently had a vision that I should take the stance of a bullfighter who can smoothly focus on any rajasic bull headed his way and easily sidestep the impact and thus remain safe. It is a skill that demands presence and awareness, and then ultimately forgiveness of self and others. Or possibly it is wiser to be out of the arena in the first place.

"Time is short for these reflections because you requested us to have our comments and questions in by tomorrow, so I have decided to list other parts of these lessons you gave that have expanded my understanding and awareness of the wisdom path. They are:
• To practice the presence of God, 'a constant vigil is kept wherein the mind, ego and intellect are kept pure and free from subtle contaminants.'
• 'The misuse of power does not really begin on the political, social, and cultural levels of existence at all; it just foments and erupts there. It really begins in the very principle of perception itself (called misperception in this regard) via the human mind and senses.'
• 'We find concentration enjoined upon the yogic aspirant, and the method being advised is single-mindedness – not many methods thrown at the obstacles in turns, but one authentic, self-actuated practice which is advised by the seers of spirituality.' For myself, concentration on an illumined sage is my preferred method. It is a form of the Divine Mother, usually starting out as Ammachi since her image is so readily available, then she morphs into Sri Sarada Devi and sometimes the so-called Virgin Mary, who is not the passive female portrayed in Christianity, but a figure brimming with Shakti power.
• 'Unfortunately and from the standpoint of pure, original Mind, the separation of Spirit from Matter is a move that should never have to happen. That is, since the soul and nature are eternally interconnected, yet each has its own place, an illumined mind would naturally assume this truth and get on with the play called life in full cognizance of its supreme nonmaterial status. But ignorance and delusion have crept in, obscuring the greater picture, decentralizing the mind, and causing the unreal to seem real.

"This last clarification held special importance for me because it healed a schism wherein I was thinking that the need to divide the sentient from the insentient in order to be free was because there was some inherent division between the two. This extended to the idea that one must believe that Spirit is essentially separate from the body. I have read that one cannot gain Moksha if one believes that he/she is the body. I can understand that from a purely intellectual point of view, but in actuality I cannot get how I am not my body. I know that I am much more than the body, but it seems that in the embodied condition, mind, body, spirit, are so intertwined and interconnected that all have to work in tandem to create the perfect environment for direct divine experience and ultimately merging into pure conscious divine awareness, Brahman. Then, nothing else is real including our individual souls or spirits. Renunciation of the unreal, then, seems to be renouncing our own bodies since they are just a

mass of vibrating particles and products of the thoughts of the mind. I would appreciate if you would comment on the following statements?"
POINT 1: "Sharanagata, self-surrender to the Lord, is key to the path and crucial for both meditation and Samadhi. Have you stood at the precipice of egolessness, with the borders of the unknown suddenly in view, and then successfully entered in where most would never want to venture? This is another subject I could spend weeks contemplating and understanding."
RESPONSE: The statement was made in the context of the import of self-surrender, usually thought of as a Bhakti Yoga component, and to indicate the many souls who are devoid of both understanding of and devotion to the Personal God. There are certain dangers in meditation on the Formless which are almost entirely overlooked by hosts of precocious practitioners. Even the scriptures and the seers of them only infer them (*"Much more difficult is the path of those who take to the Formless."* Sri Krishna). Making peace with the Personal God by knowing rituals, sacrifices, modes of worship, and taking of refuge, both saves the aspirant from these dangers, and paves the way to realizations which court perception of the Formless Reality. That is why Jesus declared that *"No one gets to the Father but through the Son."* As I have been saying lately, in empathy with this teaching, "One needs friends in high places." This is especially true of the spiritual path, the "razor's edged path."
POINT 2: "The Four Beneficial Attitudes"
RESPONSE: We have been graced by the repetition of this teaching over time from the likes of Krishna, Vasishtha, and more recently, Sri Aurobindo and Sri Sarada Devi. It is a teaching that all levels of seekers would like and it especially appeals to those who are at that potentially onerous stage of turning the obviously flawed world and mind into outright positivity. For, who would not proclaim and acclaim the qualities of: Maitri, friendliness to all beings; Karuna, compassion for their sufferings; Upekshanam, indifference; and Mudita, joyfulness. As one Jewish song sings, *"Friends do not despair, for a difficult time has come upon us; joy must fill the air."* And note the close proximity of indifference and joy, as if to caution us not to deny or denigrate teachings which proceed by a negative ambiance. And this segues into your next question nicely:
POINT 3: "....clarification of indifference and equanimity and our right to make the world 'back off' so we can achieve balance and get on with spiritual life."
RESPONSE: The word, "indifference," carries a negative connotation with today's western practitioner, while "equanimity" carries a positive one. But who is there who can retain their composure, inside and out, in the face of evil-minded beings? Thus, indifference is a handy tool to have and employ with regard to such beings and the situations that rise around them. Sri Krishna gives his own list of beneficial attitudes in the Gita, when He states that *"....one should be reverent to the sages and seers, happy for those who are joyful, compassionate for those who suffer, and indifferent to those who are demonically influenced."* The word, indifference, is not meant as a conclusion, that is, to walk away from evil beings so that they can perpetuate more of their violence. It can be either a way of example, a stopgap measure, or an indicator of future

action to be taken. For instance, one should never be quick to strike out, or go to war, especially knowing what karma will be wrought on "saint and sinner" alike in the offing. I heard that Dalai Lama wrote the President just after the 9/11 calamity, suggesting that he take time to think over what his reaction might be. The advice went unheard, of course. Both indifference and equanimity are necessary here, which is why the world is constantly engaging in violence and experiencing unnecessary suffering, because they listen to political leaders instead of spiritual ones. In ancient India, the kings and queens took counsel of the Holy Beings, and measured all decisions upon their deep-seeing, "sage" advice.

With this said, we can look at the word, "equanimity," in its own light. It is more than just composure, or even-mindedness, as grand as these are. In Sanskrit, upeksha, used readily by both Buddhism and Vedanta, indicates a peaceful imperviousness to all of the vagaries and vicissitudes of life and mind, of matter and nature, of people and situations. With the attainment of upekshanam, an abiding peace pervades the mind. This, again, impinges upon your next question:

POINT 4: "Reminder of the importance of self-inquiry; Who Am I?"

RESPONSE: Atma-vichara is one of the Four Sentinels, the other three being Santosha, Shanti, and Sadhu-satsanga. Depending on the seeker's disposition, karma, samskaras, and a small host of other considerations ("know thyself!"), the four work individually or in tandem. That is, it would be well, as far as the seers are concerned, if all sincere seekers began their sadhana with inquiry into the nature of the Self ("Who am I?"), for contentment, peace of mind, and the company of the Holy would follow as a matter of course, thereby. But, as is often the case, living beings seek contentment through the things of the world, through personalities, and through ownership and agency in action, which are long slow roads to finding out "Who am I?"— if they even lead there.

Whatever the case might be, the comprehension and practice of Atma-vichara is far more than asking a question. One can go on saying "Who am I?" over and over again for days, and end up only sounding like an owl. The parrot got the mantra from the householders, did he not, but when the cat finally grabbed him at the time of his death, and though he had repeated the mantra many thousands of times, he only reverted to his death squawk, forgetting the essential saving seed syllable. Case in point, so we ought to go deeper with this powerful question, and unwrap it like we would do a sloka from the Upanisad, the word, AUM, or a sutra from Patanjala, as we are doing in these lessons. Then, the Jnana Matra, particle of intelligence, will be engaged in the process, ending in definitive wisdom and comprehensive conclusions.

My way of transmitting the best method for attaining these salient ends is through the accompanying statement, "To know Who you are, you must first know What you are not." Matter, for instance; you are not that. Which means the body must be struck from the list of possible candidates for Reality. Both in Yoga, and in Vedanta, and in other darshanas as well, the involution process under the practice of meditation dissolves the gross into the subtle, and the subtle into the causal, i.e., the five elements have to be assigned to the tanmatras (subtle elements) from whence they sprung, and the five senses to the subtle senses, etc. This is not so hard. One can envision the dream state, and how one uses the subtle elements and senses to create dream worlds, dream objects, dream experiences. This is one level of your consciousness. Beings are just not seeing it as such, and base their sense of reality upon the waking state alone. And so, matter becomes their God, their self, their very being, occurring over lifetimes. Thus, as Sri Ramakrishna says, *"Through a succession of births and deaths man comes to believe that the world is real."*

When asked, "Who are you?," then, a man would declare adamantly, in effect, "I am the body, " or "I am my name," or most often, "I am the personality." Possibly, and further up the transmigrational chain, he might say, "I am the intellect." But few would jump closer to the Truth and say, "I am intelligence," thereby drawing the subtle but sharp distinction between a container (upadhi/kosha) and its contents (svarupa/essence). This draws near to the greatest fact of all, and vastly overlooked — that the embodied being is really pure Consciousness, nondual Awareness, through which Its own intelligence projects worlds of name and form in time and space based upon causation.

Here, then, the question, "Who am I?," finds its answer. *"Tat Tvam Asi, I am that (Brahman);" "Aham Brahmasmi, I am Brahman." "Prajnanam Brahma, I am Pure Intelligence."* And along with this final and most crucial confirmation, the question of "What is Enlightenment?" gets answered as well. As the Upanisads tell us, most graciously, *"It is the conclusion of the Vedanta that all is Brahman — time, space, living beings, and the world. Living in constant recognition of this fact is what is called enlightenment."* The slokas go on to instruct that the revealed scriptures are the sure and certain proof of this statement, which leads us to implement their study into our ongoing sadhana so that the mental movement of Atma-vichara meets with a similar, definitive, and blissful conclusion.

Akshaya Bhakti from New England writes:
COMMENTS: "Avinashi's question about the bijas Aum and Hrim in Lesson 66 has inspired me to put more heartfelt energy back into my japa / mantra practice, realizing I had become complacent over the years and had forgotten the significance of those mystic syllables. I am also trying to recite the mantra more often throughout the day to build up its power, and also to develop its capacity to bubble up naturally. In regards to my own question on Shankara's version of Yoga, I have not yet purchased a copy of the *Aparokshanubhuti* itself, but your article in the Winter 2003 Nectar entitled 'Advaita Yoga: Patanjali as Revealed by Shankara' to which you referred me, really blew me away! These clarifications by Shankara are just what I was looking for to coordinate all the teachings with which I have been blessed — such as on how to perform pratyahara: *'When all that is seen is nothing but Brahman, what is left to withdraw from?'* I realized that I did not really understand the meaning of Advaita Vedanta, thinking it just referred to the fact that we finally become One with

God in Samadhi. It isn't that you hadn't already taught us that God is the substratum for everything (many times, in many ways) and that we have actually been Brahman all the time, but I guess I just couldn't fathom the implications at the time. I have definitely become an admirer of Shankara and will be reading his text on the nature of the Self — *Vakyavritti* — which I actually bought by accident, but it will tie in so nicely with your encouragement to practice mental asana, such as 'Thou Art That,' which it elucidates. Any comments or additions to the above would be welcome. Deepest appreciation, as always."

QUESTION: "On the chart, *Stages of Dissolution of the Mind in Yoga,* there is a list, 'Practice the 4 Aids' under 'Seven Methods for Mastery.' Could you please list these 4 Aids, dear teacher? It seems like they would be very pertinent in preparing the mind for Pratyahara and beyond."

ANSWER: On that particular chart, under the Seven Methods for Mastery, appears the Five Aids to Steadfastness. They are: Utsaha (enthusiasm); Sahasa (courage); Dhairya (steadfastmess); Adhyatma-vidya (seeking wisdom); and Mahat-seva (service of the Great Souls). The list is designed to aid in mastery of the fifth and sixth limbs of Yoga by further helping to calm the restless mind.

## Pada III, Sutra 15

*kramanyatvan parinamanyatve hetuh (krama,* series; *anyatvam,* shifting cycles; *parinamah,* transformation; *anyatve,* particular cycles; *hetu,* purpose).

*"This series of changes, in shifting cycles, is responsible for all the transformations of nature."*

Patanjali has already established, in III:11, that when the mind transcends the lower state of considering many objects and their meanings and functions, and takes up instead a single-pointed concentration on one only, then the mind stuff receives the impression called samadhi upon it. From that state, the modes of maya such as name and form, time and space, etc., are clearly seen, and known for what they are, and the mind comes under further control as a result. The soul feels as if all these many changes are flowing by, but has the established sense that it alone remains unchanging amidst all movements. Settled deeply in this matter, and able to measure change and nonchange via study of its own samskaras, a more intense power presents itself — that of samyama. What follows now in the sutras is a tour-de-force in Samyama.

## Pada III, Sutra 16

*parinama-traya-samyama-atitanagata-jnanam (parinamah,* transformation; *traya,* triple; *samyama,* comprehensive awareness; *atitanagata,* past/present/future; *jnana,* wisdom).

*"By focusing comprehensive awareness on these changes, wisdom regarding the three phases of time is gleaned."*

Subtle imports infill this set of sutras we are presently contemplating. Swami Vivekananda's commentary, clear and succinct, brings out the hidden stuffing in them. It is all a matter of learning to read the samskaras of one's mind so as to facilitate the two-sided view that will reveal all things, all events, all intentions, all occurrences within the three phases of time. All of that is one side. The other side is the Akshara Brahman, the Unchanging Reality.

The inner dynamics of this, inferred by the sutras and their commentators, is most difficult of description, and must be left to the aspirant's own internal work. Suffice to say that most beings, when they do finally come upon the presence of their underlying samskaras, either overlook their deep significance or try to transcend them. But, "lo and behold," they are the reflectors of everything that has happened to you, and of everything that might happen to you in the future, especially if left unstudied and not utilized properly.

Going a little deeper by way of mere description, the impressions left on the mindstuff (chitta) represents a host of helpful information, especially when impediments such as ignorance, attachment, aversion (the kleshas and viparyayas), and the like are left behind (which demonstrates the importance of taking Yoga limb by limb, and not transgressing/skipping steps). It is the witness consciousness that, standing back to observe, both sees and then sees through the samskaric membranes, not forgetting to note what is seen there. This is the real import of the triputi of seer, seen, and seeing, at least at this lofty and subtle level of Yogic practice.

When this element of seership gets infused into the practitioner's inner process, the observer can begin to measure both life and Eternal Life through the changes that are taking place in the mindstuff reflected via the samskaras. This two-sided view reveals a supreme psychology, affording insight of a previously unimagined profundity. The mutable world, previously so problematic, then becomes a matter of easy transcendence and "ho hum" knowledge, while in its place comes that special perception and overseership of more abiding principles (shuddhashuddha, mixed pure/impure) like the changing maya, the changing mind, the changing gunas, and, most importantly and contrasting, the unique Unchanging.

To put it in terms of integration, it is the contrast between the Real and the unreal that shows up most strikingly. In line with Patanjali's Yoga and its teachings, one could then explain the appearance of a samskara that both outstrips and outlives all other samskaras, that being a Samskara of Samadhi. Like a tidalwave that sucks up all other waves on the ocean, this fully benign Impression absorbs all other impressions on the sea of the mind, neutralizing all poisons present there, and forming what is left over into one cognitive mass of pure intuition. This is how the once-upon-a time seeker transforms into an observer-of-time adept and eventually becomes what he always was but did not realize it — a knower of that which is beyond all phases of time. Thus, the Svetasvataropanisad states, *"Practicing the yoga of meditation, they perceived the Devatmashakti, Who though ever One, was nevertheless hidden by Her own modes of nature (gunas), and who had remained unseen previously due to the limitations of their own intellects."*

Those looking ahead a few sutras will see that all things become known through this inward march of samskaric evolution. One can easily know what a bird is saying, or an animal, or even people, as confused as they are, and many other things. But we will leave that for our next lesson. There is certainly enough here in this powerful lesson to keep us happily involved in a type of rare svadhyaya that was only hinted at earlier in the practice of the initial limbs of Yoga.

## Lesson Sixty-eight, 2/28/12
### Pada III, Sutra 17 & 18

Judging by the host of responses, and the many questions and discussions that have come in and cropped up, lesson 67, with its sutras on samyama and samskara, definitely perked the interest of those of us who are deep into the study of Patanjali's Yoga Sutras. The unique way that a yogi/yogini uses the impressions of the mind to read life, on all its levels, and to assist other beings, represents a particular contribution of Yoga to spiritual knowledge and lore. The role that time plays in life, in suffering, and in transcendence, gets accented in the process as well. Whereas most beings either take time for granted, and others attempt to use it for occult purposes, the yogi utilizes a combination of detachment and inspection to afford him a multi-dimensional reading of cause and effect This places him in a singular position to move with unimaginable facility to satisfy the needs of embodied beings suffering the mind-numbing effects of ignorance, avidya — the first and foremost of the five kleshas. The result outlines the eternal pathway to freedom, or opens it up once again for those who have wandered off of it.

Following are the list of questions and answers, in Atma-vichara form, that have been presented for our own inspection of the Yoga Sutras, followed in turn by the sutras up for study in this lesson. I hope that you will benefit from the concentrated "samyama" I have attempted on all of your fine questions.

**Questions and Answers for Lesson 68**
KD from Hawaii writes:
QUESTION: "I have read and reread lessons 27 and 28 and do not have any questions or comments at this time. The lessons were pretty straightforward and I understood them. I do have a question on lesson 67 however. You wrote: 'There are grave dangers in meditation on the Formless which are almost entirely overlooked by hosts of precocious practitioners.' Can you please elaborate on these grave dangers?"
ANSWER: The main danger in meditation is twofold, one for the novice and the other for the advanced practitioner. In the beginning, and after guidance from a meditation master has been received, the novice must proceed in gradual fashion to satisfy the aims of control of mind and senses, and must do so without forcing the issue. Here, short, concentrated periods of practice, rather than long periods of sitting, are best. The modern trend today is to take a host of untrained persons who are interested in meditation, and place them in a large group for days at a time. The point is for making money, for charging for the

chance to merely sit, uninformed, with others who are as uninformed as you are. Part of the group is sick and coughing, others are shifting about constantly while the noisy mod clothing they are wearing makes all manner of noise. It is the hatha fad with all its ills turned now towards the arena of meditation as fad and phenomena. With no point of focus, like Guru, Ishtam, mantra, mind-dissolution, or jnanam, these souls fall into states of dilution of consciousness that bears no resemblance to true meditation whatsoever, nor does it follow or come close to the real and actual aim of meditation.

Mastering a degree of concentration is to the point. As one great singer of wisdom songs puts it, *"My mind is a jungle of contrary and random thoughts. My guru has instructed me to clear just one acre of thought-vines and then build a temple there to meditate in. Once this is accomplished, I am to clear the rest of the jungle, acre by acre."*

So this is the danger for the beginner. It could be summated by lack of a guru and instruction, ignorance of the purpose for meditation, and lack of knowledge regarding the steps leading up to meditation proper, or in other words, qualification. The Raja Yoga of Patanjali is the definitive measure for qualification, listing as it does some six limbs or levels of practice to be attained prior to consummate meditation, and one level beyond it. To make a long story short, the yamas and niyamas are to be learned first. These alone will place the practitioner in a state fit for early meditation sessions. With facets such as devotion to God, scriptural knowledge, austerity, and contentedness in place, even a half hour of sitting will yield beneficial results — this, as contrasted to blowing oneself out of the water by hours of ungrounded, unguided sitting amidst a group of other uninformed and uncontrolled minds. Some would say, 'Well at least it is an introduction.' The authentic teacher, guru, would respond, "Sadanga Yoga, the six limbs of Yoga as taught by an illumined soul, is the introduction." In short, the tradition is to provide the ground for spiritual practice, not the general money-making public.

For the advanced practitioner, failing to come full circle with meditation practice is the danger. That is, the tendency to head for formless realization, heedless of the value of meditation on God with form along the way, and ending in the inability to be of service to others, forms the problem. As per the tradition, here are the warnings with regard to meditation practice:

1) Can imbalance the mind if initially overused, particularly without guidance
2) Can contribute to the growth of a spiritual ego
3) May lull the mind into the habit of complacency
4) Might disturb or stymie the path of action
5) Can keep the meditator from full realization

Holy Mother has mentioned another risk in meditation, that one should not force the mind to meditate when it is resistant. One is to do other spiritual practices at that time, and gradually bring the mind back to compliance.

Avinashi from Pennsylvania writes:
QUESTION: "I often imagine the Master's face breaking into a smile so broad

and brilliant and beautiful that it would put the shining of the sun to shame... and yet I've never heard any of the direct disciples or those who knew him personally saying anything about this. How strange! Any comments?"

ANSWER: You have not read deeply or widely enough, then, or have kept to the wisdom side of the readings and missed the devotional books. There are many books and songs, and many accounts by both the direct disciples and the extended spiritual family of Sri Ramakrishna who have attested to His divine beauty and spiritual charm. A whole contemporary Upanisad has been composed which is full of such references and descriptions. Read on......

QUESTION #2: "I came across an idea which expressed that Kapila, in the Tattva Samasa Sutras, used the word 'Purusha' in a singular way, whereas Panchasikacharya, his grand disciple, began using the word in the plural and subsequently taught that there were many purushas, which, I believe, is the official Sankhyana stand. I'm not sure my facts are even right, but if I am correct, I find this intriguing because it could mean that Kapila was a true Advaitin. Any comments?"

ANSWER: I have always felt, on an inner level, that Kapila was an illumined soul and a knower for nondual Truth. One might say that it is a certain drawback for one composing or outlining Truth in a particular fashion (like a darshana) that one's realization gets limited and pinioned under that one system, therefore causing others who come after him to draw conclusions based upon that darshana alone. The seer is only expressing Truth through a particular medium, for the benefit of those alive at the time of his appearance, and it does not mean or should not be meant to reflect any limitation on the part of the seer himself.

For example, who is there among the sages and seers who has not taken beings like Sri Krishna as a source and authority, or drawn from the teachings of the ancient rishis and the Upanisads to verify their philosophical offering? To set a scripture in stone is a good thing as long as the end is left open. Truth can and should be explained via religion and philosophy, but It can never be concluded, simply because It is an ever-living verity — Sanatana Dharma. If this is understood, then the systems of orthodox and unorthodox philosophy, both, become radiant roads to Reality, and all religions are seen to represent the same. Argumentation, refutation, and other doors for missing the point of spiritual realization, along with all the emotional reactions that follow, then pale to insignificance. Otherwise, the Great Soul says, "Eternal Dharma!" But those listening and who come after Him thought he said "Eternal Drama!" So they go on arguing and contending with one another, while Truth stands by, unrealized. What a waste.

QUESTION #3: "I've read that not every spiritual experience is a samadhi or takes place in samadhi, yet, a genuine spiritual experience which does not take place in samadhi, still, at the same time, does not take place in the ordinary, mundane, waking state. Would you comment on this?"

ANSWER: The problem here is that the aspirant, if he or she can even be termed that yet, has not gained any real qualification, has not reached viveka yet. They may feel love, but do not know yet That which is worthy of Love. They may feel compassion, but still imagine that if they just feel empathy or pity, that the solution has been applied. They may know a few things, from books and lectures, but they do not know yet that knowledge, when spiritualized, is a type of samadhi, and that the entire set of external and internal worlds consist of nothing less than, as Patanjali called it in a previous sutra, *"living knowledge"* — that objects are just wisdom made manifest through the medium of form.

The whole issue can be placed in terms of experience as well. If a person strives to gain experiences from life, mind, senses, and objects, etc., but never knows the Ground from which all experience rises, then life is nothing less than a march of experiences, all void of essence. Time then appears to be actual, and becomes fraught with problems. This is why embodied beings are often caught in the traps of meaninglessness, lethargy, lack of purpose, depression, and the sense of fatality. But the one who focuses in on this Ground of Existence Itself via practice of meditation and spiritual life, not only lights a fire (of Yoga) that burns away all impediments, but also, in the interim, finds a way to extract essence from these events, from those selfsame experiences that were so unrewarding and inconclusive before.

Taking this teaching in, we then turn to look at the phenomena of a powerful experience happening to us in a seemingly ordinary state of consciousness. Here, the practice of sadhana in the form of belated results is upon us. We all complain at times about our disciplines not netting us any results, but do not realize that the practice of Yoga, or mantra, or any other form of spiritual discipline we are undergoing, is always doing its work on the hidden level of the internal mind, and is also taking its own sweet time to manifest. This is why patience was Holy Mother's favorite quality in a seeker, along with perseverance. And add to this that Mother's Game for awakening us from our own little games operates with, among other factors, the principle of contrast. How great the impression of such a powerful experience is depends upon the state of mind it finds one in. If one is already in a higher state of mind, then the profound experience might seem as if ordinary. The question is, then, how impressionable is my mind to the impression? Our own revered Swami Brahmananda once had an experience where he was rounding the circular hallway of a temple interior, in a rather ordinary or "dry" state of mind, when suddenly an ocean of Light swept in on him, throwing him into samadhi. Thus, contrast is a very effective way of transforming the human mind and its thought processes.

QUESTION #4: "As I reflect on the three aspects of Kriya Yoga — tapas, svadhyaya and Ishvara-Pranidhana — I feel tempted to associate them with three central aspects of human functioning. I associate tapas with conation, ie, with will, and see its function as the redirection of our energies toward ends more conducive to successful sadhana; I tend to associate svadhyaya with cognition, ie, with understanding or comprehension, and see its function as the questioning and renouncing of old, unquestioned beliefs and the formation of views that more reflect a spiritual view of the universe; and I tend to associate Ishvara-

Pranidhana with affect, ie, with emotion, and see its function as a reorientation of emotion away from lower mayic formations and toward the Divine. As an aside, I know that worship, (Ishvara-Pranidhana), is described as an austerity conducive to self-control on the physical level, but a reorientation of emotion would certainly accomplish this. All of this is the result of an independent line of reflection, so I wonder how it stacks up against the teachings of the scriptures and sages."

ANSWER: As a set of your own reflections it is all well-thought, and it equates well with both the experiences and teachings of the seers, and the words of the scriptures. It also proves that each seeker is, like his fingerprint, unique, and will utilize the illumined souls as examples for what is possible, and the teachings of the scriptures as so many ways to realize what is in his own Self.

QUESTION #5: "Should I meditate if I'm ill? How ill should I be before I decide not to meditate? In some cases, would it be useless to meditate while ill, and are there even occasions where we might damage our sadhana by so doing? I think it might be hard to meditate if seriously congested, since the breath would not move too easily through the nose; one would have to breath through the mouth, and I wonder if this would be advisable since people, after all, breathe through their mouths when they're frightened and through their noses when they're calm. I tend to think a serious yogi will meditate even when ill, but what are the limits?"

ANSWER: A serious Yogi is a Truth unto himself, and a case all his own. For that soul, we tend to refrain from applying general statements. For all others, however, and due to a few of the points you make above, meditation should be undertaken only when general health is good. This will make good sense when one remembers what meditation really is, not just what it aspires to be. To achieve it as it is, all systems must be in good operation. A dying man, for instance, may want to meditate, but is meditation really possible for him? Possibly prayer, or an attempt at settling the mind, or centering awareness is possible and advisable. But true meditation is another matter.

However, there are other spiritual practices one can engage in while sick. So long as one is coherent, reading spiritual books, especially those which deal with divine personalities and not abstruse truisms, is good. A general repetitive mantra practice that does not require full concentration can also work, and even be beneficial to recovery. If complete bed rest is not required, then seva is even possible, so long as one is conscious of not spreading disease to others. Nowadays people go to work, and children are forced to go to school when they are sick. It is a horrible mark on our culture that we would run ourselves into the ground and get sick for the sake of work, and the money it produces.

Part of the picture, here, is that each person must learn to discriminate whether the illness he or she faces is better worked through, or rested through. I saw my neighbor out mowing the lawn the other day, and he had the flu. Obviously he was not sick enough to have to be in bed, yet was wise enough not to go to the business workplace. Certainly, in Yoga practice, the practitioner never identifies with an illness, and is never to react to it; he only observes it and relegates it to the body, not the Self. This is possibly the most important point with regard to illness.

QUESTION #6: "How do the five devotional bhavas of Shanta, Dasya, Sakhya, Vatsalya, and Madhura correlate with the samadhis of Patanjala Yoga? I believe they would all disappear in Nirvikalpa, but otherwise, what is the relation between them? I recently had a conversation with a Krishna devotee after many years, and I noticed he doesn't think in terms of the samadhis at all, but in terms of the bhavas, and later I reflected that this seems often characteristic of bhaktas, while those oriented toward Ashtanga and Advaita Yoga, conversely, tend not to think in terms of the bhavas, only in terms of samadhis. It's as if the two groups use entirely different languages and in so doing, organize their understandings of consciousness in completely different ways, too. Having 'navigated' in both worlds now, I started wondering about the correlations. Again, any comments?"

ANSWER: Bhavas, samadhis, and bhava samadhis, are all part of an integrated network of conscious states of awareness that are intrinsic to the Soul. Let us not separate them from one another due to the particular language, or the lineage we either belong to or are looking into. That is, it is not that a wisdom knower will not suddenly have a deep devotional realization, or that a bhakta will not flash forth with profound wisdom; these combinations occur all the time. Even Chaitanya, the great Vaishnava bhakta and incarnation, was both attracted to and enamored with wisdom. He sought out teachers of nondual Truth during his life as well. In the scriptures, of all kinds, Sri Krishna indicates knowledge as the supreme purifier, and Lord Siva has devout Love for Sri Ram's Holy Feet, while Rama performs sacred puja for Siva out of deep love.

In all of this, we are only to recognize and deny those whose immature religious zeal have turned them away from universal understanding of this superlative kind. They are undermining the very ideals and teachers that they profess to love and worship by their hypocrisy masquerading as religion. Sri Ramakrishna has come, in part, to quell this very tendency and its ill effects.

QUESTION #7: "I've noticed that when I share my spiritual experiences with others — sometimes even with members of the Sangha, and sometimes even with my guru — I can feel a weakening inside me; because of this, I've become much less eager to share my experiences in the spiritual domain. Any thoughts or guidelines?"

ANSWER: The advantage to remaining silent is that you will avoid the risk of both untimely remarks and poor interpretations. The disadvantage is that you may cheat yourself of valuable interpretation via the guru. My conclusion, here, is that your spiritual experiences will pale and fade away anyway over time due to the nature of the mind, so it is better to bring them out for inspection while they are still fresh in the mind. This does not necessarily apply where the meaning is clear to you, unless, of course, you have read the meaning incorrectly or incompletely.

Finally, I would say that sharing them with sangha members is not always advisable, since a sangha usually contains an admixture of beginning, intermediate, and advanced seekers.

QUESTION #8: "Experientially, what is the character of the Brahmanadi, the Vishnugranthi, and the Rudragranthi? Since, respectively, the first stands at the entrance to the Sushumna, the second precedes the Anahata Chakra, and the third precedes the Ajna Chakra, they must be in the nature of obstacles. Without knowing what kinds of obstacles these are in terms of how they're experienced, the names of them are just words and nothing more for me. So again, what is their character, experientially? So I'll recognize them, can you tell me what I'll experience as I 'approach' them?"

ANSWER: Language and words, here, will necessarily be a bit vague. About these subtle blockages to spiritual energy, one is tempted to say, "You will know them when you encounter them." But since this is not always the case, since the seeker, even the adept, often overlooks some of what is within any given echelon of consciousness in terms of its content and its barriers, we have therefore to rely upon the scriptures and the seers for cogent explanations. In that sense, I have offered to contemporary practitioners a description of these barriers, by whatever name they are called in different darshanas, as the overall "curtain of nescience" which blinds the inner traveler to his or her own Self.

Rather than undertaking the impossible task of pointing out exactly where and what these barriers are, as a surgeon might do for a form of cancer pictured in an x-ray, suffice to say that this curtain of nescience or "cloud of unknowing" consists of a combination of fear, doubt, and brooding, much of it existing at a deep, primal level. "Primal," here, means both hidden and aged, coming from and built up upon impressions from past lifetimes, many of them having to do with the memory of death, suffering, and other unsavory experiences. Man's inability to locate these barriers within, and the fact that he lives with them for lifetimes as they accumulate, is responsible for his life of ignorance, insensitivity, attachment, greed, evil doing, and, to quote Buddhism, other "unwholesome roots." Both fear and doubt lead to brooding, mostly of the unhealthy kind. The effects of these three are the reason why man does not see the Light and know himself in his deep sleep state, but only feels it and forgets upon awakening.

This curtain of nescience, at all three levels that Kundalini Yoga cites them, is difficult to pierce through. Some substantial periods of time in meditation are necessary to do so, along with some long-lived and qualitative efforts around sadhana. As these barriers are seen, and the cobwebs over our primal memory are burned away, enlightenment comes as a natural result. But one cannot really cite one especial experience, or point out any particular moment that this Light dawns. Holy Mother explained this subtle process via the train trip story, wherein a person falls to sleep between departure and arrival, and wakes up at the destination without really knowing what transpired in between. Such is the evanescent nature of ignorance, and the inscrutable presence of maya in the mind.

QUESTION #9: "There is the Witness that is an eternal aspect of Brahman, but then there seems also to be the witness that is cultivated and that comes into being through the discipline of trying to observe the movements of the psyche. It seems to me that the second eventually gives way to the first, and is only a temporary formation. I've never heard this spoken of. Any comments?"

ANSWER: Witness Consciousness, or Sakshi Bhutam as it is called in Sanskrit, has several levels to it. It is not the ultimate station of Consciousness, for no second thing such as any witness exists at that pristine level. That is why different names have been cited in relation to Brahman, such as Pratyagatman, Antaryami, Kutastha, etc. The matter, then, is not so simple as to move from savikalpa to Nirvikalpa, or a seeded samadhi straight into the Unseeded. Maybe this is why so many of the stories we read in the scriptures tell of the final phases of very highly attained yogis as they attempt to arrive at the highest station of Consciousness, some having to make several approaches to It, and others having to acclimatize to such rare spiritual heights over time. Here is where direct spiritual experience takes over, and takes the fore over all fine speculations — no matter how wise and refined they may be.

QUESTION #10: "How do Sankhya and Advaita Vedanta differently conceive prakriti?"

ANSWER: I do not think that any of the darshanas of India disagree on the principle of prakriti, nor on Brahman. Names may differ for Divine Reality and its offshoots, but the wise conception remains clear and unanimous. In Sankhya, there is just a well-developed list of evolutes. In Yoga, we see them arranged in conjunction with the Eight Limbs of ascension and the accompanying samadhis. Advaita verily stays out of the fray, focusing in on Brahman alone. To the ancient rishis, Prakriti was just an *"overflow of the bliss of Brahman."* What to say about it other than to cite its insentience. And in fact, it was only when this fact became clouded, and the seer began to become identified with the seen, that more modern rishis like Patanjali, sporting systems like Yoga, came to the rescue. Otherwise, from Sankhya to Buddhism to Yoga to Vedanta, prakriti was seen as the ever-changing product of a Changeless Reality, called Purusha, Prajnaparam, Atman, etc. What was argued about in some schools was what the mind did to create false superimpositions over these two principles — an unnatural act amidst the simple naturalness of Purusha and Prakriti.

Annapurna Sarada from Hawaii writes:
QUESTION: "While you were on the mainland this last visit, we had a chance to talk about the sutras of the last lesson. I was surprised to find that in sutra 3:15, the teaching is pointing to the changes perceived by the cosmic state of consciousness and not the individual as we usually think of it. Looking back on the commentary, I can see why, now, since the individual sees a plethora of objects/objects of knowledge, and next has to learn to concentrate and focus on one at a time. But this sutra is well beyond that stage. Would you further elucidate on how this sutra pertains to cosmic/mahat/causal?"

ANSWER: Like sparks off of the same fire, individuals possess the same consciousness as found in cosmic consciousness. As Swami Vivekananda puts it, *"Ishvara is the sum total of individuals, yet He Himself is also an individual in the same way as the human body is a unit, of which each cell is an individual. Samasti, or the Collective, is God. Vyasti, or the component, is the soul or jiva. The existence of Ishvara, therefore, depends on that of jiva, as the body on the cell, and vice versa. Jiva and Ishvara are co-existent beings. As long as the one exists, the other must also."*

In relation to sutra 3:15, and in conjunction with your question, the realized yogi is not an "individual" anymore. He has access to Mahat and the Word, and observes Unmanifested Prakriti. What is more, going beyond what is considered as "cosmic," the yogi has now had Asamprajnata Samadhi. Coming out of that state of states, samyama at the cosmic level is natural to him, so he is both informed by Ishvara and consciously part and parcel with It as well. Others are as if cells of Ishvara's body, as quoted above, but unlike the polished luminary, do not have a continual influx of wisdom information at the cosmic level. They have, at best, some surging intuitions, some flashes of insight. Thus, the ability of samyama remains to be mastered, and even samadhi may still be far off. To such as these, the deep reading of samskaras intimated by these recent sutras is still a matter of some conjecture, rather than of pat, informed conclusion.

QUESTION #2: "Another question I have has been coming up for me throughout this study. It has to do with the use of the word 'meaning.' I keep thinking that if I knew the Sanskrit words translated as 'meaning' that it would unlock the real 'meaning' of what is being taught."

ANSWER: What you are speaking of, I think, is what is referred to as an invisible truth out in the open, a secret hiding in plain sight. The Sanskrit word for meaning is "Svarupa." Svarupa means Essence. Everything points to this Essence, consists of this Essence, and reflects nothing other than this Essence. Though subtle, this secret is so obvious that it is used as a vehicle for mirth and laughter among the lovers and knowers of Reality — a cosmic joke, as it were.

You can see the irony, here. Western man, contemporary man, is so wrapped up in his modern discoveries, his technical advances, and his intellectual knowledge, that he overlooks the real meaning of everything before him and substitutes in Its place a series of external meanings which are mere caricatures of the original. This he does on all levels of his existence, if he even sees more than one.

On the intrapersonal level, he fails to see his own divinity, and gives himself to birth and death again and again — failing to realize the meaning of them as well. In the constant play between mind, senses, and objects, he overlooks the obvious again, refusing to see and acknowledge that he is the projector through which all of these manifest, and that he is the composer of this symphony of tantalizing notes that tease and taunt him throughout time. And even in the realm of religion, which should always save him and come to his rescue, he shies away from his responsibility as creator of the universe in which he lives, albeit temporarily, and places it on the concepts of God and Devil instead.

Man, himself, is living intelligence, Mother-wisdom in human form, but instead of perceiving this he *"barters his scintillating realm of pure Awareness for a paltry world of mere colored glass."* The secret hiding in plain sight is all about meaning, Svarupa, but not as he perceives it as yet.

S.B. from Hawaii writes:
QUESTION: "My first question has two parts: a) Is there a middle path between Jnana and Bhakti in Hinduism/Vedanta/Advaita? b) Would a householder's path be considered a middle ground between the two modes of God/Atman, and Divinity/Worship?"
ANSWER: The middle path you infer here *is* the path of combined Jnana and Bhakti. Few coalesce the two, falling mainly on one side or the other. As for the path of the householders, they are (or should be) emphasizing mostly the side of worship. Through that practice, mainly tantric, they will come to see the divinity, or Atman, in themselves, their children, and in all other beings.

For the most part, the householders of today, and most all other time-spans throughout recorded history, have not had the time to focus upon Divine Reality to the exclusion of all else, and so their path has been gradual, not immediate. Somehow, the ancient rishis managed it, though, and with it passed the perennial wisdom down to their children in a line of succession that remains unparalleled in human history to this day. Modern man should go ahead and take a page out of their book, then — all of their ancient books — and with these scriptures, reach the goal of human existence in one fell swoop, in one lifetime.

QUESTION #2: "Can you help me to have a better understanding of the difference between Hinduism, Vedanta, and Advaita? Is it that only a Hindu can be Hindu because he's born that, and that is his culture, and no one but a Hindu can be Hindu — that this is just a matter of birth on earth? And is Vedanta the belief that we are the creators, in that all is Atman, and Atman is all? Finally, is Advaita the same as Vedanta?"
ANSWER: You have put it fairly well, here. It can be further clarified by saying that, like little Russian dolls, each fits inside the other. Hinduism fits inside the Vedas, or the Vedanta, and Vedanta fits smartly into the overall truth of Advaita. They are one and the same in Essence, but focus on the varying modes of true existence called religion, philosophy, and spirituality. Hinduism accents the dualistic side, India's religion. Vedanta covers both all that is qualified in terms of philosophy, and acts as a doorway into nonduality. Advaita is that — Nonduality, and epitomizes all that is purely Spiritual in essence.

Kanyakali from Hawaii writes:
QUESTION: "Sloka 16 says that, while in the state of Samyama, if you want to know the past and the future, then make a Samyama on the changes in the samskaras. According to Swami Vivekananda, *'Some [samskaras] are working out now, and some [Samskaras] are waiting to work. So by making a Samyama on these [samskaras] one knows past and future.'* If, when in the state of

Samyama, the idea of time vanishes (Sloka 13), then how can you know past and future?"

ANSWER: Your question secretly answers itself. It is precisely that the idea of time vanishes that allows for the act of reading the past, present, and future, for when one is in belief of these phases as being actual, there is no objectivity. Put another way, the seer of time can see time because he has risen out of time as a limiting concept. From laboring under the belief in time, to the insight that time is a cosmic law, to the realization that phases of time merely blend into eternity — all of these steps constitute arrival into Timelessness. This would not be known without the ability to measure all these phases via a revisiting of mental samskaras. The seer must retrace his steps and enter the idea of time again if he wishes to reveal higher truth to the masses. Often he does this unheralded, and humanity suddenly has an awakening on the collective level. More often, a few awaken on the individual level. Whatever the case, the seer of time, like Siva, is to be revered.

QUESTION #2: "In studying my samskaras I have experienced the contrast between the unreal and the Real, the changing and the Unchanging. 'The soul feels as if all these many changes are flowing by, but has the established sense that it alone remains unchanged amidst all movements.' I get that far, at least on a general level. I am, at times (okay, most of the time!), caught up in my samskaras rather than witnessing them. But I practice reminding myself to be aware of them, and once I remember, I can do it. 'It is the witness consciousness that, standing back to observe, both sees and then sees through samskaric membranes, not forgetting to note what is seen there.' Taking it to a higher level, when one is in a state of Samyama, how would one turn one's awareness toward one's samskaras? Wouldn't all the mind's impressions be blown out? I think that examining my samskaras, and noting what is seen there while in such a state, would run the risk of getting swept back up in them. How is it possible to read the samskaras of one's mind, while at the same time preventing the mind from taking on modifications?"

ANSWER: We are to think that the state of samyama is the ability to take on samskaras at the cosmic and collective level. It is a special facility of the supremely illumined soul. The "blown out" phase occurred earlier. Most beings would, indeed, merge in Brahman thereafter. But some, as Sri Ramakrishna has stated, can gather the mind back from nondual samadhi in order to help others. As He said to Keshab Chandra Sen, *"Do, indeed, go to the farthest shore of the ocean of Consciousness and merge the mind in Brahman. But do not lose yourself There. Come back for the sake of these others you see about you."*

QUESTION #3: "Sometimes I feel a little lost in these sutras because of the emphasis on 'making a Samyama' on this, that, and the other. Samyama is Dharana, Dhyana, and Samadhi, so until I get into that very high state, it's difficult for me to understand how to 'make a Samyama' on something. Should I be trying to 'make a Samyama' on all of the various things that are discussed in these sutras, or should I start by perfecting my ability to get into a state of

Samyama through becoming one-pointed on one particular thing? And ideally, what should that thing be?"
ANSWER: To answer the last query first, that "thing" is Ishvara. Recitation of your mantra is practice for gaining, by degrees, the ability for samyama. In the meantime, it is just good to know that some beings have the ability for samyama, and tell us of it so that we can have some inkling of what it is and what it can do. Almost without knowing it, someday, with enough practice and adherence to Yoga, we will find that things that were once secret and hidden have become like open books to us — in the tradition of the apprentice who, by merely staying close to the yarn merchant for awhile, suddenly acquires the ability to tell the difference between a 30 strand yarn and a 31 strand yarn. It is just that subtle.

S.C. from Hawaii writes:
QUESTION: "Besides grief, what are the other two 'Great Traps?'"
ANSWER: There are actually four in all. Besides Grief (shoka), there are listed Udvega (guilt), Vishada (depression), and Vibhranti (low self-esteem). Contemplating these four is a real study in some of what has plagued embodied beings for eons, and that is even more evident today.

Ramakrishnadas from New England writes:
QUESTION: "Is it in the nature of chitta to be able to experience samadhi as well as to witness its own samskaras while in 'the presence' of samadhi? And in the state of samyama, is the chitta able to see itself in time as well as to be in the presence of Akshara Brahman, the 'timeless Essence,' or is all this beyond the chitta?"
ANSWER: The chitta, the mind's thoughts, on its own, can see very little, and is often given to mere rambling — as is the case with dreaming, brooding, imagining, fanaticizing, and other hazy mental movements. Even the chitta that becomes concentrated on worldly subjects always overlooks the obvious — the source of Intelligence. It is when the chitta gets "charged" by spiritual practice in conjunction with the buddhi, the intellect, that things really get moving. Those thoughts, previously forming in trains like lines of clouds, then accumulate great power for penetration, and can be depended upon to retain memory of samadhi and the presence of Brahman.

Thakur Sri Ramakrishna has used the metaphor of a hot air balloon that cannot rise due to the sandbags that are weighing it down. These would be weights like the Four Great Traps just mentioned. Once these are cast out of the balloon's housing, a natural rising is the result, and the marvelous views that commence from thence forth. This can also be understood from the nondual statement that *All is Brahman*, or *Brahman is pure Consciousness*. Chitta exists at all levels, only impeded at lower or grosser ones. The chitta that was at first weak and dispersed, is the same chitta that is congealed and charged up after spiritual practice. Thus, "Charge up the Chitta!"
QUESTION #2: "Can samadhi be focused on an 'object' such as a samskara?"

ANSWER: The lower, or seeded (samprajnata) samadhis, are utilized for that, and for delving deeper into subtler echelons of Spirit. It is true, that samadhi is usually seen as an end rather than a method, but in the case of these preliminary samadhis, the impetus tends to drive the soul further inward to the Source, the Asamprajnata. What one perceives via the seeded samadhis is both definitive and grounds for further qualification in this respect.

To put it simply, to end up with just a grand view of the ocean of wisdom, and the experience of the individual self's bliss in communing with it, does not complete the picture with regards to Enlightenment. At least a glimpse, and then a full immersion, in the other Ocean — Brahman — is what is sought after. That is why Sri Ramakrishna used to talk about the samsara sagara, the ananda sagara, and the Chaitanya sagara — the oceans of delusion, ocean of bliss, and Ocean of Consciousness, respectively. Hosts of beings lose themselves in these vast washes according to their spiritual qualifications, or lack thereof. And it is difficult to extract oneself from one and enter into another. Lord Kapila, of Sankhya fame, also used that metaphor, citing the stream of souls moving outwards towards material and sensual life (Samsara Prag Bhara), and another stream of souls moving inwards toward Freedom (Kaivalya Prag Bhara).

And all of this is greatly due to samskaras. In the West, we just do not have any equivalent word or theory for understanding this spiritually crucial principle, and have not explored it as anything more than a mere belief, feeling, or passing whim, about "being here before." However, from the level called samadhi, fairly transcendent, and as Patanjali is telling us in these sutras, the soul can get a good look at samskaras, not only at the individual level aligned with personal spiritual growth, but at the collective and cosmic levels which reveal the superlative design of Master Mind Itself, and beyond.

QUESTION #3: "Is the focus in samadhi dependent upon the depth or 'type' of samadhi?"

ANSWER: If you are speaking in terms of intensity, about how deep one can go, I do not see any evidence that the four seeded samadhis are gradated. The level of focus in each is practically equal, for concentration has been mastered prior to samadhi. The quality of the different samadhis varies, however, and the point of focus as well. The revelation of pervasive wisdom shifts to the bliss of knowing, then to perception and acknowledgement of the origin of both. When this occurs, and depending upon the level of adeptship of the seer, and Grace, the unseeded samadhi should occur as a matter of course thereafter.

QUESTION #4: "Can samadhi be experienced by going a step beyond meditation on our S.R.V. mantra?"

ANSWER: Yes and no. That is, pure focus and realization of what the mantra is and means is, in itself, a type of samadhi, as it places one into a high-minded state. But there may be several steps to navigate, inwardly, after the mantra has done its purifying work on the internal mind.

QUESTION #5: "Is our mantra a good starting point for experiencing samadhi, or are there other objects or subjects of concentration — then meditation, then

samadhi — that would be more natural to our western mind?"
ANSWER: Ekagra, a focused, even state of mind, ushers in samadhi. That state is assisted by mantra practice, which quells the thinking process and smoothes it out into one concentrated wave. So yes, mantra is a good starting place, especially for the western mind, that has little knowledge of true philosophy, and little time to learn its steps leading to clarification. Of course, Patanjali mentions Ishvara as well, Who, in conjunction with the mantra, is the superlative point of meditation leading to samadhi.

But put in terms of Yoga science rather than religion, the preceding limbs of Yoga ought to handle all preparation for impending samadhi. One has only to look at the depth, breadth, and profundity of the yamas and niyamas to see what a wealth of preparation and qualification ensue at even the beginning steps of Raja Yoga practice.

Sanatanand from Hawaii writes:
QUESTION: "It is a joy to be back to the study of this superlative wisdom after a short hiatus. It does help to keep me inspired, though I have been diligent with my daily sadhana. By way of bringing these two together, the mind, while practicing meditation, is often much less than quiet. In reading about the objective of meditation, my understanding is that the goal is to silence the mind. Additionally, my grasp of that process is to watch the ideas flow past in a detached state, and they, of their own weightiness, will eventually grind to a halt. Yet there are times when I can focus, and strongly intend that these thoughts cease, and there is a noticeable diminishing. Could you offer any insights or methods of practice to more effectively encourage that still state of mind?"
ANSWER: Whether, at any given day or phase of time, the aspirant has to force the issue a bit, or whether meditation occurs naturally according to sudden equilibrium of the gunas, determination must be made. Some more advanced methods, on the psychological level, for reducing mental waves, consist of preconsciously stilling the vrittis of the mind prior to meditation, or slowing down the rate of thoughts before sitting for practice. This is much like the practice of taking up the morning's meditation where one left off the night before, as if there was no break in between, as if Consciousness was seamless — because It is. These tools of the mind, to be used against the mind for the mind's benefit, are employed by adepts who have begun to either suspect or pick up on the nature of Consciousness prior to Its realization. The seeker begins to know how to attract Consciousness to him or her. In Bhakti Yoga, the same end is accomplished through what is termed the Three Alluring Offerings — arati, bhajan, and puja. However it is to be done, they do it.
QUESTION #2: "Related to practice again, I have been doing japa daily and working on bringing the image of my Ishtam clearly into view in my heart. Yet, the clarity is vague at best, and further, shifts and morphs into various other images. I have found that I am more able to keep the feeling of the Ishtam in the heart center, and it is much more sensible than the visual image. I do keep

a photo in front of me and refer to that as well, but can you offer any suggestions of how to better invite this presence into my Self to fructify this practice?"
ANSWER: Other than what I just suggested in answer to your previous question, there is the practice that Hindu devotees utilize, and which the Westerners are seldom taught (perhaps because our devotion to God with form is so lacking). That consists of putting together the form of your Ishtam in the mind's eye, piece by piece. Starting with the feet (a good place to begin), one adds on the legs, then the torso, the chest, neck, and finally the head. This process may have to be done over some month's time, since what one visualized the past day may become foggy in the interim. Soon, however, one can construct, *"...out of Consciousness alone,"* the form of the Chosen Ideal in one's inner vision. This is visualization par excellence. Along with the result, the practice also hones the mind's powers of visualization, and brings time and devotion together in a happy marriage of adoration.

Anurag from Portland, Oregon, writes:
COMMENTS: "Raja Yoga Sutras III: 15 -16, in conjunction with the last two retreats (Wood Valley and Portland) and the classes in Portland, compounded with my own sadhana, are building into a 'perfect storm' of Advaitic impact. A deeper, more comprehensive dawning recognition of the apparent process of projection of time, space, and causality is being viewed from the blessed rock solid Eternal Unchanging perspective. Yes, from that timeless perspective this two-sided view is one of 'unimagined profundity.' You have described this dynamic so well in your commentary on these sutras that there seems little that can be asked in the way of questions. It seems fitting to only absorb and hone this knowledge in the interest of opening up the inner channels leading to the Atman. Besides, you have stated outright that 'The inner dynamics of this, inferred by the sutras and their commentators, is most difficult of description, and must be left to the aspirant's own internal work.' Fair enough. I ask the following question with the knowledge that the answer has already been provided."
QUESTION: "Immersion in these teachings yields occasional extraordinary moments of transcendence as this element of seership gets stronger and more stabilized. Although I cannot say that I have any samskaras of samadhi, there are more samskaras of what I can call peace and clarity that are subsuming old and stale samskaras of brooding. So, the question for which the answer has already been provided is this: How, in the midst of 'all of this' do I increase my intensity and ability to stay awake, and catch myself from falling into ignorance? How to more quickly and definitively remove ignorance so as to swiftly be done with it and abide in the higher precincts and atmospheres which I have visited, but into which I have not been granted permanent residency?"
ANSWER: This is the cry and plea of every sincere seeker who finds his or her way to the upper limbs of yogic practice. The richer one becomes in possession of the properties of his own pristine Awareness, the more he wants to own the entire landscape. And the fear of not attaining is also echoed here in your ques-

tion, the very real consideration that one may fall back asleep into maya's arms before the definitive awakening has matured into full enlightenment — or at least the death of ignorance.

I would say that this is where the Ishtam (Ishtams in our case) comes into fuller play. Awareness of Sri Ramakrishna, driven deep into the sleepy and forgetful mind's recesses through hours of mantra practice, counts for the missing element in the sincere seeker's consciousness. Something about the Divine Personality, as opposed to all the service, study, philosophy, worship, etc., that we can muster, is heartening, soothing, and confidence-boosting, all at once. The words to Devendra Mazumdar's devotional hymn, *Gurustavastaka*, expresses this well:

*O Lord, it is by austerities offered to Thee that the mind comes under control.*
*You embody Yourself on earth to show us the way.*
*Even the Gods and Goddesses praise You with divine hymns.*
*O Teacher Divine, kindly grant compassion to Thy humble devotee.*

*The powerful spiritual force at the base of the spine awakens at Thy touch,*
*and desire disappears when You grant detachment & discrimination.*
*But my mind remains restless despite these supreme blessings.*
*O Teacher Divine, kindly grant compassion to Thy humble devotee.*

*At Your auspicious approach, ignorance and egotism vanish.*
*The poor and humble rush to take refuge under Thy protection.*
*Even still, my devotion to Thee is often unaccountably missing!*
*O Teacher Divine, kindly grant compassion to Thy humble devotee.*

You see, *"my mind remains restless despite all these supreme blessings,"* and *"my devotion to You is often unaccountably missing."* Restless activities (karmas), old habits (samskaras), and the like, are at play in the human mind and body. Notwithstanding our spiritual practices, they seem to persist, or recur. So long as you see form, and sport this human form, so long will you need to look to the highest Form for inspiration and power. Then you will certainly be granted permanent residency within those higher precincts and atmospheres of awakened Consciousness — even if they be called Ramakrishna Loka, rather than Brahman.

**Pada III, Sutra 17**
*shabdarthapratyayanam itaretaradhyasat sankarah tatpravibhagasamyamat sarvabhootaruta-jnanam* (*shabda*, word/sound; *artha*, meaning; *pratyaya*, concept; *itaretara*, in conjunction with one another; *adhyasa*, superimposition; *sankarah*, admixture; *tat*, those; *pravibhaga*, differences; *samyama*, consolidated upper limbs of Yoga; *sarva*, everything; *bhuta*, physical things; *ruta*, utterances; *jnana*, wisdom).

*"The admixture present in the mind's reckoning of word, meanings, concepts, and physical objects as superimpositions gets clarified via samyama on the differences inherent in them, with the result being wisdom regarding all utterances pertaining to the realm of sound."*

Additional information on the principle of samyama is given in this sutra, as well as the next, revealing the import of its understanding and application to spiritual life. To comprehend the real meaning (svarupa) behind all the vibrations in the universe, leading to perception of the nature of the Word, its connection with ether, and its origin — as in the profundity of meditating on the three matras of AUM — gives the yogi abilities that are far beyond those of ordinary living beings who merely hear sounds. Some of India's wisdom songs also take up this fine truism for contemplation. Ramprasad sings, in his famous offering to Mother Kali, *"All sounds you hear are prayers and praises, mantras arising spontaneously as the whole universe worships Her."* Speaking to the One who has realized this integral secret, the Guru Stotram states: *"More subtle than the ethers, eternally pure and impossible to taint, You embody that essential part of Consciousness that is indescribably peaceful and serene. Beyond the initial seed, the primal vibration, and the web of time, reverent salutations to the Ultimate Guru."*

Words, their meanings, the concepts they come from, and the physical worlds and objects they transform into, when left to their own devices in the ordinary human mind, turn into a host of mundane levels of expression. In the benighted mind they become ways of veiling and obstruction. In the devious mind they are wielded as weapons of grave harm and evil. The enlightened mind, however, makes the necessary connections that render them into revelatory power that penetrates deep into the nature and origin of sound itself, uncovering the *Shabda*. It is the *"Word"* that was *"in the beginning,"* and that was *"with God,"* and then *"was God."* We should note the order of Jesus's statement to John so as to understand the meaning of Genesis, or Origination.

For, Jesus never intended that Genesis be the final "word" in Religion. The Origin of all things would necessarily be the Cause of all phenomena in the realms of name and form. That is, The Word, the Primal Vibration, or Unstruck Sound as the Vedas refer to it, is that Cause. This tells us two important things for our philosophical understanding: first, that all manifestation emanates forth from vibration, and that this vibration is AUM, the Word; and second, that God, or Brahman, is not the origin of things; It cannot be the cause of an effect since It is Formless and beyond cause and effect. In short, God is not a Creator; His Word produces everything. And mind uses all that for projection, sankalpa.

Thus, *"In the beginning"* (God has no beginnings, middles, and ends) of time (but God is timeless) *"was The Word"* (Shabda, Nada, Sphota, Logos, Pranava, Om), and *"The Word was with God"* (was separate from God at this time, and acting as His vehicle), *"and The Word was God"* (merges with Him when everything — all effects and their causes — get dissolved in pralaya).

This internal secret, *Sristi Rahasya* as it was called by the Tantras, is what everything in the multi-leveled universes of name and form is reflecting, even shouting out loud, as it were, to the yogi in possession of the meaning of manifestation uncovered by studying the samskaras on an individual, collective, and cosmic level via the samyama process.

So, when the yogi hears the sounds of animals, overhears the words of human beings around him, listens to the music of the spheres as planets spin around in orbits through space, or hearkens to the lucid utterances of the saints, sages, seers, and saviors, he knows. Even the language of the gods, the decrees and dictates of the Trinity, and the abstruse, transcendental communications of the Supreme Will of the Divine Mother are known to him. Only Formless Reality is vibrationless, beyond Its own Word, and therefore is going to require, at the proper and auspicious time, replacing samskaras, not just studying them. And in the sweep of this more subtle process, other salient spiritual facts become known to him as well.

**Pada III, Sutra 18**
*samskara sakshat karanat purva jati jnanam* (*samskara*, mental impressions; *sakshat*, witnessing; *karanat*, direct perception; *purva*, preceding; *jati*, birth; *jnana*, wisdom).

"*Along with this (aforementioned, previous sutra), and in addition to the ability to witness samskaras, comes the direct perception of previous existences.*"

Being one of the more famous of the Yoga sutras, and certainly very intriguing to the psychologist, metaphysician, and philosopher, this statement both provides the seeker of truth entrance into the domain of past lives, and proves, via the authority of one of the world's greatest 'spiritual geniuses', the sure existence of them based upon an interconnected series of mental projections belonging to the mind stream, or flow of consciousness.

Just as by utilizing objects in nature as alambanas, as supports for meditation early in the practice of Yoga, and thereby uncovering the subtle connections between earth and smell, water and taste, fire and the eyes, etc., similarly, at this advanced stage of Yoga, can the yogic adept use the newly acquired ability to fathom the nature and contents of his own samskaras to retrieve valuable memories pertaining to his own series of past incarnations in form. This is called *daiva smriti,* divine memory, and it is something that all illumined souls bring with them when they have to enter the realm of embodied beings to accomplish the various works of the art of enlightenment. And, in fact, and as an important aside relating to samyama, they have in their facile minds a samskara based upon divine memory, having honed it in every previous lifetime via spiritual practices, while others were only busy wasting time perfecting the art of forgetfulness — avidya (the first impediment in Yoga, if you remember, and the first of five personal hells).

As I have often asserted, and to caution against seeking it for sensationalist reasons, this knowledge of past births has little to do with what particular personality the soul took on, or what body/ego complex was assumed, and much more to do with why he did not espy his true nature at the time, and what caused him to forget it in the first place. For, such wisdom signals an end to ignorance and the demise of maya's control and influence over his mind. With such knowledge, far from bantering it about to his friends by boasting about what great personage he was in the past, what nonsense he spoke then, and what futile acts he accomplished which all came to naught at the time of death, the wise yogi now clearly perceives the origin of his own birth process. This vision reveals to him his initial birth in form, what caused his separation in ignorance from Brahman, and what were the results of his incarnations up to that point in time, both beneficial and detrimental. As Swami Abedhananda, one of Sri Ramakrishna's direct disciples, puts it is his Hymn to the Divine Mother, Sri Sarada Devi:

> *Through tie of Love Divine,*
> *bound thou hast this heart of mine,*
> *granting forever Thy Presence benign.*
> *O wonder, how Thy mercy doth shine upon us.*
> *Thy Grace has made us holy,*
> *changed to virtue our endless folly.*

About this sutra so much more could be written. To get this wisdom (Yoga) from a living master, however, is better, and to meditate upon his words and realize them in the depth of one's own heart is superior to that. As Shankara has stated, *"Hearing about Brahman is good; taking teachings on Brahman is better; meditating upon Brahman is better still, but best of all is that meditation in which all doubts about the nature of Reality die away forever."* So, what better way to destroy *"all doubts about the nature of Reality"* than to destroy one's death grasp on relativity? Perceiving one's series of births will accomplish precisely that.

But along with the warning not to follow sensation pathways that are only sidetracks or detours, there also comes the caution that one should not search mainly for seeking a vision of one's past lifetimes. Focusing upon Reality via the mode of yogic practice prescribed by the illumined guru will naturally reveal such hidden caches of pertinent information. One need not seek it out specifically and thus throw up another barrier to consummate realization. Path, practice, mind, desire — all of these, and more, are very subtle and potentially precarious balances to be maintained. Only the adept emerges successful and unscathed, and he does so by following the tradition with exquisite care and unflagging devotion.

In this regard, the clarification that takes place at the level of samskaric scrutiny and samyamic ability has its own shade of subtlety, much of which has been fairly well documented by Patanjali and the host of fine commentators who have taken up his superlative darshana.

## Lesson Sixty-nine, 3/26/12
### Pada III, Sutra 19 & 20

We all send our gratitude and encouragement to all the students of this Raja Yoga email class who sent in questions for the last lesson. This increased participation adds a unique energy into the flow. And as new students join the list, and see others fully engrossed, it sends a message of support to them, knowing that Vedantists, as my guru once said, "Go hand in hand to the Goal."

And that selfsame Goal, called Samadhi in both Yoga and Vedanta, has been receiving our rapt attention for several classes now. Patanjali is at his best, and on firm and familiar ground around this superlative topic. It is as if he lives on the eighth limb, specifically, only coming down the tree of Yoga to its lower levels to transmit salutary teachings that will reveal the path leading back to the topmost branches of spiritual realization. By the nature and content coming from the previous lesson's questions, it seems that many souls are anxiously engaged on that path leading to samadhi. What could be better? Let us continue the climb, then.

**Questions and Answers for Lesson 69**
S.C. from Hawaii writes:
QUESTION: "Included in the eight fetters, there is one called 'lineage.' Does that mean pride/attachment to one's family lineage?"
ANSWER: Usually, the fetter called "pride of lineage" refers to spiritual heritage rather than family. This is because spiritual life, the caste system, and family life in India, from time out of mind, have been all tied up with one another, inextricably so. There has been time, therefore, to develop such a thing as pride of caste and pride of lineage, whereas in the West, today, the only equivalent one might cite as a similarity is the pride that an individual might take in belonging to his or her religion. To the Westerner this is more of an earthly affair, whereas caste and lineage, in India, has to do with long-standing adherence to a lineage (like shaivism, vaishnavism, etc.) that the family line has established and occupied for many generations, in unbroken succession. There has also been a priest class in India as well, equally long-lived, and unlike a preacher's vocation in the West, to the Brahmin priest it is more than a vocation; it is a devotional calling, a wisdom pathway, and a door to the heavens, all three, providing attendance upon the gods for him and his family.

However, and the Brahmin priest class of present day India is a good example of this, when pride in this great boon of a higher calling develops in the heart and mind, and unless it is guarded against, there comes a tendency towards the feeling of superiority, a monopoly over religion itself, and, as a result, the abandonment of the honorable priestly vow to help the people gain liberation through religious precepts and proper worship. This type of spiritual ego is the worst kind, and the result is a trading away of true religion for mere money-making via coveting of power — what Swami Vivekananda abhorred, in his country and ours, as "a mere shopkeeping religion." Thus, the "fetter" of pride of lineage is aptly named, and bluntly brought into view.
QUESTION #2: "What is the meaning of annam?"
ANSWER: Annam is a particle, usually one of food, but also used philosophically in correlation with prana, intelligence, and other particles that flow. And all of these are interconnected, as we have been studying in SRV classes for many years. Let's all bring our particles together, then, and make them flow towards healing, then spiritual awakening, then enlightenment. Then, "let it

flow" will become "let it be" — which is the true meaning of that statement.

Akshaya-bhakti from New England writes:
COMMENTS: "In Lesson 68, when Kanya asked on what we should become one pointed if we want to attain the state of samyama, the answer was, emphatically, 'Ishvara.' For me, Sri Ramakrishna is none other than Ishvara, but I wonder if during my japa / mantra practice, I am allowing myself to focus on this most subtle aspect of His nature, or if I am still concentrating on His advent on earth alone. In Lesson 20, there was a beautiful elucidation of Ishvara which I would like to incorporate into my awareness of Him: ".... the cause of all which stretches beyond the Sankhya list of evolutes. Ishvara can be thought of as the Cosmic Mind, or as in Vedanta, the possessor of it. Ishvara is greater than the greatest in the sense that it possesses more of the essence of Consciousness than any other principle, but is smallest than as it is closest to Brahman which alone is so infinitesimal as to belie the increment of space and transcend the passage of time. When we look at Ishvara, we are really looking at form on the verge of nothingness. It knows both presence and absence, and the eternal subject that underlies them both."
QUESTION: "How can my vision of Sri Ramakrishna's compelling form be transformed into experiencing Him as Ishvara? Does this happen through samyama on His Name alone?"
ANSWER: Mental preparedness also sets the ground for this great inner event. One must install the Great Master on the Throne of Ishvara and meditate upon Him there. It is not hard to do, because there is no competition in this day and age for an Ishvara figure like Him. Other "jagadgurus" with large followings, when examined, are seen lacking, being inextricably involved with either fame or money. The Great Master would not touch either of these. Then there are those popular pretenders to the throne of authentic spirituality who mix and mingle with occult powers. They, too, fail the test, obviously, setting a poor example. The Great Master would have nothing to do with the occult, and warned us away from it, like Sri Krishna does in the Bhagavad Gita Then, others who posture pretentiously, stumble by succumbing to scandal. All of these unfortunate cases have been seen and recognized in the so-called "great teachers" of our time. Finally, those who are Avatars do not proclaim themselves as such in their lifetime, like these pretenders have done, the latter even putting out books, like "autobiographies," which proclaim themselves as such. The Great Master only said so, definitively, on the occasion of His Mahasamadhi, and only to Swamiji, i.e., *"He who was Rama, and He who was Krishna, is now here in this Ramakrishna form."*

So, install the real item on the shrine in your heart, feeling assured of the Truth, and meditate there with constancy. If you can manage a samyama on His name, all the better, but do not leave out His august form either, nor His ignorance dispelling words.
QUESTION #2: "Also, in Lesson 68, in a reply to Avinashi, you noted that a contemporary Upanishad has been composed on Sri Ramakrishna, but I could

not seem to find any specific reference to that further in the lesson. Were you referring to the *Gospel of Sri Ramakrishna,* dear teacher, or if not, what is that scripture?"

ANSWER: A small paperback book was brought out in 1950 by the Madras Ramakrishna Math, written by C. Rajagopalachari, called the Ramakrishna Upanisad. It is really a series of articles about His stories and His life. It can probably be found and ordered online from this Math. As well, there are a number of little books that praise His name and glories. These are little treasures one comes upon only in India, which are often not present in the West, and not shown online either. "Child of the Mother" is one of those, which is a rare poem written on Him by an Indian devotee. Of course, there is the rather unknown but sweet, powerful, and voluminous work by the Master's direct disciple, Akshay Kumar Sen, entitled "A Portrait of Sri Ramakrishna." The lover of the Great Master will find a lot there.

Some of us will be going to India in late December to be present for the 150th anniversary of Swami Vivekananda's birth. It will be a good time to explore and gather treasures like these, and to feel His presence, since most all of our time will be spent in Kolkata — a Sri Ramakrishna "hotbed."

QUESTION #3: "Having found the Sankhya system of Kapila so fundamental to the Raja practice, I feel ready to experience it at the source. Which translation would be best? Much gratitude as always for your wisdom teachings."

ANSWER: All the scriptures of Sankhya have been lost or destroyed over the long expanse of time since they were composed. The Tattva Samasa Sutras, probably written by Kapila's close devotee, are available in English. That is the closest we can come. Taking a retreat on Sankhya Yoga is better, however.

K.D. from Hawaii writes:

COMMENTS: "First I would like to acknowledge how much I value the comments and questions of other members of this Raja Yoga online sangha. Lessons 29 and 30 on Savitarka Samadhi have held valuable insights for me, especially concerning the relationship between merging and separation. On one hand, in lesson 29, in answer to Kanya's questions about meditating on the unmixed word, meaning, and knowledge process, you write: 'Plumbing these depths for a time..., a time will arrive wherein the mind melts all distinctions, including the triputi you mention here, of word, meaning, and knowledge.' In the savitarka samapatti stage of Savitarka Samadhi, you write that word, meaning, and knowledge are mixed together, and when the nirvitarka samapatti stage is reached, these 3 elements are singled out and experienced individually in their essence 'devoid of imagery, cognition, and linguistic misconceptions.' Contemplating these statements has led me to observe my reactions not only to words, but any and all sounds. I don't think it is possible to differentiate a sound from the vibration that sound creates as waves, since I cannot perceive the sound until it has set up vibrations within the ears and the brain and the mind interprets it."

QUESTION: "How does one separate the sound from the wave it creates?"

ANSWER: The wave, as far as the physical ears are concerned, is on the surface, even though unseen....and unthought in most peoples' cases. What the yogic practitioner is going for is to notice the nature of the sound vibration and trace it to a subtler source, in this case the subtle senses. That is why we have a list of tattvas, cosmic principles, so that we can pinpoint this source and name it. Finding that the emanation really emits not from the physical sound, but from an inward plane, is key to tracing it deeper — all the way to AUM, The Word. So, it is not a matter of separating so much as it is a task of connecting.

COMMENTS #2: "However, it is possible for me to slow down and observe reactions to sound including base emotional defensive reactions, as well as lower and higher forms of knowledge. For instance, instead of getting annoyed and even angry at the coqui frog that likes to hang out right outside my window at bedtime, I am observing my reactions to that sound and noticing that even this little stimulus gets me traveling down Broodway Boulevard, heading for Attachment Alley, Deadend Desire, and Anger Alley (I love your humor here.) I focus on being neutral towards that sound and distancing myself from these so-called negative reactions, since I don't want to end up in the Delusional Detour headed for Ruined Reason Road. I observe my reaction to the neighbor's diesel truck starting, the neighborhood dog choir, and sounds I label as pleasant such as the early morning song of the birds. Observing these reactions has helped me when things get fast and furious in conversations with others, especially where there are habitual defensive reactions involved.

"Like with meditation on the alambanas, the goal is to experience the oneness of objects, senses, and mind. I liken it to my experience practicing scales. For a number of years I have focused musically on arpeggios of all scales in all keys — major, minor, diminished, blues, etc. There have been some moments where I had a brief insight into the artificial nature of scales, that basically there is only one scale composed of all 12 notes. I was aware of the illusory nature of scales, yet at the same time cognizant that each scale is its own unique order of notes.

"The following statement was most helpful: 'The knowledge of the oneness of all things, based upon their simultaneously interdependent yet intricate and respectively independent workings, is a powerful ground for Samadhi.' Also, this one: 'Distinction or discrimination of the differences in subjects and their operations is important, so that a sort of surface idea of oneness (as in intellectual knowledge only) is avoided, and a truer oneness based upon underlying interconnectedness is gained so that a final withdrawal from name and form becomes possible.' It seems a paradox that by contemplating and experiencing the 5 elements and their evolutes, and word, meaning, and knowledge, in as great a detail and variation as possible, we can experience the interconnectedness of all things, a true Oneness."

QUESTION #2: "Can you please expound on these thoughts of mine with special attention to the following questions:
• "Is it always necessary to contemplate elements, evolutes, and other objects and concepts in all their aspects and relationships in order to experience that

underlying oneness?"

• "Do you think my analogy of musical scales is appropriate to the subject at hand?"

ANSWER: Taking your first question first, it is not necessary to spend huge amounts of time in meditation on all these alambanas. However, if the practitioner has the time, it is a very informative process. Thoughts and connections long forgotten come to light again, and whereas these hidden facets may or may not impede the forthcoming samadhis, they quite often enrich life and mind, eventually making samadhi either sweeter or, sometimes, more complete.

The musical scale analogy is a good one. Being a musician myself, I have often used such analogies, though for different applications. You are speaking of becoming aware of inner connections. To note, for instance, that notes, scales and arpeggios are always present in pieces of music, though not apparently, is akin to finding out, for instance, that all five elements are in every object in different proportions, or that the subtle senses are behind and supporting all gross senses, or further, that prana is supporting all ten senses, etc. Simple facts are clarifying in matters of abstruse cosmology and philosophy.

COMMENTS #3: "You write: 'Rare is the one who ventures through that inner passageway (of direct spiritual experience), for entering there signifies a change of conceptual and psychological perspective which transforms life on the spot and then demands transformation of human nature as well.' In contemplating this statement, it seems clear that all desires and attachment to any 'model' of the world we hold in our minds must go out the window. Even subtle models like 'I am a person seeking direct spiritual experience' would interfere with the ability to actually have that experience. It seems that all of my actions are desire-driven, from the simplest action like eating dinner, to wanting liberation from all bondage. Faith that this is even possible has to also be present, since this is indeed a tall order to fill."

QUESTION #3: "Is this what you mean by 'transformation of human nature?' We must actually give up all natural inclinations to want anything other than being aware of Awareness, conscious of pure Consciousness? Or is it a matter of being able to go there at will in meditation, and at other times sport in Lila and simply be aware of desires and attachments without identifying them as 'mine.' Isn't coming from the heart instead of the mind a big part of this direct spiritual experience? I think that these are answers, but would appreciate an elucidation, because I need to hear these truths over and over again to gain a deep understanding of them."

ANSWER: Your final sentence here is a mouthful. Repetition is the spice of spiritual life, at least until the mind becomes sensitive and receptive — impressionable to spiritual input. For, transformation of base human nature is a gradual process; often times it cannot be rushed. Qualification is the name of the game until maturation has dawned. So, and as you mention here, there are two ideal levels to occupy: first, one of spontaneity wherein one can attach and detach at will; second, absolute renunciation.

As for "coming from the heart," I am not a big fan of it, not until the senses have been purified, the mind has transcended attachment to dualities, and the informed intellect has come into play. There are just too many errors and oversights being committed in the name of love, too many charades going on in the name of bhakti — especially in our as yet spiritually immature culture. The idea here is to first cultivate higher intelligence, then allow it to counsel daily activities, devotional life, and meditational practice. It is a very good plan, and sincere seekers should give it a chance.

QUESTION #4: "In meditating on the alambanas, I feel blocked at the level of Ahamkara. I have had very brief glimpses of how it might be true that all elements and evolutes come from Ahamkara, but doubt creeps in here, since I don't understand this. Why does the manifested world made up of the 5 elements come from Ahamkara and not another aspect of the fourfold mind? I then play lip service to prana, the fourfold mind, Buddhi as individual manifestation of the Cosmic Mind, unmanifested Prakriti, and Purusha. I realize that deep concentration on these subtle realms is essential for Samadhi, and know that intense practice is required to reach the state of ability to directly perceive these subtle truths. Can you offer some suggestion as to how to pierce this veil of doubt? Isn't perception of these subtle realms a matter of direct spiritual experience which requires transformation of human nature?"

ANSWER: When the mind is purified, it automatically means that ego is rendered pure, or ripe, along with it. For the mind is fourfold, as we have learned, consisting of dualities (manas), trains of thought about them (chitta), the misinformed intellect's manufacturing of them (buddhi), and the ego's possession of them (ahamkara). All of these four are difficult to calm and rectify. That is why we take an ideal, a seer with a perfected mental body, and meditate upon Him/Her. They have managed the task, and encourage us to do the same. Real change often only takes place when the narrow, selfish ego is put in the same place, atmosphere, and proximity with a ripened ego. The former then sees its gross imperfections, its inflated pride, its faulty stance.

So try meditating on Ishvara, on the highest form of God your mind can comprehend, when you attempt to encounter and master the human ego, ahamkara, in meditation. For, the ego contemplating the ego will lead nowhere. Ishvara is higher court. Bring in a witness, and let It testify for you.

QUESTION #5: "How does one deify all negativities and use them to pierce through relative existence?"

ANSWER: This is a tantric method advised by great masters for qualified students. The student must be ready for such a radical approach. If he is not, he may just end up using the negativities to justify his enjoyment of what is unhealthy for him. For most, concentrating on the positivities and taking all thought away from the negativities is a better method. This is called "watering the flowers and not the weeds." Both methods have their drawbacks, but what method does not? Really, it is the quality of the aspirant's consciousness that is most important. Any method, and all methods, will work immediate wonders on that soul who has qualified him or herself. This is why Sri Ramakrishna Paramahamsa could reach the goal of any pathway He selected, and in a very short time. He is the epitome of the saying "He is a quick study." Some five million devotees have taken Him as the Ishvara form to meditate upon in this age. Count me among them.

Avinashi from Pennsylvania writes:
QUESTION: "The more I look for 'matter,' the less I can find anything resembling it, as everything dissolves into Consciousness. But people — even you — keep using the word, 'matter.' To what do you actually refer when there's only Consciousness? Is this mysterious 'matter' simply a ghostlike phantasm that arises through the course of perception? Maybe the word and concept are simply necessary, perhaps unavoidable, conventions?"
ANSWER: This brings up the matter of perspectives, which are pathways. There is the view that all is illusory (Mayavada); there is the perspective that the world is real, but only for as long as consciousness perceives it (Dristisristhivada); there is the angle that declares that Brahman transforms a portion of Itself into the universe and its living beings (Parinamavada, or the qualified nondualism of Ramanuja); another look avers that all manifestation is a superimposition over Brahman out of ignorance (the Vivartavada of Vedanta); and there is the convincing assertion that All is Brahman (Aparinamavada), which I will get at in your third question, below. Even in Buddhism, with its seventy-two (more or less) dharmas, the entire gamut gets run — everything from the Shunyatavada of Nagarjuna (nothing exists) on to the "Everything Is" view (sarvastivada) of original Indian Hinayana Buddhism. As Holy Mother says, "Oh, it is all so inscrutable!"

So take up your position and be content — religiously, philosophically, spiritually — but as Ramakrishna has told us, *"Never think that your way is the only right way."* People operate at various levels of understanding, and even lack thereof. For instance, there is also the path of ignorance (Mithyavada), and the path which thinks that the world is the only reality (Vyavaharikavada). However, the Great Master also encouraged his devotees, who are essentially Advaitists, to be able to switch positions as needed, at will. We attempt to do this with the Fours Yogas in Ramakrishna tradition, so we should also take on a similar task with regard to philosophical views. It ameliorates nicely, setting the ground for higher understanding overall.
QUESTION #2: "In doing a small review of some of these RY Lessons, I came across a statement in Lesson 59 that intrigues me no end: 'The natural state for the human mind, until it gets fully enlightened, is not manas, but mahat.' Wow! Does that ever speak to me! But at the same time, its purport eludes me."
ANSWER: Of course, by the word "natural," here, I mean a mature mind that, to put it in terms of Lord Vasishtha's teachings to Sri Ram, *"is empty of everything but its own Essence."* Ordinary mind is not that mind. Ordinary mind is manas, meaning "dual by nature." Amazingly, that very same mind, when purified by teachings and spiritual effort (sadhana), gets transformed into that which it is a reflection of anyway, at the outset — the Mahat, the Great Mind, God's Mind.

It is the same case with the intellect, the Buddhi. At first it is stunted, ego-driven, using its knowledge for base and mean pursuits. Later, it is proud and attached to its learning and its vaunted store of knowledge, as in the case of an intellectual human being. Then, when philosophically and spiritually informed, it is a spark off of the original fire, the cosmic Buddhi, *"the intelligence of the most intelligent,"* as the Upanisad says. It receives visions, then revelations.

All that is needed is to grow, or, at least, to assume the position of growth. When "natural" mechanisms kick into operation due to this better and well-informed stance, man finds that evil, ignorance, base passion, etc., are all empty of substance; they cannot harm or impede him, and this is where and when he becomes more like his true Self. A sojourn away, and a timely return — that is all that has happened. Further, when looking back on the journey, and all that happened, it is seen to have been a dream, or dreamlike. It is gone, correct? As Sri Ramakrishna has said in this regard, *"Once a sweetmeat has gone down the throat, one forgets what it really tasted like."*

So enough of the past, present, and future. It is the Eternal Moment that characterizes the true Self, Atman. As far as the three phases of time are concerned, he only needs to extract the essence from what he experienced there, and be. Whether he is inhabiting a form, then, or gives it up into formlessness, it is really a "matter of little moment."

QUESTION #3: "The concept of aparinama asserts that Brahman is free of transformation. I understand that to mean Brahman is free of transformation by nature, so there can finally be nothing but Brahman. And, at present, I infer it's simply sense perception which creates the illusion that 'substances' change in their natures. Someone on a boat, out at sea, dreams on the waves and the foam of the waves, seeing veritable worlds in the patterns of the water, but really, there's only water and foam, the foam also being nothing but water. However, there is movement of the water; in the same way — in this Existence — doesn't Brahman 'move' in some manner, the intelligent particles, like waves in the Sea of Consciousness, maybe changing their positions in relation to each other? Then, because of sense perception and erroneous conclusions drawn by the buddhi, do we imagine there are actually such things as clouds, trees, mountains, and people, when really, there's only Brahman and the intelligent particles moving under impulses from sankalpic tides? But still, it must all move, even if it doesn't transform, mustn't it? In some of what I've read, it's seemed to me that aparinama implies there isn't even movement!? Maybe this is the truth for a person entering Nirguna Brahman, while a person in Saguna Brahman would see movement without change in nature — like gold being formed into different kinds of jewelry, but without ceasing to be gold?"

ANSWER: Yes, you are reasoning aptly here. Of course, it is not the senses that create the illusion of change; they are only the observers (which is why when they get purified by devotional sadhana, they imitate the witness Self adequately). So, we are back to the mind in maya, at all its levels, as being the main culprit in the projection process. And it is a process. And all processes get stilled in Brahman, or as you say, in Nirvikalpa.

So, there is no movement in Brahman, because the idea of movement never occurs to It. Unlike everything else, even the Word, It neither seeks to, nor needs to, nor wants to. Further, because of its all-pervasive nature, It does not have to. As Sri Ramakrishna has put it, *"Brahman is the one Principle that remains ever untouched by the mind and the tongue of man."* To put it in Swamiji's inimitable words: *"The earth moves, causing the illusion of the movement of the sun; but the sun does not move. So, prakriti, or maya, or nature, is moving, changing, unfolding veil after veil, turning over leaf after leaf of this grand book called life, while the witnessing soul drinks in knowledge, unmoved, unchanged."* And this is good news, to be sure, especially for the peace lovers, or when world-weariness strikes the satiated soul. In terms of living beings, then, this nonmovement also gets at the root problem with regards to love, compassion, and even wisdom and its end. As Swamiji puts it, *"All souls that have ever been, are, shall be, are all in the present tense, and — to use a material simile — are standing at one geometrical point. Because the idea of space does not occur in the soul, therefore all that were ours, are ours, and will be ours, are always with us, were always with us, and will always be with us. We are them. They are in us."* This statement of his consummates the conclusions of the ancient rishis, and has been the origin, justification, and impetus for all the recent new age movements, whether it is known or not.

The Aparinamavada is rather unforgiving in this respect. It is radical, as any nondual perspective, or axiom, must be. Ironically enough, the word Brahman comes from the root, "bhr," meaning "to expand." Fortunately we have words in English like "apparently," "seemingly," and "supposedly," to explain the possible dilemma. "Apparently," a "supposed" thing can "seem" to change without ever doing so.

As for your ocean, wave, and foam analogy, and relative to all that is being questioned here, we can look to Vivekananda for some more clarification: *"As each individual can only see his own universe; that universe is created with his own bondage and goes away with his liberation, although it remains for others who are in bondage. Now, name and form constitute the universe. A wave in the ocean is a wave only in so far as it is bound by name and form. If the wave subsides, it is the ocean, but that name and form have immediately vanished forever. So that the name and form of wave could never be without the water that was fashioned into the wave by them, yet the name and form themselves were not the wave. They die as soon as ever it returns to water. But other names and forms live in relation to other waves. This name and form is called maya, and the water is Brahman. The wave was nothing but water all the time, yet as a wave it had the name and form. Again this name and form cannot remain for one moment separated from the wave, although the wave as water can remain eternally separate from name and form. But because the name and form can never be separated, they can never be said to exist. Yet they are not zero. This is called maya."*

The mind in maya, then, is a force to be reckoned with. Enlightenment has all to do with this reckoning, and those who desire God and Freedom first and foremost will get on with the contest. Though helpful and interesting, perhaps movement and nonmovement are less important of contemplation here than dichotomous dualities such as existence and nonexistence, form and formlessness; they are "huge." So, until this dichotomous hippopotamus is brought down to size, we have to take the word of those rare few who have actually experienced Reality — the Unmoved Mover.

Kanyakali from Hawaii writes:
QUESTION: "Your answer in response to my question about being able to know the past and future by making a samyama on one's samskaras (Sutra 3:16) really struck a chord with me, and I've been pondering it ever since. You said, 'It is precisely that the idea of time vanishes that allows for the act of reading the past, present and future, for when one is in belief of these phases as being actual, there is no objectivity. Put another way, the seer of time can see time because he has risen out of time as a limiting concept. From laboring under the belief in time, to the insight that time is a cosmic law, to the realization that phases of time merely blend into eternity – all of these steps constitute arrival into Timelessness.' When I remind myself that time is of the mind and not ultimately real, I get some objectivity around it, and I become aware of the fact that much of my daily stress is because I'm 'laboring under the belief in time.' So often, the stories running around in my head are about not having enough time, not making good use of my time, time flying by too fast, needing to find more time, etc. But when I 'rise out of time as a limiting concept,' I can relax and be at ease. Since I've been taking a break from the daily grind of working full time, I've had to readjust my relationship with time. With so much 'unstructured time' at hand, self-discipline has become even more of a struggle for me. But I am persevering. Having these teachings to ponder throughout the day, and applying them, is definitely a worthwhile pursuit. I'm reminded of the verse I recently memorized, '...*then meditate on this state of awareness, pass your time contentedly, and be free.*' When you taught us this chant, you related 'passing our time contentedly' to spinning off the last of our karma in equanimity, while not creating new karma in the process. I now see how not limiting myself with the mental construct of time will increase my contentment – but it might make it harder for me to turn my homework in on time!"
RESPONSE: The phrase, "utilizing time wisely," is interpreted variously by different types of persons. For yogic aspirants, it most definitely has to do with focusing in on teachings and meditating. These two things define real sadhana. Devotion and service are more obvious than necessary. As Ramprasad sings, "*Practice meditation and cut time down.*" So, 1) utilize time to your advantage, spiritually; and 2) experiment with transcending it in meditation.

## Pada III, Sutra 19
*pratyayasya parachittajnanam* (*pratyayasya*, focused mental processes; *para*, the other; *chitta*, mind-stuff; *jnana*, knowledge).

*"When the yogi focuses his mental processes (performs samyama) on the appearance of another, the general makeup of that person becomes known."*

Long known over countless ages, the rishis of India were familiar with the art of reading the basic character of living beings. Though nowadays this art — called clairvoyance, mind-reading, occultism, etc. — has been cheapened due to novices turning it towards money, fame, and power, its original function was simply a way of measuring character, ability, readiness for the spiritual path, and other wise uses. And in fact, as Vivekananda reminds us, Lord Patanjali himself — and every great soul from Krishna to Ramakrishna — warned against the impediment of using the occult powers. To quote him: *"Says Patanjali, the father of Yoga: 'When a man rejects all the superhuman powers, then he attains the raincloud of virtues.' He sees God. He becomes God, and helps others become the same."*

Obviously, there is a difference between occult power based in "the tricks of prana," and virtue based in dharma and spiritual practice to gain enlightenment. What is more, when occult powers do come onto the scene, the intention for citing them and the quality of consciousness of the one dealing with them is on another level as well. With Vivekananda it was a matter of a mere cursory look at a man or woman, and he could immediately tell them of their past and potential future. He was quick to let them know, as well, that there was nothing mystical or hidden in this art; that it was natural to him.

This gives us a clue into the above sutra. It also introduces the next sutra, below. In the former, we can even apply an English word, that being "physiognomy," which means "....judging character by appearance." In this way, the facial features hold and show up the nature of the mind and its tendencies. In India, and in spiritual masters, however, this is not just a matter of "I see your eyes are red, so that means you are not sleeping well." It goes much deeper, being an overall look at everything the man or woman has experienced in the past — "the past," here, meaning, past lives, not just early life. A vast amount can be determined by this general reading, and not for purposes of impressing or manipulating people, but for reasons of aiding them on their spiritual journey. So this is the main difference between the science of physiognomy and the ability to implement samyama — the main criterion being the quality of awareness of the one utilizing such abilities.

And samyama goes deeper, as the next sutra explains. That is, in sutra 19, above, it is a general rendering of facts based upon outer appearance of a man that is being assessed. That is explained in sutra 20, next under consideration.

**Pada III, Sutra 20**

*na cha tat salambanan tasyavishayibhutatvat* (*na,* not; *cha,* and; *tat,* that; *salambana,* foundation; *tasya,* its; *avishayin,* imperceptible; *bhutatvat,* being so).

*"But not the deeper contents of it, which remain imperceptible, requiring a different foundation."*

The hidden contents of another's mind will require a deeper foundation, as well as more specific abilities in order to fathom them. Again, since most beings do not know their own mind, what to speak of the karmas from past lifetimes that are still inhabiting it, what to speak further of the samskaras already in place there that have already settled in and are difficult to move and dissolve, the yogi, guru, preceptor, seers, etc., will need to delve deeper. Samyama takes on a different dimension here, one of in-depth internal scrutiny, rather than of general outward observances.

And it is here that spiritual life, with sadhana combined, takes on greater import. Here is no walk in the park — no applying salve or herbs to the body, no reliance on food fads and exercise regimens, no mere advice-giving, no mystical card readings, no astrological speculations, no crystal or gemstone gazing, no seance in the parlor to contact the dead for their advice or for sentimental reasons. Here, on the teacher's side, lie countless days, years, even lifetimes, of studying the human psyche, of looking into cause and effect chains with regards to both individuals and the collective mind as well, of gathering subtle power with which to reduce the blows of karma, maya, and negative human thought and activity so that a few rays of higher understanding might visit that mind — all those minds, caught in the illusion of relativity.

And on the seeker's side, he/she must come close to the fire to get warmed. Reading the revealed scriptures and contemplating their meaning, hearing the Jnana Yoga teachings in verbal transmission from the guru, sitting in meditation with the preceptor, and serving the spiritual cause on earth of the great ones who sacrifice heavily to appear in the body out of their compassion for human suffering — these are a few ways in which the student will participate in the samyama process, naturally.

In other words, the aspirant must be present so that the powers abiding in the guru can be both applied and benefitted thereby. Then it is just a matter of consistency, and of following through. As Vivekananda states in this regard: *"Know for certain that without steady devotion for the guru, and unflinching patience and perseverance, nothing is to be achieved. God, though everywhere, can be known to us in and through human character."*

So, the building of character, as Holy Mother has said, constitutes real spiritual growth, not dancing, singing, celebrating, gaining visions, and the like. Even just being in the presence of holy company will do, and undo, a lot. When resistance impedes the mind, when laziness or boredom come, when doubt visits the thinking process, when individual pride and stubbornness arise, even when problems arrive, along with the fear of one's mortality, these are all signs that hidden karmas are being operated upon by the subtle scalpel of applied samyama and its highest intention by the guru.

Many have felt samyama's freeing touch; others have only felt the anguished touch of their own selfish egos. The benefits of spiritual life will only apply to those who take definite steps to partake of them. Otherwise, everything aforementioned — positive and negative — only fall on the human head like hammer blows on an anvil, leaving no beneficial impact or impress.

In the forthcoming sutras we will scrutinize some other great effects that the principle of samyama bring into potential for the striving and aspiring yogi and yogini.

## Lesson Seventy, 5/5/12
### Pada III, Sutra 21 & 22

On the cusp of April's Dharma visit to the West Coast, we find ourselves well-launched into the third pada of Patanjali's Yoga Sutras, and specifically those sutras that are dealing with and explaining the principle of Samyama in Yoga. Time spent in this type of study is sparse for contemporary people, as is time given to actual practice of Yoga — what to speak of access to wisdom via a living representative of the tradition. As a result, the present-day practitioner is rather forced to live the teachings in everyday life, and that becomes his or her practice and proving ground, both.

This is a good path so long as we remember that activities done after adeptship in the yamas and niyamas has been attained have an entirely different effect than those perpetrated prior to it. In Vedanta speak, that would mean Shruti, Yukti, and Anubhava — hearing the Truth (about the Atman), contemplating the Truth, and then getting some direct experience of It. In both Yoga and Vedanta, as well in all other authentic darshanas, Qualification is King, and the destroyer of suffering and misery coming from acts done in ignorance (karmas). And soon to follow qualification is the ability for samyama, as we are studying at present.

The worldly saying supporting intellectualism is: "Inquiring minds want to know." For the devotees, this selfsame inquiring mind is focused on the Atman (atma vichara), and therefore searching in a very distinct and different area of inspection. Let us continue with this singular and salutary mode of intense and in-depth scrutiny. Here are our host of questions for this past lesson, #69.

**Questions and Answers for Lesson 70**
S.C. from Hawaii writes:
QUESTION: "Would you please explain qualified non-dualism?"
ANSWER: It is one of the three steps or stages in Indian philosophy given by the three major establishers of these three schools. Madhva proposed dualism; Shankara championed Nondualism (Advaita); and Ramanuja put forth Qualified Nondualism. These are called Dvaita, Advaita, and Visishthadvaita.

Qualified Nondualism's distinguishing features lie in the teaching that the universe of name and form qualifies Brahman; or, put another way, God has become the Universe. Neither Dualism or Nondualism could really accept this unconditionally, could they? For, in dualism, God and the universe are eternally separate entities, while in Nondualism, there simply is no separation between God and the world; All is Brahman.

Thus, and to benefit by all of these three in a harmonious fashion, Swami Vivekananda shares his great discovery with us in this day and time by stating that these three are steps or stages to higher understanding. Further, I would venture to say, that as one ascends along these steps, leaving each behind in succession, one does not burn bridges so that return would become impossible. Each of these three platforms are to be used to climb and to descend in turn, ushering in the potential for realized souls to come back from Nondual Awareness and assume conditional positions that will benefit those who are still practicing and striving. Great Souls like Buddha, Christ, Ramakrishna, and others have illustrated this very thing in their exemplary lives. A study of these three steps is very helpful in one's spiritual life, especially if one holds the ideal of Sarvamukti — liberation for all beings.

QUESTION #2: "Is the guna, tamas, below or less conscious than rajas? Is there no tamo-sattva?"

ANSWER: Yes, tamas is blind, whereas rajas is only misdirected. Tamas binds, and rajas deludes. To give an example, action done in rajas makes one think that progress is being made, despite the frantic nature of it. Action done in tamas is a misnomer, really, for there is no energy in tamas with which to get any action done. Thus, rajas is a better vehicle to make the march towards sattva than tamas is.

As for a combination of tamas and sattva, yes, it is possible. Actions done in sattva sporting misguided intentions might be an example of the influence of tamas on a sattvic state of mind. In nature, take for instance a beautiful multi-colored sunset whose colors are not natural, but "photo-chemical." Beautiful, yes? But it is hiding a hideous secret.

QUESTION #3: "What is the difference between sannyas and avadhut?"

ANSWER: Sannyas is a state of Consciousness, where as an Avadhut is a class of illumined being. For instance, an Avadhut might take a vow of sannyas, to renounce the world.

MORE QUESTIONS: "What is the meaning of: antaranga, purnakama, gita, jivatman, ki-jai, kutashtha, kshatra, mundamala, prama, sahavas, sahibs, samsaris, sangraham, uparama, veena, vidyadharnis, Ishan, dharmis, svara?"

ANSWERS: Antaranga, specifically, refers to a set of pillars in a natmandir, or an open pavilion. Used spiritually, the expression means an inner set of disciples who support the Guru and His teachings.

Purnakama refers to those who have had their desires fulfilled, and are no longer laboring under desire and the karma it causes.

Gita means "song," the most famous of which is the Bhagavad Gita (Song of God) of Sri Krishna, out of the Mahabharata.

Jivatman is the embodied soul, as compared to the Paramatma, or Supreme Soul.

Ki-Jai is an expression of conclusion around the victory an enlightened soul achieves over world, ignorance, mind, and all other impediments to Illumination.

Kutastha denotes the underlying substratum for all of Existence, relating directly to Brahman and its All-pervasiveness.

By kshatra is meant the warrior caste, or Kshatriya, one of the Four Castes of Indian life.

A mundamala is a "garland of skulls," seen around the necks of the images of most wrathful deities. The spiritual significance here is to illustrate the unity of all races, all beings, particularly via the surrender of the mind/ego complex to God.

Prama means "proof," as in pramana, it being one of the foremost criterion for ways of discerning and proving the existence of God in philosophy.

I am not sure if you have spelled "sahas" correctly. The only thing I can think of is sahaj, which means natural — as in sahaja samadhi, or natural realization. If you can cite where you found it, I may be able to help further.

Sahib is a word used in India in colonial times. It is not Sanskrit, but has Arabic roots, I believe. It means everything from master to friend. Its wider use originated from the Punjab area and was directed towards the English "masters."

Samsaris are those most unfortunate ones who dwell in samsara — cycles of birth and death in ignorance of their true nature. Jumping ahead in your list, dharmis are those who have transcended samsara, and who live in the land of righteousness and true religion.

Sangraha is a beautiful term in Sanskrit which means "highest and best." It usage is with terms like "loka," as in Lokasangraha. Sri Krishna uses this terms to describe his attitude towards all beings in all the worlds — one of striving for their highest and best good.

Uparama is the equivalent of, and another word for, vairagya, or detachment.

A veena is a very sweet, and somewhat rare and ancient musical instrument, set up similarly to the sitar. Mother Sarasvati is seen holding one of these,

Vidyadharinis are female deities of the highest wisdom order. The word can also mean, "holder of wisdom."

Ishan, and Ishani, are given names in India. They refer to the Chosen Ideal, or Ishvara/Ishvari. Isha also means "Lord."

The svara, as insignia, is the independent matra of AUM. It represents formless Reality, or Turiya. I like to call it the "one-eyed smile....."

K.D. from Hawaii writes:
COMMENTS: "Lessons 31 to 33 held important realizations for me. I continue to deepen my understanding of the relationship between analysis of parts and sense of oneness or unification. You wrote: 'One who can divide and unite at will, free of any of the miasmic effects of maya's influence, is the one who is spontaneously reacting to meaning as knowledge as it flows in currents of living wisdom within the fully spiritualized body of living humanity.' That is a sentence worth contemplating. The birdbrain analogy in which the chicken is hypnotized and paralyzed by a black dot really drove the point home to me.

When I start to brood, obsess, worry, etc., I picture myself as this dumb chicken and I snap right out of the doldrums. I continue to be drawn back to Raja Yoga as if in a dream, but the actual dream is my life which usually exists only as concepts in the mind. Raja Yoga, like Vedanta, Tantra, and Buddhism, sometimes seem like they come from another realm, yet they are the Reality and I accept that and work towards full realization. I do not read much at a time because Raja Yoga is so rich and thick that I could spend months just on singular subjects, like good actions going bad, and bad actions reaping good results. So that is where I will start. We covered this in class but I need further elucidation. You write: 'Good leads to bad and back again; the result of such cycles is a belief in the actuality of good and bad, and other pairs of opposites....Good actions sometimes end in poor or even negative outcomes, and the opposite is also true.' Also: 'Serving the society with the sense of benefiting it, dharmically speaking, is one of the acceptable modes of work and action. This purifies the mind, as I wrote earlier, and that is also a valid reason to keep working.'"

QUESTION: "I know you said in class that one must always choose to act out of compassion and not use any of the above as an excuse to refrain from helping another, to ease suffering where possible etc. My question is, to avoid creating any unwanted karma while 'doing good,' is it necessary to be completely detached from the fruits of action? Is it required to act out of zero egoic concern for oneself? Or does the complete nonattachment to results afford immunity from consequences, whether construed as negative or positive?"

ANSWER: I do not see the either/or scenario in these two questions. In other words, yes, to both of them. Detachment from the fruits of action is the same as nonattachment to the results. As far as dynamics go, vairagya (detachment/nonattachment) is the only immunity that is reliable and long-lived. As Vivekananda put it, *"Only renunciation is fearless."*

Put another way, the fruits of action and the objects that they are associated with are both empty. To grasp after empty phenomena is futile. For the enlightened, and required for the karma yogi and yogini, the fruits of action are not even considered. Ultimately, there are none. If there are, then the ego is still measuring this for that, getting and losing, success and failure. Serving God in mankind is the goal-less Goal, free of the concepts and overlays of loss and gain.

COMMENTS 2: "In discussing Ahamkara, you write" 'There is Ayam, the true I that passes from the individualized ego to the knowledge-filled ego to the witness ego. This ripe ego, as witness, is what is present as the advanced seeker strives to go into nondual meditation, and is what is present as the adept luminary ascends the stairs of birth and death, to return out of mature compassion.' So I understand that the individualized ego tends to brood and be concerned with all the little mundane aspects of life, being especially concerned with self-image; the knowledge-filled ego contemplates the eternal truths of the scriptures and has gained an entirely new orientation to life; and the ripe ego, the witness ego, has begun 'to think on the level of the cosmic ego, which is Brahma, the Creator, the source of all knowledge, 'God's Mind,' as you put it.'"

QUESTION #2: "I want to understand more of this ripe ego that thinks on the level of 'God's Mind.' If I were in Sasmita Samadhi, would the sense of I-ness be a sense of pure existence that was witnessing the world of relativity with compassionate detachment? Would I actually be 'thinking' like 'God's Mind,' the Great Mahat? Would there be any thoughts at all? I have a hard time grasping this. Is this 'I-sense' the Self that is always referred to? If it is Atman, are not Atman and Brahman one and the same, so would that not be a complete merging in which no sense of 'I-ness' was left?"

ANSWER: What you ask in the beginning of your paragraph, and what you ask at the end, refer to two different levels of samadhi. In Asamprajnata, the world of name and form will be transcended, and the sense of personal or individual mind would be absent, placed in abeyance. Further, God's Mind, Mahat, does not experience Asamprajnata; if it did, the great dissolution, Mahapralaya, would have begun. Samprajnata is the state going on at very high levels of awareness, but short of dissolution. This is true of both the individual mind and the Cosmic Mind. One could say that by meditating on the Mahat as per Patanjali's instructions — as in alambanic quintuplication (i.e., the fourfold mind with the cosmic mind) — all that is available in that Great Mind becomes accessible to the individual meditator. This will grant experience of all four of the samprajnata samadhis with their respective counterpoints (i.e., savichara with savitarka; nirvichara with nirvitarka, etc).

As to how the individual will "feel" in this experience, the components of ego and mind will be ripened by it — probably had already been ripened to a certain extent prior to having that level of awareness. The tradition teaches the three types of egos: dehadhyasahamkara; sakshahamkara; and paramahamkara. Below, please see them laid out for consideration:

In the first, dehadhyasahamkara (ego identified with body), no samadhi is really experienced, unless it be only a matter of momentary flashes. Sri Ramakrishna has mentioned that ordinary people experience samadhi once in a great while, say, when their karmas recede for a time and when cycles (of the gunas) turn fortuitous. But they cannot hold onto this state, since the world intrudes upon it at every little opportunity. The analogy he used was of the delicate blue lotus, that when the sun is out it remains open, but as soon as a cloud passes over the sun, it closes, unable to bear that change. The word "change" here means intrusions such as bad news, frustrated expectations, and things of that ilk. The holding of the state of samadhi — any type of samadhi — is difficult, which is why the seers prescribe gaining "sthiti" samadhi first, which is a state of steadiness that no worldly alteration or altercation can influence.

In the second, sakshahamkara (ego calmly observing all from a detached state), the sense of witnessing takes over, transporting the mind up and beyond ordinary consciousness. It is like Sri Ramakrishna's story of the man looking upon the city with all its problems and pollution, but then getting into a hot-air balloon and rising high in the sky, where the city and its concerns simply disappear below.

In the third, paramahamkara (the Supreme I), the apparently separate "i" has become one with the transcendent "I." Lines of demarcation between worlds, beings, and states of awareness, are not just blurred here, but get dissolved completely. It is like the Great Master's saying that a line drawn on a pool of water causes a seeming sense of two bodies of water, but only momentarily. This is the "ego" of the realized soul in high samadhi. But if one places a long stick across the pool of water, the sense of two separate portions of water remains for a time, until the stick gets removed. This is the case of the bound soul's ego. It persists, even beyond death, causing return to the embodied condition in ignorance.

S.B. from Hawaii writes:
QUESTION: "My question from studying Raja Yoga lesson #6 is, if one does not make it to enlightenment before death via harnessing the mind using Sadhana, Pratyahara, and Dharana (and probably further techniques, too), then does all the work done just become prep for death and a better station in the next incarnation?"
ANSWER: Yes, and as Sri Krishna says in the Bhagavad Gita: *"....even a little effort toward attaining Yoga is never lost. The practitioner just picks up the thread of this Yoga in the next lifetime."* But what is not often pointed out is the positive effect a little yogic practice has on this present lifetime as well. Lord Buddha mentioned *"drops in the dharma bucket"* in this regard, relating that every little bit of practice one can muster in this life — unlike all the daily activities one does often absent-mindedly — accumulates, and adds benefit to the world, impetus to spiritual life, and merit to the soul. And if principles such as Pratyahara and Dharana are mastered (but not Dhyana), the future life will be more than a matter of merely "picking up a thread"; it will provide an entire series of strong ropes with which to pull the soul up and into levels of samadhi. Such is the grace that performing sadhana avails the transmigrating, but aspiring, soul. As my teacher, Swami Aseshananda used to tell us, *"Grace and self-effort are one and the same; they must go hand in hand."* Which means that those who are holding out for grace to descend upon them have a long wait in store. The answer, and all the spiritual advancement that comes with it, lies right in their own hands.
QUESTION #2: "What else is gained by the doing of these mind-harnessing techniques, if enlightenment is not attained?"
ANSWER: Of course, I just answered this question, above. Suffice to add in, that fulfillment in the dharma is a boon unto itself, for qualities such as proper orientation, selfless service, and compassion free of egoic romance and sensationalism come to the aspirant. The Four Fruits of dharma, artha, kama, and moksha are assured. Someone once asked Swami Brahmananda that if he found out that everything he knew about God and God's existence were untrue, what would he do? He replied that he would not live any other way than the way he was living at present — dharmically, spiritually — for that is undeniably what is wisest, best, and beneficial to all beings.

Avinashi from Pennsylvania writes:
QUESTION: "About pratyahara: how does pratyahara in fact show itself? Does it necessarily have to involve losing awareness of the sensory world? I have been assuming that a certain degree of unconsciousness regarding the external world is an aspect of it; have I been assuming correctly or incorrectly? Can a person enter it while remaining aware of the sensory world? Is it the case that losing sensory awareness is a secondary factor occasionally accompanying pratyahara and not essential to it? If this is true, what is essential to it?"
ANSWER: As a limb of Yoga, the fifth, pratyahara is a practice rather than a goal. It later becomes an underlying support for the entire tree of Yoga, and a preferred mode of living in the body and the world for illumined beings. Along the way to this pinnacle, and for the yogic aspirant, it is close to as you describe it above. That is, it is a way of both proposing and proving to the as yet attached human mind the illusory nature of relativity.

Pratyahara's outer application is used for detaching from objects, *"....allowing the seer to detach from the seen."* This would not be necessary if the seer had not forgotten his seership in the first place, thereby attaching to and identifying with nature. Associating with nature is okay; identifying with it is not, for well-known and oft-cited dangers accompany this dynamic. Losing its foremost ability — that of looking inward and espying its divine nature — the mind follows the senses outward and gets attached to the world of objects it has created. But great pain is in store for it on this outer journey, called the Bhogamarga, the path of enjoyment and pleasure. So, the wise seek Yoga, not bhoga. This is a fact that most beings, even many so-called yogic practitioners, have not learned. Thus, pratyahara, the stumbling block, the slippery limb, is the hardest one for current day man to climb and master, and the easiest one to compromise with.

As if attachment to hatha and preoccupation with pranayama — for all the wrong reasons — were not enough, this compromise with the limb of pratyahara causes a further backsliding on the path of authentic Yoga (please study the impediments of alabdhabhumikatva & anavasthitatvani). And what to speak of the problem of detaching from outer objects and temptations, the practitioner has not yet even found the deeper import of pratyahara, that of viewing subtle objects within and tracing them to the cause of their appearance. The sixth and seventh limbs of concentration and meditation will hardly offer up their benefits, then, until this fifth limb is accomplished inclusive of all its subtle concomitants.

Since I see that other questions around this subject are forthcoming below, I will stop this tract and continue hereafter.
QUESTION #2: "Is a deepening of vairagya, even if only temporary, an aspect of pratyahara? What is the relation of vairagya to pratyahara?"
ANSWER: Vairagya is the second treasure of the Four Treasures and Six Jewels of Vedanta. Pratyahara is the Fifth Limb of Yoga. Many great souls have looked into these two great darshanas (as is instanced by our present study via this course of lessons which uses the Father of Vedanta's commentary on the

Father of Yoga's system) with a view to combine or integrate them. And if the truth be known, the two can hardly be separated out. As I have offered before, Vedanta barely mentions any type or system of practice for its adherents, directing itself instead towards nondual Truth in straightforward fashion. The Four Treasures and Six Jewels only provide a semblance of the art of practice, and its "practice" begins at an already rarefied level of mind. Observances and practices such as yamas, niyamas, asana, and pranayama do not concern the classical Vedanta, for it considers them already absorbed and implemented into the well-informed and facile spiritualized mind — a mind that is rapidly becoming nondual, an "eye" that is already becoming "single." Even the system of Kundalini Yoga by way of Upanisad begins, ideally, with mind rather than with exercises of breathing, for prana is already controlled and taken up by the mind in that Yoga, and watching the breath and collecting the prana has long since been accomplished. It is as if Vedanta is a philosophical finishing school, to be applied after spiritual practice has been accomplished earlier, or at least nearly so.

With this said, vairagya, detachment from all that is unreal, nonessential, and "immaterial," and pratyahara, withdrawing the senses from their objects, both external and internal, only differ in the level at which they are operating and the condition they are aiming to allay. Respectively, the former works from the mind inward towards intelligence, and the latter is working on the mind outward towards the senses. Blocks and impediments are thus of differing subtleties. Vairagya is a sweeping away of everything that Viveka, the first Treasure of Vedanta (via adhyaropa and apavada), has pinpointed, while pratyahara is focusing on base or weak attachment to objects and thoughts of objects/concepts which should never have occurred in the first place.

In other words, concentration (dharana, the sixth limb of Yoga) is the God-given right of all human beings, but they misuse it for a life of pleasure seeking (bhogamarga) or sacrifice it outright via scattering the mind and its precious power of attention amongst the various sense objects. Thus does Patanjali give out the teaching of the five types of mind — scattered, dull, gathering, one-pointed, and fully transparent.

QUESTION #3: "Could it be the case that different people experience pratyahara in different ways — its salient, defining characteristics of course remaining present — but other factors shifting from individual to individual?"

ANSWER: Yes, it certainly is. However, real and authentic yogic pratyahara cannot be changed or compromised. Either it is accomplished or it is not. One applies it and finishes its mission, or fails it and falls away. The proof of the pudding in this matter is seen in the way the aspirant conducts him or herself before and after, particularly after. In the case of so many who fail limb five, even if pretended otherwise, a return to reliance on earlier limbs only is seen, and the failure, even over years, to meditate properly and with the attainment of expected results.

QUESTION #4: "If someone presents an experience to you, as I have, and asks, 'Is this pratyahara?' what do you look for in order to determine your answer?"

ANSWER: This depends upon if the person is a student or an initiated disciple. The guru cannot do much for the mere student, for commitment to a single spiritual path has not been secured and mantra diksha has not been given. The mantra, you see, is one of the powerful agents that will help distill the mind's powers and center them on the very same problems that vairagya and pratyahara are attempting to solve.

Sanatanand from Hawaii writes:
COMMENTS: "This is a most interesting discussion of the conditions of the mind and the state of Samadhi. Considering the continuity of the gross states to the subtle states gives one pause to consider not only that there is a progression toward this consciousness, but also of the spectrum of conditions that stair-step to that state where no mind manifests to this most subtle form. Sometimes it seems to be such a long road, while one wants to make that leap and just be there. Yet knowing that this journey requires effort and perseverance gives one motivation to continue."
QUESTION: "I have been working with the meditation that works to clear the mind of thought by focusing within. There are times when things get fairly quiet, but still I wonder if there are some other aids that might assist me in reaching to the higher state. I remember that there have been discussed some methods of discrimination that help one to put aside this distracting mind stuff. I am wondering what other method there might be to move more efficiently toward the goal, or is it better to just stick with one method doggedly and work through the distractions."
ANSWER: Flexibility is, of course, a great thing, but that flexibility should be exercised within the areas of the path and method the guru has given at the time of initiation. This is a great thing to understand — spontaneity inside the perimeters of one's avowed practice. I hear it often, that practitioners want another mode of study, a different method of worship, another mantra, etc. It could be that only a couple of years have gone by since they received the mantra, and they have not used it every day, nor tried to comprehend its meaning and efficacy. Perhaps it is not being connected to the Ishtam in meditation practice, and so on. So, the guru encourages the seeker to stick to the tradition, adhere to the practice, yet use one's natural intelligence to "switch things up" so that the practice will live.

As for distractions, they will be there for everyone, at all stages of practice and perfection. If one studies the lives of the great ones, plenty of distractions will be seen therein. Distractions are there in every path and practice, then; might as well accept that. Now, to get to the core of the practice and be free in this very lifetime.

## Pada III, Sutra 21

*kaya rupa samyama tad grahya shakti stambhe chakshuh prakasha asamprayogen antardhanam* (*kaya,* physical sheath; *rupa,* form; *samyama,* triple focus; *tat,* that; *grahya,* perceptible; *shakti,* force; *stambhe,* withheld; *chaksuh,* perceived by the eye; *prakasha*, revealed; *asamprayoga*, withdrawn; *antardhanam*, transparent).

*"When the yogi performs samyama on his own physical sheath, the power of transparency gets revealed, and what is otherwise perceptible to the eyes of others becomes withdrawn."*

Though skirting the precarious subject of occult powers, this sutra (listed as sutra 20 in some renditions, with sutra 22 being absent in others) only goes to show that the quality of consciousness of the one considering the teachings is crucial. Some, the sensationalists, will immediately rush to the assumption that the yogi is an occultist and an entertainer, a phenomenon that has manifested among the curiosity seekers of India's cross section of hatha yoga adherents. Lying on a bed of nails, disappearing at the top of a suspended rope in midair, the charming of cobras, twisting the body into pretzel-like shapes, and other acts of egotistic showmanship are what pseudo-spiritual surface dwellers have come to think of as being Yoga. What this sutra communicates could easily be lumped together with pretenses, side-tracks, and illusions such as these.

But in his commentary, Swami Vivekananda tells us that the body of the yogi who wields this particular aspect of the power of samyama does not actually disappear. It simply becomes unnoticeable to those around him, much like an unpopular person at a party might be easily overlooked by others present. The difference is that the unpopular person is avoided purposefully, while the yogi is assuming the power of transparency consciously.

This physical and mental transparency is akin to emptiness in philosophy, a unique ability won via a certain kind of objectivity that the yogi has sought after and found, and now utilizes for the gathering of facts and knowledge to be used wisely for the highest good of others. In other words, being transparent and moving about unnoticed through the atmosphere of people's vibrations allows for a type of perception that, for instance, is far beyond the minimal surface insights of clairvoyance, especially for one who is both spiritually illumined and compassionate about the suffering of others.

With all this said, noted, and taken to heart by the sincere devotee and practitioner, other implications of this sutra, and the next, can be taken up.

**Pada III, Sutra 22**
*etena shabdadi artardhanam uktam* (*etana*, through this; *shabdadi*, sounds; *antardhanam*, transparent; *uktam*, becomes clear).

*"This power of transparency (gained via samyama) also clarifies why sounds and other sensual instruments become useful to the yogi."*

This special ability of the yogi to "move without moving," or, be a "walker of the skies," applies not only to the body and the sense of sight, but lends itself to the realm of the other senses as well. Sounds and hearing *(shravenindriya)*, for instance, become important, and offer up their secrets in relation to true meaning — both of what is being heard and what is being said, as well as what is being inferred. In past masters, beings who have manifested on earth to serve God in all beings, they have consciously descended from inner worlds *(chittakasha, jnanakasha)* where everything, even the subtle body they occupy there, is made of sound.

This body they have gained is the *baindava sharira* (literally, made of *bindu)*, and consists of vibrating particles of intelligence, an enlightened intelligence that emits the sound of wisdom and exudes the pulse of transformation. This is why, when they take a physical form *(linga sharira)* here on earth, they are able to attract souls to them, subject them to the purifying teachings, and help transform their minds so that ultimate freedom, *moksha,* may be reached — in this lifetime, or eventually.

This same wondrous power, afforded to the yogi via the attainment of *samyama,* also visits the realm of the sense of touch/feeling *(sparshendriya —* please study your twenty-four cosmic principles to be able to access the Sanskrit words for the five elements and five senses). Of all the many potentials for such a power in the realm of action (feeling/touching is connected to handling/acting), nowhere is it more powerful and beneficial then in the principle of *Diksha,* Initiation. When an illumined soul touches the disciple — with either the hands, his words, or even his thoughts — immediate changes are wrought. This is where karmas either show themselves so that the aspirant can deal with them, or get destroyed outright by the power of emanation abiding in the transmission, all depending on the adeptship and intention of the luminary involved. *Mantra-diksha* is the usual, and blessed mode of preference for this transmission, as it allows for the aspirant to purify himself, to cut himself in the image of God, as it were.

Our next lesson will continue on in this vein of Samyama, as Patanjali completely informs us as to the existence and efficacy of this unique yet obscure principle of authentic Yoga.

## Lesson Seventy-one, 5/30/12
### Pada III, Sutra 23 & 24

With the advent of lesson #71 comes more teachings on the ability of the Yogi to apply samyama for the highest good of all beings. The quality of samyama has elicited many comments and much curiosity from the ranks of the present study group, some of which has found its way into the questions for this particular lesson:

**Questions and Answers for Lesson 71**
Sanatanand from Hawaii writes:
QUESTION: "This has been quite interesting. I have been contemplating the qualities of the various samadhis. I can understand the progression of the seeded to the unseeded asamprajnata samadhi. Like many of the other progressions, it follows a path from the relative to the highly refined. Though I grasp this overview, and have read the *Gospel of Ramakrishna,* so clearly illustrating Sri Ramakrishna's spontaneous way of entering into samadhi, I still lack a deeper

understanding. Perhaps you could explain further how one might perhaps see evidences of this consciousness, even as passing glimpses, in one's own life, that might inspire and even assist in realizing this exalted awareness in one's own life. Thank you again for transmitting this superlative teaching."
ANSWER: Through constant practice, called *"abhyasa yoga,"* experience of samadhi dawns over time. It can hardly be explained, or even spoken of with any real clarity. Unlike all other teachings, it escapes description. It is Patanjali who has placed it into such a comprehendible context in the Yoga Sutras, availing all practitioners of both the knowledge of and the desire for direct spiritual experience of it.

Still, as you intimate here, there are signs of it. These range from subtle changes of expression rolling almost imperceptibly across the yogi's face, to inner feelings playing in the heart and mind of the recipient of samadhi. I say "recipient," here, so as to express what so many say about the advent of samadhi — that it seems to come from no particular effort on the part of the practitioner, though practice ushers it in, and seems more to be a manifestation of hidden grace. This is why we feel that we are in the presence of God when we come into the atmosphere of a luminary, for his/her entire being has been co-opted for God, has been taken over as a sort of laboratory for experiments in samadhi and its experience.

Other than this rather cryptic explanation, I can advise assuming samadhi, even before it comes upon us. Peace is a sort of samadhi; wisdom, too, is a type of it. Intense devotion can bring about bhava samadhis. Of course, there is nothing like nondual meditation on a good "mind day" for getting the gist of what it is about.

S.C. from Hawaii writes:
QUESTION: "What is the difference between Ashtanga & Raja Yoga?"
ANSWER: Ashtanga means "Eight-limbed," and refers to the Raja Yoga of Patanjali. There are many beings and groups which use the word or title "ashtanga" without even knowing its meaning. One can walk into hatha yoga centers, or call up numbers from flyers that advertise "ashtanga yoga," and find that they have little or nothing to do with eight limbs at all — those being yamas, niyamas, asana, pranayama, pratyahara, dharana, dhyana, and samadhi. Another name for the authentic eight-limbed system is Patanjala. In other words, it is named after its systematizer, Patanjali. These three titles, then, are all names for authentic Yoga, but in order that ashtanga be true, it must include teachings of more than just one or two stages or limbs.
QUESTION #2: "What is the meaning of: Abhishek, Bhunkundas, Anahata-dhvani, Vedavakya, Kamarpukur, Jaya, Shree, Sadgurunath, ki, jay, maharaj?"
ANSWER: Abhishek, or Abhishekam, means consecration. In Hinduism it revolves around anointing temples via cyclic rituals that have to be performed every so often, like twelve-year periods. In Buddhism, the word takes on an extended meaning, referring more to transference of power from guru to disciple, as in initiation. There are four types of abhisheka in this regard: base ini-

tiation, secret initiation, wisdom initiation, and final or fourth initiation.

Correcting your spelling, Anahata-dhvani refers to the sacred sound of AUM heard by the spiritual aspirant at certain more advanced stages of meditation practice. And this expression intimates that there are more mystic sounds than just the primal Aum going on interiorly; the yogi perceives others as well.....".....*the tinkling of running water, the lilting of flute-like sounds, the rumbling of kettle-drums....,"* etc.

Vedavakya, unless you are meaning Vedavyasa (the "Father" of Vedanta), refers to the sacred words of the Vedas, particularly the Mahavakyas — Tat Tvam Asi, Ayamatma Brahma, Prajnanam Brahma, and Aham Brahmasmi.

Kamarpukur is the holy birthplace of the Kali Avatara, Sri Ramakrishna Paramahamsa. It is still a nice rural village, but thousands of pilgrims and devotees visit it throughout the year.

Jaya means victory; Sri is a term of reverential respect; Sadgurunath is the superlative spiritual teacher, suited to teach on a world level; ki jay means "victory to," and maharaj means great king, or great soul.

QUESTION #3: "Were the Jains the 1st religion in the Indus Valley before invaders, before Hinduism?"

ANSWER: The Jain teachers, or Tirthankaras, came later in India's recorded history, so as a formulated and organized religion, Jainism did not appear all that early. However, the Jain emphasis on ahimsa, nonviolence, was a part of India's earliest philosophy. In this way there was less of an "invasion" in that sacred land over cycles of time, and more of a series of gentle incursions. Later, violent dominators such as Atila the Hun, Alexander the Great, Napoleon, the Romans, and the English, all had their dealings with Mother India and were more or less, and ultimately, stopped in their tracks due to Her nonviolent stance. Hers was a "resist not evil" religion.

Christianity, a violent religion, entered India in the first century after Christ's passing via the apostle, Thomas, and to this day has a sound footing in the South of India. Its successful presence there is mainly due to the peaceful nature of Christianity before the crusades kicked in, or before the Church and its post-apostle founders turned warlike and proceeded to insinuate themselves on other cultures and countries via mindless violence and proselytization. What to speak of Christianity, true religion is rare in a world such as this because it fails to focus on God alone and instead gets mixed up with politics. That is its downfall, and it quickly becomes a mere caricature of its intended self and gets corrupted by the world and worldly people. *"Grant unto Caesar what is Caesar's but take unto thyself what is the Lord's,"* was Jesus' way of relating this. During his lifetime He was already chasing the money lenders away from the doors of a fallen Judaism, but His shining example did not last for long.

The world insinuates itself on all religion, but in India there was a personage called the sannyasin who was completely free from money and possessions. He was not just a monk walled up within the confines of an institution, where goods and attachment could gather and fester, but was a free, wandering soul who possessed only the Truth. The royalty of the land looked up to this liberated soul, and venerated him. Further, counsel was taken from such a being so that the kings and queens developed both a relationship with this great soul, and a spiritual life as well. A model for a working religion in the world was thus established, and can be seen and emulated even today, in thoroughly materialistic times. Unfortunately, this has not stopped modern India from succumbing to human insanity by gathering weapons and firing them across their borders at neighboring countries. As Sri Krishna says in the Bhagavad Gita, *"From age to age I embody myself forth to resurrect the fallen dharma."*

S.B. from Hawaii writes:
QUESTION: "In the last Q&A, you explained that 'Samsaris are those most unfortunate ones who dwell in samsaric cycles of birth and death in ignorance of their true nature,' and continued to explain that 'dharmis are those who have transcended samsara, and who live in the land of righteousness and true religion.' What then is the 'true religion' beyond 'All is Brahman?'"
ANSWER: The statement, "All is Brahman," *is* true religion. The only thing that lies beyond it is to live it daily. That is the great challenge, especially for the householder, the one who has to live in the world in a detached manner. *"The duck gets in the water, but water does not get into the duck."* Just like this, the householder must use the feathers of discrimination to ward off the poisons and negativities that naturally attend life in the world. Like a duck shakes water off of its feathers, the aspirant in the world must use daily sadhana to shake off all insinuations of maya. Only then can the masterful householder say and mean a nondual statement like *"All is Brahman,"* which is usually and otherwise reserved only for those free souls -- sannyasins, avadhuts, seers, etc.

Kanyakali from Hawaii writes:
QUESTION: "So much is made, in 'New Age' thinking, of cultivating the ability to manifest the fulfillment of our desires. When I read about the "laws" they are utilizing, such as: 'Our thoughts create our reality,' it sounds almost Vedantic. In these Raja Yoga lessons, we are also learning how we will ultimately conquer nature and verge upon omnipotence. However, only the yogi/yogini who has achieved a spotlessly pure mind and has ascended to a very high state can claim that 'everything comes to him naturally.' This seems to run counter to our precept of renunciation – we are meant to give up the world, not seek to satisfy our desires in it. I find it ironic that once we approach the pinnacle of spiritual life we may receive omnipotence, and yet in order to reach our ultimate goal, we must give it all up. In the meantime, as spiritual beings apparently associating with these physical minds and bodies which are naturally filled with desires from sunup to sundown – aside from the obvious risk of being overly distracted by worldly attainments – is there anything wrong with utilizing certain powers of thought projection to manifest a more comfortable life for ourselves and those we love? In other words, spoken from a truly Western perspective: Can I renounce my cake and eat it, too?"

ANSWER: Words like "comfortable" are red flags in the spiritual world, among the gurus and preceptors. The tendency to compromise the truths of the scriptures, to misinterpret the real meaning and import of renunciation, and to prevaricate around one's spiritual practice, is all too common, especially among the Western peoples. If one were to manifest a more austere life, that would be lauded by the knowers of Truth. Why do people always think in terms of comforts, and not see the value of renunciation? The former breeds bondage, the latter leads towards freedom. Renunciation builds character, and that is what strengthens spiritual life. Pleasure and comforts, praying for and manifesting all that you want, only short-circuits spiritual life, which is contrary to popular thinking.

The expression, "New Age thinking" is a contradiction in terms. For the most part they do not think, these world lovers, these sentimentalists, these believers in birth and death, these materialists masquerading as enlightened persons. Buddha thought; Christ thought; Shankara thought. These are the true luminaries, and they did not own a stitch or covet a thing. They said, respectively: *"Suffering Is"; "Birds have nests, foxes have holes, but the son of man hath no place to lay his head"; "Everything, from unmanifested nature on down to the element earth — it is all the nonself."* If these are the world's true luminaries, and these are their words, then does it behoove the seeker after Truth to seek, own, and covet the things of this world?

So, I say, along with them, use the powers of your mind to put an end to mental projection — called sankalpa/vikalpa, imaginings in time. Live in the world as a turtle does, who swims in the waters of the ocean but keeps its mind always on its eggs buried in the sand. If one can do this, all preparation is made — for contentment, for peace of mind, for bliss, for ultimate freedom. And, if the truth be known, prior to the arrival of all these, desires will get satisfied naturally.

Sri Ramakrishna has used the analogy of a rich man's country mansion. It lies uninhabited for months, with little or no activity taking place in it. But one can know of the zemindar's coming for a visit when all of a sudden there is a flurry of activity, with many servants moving a host of furniture and eatables into the place. The master is about to arrive. Just so, when qualities like contentment, peace, and subtle bliss attend upon the aspirant, it is not long before enlightenment itself will make its appearance.

And the preparation for this is not longing for wealth, or goods, or pleasures, or comforts; it is longing for God, for Reality Itself. The more desires and possessions one has, both in one's life and in one's mind, the further away will Divine Reality keep Itself. So do not collect trash. Take refuge, not refuse.

So, if one truly wants freedom, and has tasted it so that one knows a little of what it is, and what it actually feels like, one must manifest in life the "desire for desirelessness' — nirvasana. Be content with contentedness. Even if you have home, spouse, possessions, etc., do not own them; do not even think about them as your own. Renounce them daily, if you have to. Even the custodianship of these, though it teaches many lessons, eventually turns onerous.

The one final lesson it teaches is "I want none of this; only freedom." As our priceless eternal friend, Swami Vivekananda has put it:

*Have thou no home, what home can hold thee friend.*
*The sky thy roof, the grass thy bed, and food what chance may bring,*
*well cooked or ill; judge not.*
*No food or drink can taint that noble Self which knows itself.*
*Like rolling river free thou ever be, Sannyasin bold, say "Om Tat Sat Om."*

Is there a compromise, or a half way measure in all of this for the non-monastic temperament? I think not. The householder must be more on his/her guard than the monk, who is already courting freedom. Otherwise, the insinuation of maya comes full bore, destroying spiritual life and undoing the fiber of inner character outright. Before one knows it, lands, wealth, relationships, children, pets — all of life weighs like chains on the soul. To quote the luminaries, it is all empty, lacking in real substance, constantly changing, permeated with suffering, and will ultimately turn sour. Renounce it all now and save yourself much suffering later. People may think, "I can enjoy it now, and later easily give it up." But these shortsighted beings are not accounting for the subtle onslaught of habit, attachment, complacency, and the sapping of inner strength over time which a life of insouciance results in.

Moreover, what to speak of compromise, turn it all into Brahman's manifestation. Why manifest things for oneself? Leave it as it is, Brahman's already perfect manifestation, and enjoy it all immensely without the bindings of ownership and personal agency, ever free of the mind's urges towards creating more. One must live like a sword — constantly cutting away, never accumulating for long. Beautiful! Beautiful!, this life of well-tended freedom, this superlative view of inner terrains, this rare breath of spiritual heights. Let us never risk spoiling it with mental or physical clutter. As Sri Krishna advised Arjuna, *"Be content with anything."*

Avinashi from Pennsylvania writes:
QUESTION: "Pratyahara opens the realms of the samadhis, and the samadhis allow forms of knowing that aren't possible in the domains of dual experience. Are we, therefore, automatically awakened, at least to some slight degree, to chakras four and above by moving into pratyahara?"
ANSWER: The spiritual vortexes associated with the regions of the human heart and throat will open only after spiritual mainstays such as pratyahara are mastered, at least to a certain degree. Consciousness rising and consciousness remaining are two different things. That is, certain practices will open channels, but will not necessarily maintain them in an stationary condition. This is the reason why so many souls have marvelous spiritual experiences, but are never really transformed by them. Viparyayas eight and nine, mentioned by Patanjali in the Yoga Sutras speak to this unfortunate fact. Backsliding and the inability to maintain spiritual progress form a habit of failure in the practitioner's mind, a mental samskara of lack of self-worth, a disbelief in one's ability to succeed, spiritually speaking. In other words, Kundalini may "rise" to higher

centers, but She may not reside there for long if that strong foundation of strength and resilience is absent.

And the resultant plummeting of "raised" consciousness back down to lower chakras is a problem unto itself, an area of discomfort and confusion never intended in the first place. It causes unnecessary disorientation. Referring back to your point, then, pratyahara, well-matured, will prevent such calamities from occurring, will take away the errors of the yogic practitioner before they can even manifest themselves.

To flesh out this dynamic, the sixth and seventh limbs of Yoga will accomplish all that they promise to do if pratyahara is fully developed and in place prior to having spiritual experiences of a higher nature. Sound a bit impractical? The alternative is what one sees and hears about in modern day practitioners, revealed by the overall lack of success, and of enlightened souls in this country. For the most part, and with a few rare exceptions, possibly, we are knocking at the door but cannot enter yet. Pratyahara, as far as can be seen, is this doorway. It is the limb that no one wants to venture out on, the limb all fall off of.

No one wants to give up the world for Union with God, Yoga. The mind clings to forms, gross and subtle, physical and mental. We must study the life and mind of modern-day beings like Sri Ramakrishna Paramahamsa and Ramana Maharshi to both understand and emulate samadhi. In the meantime we must go to authentic gurus to receive spiritual teachings, over and over, until the mind's penchant for objects and thoughts of objects diminishes, affording a wondrous glimpse of our formless divine nature. From this glimpse — a look at the fourth and fifth chakras — the fifth and sixth limbs of Yoga will get scaled, acting as firm footholds thereafter for all that is to come.

QUESTION #2: "Is pratyahara synonymous with ekagra? I'm thinking here of the fivefold scheme of mudha, kshipta, vikshipta, ekagra, and niruddha which was presented very early in the Raja Yoga Lessons, but that has remained significant for me."

ANSWER: Again, not until it is fully mastered, and no return to old thinking patterns/thought patterns can recur. Ekagra is an exalted state of mind, whereas pratyahara is a mere practice. The former, once attained, brooks no return to the worlds of name and form under old and worn out circumstances ever again.

Akshaya Bhakti from New England writes:
COMMENTS: "When I think about Samyama, and especially when I contemplate its first step of Dharana during seated practice, I am somehow struck by a sense of awe. On the one hand, Samyama can be defined so simply (as in what Swami Vivekananda explains at the beginning of Chapter III), that Dhyana and Samadhi are just an extension of Dharana, and that once the object of concentration has been chosen, one just needs to maintain that focus for longer periods (my own words). While Shankara, in his elucidation of Patanjali's Yoga, has emphasized that Brahman is the substratum of all of Raja Yoga, and therefore gives sanctity to its practice, it feels that this is the point at which I must truly

surrender all my thoughts and feelings to my chosen goal, to intensify my concentration on That alone. I am even intrigued by the way it is expressed as 'make Samyama' or 'perform Samyama,' as if it is a holy rite."

QUESTION: "If I choose Sri Ramakrishna as my goal of Samyama, is there a special prayer I can memorize to offer Him at this point of Dharana in addition to any I may have offered at the beginning of my sadhana? We have His own prayer to the All Blissful Mother, but now I wonder what special offering I can make to Him in the same vein to enhance my intention?"

ANSWER: This prayer you ask about, it is lying in the innermost depths of your own heart, waiting to be drawn out and made an offering to Him — the Lord of the Universe. I would not venture to bespeak it for you. But I do encourage you to look within, in a deep moment, or hour, and draw it forth into sacred words. I am certain that He will delight in both — your concentrated effort, and your offering. Both already exist within Him, therefore in You.

QUESTION #2: "It seems so difficult to integrate the various darshanas, or to see them in their historical light; therefore, I am always grateful for your elucidation of them. Since you referred to the combination of Yoga and Vedanta in regards to vairagya and pratyahara in your reply to Avinashi, could you offer any such reflection on Samyama, i.e., how Bhakti and worship may be infused into the Raja practice, particularly, at the stage of Samyama, and any background that may inform the practice? With deep appreciation as always."

ANSWER: Well, that is what the sutras and their commentaries are for. So let us dive into the Samyama study further, with Vedavyas, Patanjali, Vivekananda, and whatever thoughts I may come up with in the Light of Their incomparable inspiration.

**Pada III, Sutra 23**

*sopakraman nirupakraman cha karma tatsanyamad aparantajnanam arishtebhyo va* (*sopakraman,* immediate; *nirupakraman,* delayed/slow; *cha,* and; *karma,* fructification; *tatsanyamad,* that samyama; *aparantajnanam,* knowledge of death; *arishtebhyo,* foresight; *va,* otherwise).

*"Results of action come either swiftly or slowly. By studying these types of karmas via samyama, the yogi can foretell the time of his passing from the body."*

Few beings can attain, or even think of attaining, the boon of victory over death, Mrtyunjaya. Most beings have no idea, even, that they live more than one lifetime. The way to such rare attainment is via samyama after the 6th, 7th, and 8th limbs of Yoga are individually mastered. The Sanskrit word, samyama, means "perfect restraint," and figures most highly at the level of release from form. While most beings love to sport in form, few realize the consequences — forgetfulness of one's formless nature being the most essential.

In conjunction with this sutra, Swami Vivekananda focuses in on the Sanskrit word, "arishta," and defines it as "portents." This refers to the contents of the mind or, in this case, the actual ingredients of one's karmas. One has to study, then, with intense scrutiny, the makeup of one's past actions with a view towards reviewing the action itself, seeing what was wrought by that action, and noting, as well, the series of effects that arose from such action, and the effects that all these effects wrought as well. It is the snapping of the chains of karma around any given samskara. Not only will this reveal much about one's choices and character, it will also lay out a map for release from any residue that still remains around that complex and its concomitants.

All that is said above refers more to the advanced practitioner, the one who is coming into possession of samyama, perfect restraint. Past masters are through with all that, or, in other words, are long past having to deal with residual effects from old karmas. For such as these, the entrance and exit from the body is being masterfully effected by maintaining a constant reading of the flow of karmas going on — not just for themselves, but for the benefit of other beings as well. This is why, for instance, certain Tibetan masters can guide the soul at the time of death. This is not based in mere advice, or automatic response due to the dictates of tradition, but on personal experience of all the shifting modes that consciousness is capable of and subject to.

Here is real psychology, real hands-on knowledge of the workings of the human mind and psyche. Others only pretend. Most psychologists do not even read the contents of the mind based upon knowledge of past lifetimes — theirs, or that of others. Thus, little progress is ever made in such circles. But spiritual progress of the authentic kind is being made, and has been made, in thousands of cases with regards to Yoga and its practice. Enlightenment is the result, and of the kind that not only attains balance and equilibrium, but that allows for the transcendence of form itself. Yoga does not just cure the headache; it takes the head. What it leaves in its place, at least as long as form is consciously maintained, is described by Lord Vasishtha as *"...a mind that is empty of all contents, but that simultaneously retains its spiritual element."*

## Pada III, Sutra 24
*maitryadishu balani* (*matri*, friendliness; *dishu*, brings forth; *balani*, power).
*"Performing samyama on friendship brings forth hidden powers."*

Great teachers of the past and present have brought out the teaching of the Four Beneficial Attitudes — maitri, karuna, mudita, and upekshanam. Of these four, the first, maitri, is being spoken of in this sutra. It is an echo of the Yoga Sutra I:33, and has its correlative in the Vedanta with the teaching of pratipakshabhavanam — raising an opposite wave. In this context, all traces of enmity must be destroyed in order that friendship flourish.

And spiritually speaking, it is not just the negative effects of hatred and violence that are to be rued; it is more that all the hidden powers for positive good in mankind fail to surface and manifest themselves if an attitude of friendliness towards all beings is not cultivated and attained. This is the reason for ahimsa as well. Nonviolence is really a practical matter. If it has to be proven via qualities like compassion and sensitivity, it is only second best. These qualities should never have had to be brought into the equation. Mankind, out of good sense alone, should naturally sport an attitude of friendliness towards all beings. As Vivekananda puts it, *"Oh, when will man finally be friend to man."*

Speaking on an entirely different level, for the luminary, the past master, it is more a matter of joy that every other illumined soul in the cosmic sweep of things has his highest good in mind. What has he got to fear, to attain, if all the enlightened ones look upon him with love and good feeling? Thus, joy, mudita, figures into the picture. The result is an equanimous mind, upekshanam. Thus, the art of higher attitudes is the epitome of success.

What the wise person seeks, then, is not occult powers; fools and manipulators seek those. Hidden powers for revealing the inherent goodness in each soul speaks of a different attitude entirely than that of controlling or saving. Each soul must become a master in his or her own right, not a bond slave to any other soul — no matter how great that soul may be. *"Be thee perfect as thy Father in Heaven is perfect"* says this adequately enough. A personal savior? You are that unto yourself.

In the meantime, while you realize that, do certainly take unto yourself the Eternal Friend of all beings, but practice the intention of friendship, not the convention of it. And do not be a weight on the broad shoulders of free souls, or have them have to shed their life's blood for you. Rather, complement them in kind by contributing to their great mission — to *"awaken all beings from the illusion of finitude."*

## Lesson Seventy-two, 8/2/12
### Pada III, Sutra 25 & 26

After establishing a new ashram in Hawaii, and switching ashram locations in Oregon, we return to the Raja Yoga studies, and lesson #72. The current subject is still the spiritual phenomena of samyama, which Lord Patanjali has taken up using an ongoing line of sutras designed to impress upon the minds of the aspiring yogi and yogini the profound import of increased and intensified concentration and meditation. These represent the upper limbs of the refined sacred art of Yoga, and so are to be considered more of the essence of the practice. The following set of questions coming from our list reveal the level of practice and study that current day practitioners are arriving at, and demonstrate to what degree the contemporary devotee and disciple is committed to and resolved towards the realization of the Atman.

**Questions and Answers for Lesson 72**
S.C. from Hawaii writes:
QUESTION: "Who is Adishankaracharya?
ANSWER: Adishankaracharya, or just Shankara ("adi" means original, and "acharya" means superlative teacher), was a fully realized Advaitan, as well as being a consummate devotee of the Lord and Mother. Living in the seventh

century A.D., he was said to have been in full memory of the different darshanas of India by the time he was ten years of age, and after leaving home at twelve to find his guru (Govindapada, student of Gaudapada), was seen to be teaching the elderly and advanced sadhikas in his teens, while composing many of his own scriptures in his twenties. His famous commentaries on the Prasthanatrayam (Upanisads, Gita, Brahma Sutras) formed the basis for a new age of Vedanta, or Neo-Vedanta, which he resurrected again in India during a period of stark decline and religious degradation. He passed away into Mahasamadhi at the age of thirty-two, leaving behind not only his prodigious volume of works and several famous Maths, but a reputation for being one of India's most illumined of souls.

QUESTION #2: "What is bhur, bhuvah, svaha?'

ANSWER: Being the first three words of the Gayatri mantra, they indicate three of the seven worlds, or lokas, in Hindu Cosmology, the other four being Maharloka, Janaloka, Taparloka, and Brahmaloka. The lower three of the seven, they represent the worlds of return for all transmigrating souls who have not reached liberation from name and form. The first of them corresponds to earth, or the Bhutakasha, while the other two can be said to roughly coincide with the heaven of Christianity, but of lower and higher character and quality.

QUESTION #3: "What are Yajur, Atharva, Gandharvas, Pitris?"

ANSWER: Yajur and Artharva are two of the Four Vedas, the other two being Saman and Rig. Gandharvas are celestial musicians, who inhabit worlds such as bhuvah and svaha, or the Pranakasha and Chittakasha. Pitris are the ancestors, who are the pool of souls from which are drawn the myriad of human births here on earth, or Bhutakasha. They inhabit the pranakasha and rarely break through to deeper and subtler realms of existence, being attached to heavenly pleasures, both in heaven and here on earth.

QUESTION #4 "What is the 5th ether, I've got physical, mental, intelligence & spirit?"

ANSWER: The realm of subtle life-force, called the Pranakasha, or realm of prana, is the other. It is connected strongly to the earth plane, like humans to ancestors, life force to nature, the senses to their powers to see, hear, touch, taste, and smell, etc. All that is of the brain and lower mind — psychic, occult, and sensational — also connects there. In spiritual life here on earth, then, it plays an important part along the lines of purification and transcendence. Mastered, it gives powerful impetus to the aspiring soul. Left unmastered, it becomes a limiting bond which binds the soul to matter, energy, contention, and lower levels of existence.

QUESTION #5: "'Switch off all powers at the source' — would you explain this from your last writing in the last paragraph of Sutra III:1?"

ANSWER: This is in reference to meditation and thought, as well as what proceeds after thought occurs via the senses and their objects. Ineffective methods seek to treat the effect, and attempt to stem attachment, desire, greed, lust, etc., by dealing with the senses. The mind is the controller of the senses, the chariot to which the five horses of the senses are tethered. Shutting the mind down in meditation is therefore an ultimate solution, and brings about mastery in self-control speedily and with finality. With mental control attained, the human being can live a good and balanced life, effortlessly, and also more easily gain the higher limbs of Yoga with regards to spiritual adeptship.

QUESTION #6: "I have a building that carpenter bees are eating, I worked with them for 8 years with sprays, caulk, foam, but to no avail. Now I catch them with a net and kill them. This is violent, I don't like it, but they are destroying this beautiful building that I built. Krishna seems to say in the Gita that killing doesn't matter since we aren't bodies. Help."

ANSWER: The example of Sri Krishna, Arjuna, and the battlefield of Kurukshetra as portrayed in the Bhagavad Gita is not adequate in this regard. Human beings and insects are very different beings, the former being souls and the latter being mostly prana. I remember an example told in our tradition of someone walking in on Sri Ramakrishna while he was sitting on his bed killing bed bugs between His fingernails (bugs should be so lucky!). The question about nonviolence was posed to Him, to which he replied that the bugs had become a nuisance and had to be dispatched. I am sure He was sending them back to their pranic source in the most calm and even-minded fashion — an object lesson here for you. In other words, no anger, no insensitivity either. All that is needed is a sure solution accomplished in nonreaction which both saves your building and deals with the infestation in a practical way.

QUESTION #7: "What if you pick a partner that appears to be spiritual, but then isn't?"

ANSWER: There are many possibilities here. The spirituality of one person may be different than that of another. That is, one person may express it in an overtly religious way, and the other may do so silently and contained. Also, Swami Vivekananda said that he had met atheists in his life who were more spiritual than some who professed to be religious. But whatever the case may be, if the relationship is truly one of convenience only, or if the time for factions to separate has come — and one still wants to be in relationship — then one must only learn from the mistakes of the past and choose more wisely next time. As both Lord Buddha and Sri Ramakrishna have said, it is better to remain alone, but if that is not possible then husband and wife ought to agree on religious matters before they join in matrimony. Christ was of the opinion that it is better to marry than to burn, but it must be said that there is a type of burning that happens during marriage as well, and that destroys one's peace of mind and leads nowhere but frustration.

QUESTION #8: "What is jyoti-rupa?"

ANSWER: The form of Light, probably in reference to the formless form, as in the case of Ishvara/Ishvari who have form, but who are also so filled with Light that they are as if formless.

QUESTION #9: "Would you tell us about Ramachandra?"

ANSWER: The Avatar of the Treta Yuga, one has only to read the Ramayana for all the facts, and read as well the Adhyatma Ramayana to get the nondual teachings from Him, and the knowledge of His Avatarhood. Even after so much time has elapsed since His presence on earth in that particular form, he is still loved by millions of souls. He was born again as Sri Krishna in the following yuga, and as Sri Ramakrishna Paramahamsa in this present Kali Yuga.

Suprema from Pennsylvania writes:
COMMENTS: "I go again and again to the Complete Works of Swamiji in conjunction with your lessons to amplify my understanding of what is written, and again I go for Sutra 3:24. Samyama on the karma which is 'waiting' to work, and the knowledge of this exposing the time and death of the body, is a fascinating knowledge of self. What the world calls 'pop-psychology' can never reveal it. I go to work daily in this field, not as a hypocrite as I used to feel, but as a witness. I remember when we told our patients to hit pillows till they burst! Now, will that cure ya!? It's just another way I can remain in householder role while knowing it all for the game it is. Swamjii said to 'think of death always.' It helps to keep proper perspective for me. He says little on Sutra 24 in the works here, and refers back to chapter 1:33. Along with friendship, mercy, and gladness, what shouts at me is the need to remain indifferent to evil — upeksha — and thus sustain that energy for good."
RESPONSE: Since evil has no substance to call its own, and is gone instantly like darkness in a cave once a torch has been introduced, I would say that you have a good plan here. Add to that your opportunity for bringing equanimity into your field, and thereby building character for yourself while simultaneously serving God in mankind, all would then be in perfect accordance with Swamiji's plan for the world in general.

Avinashi from Pennsylvania writes:
QUESTION: "In a previous email, I had written to you suggesting that pratyahara involved an inevitable loss of sensory awareness; but from your reply, I'm thinking I may be mistaken. It seems to me that pratyahara, far from involving a necessary loss of sensory awareness, might actually enhance it in clarifying ways, since all that quintessentially appears to be involved is the suspension of attachment, (and I would assume, its companion, aversion), through the utilization of yogic technique? For someone sitting on a cushion, deeply and inwardly focused on the Ishtam, maybe this would involve the temporary loss of sensory awareness. But from what you've written in one of your recent emails to me, it doesn't appear it has to, since pratyahara becomes 'a preferred mode of living in the body and the world for illumined beings.' I am thinking, now, that pratyahara may be more a state of the heart, in the sense of a state of the affections, of freedom from raga, dvesha and the klishta-vrittis, than a state involving some necessary disconnection of the senses. The notion of a karma yogin abiding most of the time in pratyahara without the quality of his performance being in the least diminished strikes me as a possibility when I think along these lines. In fact, might that yogin's performance actually be improved by this due to the freedom from raga and dvesha which it would provide?"
ANSWER: Most certainly, and I like your line of reasoning on this area, and the evolution in understanding it has undergone. Further, there is no doubt that

pratyahara has inner and outer aspects. If one can master and effect the former, then the latter becomes a matter of ease. That is, aspirants and beginning sadhikas who hear the preliminary teachings on detachment, then go on trying to strip the senses and mind of their tendency towards encountering the objects. How is that? We live in a world of objects, and mind is dual by nature. The senses will follow where mind perceives duality. So, to move among the sense objects without fastening to them, or better yet, and a more advanced level of adeptship, to move among the sense objects while attaching and detaching at will, is the greater attainment.

This is the outer mastery. It becomes a habit, albeit a good one. Just as negative habits form (klishta vrittis), positive ones (aklistha) should as well, and it is up to the practitioner to make sure that they do. However, and this is to be known as well, the inner mastery, the like of what we see in the illumined souls who happen to be on earth when we are embodied, skirts all need to withdraw or engage. It partakes of the "nectar of naturalness" that the nondual scriptures speak of. For, there is one thing that the illumined soul knows, with a certainty, that the worldly and the practitioner do not yet know (though the latter are suspicious about it), and that is that the world is "unreal" — as empty and void of substance as the hallucinations of a sick and feverish child. Those who think otherwise, and who rush towards it as if it were their oyster, as if it had any meaning, as if God had a plan for the soul in it — are like apparitions eating cotton candy in a dream carnival in the sky to satisfy hunger.

Therefore, it is only through viveka, discrimination between the real and the unreal, and vairagya, detachment from the unreal, taught in Yoga via twelve levels (a twelve step program for the aspiring luminary), that one can transform this world of appearances into nothing other than an expression of Brahman. Then the luminary emerges as the true karma yogin.

QUESTION #2: "I wonder, secondly, if the distinction between pratyahara and the samadhis that follow might not be a little artificial? I mean, where does pratyahara end and the samprajnata samadhis begin? When driving across the U.S., I might not notice the boundary lines between states that are drawn on the map for the simple reason that they aren't really in the world; they're only drawn on the map for convenience, so we can find our way. In like manner, might the distinction between pratyahara and the samadhis be similarly artificial? For that matter, might the distinctions between the samadhis themselves be artificial too? It has occurred to me that 'samyama' might be a name for the samadhis when the artificial distinctions between them are abolished so that they're viewed wholly, organically....maybe in the seamless way that they really function in the highly realized adept? If viewed this way, samyama would be comprised of dharana, dhyana and samadhi, as is described, and the use of the term 'samyama' would simply represent a more advanced and unitive understanding of those last three limbs of the Ashtanga Yoga system. Would you please critique this idea?"

ANSWER: Yes, your case for this point is well taken, and rightly expressed. And this is the case with anything for the Advaitist. The taking apart and the resultant designation of an object, situation, relationship, and experience is really only for the aid of the mind's understanding, to remove its self-superimposed ignorance, so that it can live in constant and eternal samadhi.

However, the wise have returned from the Absolute State to tell us of the steps that lead inwards and beyond — *gatam, gatam, paragatam.* The borders of the states may be invisible to the driver who crosses them, but the respective beings dwelling in these states, operating under the oft times differing laws of each, may object and impose their influence there. The intrepid spiritual traveler may find that he or she has to honor both the "guardians at the gates" and the pertinent rules of passage in order to find That which has no boundaries and borders. I was riding in a car recently with a person who got pulled over for speeding. Her excuse, when asked about it, was: "I was just flowing along with the rest of the traffic." The officer did not buy it, and a ticket and fine was inflicted. Just so, on the freeway of inner life, there are laws and their upholders, and it behooves the wayfarer to be aware of them. In our context here, Patanjali and his eight-limbed Yoga will assist us in arriving at Asamprajnata Samadhi not only detached and spiritually unencumbered, but free of the ticket of karma and the fine of reincarnation.

Sanatanand from Hawaii writes:
QUESTION: "It seems as though the fog of maya is somehow coalescing and coming down as the rain washing away the mists of mystery as a vision is beginning to emerge. It may just be a case of synchronicity. In this particular lesson on Raja Yoga we find that, though the wisdom of the seers helps one find one's way to the edge of the abyss, one must finally transcend it all and make the great leap. The path has been elucidated, following the trail of breadcrumbs, from the gross objects to the subtle mind. Concurrently, in our last class, we are looking into the forms of meditation where the same path is viewed from a different vantage point. What is seen is that one courses along this path directing the mind ever inward where one focuses on objects continuing to ever more subtle realms until again, one approaches the point where all this must be abandoned, and only Divine Grace can descend to grant final liberation. While this pot is rapidly heating up, in the depths, I have this niggling question about the nature of freedom, which seems to be so connected with these glimmerings. I am inspired that a vast soul like Vivekananda would value Freedom above all else. Freedom has always been something I have valued as well. Yet when I contemplate it, and especially when I read how the seers explain it, I am a bit perplexed. On the one hand, freedom would seem to imply the lack of any constraints. Yet, as one ventures within, one learns that perhaps all of the real limitations are within. I think maybe the idea that seems the most difficult to wrap my mind around is the statement by many illumined beings, that ultimate freedom can be best, or even only, achieved by complete surrender to God. Though I have an inkling of what the implication of this might be, I would humbly appreciate your elucidation on it."
ANSWER: Self-surrender, sharanagata, is invaluable and indispensable to any

spiritual aspirant who sets foot on the "radiant road to the realization of Reality." Sri Krishna tells Arjuna this in the Gita, after Arjuna asks a similar question, and voices a similar concern. He tells that the path of those who seek God beyond form is much more difficult than those who seek via reliance upon form. So, until the soul is well-qualified in the nondual Truth and its axioms, it must seek grace through self-effort.

But reliance here does not mean dependence, or have anything to do with weakness, etc. Weakness is what leads to mass ignorance, to using the Savior (God with form) as a doormat rather than a doorway. It is to be pointed out and taught, then, that grace will not come without self-effort; that is, that it will not be realized, even though it is all around. *"The wind of God's Grace is always blowing,"* said Sri Ramakrishna, *"but one must raise one's sail to catch it."* This quote, and a related image/cover, "graced" the first issue of our advaitic journal, *Nectar of Nondual Truth,* back in the Fall of the year 2000. Thus, we are advaitists first and foremost, sadhikas next and (at this seeming juncture) necessarily, and devotees of the Lord and Mother throughout. *"None else but Self, none other than Mother,"* as the consummate Shakta puts it. Or, Shakta-advaita-vadists. In this, our way, there is no fear, nor any competition with other paths or faiths. We have found our "niche"; that is all. And from its protective atmosphere we will serve — *"Atmano mokshartam jagad hitaya cha."* (Rig Veda) For, the Upanisads have taught us that *"Higher than the Personal God is the infinite Supreme Brahman who is concealed in all beings according to their bodies, and who, though remaining single, envelopes the entire universe of form. Knowing That to be The Lord, one becomes Eternal."*

And, even more pertinent to your concern, which includes both our feeling for and necessity of transcendence, there is that Sanskrit sloka by Shankara which I have culled out for memorization (svadhyaya), and which, repeated below, will help us immensely in the realization of the total Brahman:

*Om drishyam pratitam pravila payan san*
*sanmatram ananda ghanam vibhavayan*
*samahitas san bahir antaram va*
*kalam nayetah sati karma bandhe —*
*"Brahman is an indeterminable mass of pure, conscious Awareness,*
*Therefore, taking what is external, and what is internal,*
*render them both into one, Indivisible State.*
*Then meditate upon that State, pass your time contentedly, and be Free."*

The more time one can spend in the contemplation (manana) and realization (nididhyasana) of chants like this one, the better it will be for the mind/soul dwelling temporarily in the world. There can be nothing better than this, both for our terrestrial well-being, and our concerns around transcendence. COMMENTS: "This morning I think another veil lifted. I have been aware of this intellectually, but somehow it has rounded the corner and dawned on my sensate higher Self. This involves the idea of maya. What has come to me is that how can what we call reality be anything other than maya? How do we perceive it? It is through our senses. It would be like calling television reality, which some people do. Everything we see, hear, touch, smell, and taste flows through interpretive filters. Further, we know that what we perceive is only a small fraction of the wavelengths of light, frequencies of sound, etc. This, then, relates to the current aphorism where we see that it is the mind that needs to be calmed and quieted to reach the inner spirit which is beyond the illusions that we think of as reality. It is only in this inner sanctum of the spirit, past the impressions, the samskaras, that this state, ascendant of all duality, can exist."

RESPONSE: I have always been extremely grateful to the Indian rishis for espying the foremost of insidious influences in this life and world, and for "coining" a word for it — maya. From Tantra, to Veda, to the recent Avatar, Sri Ramakrishna, so much (from a distance) has been seen and related about the subject. For instance, after finding it out, then to know it is insentient, it is the cause of the worlds of name and form, and it is eternal (up until the moment moksha is realized) frees the aspiring being in advance, right where he stands. One has only to look and see.

C.S. from Toronto writes:
QUESTION: "I have been reading and contemplating your new book, *Reclaiming Kundalini Yoga,* and contemplating the Raja Yoga lessons together. I have been meditating on the yamas and niyamas to understand their obvious as well as subtle implications as they are mastered. I also see how their mastery and practice must happen in all areas — mental, physical, emotional, and spiritual — which then transforms into spiritual understanding and desire for continuous practice and awareness. It has occurred to me that if one truly masters the yamas and niyamas one would be about as close as humanly possible to practicing unconditional love which, in my explorations, seems to be Divine Love, a state impossible to attain as an unconscious being, and nearly impossible even as a spiritual seeker. I would appreciate your comments on my thoughts if they have any validity."

ANSWER: It is to be hoped that Divine Love is the real impetus for seeking God at the outset, even before practices like Yoga, with its yamas and niyamas are discovered, outlined, and engaged in. If that is not the case, or if the seeker has still not identified Divine Love as the real instigator, Patanjali (and others like him, like Lord Buddha) feel that this prime element will come to the fore naturally once the practice is engaged in. In this regard, then, the contemporary mantra, "just do it" can be borrowed from the billboards and applied to putting on the tennis shoes of sadhana and running the real race of spiritual emancipation. For, what is truthfulness if not for the love of it; what is nonviolence if not for the Love of it, etc. And certainly, the niyama of Ishvara-pranidhana will bring Love forward, if it has not already revealed itself as the determining factor of all sadhanas. Thus, as you reckon here, the first two limbs of Yoga are aligned with Love, and must be practiced in it to ensure real success.

QUESTION #2: "Referring back to lesson #70 and Sutra III:21, it occurs to me that the mastery of pratyahara could be a contributing factor to achieving the invisibility the sutra speaks of. By controlling the outward seeking of the organs completely, one would also, consequently, reduce the vibrations extending to others. Therefore, others would find no stimulation from the yogi. Hence, as we know how active we are in seeking stimulation, and none would be found in the yogi's presence, the senses would go elsewhere to find stimulation so that the yogi becomes as invisible as he is calm and contained. I was so interested in your response to question 1 from Avinashi. It clarified and explained some of my own personal observances regarding my own spiritual experiences. It is as if Ramakrishna graciously granted me wonderful experiences just from reading accounts of his teachings in Great Swan, and these teasers encouraged me to follow the path he laid out so beautifully. What I have discovered is that laying the foundations beginning with yamas and niyamas supports everything else in spiritual practice. Practicing tushti somehow douses the flames of desire in many areas, while at the same time the relentless desire to make spiritual 'progress' remains the same. Could you help me understand the practice or application of saucha? Jai Sri Ramakrishna!"

ANSWER: Saucha, purity, is essential for success as well, and interfaces perfectly with all other yamas and niyamas, and definitely with Love. The fundamental teaching on it, in the Vedic and Tantric traditions, has to do with its three types — purity of location/atmosphere, purity of deed, and purity of thought. These are titled dravya shuddhi, kriya shuddhi, and chit shuddhi, respectively. A unique way of teaching these is to bring out the point that if the mind is pure to begin with (upon embodiment), then the other two — atmosphere and actions — are already in possession. Meditating upon this fact, particularly in connection with the illumined souls we meet and learn from, establishes in the mind several crucial facts: 1) that there is perfection; 2) that we have lived other lives; 3) that limiting karmas have accumulated from past lifetimes that inhibit our awareness and knowledge; 4) that neither God nor devil are responsible for our present situation, etc., etc.

Meditating on just purity alone, then, reveals all manner of helpful hints that are pertinent to our spiritual life and practice. This is where the niyama of svadhyaya comes in, for instance, for if the sadhika ruminates on the thoughts, concepts, and aspects — negative, secular, and sacred — contained within his or her mind, and in the way prescribed by teachers like Patanjali, revelation is bound to come. With this, the human being lifts the lower self into the atmosphere of the higher Self, and thus, purity of act and location become a given. There are these quotes in relation to this divine effort:

*"The Self is master of the self. Who else would the master be?" Lord Buddha.*

*"Following only in the footsteps of the wise, I merge you both (mind and intellect) into the ancient Brahman by meditation. May that glorious One manifest Itself! May the children of Immortal Bliss hearken unto me — even they who occupy celestial regions." Svetasvataropanisad*

S.B. from Oregon writes:
QUESTION: "Are reading and learning not a part of Svadhyaya?"
ANSWER: Yes, two essential parts of it. They are to be followed by

manana/yukti, rolling what one reads and studies over and over again in the mind's thinking process; and then going forth to realize the Atman.

QUESTION #2: "Would fasting for purification of body and mind fall under the niyama of purification, or under the heading of tapas? And if austerity means fasting, why would Swamiji quote the Gita saying that one that fasts cannot become a yogi?"

ANSWER: Both, though fasting of the body would be reckoned more for the purposes of purification rather than as high-yield tapas. For the mind, fasting would mean refusing to take in all that is ordinary, conventional, and certainly all that is negative. Otherwise, the mind should be fed regularly with spiritual wisdom so it can gain purification of the highest and best kind, as is outlined in the previous question, above.

Regarding your reference to Sri Krishna's words and the Gita above, care must be taken not to misquote or take such words and meaning out of context. Lord Krishna said that fasting *too much* and feasting *too much* were not conducive to Yoga, not that fasting is not for the yogi. It is just that many beginning aspirants are still under constraints and limitations around food intake, and many even suffer from what Vivekananda has termed "food-faddism" — thinking that food has anything at all to do with realization. It has to do with the practice phase only, and has only a small part to play there as well. Once proper diet has been observed, and desire for food and pranic energy has been controlled, one can and should proceed towards much more important and essential aspects of the practice of Yoga. This is real tapas, the attaining of which leads to the realization of the Atman. As Swamiji states, that *"No food or drink can taint the noble Self that knows Itself....."*

K.D. from Hawaii writes:
COMMENTS: "Lessons 34 and 35 have acted as a catalyst that has brought together various threads of thought and experience concerning the importance and relevance of devotion on the spiritual path. Raja Yoga sutra II.I, states that *'The yoga of conscious action is performed via austerities and study of scriptures – all performed in an atmosphere of devotion to God.'* Devotion to God has been something I have not been able to relate to, so therefore I concluded that it was not essential. However, the appealing nature of Ishvara and analogies such as *'Doing austerity and study devoid of this beneficial atmosphere (devotion) would be likened to growing crops in depleted soil, lacking in nutrients.'* I am realizing that devotion is the ground of being of sadhana, a foundational attitude toward the path to liberation. I just have not been able to understand how to have devotion for Pure Consciousness, Awareness, Bliss, otherwise known as Reality."

QUESTION: "In lesson 35, in answer to the question 'Do you believe in God,' you so succinctly responded by listing all the Gods you do not believe in; and then you wrote: 'God is consciousness, nameless and formless, existing beyond time and space.' Even more clarifying was the following explanation as to who God really is. 'God the true Reality, dwells in living beings, especially and most consciously in human beings – not as their forms, or body/mind mechanisms, but as their very Consciousness. Therefore, with awareness rendered pure, and karmas destroyed by higher wisdom, this very God/Reality can enter into the human form as Consciousness and, unimpeded by ignorant overlays and false superimpositions, perform the purely selfless and most beneficial work possible only to Him/Her (Ishvara/Ishvari). This is the God we most need and love here on earth, who, though ever-transcendent and ever-pure, can enter and exit the realm of form and formlessness at will, transforming it into nothing less than the reality of Brahman.' How can I make this 'God we most need and love here on earth' more real to me so that I can experience devotion? If the scriptures are only the 'finger pointing at the moon,' and if direct experience is the only way to know Truth, and this Truth can only be the result of a transmission from one soul to another, is devotion truly necessary?"

ANSWER: It depends upon how one defines the word devotion. Of course, most of what we see around us that is termed devotion is only mockery, or show, convention, or selfishness. Even at best it is just an immature form of the original. And that is why we repeatedly cite the Vedantic phrase, "Pure Love, Pure Knowledge, and Pure Devotion." In order to be pure, devotion must be pure, i.e., free of selfish motive or any want for itself, whatsoever. If a soul can develop this rare type of devotion, then the god and goddesses of everything and everywhere come running, what to speak of The God, Ishvara, The Chosen, The Archetypical Soul.

If, after consulting the guru, the scriptures, and gaining some direct experience for yourself via self-effort over time, you still do not feel devotion for God, then you might conclude that you are a soul who is more attracted to the Formless. But from what you wrote here it seems more that you have an inner yearning for both that deep feeling and the Ideal who stands at its root. So remember, then, that a sincere yearning for Freedom -- Mumukshutvam -- is rare, is a rare bird.... *"like the famed chatak bird who will not drink water from brooks and streams, but only from pools formed by rain that falls only when the star Svati is ascendent in the night skies,"* — and that is also a rare occurrence.

Personally, I cannot see how any true seeker can turn away from either highest wisdom or the path of devotion. The two are the two wings of the bird by which it takes to the air for successful flight. Developing both Yogas, plus the yogas of action and inaction as well, is the way to Enlightenment in this day and age — the Kali Yuga, or Age of Darkness.

QUESTION #2: "Can one have a deep commitment to Truth to create that beneficial atmosphere without actual devotion to a personified God? I am on a search for devotion, and the closest I've come is an experience of something deeply and awe-inspiringly sacred. It was not Ishvara, but a space, a place, more of a location — like the inner sanctum of a most sacred temple or a forest glade where Krishna may have played his flute. I try envisioning great Avatars like Ramakrishna, but I do not experience devotion, although it would be closely linked to deep gratitude if I did have that experience. I pondered that possibly this 'beneficial atmosphere' could be correlative to rhythm in music. A musician could produce a beautiful tone, know scales inside and out, and read expertly, but if that musician lacked a sense of rhythm and could not keep a beat, the music would lack vitality and interest. Do you think that is an appropriate analogy?"

ANSWER: Yes, it is a good one, which makes me return to the point that you obviously have a deep inner yearning for the Divine with Form. And in fact, your experience cited here contained an atmosphere that was sacred. The Deity was the presence of that atmosphere, and produced it, and was holding it for your visitation to it. That particular Deity was invisible to you, meaning that Ishvara really is a formless Entity, a manifestation of Brahman, and will only take form to satisfy the deep desire of the devotee to actually see the expression of God in human form. This is a classic appearance, and one that thousands upon thousands of beings have sought and attained throughout periods of immeasurable time. This superlative vision is well-worth seeking and having, and forms the basis for a very significant introduction to the timeless, spaceless atmosphere of Absolute Reality. *"One comes to the Father through the Son."*

**Pada III, Sutra 25**

*baleshu hastibaladini* (*baleshu,* strength; *hasti,* elephants; *baladini,* force).

*"For imbibing strength, the yogi performs samyama on the force of an elephant."*

Along with being a metaphor for many things, this is Patanjali's version and advice to the yogi and yogini who would "think big" in order to overcome weakness, indeterminacy, lack of self-worth, and other obstacles, which are called antarayas and vikshepas in Yoga. To think small is also an option, at least for those who have mastered slothfulness, solicitousness, and pusillanimity. As Sri Ramakrishna has mentioned, *"A tiny germ kills a huge elephant."* Often, then, to find the source of things, we have to utilize "small" after mastering "big." All of today's suffering and ignorance can be traced to the inability of the present-day culture, race, and humankind failing to search for and uncover the microcosm in order to truly understand the macrocosm.

And it is not just a matter of the astronomer's focus upon outer space in contrast to the scientists inspection of minute particles, in further contrast to the medical practitioner's look at the world of germs and biologists peering into the realm of microorganisms. All of these are taking place only in matter. What is missing is scrutiny of the truly internal, what Christ called *"The Kingdom of Heaven within."*

And this is where the psychologist has the advantage, for he or she examines the workings of the mind, called the Antahkarana, or inner cause, in Sanskrit. As the revealed scriptures, the Upanisads, have stated: *"From the internal (the mind), the infinite, the external (nature), the finite, has come, yet being infinite, only The Infinite (Brahman) remains."* It is in the mind, then, that all errors get rectified, all questions get answered; for it, the mind, has produced all the mistakes and problems.

However, if one's psychology and its practitioners have all been born and raised in a society and world whose overall philosophy is that of materialism, and its astronomers, scientists, doctors, and botanists have all succumbed to this limited, often stunted arena and view, then the art of mental examination will focus in on the mind's infirmities rather than its potential, on its imagination rather than its infinite store of wisdom, on its penchant for dualities rather than its nondual Source.

And here is where Yoga Psychology comes forward to inform, teach, and deliver the materialistic mind from its otherwise ongoing conundrums and eternally cyclic predicament. This is also where true Philosophy has its rightful and permanent seat — not a philosophy founded upon lower knowledge and prideful position; or one of constant debate and argumentation for proof of superiority over others, temporary at best; or a pseudo-philosophy of posturing and pretense for the sake of mere money-making and pleasure seeking. Philosophy to both prove the existence of Existence, if any should ever even be needed, and to ensure the transmigrating human soul, temporarily sojourning in the finite realms of time and space, that his and her true identity is always and ever one with Reality.

This is the work of enlightened luminaries such as Patanjali, Vedavyasa, and Vivekananda -- our systematizers and commentators in this study. They have meditated on the strength of the elephant, and the subtler strength of the germ that destroys it. Finally, they have glimpsed a finer force, called Shakti (Chit-shakti in Yoga), that underlies everything, and that is both sentient and beyond creation, preservation, and destruction. By meditating upon Her they received the boon of samyama and used it to plumb the very depths of relativity — both the seen and the unseen — going beyond them both to realize themselves and all others as The Seer.

## Pada III, Sutra 26

*pravrittyalokanyasat sukshmavyavahita-viprakrishtajnanam* (*pravrttyah,* refined vibration; *aloka,* appears; *nyasat,* samyamic concentration; *sukshma,* subtle; *vyavahita,* obscured; *viprakrista,* far away; *jnana,* wisdom).

*"Samyama assists the yogi in gaining awareness of all wisdom that is subtle, obscured, and far away (deep within)."*

Another important triputi emerges at this juncture of exposure and exposition of the Yoga Sutras, falling under the intense scrutiny of our ongoing study. Lower knowledge (aparavidya), wisdom (jnanam), and higher Wisdom (vijnanam), all stand forward to reveal their respective places in the spiritual evolution of the aspiring soul. Important of note, is that all these levels of knowledge lie within the vast human mind, and can be accessed at any time by the one who both opens and intensifies his or her concentration. For, one of the Seven Laws of Yoga states that "All knowledge lies within," and this has been proven by the luminaries by their own direct spiritual experiences. The Yoga sutras alone, for instance, are proof of this. Both their revelation and their exposition are a matter of Patanjali's internal meditative processes.

As has been read about and studied previously in the preceding sutras, the samadhis of wisdom which occur prior to the "self of bliss" samadhis and the Unseeded Samadhi, open the seeker's inner eye to the presence of the Eternal Truth. Like an armada of ships resting upon the vast waters on an ocean, all this wisdom is spread out across the ocean of Truth. Another analogy is of the many millions of wisdom particles that make up this Ananda Sagara, or Ocean of Bliss, each termed an "Atom in the Sun of Knowledge" in the Sufi tradition.

To conclude pertinent to the sutra presently under study, it is as if Patanjali is giving the practitioner, we ourselves, the opportunity and permission to go ahead and begin to fathom the depths of our own Consciousness — the granting of a boon for a lost ability which we should never have had to recover in the first place, but that became available to us once again after avidya, forgetfulness of our true nature as Atman, overtook us in the succession of our lifetimes in relativity, and we finally recognized it. For, all is Divine, the only real calamity around this is the presence of human forgetfulnesss.

Thus, and with very good reason, we pay homage, with reverence, to the rishis, modern and ancient, and, do our rishi-yajna — the sacrifice of study, memorization, chanting, and spreading of Wisdom — daily, for the highest good of all living beings.

## Lesson Seventy-three, 8/18/12
### Pada III, Sutra 27 & 28

Continuing on with the sutras on samyama, the subject has brought forth a host of responses and questions around that principle, that uppermost aspect of Yoga. Of course, there are still many who, having started into this course later than others, are still studying in earlier lessons. Therefore a healthy mix of queries is being created in later lessons such as this one, giving all of us recourse to that most beneficial of teaching qualities called repetition. By it, many connections that might have been lost are made, and the subject at hand is enhanced greatly as well.

Below please take in the questions and answers, leading up to the two sutras for this lesson around samyama.

**Questions and Answers for Lesson 73**
S.C. from Hawaii writes:
QUESTION: "Can you explain more about adhiyajna and adhyatma?"
ANSWER: Add in adhibhuta and adhidaiva and you have some of the content of Arjuna's famous question to Sri Krishna in the Bhagavad Gita. Basically, the four are the supreme sacrificer, the supreme soul, manifest nature, and the host of divinities, respectively, as listed in order of appearance above.

The Sanskrit prefix, "adhi," means original; it can also mean additional, as in add-on or expanded list. Suffice to say that there are four main levels of existence in this regard, which match up with other triputis (triple teachings) and the ultimate Goal or Principle that they indicate. So, and placed in an order from gross to subtlemost, lower to higher, they are:

Adhibhuta is nature, and all the forms it contains and supports.

Adhyatma is the Soul, or Self, and the science that reveals and guides one to It — if it has ever been lost in the first place.

Adhidaiva indicates the host of celestials, suras, gods and goddesses and other deities that preside over the many realms of name and form — not just the earth realm, but other lokas as well.

Adhiyajna is all about the great sacrifice that Ishvara, Avatar, Jivanmuktas, Bodhisattvas, etc., take on when coming into the body to aid others. For ordinary beings, life and embodiment is perpetrated in ignorance, behind a series of masks or coverings. For the illumined soul, life is a mere visitation, or sojourn away from the Source, Brahman. The only reason to come into the body, into the realm of adhibhuta, is to convince and help free others from ever doing so again. In short, suffering cannot be destroyed in the embodied state. Thus, it must be transcended.

Another helpful designation for this triputi is to indicate the Threefold Sorrows of Existence. It is a teaching of Lord Kapila who, millennia before Lord Buddha and his Four Noble Truths teaching, had summarized the gist of it in this way. Ironically — or better yet, symbolically — Lord Buddha was born in what was then known as the city of Kapilavastu, Lord Kapila's birthplace. This indicates the oneness of such souls, both by way of teachings and personality.

In this regard, then, the teaching runs in terms of adhibautika, adhidaivika, and adhyatmika. The first signifies all the dangers present in relative existence, particularly in nature, such as floods, earthquakes, plagues, famines, etc. In more enlightened traditions like our Vedanta, these are not acts of God, by the way. They are purely of nature and, of course, its connection with the human mind. God is neither matter, energy, nor thought; so we must leave That out of the quotient. Illnesses and threats coming from insects, animals, plants, and microorganisms also form a part of this level of suffering.

Adhidaivika represents the dangers coming from lower realms and higher realms, demons and angels, if we must name them in accord with our present understanding in the West. These are what are called transpersonal dangers, as these beings have a design on our life and its energy, so we must be on guard with our discrimination as to what can be accepted and what must be rejected in this realm of potential suffering.

Adhiyatmika indicates dangers coming from our own mind/ego complex, and those of others as well. Even the dangers potential within our own bodies are always threatening, though the body only comes from the mind, and therefore can be purified and become an expression of a healthy mind. Practice of Yoga, then, is paramount for neutralizing the impurities present and potential at this level of existence.

The three listed above, then, are used to teach about the three great dangers, or Trividham Duhkham. Mastering them is called attaining the Three Great Accomplishments, leading to the attainment of five others which are "secondary" — meaning which can only be possessed after these forms of suffering are transcended. From ancient teachings like this have sprung the practice of chanting "shanti" three times — to save us from the three types of dangers and transcend the three sorrows present in the Three Worlds.

Avinashi from Pennsylvania writes:
QUESTION: "With something of a shock, I came fully awake to something a few days ago. I used to believe, (and this is how I put it to myself), that 'the River of Nature leads to the Ocean of Enlightenment.' In other words, relax, go with the flow, if this is rightly done, Nature itself will take us to illumination. But my view shifted. Now it seems to me that nature is important in that it constructs and holds forms together, including those forms (or should I say 'tattvas'?) that allow discrimination and sadhana, (namely, the higher tattvas of the antahkarana, though the health of the body, wholly, is also, of course, important). So there needs to be a good, dharmic relation with nature (which would also mean our appetites) so the faculties we use to gain illumination are strong, but to gain illumination, we follow the path of the sages and scriptures, not nature, correct? In fact, illumination involves the experiential realization of what is beyond (or behind) nature, so it's necessary to engage in austerities to take attention and energy away from nature and turn it toward Spirit, is this all correct? In the end, (or as we move along), nature and all its beings are even deified, but this is still not the same as following nature through any form of 'going with the flow.' It strikes me now that it is shamanism that goes along with nature; it seems to me that shamans seek communions and unions with nature for purposes relating to different kinds of pleasures and powers; but intrinsically, shamans aren't seekers of self-knowledge and the shamanic path isn't a self-knowledge path, and once again I'm left with this very clear, unambiguous understanding: for true illumination, follow the scriptures and the sages, not nature. It is seeming to me now, as I have been thinking all this out, that even tantric techniques involving sexuality have as their purpose the turning of our whole selves toward Spirit. But the view I've arrived at on all of this is so unequivocal that I fear it may be unbalanced. Your comments?"
ANSWER: I would say that you have ascertained correctly regarding Nature and Spirit. As I have put it, and I have done so in several ways over the years, there is a relationship of Spirit with Nature, an association, but there should not be an identification — not if said identification leads to fascination with, bondage under, or dependence upon it in any way.

In Sankhya, Yoga, and Vedanta, the same idea gets conveyed. In the first, Lord Kapila marks definitively the distinction between Samsara-pragbara, the river of souls flowing towards rebirth in form, and Kaivalya-pragbara, the stream of consciousness flowing into liberation, away from Nature — isolation from Nature, he calls it. Patanjali, too, uses the term isolation from Nature, and cautions against the Seer (Consciousness) becoming identified with the Seen (Nature). And in Vedanta, from Vedavyas to Shankara, and onwards to Vivekananda, the listing of Sankhya's Twenty-four Cosmic Principles (tattvas) are utilized to indicate everything that is a part of the nonself, leaving one with that essence that is left over as Atman.

Indigenous "religions" such as Shamanism are centered most often around nature, and particularly around the hidden energy (prana) that flows in It. This would be all right as a pathway (like Tantra practices) except that the sensational side of subtle energy gets taken up, and a sense of the mystical and the occult — as if nature is somehow sentient — gets projected over everything. They also often emphasize the ancestor realm as if it is the highest, a lower tendency that Christianity has played with over the centuries in its heaven-seeking philosophy.

Suffice to say that, over millennia, wherever Nature was used as a metaphor for spirituality, a partnership for enlightenment was enjoyed, but whenever Nature got the upper hand, and became the thing to be worshiped in and of itself, trouble and mischief followed, and a stunted effect was seen on the progress of mankind towards the Supreme Goal.

QUESTION #2: "Since the time of my initiation I've worked hard at visualizing the Ishtam, in synchrony with chanting the mantra. I've used the classic method of working with parts of the Ishtam's form, then putting the parts together. Now I'm at the point where I can see the whole form at once. While, of course, visualizing the Ishtam in the heart, I bring the focus of my inner vision to the Master's hands and let my focus rest there. While doing this, the entirety of the Master's form congeals in inner view. Every once in a while, I need to open my eyes to re-impress the image on the chitta; I only open my eyes ever so briefly — like taking a snapshot with a camera — and this serves to rather vividly bring the image back to clarity inside. My question concerns the degree of clarity I should strive for. If I do what I just described above, I can, at this point, get a nice, steady flow of attention moving toward the Ishtam. However, if I continue to work at visualizing parts of the Ishtam's form, for the sake of greater, inner clarity, I cannot get that steady flow going; the steady flow is broken up. The sense of ease that goes with the steady flow also goes away. So here's the dilemma: if I continue to work at visualizing the Ishtam in its parts, I can develop an ever-greater clarity in regard to detail. I could, for example, get to the point where I could even accurately visualize the detail of a hair in my inner vision. But I think this could be carried too far. How far should I carry it, seeing that this endeavor breaks the easy, steady flow of attention up?"

ANSWER: This question cuts to the point of why we use visualization in the first place. Of course, any congealed image we have fashioned with our mind — even that of Ishvara — is not the real item. It serves only as a facsimile. The formless Essence stands behind all, and we are to attempt to dissolve into that. Only by that move can we have samadhi of a definitive kind — Asamprajnata. This is active Yoga, the *"getting to the Father through the Son."* Also, along the way of this inner trajectory, we can replace the constructed image with the real Station of Ishvara, and have a communion that not only facilitates ease of flow, but actualizes real darshan with Him/Her. The realization of the statement by Sri Ramakrishna Paramahamsa, that *"Brahman and Shakti are One,"* will be the result. In other words, in all-pervasiveness there is no need any longer for "flow."

QUESTION #3: "The difference between dharana and dhyana isn't clear to me. What is the difference?"

ANSWER: Dharana, concentration, is the mechanism (after pratyahara is mastered) by which one can get into meditation, dhyana. The line between them is fine, but when the aspirant feels the need for focus slipping away, and a natural ability to rest with meditation sets in, then one can be said to have attained the seventh limb. Then, dharana slips to the background as an already mastered fact and quality. Another way of telling is that the meditator can sit and immediately go into one-pointed meditation, leaving off where the previous meditation ended, with no impediment or deviation from spontaneous abidance. This is meditative life per se, and a wondrous boon and blessing. Samadhi cannot help but "happen" after this level is reached.

Ekendra (earlier R.W. prior to recent SRV initiation) from South Carolina writes:
QUESTION: "First, I would like to say how fortunate I feel to have made my way back to this study. It has been some years since I've participated or even read the email attachments. In reading through the last class Q&A it dawned on me how much I have missed out on. If it is alright with You and the rest of the class, I would like to re-visit something from Swamiji's prelude to Raja-Yoga, from His chapter on 'The Control of the Psychic Prana' On pages 60-62 of the red paperback edition of *Raja Yoga* (pages 604-605 in *The Yogas and Other Works*), Swamiji explains several practices, one of which I have incorporated into my daily sadhana. The one that I use is the inhale (puraka) for X number of seconds, hold (kumbhaka) for double that amount, and exhale (rechaka) for half of the time held. I used this one because it most closely resembles the one that you showed us at the last SRV summer retreat. My questions: Do the specific numbers of seconds that Swamiji mentions have some hidden or sacred meaning to them, or are they simply used as a starting point? If not, then should I keep increasing the number of seconds over a long period to the maximum that the body will allow? Does there come a time when we discard counting and concentrate solely on drawing the Kundalini upward through the Sushumna?"

ANSWER: Yes, you have surmised correctly. There is no real esoteric meaning to counting. As Holy Mother has said, that is only to help the beginner to stay engaged. The same is true of repeating the mantra and counting the number of times. All that falls behind when concentration is attained, what to speak of the vision of God within.

Regarding increasing the time of puraka, kumbhaka, and rechaka, that is applicable only if the aspirant does not progress rapidly. If there are areas of the mind that are shut down, and blockages in the nadis, then he/she may have to prolong the phase of pranayama in order to purify these. Otherwise, if concentration begins to happen naturally, one can do less pranayama and get on to the point of Yoga practice. The "professional student" syndrome — we want to avoid that. There are countless hathis in India, and a number of schools, that center, even hover, around these preliminary practices as if they were paramount. They are useful only in early practice. If extended too long, the mind gets imbalanced, and the Goal is never reached — becomes even forgotten, or replaced with a vexing show of outer sensational pursuits and "attainments." In my own case, I practiced asana and pranayama only for some two years, early on. I occasionally referred to them as temporary tools later, but seldom ever needed them again.

So, this is one great stumbling block to Yoga, the preoccupation with asana and pranayama. The other, which when reversed would also act as a solution for this problem, is failing to master the yamas and niyamas (limbs one and two) prior to entering into asana and pranayama. Take ahimsa, for instance, nonviolence in thought, word, and deed. If there is still the penchant or tendency in the aspirant for violence, what do you imagine will be the outcome of doing asana and pranayama in that state of mind? The presence of violence will only get fueled, its flames fanned. And just ruminate a minute on the effects of asana and pranayama before the qualities of brahmacharya, purity, and austerity are attained. Now imagine a whole hatha yoga culture playing with the fire potential in Yoga prior to gaining a grasp on the first two limbs of Yoga!

QUESTION #2: "When I was reading over the slokas leading up to the current study on Samyama, and about the powers that accompany its intense practice, I could not help but think that some of the powers mentioned could be detrimental to one's attainment of the 'actual' Goal. Do people get hung up on these powers, and are some of these the occult powers that I have heard mention of so many times? Or, is it that by the time one reaches these more advanced stages in their practice that they are already set firmly enough on the path as to not be tempted by the cultivation of these powers for material gain? I myself have no use or desire to be as strong as an elephant, or to know who I was in a past life, or to gain any powers that won't necessarily lead me to Atmajnana (right now I would be happy to have the power to remain focused in my concentration for more than 15-20 seconds). There is however the question of where some of the images that bubble up, seemingly and suddenly out of nowhere, when I am sitting and absorbed in concentration for those short periods. Some are positive, but most are negative in nature. I can recall the source of some of them, but there are others which "feel" familiar but that I have no recollection of. Is it possible for a fledgling yogi to somehow stumble into Samyama for short periods of time? Do you think that perhaps some of these thoughts and images are old samskaras from previous lives? What do I do about them?"

ANSWER: First, as to the question of powers, there is a need to discriminate between the eight occult powers (asta-bala siddhis) and the powers which come to one naturally via sadhana. We know that Sri Ramakrishna, Swamiji, and Holy Mother (what to speak of Sri Krishna in the Gita) have all warned us against the seeking of the occult powers. In contrast to these, which are sought by power-hungry beings in order to gain both pleasures and domination over others, there are those powers which come to the seeker who is pure, dedicated, and properly oriented in Yogic practice — with the right intention. Keeping the mind on the Goal and its prescribed practice, both the gaining and usage of such power will be easily avoided by the sincere aspirant.

  Both the positive and negative images that come to the mind in meditation practice are to be witnessed and put behind you. Some of them are mere phantoms, called the "1000 imbecilities of the mind." Others come from previous existences, from actions perpetrated or performed there. Some even come from this lifetime, from early childhood and young life. They have been spirited away, out of sight, and come up in accordance with actions and events we are presently engaged in. The rule with them is to water the flowers, not the weeds. For, even the flowers will need to be transcended at some point, as they may act as influences of attraction and attachment in the near future. And yes, they are part of the samsaric makeup in the mind. When we get free of them, the practice continues in the form of making sure that no new samskaras will be formulated. Patanjali states that only samskaras of meditation and samadhi can be allowed to persist thereafter. Samyama is a matter of absolute mastery, and still a far cry yet.

Akshaya Bhakti from New England writes:
COMMENTS: "Over the last several months I have somehow been neglecting to include Raja practice during sadhana, letting even Pranayama slip away, defaulting to my Japa / Mantra routine. I must admit this is due, partly, to inconsistency in practice and thus relying on what comes most easily to me. But once I feel the Peace and happiness in Their Holy Company, I find it difficult to move on! I want to be able to surrender my heart but focus my mind on the principles of Raja. I don't want to forfeit the blessing of this intensive study. I realize that although Bhakti and Raja lead to the same goal, they do have separate 'rules,' just as within the 'state borders' that you and Avinashi discussed. There are so many choices offered to us as to what we can reflect upon. I could use some help re-establishing how I should direct my mind, especially in seated practice. Deepest gratitude."
ANSWER: Yoga practice, in this day and time, among the busy people of the Kali Yuga, is for the few rather than the many. This is why the practice is japa, and bhakti, mainly. Therefore, sitting and repeating the mantra will surely suffice, and it should never be given up. Even at the time of passing from the body, and that of others' passing, it will assist immensely.

  But it is a great soul, and a truly aspiring mind, who wants something more than salvation, and seeks to liberate the mind from all fetters, forever. So suffice to say that, as you do the prescribed mantra practice, and deepen it through attending retreats, pilgrimages, studies, meditation, and the like, you can add in a few hours here and there for mastery of other areas of Yoga overall. As Sri Krishna says in the Gita, *"Even a little practice of this Yoga of Mine,*

*Arjuna, will free one from the Great Fear. Nothing is ever lost in its pursuit."* Thereafter, and as Shankara advises, just *"....meditate on the state of oneness and pass your time contentedly."*

QUESTION: "I wonder how to transfer my mind from the devotional mode, (understanding that I will still be maintaining that connection to the Holy Ones) to reflection on the inner self? How do I get to the alambanas of the 24 Cosmic Principles? How do the final 3 steps progress?"

ANSWER: It is like shifting gears, or adjusting to climate changes as one moves higher in altitude up a mountain slope. From alambana, to subtler alambanas, to Ishtam, to Formless Reality, then back again, we need to get well versed at such inner movement. After hearing of this esoteric teaching, there remains only left to do it, to practice it, to repeat it again and again. It is like each time up a mountain slope new things get discovered. One may even run into a partially buried treasure on one such ascent.

QUESTION #2: "Concerning the translation of the prayer, *Om drysham*, dear teacher, I would like to know which is the Sanskrit word for 'mass' (of pure conscious awareness) and to know if there are some other meanings of it. Whenever I recite it, the connotation of 'mass' seems to conflict with my feeling of the lightness of God so I like to substitute the word essence. Does that seem acceptable?"

ANSWER: Whatever works for you. But I advise not eliminating the word from your understanding. Rather think, "mass," *"ghanam,"* not in the way that geometry and science means it, as weight and density, etc., but as an infinite conglomerate, a boundless sea of Bliss — *Anandaghanam*. The profound Sanskrit word, *Ghanaprajna*, for instance, means "massive and undifferentiated Consciousness." Maybe think of the word "boundless" rather than the word "bulk," or "density." To coin a pun, it is not heavy; it is "Light."

Sanatanand from Hawaii writes:
QUESTION: "These sutras were also most enlightening for me. Though the preceding sutras were very informative and helped to outline the overall vision of the pathway to travel, the practices really go to the heart of the matter. The elucidation of these practices are really the most precious part, for when one becomes convinced of the purpose of one's life, which is to realize God, what is left is to avail oneself of the procedure. Your description and clarifications of these methods is very helpful in fine-tuning one's focus. As one comprehends the general idea involved, a picture is formed which yet lacks specificity. To apprehend the specifics greatly assists in where to best invest one's time, intention, and devotion. On that note, though it has been a point in my practice that I have put my attention on, perhaps you can suggest a way to help me increase my sense of devotion with regard to japa, Ishvara-pranidhana, and meditation. I do work at intensifying these, yet I feel that this could be the pranic force to best help break through to a deeper level. I remember in the Gospel where Ramakrishna is in front of the image of Kali, weeping and imploring Her to come to Him. Perhaps I am not quite capable of this level of intensity, yet it

did facilitate a profound breakthrough for Ramakrishna."

ANSWER: I was just speaking of this very subject in a meeting with a student today. Rapt participation in one's own spiritual awakening is a way of saying it. Yet it takes a kind of spontaneity, and some deep yearning — both which the aspirant has to keep alive and burning daily. A complete abandon is another way of describing it, which is probably what is really inferred by the Sanskrit word, *sharanagata* — self surrender. In one of Ramprasad's wisdom songs, he puts it nicely by singing, *"Drive me completely out of my mind, oh Wisdom Mother."* This very idea must have inspired Sri Ramakrishna Paramahamsa all the more to make deep and certain contact with Her, Mother Kali, no matter what the outcome in terms of mental states and ego survival.

In terms of actual advice, or instruction around this, it is very personal, particular to each striving soul. The best guideline, however, is the knowledge and foresight that the mind goes through periods or phases wherein devotion becomes inexplicably dry and cold. Then, suddenly, as if some unseen force had lifted a floodgate, the whole mind becomes wet and hot with increased devotion. All that can be said is that the devotee must work, as consciously as possible, towards these intense phases, finding ways to usher them in, to attract them. A sort of subtle anticipation is advised in daily meditation, as if just sitting each morning will itself produce the onslaught of such intensity. One should practically taste the advent of such devotion, or catch an aroma of it in the subtle ethers, for all of life becomes a flow when living under such a force. As the Upanisads say, spoken by those who have tasted this nectarlike bhakti: *"Godspeed to you in crossing over the farthest shore beyond all darkness."*

Kanyakali in Hawaii writes:
QUESTION: "I want to delve deeper into the process of samyama because it leads to the dissolution of the mind in samadhi. Once one is able to sustain meditation, the mind is concentrated and highly focused, however, it is still acting. When one goes further, at some point, the mind gets absorbed into the object of meditation, and one leaves off the mind and enters samadhi. I would like to know more about this point of transition, and I think hearing more about meditating on alambanas vs. samyama would help. For example, it seems that one could meditate on an elephant either as an alambana to aid meditation, or as an object for samyama. Could you explain how the processes of meditation on alambanas and samyama differ?"

ANSWER: The first is still a move towards clarification, and thus a means to a fuller inner knowing. The latter is a marvelous tool used by a master to reveal anything he wants to behold. Again, the former facilitates an intense and far reaching look at inner worlds and their populations for the purpose of observing and noting them. But samyama in the hands/minds of illumined souls causes profound shifts and changes in these very realms and the souls that inhabit them.

It must be noted that there is no personal or intentional will on the part of the luminary when samyama is employed; it is not a power to level against relativity. Rather, it is perfect restraint. Samyama, beyond the eight limbs, is defined as limbs six, seven, and eight — concentration, meditation, and samadhi — conjoined. Limbs six and seven facilitate a deep look at all that is within the gross, subtle, and causal realms. Samadhi is the result, and involves separating oneself from these three worlds (kaivalya) and merging into Bliss. This separation owes its power to limbs six and seven effectively revealing that all worlds are unreal, are fabrications of Mind at cosmic, collective, and individual levels. Knowing that all realms where name and form persist infer maya, why would the realized soul utilize samyama for personal or transformative reasons? Will he invest in such folly? No. But he may leave a hint, a clue, or a bit of treasure for those who are to come after.

In short, saving the world is not an option. It was never real in the first place. Convincing souls to give it up so as to perceive it as nothing other than Brahman — now that is an undertaking worthy of the effort.

K.D. from Hawaii writes:
COMMENTS: "Lessons 36 and 37 on the kleshas were most illuminating, and came at a very auspicious time when I was aware of the bondage created by attraction and aversion. I was noticing that I was clinging and grasping at that which I thought would provide a sense of security, only to find that it morphed into something that I was adverse to and wanted to run away from. Clinging and grasping at human relationships out of a fear of being alone cast shadows all around, and left me feeling even more insecure and lost due to the fact that I had lost my own internal anchor – the knowledge of and hopefully direct experience of the Self, Atman. So to have the kleshas explained in greater detail than they were presented formerly became key to being the witness of the drama, and not mistaking it for what is real. Also helpful and interesting was the following: 'One can avail oneself of all manner of facts, and should do so if knowledge is duly sought, but if the realization of the thing studied is replaced by the mere study itself, no real facility will manifest from that effort.' So it is not enough to understand the kleshas and know their names in Sanskrit, but to almost constantly contemplate and monitor the situation for their presence and adverse effects. Since I am usually (always) acting out of egoic perspectives, it is essential to question: "What kind of egoic impulse is this? Is it verging on the mature? Is it ripening into an ego which is of benefit to self and others? Is it 'giving birth to qualities such as the tendency of inner study, the desire to meditate and transcend and the wisdom to do selfless works?' Or is it a puffed up masquerade looking to draw attention to itself? You wrote: 'Attachment neither frees nor sets free, and without freedom, as we all should have learned by now, there can be no real love.' Thank you for the reminder."
QUESTION: "To rid oneself of the 5 kleshas it is advised to raise the opposite wave and, of course, be aware of the siddhis so as to avoid even a semblance of their manifestation. When we raise the opposite wave we are dealing in pure duality, are we not? You wrote: 'The separate I-maker captures the mind's awareness and points it in the direction of those deluding pairs of opposites.'

I know and understand the value of replacing love with hate, and confusion with clarity, so it must be the state of the ego which is raising the opposite wave that makes the crucial difference. If it is a mature or maturing ego, it is engaged in a process of purification by raising the opposite wave. But if it's a little ego seeking self-gratification it will create the negative by seeking the alleged positive. Is this correct?"

ANSWER: Yes, it is the state of the ego involved, or, as I often say, it all (success/effectivity) depends on the quality of consciousness at any given time. And you coined a good term for it when you wrote "pure duality." When one engages in practice in order to rid oneself of impediments, it is a different orientation around duality that is taking shape than when one only suffers the results of dualistic living and thinking, not striving to purify. The yamas and niyamas of Yoga, and the Eightfold Path in Buddhism, are good examples of methods that transform the mind's thinking process early on into a way of skirting unwanted effects. Many and legion are the beings who fail in their sadhana by not committing to paths such as these, and failing to listen to the guru around them. So many enter in without the means and the instruction. No wonder there are so few illumined souls amongst us.

QUESTION #2: "In going over the more common manifestations of the Eight Occult Powers, such as nonresponsibility, obsession with thinness, meddling, beautification, allurement for selfish motive, enjoyment of material objects, I can understand why most are harmful egoic expressions. However it seems that motivation is more important than the actual action taking place. Is that not true? Is the Power of Enjoyment also Raga, attachment? If one is enjoying food and beautifying spaces out of a sense of appreciation for the wonders of nature, and not to gain power and control over others, is that not beneficial?"

ANSWER: If there is no selfish grasping present, and no sense of fear or foreboding of such pleasures and vistas being taking away, and full knowledge of the ephemeral nature of all forms, then it may be said that the soul has become the "Supreme Enjoyer," and is free from the dangers of attachment, and the risks of raga, attraction.

It may be added that if the witness of such wonders "of nature" is fully aware that all these wonders came out of the human mind and soul, and that in that sense they can never be destroyed, then a state of naturalness has been attained, This is a hard measure, a harsh task master. For, in most all cases, it will be found that the soul, either then or later, begins to lean towards enjoying and relying upon pleasure, and cannot then do without it. That is why tapas, austerity, is recommended and practiced. For hopefully, via such singular practice, the soul will find in itself that superlative quality and unsurpassed power called renunciation, tyaga, which no pleasure or pleasing vista can equal. When one has that, one has everything. Beings like Christ, Buddha, and Sri Ramakrishna had that, and having that, had authentic Freedom.

QUESTION #3: "It seems the hallmark would be to examine what is a selfish act and what is a selfless act done out of service. But then you wrote: '[Should] the world, changing constantly via its own nature as change,…even be saved or bettered at all, or must the soul only strive to realize the changeless Divinity within...?' Of course the world would be bettered and maybe even saved if everyone was striving to realize the changeless Divinity within, so my question is, "Should we not just harken back to the Yama, Ahimsa, and as long as no one is being harmed in any way by any actions taken, assume then we are in the safe zone?"

ANSWER: Better to harken ahead to Samadhi and Samyama; they are the only safe zone. Ahimsa, or any yama or niyama, is a ground rule, and thus important for the correct start and orientation. But one will always encounter those who preach and live by the rule of himsa, violence. What to do then? They would rather dispatch you outright rather than listen to your perspective. In nondual samadhi, there is no second person to disagree or cause conflict. This ultimate station is thereby advised by the luminaries.

COMMENTS: "Your comments about family were also interesting and valuable. 'One cannot get to an illumined state while one is still attached to family and the world. It is like the case of a captain trying to put out from port while the lines of his ship are still tied to the dock.' I was glad others questioned this wisdom, for your further elucidation shed more light on the subject. The key word of course is attachment, and like stated above 'Attachment neither frees nor sets free, and without freedom there can be no real love.' I work on detachment, and sometimes it is easy and sometimes not so easy. Sometimes I resort to 'don't care,' which feels more like numbing out rather than true detachment. Detachment must be aware, aware of the suffering that one wishes to detach from. It cannot be a running away. It must be a state of total acceptance of what is without any attempt to change the situation and make it better."

FINAL QUESTIONS: "What does true detachment actually look like? Is there never suffering in detachment, or can there still be pain but no one believing the pain is real? It seems unrealistic to never experience suffering, so possibly detachment means remaining in the witness mode with a certainty that feelings are fleeting, impermanent phenomenon, and that any uncomfortable emotions will surely pass. Grief is one of the 8 fetters, but does that mean wallowing in grief or experiencing it like in the case of a loved one's death, and then moving beyond it to a deeper understanding that the soul never dies?"

ANSWERS: A positive "yes" to your final question, though a "wallowing in grief" would not be advisable if it could be avoided. Grief is also one of the four great traps. It has to be watched carefully, for the wallowing tendency of the ego can become a sort of perverse enjoyment for the soul, giving way to its tendency of feeling sorry for itself — a sort of mental hypochondria.

As for your observations on detachment, they are well expressed. Yes, suffering comes to all embodied beings. We recently witnessed the Mother of the Universe embodied in Sri Sarada Devi, and how She suffered at the loss of Swami Yogananda (Yogin) and others, what to speak of Her divine husband, Sri Ramakrishna. Still, She went forward and saved thousands of souls, liberated others. In SRV we used to have a saying around this, that "pain is inevitable; suffering is optional." It means that much of what beings have wrought upon themselves can be undone with a little effort, mentally and spiritually, but the six main transformations — birth, growth, disease, old age, decay, and death, must be endured. From ant to Avatar, all must "suffer" them. Such is the nature of the embodied condition. Now, to make that optional as well.

ADDENDUM: "I found it ultimately cool to watch you today on the Live Stream. Amazing technology!!! I did not hear your whole lecture, but most of it, and I will watch the remainder as well as other classes on your channel. I suppose I'll figure out how to do it. It reminded me of how important it is to be in touch and constantly reminded of Vedantic wisdom. Thank you so much for uploading your wisdom and making it accessible to anyone, anytime. About the Jnana Matra teaching you gave, I was wondering about sentiency. You said that these wisdom particles were pure sentiency. Well, I know you are very familiar with the work of Masaru Emoto and his work on the intelligence of water. Surely he has proven that water is intelligent, and responds positively to positive loving input. So is not water full of Jnana Matra, and thereby sentient?"

RESPONSE: Full of jnana matras (unawares), yes, but not sentient — because water does not have the intelligence to cognize and utilize jnanam. Only the human mind has that capacity. Therefore, I would not say that anything in nature is sentient. Prana in the elements "looks" sentient; preservation in insects would seem sentient; instinct in animals "appears" sentient. But it is only consciousness in humans which is actually sentient, and we know that for this to be so, Consciousness has to be realized. Otherwise, misconceptions (like nature being sentient) remain in the mind, and it never gains true clarity.

Still, the intelligent particles are in everything. The reality of the situation is that they emanate from human consciousness. We place them in earth, water, fire, air, ether, etc, when we concentrate on them. Even a mere glance at them by an ignorant person, like at clouds, causes a reaction in the clouds. Thus, they all appear sentient. In short, Consciousness authored nature. Consciousness animates nature. Consciousness changes nature. Consciousness dissolves nature. All things in nature are only responding to the mind's power of awareness placed upon them by the soul — sort of like vegetables in a pan of water "dancing" — not of their own accord, but due to the heat in the burner. Sri Ramakrishna, therefore, used to tell the story of the little boy who entered the kitchen and cried out to his mother, "Look, ma, the vegetables are dancing; they are alive!" And the mother had to explain that the vegetables could not move of their own accord, but were animated by the power of the heat radiating underneath the pan.

Following this story, and at the request of one of my students, I was asked some years ago to make up a poem for the children around this story of the Master's, so that the lesson in it could be taught. That poem is placed below, both for demonstrating the phenomena of the appearance of sentiency all around us, and for giving us the will and wisdom to seek out the true Source of all phenomena — Brahman, the "Inactive Agent," which is pure Sentiency Itself:

### The Kid in the Kitchen

*The kid in the kitchen
while dinner was fixin'
looked toward the oven,
the kettle there bubblin'.
He said to his mother,
as he began prancing,
"I think I can see
the veggies are dancing!"*

*"My son your' mistaken,"
said Mother, a-bakin'.
"That food cannot move
of its own undertaking.
It's the water you see,
at least it's my notion,
which boiling so freely
causes the motion."*

*Then Dad at the table
upon hearing his wife,
said, "Water's unable
to bring them to life.
The squash and potatoes
and carrots and beet –
they all are a-dancing
because of the heat."*

*Then Grandma walked in
her eyes in a squint.
She looked at them all
and said, "Well, here's a hint.
My decision is such
and it could not be firmer
They're dancing so much
from the fire in the burner."*

*Then Grandpa stepped in,
with the hair on his chin,
and said, "By my word,
It's part true what I've heard.
For back in my day,"
he said slappin' a knee,
"I once worked for my pay
at the gas company."*

*"And there in a tank
is an endless supply,*

*which all beings thank
but never think why.
It was there that I found
gas flows underground
in pipes 'neath the street
which brings us all heat.
Thus the vittles in water,
the flame on the coil
Is caused by the gas
and that makes water boil."*

*So to find this life's purpose,
my sisters and brothers,
you must look 'neath the surface
declares our Great Mother.
And then you will see
upon taking some pauses
there It will be
the Cause of all causes.*

*And that Cause is Brahman,
or God if you will,
It really does nothing
but stays ever still.
So next time you say,
"I think I see God,"
you might just delay
and think it quite odd,
that here on the outside,
where all things are dancing,
the real Cause is inside
and ever-enhancing.*

## Pada III, Sutra 27

*bhuvana jnanam surya samyamat* (*bhuvana*, subtle atmospheres; *jnana*, wisdom; *surya*, the sun; *samyama*, concentration, meditation, and samadhi conjoined).

*"By performing samyama on the sun as a symbol for inner wisdom, subtle atmospheres become accessible."*

As we have long contemplated in SRV and its prevalent, pertinent, teachings, all of nature is a symbol for spiritual life; it has all come out of the mind via the twin mechanisms of thought and prana and their combined work. The entire universe is intelligence made manifest. All objects are thought concretized. Universes and their objects have not been created out of nothing, but exist, eternally, within the mind's marvelous scope. Of course, this mind, or Mind, is cosmic, collective, and individual, all three; but nevertheless, it projects of its own intelligence, of the nature of emanation, all drawn from The Word, AUM.

With this "mind-only school" teaching, or truism, the seeking soul can go forth and make so much more sense out of life and the world. This involves, as I just stated above, beginning to see the symbology in nature and all the objects it produces. The sun is one such object, possibly the most important and obvious to living beings here on earth. But let us not conclude that there are no other worlds within; they also being accompanied by suns. And here is where the meditator can utilize such suns, and the light coming from them — whether it be gross or subtle (sun rays or wisdom rays) — to uncover or unveil all that is hidden amidst the "Kingdoms of Heaven within."

A samyama on the sun consists of first meditating on the nature of fire. That can start as focusing in on a candle flame, as Westerners used to do in the 60's. Eventually, black light posters were not enough, evidently, and not a fitting representative of the grand magnitude that an actual fiery orb in the sky possesses. The moon was also used as an inspiration, but its light was only borrowed. It was not "self-effulgent," svayamjyoti. Still, by the time the nature of fire and its light were cognized, the sun was effectively being taken inside and used for an example of the absence of darkness, both in the world and in the mind. Early on, in Patanjali's time, and philosophy, it was one of the superlative alambanas to benefit by in meditation.

What happens to the sun in meditation at the time of the soul's yearning for Truth forms an altogether unique turn in its understanding of its own consciousness. And that is the point, here, that the shift of orientation from matter to consciousness evinced a turning towards a desire for transformation of mind, and it also facilitated a turn from worldly life and mundane human convention, to a life of spiritual practices leading towards striving for Self-realization. This manifested for the seeker via the insight that the physical sun is an expression of Wisdom, or intelligence — really, all that reveals, illumines, uncovers, and provides comprehension and clarification.

The result of using the sun for an object of meditation, then, was a vision of internal worlds. As Patanjali's sutra states, these subtle atmospheres became visible to the single eye of the meditator located in the mind, just as surely and certainly as the outer world for the human being with its two eyes located in the head. Thus, it was not any more a matter of the universe of outer space being the "final frontier," but more the boon of inner space being the Eternal Kingdom.

Following that Light of Intelligence to its inmost Source, then, the meditator, armed with wisdom teachings from the seers, penetrated the imaginary line between matter and Spirit and arrived Home. Just as the infinite number of suns in physical space represented matter to the earth-bound soul, so too did the infinite number of suns within show themselves up to be atoms of Wisdom to the illumined soul, all radiating Truth, not mere appearances or illusions.

All it takes, then, to join the ranks of the truth-seekers, is a transcendence of both mundanity and imagination. The first fastens the mind to tired conventions and rituals with no meaning, and the latter takes one into the many misleading fancies of the mind which are substanceless and devoid of fulfillment and consummation. The following sutra reveals this nicely.

## Pada III, Sutra 28
*chandra tara vyuha jnanam* (*chandra,* moon; *tara,* subtle regions; *vyuha,* order; *jnana,* wisdom).

*"By performing samyama on the moon as a symbol, an internal map for the subtle regions can be gained."*

As Sri Krishna states it in the Bhagavad Gita, *"The solar path and the lunar path, both of these are called My Two Eternal Pathways for mankind."* Taking a clue from this Great Master, Patanjali both brought out and emphasized the import of taking the external and utilizing it to reveal the internal. Ideally, the intelligent way of proceeding is to know the internal first, and then see the connections spinning out as a result.

But life in the world, and embodiment in the Kali Yuga, resists this right orientation. Beings born here on earth, thereafter identifying themselves with the physical body, have to reverse the karma of a birth in ignorance (according to Buddhism this process of reawakening takes three lifetimes) and begins the quest of finding themselves again via the spiritual path. This has been described by some, somewhat blithely, as a play, or a game of tearing off masks. Unfortunately, the triple imposition of matter, ego, and maya is difficult to see through, and the so-called "game" turns into an extended series of births in the realm of suffering. Added to the task are several other impediments, such as poor upbringing, a materialistic society, a religion that has failed to pose freedom as the highest goal, and a world that holds money as the purpose for life and existence — the seeking of Mammon instead of Spirit. No wonder Vivekananda has described the situation here in relativity as one that *"piles more gloom on gloom."*

In Vedanta circles, the idea that the moon shines by borrowed light is conveniently posited in order to demonstrate metaphorically the difference between Atman and the mind/body complex. The idea is that the Eternal Witness is self-effulgent. It illumines and witnesses all else, but nothing witnesses It. The Katharudra Upanisad concurs, and states: *"Food is pervaded by vital energy; vital energy is pervaded by mind; mind is pervaded by intelligence, and that ever happy intelligence is pervaded by Bliss. This self of Bliss is pervaded by Brahman, the Witness, the innermost of all. Brahman is not pervaded by anything else. Neither by action, nor by begetting children, nor by anything else — only by knowing Brahman — does one attain Brahman."*

In case the student does not recognize it, this sloka is referring to the Five Sheaths of Vedanta, or the Adhara System. These five coverings, called upadhis, veil our Formless Essence from view. This is not a matter of randomness, accident, coincidence, sin, evolution, or negative forces such as a devil. It is the nature of form to obscure the Formless; that is all. Referring back to the above sutra, the truth-seeker of olden times learned to look upon lights like the sun and the moon as distractions that pulled the attention of the inward-moving aspirant away from the Light of the Soul. When we look at the present-day culture and its contemporary soothsayers, we see that ignorant souls, worldly souls, educated souls, intellectual souls are all looking at the sun and the moon as if they were real, as if they themselves were the goal, and with an eye to inspect them for some hidden content they are supposed to possess, and to thereby "conquer" them. Under this veil of delusion, and failing to see the Reality behind and beyond them, it is sun and moon that have conquered mankind, grabbing and stealing away with its consciousness. What to speak of these external lights in the skies, even the mere light of a television has captured most beings. It is this that our champion, Lord Patanjali, seeks to reverse and rectify.

In this regard, one sloka in the Ishavasyopanisad has the awakened soul praying to Ishvara so that the real Light could be revealed unto him: *"Like a lid, Thy shining golden orb covers the entrance to the Truth in Thee. Therefore, oh Lord, remove the sun so that I who am devoted to what is True may behold That."* Thus, we must learn to look upon the sun and moon, upon the entire earth and its various objects, as symbols for an internal and transcendent Reality. Soon thereafter, samyama will become natural.

## Lesson Seventy-four, 9/28/12
### Pada III, Sutra 29

On the eve of Navaratri, 2012, as we are, the import of Patanjali's Raja Yoga system in the scope of spiritual life takes on a more pronounced import. The single sutra taken up in this lesson bridges the gap in our conventional knowledge and brings into focus the very real presence and existence of the subtle worlds within — not just in the sense of realms and lokas, but more importantly, as the emanation of Shakti power and its (Her) predominant place in all Yogas. Thus, a third element, that Patanjali called "Chit-shakti," takes its place, forming another important triputi for our collective contemplation: deities, principles, and Kundalini. It is not only the purely Tantric systems, then, that know, speak, and teach about Her; it is also the Upanisads and the Yoga Sutras.

Many of the questions sent in from the last lesson are as if in anticipation of this superlative area of spiritual life. They act, then, as a fitting introduction to the content of the sutra.

**Questions and Answers for Lesson 74**
S.C. from Hawaii writes:
QUESTION: "What exactly are celestials, & gods and goddesses?"
ANSWER: Vedanta teaches that those are deities, but not in the sense that they exist outside in an exterior world, like in space, but rather within, and related to different grades of consciousness. Wisdom principles (tattva-jnan), and wor-

ship of deities (upasana dhyana), are to be combined in order that the fullest maturation of comprehension of both mankind's heritage and gradation of consciousness be attained. This then leads to nondual understanding and realization. This also helps embodied beings to better cognize dreams, visions, and other unusually subtle occurrences in consciousness. To find all beings within oneself is thus a fulfilling way to both integrate (if one's knowledge has fallen apart) and realize the nature of Awareness.

Akshaya-Bhakti from New England writes:
QUESTION: "As we study these later sutras of Raja Yoga that deal with advanced realization, I have been thinking again about Turiya as the 4th state of consciousness that would come in samadhi, vs. deep sleep. It is disturbing to me that although we awaken refreshed from deep sleep, we don't seem to retain that awareness. Is it just that we don't remember deep sleep, or are we not even in awareness of our True nature then? Does awareness of Turiya come only after Samyama?"
ANSWER: Deep sleep is that level of consciousness where all things external and subtle (elements, senses, sense objects, worlds, etc.) are returned to an indeterminate state and stored there in potential. It is similar to dream, wherein we remember and review what we experienced in the waking state, but with even less of the usual cohesiveness that dreaming has. That is, Brahman is a mass of pure Consciousness, with no cycles or phases. Continuity is not necessary in It. Deep Sleep, sushupti, is somewhat more connected, but still widely dispersed and far flung. The trace or mere semblance of objects that are there is just a hint or a flavor of future manifestation. This causal array is vast and peaceful, very expansive, spread around the limitlessness of Consciousness — resting somewhat like the presence and distance between planets in outer space. This is why the soul gets awed and falls into a deep reverie there. In that indrawn state of trance it rests, rejuvenates, heals, and refreshes itself in the light-filled space that is humming with the sound of stored up power.

  To become aware of what is happening to it on these multiple occasions (sattva, peace, and the grace of God are rare, but sushupti is plentiful of access), the soul (transmigrating mind) must develop the ability to abide in one-pointed focus all of the time. Samyama is this ability intensified manyfold, and all of the experiences of life provide the opportunities to possess and refine it. This is why it is a great waste to do anything, any act, heedlessly, or to think any thought mindlessly. There is not just karma to bear for these oversights; one sacrifices the chance to live in Consciousness, and that is the natural and intended state of the human being. In actuality, being aware and focused is the simplest of all modes. It requires the least amount of energy. In this way awareness is much like deep sleep, for there the soul expends nothing and, if aware, realizes everything that is beyond loss and gain.
QUESTION #2: "Could you review the nature of Turiya, at least as far as words can describe it, and how it relates to Samyama and deep sleep (including our other bodies)? Regarding Samyama, for a long time now I have been unsure of

how to deal with these sutras about the 'powers' that come from focusing on various objects in that state — like the moon, as in Sutra 28. As other students have stated, not only do I not seek them, but would fear becoming attached to them. Suddenly, however, I had the thought that these are just another way of looking at the stages of the Word, using concepts that are approaching the Inner Self, specifically related to the cosmic laws, enabling us to see through to the true nature of their essence and their origin. Could you please comment on the appropriateness of this line of thinking, and how I might utilize it further in practicing involution of these higher principles? Deepest gratitude as always."
ANSWER: Turiya is the Advaita Vedanta way of labeling the highest state of Consciousness (also, Turiyatita). Patanjali calls it Asamprajnata in Yoga. Vedavyasa titles it samadhi, and Vedanta in general calls it Nirvikalpa. It is of the nature of Formlessness, but not the formlessness of deep sleep wherein there exists an abundance of "formless" forms, i.e., everything in potential (seeds) waiting to be brought out into manifestation. Besides, sushupti's formlessness is covered over by nescience, while Turiya has no covering. This is why Sri Krishna makes the distinction between form and formlessness (physical world/body and subtle/causal world/bodies), and Ultimate Formlessness. To make it easy to understand, we need only think of how dense the mind is when it thinks of and cognizes nothing. This could be blank mind, sleepy mind, vacant mind, wandering mind, dull mind, comatose mind, or the mind in deep sleep. There is little or nothing to it, and certainly little benefit coming from it. Even deep sleep, though it refreshes, has to be repeated again and again, in cycles, in order to confer benefit. This is not true of the mind in Turiya, which experiences what is everlasting and of infinite value. If the meditator comes out of that state at all, ever again, he/she demonstrates all that the seers and sages are known for — Peace, Bliss, Wisdom, Transcendence. Thus is the nature of Turiya explained, and its difference from sushupti — what to speak of waking and dreaming (jagrat and svapna).

Regarding the powers of the Yogi, they are vastly different than occult powers. As Swami Vivekananda was so fond of stating, by quoting Patanjali himself, *"When a man renounces the occult powers, he attains the rain cloud of virtues."* It has to do with the true meaning of the word, *"siddha."* In our Raja Yoga commentary, Swamiji clarifies it somewhat by stating: *"The Siddhas are beings who are a little above ghosts. When the Yogi concentrates his mind on the top of his head he will see these Siddhas. The word Siddha does not refer to those men who have become free — a sense in which it is often used."*

Further, your thoughts are running in a sensible line when you bring in The Word and the Cosmic Principles. Everyone uses these in life, and the shakti power and prana that infuses them. The real difference lies in how they get used or, maybe, whether they get "used" or utilized might be a good way to say it. Even a mere occult power can be impressive in the hands of a luminary, while any power — occult or divine — will be wasted and misused when wielded by an insincere seeker or practitioner.

Avinashi from Pennsylvania writes:
QUESTION: "I don't see the relation between renunciation and deification, though you mention it frequently. Would you explain this?"
ANSWER: I was speaking from that great statement that I heard my teacher express many times, that of *"Renunciation is not condemnation; it is deification."* Since he was a lifelong monk, the profound utterance takes on even more significance. That is to say, there are monks who might renounce out of aversion, out of tradition, or out of realization of Formlessness as being the final beatitude, and so forth. The way I would explain it is that to renounce out of love is higher, and that is what this statement confers. In other words, when one sees through all earthly attractions as being secondary at best, and even troublesome due to the accrual of karma associated with them, one is then a candidate for loving God first and foremost. That is the meaning of the greatest of all commandments which states *"Thou shalt love thy Lord, God, with all thy heart, all thy mind, and all thy spirit."* To put it even more directly, when one loves God after seeing God, the world turns into nothing other than God, and then there is no need to renounce it in the usual sense of the term. *Sarvam khalvidam Brahma* is how we say it in Vedanta — All Is Brahman. My own view pertaining to such a realization is that it comes about via the integration of yogas such as devotion and wisdom, plus action and inaction. As Vivekananda put it so nicely, *"I want to give Truth dry hard reason, softened in the sweetest syrup of love, and made spicy with intense work, and cooked in the kitchen of Yoga so that even a baby can easily digest it."* Let's eat!
QUESTION #2: "In the great spectrum of akashas and matras, where does physical light fall? and more particularly, what is it?"
ANSWER: It is a symbol of light that is of a different dimension and a subtler particle and vibration. You have heard that the yogi's business is to see through all false superimpositions, all ruses pulled by the world-enchanting maya in conjunction with the worldly mind. Well, it is also his business to find the meaning of these overlays, and this is the stuff of greater realization — which is why there are differing levels of realization in the various luminaries of the spiritual realm. There is a beautiful sloka in the Upanisads which states, *"Oh Lord, I see the sun in the sky. Please remove this shiny orb so that I can see your true Light."* The idea is that the physical sun is an appearance only, and is also potentially distracting to the truth seeker. Just see how thousands of sun-worshippers, astronomers, sun-tanners, and other beings fall victim to the sun's various allurements, but never see through to its real meaning. To make this fact even more evident, even obvious, the "Creator" God has placed billions of suns in the night sky, as if to say, "It is nothing! Get over it." So, there is a subtler light, call it the light of intelligence if you will. Everything "out here" is an expression of all that is "in there" — *"....from the infinite the finite has come."*
The same is true of everything in this universe, and some beings are fast and hard on the trail to uncovering its "mysteries." Let us count ourselves as being among them.
QUESTION #3: "Can you speak about the state and development of integral

Yoga in India before Sri Ramakrishna, Swami Vivekananda, and Sri Aurobindo?"

ANSWER: To the former two beings, the expression "integral yoga" is a redundant one. They are always living in and espousing the Universality of all religions, not just synthesizing Indian Yogas. To bring the idea of integration forward, some souls introduce it into other cultures; but it is nothing new. Both the Synthesis of Yoga and Universality have been there in the Vedas from time out of mind. Sri Krishna, possibly the most ancient of all Great Teachers, speaks of the Four Yogas in the Bhagavad Gita, Chapter 13, slokas 24 and 25, and Chapter 18, slokas 50-57. You may view them there with commentary for elucidation, but best to use the versions of the Gita by the Ramakrishna Order.

QUESTION #4: "I doubt that exercising upekshanam in regard to evil means being apathetic about it. Gandhi, for example, wasn't apathetic about the abuses visited upon India by the British, yet it seems to me he exercised upekshanam consummately. So what's the difference between the healthy exercise of upekshanam and an apathy which would allow evils that should be confronted, to instead burgeon and flourish?"

ANSWER: Having just mentioned the Gita above, the predicament of Arjuna is an excellent advantage of this. There have been commentators of the Gita who denigrate Sri Krishna for encouraging Arjuna to enter the battlefield. But what do they know? They have 1) probably never been in battle, and 2) have never comprehended that the Atman in all beings is birthless and deathless. If one reads the Mahabharata, wherein the Gita is contained, one will see that Sri Krishna made every effort to mediate between the two warring clans in order to offset the war in Kurukshetra. But there was a definite evil party involved (Kaurava Clan), one that wanted lands, wealth, fame, power, and enjoyment above all else. It is an old, old story. Even God is helpless among evil beings.

So what to speak of apathy, there is the crying need that comes due to unavoidable circumstances in this world which will compel every being to stand up for what is just and righteous, as Gandhi did, in his own way. It could be, that when you have the fate of nations hanging in the balance, rather than just a few hundred-thousand chariot drivers and foot soldiers, and you want to stop nuclear-tipped missiles from destroying an entire world instead of one battlefield, you may want to employ a subtler technique and some diplomacy.

But it all should be done in equanimity, upeksha, not with anger, revenge, or lust for power in the mind. Otherwise dire karma will develop, and that will show up in the nation's near future, affecting its prospects.

QUESTION #5: "As you describe, there are four major Shaktis; but is the Kundalini a fifth? Or is it an expression of one or more of the other Shaktis?"

ANSWER: Rather, Kundalini Shakti is the foundation for the other four. She is their wielder.

QUESTION #6: "You sometimes speak of beings who are 'past Masters.' What is the full sense of this term?"

ANSWER: They are beings who have attained enlightenment many lifetimes ago and, additionally, beings who are "Ever-Perfect," called *Nityasiddhas*, and who never erred by way of karma and ignorance in the first place. According to Sri Ramakrishna, an *Avatar,* His chief disciple, Swami Vivekananda, is one of these — a Nityasiddha. These are usually *Videhamuktis,* beings who will not enter form again. But if a great Soul, such as an Avatar (whose business it is to return to earth periodically), can talk a Videhamukta into coming to earth, then one sees a remarkable soul such as Swami Vivekananda. There are several beautiful songs about this relationship and how Ramakrishna convinced Vivekananda to enter form again for the *"highest good of all sentient beings."*

QUESTION #7: "In one of your talks, when speaking of meditation on Ishvara, you say that one must also be able 'to know when the gaze of the Ishtam' is upon one. How does one know or sense that?"

ANSWER: What it is not, is sattva. Sattva is a fine state of mind that comes upon the meditator due to his or her own doing — like an ebb in festering mixed and negative karmas, or a fructification of positive karmas — all blended with the mind's natural tendency towards occasional balance, etc. No, the "gaze" of the Beloved is unmistakable. It confers deep Peace, Bliss, and a Grace that cannot be accounted for by "ordinary" spiritual means like sadhana. Having this gaze fall once, the seers say, causes the embodied being to *"....cut oneself in the image of God,"* to make oneself a candidate for highest Realization.

T. H. from Oregon writes:
QUESTION: "What is the relationship between the Four Noble Truths and the Eight-fold Path?"
ANSWER: The fourth Noble Truth *Is* the Eightfold Path. Please review this great system for clarity.
QUESTION #2: "What does it mean to have an unripe ego?"
ANSWER: Selfishness is the key word here, along with the inability to actuate self-surrender to God. All the ugly manifestations that rise out of a selfish person are sure signs of immaturity and, if left unchecked, give rise to the tendency to actually commit violence against other beings — they who are the children of God, awares or unawares. But the increasing ability to serve God in all beings (Karma Yoga) gradually matures the ego, and that ego then transforms itself further into a ripe ego that eventually surrenders itself to the Lord.

Sharanagata, self-surrender, is thus an important element in the bhakti yoga path, and really, in all the yogas. A jnani must surrender his learning to God; a karma yogi/yogini must surrender the fruits of his/her works; and the meditator has to surrender all progress along the path of contemplation in order to transcend or sidestep that rascally ego that pops up just prior to the greatest spiritual achievement of all — the merging of the apparently individualized self into Brahman, called Nirvikalpa Samadhi.

QUESTION #3: "Who am I to pray to?"
ANSWER: Good question. Since the Formless Reality is beyond prayer, praying, and prayee, that only leaves Ishvara/Ishvari as the recipient of our inmost prayers. That is our Chosen Ideal, the one we select as our highest expression of God with form. A point should be made, though, that Ishvara is beyond

idols, gods and goddesses, guardian angels, and beings of that ilk. And it is certainly of a much different character than that rascal that most beings pray to, whether they know it or not, the personal ego. Finally, one can pray to the higher Self, Atman, but that is where meditation comes in. When one sees that all has come out of the Self, what reason will there be to pray for things?

Thus, the happy meditator gazes with delight upon the fullness of his/her own Being, content with what is, while others only languish foolishly in maya, running after and wishing for wispy dreams.

QUESTION #4: "Why is it that so many beings are born in animal bodies, and so many others are confined within the realm of disembodied spirits? Is all this by choice? Or is it that Spirit remains unknown to them as they occupy these stations. Or is it their stubbornness that makes them fall into these lower realms?"

ANSWER: All three! To embody is indeed a matter of personal choice, being that it is accomplished by the individual. And they embody, for the most part (the illumined excluded), because they think there is something that they have not got in their original state. After they enter form, the various enticements there, though not comparable to the Bliss of Brahman, attract them to mere imitations of Reality.

But as for animals, that is another matter. There are differing opinions. It is evident that the more advanced animal forms take on similar characteristics as the humans. Such apparent evidence has given rise to the idea that man came from animals via evolution. Vedanta, and other refined systems of Enlightenment, make it clear that this is untrue. Even Christ made the distinction between the two realms when He said, *"Birds have nests, and foxes have holes, but the son of man hath no place to lay his head here."* Vedanta has it that the human being is divine by origin, and actually is originless. Pure Consciousness has no birth. It is eternal. The body it takes on may go through changes, but it is suspect whether those changes include taking animal bodies at all. One wonders when seeing a dog, or a close pet, and thinks there is a soul in there. There is no doubt a more developed brain there than in most other animals, and that gives us a clue. The human brain harbors memories; the dog's brain contains instincts and other conditionings. The idea that it can evolve to human status is a popular one among those who believe in rebirth.

But whatever the case, the real point is the human being — *"....man, the highest form, meaning in Sanskrit, manas, thought — the animal that thinks, and not the animal that senses only."* Dogs dream about chasing rabbits and such, but man can dream about heaven, education, refinement of all manner. At the time of death a human being can (and should) direct the mind towards God, towards higher Consciousness. He can do so because he has learned from his/her master to study wisdom teachings, to practice devotions, to meditate, and to reach for Enlightenment.

About disembodied spirits, they are mere fragments of consciousness. As such, they are illusions, really — vague dreams in the process of working themselves out. They will move to their source, and when they merge there it will be as is they never existed, for they never truly did. "Projections from somewhere else" is a fitting description for them.

But please do not conclude from what I am writing at present that there are not animals or disembodied spirits that are a unique variety. One wise Lama told me once that when he lived in Tibet as a young boy, he was very friendly and compassionate to the farm animals he lived around. In his older age he said he saw those souls in some of his students many decades later. Well, the question arises, what is it that gets embodied? Conditioned awareness, no doubt. So what occurs when such conditioning gets unconditioned? Empty mind, Pure mind, Buddha mind, No mind. Humans, animals, insects, plant life, spirits — they are either all Brahman or they are as if nothing.

QUESTION #5: "Would you agree that as long as we live in the world, the saying 'my heart belongs to God and my hands belong to work' is a good one?"
ANSWER: It is as good a motto as any for proceeding in the work of the refinement of our being. But add to it, "My mind and senses must belong to me!"

Sanatanand from Hawaii writes:
COMMENTS: "This new chapter offers to me an opening of the door to an actualizing and deepening of yogic development. The previous chapter, while comprehensive in its explanation of the philosophy and engendering an understanding of the overall underpinnings of Yoga, didn't really help as much in defining and explaining the techniques of the practice. Though this new chapter has only just begun, already I see the steps to be taken and the work to accomplish the unveiling of the inner light being offered. I have come to see the importance of the five kleshas mentioned in this current reading. They are something I consult frequently in my daily life. For the most part, I feel I have a pretty good handle on them, yet it is most useful to hold up the mirror to reveal the work within yet to be done. Your explanation of the aspects to focus on with regard to the study of scripture and the practice of contemplation are good pointers to help hone my own sadhana."
QUESTION: "My question, though, is in regards to something I have been contemplating. It is interesting that today in class you made a mention of the paths of Vedanta and Tantra merging, and also the enrichment that occurred in Buddhism as it was introduced into Tibet, and the value of that synthesis. I have been exploring the spiritual and monastic tradition of Shaolin Kung Fu. I originally began the practice in wishing to adopt a spiritual discipline. It does have its physical aspect, yet at its core it springs from deeply spiritual roots. In my study and practice over the years I have done some reading about the spiritual aspects. Where I studied the actual practice, not much of the actual philosophy was taught. It was experiential, and I learned much useful to spiritual life. Recently I have encountered a book written by a group of expatriated Shaolin grandmasters who go into great depth in the explanation of the methods of Kung Fu and its relevance to Buddhism and Taoism. I wish to increase my understanding of this aspect, as it is the focus for why I wished to study it in the first place, and it is the essence of what I wish to pass on as I teach others. Now,

what came to light, which I would like to inquire of you is this. First, to maybe put this in better context, I should mention that the type of Buddhism that was practiced was Chan Buddhism. And I do remember you stating that Vedanta and Buddhism are really much the same thing. What was mentioned in the book was that though they believed in reincarnation, they did not believe that the soul reincarnated into another body. I would very much like to rectify my understanding of the nature of this belief, and how these two different ideas might merge in an encompassing overview. As always, I appreciate your penetrating insights in helping me along my journey."

ANSWER: Knowing little about Shaolin Kung Fu, I cannot speak for their belief in reincarnation, and what that entails. But it sounds as if you have a good source or sources to refer to in your search there. Suffice to say, however, that Yoga and other Indian darshanas, including Buddhism, sport not only "belief" in reincarnation, but vast knowledge of it. Then again, there are different schools and interpreters of Yoga, Vedanta, and Buddhism. so their views and stances vary, and sometimes even stand against one another in the actual dynamics of it.

When you state here that the Shaolin belief is that there is reincarnation, but not into other bodies, it does not seem sensible. Where else is the soul to reincarnate if not into other forms? Otherwise, there is only formlessness, wherein the soul ceases to incarnate completely, i.e., Moksha or Mukti. In other words, where is this myriad of souls coming from if not from other forms — so long as they are interested in or bound into the worlds of form, anyway. Some Buddhist schools aver that there is just rising and falling, rising and falling, endlessly, but that no soul/personality is constant in this process. Possibly this is what is meant by the statement you referred to? Whatever the case may be, if you would like to read more and write back with clarification on what the Shaolin monks believe in this regard, that would be interesting.

Ekendra (formely R.W. prior to SRV initiation) from South Carolina writes:
QUESTION: "In contemplation of these verses, for some reason I think of the chakras. The sun appears to rise and set each day, so too does the moon. Yet they don't really move, it is the earth that moves. The sun brings light, warmth and nourishment to the plants that give food and oxygen. And, while the moon merely borrows light from the sun, and helps us by controlling the ebb and flow of tides, cycles, etc., to me there appears to be a correspondence, or representative quality of the way that Kundalini energy rises through the chakras, bringing light to those centers as it does. Somehow, too, all this reminds me of the moon as it waxes and wanes, keeping the cycle going. Because I am a novice aspirant, it is hard for me to put into words all of the thoughts and impressions that these two verses bring forth. I guess my questions would be: Are there any correlations here to speak of between the sun, the moon, and the chakras? If so, is it implied that by practicing Samyama on these heavenly bodies that the corresponding subtle centers will open up for us?"
ANSWER: There are symbolic correlations, of course. The Ida and the Pingala

nadis that circulate around the Sushumna are likened to the sun and the moon, and to the male and female energies. Meditating upon these, utilizing breathing exercises and other pertinent spiritual practices will be somewhat effective in helping to open the chakras. But soon the aspirant will move beyond symbology and want to face off with the Reality. The analogy you have called up of the sun is of nonmovement — something to be deeply contemplated in the scope of all this.

**Pada III, Sutra 29**
*dhruve tadgatijnanam* (*dhruve*, pole star; *tad*, their; *gati*, movement; *jnana*, wisdom).

*"Utilizing samyama on the pivotal star allows for knowledge of the movement of the inner cosmos."*

The past two sutras, numbers 27 and 28, and this present one, number 29, have brought in the sun, moon, and stars for contemplation. Knowing what we do about Patanjali's technique of using alambanas for gaining knowledge and destroying ignorance (fear, doubt, brooding, etc), this should not catch us off guard.

For here, references are shifting from a type of Sankhya Yoga method and procedure, to the spiritual art form of Kundalini Yoga, which begins to show up the hidden interconnectedness of all of these systems. Whereas sun, moon, and stars were a part of the meditator's inspection of the outer universe — albeit that inner symbologies were inferred — here, the inner symbologies are not only inferred, but brought forward and posited as spiritual principles of the marvelous human Consciousness. Here is not mere imagery, but visions of inner terrain that celestial bodies like the sun, moon, and stars can only hint at. We are reminded of great devotional wisdom songs, sung by luminaries who have explored these realms called lokas. Sings Ramprasad Sen of Bengal: *"Bathe at the sacred confluence of holy rivers found within the precious human body where the three spiritual nerve channels meet."*

The major Sushumna nadi with its circling nerve currents called Ida and Pingala are sun, moon, and stars in one conscious nocturnal sky. The "Milky Way" in our own solar system is an outer physical representation of that Milk Ocean of pure Shakti Essence that flows up the Sushumna towards the Sahashrara at the crown of the "precious" human head. The yogi/yogini uses a special type of honed and refined concentration called samyama to make an entrance into the Brahmanadi at the base of the spine. The effects of this move and its passage escape description via ordinary words, and even challenge the limits of an inner wisdom language like Sanskrit. In the Yoga Kundalini Upanisad there is a fine summation of this final journey, at least:

*Kundalini, heated by Agni (subtle fire/sadhana) and blown forth by Vayu (subtle wind/prana, enters the mouth of the Sushumna (Brahmanadi aperture) and pierces the form of root ignorance (Brahmagranthi). Then it ascends and pierces the second veil of Vishnugranthi at the heart, and ascends further to penetrate the subtlemost veil of Rudragranthi above the middle of the eye-*

*brows. Her powerful rise heats the blood (life-force) via contact with the sun, and dries up the moisture produced by the moon. The residue left from this purification is taken by the practitioner and imbibed. Chitta (mind and its thoughts), previously moving amongst sense objects, is now restrained there, in a high state of Peace (Ananda) and becomes devoted to the Atman. Kundalini next assumes the eight forms of Prakriti (matter) and attains Siva by encircling Him, and dissolves in Him. Rajas-Shukla (seminal fluid) thus rises up and goes to Siva on the Vayu. Prana and Apana become equal. Prana flows in all things, great and small, like fire in gold. Then the body called Adhibhautika (composed of elements) becomes Adhidaivata, focused on the tutelary Deity. Then, pure, it becomes the Ativahika — the Ultimate Vehicle that can conduct itself and others anywhere in the Three Worlds. It is free, stainless, or the nature of Chid, and becomes the Chief of all, being of the nature of Tat, That. It is released from life in samsara cycling in the delusion of time.*

By now we must acknowledge the meaning of sun, moon, and pole-star as being more than just symbols, even more than mere alambanas for our foundational meditation. Yet, it is through such principles and their cryptic references that we are given, or even stumble across in the esoteric portions of ancient scriptures, the keys to participating in our own enlightenment.

To conclude in a somewhat more simple fashion, there is an inner cosmos from which the outer cosmos has proceeded. Once knowing of it we must find it in meditation and study it in order to: 1) find the meaning of our lives in the universe; 2) to develop the ability to connect with such important truths as origins, deities, and formlessness; and 3) to reach the goal of human birth. This latter facet, called Enlightenment in this day and time, proceeds via perception of Light and Sound, or Vision and Vibration. If there be enough light emanating off of one physical sun to illumine an entire planet, then we must envision to what extent the subtle light of the inner sun, moon, and stars mentioned in these past three sutras can illumine the mind — the minds of billions of souls.

In the next lesson, set for early November after Navaratri, we will take up the subject of samyama as pertaining to parts of the body, along with their respective significances.

## Lesson Seventy-five, 11/13/12
### Pada III, Sutra 30

Poised in the middle of a host of sutras on samyama as we are, this subject, most esoteric in nature, is being exposed for our inner view, and as it is, the soul is remembering its inherent powers with regards to Yoga. Now, after comprehending the soul, its coverings, and its power of revelation, the accomplishment of putting samyama into practice remains to be done. Darshanas like Yoga and Vedanta are precision mechanisms of a philosophical nature. We have to understand them before applying them to life — both inner and outer.

And when inner and outer have been seen as two facets of one Reality, one Existence that includes all apparently separate existences, the practitioner of Yoga and the seer of Vedanta come together with immeasurable results, the signs of which indicate the end to problems that stymie spiritual progress.

In regard to these questions coming from our growing list of yogic practitioners, please find them just below, along with their respective answers:

**Questions and Answers for Lesson 75**
Avinashi from Pennsylvania writes:
QUESTION: "Clearly, certain attitudes are necessary or at least helpful in doing karma yoga. We might, for example, understand that it's mainly for our own good and not for the good of others that we practice it; and we might understand the importance of serving God in human beings rather than the apparent human beings, as they present themselves to our outward-seeing senses. My question is: what attitudes, in general and across the board, are necessary to lay a good foundation for the practice of karma yoga?"
ANSWER: Better than attitudes are actual practices, and these practices are attitudes. If we adopt the rule of engaging in all work without desire for any fruits or specific outcomes, then that is both a superior attitude and an ongoing practice. So we can learn the basics from the consummate karma yogi, Sri Krishna, as outlined in the Bhagavad Gita.
QUESTION #2: "Are different forms of work, as karma yoga, good for offsetting certain weaknesses and for developing certain aspects of ourselves? For example, very simple manual work might be good for working on basic elements of karma yoga such as attention to detail and a non-hurried manner. Direct work with the dying in a hospice, however, might not be so good for these purposes but might be helpful for other purposes. What forms of work are good for what purposes and is there a way a person can know which form of work he might best adopt if he wishes to move into the practice of karma yoga? Surely one could exercise more intelligence in this than is commonly exercised?"
ANSWER: The basic rule here, overlooked by the greater percentage of beings engaging in work, (even so-called karma yogis and yoginis), is to destroy ignorance with knowledge before entering onto the field of action. This may sound impractical to most beings, especially beginning practitioners of spiritual life. They would object and say that work itself is the best way to destroy ignorance, as it grants direct experience in the field. The problem with this opinion is twofold: first, there is the additional press of prarabdha and kriyamani karmas, which are operating and formulating more effects even as the karmi is engaging in work on the field to gain experience and expunge existing karmas. The result of this double press is seen all around us in the form of beings, even spiritual practitioners, who end up spending most of their time working and very little time in study, meditation, and worship. This results in what the Father of Yoga calls one of the nine spiritual impediments (viparyayas), anavasthitatvani — the tendency to move forward a little but fall back twice as much simultaneously — the old one step forward two steps back dance. Maya attacks from all sides,

just as green scum covering a lake returns after a few seconds after it is spread apart by the hands. In other words, one hardly notices the accrual of new karmas, as well as the surfacing of karmas from past lifetimes, as one is busy attenuating the karma in this lifetime. Thus, acquiring jnanam before entering the field of works is advised most vehemently by the seers.

The second reason why mere work is ultimately ineffectual in destroying karma is that the experiences that one receives on the karmashaya/karmakshetra are themselves colored by rajas. Action begets more of the same. It is only the wise one who, having learned of the utter futility of action in the end, has destroyed ignorance by gleaning wisdom and can thereby both act and not act, simultaneously. This is why Sri Krishna states that oft misunderstood teaching in the Gita, saying: *"Those who see action in inaction, and inaction in action, they truly see."* The wise one here, who "truly sees," is either: 1. a past master; 2. a soul who learned the dharma well in a previous lifetime and is now reborn to help others; or 3. a soul who has awakened to the superlative ways of yoga in this lifetime and is busy perfecting its means on the field of karma. The scriptures and the host of sayings of the illumined souls are replete with examples of this primary teaching of mastering Jnana Yoga before attempting the Karma Yoga. What we see in the enlightened beings on earth as that easy abeyance with the flow of works, and the ability to remain free despite shouldering a heavy burden of activities and the karmas of others, is only the result of having mastered Jnana Yoga first before entering the frantic fray of the field of karma. As Sri Ramakrishna put it, *"The expert swordsman fences with two swords — one of knowledge, the other of action. Most beings only try to heft the sword of action."*

In traditional Yoga, and sorely indicative of shortcomings of modern times and its surface practitioners, the teachings of the yamas and niyamas reflect this sound rule. Svadhyaya, alone, represents the need for the beginner to study and memorize the teachings in the scriptures in order to glean knowledge early on. A host of other problems, and the kleshas themselves, will be avoided if this is done properly under guidance from the preceptor — problems springing from the results of the nonobservance of yamas such as asteya and aparigraha. Aparigraha is not mere refusal of gifts due to strings being attached, or not owning anything; it is more that the receiving of gifts places the mind on the world and thus takes the mind off of *"thoughts of God alone."* The result is the forgetfulness of one's past lifetimes, engendering further exacerbations such as believing the world to be real and determining therefore that God does not exist. Does this not sound like the state of things today? So, Jnana Yoga — *"the greatest of all purifiers"* — first, the other yogas thereafter. For, how much can we trust the heart's devotions and the mind's meditations if there are still the defilements of ignorance in one's thoughts and emotions?

QUESTION #3: "You speak of resting in the Atman when the mind falls into the lower gunas. How is this done? Apart from realized seers who always rest in the Atman, what does this mean to the rest of us who have no easy access?"

ANSWER: Arrest the prana. Even the illumined sage cannot have darshana of the Atman very often, what to speak of the advanced practitioner. Nonduality is not candy to be given away for free. It is the highest state of Awareness, the singular one in which there is easy abidance with Formlessness. Therefore, in the name of preparedness and readiness, the seeker learns to rest the mind, its thoughts, its intelligence, and even the ego, in the all-pervasive prana, and that acts as a default zone. This is also the raising of the bar with regards to the intermediate practitioner who must learn that a few visitations to the realm of sattva are not going to be enough — not for enlightenment, not even for satisfaction. Thus does the Holy Mother, Sri Sarada Devi, advise us: *"You need peace of mind first and foremost."* To get this, as well as the *"Peace that passeth all understanding"* to come, one needs to practice, and the sign of attainment of this level of practice is the steady resting of the mind in the all-pervasive prana, called vyana. When it rests there it can then perceive the upward moving prana (udana) that, when mastered, will destroy the mind's tendency to brood, imagine, dream, desire, and otherwise drift in the many-faceted realm of sankalpa/vikalpa.

     These and other more esoteric teachings on the five pranas are entirely overlooked by today's hatha exponents, who relegate the prana to physical functions and health only. The true ashtangi (practitioner of the eight-limbed yoga) goes quickly beyond this base level of body-bound vital energy where so many beings get stuck, and realizes the immense import of the prana. The udana form of prana is the one that takes one out of the body at the time of death, so one can clearly envision the tremendous facility that its mastery implies and delivers to the freedom bound soul. Should the vyana be used only for abiding happily in the healthy body? Should the udana be utilized only for producing a few inbreaths and a couple of nice sneezes? Is that where our yoga has brought us? Is that what the Father of Yoga wants for us, for his ingenious philosophical system?

QUESTION #4: "It seems to me that becoming the witness to one's internal movements without simultaneously connecting with a higher purpose only leads to a state of drifting that is sterile at best and that, at worst, delivers us to the impulses of the senses and the power of negative samskaras. Any comments?"

ANSWER: The problem with the word "inner" is that it creates a duality wherein the all-pervasive homogenous Awareness seems to be divided into two factions — a tendency we are always trying to alleviate in nondual philosophy. Thus, "inner and outer" become a convenient way of explaining and delineating between what is gross and what is subtle or, more specifically, two of our three bodies. Stula, sukshma, and karana — the three bodies of the human being — are well named. If one meditates on the primal Word, AUM, rather than merely reciting it without knowing its meaning, one will effectively connect all outer and inner apparatus, phases, and meanings to a higher Source. One of the real excellent direct quotes from the scriptures (the rishi, Pippalada, in the Upanisads) that illustrates this perfectly, goes: *"The ignorant soul imagines the three lower nadis to be separate, and thus wanders in bondage, while the aware soul, getting wisdom from the Vedanta, does not suffer delusion from the lower states, realizing the oneness of all four of them."*

The fourth here is, of course, Turiya, beyond the waking, dreaming, and deep sleep states of a human soul. It is samadhi. By leaving the three matras of AUM separate, then, by not connecting them in meditation and therefore not "making thine eye single," the soul wanders about the three worlds (gross, subtle, and causal), ignorant of its true nature. Then, the power of the earth-bound senses, as you say above, and the construction of negative and mixed samskaras around the skewed experiences gotten from them, mount, and suffering in samsara is ongoing and hard to remedy. Thus, we must be careful to connect the dots, as well as defining terms like "inner" and "outer" in a way that is destructive of misconceptions and conducive to higher understanding.

Savitri (formerly C. S. prior to SRV initiation) from Canada writes:
QUESTION: "As I've contemplated this lesson, I see that my own experience, and something I've recognized in these last several weeks, is also contained in this sutra. It has been apparent that the Mother has been providing the perfect situation where my only course of action to avoid suffering is to go within, to seek the kingdom of heaven within, and to find the answer of alignment for my own particular Dharma. So, is the 'Polestar' that which does not change? Samyama on that should lead to the eternal Self, correct? It is the recognition of which allows one to act in alignment using jnana, and the yamas and niyamas? Meditation on this pivotal star, observing the stillness and unchanging nature of that allows understanding of that which changes around it, correct? Is the deep joy I feel underneath this Polestar peeking out into the relative world? Is the samyama you describe starting at the Brahmanadi something one does consciously? If so, it would seem this should be guided by a teacher? How do we know when we are ready to attempt this journey?"
ANSWER: Yes, it is guided by close proximity with the teacher, is to be done consciously, and anyone who has been in the atmosphere of holy company and taken the wisdom teachings is already launched into the precious journey. The only problem there being whether or not they take deeper commitment to the path through initiation, and whether they avoid the old pitfall of giving up along the way — of changing horses in the middle of the stream, as they say. Inadvertence, or that on again off again, fits and starts, kind of procedure bears disastrous results for one's spiritual life, and the quest for Enlightenment.

About doing this consciously, it begins by doing all things consciously — rising in the morning, washing with (sacred) water, preparing (holy) food, moving about the house (temple), serving others (as God), even at the workplace — everything is to be done in the dharma and with full consciousness brought to bear. It is "practicing the presence," as it has been called by some, and attempting thereby to *"see God in everything."* It is worth doing even if the beneficial results come or not, just as a purifier of everyday life and of mundane mind.

And yes, the Polestar, being Atman/Brahman, will only come into view via the huge "hubble bubble" telescope of the dharma, and the mind's adherence to it. Align the mind via the dharma, then, and look with honed intelligence and keen awareness at the Self. Inner scrutiny is demanded of the practitioner, the kind that we are engaging in utilizing this ongoing Raja Yoga study course, for instance. Also, and to cap it all off, affirm for yourself daily that you are on the path, are a practitioner of the dharma, and will soon see the death of all types and levels of ignorance in this lifetime, for that is what is happening, though we often are not aware of it. As Holy Mother has said, *"If one takes a train from Kolkata to Benares, and falls asleep along the way, all the scenery goes by unnoticed."* This is Her way of telling us that ignorance passes away unbeknownst to us; we only have to adhere to the dharma and follow through with daily practice.

Kanyakali from Hawaii writes:
QUESTION: "When I contemplate your statements regarding nature being insentient, questions often come up for me. I understand that the physical matter that makes up nature is to be considered insentient, but at the same time it seems like there is a perceptible sentiency or consciousness that permeates nature, and I wonder about that. I recently asked you this question during satsang: Since there is only One Consciousness, is it possible for one to perceive one's own sentiency flowing back from nature? And you gave me the most wonderful answer: You said, 'That's all we ever perceive!' It was so helpful for me to hear that. When that question came to me, I was thinking about the sentiency I perceive when I look into the eyes of an animal. There certainly does seem to be some level of consciousness there, but I had never really put it together before, with the One Consciousness that permeates us both, which must flow from my higher Self and return to me through the eyes of the animal. Now some of the other things we're learning about in Raja Yoga also make more sense. I can more easily comprehend how things like knowing what animals are saying, or remote viewing, etc. are possible for one who engages in samyama. And it also leads me to another question. A long time ago, when I lived in a commune in the Oregon forest, we spent a lot of time attempting to communicate with the so called "devas" or nature spirits (residing in the astral world) who are the architects of certain forms of nature. So, for example, when we wanted our carrots to grow better, we would contact the Carrot Deva, etc. (a la Findhorn). When I started learning from you about the insentiency of nature, I began to pooh-pooh all that. Now I just have to ask you, do you think it's possible that there are conscious beings who are in some way overseeing different aspects of nature, and in this manner are able to lend nature a sort of sentiency?"
ANSWER: Yes, but these beings are just like basic humans, only on a different plane of consciousness. Terms like "elementals," "intermediate plane of existence," "nether-worlds," and such, come to mind, and mentions are found of them in the Itihasa (mythological) portions of the Hindu scriptures. They are much like the gods, only on lesser planes of existence. Their realm is prana,

mostly, and they are identified with it just like materialistic people here on earth are identified with matter only. A mind could focus there, on insects, or animals, plants, etc., but consciousness focused on these levels tends to gravitate to them, and think like them, and relate there. It is a dim light that abides there, and no real answers are found in them in and of themselves. These are not really the "architects" of nature either, but rather overseers of slim veneers of it, presiding over the lesser lights of the gross pranic realm. The fanciful flights of human imagination are drawn from glimpses of these worlds and beings.

But when I hear the seers state things like *"We will crush the stars to atoms, and unhinge the universe;"* or *"I have a clear light now, free of all hocus pocus";* or *"The unreal never is, the Real never ceases to be,"* I get a whole different comprehension of Consciousness that quickly abandons the precincts of these "lesser lights and distant glares" and yearns to be free of the formative mold of nature and its endless products. Perhaps whether nature is sentient or insentient is not the real question to ask. Better than that is, where is the Source of all Light that, once beholding, man is free forever from the onerous press of name and form in constant cycles?

The Great Ones — Christ, Buddha, and others — they gave up their forms willingly. They never wanted to come into the realm of name and form anyway, and when they did they suffered considerably. To *be* Consciousness means that one never has to try and look through limited, fleshy orbs into the glazed eyes of another form of nature and attempt to recognize what is there, pondering "sentient or not?" It is all Sentient or it is not; it depends on the extent of realization of Consciousness that one possesses, or not.

But one thing is certain, they tell us: we will never fully possess our own Awareness so long as we fail to concentrate on the Essence of that Awareness. Focusing in on all manner of projections, pretenders, and posturers will only lead one astray. *"Sharpening the arrow of mind with thoughts on Reality alone"* will alone facilitate the highest end. To quote Ramprasad, *"The shimmering surface of the waters of mundane existence is hypnotic, and it is there that death is granted his fishing grounds. Quick, dive deep into the depths of your own Awareness, where death cannot go."*

To put it in another way, we should give up trying to gauge, measure, or comprehend Absolute Reality with defective and ineffective mechanisms such as the ordinary mind and senses. As long as there is dog, the mantra is "beware of dog." But as soon as there is God, the mantra becomes, "Be aware of God." In the meantime, until that Awareness dawns, let us go quickly and directly to where Awareness is refined and realized — to the illumined seers and holy company.

Akshaya Bhakti from New England writes:
COMMENTS: "In Lesson 74, I especially enjoyed the description of Grace and the elucidation of Turiya (in the reply to my own query) which I found very helpful. The chart on the 'True Meaning of Siddhi,' with the section on 'The Three Kinds of Sufferings,' ties in well with my recent efforts to overcome (not

very successfully, I must admit) a particularly long bout of sinus distress. It has been my personal "Achilles Heel" over the years. As usual, I felt really overwhelmed with tamas, not only physically, but mentally, making it even harder to find a positive frame of mind. Even thoughts of the Holy Ones seemed to be too exquisite to bear — not that I had lost faith, but that I felt unable to open the door to comfort."

QUESTION: "A thought that seemed to soothe me was that one has to endure the results of one's karma as long as one has not reached illumination. As Holy Mother has said, even her children may have to bear the burden of their karmas, although they may be greatly mitigated, like not losing a leg but feeling a thorn prick, for instance. Was I just trying to justify my lack of transcendence, or could I have been burning off some negative karmas?"

ANSWER: The embodied soul, no matter who it is, has to bear the suffering of this world whether or not they gain illumination. In fact, it was Sri Sarada Devi who said that all beings suffer, but the enlightened suffer more. That is, the enlightened are aware of two painful facts, whereas the unillumined are aware of only one. First, they are cognizant that suffering is in the nature of creation/nature/life; and second, they are keenly aware of their separation from God as long as the physical body persists. Thus, as She said, *"Forbearance is the default zone of the wise."*

With regard to karma, it is of various kinds. The enlightened still have their prarabdha karma to deal with, which is that which formed their bodies. An arrow shot from the bow cannot be called back. But all other karma has been neutralized in their case, and many of them have taken up the karmas of others in the interim.

Therefore, it might be good to know, and by way of encouragement, that thinking of the Holy Ones when we are suffering the results of karma and illness actually mitigates the intensity of it. It is also a good lesson, in that one realizes just how much power one actually has over pain and suffering, physical and mental, inside of this process. I bring this up in correlation to your next question.

QUESTION #2: "I know that lack of consistency in my practice impedes my spiritual power, that I don't have enough control of my mind yet. So if one cannot transcend, one must forbear as listed as one of the cures for physical suffering. I understand this in the worldly sense as 'toughing it out.' Would you please explain more about how to practice forbearance in a spiritual sense? Is there any particular advice you have given to others that helped them maintain peace of mind despite pain? I ask this humbly, knowing how much some of your other students have had to endure."

ANSWER: Forbearance is not all as bleak and glum as it sounds. When honed and mastered it acts also as a form of concentration that allows the mind to lift off of its troubles and sufferings. It is all a grace of the mind, since the senses that feel the suffering in the nerves are connected to the mind; otherwise, like in deep sleep, there is no pain even in a thoroughly diseased body. To control the mind and senses, then, is the best course.

Another point to factor in when considering the mind's abilities, is the power of taking time and condensing it down. As this pertains to disease and its pain, is the shortening of the duration of any given period of ill health, simply due to the mind's resilience and persistence. If the mind decides to practice forbearance in the form of transcendence, and refuses to give in to the effects of a cyclical illness, then the body responds and the result is a shortening of the actual span of the illness. A two week head cold can then be turned into a few days of experiencing the effects. One becomes aware, too, that the main brunt of the illness passes in the atmosphere of this higher mental attitude, and only some mildly adverse effects persist for the duration of the cycle. Otherwise, without forbearance and transcendence, when the soul gives way to surrender and invasion, the full brunt of the illness will pervade, and healing is also slow and impeded.

Generally, forbearance is a putting up with adverse circumstances, and results in strengthening our patience and resolve. If it is relegated only to daily life and physical suffering, then the subject becomes numb or, at best, "stoic." What we want is mastery bridging on transcendence, and for that we need to practice and bring a refined form of forbearance into our mindset, coupled with a spiritual life and practice. At that level it will mature, and thereafter not only carry us through periods of trial and challenge, but usher us into that blessed space of exaltation where suffering becomes a thing of the past.

K.D. from Hawaii writes:
COMMENTS: "In lessons 39 and 40, there are a few references to transformation that I have been pondering. They seem to contradict each other so I am seeking clarification. Here are quotes from you as well as one from Sutra II:15. 'The ability to both encounter, transform, and transcend suffering are to be studied next...' 'As far as we Vedantists are concerned, the greatest miracle is transforming the mind (not just the brain) and the character of a human being, for that mental complex...goes with one after death.' And: 'Nowhere in all the Indian darshanas were the imperfections of mankind seen as other than temporary inconsistencies in need of modification, even this transformation accomplished only at the right and auspicious time...' Then, in Sutra II:15 'The discriminating being sees pain and suffering everywhere, in the modes of nature, in the oppressive heat of ongoing transformation...' 'The principle of Aparinama...means that all transformation is illusory and does not occur in actuality. Since Brahman is birthless, deathless, and changeless, the only Reality, then no transformation is possible.'

"Everywhere around me I see transformation taking place in prakriti. A seed becomes a tree, then dies and decays into the soil. Fire turns wood to ash, lava destroys and then builds new land. And you might say that these transformations are occurring in insentient matter and the above quotes are referring to transformations in the minds and characters of human beings. Are all transformations illusion because they are all temporary and impermanent? Then, if that is the case, it seems there is nothing but transformation taking place in this world of relativity. Websters has two relevant definitions of the verb, 'transform:' 1) to change in composition and structure; 2) to change the outward form or appearance of. So an alcoholic who quits drinking may have only the appearance of transformation because the seed of alcoholism is still within the unconscious. However, a person whose mind and character have been transformed through austerities, devotion, and study has changed in a more fundamental way leading to transcendence defined as having 'risen above ordinary limits, being prior to, beyond, and above the universe or material existence." (Websters)

QUESTION: "I suppose my comments revolve around the familiar need to discriminate between what is real and unreal. Even though all of nature is simply whirling vortexes of minute particles which blink in and out of existence, and all matter is almost entirely empty space, I still walk on the earth, climb concrete stairs, drive cars, and interact with other beings who are experiencing the seeming solidity of matter. Brahman is Real, and the world is real too. Isn't that what one of Ramakrishna's disciples said after suffering some kind of accident? Isn't it our limited perceptions that create illusion, and not matter itself?"

ANSWER: Yes, precisely. Since all of the universe is mind made manifest, is thought concretized, that selfsame universe becomes good or bad, finite or infinite, real or unreal, due to the condition of the mind that projected it. The real meaning of the word "unreal" in the Vedantic estimation, is "ever-changing." Nature is the ever-changing hub, the city of the soul that rests in the boundless surrounding countryside of Brahman. It is only that we must not grasp onto what is ever-changing, but only move through that, unmoved. We must become like Brahman, the Unmoved Mover. This is the lesson that the world teaches naturally. If we do not learn this lesson, the seers have to come among us and remind; that is all. They will do so by saying that it is all a procreation of the mind, or all dreamlike in nature, or without substance, or an outright illusion, or is ultimately unreal, or is real as long as the benighted mind and senses behold it, but not thereafter — whatever it takes for us to let go.

So, all of what you write and what we read must be compared to the nondual experience of the seers. We laugh, sometimes, at the reaction of worldly people to the famous Vedantic statement of Truth which declares that *"God is Real, the world is unreal."* People immediately chafe at the idea of the world being unreal; they do not, however, breath a sigh of relief, or even jump for joy, to find out that Brahman is Real! But follow this up with the other famous statement that *"Brahman is the only Reality,"* and what is left? Only to rejoice in all of Existence as being nothing other than Brahman. To the soul doing this, both this world and the next are Brahman. In their case, however, and unlike the disbelieving soul, they are not going to get caught in the solidified world of the ever-changing Brahman. This is the one difference between the nirvanis and the samsaris.

Testing one's attachment to the worlds of name and form, then, is the effective measuring device by which a freedom-loving soul remains in a state of eternal emancipation — Moksha.

QUESTION #2 "If all transformation in Maya is illusory, then what is the Sutra II:15 referring to by stating 'the oppressive heat of ongoing transformation, all due to constant conflict residing in the mind full of unresolved mental impressions'? The words, 'oppressive heat,' are especially intriguing as a way of describing the relentless pleasure/pain cycle that ignorant beings are continually caught up in, such that even pleasure is a form of pain. Is that the only transformation that this sutra is referring to? This sutra must be referring to a discriminating being who is witnessing this oppressive transformation. Has not this being transformed his mind and ego complex into witness consciousness?"

ANSWER: Of all transformations happening here in maya, the one we are most interested in, as stated before, is that one in which the mind changes from worldly to spiritual, from earthbound to God-realized. The alchemy of this particular transformation cannot be seen with these physical eyes, like that of an admixture of chemicals in a laboratory. *"Only that one knows Brahman who becomes Brahman."* It is an inner mystery. As far as we can see, it is world-weariness that causes this change; otherwise, not even the presence of God in human form, Ishvara/Avatar, can effect such a change in very many cases. In most cases, in fact, people only fall back to sleep after the Great One "departs" for nondual climes. In other words, He did not come to cleanse the soul with His blood, to expiate our sins; He came to awaken souls to their ever-perfect nature. The former phenomenon, if it did occur to some souls, only happened on the level of transformation, not on the level of Truth. As Swamiji says about higher transformation, *"....it is less and less in the body and more and more in the mind — in man, the highest form, meaning manas, thought — the animal that thinks, and not the animal that senses only."* Unfortunately, many human minds still occupy the realm of the bestial. The transformation called death, for instance, is real to them, and brings about an end to existence — a contradiction in terms, really. Existence is eternal. Have we ever seen an end, even to the ever-changing maya and nature?

QUESTION #3: "Swamiji writes: 'It is only by giving up this world that the other one comes, never through holding onto this one.' Is it only the ego that needs this kind of clarification? Does it really matter if my mind wants to believe in transformation? Does it even matter to ultimate realization that there is any discussion of whether or not transformation takes place anywhere?"

ANSWER: It matters to that mind that is still in doubt about the Real and the unreal, the changing and the Unchanging. For instance, most beings have never heard of the Unchanging Reality. To them it is not even a consideration. Are we to say that, for the enlightenment of these souls, the lack of clarity around existence and nonexistence, reality and relativity, transformation and nontransformation, does not matter? Is not realization itself made up of such essential insights?

What to speak of this main distinction (a duality), what of the difference between the changing, the unchanging, and the Supremely Unchanging (a triputi) that Sri Krishna elucidates upon in the Gita. I know that it was a main key for understanding in my own spiritual journey, and that without it I would not be able to explain the process of enlightenment for myself, or for others. To lift off of the attachment to this world must have some distinctive markings for the aspiring soul, yes? Otherwise, what, indeed, would be the difference between the illumined and the ignorant? The scriptures and the testament of the enlightened beings throughout endless time would then have no benefit, would be useless. Enlightenment, in other words, is not a matter of unknowing, or noncaring; it is, rather, finally, that *"I know, and I know that I know."*

COMMENTS: "I have also been contemplating certain statements of Swamiji pertaining to desire and focusing on one idea. I have re-read most of the first eight chapters of Raja Yoga and two statements became leading lights and began to become interconnected. Swamiji's advice became valuable to me. He writes on page 79, *'Take up one idea. Make that one idea your life – think of it, dream of it, live on that idea. Let the brain, muscles, and nerves, every part of the body, be full of that idea, and just leave every other idea alone. This is the way to success and this is the way spiritual giants are produced.'* The other quote, from page 93, is: *'To him who desires nothing, and does not mix himself up with them, the manifold changes of nature are one panorama of beauty and sublimity.'* I came across this quote from the Rig Veda 10:129:1-7, in Yoga International magazine, and it has also broadened my understanding of desire which is a major focus of chapter 40: *'In the beginning there was neither being nor non-being, neither movement nor lack of movement. There was neither death nor life nor day nor night. Darkness alone existed and that too was veiled by darkness. Kama (desire) was the first thing to come into being. Desire is the very essence of the mind. Desire is our friend, the ground of our existence. Its light spreads in every direction. Desire is the seed of creation, the force behind every action. The knowledge from whence it came, of what it is made, the power that presides over it, and the space where it ultimately subsides is the exclusive domain of the sages.'* I decided to focus on the idea of AUM and contemplate emergence/creation/projection on the inbreath, sustenance/existence/maintenance on the held breath, and dissolution/destruction/withdrawal on the out breath. Well, I found that it is difficult to focus on only one idea, because that idea becomes connected to all other ideas. AUM is connected to everything in the universe and acts as a portal to Brahman. The unstruck sound, as the first manifestation of a desire from a formless, blissful, pure awareness, set all in motion as becoming, existing, and dissolving. So this Shakti power whose essence must also be bliss, love, and peace that has no opposite, was desire according to this interpretation."

QUESTION #4: "Was it this desire that created Mahat and Ahamkara and gave rise to the other 24 cosmic principles? Was it desire for stability, liquidity, luminosity, homogeneity, and all-pervasiveness that gave rise to the world of name and form, space, time and cause and effect? If desire is so indigenous to the mind and to existence, how can we hope to escape desire except to have the desire to have no desires? I know you listed several ways to minimize and even eliminate desire, but short of Asamprajnata Samadhi, can we safely conclude that desire is our friend as long as we only desire that which leads to dispassion as outlined by Sri Sarada Devi in chapter 40? If we identify with the seeker, are we not just falling into another egoic trap?"

ANSWER: Desire, in its primal or original form — very sattvic — is the "friend" of the realm of name and form, the manifest Brahman. In Tantra the word is *vichikirsha*. This is no base desire, as in lower existence. It is the driving force behind the union of Siva and Shakti. It is pure Love that produces pure Mind, the Mind that the Vedas are speaking about in your quote above. To paraphrase from the Tantras: *"When Shakti, the force of creation (Tattva), approaches the light of Siva (Chit), who is all Intelligence, there arises in Her the intense desire to create (Vichikirsha). This union forms the Bindu, which bursts and gives rise to Nada and Bija."* Elsewhere, we find: *"When the Bindu bursts there arises the primal sound, called Shabda Brahman, which is pure Consciousness that pervades all of creation, and which is the source of all alphabets and their letters and meanings."* It is from this Shabda that we get other tattvas, which eventually come to us as air from touch, fire from color, water from taste, earth from smell, etc.

Of course, there is much more to this process and its description, called Sristi Rahasya in Tantra, or, "the Secret of Creation" (Projection). But suffice to say, and in connection to your queries above, that we must not take words like "desire" in the conventional sense only, especially when they appear in the nondual scriptures. That is, the desire of the husband and wife for offspring comes from this same desire to create anew, but the mind and consciousness of the parents must be pure (like Lord Brahma's) and refined in order for higher qualities to manifest in/as the children. If desire is base, and acts of union are unconscious, then such desire can hardly be called a "friend," especially seeing what troubles and horrors emerge from the womb in the form of so many ignorant and evil embodied beings.

Beyond desire as the friend of creation, is desirelessness as the friend of the wise. As Holy Mother has said, *"What should we pray for? The one thing to be prayed to God for is nirvasana — the extinction of desire. That will be the last lifetime of suffering when one gets rid of desire."* So, we can call desire a friend and an enemy in the same breath, the same sentence. It all depends on what level, and in which realm, we are speaking.

FINAL COMMENTS: "I can't help but think that the whole conundrum can only be solved by understanding that life is paradoxical. There is only one Reality, Brahman, yet the world is real also, if only in a relative sense. Desire seems to fuel existence, yet only in its absence can one achieve ultimate liberation. Everything is constantly undergoing transformation in maya, yet that transformation is illusory, but only in an absolute sense. I would appreciate your comments on these final comments of mine."

RESPONSE: Here is a set of excerpts selected from the *Gospel of Sri Ramakrishna* which places the conundrum of the "Real and the unreal" in another perspective: *"In the light of Vedantic reasoning the world is illusory, unreal as a dream. The Supreme Soul is the Witness of the three states of waking, dreaming, and deep sleep. The waking state is only as real as the dream.*

*This is the realization of the jnani. But the bhaktas accept both states — the Relative and the Absolute. Still, their realization can be somewhat incomplete. It is much like the milk from a cow that eats everything in the field, indiscriminately; that milk can taste a bit funny. Therefore, the supreme devotee of God strives to know the Absolute and the Relative, the Nitya and the Lila. If the milk of your realization tastes a little funny, then simply boil it over the fire of knowledge."*

Thus do jnana and bhakti work together to bring about the ultimate synthesis of Yoga in the mind of the seeker. In order to be able to see God everywhere and in everything, the aspirant must do some extraordinary things, must pull out a few amazing tricks from the respective realms of religion and philosophy. What is more, practice is necessary thereafter and in the interim. That practice is Yoga, Patanjali's Yoga. We are in the midst of utilizing it now, in correlation with all that we are learning in weekend classes (jnana) and in weekly pujas (bhakti).

**Pada III, Sutra 30**
*nabhichakre kayavyuhajnanam* (*nabhi,* navel; *chakra,* vortex; *kaya,* belonging to the body; *vyuha,* system; *jnana,* wisdom).

*"Utilizing samyama on the navel provides knowledge of the entire body."*

Fascination with the region of the navel occurs at all levels of existence — for those seeking health and longevity, for those desirous of having children, for those wanting to tap psychic powers, for those seeking to control or increase their prana and "chi," etc. In spiritual life as well, the region associated with the navel, called the Manipura Chakra, has profound ramifications. That center *is* center; that is, it is at the center of the body, and of all bodies. To explain this statement further, the centrality of the Manipura Chakra at the navel is noted due to its pivotal function in the principle of the transition of souls after death to other levels of existence. Hundreds upon thousands of physical channels, such as nerves and vessels, connect to it, and this is true on gross and subtle levels. Nerves and blood vessels in the human body are symbolic of (and manifestations of) nadis and subtle channels of sustenance running through the spiritual body. This network, or plexus (chakra), is key to movement of all types — physical, mental, cosmic, and spiritual.

Thus, by Patanjali's mention of all that belongs to the realm of the body (kaya) and the functioning of its systems (vyuha), we are to infer that there is more to the human being than the physical aspect. The temptation, which the hathis and health-oriented beings have fallen victim to throughout the past seventeen or so centuries since Patanjali masterminded the Yoga system, is to focus in on the rasas and the dhatus — the hormones, gastric juices, and fluid essences; and the blood, flesh, bones, air, bile, and phlegm, etc. — as if it were the only area of Yoga worth considering. But what about the karanas? These are the five active and five cognitive senses and the mind. Are they only physical as well? Do the senses operate by themselves, or are their subtle "indriyas," little gods and goddesses, animating them? Is the mind only a brain? Or does thought, ego, intelligence, and memory go on after the brain decays? Put another way, if there is only one life, and the physical body is the only body, then why take the trouble to scale the eight limbs of Yoga and accomplish the abilities of samyama at all? Only to contemplate one's navel?

More likely, it is that the health of the body is important so that a human being has more time to master the eight-limbed Yoga and gain Enlightenment, which is the supreme prize of Yoga — and Vedanta, and Tantra, and Sankhya, and Buddhism, and all other religious and philosophical systems of India. For, buried beneath the search for abiding health of the body is the secret of Immortality — a superlative kind of longevity that outstrips all things physical. It even transcends mind and intellect. It even outlives the gods in their heavens. Importantly, and pertinent to this particular sutra, it transcends the ancestors, whose multi-faceted set of lokas is directly in accord with the navel center and all that it implies. As one Yoga commentator has written, *"Thousands of energy systems operate through this center, and thus samyama on that center reveals the nature of those systems. These are to be encountered, experienced, and set aside via non-attachment so as to uncover the abiding grace of samadhi."* Another commentator adds in more: *"As with all experiences under the Yogic mantle, the contemplation of this center is seen to represent both an attainment and an obstacle, and is to be duly set aside using the practitioner's power of non-attachment."* Please note the teachings in sutras 1.15 and 3.38 for more corroboration.

## Lesson Seventy-six, 12/12/12
### Pada III, Sutra 31

Our ongoing study of the spiritually beneficial and philosophically comprehensive system of Truth called Patanjala, named after its founder, is Yoga. Substitutes, there are none — particularly not the set of physical exercises and postures that people are glibly referring to as Yoga today. Our recent lessons on the principle of Samyama should make this imminently clear, in case it was not earlier, in our spiritual infancy.

Samyama is inner focus of the purest kind, intensified three times (dharana, dhyana, samadhi combined). As you know from my teachings, triputis, or triple structures, are both legend and legion in Vedanta and other Indian darshanas.

But this triputi is distinctively Yogic. In the present sutras under study, more will be gleaned from it. As it pertains to questions, placing the ability of samyama on queries such as those that follow is what brings clarity, a clarity that can be used to go deeper into subtler and subtler realms of realization. Please observe carefully and consider these questions and their answers in that yogic light.

## Questions and Answers for Lesson 76

S.P. from Oregon writes:

QUESTION: "My feeling and sensing is that Brahman and Ishvara are one, i.e., the wetness, (Ishvara) of water, and the Ocean (Brahman). And in this I sense the beauty, love, and wisdom all around and within. Yet, such a knowing should not justify or imply tamas or lassitude — an attitude such as 'if it is all God then why make choices or disallow anything?' Constant vigilance is necessary, and application of will. So both a self-surrender and a self-vigilance are required to realize our inherent perfection and the perfection of all that is. Is this correct?"

ANSWER: It is well written, and to be taken to heart. There is a vast difference between a worldly person and an intellectual, and between the intellectual and the awakened soul. Further, a substantial difference is also noted between the awakened and the practitioners, and between them and the adept. Masters and Past Masters are an entirely other league unto themselves. So it goes in this world of apparent becoming.

COMMENTS: "Yoga is the process of transformation from dull ignorance to awakened, non-dual experience, developing and refining the tools, our bodies and minds, to be clear receptors. These practices are about purification, alignment, balance, and awakening. In so doing we connect with/realize the all-pervading prana and learn how to consciously work with it in its five aspects, specifically in our own body/minds. This learning is all to better realize God. I have many mental questions and excitements around akasha, prana, prakriti, Shakti, Shiva, Ishvara, and there are many answers in Swamiji's chapter and your lessons. But I feel like it is best for me to focus on the practice and the purifications and allow the mental understanding to grow over the course of the class. I think I feel most nervous over how to both honor the "austerities" of practice, and develop a commitment to this path as you are offering it, while being true to the living understanding of my life so far (60 years) — how to integrate them all. I know that if I don't honor both, I will lose my constancy."

RESPONSE: It is well thought again. Perseverance is the main component of success in spiritual life, at least any long-lived success. The only other serious consideration that we (teachers from India in the West) have noted amongst the Westerners is the lack of qualification before one sets foot on the path. Ideally, our "dream" devotee, our avowed aspirant, would combine these two — proper orientation at the outset, and long-lived self-effort until the goal is reached. It seems that everything else — distractions, attachments, allurements, karmas, samskaras — would be effectively eliminated, in turn, if these two elements were present early on.

Since that is not the case, in most cases, we (teachers) try to undermine that which is doing the undermining, or turn maya back upon itself. The Tantric element is helpful here, like turning anger into anger at the lack of realization, or transforming lust by lusting after Truth, etc. The Vedanta, being sword-edged, this hard to rise to, needs some time to work its magic in the West. That time is bought and well used by implementing tantric teachings into the mix.

God knows, that Sri Ramakrishna was always doing so, as instanced in the *Gospel of Ramakrishna.*

Nischaya from Oregon writes:
QUESTION: "In our SRV prison ministries I have undertaken we are still studying Chapter 2 of the Gita. I have a question about sloka 25 and the commentary by Swami Chidbhavananda. Essentially it is addressing the nature of Atman and how it is beyond the perception of the senses. Since Akasha is the only element that does not undergo modification, then logically it would be the best element to study in order to attempt to understand the qualities of Atman. Swami states that "Elemental Akasha" is insentient, and Atman or Chit-akasha is sentient. First of all, Chit-akasha, being synonymous with Atman, is a mind-expanding concept and worthy of contemplation. So what is the connection between elemental Akasha and Chit-akasha? One idea comes to my mind concerns vyana, or all-pervasive prana. It also struck me that the Sankhya system and it's 24 cosmic principles does not explicitly mention or list prana. Would you say that the concept of prana is a missing link in the Sankhya system?"
ANSWER: "As to your question, the connection between the bhutakasha and the chittakasha is similar to connecting up the elements to the senses, then to the subtle senses, then to mind. The thing is, is that these connections have to be made consciously, then enforced over time via meditation (and samyama) until the entire system works together. Prana is very definitely the connector, which is why we need control of it first, if possible. Who can transcend the gunas, for instance, without controlling the prana?

The prana is inferred in the Sankhya system, though not included in the list, and that is why we must go to Yoga and to the Kundalini system in order to find out more about our subtle energy and its impediments. A dinner table setting may be missing one or two items, and so we look into our old dinner setting to find that missing spoon and fill it in before company arrives. Thus, philosophically, we study several systems, and must have the mental acuity and spiritual flexibility to overlap systems and come forth and find just what we need for consummation.

As you know, I have called the lack of understanding of prana a missing link in today's living being, and in our western culture overall. Revealingly, it is deeply connected to the emotional level of existence (ancestors, loss/gain, dying, etc), and it is the emotions that will receive the first benefit from the act of controlling the prana. But do not stop there, oh practitioner, else you will run the risk of stumbling and falling into the realm of the occult. For, when one masters a little of the prana, then is when those little "miracles" occur, and the novice gets fascinated with them. Resist that temptation and plum the depths of the mind in order to master the psychic prana. It is there that higher visions begin to show themselves up. Go beyond them as well.

In this yogic/sankhyic methodology the links will become clear, and when they do one can easily see the lack of sentiency in matter, like in objects and in space. What to speak of physical space, the akasha will soon come up for examination and found to be lacking its own Light as well. Oh, reflected light there will be; that is what fools the onlooker into believing that the elements are living — a mistake which will then give rise to believing the world itself to be real, which then turns into the forlorn conclusion that God does not exist; that the world and the body and its one lifetime is all there is. Rubbish! There is too much real meaning in everything to fall for that old trick of the maya-influenced mind. Even the very object one rejects as being insentient holds the secret of Reality in it. It only has to be inspected properly, and with detachment. That is why the Vivekachudamani states, *"It is the apt and final conclusion of the Vedanta that all is Brahman, time, space, living beings, and the world...."* Brahman is in everything, but can never be limited to any thing. Find the truth of this through your yogic practice, then find Enlightenment already within you upon realization of that truth.

Avinashi from Pennsylvania writes:
QUESTION: "What is the difference, if any, between jyoti as intelligent light, and Shakti? If there really is no difference, will you unite these two in my understanding?"
ANSWER: The Ultimate Shakti, called Mahashakti, is the owner and purveyor of that Light called Jyoti, the Light of Consciousness. As the Tantras state, *"It is She who placed the Atman in all beings, all things."* If She, as Sri Ramakrishna said, is the wetness in water, the light shining in a gem, the heat in fire, then why not take this as an invitation to experience Her cooling "wetness" in the roiling Sea of Dynamism, Her scintillating Light in the boundless Ocean of Awareness, Her comforting warmth in the dazzling Fire of Yoga.

As this pertains to "intelligent" light, again, it is Hers. Just as you see and feel nothing but intelligence emanating off of the seers, the sages, and your guru, just so does this selfsame intelligence radiate off of Her august Presence. One can hardly find a difference.
QUESTION #2: "In the Sanskrit term, 'kamini kanchana,' or 'woman and gold,' which word refers to woman and which to gold? And since good pronunciation is important to me, which syllables are stressed in pronunciation?"
ANSWER: This is the Bengali phrase, really meaning lust and gold — never meant to be a denigrating term about women, who are Shakti. Of course, many women, who are not real women yet, are avidya-shaktis, who are themselves not only addicted to lust and gold, but who are walking emanations of them. One has only to walk through the shopping malls of this country to see them in droves, going about the business of "storing up for the future" and amassing possessions. In that way, Swami Nikhilananda's choice of the translation, women and gold, in the Gospel of Ramakrishna, is not inaccurate.

As to pronunciation, the accent falls on the first syllable — KAmini KANchana. Kamini is lust (kama); kanchana is gold/wealth.
QUESTION #3: "In the last RY Lesson, you write that 'By leaving the three matras of AUM separate, and by not connecting them in meditation, and therefore not "making thine eye single," the soul wanders about the three worlds

(gross, subtle and causal) ignorant of its true nature.' A little further on you write we must be careful to 'connect the dots' or 'suffering in samsara is ongoing and hard to remedy.' I'm not sure I see why connecting the matras, (which must of course mean connecting what they refer to or signify), can bring realization and release. Is it as basic as finally connecting everything we experience to Consciousness/Brahman, so as to be released by realizing that 'Everything is Brahman?' Or is this answer too simplistic or brief?"

ANSWER: No, it is a good answer you state here. But, as you say, it is too "simplistic" for most people to accept, or to satisfy the soul seeking nondual Truth through profound means. If one were really qualified, prepared over time to really receive the intended impression, on the spot, then the statement "All is Brahman" would throw one into Samadhi, no doubt. Two farming stories of the Great Master illustrate this conundrum. I call them Complexity, Profundity, and Simplicity.

"*A farmer once bought a track of land, and needed to irrigate it for his crops. He faced many days, even weeks, of hard labor with the shovel. As he was inspecting his newly acquired land one day, he accidentally bumped his foot against a hidden hose that was jutting up slightly from the earth, and water started flowing out in gushes. His problem was over, as was his forthcoming effort.*" This story illustrates the condition of that mind that has accomplished much practice in a previous lifetime(s). In the present existence a slight occurrence will be all that it takes to bring the fruits of this effort to the fore.

The second story is: "*a farmer once spent many days digging irrigation ditches from the river to his field. He dug them, but left them blocked at the river end so that no water would flow in as of yet. Then, when he had all of the ditches dug, he simply walked about and knocked down those blockages of dirt with a stick, and water flowed readily into the whole field.*" This story relates how intense self-effort leads to the final and simple effect of Truth flooding the entire land of Awareness. In the first story, all is simple. In the second, all is profound. What we do not want is for confusion or complexity to invade our lives — not by undue labor or by wrong method with its ill-advised instruction. This pertains to the last sentences of your question above.

As for the three matras of Om, it is not hard to draw a correlation here. It is certainly one of our favorite teachings in the scriptures, this instruction about the A, U, and M and their connection to Turiya.

If we speak in terms of precious connections, how about A stands for "action;" U stands for "understanding;" and M stands for "meditation." According to Gaudapada and others, the A is our waking state (action) and it must be mastered before we can perceive that "this dream has come from that dream — dream #1 from #2" When we know this through mastering our waking state, then we can begin to invest our dreams with a stable consciousness rather than a restless one, and dreams become lucid — reflectors of Light. Thus, the U of AUM gets taken under inspection in a new light (understanding), and so many insights come to the fore! — not the least of which is the real point — that there is an observer of both states, and "Thou Art That."

This understanding will attract one more towards meditation, towards spending more time inspecting both the nonself and the Self, and noting the distinction there. From the position of a calm and deep meditation, one can look both outwards towards the worlds of becoming, and inwards to the Light of Brahman — signified by, what else, the Word, AUM.

Sadhana in this lifetime is to be based upon understanding that *"....In the beginning was the Word,"* revealing that the Soul, Atman, is beyond the Word, transcendent of the beginnings, middles, and endings that "originate" there (A, U, & M).

Almost no one knows this — traditionalist, philosopher, aspirant. And by not knowing it they *"leave the three matras of AUM unconnected, and wander about the three worlds (A, U, and M — waking, dreaming, and deep sleep) in ignorance."* This most precious teaching of the dharma is the superlative realization of the Nondualists, like Gaudapada, and why my own guru, Swami Aseshanandaji Maharaj, began many of his discourses by stating, *"I salute Gaudapada, for he was an illumined Soul."*

QUESTION #4: "When effecting involution through meditation on the alambanas in Sankhya, I find little problem is returning manas to buddhi, buddhi to ahamkara, and so on; in other words, I have little problem working with the higher alambanas. But working with the lowest ones elude me. I've worked at returning both the bhutas and the sense-organs to the tanmatras in order to 'involve' them upwards, and when the tanmatras have been the unifying element, this has seemed to work well. But directly 'involving' the panchabhutas, from the lowest to the highest, (earth to water, water to fire, fire to air and air to space), has not worked for me. It is difficult for me to see how these 'elements' could come out of the highest one (akasha) or be reabsorbed back into it. Sometimes I've toyed with seeing these 'elements' not so much as elements per se, but as states of elements, which has yielded results. But truly speaking, I'm still stuck. Will you offer me necessary understandings?"

ANSWER: It is a matter of gross to subtle, even on this basic level. If we agree that everything evolved out of the subtle, then it stands to reason that everything can be traced back to its source in the subtle. As we know, the gross elements have subtle components, as do the gross senses. In the case of the elements, they all exist in the Bhutakasha, the space of objects. If we look back in lesson #64 of this study course, we can observe the five akashas and see how each one is stored back in the other, gross back in to subtle back in to causal, like little Russian dolls. Think of the gross elements in that way, and meditate in that fashion.

Lord Kapila has stated in his Sankhya philosophy: *"Sancharah prati sancharah — There is a chain of transition from unmanifested or nonevolved prakriti to manifest prakriti and its evolutes, ending in the grossest element, earth. There is also a reverse transition of evolutes ending in dissolution into unmanifested prakriti."* It sounds as if you have little problem with the upper echelon of this transitional process. So, taking that as your clue, simply apply the same rules to the five elements. That everything here comes out of space is not hard to understand, especially when science and astronomy are thinking in terms of the function of black holes and their power to produce and withdraw forms of matter. Space carries all, envelopes and pervades all. What we call ether nowadays is actually a powerful clue to not only the transitional process (evolution), but to the reverse transitional process (involution) as well — something we tend away from due to fear of death, belief in a void, etc.

Meditation of the essential function of each tattva, then, is not only scientifically practical, but also cosmologically revealing. The as yet "far cry" of Enlightenment in this context is brought closer to bear on the human mind when it contemplates and comprehends the order of things from the causal to the gross — from The Word on out to a mountain of earth and stone.

QUESTION #5: "At nearly 59 years of age, I have almost no experience of the deaths of close loved-ones. People who I was not close to have passed, but the people I feel a deeper love for are all still here. This is a little bizarre for my age, but it is the case. So please clue me in on ideas and attitudes that will help me keep my balance when inevitable bereavement comes. The practice of doing mantra with the loved-one in mind will be helpful, I'm sure, not just for the loved-one, but for me, too, since this will allow me to give and express my love rather than suffering helplessly. But any other tools you can offer me, that I can use when the time comes, would be appreciated. Above all, I do not want my sadhana to be interrupted and, without adequate coping skills, I'm afraid this might be the first casualty."

ANSWER: This is a question that eventually comes forth from the mouths of many aspiring beings. That is, when real love for family and mankind visits the heart, rare and seldom seen in this world, then the considerations turns towards the higher good of others more than oneself. Such concern brings the likes of a Vivekananda to earth, and causes him to linger long after the body falls away, i.e., *"I will be reborn a thousand times if I can but help one soul to get free."*

And in this process of all moving towards death — actual death for the ignorant, assumed death for the enlightened — the sensitive soul also feels the need to ground him or herself in a method and/or mindset that is as impervious to the insinuation of death as is possible. The mantra is excellent, to be sure, but unknown to many, its benefit is really to help souls who have departed. That is, if one grounds himself in mantra practice early on, and death makes a close visit to one's family or circle, the practice will stand him in good stead.

But the real facility is to use the living mantra to send healing, peace, and light to the departed. Breaking down and weeping, though human, and perhaps natural in a sense is, well, lets admit it, a bit selfish. They say such grief even holds the departed soul back from its intended trajectory inwards. Whatever the case, in any given case, the time for grieving must end. The problem here is that by the time one's grief subsides, so has the auspicious time to help the departing soul reach its highest and deepest destination. Therefore, to steel the mind with the singular teachings — everything from the teachings of impermanence, to instructions on the birthless, deathless nature of the Soul, or Atman — must be accomplished early on. When the time comes to face bereavement, then, not only will the mind be able to forbear, it will also be able to be of service to the freshly departed soul (mind) of the loved one.

Great souls, they say, do not have special feelings for any individual; they love all, and love them equally. As Swami Aseshananda sometimes said, "We do not have sweethearts in Vedanta." Thus, these souls are not hampered in their service of God in mankind by emotions and personal sufferings. This does not mean that they do not have feelings, or that they do not feel the loss and absence of their closest companions; they feel them more keenly than others. It is more that their wisdom and their realization — what to speak of their insight into the internal movement of souls — is informed and intact. This is the best way to live in the realm of death, and better still is to be born with such attainment. And that all depends on how we act, or react, to the challenges we face in the present lifetime, the deaths of our loved ones being one of them.

May the Divine Mother of the Universe be gracious to us, and grant us the double boon of auspicious timing and great strength and balance in the face of bereavement.

QUESTION #6: "What is the difference between rasa and bhava. They seem like synonyms, but I feel they are not."

ANSWER: These two words, and words like them, have a very wide scope, and can be used from everything from the superficial to the sacred. Rasa, for instance, refers to the taste in foods, the sound of music, and other sensual occupations. In this way it accompanies worldliness, and forms the justification and the excuse for humans to engage in trying to satiate appetites for the sake of pleasure. On the other hand, rasa has connotations that associate it with everything from the power in the senses, to the exquisite bliss of Awareness (samarasam). Here, it can be used as a foundation for meditation (alambana) that not only helps the mind trace origins, but also clears up the very habit of enjoyment that it created. The meaning here is that there is a power in taste which, when contemplated and employed for higher purposes, leads one beyond mere enjoyment of the senses and introduces one to the realm of the subtle.

The word bhava can also be treated in this fashion. It can be a mere passing mood, or the profound effect of a devotional experience. One can take it as a name, as in, "Hello, my name is Bhava," or it can be the name for a particular kind of samadhi itself — as in Sri Ramakrishna saying, *"I was in Bhava Samadhi at the time....."*

Savitri (formerly writing as C.S.) from Canada writes:

QUESTION: "Thank you for Lesson 1. I read it with great interest several times. Swamiji talks about the value of experience in spiritual life. I am so happy to read this! He speaks about how it is not just for some, but for all to experience spiritual truths, and then use the rational mind (and Heart I would say) to validate the wisdom of the ancients. Perhaps what I experienced when I awoke and remembered where I had been, is I had been in one of the lokas described in your chart – maybe Mahar Loka? The experience has stayed with me and allowed a kind of detachment, while still being able to be responsible

in the material world. Is this possible?"
ANSWER: Is it possible to be in Mahar Loke, or is it possible to have detachment and still function well in the material world? — I am not sure which you mean here. I can say about both, however, that worlds (lokas), spans of time (kalas), levels of space (akashas), and series of happenings (karmas) should all be seen as intersecting and overlapping, like the case of a layer cake as opposed to a line of cookies. The linear view of things and events is an inferior view.

When we sleep we leave the Bhurloka, the realm of physical objects, and often have profound experiences, many forgotten upon waking up. Where does the mind-soul go then to experience these? In order to know, we must study and meditate to hone the intellect and reveal the true Self within. Sleep and dreams do not satisfy the soul; do not convince it of deeper realities. They are as wispy, transparent, and undependable as the waking state of this outer life.

So, outer and inner form another problematic duality for us, the only solution for which is wisdom and meditation. We must move from the stage of practicality to the station of practitioner. Then, and then only, will dreams and experiences translate themselves into realization. We will see all in One and the One as all. All lokas, then, are now. All beings, are here. All of time exists in one, eternal moment. All karma is relative.

QUESTION #2: "You speak of how yoga brings not only 'good,' but also 'bad' experiences. My experience has brought me to valuing both as seemingly equal in what they cause me to examine in pursuit of Self. I recently had a perception shift of seeing my whole experience with a close friend as Mother acting through him to give me experiences I needed for spiritual growth. At the same time, while I don't condone all the actions that this friend took on the worldly plane with others, I am grateful for the 'mighty whack' – a term that often comes up in poems. It is the play of light and darkness. I more easily and quickly am able to return to a place of equanimity these days, and have a look at what happened in relation to scriptures — the few that I know or have access to. Reading the 18 chapters of the Gita have helped immensely. And here I have a question about purification. If very little comes from outside oneself, repeating the mantra or Divine names increases the higher vibrations within the self, slowly working to cancel out the negative vibrations within from samskaras, karma, or negative deeds, thoughts etc. from this life? Is purification possible from without?"

ANSWER: Not only possible, but necessary, especially at the beginning And in natural dharmic life, such purification is less of a task to be accomplished and more of a boon to be engaged in. The young Hindu child joins in gleefully to perform puja, worship the gods, and learns how to sanctify the food and turn it into prasad before consuming it. All the while she is purifying the senses, and with senses rendered into a pure state, she is already far advanced over most souls as she beholds the world as nothing other than Brahman in form. Whatever naivete and immaturity that is in her at that time will get refined later, as she encounters higher wisdom, deeper sacrifice, nondual worship, and intense sadhana. From the outer to the inner to the transcendent — it is an ancient process guided by eternal principles, and equally ancient beings.

QUESTION #3: "With regard to the fourfold mind, does jnana yoga take place in the Buddhi alone? What allows Ahamkara to experience detachment? When it does experience detachment, does this leave a space for compassion?"

ANSWER: In order of your questions, Jnana Yoga mainly pertains to the buddhi, though manas and chitta are obviously included. Mind, its thoughts, and its intelligence are a major triputi, while the ego is just "along for the ride," as they say. But even the ego, if it is ripened via worship and sadhana, takes a liking to jnanam. When that occurs, the last resistance to what is entirely good for the mental complex breaks down, and the usual result is peace, bliss, and realization — quite often in that general order.

And about the ahamkara, it is, again, when it is ripe, that it feels both the need and the value of detachment, vairagya. At first, this detachment is at its early stages, and compassion is not so much its concern or focus. The personality is still working on itself. Please look back to see the chart, The Nine Levels of Awareness (detachment) in Aspirants, in Volume 1 of this literary work.

QUESTION #4: "It occurs to me that self-surrender, self-effort, and Grace somehow go hand in hand? Is this an accurate statement, and are there any scriptures that support this?"

ANSWER: It is more that the direct words and experience of the seers state this. You have probably heard the saying via me, since I often repeat it, as it was a teaching given by Swami Aseshanandaji all the time in his discourses. It goes along with the teaching that self-effort is grace, which is what becomes clear once the aspirant gets further into his or her practice. Looking back, and deepening more and more as the nondual state of mind settles in, the aspirant simply cannot remember a time when the grace of Guru and Divine Mother were not present, guiding and fulfilling. As Swami Vivekananda has put it in his beautiful poem to the Divine Mother, which Swami Aseshanandaji also used to recite by heart at his pujas:

*She who, since birth, has ever led me on*
*Through paths of trouble to perfection's goal,*
*Mother-wise, in Her own sweet playful ways,*
*She, who has always through my life inspired my understanding.*
*She, my Mother; She, the All, is my resort,*
*Whether my work o'erflow with full fruition, or with none.*

QUESTION #5: "Are emotions also part of the puzzle of vrittis? I see how mastering the yamas & niyamas decreases the control emotions exert on us from personal experience. Arjuna was reacting with emotion in the chapter Arjuna's Grief. Does Krishna impart the highest knowledge which dissolves the suffering resulting from only moral teachings and emotions?"

ANSWER: Highest knowledge is not meant for dissolving emotions, since people with uncontrolled emotions do not comprehend higher knowledge when it is given to them. It is meant for dissolving hidden things, like subtle karma and samskaras. Still, one can see how Arjuna's mind clears up, and his depressed state (vishada) passes swiftly at the Great Master's instruction and discourse. Usually, however, and in people less valorous than Arjuna, some basic work on the ego and emotional body have to be undergone before wisdom of the non-dual type can be digested properly. This is the reason why so many in the West today are as if deaf when they hear higher instruction and Vedantic teachings. The emotional body is still too weak and raw from matters such as root ignorance, poor upbringing, egotism, immaturity — in short, traumatic turmoil and dire drama in their lives. They need dharma, not drama. But how can they recognize the former from the imbalanced emotional states they are always in? It will take some lengthy work on the outer level before the inner world can be approached with any success.

QUESTION #6: "I notice that detachment from Ahamkara assists the mastery of Yamas, Niyamas, and Asana. Then it's a piece of cake after that. Does the mastery of Brahmacharya in thought, word, and deed ultimately have to do with not creating desire from the gross to the most subtle in any aspect of the material world?"

ANSWER: Not really. Desire is much more than sexual in nature. There are souls who have no real desire for sexual activity, and for whom lust is not a problem. Brahmacharya has mostly to do with steadiness, with faith and fealty to a high Ideal. Giving up the sexual act is only a cutting down of possible distraction from that. All beings, not just monks, can benefit from brahmacharya. If sexual energy is not squandered, steadiness is the result. The "piece of cake" part is then taking it up the spine via pure food, mantra practice, and spiritual exercises — sadhana. With steadiness on one's side, the fruits of one's spiritual life should come swiftly. That is why Swamiji states that "....*one should be able to become a yogi in six months....*" He is presuming that you are maintaining celibacy, for a time at least, as you practice Yoga.

Sanatanand from Hawaii writes:
QUESTION: "In the Raja Yoga study, it is pointed out that ignorance is the field of all error. It is explained that this ignorance is the source of egoism, desire, attachment, aversion, and clinging to life. This error is a result of our confusing the body for the Self, believing that death of the body is the end of the Self, and that these and other illusory aspects are from the lack of understanding of the true nature of how things are. My understanding is that Vedanta doesn't affirm that there exists an evolutionary process, at least as far as humans are concerned. My question is, then, as our nature is that of bliss and purity, how is that we formed these samskaras that are blinding us to our true nature? It would seem that the fall from grace concept would fall short of revealing the truth of the matter, yet were we originally pure or were we originally flawed from the beginning? And further, from my understanding, it seems that there is the opportunity to transcend the material plane as one is able to become illumined. Does this suggest that there is a continuum of consciousness where one starts out fresh as ignorant and has the possibility of transcending this state? And

would this suggest that the Self is eternal but perhaps not individuated? Much to ponder."

ANSWER: Advaita is given first; and then all else — like the questions you propose here — are taken up after that. The conclusion the seeker comes to in this order of spiritual business is that life is dreamlike, i.e., not really actual. We note that all experiences are here and gone in an instant. Birth, childhood memories, tastes, pleasures — they can hardly be remembered over the sweep of our lives, and this is certainly true of the series of lifetimes that we have forgotten. Thus does Swamiji write in one of his letters, *"This life's a dream, though true it seem; the only truth is He, the living. The real me is none but He, and never, never, matter changing."*

    The realized soul is God; there is no other God here but he/she. The idea of starting out in ignorance, of falling from grace, of becoming perfect over time — these are greater dreams inside of lesser dreams. There can be no change in Brahman, and *"Thou Art That."* Shankara states that you have no death because you never really had a birth. This relates to that "continuum of Consciousness" you refer to here. It is never divided by birth and death, by coming and going, starting and stopping, evolving and involving; these only take place in show, in mock play. It is all *chaya,* a shadow play the soul is enacting. But if the soul begins to believe that its shadow play is real, it covers the truth under a false superimposition. It *"covers its Light under a bushel."*

    Swami Vivekananda wants us to come out from under all these self-imposed coverings. Almost everything he said or wrote was about this act of self-revelation — Self-revelation. *"I have a clear Light now, free of all hocus pocus."* We, our minds, are great magicians. We hide the truth away as we play with hosts of shadows of our own devising, and blame all the suffering we undergo in the interim upon god, devil, other beings, our karma, etc., instead of placing the blame on our own self-constructed ignorance. He will only call us true men and women if we cast all this off and return to our eternal divine nature. Finally, a man worthy of following! He is the original, not an imitation. So he will not accept pallid imitation from us.

QUESTION #2: "I would like to express appreciation for all the charts you provided. I particularly valued the one dealing with the preliminary practices to mantra meditation. I had already copied the essence of that one from class and made a small 4x6 card with the points listed. I particularly like integrating the teachings into practices. In going through the list there was one that I would appreciate an explanation of. It is nityasarga, waking consciously every day. I am not sure really what this involves. I do awaken and feel conscious, yet something more seems to be implied. What might that be?"

ANSWER: Nityasarga, defined in Sanskrit dictionaries as "daily creation," and "awakening the divinity every morning," speaks for itself, and calls all beings to affect certain accomplishments that are in keeping with the perfect nature within, the Atman. For one thing, we must awaken from sleep in a conscious state, ready for the day, and not give in to drowsiness, lethargy, and a falling back into sleep. The teachings are not suggesting here that you do away with sleep, like pseudo yogis pretend to do, or try to do. Sleep deep and well when you sleep, but awaken and be alert when that mode presents itself; that is all. This is a part of the reason one goes straight to meditation after one rises every morning. It forms a habit of being awake, of convincing the mind that it does not need so much sleep. Eventually this turns into what we call yogic insomnia, wherein the mind remains ever-awake — even when the body sleeps. Is not the mind awake when the body sleeps anyway? Dreaming and moving about internal worlds? Thus, the favorite poem:

*A man has come to me from a land that never sleeps.*
*Now all my dreams have been transformed into radiant meditations....*

Or, from another masterful song by Ramprasad Sen:

*O dreaming mind, awaken now!*
*And remain awake!*
*Sleeping with eyes open as you walk the world is the strange sleep of delusion.*
*How long will you remain deceived by egocentric projects and projections,*
*your original awareness remaining veiled by dreams imagined to be real?*
*This dream-life of empty repetition, this constant drive for gratification,*
*wastes your precious powers, O mind.*
*You are dreaming!*
*You dream away your existence!*
*Your dreams are fueled by selfish desire.*
*Replace the darkness of this deluded sleep with genuinely peaceful repose,*
*selfless concentration on Kali's Feet of Light*
*This is the radiant treasure that you truly desire.*
*The essence of your being will awaken through this devoted contemplation,*
*and you will be enlightened by Her Light,*
*experiencing ecstatic Love and transcendent insight.*
*O mind, your life is the life of the entire universe.*
*Awaken into perpetual meditation and every dream-veil will dissolve.*

## Pada III, Sutra 31

*kanthakupe kshutpipasanivrittih* (*kantha*, throat; *kupe*, base; *kshut*, hunger; *pipasa*, thirst; *nivrittih*, cessation)

"*Samyama focused at the base of the throat of the yogi brings cessation to hunger and thirst.*"

Samyama, as has been seen thus far in this ongoing set of sutras, is a profound and powerful yogic ability. But the power here is not of the occult variety or level. If that were the case, then the ability cited here would be used by well-intended but ignorant souls to remove the hunger of the world. It has been tried, but the physical world ever comes up revealed as being dual by nature, wherein gluttony and scarcity, feasting and fasting, and other pairs of opposites exist side by side eternally, always shifting their balance from one extreme to the other.

Learning this lesson well, authentic spiritual beings such as yogis and yoginis turn their focus on complete mastery of such problems and limitations. Mastery, here, is defined as freedom from fear leading to Freedom itself; the bound only remain bound, either to failure or to endless futile activity. For, as long as fear — of wont (starvation) or of loss (pleasure) — is present in the mind, just so long will abilities such as samyama escape the unawakened soul. Such souls will simply go along their merry but muddled way, posing inferior systems such as politics, social reforms, and altruism as solutions.

Yoga — at least until Samadhi is gained — is control of the mind, as I have said before. To repeat again, in Yoga, one accomplishes this control through two accepted ways: control of the prana (lesser way); and control of the mind (greater way). Taking this to heart, then, envision if you will the mental state of that masterful soul who, if needs be, can go for days eating or drinking but little. Imagine how little expenditure, how little wastage there will be in such a being — not just on the financial level, where everyone focuses in this world, but on the physical, mental, and psychological levels as well. The inevitable wearing out of the organs will be delayed; the power vested in the senses by the prana will wane only very gradually; and the potential for stress and brooding in the mind will cease completely, leaving a pure and stainless mind with which to return to Brahman. In short, there will be more time for the yogi to implement two main things: to live a divine life that is a shining example for others, and to serve God in mankind. Thus is Yoga utilized by the luminaries for the highest ends, while showing up the limitation or hypocrisy, as the case may be, in the attempt to utilize it for inferior means.

Hunger and thirst, then, they are part and parcel of life, listed among the constituents of both The Six Transformations and The Six Billows in Vedanta and Buddhism, respectively. The hard lesson for aspirants to learn is twofold: to learn to accept, and to learn to forebear. The hard lesson for naive souls is also twofold: to learn to recognize fascination with the occult realm, and to learn to leave it alone. Case in point is Swamiji's brief commentary on a forthcoming sutra, number 33, which will be taken up in future lessons. He states: *"The Siddhas are beings who are a little above ghosts. When the Yogi concentrates his mind on the top of his head he will see these Siddhas. The word Siddha (here) does not refer to those men who have become free — a sense in which it is often used."* Those seeking siddhas, occult powers, then, are occupying very inferior worlds, not much higher than wandering spirits. The sincere yogic aspirant is meant for much nobler pursuits and accomplishments.

So the point is accented here, that mastery of such things as desire, habit, attachment, obsession, outright addiction, is one area to be neutralized. These things are as unnatural to the pure human soul, and are thereby overlays that have accumulated over lifetimes which are to be done away with — if they appear at all. But the six transformations come to all, to the evil to the ignorant to the illumined; all have to deal with them. In this sutra, and due to the attainment of samyama coming forth from intense and long-standing practice of the three upper limbs of Yoga — only after the preceding limbs have been mastered — the yogi takes the higher pathway and destroys hunger and thirst thereby.

*"Man does not live by bread alone."* Along with other potent sayings of Christ, this one has scarcely been understood by humanity to date. Jesus was a yogi, was a sannyasin, was an essene, was an awakened Jew, was the ideal Christian, was the Avatar of His age. Through all the shades and modes of His practice, his great success in spiritual life was greatly enhanced by His mastery over the prana. He knew, then, that it is the prana by which man lives. It is found in food, obviously, but is seen in nature, is felt in the body, is key to one's energy body, and is the power running through the subtle nerves (nadis) along which the thoughts of the mind course. It even carries the soul out of the body at the time of death, and back into the body at the time of rebirth. In the interim, it is thoroughly pervading the realm of the ancestors as well. It is akin to shakti power, and is therefore the power of the Mahashakti Herself. Enough said, right there! The yogi wants to master the prana, and thank God there is a system of philosophy and practice that allows him to do so.

Concentrating at the base of the throat, then, Patanjali and other beings, in the midst of their practice phase, found the hub and the vortex of all the above stated levels of existence. Just as the manipura chakra at the region of the stomach is more than just association with digestion of food and production of the fetus (it also correlates to the realm of the ancestors, the Pitriloka), the region of the throat is more than association with eating, swallowing, speaking, and breathing. Ordinary beings engage the mind, body, and senses in such actions daily, but most are unconscious of both the meaning and potential of such principles. This is why, as alambanas, the Father of Yoga asks us to meditate upon them. Soon we will "samyama" them! For, our unconsciousness is based in both the lack of reverent attention upon what we are doing (mindlessness), as well as the lack of knowledge of how much power exists in a human being, a human mind, a human soul — even the "precious human body." To awaken this power is a main theme in Yoga. May beings come alive with the subtle awareness of what lies within them.

## Lesson Seventy-seven, 1/23/13
### Pada III, Sutra 32 & 33

Our present lesson, coming at the end of SRV's latest pilgrimage to India, follows the course set for us by Patanjali that traces an ascension of conscious Awareness towards the crown of the head, and beyond. The avid and informed student has already been making connections between classic Yoga and the Kundalini Yoga system for, as Sri Ramakrishna has said, *"Nothing happens in spiritual life without the awakening and raising of Kundalini Shakti."*

And this is where a guide like Swami Vivekananda is most valuable to the seekers of this day and age, shrouded as they are in so much darkness, their present day evaluations open to so many loose interpretations. Case in point, of some five or six versions of Sutra III:33 that I checked into while formulating this lesson, I found that only Vivekananda's interpretation made the distinction between lower occult attainments and higher inspired tendencies — between the host of siddhas that occupy the region just beyond the humans, who are *"not much higher than ghosts,"* and the real Siddha, the perfected soul, like himself. Please note this closely, especially when studying Sutra III:33 at the end of this lesson, for it stands in line with Tantra's higher teachings on the seven chakras, which declares that not only are there nectars presiding at the higher chakras, but there are also poisons. It is these poisons, or the lack of discriminating wisdom — of the mental ability in many ascending souls to mark the distinction between these poisons and count them as undesirable instead of desirable — that waylays one's spiritual progress and thereby causes souls to fall from the path.

And speaking of the path and the surmounting of obstacles, kindly study the questions of your brother and sister sadhakas below, learning well from their experiences in the realm of Yoga practice.

**Questions and Answers for Lesson 77**
Avinashi from Pennsylvania writes:
QUESTION: "I seem to spend a lot of time remembering the past. I remember or ruminate on it in a way that's undoubtedly very common, my processes of attention running and re-running over mistakes I made, or over experiences of humiliation. I became curious what would happen if I refused to do this anymore. Accordingly, I swept the past completely off the table every time it arose, not bothering to ruminate on mistakes or humiliations or on ways that — in the future — I might correct them. But I began to wonder, that if I ignore the past, (and the projected future that comes out of it) as completely as I've described here, will I lose the ability to learn from my mistakes? Maybe I will cease to perceive my shortcomings and therefore lose the ability to correct them. I think this must surely happen if ordinary people, bereft of dharmic guidance, ignore the past, since all that these people really have, in regard to straightening themselves out, is their retroflections. But I wondered if a fierce devotion to my Path and the Dharma of Sri Ramakrishna and the Way he teaches might allow me to indeed move forward without looking to my past or future at all. In other words, maybe the teachings could supply the corrective factor in a way that would completely negate the need to retroreflectively examine the past? Now I feel a considerable release from anxiety, and a large measure of peace when, transferring all that freed energy into walking the integral path of Sri Ramakrishna, I just open into a Spacious Present. But can I safely ignore the past as completely as I'm contemplating doing?"
ANSWER: Yes. After seeing it as it happened, and reflecting on it as it now is, one can and should just let go of it. Among other positive results that occur from this method will come the readiness to let go of all projected phenomena at the time of death. But to fully graduate to such a level means that one must not only let go of the past as a phase of time, and as a host of seemingly real occurrences, but also let go of the brooding that goes on afterwards — just as you describe here. Noted, that you are really asking your guru a question here.

But it sounds like it may border upon the habit of brooding, so one must take care.

This question of yours also brings back to us the yogic teaching of alambanas. The three phases of time are more than fit foundations for an aspirant's meditations, For the evil-minded soul, they are a source of karmic pain; for the worldly person, a reason for fear; for the imaginative being, an excuse for mayic projection and fantasy, assumed to be real. But for the yogi and yogini, they form a powerful and revealing basis for meditation. Only this latter usage will cut time down and allow for its transcendence.

The past is even less than a dream; it has become an illusion. The problem with such illusions is that they recur in the form of karmas that were formulated via actions done in this so-called past. Brooding on them in the present only furnishes them with nourishment for their sustenance, and also re-seeds them for further fructification in the so-called future. That is why Shankara sings, tongue in cheek: *"Exceedingly wonderful is this empirical process."* The triple strands of maya are alive and well in the doubting human mind. As my guru, Swami Aseshanandaji Maharaj, often said to us, *"The past is an illusion, the present is a dream, and the future is an imagination."*

The longer the aspirant can hold the mind in an indeterminate state, in a condition of positive emptiness that both places the present karmas on hold and leaves past karmas bereft of sustenance, the more chance there will be for the outright death and disappearance of negative samskaras to take place. As you are doing here, I advise everyone to give this method a good try, and learn what it is to experience a steady mind for a time. Then, with this steady mind as your compass, place its needle in the salubrious direction of the wisdom teachings combined with nondual meditation and, as Ramprasad sings, *" ...sail easily across the blissful ocean of Absolute Existence...."*

People do not know of this yogic way. Thousands of souls spend time in woeful prayer, a type of brooding that hopes for some savior to come and rescue them from self-actuated karma. But Jesus is in you. Buddha is in you. Sri Ramakrishna, too, is in you. They will seldom come to you from the outside — only when the soul is so lost as to have forgotten its own Essence. Call upon Them, the true Siddhas, in a manner that follows the rules of yogic qualification. Then just see how swift and sure your spiritual progress becomes.

G.S. from Madras, Oregon writes:
QUESTION: "You have stated that the mind is a mechanism; that it is not the sentient Self, or Atman. This I understand and believe totally. My question revolves around those who have damaged brains and impaired faculties., either from birth, or acquired in their life, say, via imbibing drugs and intoxicants, etc. I have done some damage to my brain in this way, but I do believe that it is healing and getting better. Is it possible to heal in this way, and thereby change my past karmas around it?"
ANSWER: First, let me say two things: The spiritual Goal is a high one – the Highest – and so the criterion to satisfy it is often demanding. All beings, once

knowing of it, ought to proceed to follow the tradition of choice in a fully resolute manner, and all else will fall into place.

Second, often times, the seers of the ancient past were very explicit in their descriptions, and very conscious of the human mind and its failings. They knew how much it takes to reach Enlightenment. Therefore, in that context one finds these precious teachings that take the mind to task – and that is a good thing. So do not think so much in terms of success and failure as you study and meditate, but more in terms of keeping up the practice.

As to your question, many beings in this day and time, and especially in this culture, have had their flings with drinking and intoxicants. A mere fling does not necessarily leave lasting impressions, and therefore is not so detrimental. But where addictions and obsessions are concerned, it is another matter. One has to be very careful not to mix desires and habits of that nature in with ongoing spiritual practices, for all manner of delusions will rise as a result. Then, excuses to continue on in one's deluded actions will rise up, and these will spoil all progress along the spiritual path — even thought the aspirant feels that he or she is making headway.

Those who, having heard of the Truth, and who begin to follow it while still holding on to detrimental behaviors, only risk losing memory of that precious moment of recognition in their succession of lifetimes. The scriptures compare them to a drowning man who reaches out and grasps a crocodile, thinking it to be a log. Others, who hear of the Truth, and who thereby immediately give up their delusions and misguided actions and take to dharmic practices that lead to realization of the Truth, can and do change their karmas. The scriptures are full of records of such beings who have done so.

Using this guide and example, then, we must get onto the path and not look back, and start doing all those things which comprise a truly dharmic life. Then we must not deviate. If we fall because of the weak mind, we simply put ourselves back on the path and strive for steadiness and constancy — but never in the unwise company of those poor behaviors that caused our fall in the first place. The admixture of compromise may be allowable in worldly life, in certain situations, but it is never advised in spiritual life. For, only the Pure can reach the Ever-Pure.

M.E. from Salem, Oregon writes:
QUESTION: "I want to attain the fruits of spiritual practice in order to enhance my self-defense skills. Yet, I am unable to make progress in pranayama practice, the main practice that will allow me to do so in order to attain nadashuddhi, self-purification. Can you say anything about this frustrating situation?"
ANSWER: I find that you want to receive benefits from your pranayama practice that are not in line with yogic precepts, principles such as nonviolence, etc. We should be clear that Yoga is for enlightenment, not for the gaining of occult powers. Those who use Yoga in this latter way are the ones that get off track and suffer, and act as bad examples for others as well.

As far as progress along the path is concerned, one needs to practice yoga, all of its eight limbs, with a mind that seeks purification. This is what *nadashuddhi* means – purification (shuddhi) of the nadis (subtle passageways in the inner subtle body, i.e., the mind). So, we are to strive for a pure mind. We do not need to dominate over others, not physically or in any other way. Also, one should not seek to measure progress along the path. One must only do the practices as the guru advises, and then move forward without expectation.

So these are the few things I can begin with, in order that you might gain right orientation along the path of yogic sadhana.

S.B. from Lakeview, Oregon writes:
QUESTION: "I am enjoying immensely the various books that you have made available to us through our library. But I have heard it said that books can never bring us enlightenment, and words are useless in bringing about illumination. How do I justify, then, my love of spiritual books?"
ANSWER: Regarding books overall, they are not to be discounted, especially spiritual ones. These actually increase the soul's tendency towards renunciation which, in turn, will lead to the attainment of Enlightenment. Everything in spiritual life in this world happens in stages, not all at once.

And regarding spiritual books per se, when Sri Ramakrishna speaks of *"mere book learning"* in His Gospel, for instance, he is referring to intellectual and worldly material. Books that quicken our dispassion are an entirely different matter. So do not feel indeterminacy or aversion on this score, but rather feel joyous that you have found these treasures. If the seers did not value books and scriptures, they would not have taken the trouble to incarnate, hone their knowledge base, and forebear suffering — all to bring you a few sterling written and spoken examples of how to follow the way of Enlightenment.

Those who say that books and discourses are just words are the very ones who are pretending to be spiritual via inferior means. They really are only trying to skirt the strong effort and groundwork that is the preliminary criterion for Enlightenment. No one gets to that Supreme Goal without using the mind, and those who say they are proceeding via the heart do not know that mind is heart in Vedanta. For where is the heart? What is the heart, really? Is it an anatomical organ? No. It is the Atman, and therefore cannot be a location in the body or a set of emotional feelings. The store of emotions and devotions, feelings and insights, all reside in the mind. So, the real heart is Atman, pure and perfect. It does not need purification. The mind — that needs purification, and the way to purify it is via the imbibing of wisdom. The drop of this wisdom nectar occurs through studying the scriptures and hearing the Guru's words via direct transmission. Words and books, then — there is no replacement for them.

## Pada III, Sutra 32

*kurma nadyan sthairyam* (*m*, turtle; *nadyan*, passageway; *sthairyam*, steadiness)

*"Simulating the steadiness of the tortoise, the yogi meditates on the kurma passageway adjacent to the throat, in undisturbed fashion."*

In the Bhagavad Gita, Sri Krishna transmits the importance of steadiness many times to Arjuna — a man who is facing a host of problems that would duly deter many a soul from moving forward along the prescribed pathway. Arjuna is yet to find out what marvelous kingdoms of heaven exist within him, in his very own soul. Intersecting the upper trajectory of this host of kingdoms lie two spiritual vortexes represented by the throat and forehead (third eye) regions of the human body, the physical form really only being a template or external map indicating the presence of inner Reality.

It is these two regions, and their connection with the "crown of the head," that Patanjali speaks of in his own special way in the two sutras up for study in this lesson. Known as Vishuddha and Ajna, they represent, respectively, wisdom and its transcendence, or purification and entrance into the realm of formless Reality. Few venture here, especially to the latter summit, and even fewer make these their permanent place of abidance. It is those few great souls who prepare and set down a transcendent asana in the Ajna Chakra and, from its causal depths, radiate pure conscious Awareness to the denizens of multiple lokas lying below — doing so through the medium of the Vishuddha Chakra. As Lord Buddha put it, in regard to such a precipitous and successful inward climb: *"Wide awake among sleeping souls, the wisdom-knower forges ahead of them as a powerful steed outstrips a mule. And when the wise one, having ascended to the high tower of inner perception, looks upon the world of suffering beings, he does so with an afflicted and compassionate heart. He beholds the ignorant masses as a mountaineer on the slopes espies people down in a valley."*

"Down in a valley" can mean several things here, for there are many lowlands, or sunken grounds *(patalas)* in the vast projected realm of the mind's consciousness. That is, in case we are thinking that the hosts of suffering beings represent the only type of patala, we should stop to consider that anyone, in any sector of awareness, at any level of consciousness, who is still laboring through life devoid of the knowledge of the Eternal Soul, Atman, and bereft of the nondual truths of Existence in all its many facets, is still dwelling in the fetid marsh of delusion and misconception. Western psychology, modern medicine, quantum physics, contemporary politics, today's secular educational systems — all of these are like steaming marshlands to the illumined yogi who has arrived at the summit of all prime experience. So long as these sectors of still benighted consciousness proceed with their undertakings via the mantle of ignorance, still believing that the worlds of name and form are real, so long will they lead multitudes of beings away from Truth and, as the Upanisads say, *"towards a deeper bondage still."* That is why these nondual scriptures reiterate phrases such as *"....and not that which people worship here"* again and again, to indicate the real place of worship within — which, again, is why Swami Vivekananda taught his disciples, through poems, songs, and scriptures, *"This world's a dream, though true it seem; the only Truth is He, the Living.*

*The real Me is none but He, and never, never matter changing."*

All of this wisdom, which is of higher merit and deeper thought, radiates from the "throat" chakra like rays beaming from the sun. As Patanjali's sutra intimates, then, the yogi perceives the existence of this higher wisdom and proceeds towards its radiant warmth, and once arriving there, settles, like a huge turtle, in the very midst of it. He thus escapes distraction for all time. For, death is not there; darkness cannot penetrate; of fear, there is none in that place, and doubt has died there. As Swami Aseshanandaji Maharaj used to say to me, *"You must make fear afraid, make doubt doubt itself, and put death in its own grave."* And this will only be possible if the yogi arrives at the space of higher wisdom to stay. A mere glimpse of that shining realm, followed by some proclamations and pretenses of mastery, will not suffice and, in fact, a quick look followed by a fall conjures up dangers which are better skirted altogether.

Thus do the authentic yogis, like Patanjali, advise us, revealing to us both the existence of and the methods for becoming steady in realization. After all, Brahman is immovable; Siva is ever-stable. Consciousness neither transforms nor transmigrates. About things that change, *"All of that is mere nonsense."* To become fixed and motionless, then, like a masterful meditator, is the aim; the end of all forms of foggy thinking is the result. Then, clarity, *khyati*, is no longer the yogi's need; it is his mead. He is then the consummate teacher of the worlds, whether he is acclaimed or not. As the Katho Upanisad puts it, both with regards to the guru and the path: *"Arise! Awake! Realize the Atman after having approached the excellent teachers. Like the sharp edge of a razor is the path, difficult to cross, and hard to tread — so say the Wise."*

Thus far we have taken a brief but good look at the throat center, the blue neck of Lord Siva — King of Yogis. The following sutra introduces us into the realm of transcendence, and the first solid evidence of the formless nature of Divine Reality.

**Pada III, Sutra 33**
*murdha jyotisi siddha darshanam* (*murdha*, crown/peak; *jyotis*, spiritual radiance; *siddha*, perfected; *darshanam*, communion)

*"When concentration gets centered at the crown of the head, the yogi sees the spiritual light and has darshan with the illumined souls abiding there."*

In Sutra III:31, we found that there is a space for meditation at the "hollow" of the throat. In the previous sutra, we moved upwards, rather inwards, and found a subtle area that is the junction between throat and third eye via the kurmanadi. Since Patanjali and the commentators have moved on to the "light emitting from the top of the head," it seems that the third eye region has been underemphasized. This is not the intention. As solid filler for this apparent oversight, the commentary here under construction will linger more on the third eye area, notwithstanding the full acknowledgement that it has a primal connection with the "crown" chakra that is being brought forth in sutra 33. In other words, it is as if to say that, when the aspiring yogi reaches such an elevated level of consciousness/Consciousness, there is almost no distinguishing the third eye from the crown chakra, the only trace of difference lying in the fact that some semblance of form still remains for the yogi whose consciousness dwells at the third eye area.

The interested and enthusiastic devotee can find a full scope of references and teachings centering around the third eye chakra, otherwise called the *Ajna chakra,* or *Jnana Chakshu* — the "Wisdom Eye." As was written previously, this is where form begins to disappear for the inwardly ascending yogi and yogini, and the "Light of Awareness" comes into view and within reach. The world does not much matter anymore to such a soul, and the long-standing question of the embodied, suffering soul as to whether the world is real or not gets firmly answered. Classical Vedic wisdom states it is not, while a more refined level of comprehension, also attained at this level, reveals that it is not unless it is perceived as being one with Brahman.

Thus, *"Brahman is real, the world is unreal,"* is the truth of the matter when higher wisdom dawns, and *"Brahman is real, the world is also real,"* embellishes that rare insight when higher wisdom gets transcended in nondual samadhi *(asamprajnata).* Since renunciation of the world and the complete absence of any world in nondual samadhi are both rare views, the higher percentage of beings gravitate, inevitably, to the erroneous belief that the world is real, and most of these even decline further into that pit of delusion that considers the world to be the only reality. Thoughts that therefore originate in the top of the head, called the brain, may not ever or even imagine that the Light of pure, conscious Awareness also has its habitation at the top of the head — though in a completely different way. As Sri Ramakrishna has said, *"The eyes lie in the forehead, where subtle wisdom hides, but their gaze is always fixed downwards on the three lower centers, where eating, drinking, and sex life take place."*

Illumined souls, advanced, no doubt, also occupy two areas in this subtle region, sometimes referred to as Vishnu Yoga and Siva Yoga. One group looks outward and occupies the throat region and third eye in turns, while the other group looks further inward and occupies the third eye in conjunction with the crown chakra. This latter group tends to get more and more absorbed in meditation over time, so that they will not return to an embodied condition, of any type, after a period of adjustment to formless Reality transpires. The other group of souls, each for their own reasons, will keep a subtle body in the realm of form for purposes of working with souls who are still developing their higher awareness, or even souls that are inordinately suffering and cannot manage inward ascension at all. The Avatars are particularly interested in these, called the "fallen and the lowly ones" — *patita pavana* being their savior. Thus, the sixth and seventh chakras, and their connection with the fifth, are an entirely unique region all their own, as are the three lower chakras where earth bound souls take their birth in ignorance again and again, knowing nothing better. The entire scheme can be described, then, as consisting of *"three above and three below, with one in the middle."* That middle chakra, the heart — or *anahata* — is the prime inward place to reach for aspiring souls, as arrival there puts to death all attachments that have to do with the worldly gravity which drags beings out of heaven to earth again and again. In similar fashion, if the heart chakra is only glimpsed, and then abandoned due to attractions below, the soul will fail to transcend heaven and thereby not reach those singular realms of absolute felicity that put all heavenly lokas to shame.

Patanjali emphasizes the crown of the head in this particular sutra, and connects it mainly with having darshana, divine communion, with all the illumined souls that abide there. Lord Vasishtha calls this connection and its fruit by the expression, *"Walker of the Skies,"* intimating that the soul has attained an ability to transcend earthly realms and take up residence in subtle atmospheres within — *'The Kingdoms of Heaven within."* If one changes this phrase to *"The Kingdom of Heaven, within,"* thereby rendering it singular, grammatically speaking, it refers directly to Brahman, or nondual Reality, or Oneness with *"The Father."*

It helps to know, however, that souls of differing magnitudes, and of varied intentions, spiritually speaking, both inhabit this causal state. After meditation on the heart chakra has been perfected, one's devotionally charged-up consciousness naturally rises, and begins to court higher wisdom, transcendence, and immersion, respectively. As Ramprasad Sen sings, in blissful fashion: *"Bathe at the most sacred confluence of holy rivers, found within the precious human body where the three spiritual nerve channels meet, and breathe the sanctified atmosphere of the most remote retreat, the primal lotus center at the root of awareness."*

In the next lesson we will take an in-depth look at authentic spiritual knowledge, in conjunction with Sutra 34 and its valuable but subtle hidden teachings.

## Lesson Seventy-eight, 3/19/13
### Pada III, Sutra 34

As another winter comes to a close, we enter into our eighth consecutive year of constant study of the Patanjali Yoga Sutras — the authentic eight-limbed Yoga. Since its inception in 2005, up unto its present point, many students have absorbed the timeless tenets taught by Patanjali, with running commentaries by Vedavyasa and Swami Vivekananda, and further contributions by myself. Many students have joined at various points along the way, and have added in their profound questions in that *Atma Vichara* tradition that is most beneficial to the aspiring Vedic/Tantric/Yogic practitioner. Some souls have even found their path and taken initiation into SRV and received spiritual names as, through the years, they connected with guru, dharma, sangha, and scripture.

Now, coursing along in this dedicated fashion, the following questions are listed, with their respective answers:

## Questions and Answers for Lesson 78

Avinashi from Pennsylvania writes:

QUESTION: "Dear Teacher. Remembering the manner of operation that you shared with Lex Hixon, and that you told me about, namely, 'clarification and intensification,' I would like to request further clarifying teachings from you in response to the wonderful answer you gave to my last RY Lesson question. What I am experimenting with is not reviewing the past at all. I am, through a decided act of choice and will, vigorously choosing to move only in the present and not review the past ever, at all, not in the slightest way. There are yogic techniques where one reviews one's day in the evening, etc. But for me these sorts of things are traps, because the tendency to (morbidly) review the past is strong in me, so strong that the slightest backward look can be like a sucking whirlpool that draws me in. So far, it's seeming to work ok. I seem to see what I need to do in the present much better if I throw the past out completely. But there was one statement in your answer to me that I would like to query you on: "After seeing it, (ie, the past), as it happened, and reflecting on it as it is now, one can and should just let it go." But I'm not even doing that. Even to do that can suck me in due to negative tendencies in that direction. And like I said, so far, no problems. But I am asking you here if you are recommending a little bit of consideration of the past. Are you? Or should I just continue with my present experiment of consciously choosing, in a radical way, to live in the present, to see what happens? Oh, what sweet relief it gives! But I truly do not want to go wrong. With much appreciation for your continued guidance."

ANSWER: The answer, I'm afraid, must continue to be twofold. First, yes, you can let go of the past completely and concentrate only on the present — or better yet, the Eternal Moment; secondly, there seems to be a fear in you about looking into the past, and some negative reactions to what it holds. To examine both that fear and what gives rise to it, in detached witness fashion, is what the yogi would do, so that nothing will rise up later, unexpectedly, when higher states of Yoga are being attempted. That is, if looking into the past is just a matter of disinterest, then there is no problem in assuming the preferred stance. But if there is an aversion — ragadvesha — then such kleshas cannot be allowed to exist in the mind, even and especially in the background. To quote the commentators of Yoga, it would be like living in a large cave with a bear. One could go on doing it for some time, or indefinitely, but there will always exist the possibility that one will have an encounter (a "Kodiak moment") with that undesirable roommate and, what is more, will also harbor fear of such an encounter.

QUESTION #2: "As I understand it, the pranamayakosha accompanies the subtle body at the time of death. Since this indicates a kind of independence of the pranamayakosha from the physical body, then I wonder why it needs to be replenished at all through eating? I came across a teaching that there are three parts to food: one part is expelled as waste, one part nourishes the body on a physical level, and the third part is pranic. What exactly does this third part of food nourish? I imagine it is the pranamayakosha that is nourished, but if it is independent of the physical body, why would it need to be replenished at all?"

ANSWER: None of the five sheaths are independent of one another; they are all interconnected. The Buddha and Lord Patanjali both evince this teaching, each in their own ways, called (in Buddhism) Pratitya Samutpada, or the "interdependence" of all things. This is based upon twelve links (nidanas) that condition life and mind, often in unwholesome ways. In Vedanta, a similar correlation can be drawn using the Adhara System of the five sheaths. One covering overlaps and conditions the next, all the way up and in to the ego complex, the anandamayakosha. But in Vedanta this phenomenon is explained in terms of pervasion rather than of emptiness. As the Katharudra Upanisad states: *"The bodies of beings which appear in the form of a framework of bones and sinews is the self of the nature of food. Further within is the self of Prana, split into five. Deeper still is the self of the nature of mind, different than these. Even deeper than it is the self of the nature of intelligence. At the deepest of all distinct levels is the self of the nature of Bliss. Thus, food is pervaded by vital energy; vital energy is pervaded by mind; mind is pervaded by intelligence, and that ever happy intelligence is pervaded by Bliss. This self of Bliss is pervaded by Brahman, the Witness, the innermost of all. Brahman is not pervaded by anything else. Neither by action, nor by begetting children, nor by anything else — only by knowing Brahman — does one attain Brahman."*

To apply this to your question, well, the answer is thus made obvious. The overlapping, interdependent, or pervasive effect of both the annamayakosha and the manamayakosha on either sides of the pranamayakosha condition it, and it conditions them. "Conditioning," here, is not only a psychological matter relating to karma and rebirth, but also a natural phenomenon, the study of which allows for the embodied soul to both see and note the workings of relativity and, in classic yogic fashion, engage and withdraw from them, in turn, at will. As my guru often said, when giving us higher teachings beyond conventional ones: *"The practitioner must first learn to detach, but the yogi can both attach and detach at will."*

S.P. from Oregon writes:
COMMENTS: "All of my questions or wonderings continue to be practical and kind of everyday. So far, they are satisfied in your responses to others. I hear Swamiji explaining that supersensual perception and superconscious wisdom come from awakening the coiled serpent, a form of the Mother Wisdom, and bringing it up the central column of the Sushumna. This is done by both practice and grace. When the prana comes up the nerve currents, it produces imagination and image; when it comes up the hollow canal, it evokes wisdom and knowledge. And when we feel small moments of such knowledge, we probably have inadvertently triggered this. The practice in this chapter is on realizing that one must get the energy to flow in one direction rather than be dispersed, and to have will power follow the knowledge so gained. So, my focus is on practice which will stabilize and make conscious these results, however long it takes. I appreciate the practical exercises and advice in chapter four and five. Also, thank you for the clarifications about both sides of the Ida and Pingala

receiving energy through both inhalation and exhalation. I love the assurance that the mind will become the book of wisdom."

QUESTION #1: "I am curious about the use of imagination in Vedanta. There seems to be a mixed testimony about imagination. Swamiji says that imagination aids in pranayama, yet in other places, sankalpa and vikalpa seem suspect. I would appreciate knowing where to study this in depth. Can you clarify?"

ANSWER: Imagination aids in pranayama only in so far as the beginning practitioner is completely clueless as to the presence of prana, what to speak of its vital and subtle functions. *"Man does not live by bread alone."* Prana does everything, from vitalize the body/mind mechanism, to carry transmigrating souls (along the nadis) from the embodied state to internal realms of consciousness — to *"the kingdom(s) of heaven within."* Since novitiate spiritual aspirants are not yet aware of this inward movement to any degree, or maybe only intuitively, the teacher sometimes advises imagination at the earliest stage to aid in the remembrance of this key element in life, and in spiritual life. That is why both imagination and intuition do not carry much weight in Vedanta, and must take a back seat early on to serious self-discipline and practice (sadhana) and the direct spiritual experience (anubhava) that follows in due course.

Possibly the word "envisioning" would be more appropriate than imagining, however, for the prana and its role are not to be taken in the sense of illusion, as in the apparent existence of material objects, or in the sense of fantasy, or as in the mind's broodings and wanderings, but in the sense of what you mention here — Kundalini Shakti. Prana is Hers, and is how She accomplishes that inexplicable all-pervasive presence in everything, and in everyone.

In this regard, the Mundakopanisad speaks about a spider and its web — *"As the spider emits and withdraws its web, as herbs sprout from the soil of the earth, and as hair grows on the head without any effort, so from the imperishable Being the universe springs forth."* — in order to explain Divine Reality, prana, and its multifaceted and multifarious functions. But however beautiful and expressive, words and teachings fall far short of describing or explaining both the immensity and inconspicuousness of the web of nadis — gross, subtle, and causal — that stretch inwards from the solid earth plane to the incandescent realm of Lord Vishnu's Vaikuntha. Even the Sanskrit words, sankalpa and vikalpa — mental projection based on desire — cannot convey the inwardly ascending levels of Awareness that Prana, as Shakti, reaches and merges into.

Today's imagination is tomorrow's visualization, and tomorrow's visualization is next week's realization. Thus should the aspiring yogi and yogini hear the Truth and, contemplating It, become an illumined being in this life — or in six months, as Vivekananda states.

QUESTION #2: "I am wondering about how to come into a devotional relationship with Shakti (I believe I already am, but have not fixed on a deity or form; they all attract me). I have had some experiences, but I try not to objectify them or hang on to them; yet, the study of the Divine Mother calls. She, too, seems beyond form, yet takes on so many. How does one hold both in regard to the Mother energy? Any suggestions?"

ANSWER: I do not have any suggestions; only direct teachings. From imagination to visualization to realization — it all began with objectification, did it not? Vedantists are not afraid of form, or in any way averse to it. We use it to trace Divine Reality to Its Source. It is the three step process of Sankhya to Yoga to Vedanta, and once having accomplished this, the Advaita awaits us — never having changed its insuperable position in the first place. It is all the Divine Mother's domain, the realm of Spirituality.

So, the aspirant feels the draw, determines the cause, envisions the Divine Form, and then goes to the spiritual teacher to bring that Form into greater focus. That Form has a Name, and that is called the Mantra. Receiving that precious boon, like an oyster obtaining a bit of sand, he or she dives deep into the ocean of his/her own Awareness via contemplation and meditation to perceive the diamond-like Deity. True worship then takes place, which brings in its train the merging of Deity, Devotee, and Devotion — all three — into Formless Reality. And so it Is.

Sanatanand from Hawaii writes:
QUESTION: "In Sloka 12 of this pada, I found Swamiji's discussion of the use and assimilation of energy most interesting. He contends that the Yogis can change the energy they take in to transform their bodies, even into god-bodies. He says further that the Yogis can even take in this energy directly in place of taking in food. All this is based on the acquisition or development of positive Samskaras. Further, he discusses the ability of these elevated beings to be able to transmit electricity directly with their minds alone. This causes me to ponder. My understanding is that our primary purpose, or even opportunity, is to realize God in this very lifetime. And yet it seems that, as Swamiji has pointed out on many occasions, our human potential is far greater than we realize. I would value your assessment of the purpose of these Yogic energy abilities, and how they might be applied toward that primary goal of Self realization. Would Sri Ramakrishna regard them as *'mere crow droppings by the side of the road,'* and if so, why does Swamiji provide a discussion of them? Thank you, dear Guruji."
ANSWER: It is the Raja Yoga of Patanjali that is providing the discussion of these "energies." Swami Vivekananda is only commenting on the system of Yoga. With that said, it is obvious that Swamiji admits to their existence and to their efficacy — but only if they are placed in the proper hands. The "proper hands" in this case belong to those who are advanced in their realization. We know, for instance, that Sri Ramakrishna acquired the occult powers, which He said were a natural result of his spiritual practice. That is, He accumulated them as a matter of course in the process of right concentration on the Deity and the Reality. Importantly, however, He never used them, relying instead upon complete self-surrender to the Divine Mother to bring about all highest aims and ends.

Besides, the energies that are being talked about here do not necessarily have to be restricted to or even associated with the *asta-bala siddhis* — the eight occult powers. Nowhere in the Yoga Sutras does Patanjali discourse on them, or ask the yogi to acquire them. Rather, he warns the aspirant away from them. He states, *"When the Yogi gives up all attraction for occult powers, then does he attain the raincloud of virtues."* And Vivekananda adds, *"The yogi then becomes free, and helps others do the same."*

V.B. from Hawaii writes:
QUESTION: "In lesson #77, I was intrigued by this passage of the teaching: *'Illumined souls, advanced, no doubt, also occupy two areas in this subtle region. One group looks outward and occupies the throat region and third eye in turns, while the other group looks further inward and occupies the third eye in conjunction with the crown chakra. This latter group tends to get more and more absorbed in meditation over time, so that they will not return to an embodied condition, of any type, after a period of adjustment to formless Reality transpires. The other group of souls, each for their own reasons, will keep a subtle body in the realm of form for purposes of working with souls who are still developing their higher awareness, or even souls that are suffering inordinately and cannot manage inward ascension at all. The Avatars are particularly interested in these latter, called the "fallen and the lowly ones" — patita pavana being their savior. Thus, the sixth and seventh chakras, and their connection with the fifth, are an entirely unique region all their own, as are the three lower chakras where earth bound souls take their birth in ignorance again and again, knowing nothing better. The entire scheme can be described, then, as consisting of "three above and three below, with one in the middle." That middle chakra, the heart — or anahata — is the prime inward place to reach for aspiring souls, as arrival there puts to death all attachments that have to do with the worldly gravity which drags beings out of heaven to earth again and again. In similar fashion, if the heart chakra is only glimpsed, and then abandoned due to attractions below, the soul will fail to transcend heaven and thereby not reach those singular realms of absolute felicity that put all heavenly lokas to shame.'* When you wrote, 'The Avatars are particularly interested in these, called the fallen and the lowly ones — patita pavana being their savior.' This passage really interests me in particular, can you speak more on this? What is patita pavana?"
ANSWER: The Savior of the fallen and lowly ones, Patita Pavana, is the Avatar, who comes to earth from age to age to rescue suffering souls. Ramprasad states, that He *"saves them from the illusion of finitude."* Vivekananda writes that He *"goes from place to place and helps them out of darkness, Maya's veils."* In the Bhagavad Gita, Sri Krishna, the Avatar of the Treta Yuga, states: *"Paritranaya sadhunam vinashaya cha duskrtam dharma samsthapanarthaya sadbhavami yuge yuge. For the protection of the good, for the destruction of the wicked, and for the establishment of dharma, I am born age to age."* Patita Pavana is a name primarily associated with the Avatara, Sri Ramachandra, and His Divine Consort, Sita. The term has also been brought forward to our age, the Kali Yuga, having been nicely assigned to Sri Ramakrishna Paramahamsa and the Holy Mother, Sri Sarada Devi, both by way of the creation of many wis-

dom songs by the devotees since their arrival on earth in the 1800's, and due to Their compassionate efforts in taking on and destroying the many karmas of living beings in this age. To Them, and in all their previous Forms, we pay our eternal obeisances.

COMMENTS: "My direct experience of dawning awareness has been one of concepts dissolving and of not being separate from any emergent and dissolving phenomena. What is my body other than all that is? I need not dwell on any 'object,' for it is truly just as it is. There is no fear. A sensation might emerge that I may have in the past thought of as fear, and through the illusory power of the mind I separate myself from it. But even this imagined illusory separation cannot separate one from one's True Nature. There is no seeking here. Who is it that could seek? Resting in this Samadhi, I go about the day at total ease and peace. Within this Peace may emerge an apparent conflict, but this is not truly real nor disturbs the Real. I am at Home. My actions are not my own. There is a sense of knowing but that knowing has an 'I don't know' mysterious unutterable quality to it. And if I were to grasp onto any of these concepts, even the holy scriptures, as a tangible description of the ineffable Godhead, I would fall straight into hell and samsara."

RESPONSE: What you describe here is a good mental station to occupy, a "practice" of nondualism, if such terminology could be allowed. But in Yoga there is no taking hands off of practice; it is all practice all of the time. And the practitioner makes no bones about it. The yogi does not measure his spiritual progress, nor does he claim realization or samadhi to himself. The spiritual ego is to be guarded against. In the meanwhile, in-depth study (svadhyaya), devotion to God with form and beyond (Ishvara-pranidhana), service of that self-same God in mankind, and meditation broaching upon samadhi — seeded and unseeded — is to be undertaken and fulfilled daily. This is Yoga. As the Sankhya scriptures declare: *"There is no knowledge such as Sankhya, and no power like that of Yoga."* Thus, for the consummate devotees of Mother India, Sankhya is our science, Yoga is our daily discipline, and Vedanta is our eternal Philosophy. In authentic Advaita, nonduality, we embrace and perform all of them.

G.S. from Oregon writes:
QUESTION: "What is sadhana, what is saucha, what is sankhya, and what is sangha?"
ANSWERS: *Sadhana* is self-effort accomplished in the realm of spirituality for the purposes of purification of mind and senses in order to bring about Enlightenment. *Saucha,* one of the five niyamas (second limb of Yoga), is the self-same purification, as listed in the Yoga Sutras. *Sankhya,* with its Twenty-four Cosmic Principles list, is the ancient darshana of India that influenced all other paths and ways that came after it. Finally, *sangha* is holy company, the gathering of devotees who are dedicated to the realization of the Atman within.
QUESTION #2: "You say, from pure food comes pure blood. What is pure food? What is proper diet, and proper exercise?"

ANSWER: It was Holy Mother who gave us this sequence: *"From pure food one gets pure blood. From pure blood one gets pure mind."* So it stands to reason that from pure mind comes pure thought, and from that, illumination.

Following in this sublime line of thinking, pure diet means long term study of the scriptures under the auspice of a teacher, and proper exercise means performing one's daily sadhana. If these are maintained, food and energy turn to nectar; otherwise not. In other words, in Yoga and Vedanta we work from the top and at the root simultaneously. This does not mean brain and body. "From the top" means the mind, and "at the root" means the mind's samskaras. Working on the body alone produces only physical results. Diet and exercise may even help the brain a bit, but they convey no aid on the mind. From its innate power, the mind produces the universes of name and form. From mere exercise and diet, the body only produces sweat and excrement. Which of the two (mind or brain/body) should one work on if one wants to heal one's diseases and solve all one's problems in the world? This, pun intended, is a "no brainer," as they say.

For more on the physical side of food, and its higher uses, a good read of SRV's new book, *Reclaiming Kundalini Yoga,* the early chapters, would be informative. There you will find that mantra is utilized to purify food of defects — defects which the act of merely eating organically cannot remove. You see, some beings aver that physical problems can be solved via physical solutions. This is never a sure bet, and the assumption is usually an error. As Einstein put it, and I paraphrase: Problems created at one level cannot be solved at that same level. The idea is, that one has to rise and find the answers at a higher level of consciousness.

QUESTION #3: "What are the Eight Occult Powers?"

ANSWER: Anima, laghima, mahima, prakamya, etc. — things such as levitation, disappearance, domination, and other unholy tricks of the prana.

QUESTION #4: "You stated that all imperfections are conjured up fallaciously via ignorance and then superimposed from the outside on the various mechanisms. Can you explain this?"

ANSWER: The very idea of imperfection is a skewed one, since the Soul of mankind, Atman, is ever-perfect. All these imperfections, then, are products of the mind and its thinking process. Thus they are non-actual and, rather dreamlike and illusory. Vedanta operates from the superior premise that the human being is divine, the Divine Being in a human form. As Vivekananda stated, *"It is the greatest sin to call a man a sinner."* We must look to man's perfect Nature and, by doing so, allow him to raise himself out of self-imposed false overlays to thereafter occupy his supreme station in life. As I have often put it, playing off of Swami Vivekananda's ideas, if we serve human beings as God they only turn into egotistic human beings, but if we serve God in human beings they tend to return to their Divine Nature.

QUESTION #5: "You stated that at one time we convinced ourselves that we are impure and imperfect. Why did we do this? Why have we divided ourselves up into parts? To experience life?"

ANSWER: Yes, life is division and varieties — the separating of one, indivisible Consciousness into many fragments, as dichotomous as that seems. To understand that we must meditate on the Divine Mother of the Universe. But as to the "why" of it, as in, "Why have we done this," it is based in desire for life-experience. As I wrote earlier, sometime, in a past beyond reckoning, we convinced ourselves that individual life would be better than remaining One. This was the ego's doing, called the "separate I-maker." Please understand that all beings who have taken on a form must do so through the ego mechanism. It is just that the greater percentage of them do so using an unripe inferior version or "mechanism" of that, while some rare others do so very carefully, and for specific reasons. That is, some come here (to the earth plane/embodied condition) to sport; others, to suffer. Still others come to work and purify, while others only embody to seek pleasures. All reap the respective karmas of their modes of action. Even here on the earth plane, though, there are some masterful souls who know how to act without acting, to tread the field of karma while creating none in turn. Still others can even destroy the karmas of others, like the Avatar.

QUESTION #6: "What is that one position of the mind that allows for mental stillness, leading to the ability to concentrate and meditate?"

ANSWER: It is peace, and it must not be sacrificed for any reason, for any desire. Ahimsa, nonviolence, is its mainstay. Satyam, truthfulness, is its sustainer. Non-ownership and non-agency are its linchpins. From it comes peace three times in the three worlds, called *"shanti, shanti, shanti,"* and from that comes Shanti — the *"Peace that passeth all understanding."*

R.C. from California writes:

QUESTION: "In regards to lesson 11, my question is: have you seen God? Have you had samadhi? Also, please know that the SRV livestreaming classes on weekends are helping me with my longing for God. Until I realize him, I plan to continue with the Raja Yoga lessons and practice and reflect with questions — which I have difficulty formulating, as this is all very new to me."

ANSWER: Welcome to the realm of Atma Vichara, where questions regarding Divine Reality and how to merge in It are always forthcoming. Via study of these sutras, plus the seeking out of holy company, all impediments will dissolve in time. It is the main thing that Time is good for!

As to your questions, I have never seen God here on earth, in nature, or walking around in a form. Even if I did, or thought I did, it would be a reflection only. Such is my Vedantic training, for which I am extremely grateful. We take no "wooden nickels" in Vedanta.

God is formless in Essence, and therefore one will have to enter formlessness in order to "see" Him/It. In Yoga, that means entering into Samadhi. Have I "had" Samadhi? Not of the formless kind — Asamprajnata — in this lifetime yet; but I know it is my true nature. My higher experiences have all been of peace and wisdom. Those are types of samadhis as well — called samprajnata. Thanks to Vedanta, my teachers, and these personal experiences, my ignorance is gone. Peace of mind has taken its place. It is my conclusion that the Other, Formless Samadhi, Nirvikalpa, will occur only due to Her Grace. And I can wait.

**Pada III, Sutra 34**
*pratibhad va sarvam* (*pratibhad,* spontaneous wisdom; *va,* or; *sarvam,* everything)

*"Or by the flow of spontaneous knowledge, everything may become known."*

Spontaneous knowledge that flows — it is a rare thing. Knowledge of secular subjects, of nature, of the world, etc., is rather common. Once again, it does not bring peace of mind, nor does it fulfill. As Vivekananda has written and said, *"Spiritual knowledge is the only thing that can destroy our miseries forever; any other knowledge satisfies wants only for a time."* It reminds us of that great questioner of the Upanisadic era who came among the illumined rishis and asked: *"Teach me that one Thing, by which knowing, all else is known."* All of the rishis uttered their approval of such an apt question, which is based upon deep introspection and long-standing rumination. That one *"Thing,"* of course, is Brahman, the Reality, and whereas it cannot be known via ordinary knowledge, the superlative wisdom called Atmajnan can lead the aspirant straight to It.

Patanjali is well in the know, then, about the kind of knowledge the yogic aspirant must seek. "Flowing" knowledge has to do with what the luminaries term as *"Tailadharadhyan,"* that meditation practice (dhyan — seventh limb) that is based upon the mind's full and unstinting attention towards a single subject — the Eternal Subject — and which flows, unbroken, to its beloved Source, much like oil flows from one beaker to another. Unlike water, which splashes and departs its stream, this warm healing oil of rapt attention pours easily and in uniform fashion into the receptacle that is Brahman. For, as Vedanta declares, *"All is soluble into Brahman."* Names and forms, elements, objects and their enjoyers, even subtle principles like time and space, all dissolve into that formless Ocean that is made up of Pure Consciousness alone. The only word that comes to mind, that vibrates around this Ocean, which characterizes it perfectly, is AUM.

This profound sutra has two other facets to unwrap. The first comes to light based upon the Sanskrit word *"pratibha"* which Patanjali selects for the sutra. Those of you in SRV loka recognize it, since it has long been a prime subject for discourse and teachings. It is "flint-like intelligence," meaning a "substance" whose very consistency is like fire, and which can strike sparks of recognition and revelation in the soul simply by its mere application. Metaphorically, and following Patanjali's wording, as a "flowing" substance it is more akin to earthly lava, which can find its way to the surface of existence, as well as plummet to the depths of all darkness. In both cases it lights up the atmospheres or, abandoning the metaphor, charges up the chitta, the mind's thinking process. It was Sri Ramakrishna Paramahamsa who pointed out

Narendra (the young Swami Vivekananda) as being like a flint, which though steeped in a river for a thousand years, nevertheless strikes sparks as soon as it is taken out — even when wet!

More could be said about pratibha, but suffice to say that the clueless state of the darksome mind in ignorance of its true nature, the obstacles that arise due to such inattentiveness, the power of flintlike intelligence that eradicates those obstacles at their very root, and the One who effectively holds and embodies that power, are all combined in an edifying way in it. May such flowing knowledge inspire the seeker to new heights of Awareness.

Further assistance in comprehension of the Pratibha can be gotten by looking at the entire Jnana Matra series of video classes that are now being posted on the SRV website. That series was given last year, mostly in Hawaii, and in its course undergoes a thorough unwrapping and display of the power of intelligence for the benefit of all who would take advantage of it.

The second facet of this sutra worth bringing out is the reference to "all-knowingness." The Sanskrit word *sarvam* is one of those rare and universal terms that suggests things overtly spiritual in nature. The teaching of what I have been calling The Three Om's — Omnipotence, Omnipresence, and Omniscience — form a good example of what the word sarvam infers. That is, beyond knowledge, transcendent of scriptural truths, and even deeper than spiritual wisdom, is The Truth Itself. These three "Om's" partake of It: the first by dint of the power of intelligence; the second by way of all pervasiveness; and the third, straight to the point, through all-knowingness. When this triputi is contemplated as one unit, much like the three matras of AUM, the seeker arrives at a more complete realization of the kind of penetrating power that spiritual wisdom holds, and thereafter is able to wield such power for the highest good of all beings.

In this way *"everything is known,"* not merely through a process of learning and growth so common to other forms of knowledge, but much more immediate — *"spontaneous."* Patanjali can only hint at it via words in sutras. However, his entire amassed system of Ashtanga Yoga is certainly ample proof, if any were needed, of the power of intelligence. For the rest, called "all-knowingness," the practitioner must come to know That by following the tradition with full faith. As the Upanisads state, *"When mental impurities dissolve due to yogic practice, the seer sees That everywhere, in everything, in all places — even here in this very body."*

## Lesson Seventy-nine, 4/26/13
### Pada III, Sutra 35

Responses to Raja Yoga's teachings in the recent lesson, and in previous lessons, are placed below for our consideration and deep introspection. The single sutra that ends this lesson places emphasis on the human mind, and gives profound keys to mastering it for all time.

## Questions and Answers for Lesson 79
Avinashi from Pennsylvania writes:
QUESTION: "It is said that the Master attained perfection by different paths. But once he had attained perfection the first time, how could he give it up to realize it again? There's something that doesn't quite gel there for me. He did not, after all, move backward and become un-illumined, did he? Or maybe he did. That would seem to be a peculiar ability in itself, if it could be done."
ANSWER: The answer is twofold. Put simply, it is that realized souls have gained their illumination in previous lifetimes. When they return to embodiment, each for his/her own reason, it is not under the sway of ignorance, and uses nature/maya only for projection purposes. Then, and secondly, they assume names and forms; they then go through the motions, like everyone else. Thus, the question comes up, even in scriptures, *"How does a luminary walk, how sit, how act, etc."* Well, it is basically like everyone else, only free of ignorance of their true nature. The student standing by has to get close to such a soul and spend time there to really see the inner workings of that subtle and superlative inner life going on. One of my brother devotees, gurubhais, told the story of being around Swami Aseshananda for a year or more. One day, the swami turned his head to him and said, "If you want to get warm you have to come near the fire." That was all that was ever said. The student took the hint, moved into the ashram, and spent the rest of his days studying the illumined soul.

In the case of the Avatar, like Sri Ramakrishna, this applies even deeper. Enlightenment is forever. What we are seeing in His case is the return, maybe every 500 years or so, of a soul who has to come again and reenact all that He demonstrated earlier for souls who did not "get it" before, and for a new set of souls as well.

It has to be said here, that though "All is Brahman," and that "Atman is in everyone," still, there are souls who do not go to Brahman after the body's demise, but instead go unconscious and abide in an indeterminate state, like dull sleep, until their next birth. In other words, they give themselves to the "illusion of finitude," to nature, to matter, and not to conscious Awareness. This lack of Awareness becomes chronic in living beings, until there is nothing for them but matter, and millions come to believe in it as the only reality. Just look at the state of the world today for proof of this, if any is needed.

So, what can a sensitive and realized soul do but incarnate again and again along with this mass of sleeping souls and enact the process of birth, life, and death with them — the play of relativity. The advantage to the Kali Avatar, the One who came in this recent time, is that He showed the whole of existence to be nothing other than the sport of Consciousness in the realm of names and forms, a massive Lila. Oh yes, such a being can feign ignorance if it will help Him in awakening others. As the Master used to cite, baby Krishna (Gopala) once lifted Mount Govardhan and used it as an umbrella to shelter a village from the torrential rains. Later, someone asked him to fetch the stool across the room, and He said, *"I am just a baby, and too weak to lift that."* Thus, as devotees of both the Avatar, and of the ideal that He brings amongst us, we must not fall victim to delusion and begin to think of Him as an ordinary being. As Holy Mother said, *"If you begin to look upon your Guru as an ordinary person, you will never make spiritual progress."*

Sri Ramakrishna is an example of that singular Soul whom nature could not form. What we are seeing when we look at Him is nothing but God. Thus, His picture on our altars.

QUESTION #2: "A friend and I were talking the other day concerning the nature of enlightened souls, and she asked me about the difference between the illumined and unillumined in regard to how they experience life. I started talking about bliss, but she called me on my answer and asked if they were ever stressed. I then remembered two biographies I had recently read — one the biography of Swami Paramananda, (*A Bridge of Dreams*), and the other of Swami Ashokananda, (*A Heart Poured Out*) — and they were both very stressed at times, indeed stressed to such a degree that it badly affected their health. This did not strike me as perfect equanimity. Indeed, the equanimity often seemed far from perfect, and at times it looked as if bliss was utterly absent. So a question is: are there differences in depths of illumination, of enlightenment, from illumined soul to illumined soul? If so, what accounts for those differences in the depth of illumination? Is it, for example, something concerning the depth of certain understandings, or what is it? And in what regions of the antahkarana would those differences be based?

ANSWER: Following along in the line of approach of your previous question and my answer to it, souls whose ignorance has died are never "stressed out." When I read those very same books you mention here in the past, I did not see any such thing in those two swamis. There were stressful situations, to be sure, but that is the reason for their coming — to show how to bear such circumstances and still be free, and remain free. Anger, passions, stress, are mere masks for such a person. It is not that they do not suffer. If they did not, it would seem unfair to the rest of us, and would not make any real impression on us — like the impression of renouncing the world, as they have. Would one renounce the world, then be affected by it? What sense would that make?

Another way of explaining this is that *"Forbearance is the default zone of the wise."* Forbearance is how they handle the world, but their modus operandi is peace of mind, and their especial quality is Bliss. That is why they have taken that last name, "Ananda." Since most have never had bliss of a spiritual nature, called samadhi, then they have no idea what it looks and acts like. But I have spent two thirds of my life with the Ananda family, two of my three gurus were monks, and I can attest that Ananda (bliss), Shanti (peace), and Titiksha (forbearance) are in them. So are Udasina (indifference) and Samkampana (stability).

To fill in the answer to your question, there do exist different stages of enlightenment, and that is due to varying temperaments, and even changing situations and circumstances. But more important to the nature of this question is the fact that Enlightenment is the death of ignorance, and once this ignorance is gone it does not return, nor does it have an influence any more on the illumined soul, from sage to seer to Avatar. Others just think it does, and that is due to their own ignorance; what else?

QUESTION #3: "If a person were to give an introductory talk on Hinduism to people unfamiliar with it, what points should they cover, and in what order?"

ANSWER: First to say, is that Hinduism is different than Vedanta. Hinduism is the religion of India, meaning the conventional side of things spiritual. Vedanta is more the philosophical side, but higher than that, the Nondual Truth made palatable to aspiring souls who have gone beyond to what our SRV founder, Lex Hixon, called "the open space beyond religion."

So, if Hinduism is the subject, take a college class or attend a temple. But if it is Vedanta we are talking about here, we want to take the opportunity to tell the listener about nondual axioms that are at the base of all religion and philosophy, principles such as the eternal nature of Reality, Its all-pervasiveness, Its transcendence of all processes such as birth, death, and evolution, and finally, and importantly, mankind's oneness with that Reality — the oneness of Jivatman, Atman, and Paramatman. In short, the embodied being (Jivatman) is really God sporting in a form, being the Supreme Soul (Atman) that has taken on five coverings (sheaths or upadhis) as overlays over its Formless Nature (Brahman). That is a good start for any cultured listener, and a real mind-full, yes? Hopefully this Truth of Vedanta will sink deep into them, into all.

QUESTION #4: "Does the 'stithi samadhi,' ('the samadhi of steady wisdom'), have another name? Is it possible that it embraces a range or class of samadhis?"

ANSWER: Yes, the samadhi of steady wisdom can also be called Samprajnata in Yoga, especially those levels of it concerned with savichara and savitarka, and even their concomitants, nirvichara and nirvitarka. Where knowledge of Reality begins to manifest and appear on the horizon of the aspiring human mind, there comes to it a steadiness, stithi, that leaves a lasting impression in the mind-stuff. In Vedanta, it is all wrapped up in the savikalpa level of samadhi. In other words, when wisdom and equanimity come to the fore, there stithi samadhi will abide. Everlasting peace is also a sign of its presence.

QUESTION #5: "You may or may not remember that I go to something I call 'my Saturday Morning Self-Inquiry Group.' It was started by a man, a little-known deceased sage, who probably, in my view, is an enlightened jnani. These groups are all over the country. Anyway, I've been finding the group increasingly irritating; something was just not right about it. And suddenly I began to see it a few weeks ago. There is hardly anyone there who is seeking enlightenment. Instead, they're seeking a state of individuation, almost for its own sake. They aren't seeking that which is common to and One in us all. That is why they're so obtuse, so impenetrable when it comes to really hearing, in a genuine way, anything from the Wisdom Traditions. They've turned the Wisdom Traditions on their ears, restructuring the concepts so that they serve the purpose of this individuation they seek. One of the guys there got your book, *The Avadhut And His 24 Teachers,* on my recommendation. But, my

God, how he distorts it! He took a couple ideas from it that support his own warped views and ignored the rest; mainly, he took the ideas that assert we are already enlightened, or our Essential Nature is of that character, and he uses those ideas to state that we don't have anything to accomplish because 'we're already there,' and if we engage in any kind of discipline it just shows we don't understand the Truth. Worse, he speaks and says, 'Babaji says...' and then he comes out with this stuff. And I say to him, 'Babaji doesn't say that. You cherry picked an idea you like, out of context, and then tag his name to it to lend strength to what you want to believe.' That's when the obtuseness comes in. Well, I don't mind cherry-picking, but I'm afraid I have done you a disservice in recommending your beautiful book to this man — a pearl has been cast before the swine.

"But this is America. This is what it's about, spiritually speaking anyway. My view has turned about to come much closer to yours regarding America. And what does one do in a situation like this? In the absence of worthwhile association, the advice of the Gita is the only advice worth taking, i.e., live alone and practice yoga — which, of course, I do. But that means my circle of friends is disappearing from my life, though I find I was not that attached to them anyway.

"What should I say at this point? Thank you for listening? I guess I'm frustrated. I'm trying to come to terms with the truth that this fox seems to have no den, this bird, no nest."

ANSWER: You make very good points here, for all sides, and all this falls into my area of operations in this world, i.e., an awakened soul among sleeping people. I have to attempt to correct, yet do it gracefully and with compassion. Therefore, the best attitude to use with such bare novices is one of father to child. As Vivekananda said to us when he arrived and saw our puerile spiritual condition, *"I see you are all mere babies, and babies must submit to be taught."*

This attitude towards humanity, as you surmise, has to be free of condescension. If I must say it, it must be naturally superior, since that is what Vedanta is, but cannot be smug superior; it cannot have a trace of looking down the nose in it. On the other hand, having heard the Truth, are we to let it be bantered about and compromised in our presence? That will happen anyway when we are away, but cannot be allowed to do so when we are present.

As you did in the meeting, then, you must correct where false or skewed overlays are being perpetrated, or, if you are not yet a fully fledged adept, then at least offer suggestions based upon your understanding. I can tell you one great thing. In the 1000 Questions (Prashnottara Ratna-Malika) of Shankara, he asks his students these many queries. One of them asks: *"What is the one thing to be avoided?"* The answer comes back from Shankaracharya, *"A congregation without a leader."* Where there is no guru, there is bound to be error and chaos. This is termed by the wise, "the blind leading the blind," no matter the good intentions. The Americans value democracy. But spiritual life is not a democracy; it is a theocracy lying necessarily in the hands of illumined souls. They have specialized there; others have not, plain and simple. Sri

Ramakrishna said it best: *"One goes to a doctor if one is sick, to a lawyer if one has a court case. But then not to go to a guru when one wants to learn about Truth and spiritual life? What kind of delusion is that?"*

I have seen personally what a mishmash of error exists in such gatherings as you describe here. But for you, since you possess honed discrimination, viveka, which is the one most crucial attribute for true spiritual life, and the one that is mainly missing in the West in present times, then you can go to that gathering and observe. You can start acting as a monitor too, a sort of conscience, and be more proactive, thus gaining the respect of some of your fellows there. Some will resent it; others will argue against you. They are to be seen as *"curs barking on the heels of an elephant as he moves through a village."* Or, you can cross them off and go your own way. It hardly matters. Only, if you can leave them with something to consider in your absence, and plant some seeds of higher Vedantic and Yogic thinking in their minds, all the better.

I want my students to follow after me and spread the Word, help the world where it will accept such help. The "pearls before swine" syndrome is always a consideration, however, as are two other factors: protecting oneself from negative vibrations; and guardedness against spiritual ego. With all of this said, possibly you can find the middle ground and go forward.

QUESTION #6: "I don't know if what's below is a question or comment; certainly, though, it's an expression of certain observations and reflections of mine that I've been thinking about a lot of late, and that I would like to have your feedback on — corrections, amplifications, clarifications, or editorializations. I've noticed that samskaras, catalyzed into manifestation by external or internal triggers, roll up out of the chitta if emotional charges, for or against, are attached to them, so that, considered as karmas, they visibly move from the sanchita state to the agami phase. But if I fail to catch on to what's happening so that the affective charges continue to operate, the latencies gain a grip that become increasingly difficult to negate: I take this to be agami karma moving to the prarabdha phase. Sri Shankaracharya, as we know, says that no karma needs to be finally lived out except for the prarabdha: once karma reaches the prarabdha phase, it has to be lived through, or so goes the theory. Even if its impact can be reduced, (so one suffers a pin prick instead of a sword blow), it still has to be lived out. But I notice that if I lay back, shut my eyes, and let go of affective charges attached even to firmly situated, fully operating latencies, that I can roll even these back toward the agami phase and then to the sanchita, as it were, taking the arrow out of the bow and putting it back into the quiver. And if, through effective sadhana I can keep the karma-arrow in the quiver, why should it ever have to emerge again? So I ask: at what point does karma in fact become prarabdha in the sense that Shankara described — full, strong, but above all, irreversible? I can see how karmas that affect systems external to the seer — the way, say, that a crime affects society and triggers the activity of the court system — might have to be lived through to one degree or another; and I can see how the ability to roll emerging karmas back into the chitta could vary from person to person depending on such factors as degree of wisdom attained, but the idea that there is really and finally any such thing as an irreversible karma is, for me, falling apart upon close examination. Do you have any teachings about this?"

ANSWER: The main teaching here is that karma is a relative law — and this means all karma. Since Brahman is the Reality, and there can be none other, and It is karmaless, being inactive, what is this karma, and where does it lie? It lies only in nature, and that presence kicked off by the human mind in ignorance. So, to transcend all karma, prarabdha included, is to reach illumination of mind. At that point, if the seer remains in the body, his prarabdha karma is just his body and its temporary existence. Some go into a cave and slough it off, imitating the actionless state that is to come after death, in Brahman. Others forbear, as mentioned in an earlier question, and go on acting as if a puppet moved by invisible strings. This is where service to God in mankind is a great thing, as it gives the luminary a good reason to let the arrow that has already left the bow time to reach the target — the Inactive Agent, Brahman. Or, as the Akshi Upanisad states it: *"I am no agent; the agent is God, or my own prior actions."*

Savitri (earlier C.S.) from Canada writes:
COMMENTS: "Thank you again for the Raja Yoga Homework Course. It provides a touchstone for me, as I am such a distance physically from the Sangha. Question 1 in the latest lesson from Avinashi, and your answer, mirrors my own experience with the past, and with fears. I find I have the grace to look at what I fear when I feel it rise, whether due to letting my thoughts wander to the past, or something I experience in the moment. In my experience, the facing of the fear is essential to clearing it. Somehow Grace descends and the fear is revealed to be unreal, a delusion, and the mind regains serenity. It is not that fear no longer arises, but that there is no more a fear of fear itself to cloud discrimination and discernment — at least in theory. In any event, I find in meditation the mind now rests more easily, as fear of the future because of the practice of examining fears as they arise doesn't exist. For me, much of my repetitive thought was about 'what ifs' – projection into the future. I am hopeful of lessening the possibility of a 'Kodiak' moment in the future. Two summers ago I ran into a Grizzly Bear and her cub on the trail. She was not 20 feet away. The look in her eye was mild curiosity (I was close enough to see that look). I had a dog with me. We turned and went the other way. I attribute the calm nature of our encounter to the wonderful state a deep meditation earlier in the day had left me with. Another practical reason for sadhana revealed."

QUESTION: "Knowing that mental projections are based on desire, and watching my own processes change over time and practice, I wonder, can you help me with this? It seems that mental projections are indeed based on desire. Desire seems to be so ingrained that to even notice one's subtle desires takes mature discrimination and discernment. It also seems that as one engages in sadhana with sincerity and devotion to the Ideal, the desires begin slowly to drop away. So what is the process occurring here? Is the sadhana purifying the mind, and thus the projections diminish? Grace is also at play?"

ANSWER: This question reminds me of last Sunday's live-streaming class, and the subjects covered there. You might want to look back at it on Advaita Academy's website. Also, my new book called *Dissolving the Mindstream* goes a long way into the subject of sankalpa, mental projection. That should be out within the month or thereabouts.

But suffice to say that mental projection, from the cosmic to the collective on down to the individual mind, makes the worlds turn. Another way of saying it is how Holy Mother put it, that *"The cycles of existence are going on because all cannot be through with desire. But it is the last lifetime when one gets rid of desire."* Of course, Her method for most beings was to fulfill those desires. But we also know that desires cannot be fulfilled without subjecting them to the dharma. Otherwise, *"satiation never comes,"* as my teacher said.

So, we live a dharmic lifestyle and fulfill all legitimate desires therein, naturally, without our even noticing it. It is the way of all forms of ignorance to simply cease and desist, then disappear under the power of our own sadhana. Thus, I am repeating what you say in your question above. Only, just give up brooding and cultivate a peaceful mindset in which to watch all forms of desire vanish in due time. Only certain types of beings can tear desire out by force, without leaving a void, a dangerous mark on the mind. As the Great Master has said, if one tears off a palm frond while it is still green, sap runs out and the tree is harmed. If one waits until the frond yellows and droops, however, and then removes it, no harm comes. One should treat one's desires in this fashion, which will only require some close attention as the witness. People who are insensitive to their thoughts and acts do not practice this way, and therefore run into problems and undue suffering. As Holy Mother told us, again, *"Desires? What are they to you? They come and go. My dear, go on and fulfill them. They cannot harm My children."*

QUESTION #2: "I sometimes have a hard time resolving the effortless effort, surrendering all to the Divine, and The Mother does all, and yet surrender is an action. Are we not actually helpless before the Divine? Is helplessness and empowerment a pair of opposites from which Krishna encourages us to be free?

ANSWER: Actually, the seers prefer that we act with determination rather than take refuge in any manner of weakness. Swamiji's teachings have made this imminently clear. When he found the word "bold" in the English language, he was very happy, and used it lavishly. Sri Krishna, too, told Uddhava much the same thing. In the Uddhava Gita He states that some beings free themselves by their own self-effort, not waiting around for grace to descend. He seems to like that forward moving aspirant very much. As Swamiji said, *"Get free, then turn and help others do the same."* If we merely wait around, how many opportunities for helping suffering beings and serving God in mankind will we miss?

One thing can be added here: self-surrender is not a form of weakness. It is a very hard task to accomplish, as anyone knows who has tried to accomplish it. What occurs by that act is the diminution of the ego. That is the key to your quandary here, described as "effortless effort." As the teaching of

Mahamudra in Tibetan Buddhism puts it, so nicely:

> *When focusing occurs, focus without objective*
> *When stabilizing occurs, stabilize without distraction*
> *When shifting occurs, shift without grasping*
> *When manifestations occur, experience them as reality*
> *When liberation occurs, allow it to occur naturally*

G.L. from Hollywood writes:
QUESTION: "I have so many questions about all the different kinds of practices: Raja Yoga, Kriya Yoga, etc. Which is the preferred method? Is there one? It is all very confusing. But I am meditating, and feeling a burning sensation at the base of my spine, and whenever I start the breathing I automatically refer back to my mantra given to me by Swami Swahananda. I would like to increase the regularity of my practices, and know what specifically to do each day and how to do it. I simply want to let go of all my frustrations with not getting what I have wanted in the past. I just want to feel happy. I no longer want to feel like I have failed at something, and have that bring me to an emotionally depressed state. These Raja Yoga classes, reading, and the like, all make me feel less of those anxieties, but I want to be able to just have the faith that God will do what is best for me, whatever that is, and I want to be willing to trust in that and be willing to accept whatever that brings with it, good or bad. Is this question too confusing?"

ANSWER: Not at all; one only has to put everything in its own place and address each. There are some three elements to your question here, which is good. The first is emotional, such as getting rid of frustrations, feeling unhappy/happy, worrying about failure, and the like. You can get rid of these right away. The Vedantist — every sincere aspirant after Truth — does not allow these to enter the picture, and is long done with them. They are of no help or benefit whatsoever, and fall in the category of brooding. As Vivekananda has said about them, and I paraphrase: *"Make a bundle of all of them and consign it to the fire god."*

The second area of your question is qualities and merits, along with pure desire. You want to increase the regularity of your practice, be willing to trust and accept, and have faith in God. Place your mind on this field and you will be able to conclude that you have already attained many of these desires, and now only need to acknowledge that fact. And whatever has not been attained yet, it is in the process of being attained, and will be yours soon enough — especially if you "increase the regularity of your practice." I deem that mention to be of most value to you at this time, as it is to most practitioners. It is sadhana. Just do it! For instance, you state that these lessons always make you feel better. Spend more time in study, then, and keep the otherwise distracted mind occupied.

The third level of your question falls around method. Again, and first, acknowledge that you have been given the essential method by your guru, Swahanandaji, and engage in it and "increase its regularity." One of the aspects of my teaching is to let people know about what the seers advise as *pratyabhi-jna* — recognition. Often the aspirant runs around looking for what is already his or hers, or worries about what is already in his/her possession. This is true, of course, of the *Atman*, our perfect nature, but I am not bringing that up yet. It is all the qualities that are within oneself I am speaking about. They are within, and one needs to gather them up and account for them, then move forward.

The method you have been given is the mantra of the Great Master and Holy Mother. There is none higher than it in this day and age. By using it these past years you have awakened the Kundalini Shakti at the base of the spine, and She is showing signs of rising to meet Her Lord at the crown of the head. All of this is happening in you! Are you nonexistent? a nonparticipant? or somewhere else? How can that be? So join in and celebrate the appearance of the formless Essence here in the worlds of name and form. Should She rise up and find you unwilling, or unaccepting, or full of worries and issues, will She want to remain? Prepare the ground with more of Her mantra, more study, and increase your devotion for Her exponentially. It is a great opportunity, not to be confused with other elements. Thus, my three-part answer here to your question.

QUESTION #2: "Lesson 7 brought up all kinds of interesting conflicts in me. I was told to pray to Holy Mother to have more clients appear for my psychotherapy practice to be successful. On the other hand, I feel as though it is a shallow and empty request, that what I should be asking for is Her spiritual personality in my life. I pray to Her, Ramakrishna, Swamiji, and Swami Swahananda to grant me their blessings in my life as far as spiritual strength is concerned. I have to fight off, sometimes unsuccessfully, my desire to pray for clients, good health, and a long life, etc. I feel like a hypocrite. Any insights for me?"

ANSWER: This is a good question, bringing up the subtle dichotomies of life lived in the dharma by a sensitive soul such as yourself. First of all, that you have found the Holy Trio, and been given Their mantra in life by a luminary such as Swami Swahananda, is of great merit, and simply means that you have no worries whatsoever. Salvation is there, now to work on liberation — like They have.

Holy Mother said, *"The desires of the devotees? What are they, really. The more they come and go, the better it will be for them."* So, you see, the devotees have to run out the spool of their karma in reverse fashion. It is like Sri Ramakrishna talking about burnt ropes — they still look like ropes, but a puff of wind will disintegrate them. Such are the final desire-wisps of a sincere devotee of God.

And all the better if one's final desires revolve around helping others in the true spirit of service, called Karma Yoga. As long as you keep in mind the difference between nondual attainment, and prayers for the good of others, then no hypocrisy can or should be assigned in the mind. Each apply in their own respective sphere, and need not contradict one another. That is, practice discrimination, but be of assistance to others. These others may not yet be ready for spirituality. They need to fulfill certain ends on earth in order to prepare themselves when the time comes. Help them, but do not fall into their vibration as you do; remain in the Great Master and Holy Mother. Their will be done, and we are but limited instruments. But these limited instruments are Their limited instruments. That is the difference. Thus, my first point above, that you need have no worry or reticence.

As far as prayer is concerned, it cannot equal or compare with wisdom, devotion, meditation, or selfless service. The Four Yogas outstrip it by a long measure. Yet, if the prayer is offered after higher wisdom is attained, after devotion has matured, after meditation has been embraced, and selfless service applied, then it becomes a very powerful tool for that one who seeks the highest good of all beings in all realms — Loka Sangraha.

G.S. from Oregon writes:
QUESTION: "How can we be conscious in our dream state?"
ANSWER: By being conscious in the waking state. The Word, AUM, has three matras — particles or portions. The "A" stands for the waking state; the "U" stands for the dreaming state; the "M" stands for the deep sleep state. These are the three levels of consciousness in mankind. The seers want you to first fully master the waking state. The dreams of most beings are cloudy, murky, silly, and random. It makes sense then, does it not, that they are this way because our waking state is so confused and unclear. We dream based upon how we live when we are awake. If one wants to increase the quality of the dream state, then one has to purify and perfect the waking state — life. We are first to live a dharmic life, then a divine life, then a transcendent life. One can call them the worker, the warrior, and the witness, if one likes.

Whatever the case, strength will be needed. We cannot power charge our dreams, suddenly flex some unseen muscle and turn the dreamscape beautiful and blissful all the time. It is like the waking state, full of troubles and trials, then triumphs and victories, then peace and contentment — all in turns. Constancy escapes us. Continuity avoids us. We need to master the three states, one after another, and then our knowledge, peace and bliss will be unalloyed and uninterrupted.

QUESTION #2: "How can I learn the concentration to be free?"
ANSWER: All concentration is freeing. It is its opposite, distraction, that is the problem, and has become a habit. Thus, start by knowing yourself to be free.

Both concentration and distraction have levels. In the latter, it can run the gamut between mild distraction due to everyday pastimes, hobbies, tv, etc., on to obsession with mundane human convention, into outright scattered mind that suffers continual and uncontrollable intercourse with mental horrors untold. Whatever the case, stilling the mind of *vrittis* is to be accomplished.

In the case of concentration, if one can master it in the world via secular studies, arts and crafts, and other aids (or diversions, as the case may be), then one can eventually apply said concentration in study of scripture, worship, service of God in mankind, and finally in meditation. *Samadhana* is what Vedanta calls this latter ability — the singular concentration that focuses on God, and God alone. All manner of higher good comes from that, which all other forms of concentration cannot give.

By this short explanation, one can clarify the issue. What remains is to attempt one's first experiments in the art of concentration and begin to gather experience around it. In Yoga, the initial four limbs are to be mastered first, at least for the most part. When the fifth limb (pratyahara comes up for consideration, then one will find just how subtle is the art of concentration. That is the entrance to the freeway to Freedom, right there. But the toll booth operator demands the payment of proof of mastery of pratyahara. It is a limb that is difficult of attainment, which is why the inner freeways of spirituality are as yet very uncrowded; no traffic jams there! Well, all the better for those of us who are testing for our driver's license. See you on the open road, the higher path!

QUESTION #3: "You mentioned in class that it is better to learn from an Indian swami. Why would they be better than learning from you? I have been learning from you and feel confident in your guidance. Do you doubt your ability to teach? Sorry if this question is inappropriate."

ANSWER: I am the Indian swami in manifestation. My teachers were swamis. They transmitted to me the Vedanta. I know of other teachers who venture forth in that arena, and who have never gone to an Indian luminary to learn, have never surrendered the ego there, have never taken initiation. Thus, they misunderstand the Advaita, Nonduality, and commit all manner of misfeasances and lay many misconceptions over it. Until Westerners are able to bow before true Wisdom, and leave off worshipping at the altar of intellectual knowledge alone, they will erroneously mix materialistic concepts in with purely spiritual axioms, coming forth with an unhealthy amalgam of undigested thought. They cannot help it, as that is what they were raised in, and they arrogantly hold it as the highest. That is due, in part, to the erroneous perspective that if you go back in time according to the West, you were a paramecium, but if you go back in time according to Indian philosophy, you are God.

Reality is not relativity. Reality does not transform. Reality does not evolve. The Soul of mankind is not matter, energy, or thoughtforms/concepts. The Soul of mankind does not get developed (science) or created (religion). Until one comprehends and implements maxims such as these into the mind, and meditates upon them until ignorance dies, one should not dawn the mantle of a teacher by any means — certainly not a teacher of the noble Advaita Vedanta.

QUESTION #4: "How do we learn to regulate the prana? Is it through pure food, exercise, good posture, and deep and even breathing?"

ANSWER: You have read well. Indeed, these four techniques form the beginning of the purification process, leading the soul onwards towards That which is Ever-pure. The prana, as well, is not the Ever-pure, for it moves. But that it moves in subtler regions is what the practitioner has to find out, and then using it, he must explore those regions of his/her own consciousness.

All of this, plus what you have written above, regulates prana. To master the prana is a further step. One who has mastered prana returns to embodiment later, and people say of him, "Why is it that he is so peaceful, so blissful, so contented, so wise," etc. This sublime soul has mastered prana by the mind. He does not need to observe rules around diet, asana, breathing, and the like. If he does so, it is only to teach others how to do them. He is the natural teacher. As Swami Vivekananda has stated about such a one, *"The body in which one becomes an acharya is very different from that of any other man. There is a science for keeping that body in a perfect state. His is the most delicate organism, very susceptible, capable of feeling intense joy and intense suffering."*

So, until such mastery is upon the soul, the purificatory observances and rituals are very important, and should never be underestimated, or cast aside out of pretense. Even a past master can return to them if he so wishes, just to exemplify them for others whose minds are evolving. Deep and even breathing, alone, is a key to espying the prana, so that it can be tamed and utilized for the highest good of all.

QUESTION #5: "What kind of foods must be given up for Yogic practice? What foods should replace them?"

ANSWER: Foods that increase tamas, slothfulness, and rajas, frenetic activity, are to be given up. This may happen swiftly or gradually, depending upon the aspirant's strength and capacity -- and the situation one finds oneself in as well. Much has been said about the giving up of meat, and I concur with it, generally speaking. But can we insist that the Eskimos, for instance, give up taking meat? They would die. What would we have them live on? Iceberg lettuce? Snow peas? Winter melon? If one has to labor physically, in harsh conditions, then a thicker food will be required. If one does not have to put out such efforts and energy, then vegetarianism is an excellent road. Even there, the body, accustomed to many generation/lifetimes of meat-eating will have to readjust to the lighter diet. But once there, one need never go back to eating flesh again unless special circumstances require it. Here again, the yogi can eat or not eat, as the case may be. Others may have to keep regular meals until the power of mental detachment and renunciation is refined.

Foods that can replace all the above are sattvic foods that produce lightness and well-being. They do not weigh down the system, yet produce good energy for subtle practices. Tofu and other natural proteins can replace animal flesh; fish can replace red meat. Most importantly nowadays, natural foods like rice, grains, and fruits can replace overly processed fast foods and sugary snacks. Vegetables, in greater amounts, are the very best. For those with allergies or reactions to healthy animal products such as eggs, cheese, and dairy, it is not the food that is the problem, but the body's loss of ability to take denser foods. Dairy is excellent, for the most part. The body should be strengthened so that it can process most anything without "undue residue." The flesh of birds is mostly the stuff of bugs and insects. It should be given up where possible. Occasional fasting from all food is beneficial, if not overdone.

Best of all diets, however, is Jnana Wisdom. The saying, "You know that what you eat you are," applies well to wisdom, or lack of its intake into the mind. You are not your food, because you are not your body. Though this seems obvious to most aspirants, there are still many who need to reflect deeply on this fact.

QUESTION #6: "You prescribe divorcing oneself from drugs. I unfortunately take a number of them for high blood pressure, allergies, depression, bi-polar problems, etc. What should I do?"

ANSWER: Keep the ones that are specific to the body, but give up or wean yourself off of those that are prescribed for the mind. We cannot easily reverse what has already occurred in the case of the body, its genes, heredity, and the like; we have to live with that. Modern medicine has its best role to play in helping fight inherited problems and their effects that happen over the span of one lifetime, with chemicals. For those "naturalists" who object to this, the real point, for the practitioner of spirituality, anyway, is to live a longer life so practice can be applied and Enlightenment can be gained. We are not interested in longevity so that we can merely have more enjoyment, cling to earth and the body, get old, and live merely as healthy animals gibbering in the forest of the world. Even the argument of "Quality of Life" does not make much sense to us, for where is there any quality in living whatsoever without God (Reality) and its attainment (spiritual practice)?

As for drugs for the mind, to the one who has mastered the mind, or is in the process of doing so, it is an ugly concept. No doubt this too has its place in some cases, but overall, and as the society and its people and systems are showing, drugs are being both overused and errantly prescribed. To give a child a drug, for instance, because he or she cannot concentrate, is a form of madness. In such a case the healer is more insane than the patient. There are so many other better techniques for helping anyone to concentrate — if one only has the patience and ability. But modern medicine is not known for its patience, as we know. If the case is one of mental damage that was present at birth, the real issue is what happened before birth, i.e., in a previous lifetime, that made that soul incarnate in such a way. Here, inspection of the mind, and transcendence of the mind, take on greater import. Healing such a mind is hardly possible; the arrow has already left the bow, and it must find its mark. Only the divine can change such an orientation, and modify or withdraw such a direction. As Holy Mother said, *"What the Divine Mother has written in the book of destiny, She can also erase."*

By answering a question of this nature I deviate some from my focus upon Yoga and Vedanta. Watering the flowers and not the weeds is our way. But these issues require answers from different perspectives than conventional ones. Please understand that I answer these from the Vedantic position, and not from those of a worldly person, intellectual, doctor, psychologist, or scientist.

QUESTION #7: "You state that the Bhutakasha, the space of the physical, has all sorts of beings in it, even disembodied spirits and the like. Is this something one should worry about?"

ANSWER: Not at all. What one needs to worry about is that cross-section of humanity who turns the realm of disembodied beings into things called "ghosts," "spooks," "mummies," "flesh-eating zombies," and the like. For the luminary — and he knows, for he is the seer of the realms of the bhutas (spirits) and the pitris (ancestors) — disembodied beings are just bits of consciousness, like thought and memory congealed into a loose complex, that are disoriented and therefore have not located their source, thus have not returned to their point of origin and gotten fully established there. The main brunt of original consciousness is not even concentrated there in that wisp of thought/memory, so it need not be feared at all. It can rather be released and sent back to its home of peace.

And in fact, that is what is happening — on a much grander scale, of course — to embodied souls when they gain Enlightenment and get released from the illusion of finitude that is the embodied ego/mind complex living in the physical world—as if it were the only reality.

May all beings gain freedom from all manner of misdirected thought that congeals consciousness around delusion and ignorance.

QUESTION #8: "You mentioned that the incense stick is for God, as is the offered flower, sacred water, etc. Since everything is one with God, and we are one with God, couldn't these be for us as well?"

ANSWER: They are for our elucidation, as observers, but they are not to be taken to the ego self. The reference here was to a puja, or divine worship. In the Indian puja, God is the focus. Soon, after learning to perform the puja correctly, all of life can be considered one great worship, and one will perform it (life) well, just like a puja. If we light the stick of incense for our own enjoyment, and sniff the flower before offering it to the image of God on the altar, it is rather akin to enjoying mixed aromas coming from the kitchen while sitting on the toilet in the bathroom. If we partake of the food to be offered to the divine in puja, or sip the water reserved for Him/Her, it is rather like tasting food and drink at a cafe and then serving it to others, mixed with our saliva. The idea is, that people have lost all sense of the sacred — around food, acts, thoughts, other beings, and even and especially, God. We are to be brought back to our (higher) senses via authentic rites, and this can only happen if we pay close attention to the strict rules around ritualistic worship. It is really only an exercise in brutish existence to do otherwise. Besides, withdrawing from taking objects of pleasure to the senses is much nobler, and healthy. It is Yogic.

Besides this, there is the Presence of God Itself, existing in the shrine room, coming through the altar. It is real. One will not come to know this unless that Presence remains in the atmosphere, and It will not do so if impurities are present. So, food, acts, thoughts, and other beings must all be held sacred in the puja, and all interactions with them are to be carefully observed. Once achieving success there, in the puja, one can then go out into the world and see that Divine Presence in everything, everywhere. Ironically, this is a great secret that leads one to Nonduality. As Sri Ramakrishna Paramahamsa has said, *"Everywhere, at all times, there is a Great Puja going on."*

**Pada III, Sutra 35**

*hrdaye chitta samvit* (*hrdaye,* heart; *chitta,* mental complex; *samvit,* wisdom)

"*By meditating in the heart, the entire mental complex, and other minds, become known.*"

Here is another statement relating to the deep connection between heart and mind. The luminaries do not forgo one for the other, but use both in synchronicity with one another.

Further, this is the very best bit of advice for the meditator — to focus attention in the heart, not in the head. So many beginning and intermediate practitioners get off the path, with minds imbalanced and feet gone astray, by meditating in the head. If the heart is strengthened by focused concentration there, it acts later as an inviolable platform upon which the meditator can both rise to higher levels of awareness, and keep from falling to the gross climes and the old repetitive activities of the lower chakras. These are the first things to be said in accord with this powerful sutra.

But further intrigue comes forward upon considering this sutra. It is not only one's own mind that becomes known to the practitioner — a feat that is hard enough to accomplish — but even the minds of others. Among other helpful facets, this allows the aspirant to come to know the egoistic tendencies, personality traits, and character flaws abiding in the human mental complex. Bad influences can thereby be avoided, and this applies to both seeking true friends and looking for authentic teachers as well. For, this selfsame ability also affords the seeker the keen insight to observe positive attributes in fellow seekers, and in sincere teachers too.

Finally, it is not just knowledge of the individual mind that opens to the devotee, or just the collective mind; it is also the Cosmic Mind that reveals its treasures. Part of this capacity comes about by meditating on Ishvara/Ishvari. Such primal powers that are directly involved in the universal projection are valuable to know, since the meditator will have to encounter and pass through Them in the forthcoming spiritual journey to Enlightenment. Even the return to earth in another body, for whatever reason, will be graced immensely by knowing about Ishvara, and by building a relationship with God in form. For, there is a lacking, even a danger, in those who seek transcendence only, who are one-sided in their approach and realization. And who would want to forego the wonders of God's Mind, anyway?

In short, the Cosmic Mind, what to speak of the transcendent Mind of Ishvara, is the best example of how to use a mental complex. Certainly, there are numerous examples of how not to use this great boon. The mind is one of the Six Powers of the Godhead, along with the universe that it projected, and the knowledge that this projection was founded in. Such is the great import of the mind — individual, collective, and cosmic. As Holy Mother, Sri Sarada Devi said: *"The mind is very important to you at this stage. You must keep it in fine shape, for you will have to take it with you on your way to Brahman."*

Please send in your questions on all matters pertaining to spiritual life along the precious trajectory of Raja Yoga, and these sutras and their lessons.

# Lesson Eighty, 6/19/13
## Pada III, Sutras 36, 37, & 38

Raja Yoga class #80, with its three salient sutras, delves deeper into the powers of the mind — which are classed by Patanjali and Vedavyasa as both necessary attainments and potential dangers. We are entering into the realm of psychic prana at this juncture, the understanding of which is of utmost benefit to the sincere aspirant. Many and many have deviated from the traditional course and true purpose of authentic yoga at this point in the practice. Powers, especially to the contemporary Westerner, are just too attracting, and many would cast away the *"precious gems"* of concentration, meditation, and samadhi (samyama) for *"the few useless bobbles"* that might bring them domination over the enjoyment-laden world of relative existence. Therefore, a close study of the seers and their teachings in accord with this subject and these particular sutras is enthusiastically enjoined on the practitioner.

As the study here commences, we are to first look into the queries that came up for several of the participants around the previous lesson. There were precious few responses this time around, which I hope translates as clarity rather than apathy.

**Questions and Answers for Lesson 80**
Kanyakali from Hawaii writes:
COMMENTS: "I like this sutra very much (III:35) because in recent years I have really been enjoying meditating in the heart. I am one of your students who was instructed to bring my focus of attention from the third eye down to the heart, and it has been most effective. I now feel that my heart is far more the "seat" of consciousness than my head, and I get a wonderful sense of the expansiveness of consciousness, particularly when I bring my heart together with the heart of my Ishtam and they beat as one."
QUESTION: "You mentioned that eventually, by practicing samyama on the heart, one can come to know the traits and tendencies of other people. I am really looking forward to that day. So often I have misjudged people. It happened again recently. What started out seeming like a dream ended up a total nightmare. I wonder if sometimes maya works to hide people's character flaws in case there is karma to be worked out or lessons to be learned together. Do you think it might work that way?"
ANSWER: Maya works all ways, in every way possible — both to form karma and to bring about opportunities that lead to its neutralization. It is the mind that is the active element here, however. Remember, maya is insentient. That fact is one of the ten characteristics of Maya according to the Tantra. Like green scum that covers a lake, and that forms in the waters of the lake itself, maya is latent in the mind and appears naturally as a matter of course. The wise who know this take all manner of pains and cautionary measures to hold it from manifestation, keeping the waters of the mind pure so that nothing can formulate there.

It is a pure mind like this that can see into another's mind, and notice the latent tendencies there. But even then there is always the unexpected. The human mind and character, and the ego of course, are so unpredictable. Just like green scum coming from nowhere, seemingly out of nothing, so too will invisible tendencies come forth in unexpected fashion. To know oneself, as hard as that is, is nowhere near as hard as trying to know another. Only longstanding experience combined with careful proceedings will help in this volatile area. Spiritual teachers have known this for time out of mind.

QUESTION #2: "A friend of mine produces sound tracks that are designed to influence brain waves, guiding them to a meditative state, or slowing them down to improve sleep. They have names like 'Deep Theta Meditation' and 'Sleep for Chattery Minds.' He gave me some of them to try but I've been hesitant. What do you think of this type of meditation aid? Are they helpful or harmful?"

ANSWER: They can be helpful to those who need them, and by that I mean to those who have no other recourse. As I mentioned in a recent lesson, meditation has only one true use, and that is to have direct spiritual experience, called God-vision. All other uses are secondary, at best. If such secondary methods were titled "aids to help calm the mind" rather than anything that has to do with meditation practice, that would be okay. That is, someone with a restless mind could sit for a while and listen to nature sounds, or calming music, etc., and then when they feel quiet they could go for meditation — thereby keeping it one-pointed and focused on its one true purpose. The same would be true of hatha and Yoga. They are not the same by any stretch of the imagination. If one does a few asanas, then, to relax the body, then assumes the one meditation position and practices the seventh limb, then they rightly approach Yoga proper. Admixtures are what are to be avoided in most all cases. Especially in spiritual life and practice, we must be purists.

QUESTION #3: "I read a statistic that the average cell phone user checks his or her phone 150 times per day! This sounds to me like a huge potential for forming a samskara. Is there a way, aside from the obvious 'dump your phone,' to prevent such a samskara from forming? I'm thinking along the lines of keeping one's mind on God or repeating one's mantra whilst sneaking a peak?"

ANSWER: This is an admixture that you are proposing. Distractions are distractions, plain and simple. And they enter the mind even when the cell phone, computer, or television are not in one's immediate proximity. Sri Ramakrishna used to say, *"An object kept near a mirror reflects in it."* The mind is the mirror. So, unless one either keeps objects away from it, or turns the mirror in an opposite direction, distractions will form and foster. Taking an example from the source, we all know how we feel when someone puts us on hold in a phone conversation. Imagine how God would feel by being put on hold by material objects. Well, now you know why God-realization is so rare, especially in this day and time. God/Mother will not settle for second best. He/She is either your very best friend, or no friend at all.

R.O. from Hawaii writes:
QUESTION: "I was wondering if you could clarify the vegetarian diet which is recommended. I know there are many health reasons, i.e., low cholesterol that benefits the heart, and bulk that adds to the digestive system, in addition to many others. But I recall that the main reason given is avoidance of killing animals (and the karma created?). However, are we not considering the killing of plants? These are life forms also; and what about sprouts which are young little life forms just starting out and we bunch them up and put them in our salad. Does this not create karma also or are they too low on the scale of life? Even the Breatharian Diet with water would be consuming microbes & germs!"
ANSWER: There are three levels of eating, just as there are three levels of nonviolence. Basically, they are specific, general, and personal. In the specific, the beginning aspirant, being at a very young and sensitive age, feels the effects of food its and challenges keenly. He/she has not got the strength and resilience yet to move ahead in spiritual life while transcending minor obstructions — rather like the rare blue lotus that opens in the sunshine, but when clouds pass in front of the sun it closes abruptly. At this level the giving up of foods like meat, onions, garlic, and other foods deemed to be "rajasic," i.e., giving rise to coarse energy, is recommended. Even here, in the specific, rules change due to the adherent's physique and temperament. Some beings may have to take meat in order to gain a certain type of energy that will help them get over impediments. Cultural habits also figure in here, especially when meat eating has become a habit — a day to day habit. Such a culture gives rise to negativities like war-mongering, violence, the will to dominate over others, military madness, insensitivity to human suffering, etc. Suffice to say that meat is not a necessity, can be taken once a week, like fish on Fridays, etc. Then there is the harm done to animals, which many beings abhor.

All of this gets into the general level, where one takes into consideration all the species. When considering harm done, karma, etc., it is far less productive and ensuing in the case of plants, sprouts, etc. There is no nervous system per se in plants, no brain, no senses. Even the body is simplistic, and readily regenerative. Putting aside the "sensitivity " of plants that some speak of (no doubt that they "live" on one level of consciousness), the karma associated with the ingesting of them is minimal, if at all. They are the perfect food, and since every living thing on this planet and in this world has to eat to live, and eats others as a matter of course, most animals and sensible humans rely upon the plant world for their physical sustenance. Such acts are practical, harmless, and almost completely nonproductive of karma. The only time karma comes up with relation to plants is when mankind willfully destroys forests, waters that contain aquatic life, air that sustains plant life, etc.

On the personal level, and especially if one's choices are based upon long-standing personal experience, the whole matter is rather like one's actions. That is, if one's actions do not harm others, then one is relatively free to do what one pleases. The same with food. If beings living from the level of the five senses on upwards, i.e., humans and animals, are not harmed, then one can take the food that is best for one's individual health — especially so long as habits such as gluttony, pleasure-mongering, and the like are eschewed. With liquids, all forms of alcohol are to be avoided, shunned, really. Their only use should be for sterilization, etc. Overall, alkaline diet is best, and some experts say that foods that are fermented ought to be moderated or given up.

And as long as we are on the subject of the personal, I have been a vegetarian for 44 years now. The diet is both healthy and easy on the palate. Illnesses are scarce in occurrence. Heaviness of limbs and body are never present. In fact, lightness of being is the norm. I do not take meat of any kind, but some dairy suits me fine and gives me the protein element, along with beans and nuts. Some may want to go vegan, macrobiotic, raw, etc., but aside from the need to do so because of certain problematic traits in the body due to genes and heredity, it is not necessary. Overall, the trend towards "food-faddism" can become a preoccupation, and should be avoided for sensible eating. Food is to be controlled, moderated, then used to possess pure energy so that the mind can gain the unbridled freedom that is already in the Soul, Atman. I would venture to say that the literary diet of people nowadays poses even more of a problem than their food habits. As I travel and look around, I can scarcely believe what garbage people are taking into their minds through books and various readings. This diet and what one eats mentally is to be observed, scrutinized, and changed for the better. Again, a man eats an overall meat-based diet, loses reverence for nature and sensitivity for animals, becomes violent due to the coarse nature of the food he has taken, loses control over his temper, declares war on the world, then sits for his meal with a few too many drinks after he has dominated everyone and reads novels about sex, gambling, cheating, murder, war, and overall worldliness. And it all started with how you treated your wife, children, animals, environment, food, and, of course, your potentially divine self.

To effect a beginning, we propose that human beings return to the good habit of blessing their food — whatever it may consist of — with mantra, and taking it in reverent silence and holy company. Holy Mother, Sri Sarada Devi, the divine wife and consort of Sri Ramakrishna Paramahamsa, is our inspiration for this method. Her words: *"From pure food one gets pure blood; from pure blood one gets pure mind; from pure mind one gets pure thoughts; and from this one attains Brahman."*

## Pada III, Sutra 36

*sattva purushayoh atyanta asankirnayoh pratyaya avishesho bhogah pararthatvat svartha samyamat purusha-jnanam* (*sattva*, balance; *purushayoh*, soul; *atyanta*, fully; *asankirnayoh*, unmodified; *pratyaya*, concept; *avisheshah*, free of difference; *bhogah*, enjoyment; *pararthatvat*, lived for another; *svartha*, self-interest; *samyamat*, concentration/meditation/direct experience; *purusha-jnanam*, knowledge of the Self)

*"Enjoyment springing from mental balance proceeds due to the self-interest of another (the ego), but samyama on the Soul (Purusha) uncovers knowledge of the real Self."*

Several of the main teachings that Vedantists are familiar with appear here in this sutra. There are the three gunas, with balance, *sattva,* being one of them. There is the ego and its penchant for enjoyment. Then there is the search for the true Self, and for Enlightenment. But the hidden clue in the sutra, and the two that follow, is knowledge, so often overlooked. That is, *Purusha,* the Self, and *Jnanam,* knowledge leading to It, though deeply connected, are two different aspects. It is so easy for practitioners to merely see and note that knowledge is needed, but then fail to enter into its pursuit and attainment. Thus, we find so many beings — both teachers and practitioners — devoid of it, thereby showing a mere one, or even two-sided, spiritual life.

In the Bhagavad Gita, Sri Krishna states: *"In beings, I am knowledge."* Failure, in all walks of life, is due to the lack of attainment of knowledge, in any given field. In the spiritual field, which depends heavily on what Patanjali has titled the *karmashaya,* the receptacle of the mass of actions done, the mind is cited. Both source for and cause of all effects in the universe, and in all universes — even those subtler and beyond the physical realm — the mind that is left uncontrolled, untended, and unmastered brings the soul in the end to its painful dunking in the ocean of suffering *(Samsara Sagara)* rather than its sweet immersion in the ocean of Peace and Bliss *(Ananda Sagara).* It is all because the embodied being failed to comprehend the import of the dharmic teachings and follow through with study and contemplation on their timeless message.

Such a study, according to Swami Vivekananda, might well take up one whole lifetime. *"I am strongly of the opinion that very few persons in any yuga attain jnana, and therefore we should go on striving and striving even unto death. That's my old fashioned way, you know."* But it is most worthwhile, seeing that many lifetimes of suffering may occur if such an important attainment is not engaged and consummated. As the famous song in India puts it: *"The errant and stubborn child who does not study is spanked soundly and put straight to bed without supper."* In spiritual life in the world in these times, workers, meditators, and worshippers, we have. What is missing in seekers and teachers alike is spiritual wisdom. By spiritual knowledge, we mean *pratibha,* which appears again in the following sutra.

## Pada III, Sutra 37

*tatah pratibha shravana vedana adarsha asvada varta jayante* (*tatah,* therefore; *pratibha,* light of higher knowledge; *shravana,* divine sound; *vedana,* divine touch; *adarsha,* divine sight; *asvada,* divine taste; *varta,* subtle sense of smell; *jayante,* happens)

*"When this higher knowledge, called pratibha, dawns, the five senses of perception get purified and behold their inner powers."*

The eye, the ear, the tongue, the nose, etc. — they are mere flaps of skin and fleshy orbs. It is the power in them that is most notable, and which must be located and utilized. The word, *indriyas,* used to name the five senses, rises from Indra, the Lord of the Gods. Just like knowledge, if the senses are taken for granted, left as mere enjoyers of objects, their real power is never tapped. Then they act as blocks to inward progress instead of helpmates to attain it. Thus, the yogis say that they must be purified.

This process does not take place by washing the eyes out, cleaning the ears, or scraping the tongue, etc. They are to be connected through meditation to the prana, or life force, which gives them the power to see, hear, touch, taste, and smell. Even prior to this great inward connection, and to effect the swift and easy withdrawal from their willful penchant for outward enjoyment, the five senses are to be connected in the other direction (externally) to the five elements of earth, water, fire, air, and ether. The chart on the facing page (269) demonstrates this practice and its aims. By connecting all these "alambanas" via meditation — the five senses outwardly to the five elements, and then inwardly to the subtle elements via the one prana in its five forms, Yoga, Union with Divine Reality, can begin and proceed. Otherwise, only a disconnected life resulting in a scattered mind (kshipta) will occur — so prevalent in this day and time.

What results from this double connection, and which is also the real meaning of this sutra, is the purification of the five senses, which is really the mind's ability to control or withdraw them from their otherwise coveted objects. Asteya, one of the earliest teachings in Yoga in the form of the five yamas, is noncovetousness. How do beings imagine that it gets effected? It is really by connection more than by withdrawal. This is one of Yoga's secrets, that makes it distinct as a practice and a philosophy from its companion darshanas. To attach and detach at will is higher than mere detachment, and this ability is gained via the practice of connection. It is thus that Sri Krishna advises His devotee on the battlefield of Kurukshetra, *"Be thou a Yogi, Arjuna."*

This subtle teaching of inward connection also outlines for us the actual dynamic of the dawning of higher knowledge in the human mind. We know that *"earthly knowledge satisfies only for a time,"* as Vivekananda states, while *"spiritual knowledge is the only thing that can destroy our miseries forever."* This is true because of the purification process that the yogic practitioner engages in, which takes up the mind-field (karmashaya) itself for neutralization.

In brief, senses abide with objects and then vibrate with contrasting pairs of opposites like pleasure and pain, gain and loss, thraldom and boredom. These mental vibrations, *vrittis,* cause reactions for the ego in the mind and leave good, bad, and mixed impressions therein, thereafter. Patterns form around this process and are strengthened via repetition. Human behavior becomes trapped in and dependent upon this crystallization process. Seeing this conundrum, the newly aware practitioner strives to reverse it.

But in the other direction, away from a mere life of the senses alone, lies higher wisdom — pratibha. Suffice to say, that this "flint-like intelligence," as Sri Ramakrishna has called it, comes to the yogi and yogini who seek to place the mind back in a position of mastery over senses and nature. Therefore, it is more of a natural result of human life than a special quality. That is, intel-

# Yogic Connections and Correlations in Meditation Practice

*"Utilizing the supports (alambanas), the yogi stabilizes the mind-field by meditating upon them all, from the grossest magnitude inward to the subtlest principles. Let the yogi focus upon what is agreeable, then, observing it all in waking, dreaming, and deep sleep states with detachment."*

— *Vedavyasa*

## Alambanas, in Order of Meditation

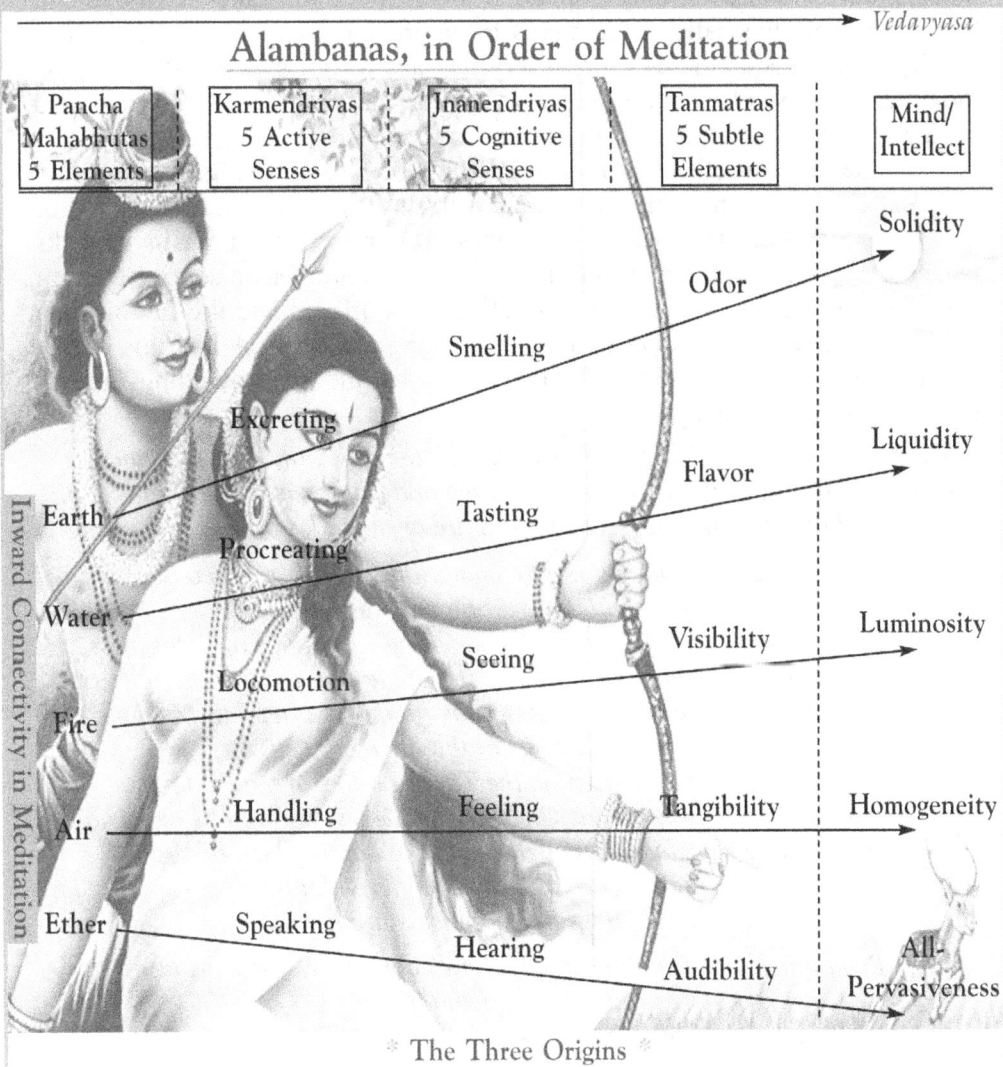

| Pancha Mahabhutas<br>5 Elements | Karmendriyas<br>5 Active Senses | Jnanendriyas<br>5 Cognitive Senses | Tanmatras<br>5 Subtle Elements | Mind/Intellect |
|---|---|---|---|---|
| Earth | Excreting | Smelling | Odor | Solidity |
| Water | Procreating | Tasting | Flavor | Liquidity |
| Fire | Locomotion | Seeing | Visibility | Luminosity |
| Air | Handling | Feeling | Tangibility | Homogeneity |
| Ether | Speaking | Hearing | Audibility | All-Pervasiveness |

*Inward Connectivity in Meditation*

### ❊ The Three Origins ❊

Ahamkara, Ego ⟶ Buddhi, Determinative Intelligence ⟶ Mahat, Cosmic Mind

---

#### Meditate Upon Each Via

- its origin
- its qualities, attributes, characteristics
- its consistency and content
- its appearance in waking and dream
- its changing nature
- its place in the mind and thoughts
- its power and hold over the mind
- its disappearance in deep sleep

*"Wisdom samadhi occurs via the process of gross thought to subtle thought, culminating in the indescribable state of 'I-am-ness.' In Abhava Yoga and Mahayoga, wherein one begins to see the blissful Self, the alambanas are absent. Thus, they are to be transcended in deep meditation."*

ligence is not intellect, just as the mind is not the brain. There are containers for Consciousness, but there are also primal compounds of Consciousness. Intelligence is one of those, and the foremost. Intellect, or vijnanamayakosha, is a sheath, both a container and a covering. A man under the auspice of his intellect and not in possession of his intelligence is really only a wise fool. Living with impure senses, i.e., senses that are attached to and see only external objects, and which seek only contact with them for the sake of enjoyment, leaves him/her physically at the mercy of nature, and mentally in the lurch of duality. On one side there is the misery that always follows pleasure, and on the other is the problem of an intended satiation that only ends in gluttony and exhaustion. How intelligent is that?

The yogi, whether aspirant or adept, is seen to be living in an entirely different mode, and heading in the opposite direction. He does not own or covet; he renounces. He does not seek pleasure, nor does he shun pain; he seeks balance. He does not attempt to satiate the senses, nor does he deprive them of their due; all that he experiences through them is offered into the fire of Yoga for both purification and spiritual impetus along the path. All of this is true pratibha in action. A song of Tibet, sung by the cave-dwelling ascetic, Milarepa, describes this perfectly:

*The tree of guidance has many branches — the guru, the disciple, and the secret teachings; endurance, perseverance and faith, wisdom, compassion, and the human form. All of these are ever guides on the path.*

*Further, solitude with no commotion and disturbance is the guide protecting meditation.*
*The accomplished guru is the guide dispelling ignorance and darkness.*
*Faith without sorrow and weariness is the guide that leads to happiness.*
*The sensations of the five organs are the guides that lead to freedom.*
*The verbal teachings of the lineage gurus are the guides which illumine the Three Bodies of the Buddha.*
*The protectors, the Three Precious Ones, are guides with no faults or mistakes.*
*Led by these six guides one will reach the happy plane of Yoga, abiding in the realm of nondifferentiation in which all views and sophisms are no more.*

*Remaining in the realm of Self-Knowledge and Self-Liberation is indeed happy and joyful.*
*Abiding in the valley where no men dwell, with confidence and knowledge, one lives in his own way.*
*With a thundering voice he sings the happy song of Yoga.*

*Falling in the ten directions is the rain of fame, brought to blooming with the flowers and leaves of compassion.*
*The enterprise of Enlightenment then encompasses the entire universe.*
*The pure fruit of the enlightened heart thus attains perfection.*

Notice in this yogic song the engaging presence of pure happiness and the total lack of solemnity, aversion, distaste, and disengagement with life. Here is true life, yogic life. Here, even the *"sensations of the ten senses"* (karmendriyas and jnanendriyas) are only *" guides that lead one to freedom."* Conclusively, then, Yoga is a path of Joy, *Mudita* — even its intense practice phase. One only has to seek to engender the spirit of uninhibited freedom and shun the weights and impediments of preponderant bondage.

## Pada III, Sutra 38
*te samadhau upasargah vyutthane siddhayah* (*te*, this attainment; *samadhi*, conditioned higher awareness; *upasarga*, impedes; *vyutthana*, externalized thought-vibration; *siddhi*, powers)

*"The effects of this attainment (called pratibha samadhi) are both an attainment and an impediment to higher realization, depending on the resultant externalized thoughts."*

The comments of Swamiji in Raja Yoga are worth repeating here: *"These are obstacles to Samadhi; but they are powers in the worldly state. If the Yogi knows all these enjoyments of the world it comes by the junction of the Purusha and the mind. If he wants to make Samyama on this, that they are two different things, nature and soul, he gets knowledge of the Purusha. From that arises discrimination. When he has got that discrimination he gets the Pratibha, the light of supreme genius. These powers, however, are obstructions to the attainment of the highest goal, the knowledge of the pure Self, and freedom; these are, as it were, to be met in the way, and if the Yogi rejects them, he attains the highest. If he is tempted to acquire these, his farther progress is barred."*

Utilizing the increased power of the senses for personal gain and glory after purification of them is achieved is the move of a worldly and insincere person. Until and unless the ego element in the human being is brought to full obedience, its willful nature ripened and its selfish outlook matured, the novitiate practitioner will only prove to be a positive danger to himself and to others. So many leave the path prematurely due to the egoic element in them, thinking that they know better than the spiritual teacher, and imagining that they can somehow maintain the world, their practice, and their newly-found powers, simultaneously.

But Yoga, and the spiritual path — the "razor's-edged pathway" — demands full attention. It will be hard enough for the householder to hold good employment, make legitimate money, maintain a dharmic family, teach their children moral values and spiritual truths, and hold to their daily practice, what to speak of avoidance of muddying the waters with powers, potentially occult in nature, that have no real and authentic worth in the end anyway, and that risk threatening one's pursuit of Enlightenment as well. The whole point and purpose of Yoga gets frustrated by such a mistake, and what is worse, massive amounts of benefit are thrown away.

How to skirt the dangers and achieve the attainment of pratibha? The challenges, as Swamiji says, are *"to be met in the way,"* a facing off that is typical of the Yoga. Nonreaction in practice, nonresistance in meditation — the art of effortlessness, as a spiritual quality, gets mastered over time and with experience. Otherwise, both the efforts undergone to purify the senses, and the wondrous powers of pratibha for illumination and overall benefit, are sacrificed.

The other facet of this sutra worth exploring a bit is the point regarding *vyutthana* — externalized thought. Pratibha, the increased power of thought, aided by purification of the senses, if focused on powers for their own sake, turns into vyutthana. The living being is then drawing forth power from within and utilizing it for outer purposes. Whereas this sounds like a positive factor, as in gathering knowledge, discovering the secrets of nature, attaining success in worldly life, healing the sick, and the like, it is not the purpose of Yoga. If gathering knowledge is only for the ego's prideful usage, if discovering the secrets of nature only leads to war, destructive power, and domination over others, if gaining success in worldly life only results in failure in the end due to the world being unreal, then of what use are any powers in the end? As my guru, with his ashram in Oregon, once declared: *"Those who want God get Peace. Those who want power get Rolls-Royces."*

Spiritual power, Shakti, granted by the Divine Mother in *Pratibha Samadhi,* directs the human mind inwards, not outwards. After perfection is gained, and true insight gathered, then the yogi and yogini can venture forth, armed with the strength of yogic equipoise and ready to serve God in humanity. This type of living soul is, as the earlier song sings, *"....the perfect guide with no faults or mistakes."* Those coveting external power, fixated on changing matter only and what it can bring, though they may presume to lead, in seeming friendship, only create negative karma for themselves and for all those involved with them. To them we must say, *"Save me from my friends, and may the Divine Mother lead me to my spiritual teacher."*

We shall course on towards lesson #81, while waiting for good questions to arrive on this lesson in the interim.

## Lesson Eighty-one, 8/17/13
### Pada III, Sutra 39

We are presently well into the third pada of Patanjali's Yoga Sutras, called Raja Yoga -- the "Kingly" or "Royal" Yoga. Those who have remained steady and dedicated to this study thus far have gained a deep training in this meditative science (also called Dhyan Yoga), which fuses the highest and purest psychology with the hidden esoteric secrets of spirituality. Such integration goes the farthest, and has the best chance of both deepening the heart and widening the mind. With a devoted temperament and a catholic outlook, the problems of life soon get surmounted, and the Goal of human existence is seen. With practice, termed *sadhana,* the Goal is met, then attained, leaving the sincere aspirant in a state of perpetual freedom, called *Moksha.* Yoga is another name for Moksha. Thus, as Sri Krishna once advised Arjuna around the many things one could aspire to be, *"Be thou a Yogi."*

The following few questions have come in from some of the Raja Yoga study list adherents.

**Questions and Answers for Lesson 81**
R.O. from Hawaii writes:
QUESTION: "I'm still pondering what you mean ( I understand the 'Forgotten Realization') by the soul straying from the true path and taking embodiment in space and time, a primal error. What choices would SOUL have if it didn't individualize itself? How does it get temporarily disoriented? What is the true path before embodiment?"
ANSWER: So long as the transmigrating soul's karmas remain unresolved, the true path before embodiment is identical with the path after embodiment; they cannot be separated. From the realms of the ancestors, or from lower and higher heavenly states back to earth, the soul moves, as if in a dream, not knowing the reason why it constantly projects itself. Its true nature, Atman (SOUL, as you write it here), is ever-stationary and does not move about. One needs to prove this to oneself via rapt and still meditation. As Vivekananda has stated, this coming and going is all nonsense. To read it in his own words: *"Coming and going is all pure delusion. The Soul never comes nor goes. Where is the place to which it shall go, when all of space is in the Soul? When shall be the time of entering or departing, when all time is in the Soul?"* This statement is profound, and the real essence of Advaita Vedanta. It imparts to us, and from the lips of a rare, illumined soul, both the mechanics of maya and the truth of Nonduality — the divinity of the Soul.

In other words, then, and to address the first part of your question, the real path of the Soul is no path at all. All pathways lie within the dreaming mind. The Goal *Is* the Soul, but not the transmigrating one (the mental complex). To travel from realm to realm is to move from one dream to another, and everything associated with such movement lies in Maya. As Gaudapada counsels us in his famous karika, *"A runner running a race in a dream goes nowhere."* On the other side of the equation, Ramprasad sings in one of his wisdom songs: *"To be born in this body composed of earth is a heavy burden for the soaring Soul. To incarnate again and again across the face of this vast planetary realm can never slake our burning thirst. The poor one who sings this song proclaims: 'No more birth for me from the womb of matter, only emanation from my Divine Mother.'"*

Now, another thing may be mentioned here, which may possibly be more to the point of your query. A fully conscious incarnation, called a divine life, is also true. Fully aware beings accomplish this when they embody. The only thing about this — and all the wise luminaries say so — is that such a "birth" cannot be classed as a birth at all, since the Essence of the Soul, Atman, is neither forgotten nor has been strayed away from in the least. In other words, a divine life is existence lived in Self-realization. It has nothing to do with seeking or finding, and has no karma to answer for. Delusion, suffering, dreaming, searching, or living for the purposes of mere enjoyment, are not found in It, are alien to It. It is not birth at all, then, as the song above explains, but only *"emanation."* An emanation never disconnects from the Source like dreaming does, for if it did, the pure ray of light would simply dissolve in space and time, in Maya. And actually, this is what taking birth, life, and death in Maya is like, what it is all about. It is running a race in a dream. Beings may look back and think that they made progress, gained substance, actually went somewhere, but there is nowhere to go in a realm of illusion. A hamster running constantly on an exercise wheel in a cage fails to move even an inch.

There is no way to make Maya work for oneself. *"It is neither real, nor unreal, nor neither, nor a combination of both."* As Sri Ramakrishna has said, *"Never study Maya; observe it from a distance."* If one studies it, like, for instance, physics and science is doing, it only sweeps one into it. Soon, one is beholding the particles of one's universe to be changing at a billionth of a second, and as a result getting hypnotized to such an extent that one cannot conclude that it is all Maya, and that it and its objects are empty — that the world is ephemeral, like all the true luminaries of the past have told us. It cannot be owned, it cannot fulfill, and the fact that even intellectuals seek to possess and gain satisfaction from such emptiness (*shunyata*) is the real definition of delusion here on earth.

The question may be asked, then: what constitutes the realization of an illumined soul who emanates bodies with minds devoid of mayic delusion? The answer is: that selfsame renunciation of all things temporal, or all things changing, of the entire empirical process. And there is another facet of this unique realization as well. The realized soul knows that 1) all phenomena have proceeded from his own mental process, and 2) that it all exists within him, not outside. *"All is Brahman."* To the realized soul, the world is Brahman. To the bound soul seeking freedom, the world reveals itself as Maya. To the one-sided intellectual devoid of spiritual wisdom and proper discrimination, the world is falsely taken to be real. To the worldly person seeking pleasure and fulfillment, the world is his or her oyster, but lost in a sea of temporality and empty appearances. To the lost soul, the world is a prisonhouse of suffering. To most beings here on earth, they do not care one way or another. They just go ahead with their practice of the "Yoga" of Apathy.

Back to the final aspect of your question, unless one sees and knows the Formless Essence underlying all manifestation, all expression, and all appearances, form may as well *be* delusion. Taking a form would then constitute bondage. Venturing into *"the realms of name and form in time and space based upon cause and effect'* (Swamiji's definition of Maya) would then epitomize disorientation. Such pointless wandering creates desires that are both connected to and a product of the soul's original desire to embody apart from or devoid of the knowledge of Brahman. Here, that familiar adage, "....don't leave home without it," pertains perfectly to the soul's exit from Formless Reality and its entrance into the realms of name and form. As Vivekananda has put it, when asked if a man should embody: *"I certainly hope he will not; not until he can do so in full Consciousness."*

Avinashi from Pennsylvania writes:
QUESTION: "Thank you for your answer to my question on the samadhis in a recent satsang. I'd like to place a follow-up question on that question. The content of the lowest of the samprajnata samadhis eludes me, yet interests me greatly at the same time, if for no other reason than they will probably be the first samadhis I experience. I want to be able to connect the 'map' of these samadhis to the 'territories' they describe so they're more than mere abstractions, but will only be able to do that if I understand the content of the lowest four samadhis better than I do. The four samadhis I'm enquiring into are the savitarka and nirvitarka and the savichara and nirvichara. My general understanding at this point is that the 'tarka' samadhis relate somehow to manas, while the 'chara' samadhis more relate to buddhi. As such, if I'm correct, then I might expect the lowest two samadhis, (the 'tarkas'), to yield more in the sense of classic visions... colorful, in form, thrilling perhaps, while the 'chara' samadhis would be more subtle and would involve shifts in the way we understand existence at fundamental levels. I further understand the difference between the 'savi' and the 'nirvi' forms of both samadhis as relating to language and how language enters into the samadhis as a part of them. I conjecture that in the 'savi' forms of both samadhis, language has a tendency to lead, while in the 'nirvi' forms of them it might tend to follow, and therefore play a more secondary role to other facets of experience occurring at the time. And for me, this would relate to conditioning, in that the forms of these lower samadhis where language is dominant would tend to be more conditioned, while the forms where it's secondary might be more unconditioned and thus offer more freedom to the unfoldment of understanding. All of this is, of course, mere conjecture... conjecture, however, that seems unavoidable when it comes to my attempts to more clearly understand the concepts of this doctrine. I am presenting these conjectures to you to hear what you have to say."
ANSWER: To begin with, we need to place the lower samadhi category in order (Samprajnata, or Sa-bija) as Patanjali has given it to us. The order thus goes:

* Savitarka (with Nir-vitarka)
* Savichara (with Nir-vichara)
* Sananda
* Sasmita

The word, *"vitarka,"* means gross thought, and the word *"vichara"* indicates subtle thought. A look back and review of the Yoga sutra 1:17 and its surrounding sutras would be good for your further comprehension. Essentially, vitarka proceeds by considering gross objects, called *alambanas,* as fields for meditation. When it is complete, it gets refined into the vichara stage where vitarka is abandoned.

Again, vitarka meditation is involved with objects and their names. Vichara meditation, being more rational, leaves behind gross objects and their names and takes up subtler objects of concentration, like mind, intelligence, and

*Mahat.* Yogis who have become bodiless, *videha,* maintain their subtle bodies at the Mahat level *(linga sharira).* This can only happen after objects have been dissolved into original *Prakriti,* which is also a stage towards final liberation, called *Kaivalya.* Then, *Asamprajnata,* or *Nir-bija Samadhi,* is close on the horizon.

So, your ruminations about conditioned and non-conditioned states can find validity here if further subjected to the traditional teachings. One can see, then, that the nir-vitarka stage of sa-vitarka samadhi, and the nir-vichara stage of sa-vichara samadhi, represent the refinement process wherein all traces of the previous samadhi are resolved, and the meditator can get into each approaching samadhi free of residues. *Sananda samadhi* will then be "rapture accompanied," and *Sasmita samadhi* be attended by the fullest and most mature sense of Self possible.

For a full rendering of this grand process, please see my chart, *The Process of Samprajnata to Asamprajnata Samadhi,* back on page 61.

Akshaya Bhakti from New England writes:
COMMENTS: "How I will welcome the forthcoming Raja Yoga text, especially since I am eager to review the 8 years (!) of lessons with which the guru has blessed us. I have been appreciating the charts more than ever as a way of reinforcement. For instance, the recent chart of "Yogic Connections and Correlations in Meditation Practice" in Lesson 80 facilitates involution when using the alambanas, which I found so helpful initially. This last year has been particularly challenging for me, but I am trying to see that spiritual life is not separate from the world: First of all, my beloved mother passed away. We had such a precious bond that I can't help but feel it was the fulfillment of a long awaited desire (on both of our part), of which Sri Sarada spoke. While I am sure I will always miss her physical presence, I am greatly anticipating the connection with her spiritual one, and know that it just requires an adjustment on my part....as Sri Ramakrishna told Holy Mother after his passing — that he was just passing "into another room". How much comfort Their presence on earth has brought, to know They have such compassion for our suffering and our weaknesses.

I realize these profound Vedantic principles also have the power to disperse my second major source of distress this year — physical pain and illness which have been intermittent, but chronic. Thankfully, they are not by any means life threatening, perhaps just the "pinprick" that Holy Mother referred to, but which I have felt at the very core of my being. In reply to one student in Lesson 79, I was excited to see you use the familiar quote, "Just Do It," as that actually had been reverberating in my own mind in regards to re-vitalizing my practice. When you wrote to me about proceeding with 'the least resistance,' it translated to me that while there might always be some bumps in my practice, I should not take them to heart, but continue to move forward. Then I began to wonder what resistance actually means in sadhana, and how we create our own obstacles through the immature ego, the sense of the little "I" — my pain, my sorrow, my expectations, my doubts. Deepest thanks for the replies to my queries below, and any comments on the above thoughts."

QUESTION: "In connection with all of this, could you please explain again the teaching that is often given about how we should not resist Maya, how darkness has no substance. I try to pray to Holy Mother as the embodiment of Mahashakti, and say, 'Oh, Mother please do not delude me with thy world bewitching Maya.'"

ANSWER: "Resist not evil" was the way Jesus put it, but this should not be taken to mean that one can become lazy and complacent in one's spiritual practice. This would be like living in a very large cave with a bear. You might not encounter it, but the probability that you might always exists. Similarly, we must adhere to our practice, for that alone will prove to us that evil, and Maya, have no real existence in the end. That is the real meaning to this statement. That poison exists in a snake proves no real threat to you, that is, unless the snake bites you. Maya is insentient, substanceless, but if taken to be real, will infill every pore of your life and being with deluding power. See also my answer to the first question of this lesson for more on this subject.

QUESTION #2: "Also, forbearance is given as the antidote for physical suffering. I know you had discussed this with Avinashi in Lesson 79, but could you give even more details on how we can master this? Does it just come automatically from consistent sadhana, or is there some special way we can foster it? I think I understand some of what is required, such as patience and the knowledge that we are not the body, but it would be soothing for me to hear it from the guru, something to which I can refer (at least until I am enlightened!) when I feel like I am being overwhelmed."

ANSWER: Ironically, forbearance is gained simply by engendering more of itself. Much like patience, that must be long-standing, *titiksha* must be maintained by titiksha. The other way is not always so desirable, i.e., having to test one's forbearance in the fires of pain, suffering, illness, the loss of loved ones, and the many other vagaries and vicissitudes that life inevitably brings to us. Whatever the case, once developed, there is nothing quite as helpful in the face of Maya, so do work on strengthening those inner, invisible muscles of forbearance by whatever means is afforded to you over the ongoing course of life and time.

J.M. from Oregon writes:
QUESTION: "Are the Six Jewels of Vedanta gradated, or is it just that some are connected — like how inner peace and self-control go together?

ANSWER: They are definitely connected, but do not necessarily arrive to the aspirant in listed and orderly fashion. As I have often repeated, inner peace and self-control usually get practiced and mastered together, as do the next two — forbearance and self-settledness. All of this, these four, allow the aspirant to meditate on Reality alone, called *samadhana,* and this leads to unshakable Faith. Therefore, if a Vedantist is asked to explain his or her faith, all he/she needs do is start with Faith and explain how the first two treasures, viveka and vairagya, set the stage for it, leading in fine succession to the practice and attainment of the first Five Jewels in order. And importantly, all of this brings only a single pure desire for Freedom, not Freedom Itself. That is how rare and difficult of attainment is this state called *Moksha* or *Mukti,* according to the *Rishis.* Salvation is relatively easy, but liberation is "as rare as hen's teeth."

Kanyakali from Hawaii writes:
QUESTION: "I have a follow-up question to the one I asked last time about judging people's character. It is indeed difficult to know another's unpredictable mind, ego, and character, particularly when those invisible tendencies come forth in unexpected fashion. As much as I want to be a trusting soul and give people the benefit of the doubt, lately I find myself thinking twice before stopping to help someone on the road, or offering to give a ride to a stranger. On the one hand, people who devote their lives to service put themselves at risk constantly. But I doubt very much that Mother Theresa ever refused to help someone because she stopped and thought of her own safety first. And yet, we also hear about unthinkable acts of violence being perpetrated on good and noble people whose only fault, it seems, was to take the risk of helping someone who turned out to be the wrong person. So it makes sense to proceed with caution. However, to some extent, I believe that my karma dictates the things that happen to me, no matter how carefully I proceed. We are instructed to be fearless. If I am birthless and deathless then there is no reason not to be fearless. I'm going back and forth on this issue. Can you help me sort through this and offer some advice?"
ANSWER: You have touched on all the main points of the issue here, and done so using words that are both well constructed and sensible.

    Sri Ramakrishna Paramahamsa used to say things like, *"To be spiritual is not to be a fool,"* and, *"God exists in everything, but do not go and embrace the tiger on that account."* Thus, we are to proceed with caution, but must also pause to assess the situation. Assessing the situation does not mean doing so just when circumstances arise, but to take a look at the nature of any given culture in any given time period, and what kinds of people inhabit these times and cultures.

    For instance, Mother Teresa was not stooping on the streets of the United States to help Westerners who once had money and were then bereft, then finally abandoned due to the callous nature of an uncaring society. She was not facing people with unresolved family and emotional issues, violent upbringing in the atmosphere of war and guns, heavy drug addictions and imbalanced minds. She was rather helping poor, helpless, hungry Indian people steeped in generations of poverty, with physical illnesses. These latter would hardly have attacked her as she bent to help them.

    Here in the West, it is risky to pick up hitchhikers and extend oneself to render aid, so one must be on one's guard. Alone, certain things should not be attempted, but in the company of others it may be possible. Pick and choose accordingly, based upon a standard of personal safety.

But over all, continue on with spiritual life seeking Yoga. Yoga, union with God, will naturally protect one — like practice of the mantra, daily. Yoga, as applied psychology will also help immensely, for it will aid one in seeing into the minds of beings around you. With time, careful observation, and experience, you will be able to assist others by uncovering and removing root causes to problems that only surface later on the *karmashaya,* the field of action. Helping beings after the deed is done proves of little help at all. This after-the-fact method should have been seen as "passe" long ago, even by conventional methodologists. What we want is the ability to see into people's minds (like the sutras under study in these most recent lessons are trying to tell us) and defuse imbalanced energies and tendencies before they get a hold of the brain and limbs and lead to unbridled wanton acts.

We will have to become students of Eastern Psychology to qualify ourselves for such subtle insight, for Western Psychology is still an infant science whose savants, like Freud and Jung, never thought outside the box of a single life span, and never had any training or experience with beings who lived and acted under the principle of a many lifetime scenario.

Placing this wider view aside for the moment, dredging up the contents of people's subconscious and unconscious minds, depending on the individual who is being "counseled," is dangerous. Devoid of the proper internal tools to deal with such poisonous mental materials (such as the guru possesses), and thereby being unable to neutralize what comes forth, the "therapist" of the day is only dabbling in things unknown to him/her. Put metaphorically, it is similar to naively taking a stroll through a mine field — or as Patanjali calls it, a mind-field. Here, "fools rush in where wise men fear to tread."

As was just mentioned, the present sutras, like the one below in this lesson, speak to this spiritual art and its concerns very well, and all from the Yogic perspective. As the sutra III:39 relates, informed entrance into another's mind first demands the acquisition of higher wisdom from an illumined soul. Where is such wisdom in the Western psychologist, in the contemporary therapist? The same place that success in true healing is: absent.

## Pada III, Sutra 39

*bandha karana shathilyat prachara samvedanat cha chittasya para sharira aveshah (bandha,* bondage; *karana,* cause; *shathilyat,* letting go; *prachara,* moving along; *samvedanat,* via wisdom; *cha,* and; *chittasya,* thought forms; *para,* others; *sharira,* forms; *aveshah,* associate)

"*Letting go of the causes of bondage, the yogi acquires wisdom of all types of forms, and can then deeply associate with the bodies and minds of other beings.*"

Swami Vivekananda tells us that, at first, the yogi *"can only work through the nerve currents in this body, but when the Yogi has loosened himself from these nerve currents, he will be able to work through many other things."* The mention of nerves and nerve currents, called *nadis* and *prana* in Sanskrit, along with the way that the yogi destroys ignorance by knowledge to gain higher wisdom, accents the inner way that is yet far beyond the understanding of most embodied beings. This is the Spiritual Way and its superlative life. With eyes, ears, nose, tongue, and sense of touch all focused outwardly on the objects of the senses alone, and simultaneously disregarding the power of thought while failing to see it as a world unto itself, the sense bound man overlooks not only the cause of his bondage, but also the real meaning of the ten senses and their connection to objects.

The theory of physical creation, and the deeper realization of the power of mental projection, have both been well documented in the long history of India's deep philosophical systems, but the secret of how life force energy (prana) moves along the hidden network of subtle nerves (nadis) remains unknown and unutilized except by only the few. Once, in times long past, beings interested in the makeup of the physical form could only guess at the functions of gross nerves in the body. By dissection and experimentation, deeper knowledge was gleaned. In current times, intelligent beings such as doctors, scientists, and psychologists are still unaware of the presence and purpose of subtle nerves/nadis that permeate and infill the gross nerves by the hundreds of thousands. Direct experience of them via concentration, meditation, and samadhi (samyama), would offer up the deeper secrets of energy, both metaphysical and psychic, revealing, among other things, the presence of prana — one of the two missing links (along with the tanmatras, the five subtle elements) in Western understanding at present. The real function and meaning of the human brain, it being a symbol for the mind (manas) and its thinking power (chitta) would then stand revealed as well.

Until such knowledge is gleaned and accepted, the questions that have haunted mankind for millennia — such as what happens to the soul before birth and after death, and where do beings go after leaving the body and the physical realm — will not get proper answers. Poorly formulated and unintelligent opinions springing from the escapist tactics of untenable dead end systems like atheism and nihilism, as well as silly theories ranging from stories of storks, to beings coming from outer space, get postulated instead. It is time for humanity to look seriously into systems such as Kundalini Yoga, making sure to find authentic realized teachers of it while staying away from charlatans who seek money and fame rather than the freedom and enlightenment of the human race.

Among authentic luminaries, Sri Ramakrishna Paramahamsa has stated that *"....there can be no spiritual progress without the awakening of Kundalini Shakti."* The movement of an adept soul's subtle energies from one body to another, or his/her ability to focus on an object, a situation, or a problem, is based upon such spiritual awakening. Letting go of his own bondage first is what is required, however. This requires the practice of Yoga on all levels — mental, intellectual, devotional, etc., all under the mantle of spirituality and its aims. You must "know thyself" before you can know another, and you must fully trust in the Self as well. This describes what must take place for authentic faith healing, which requires much more than mere belief for its success. Self-Realization, Enlightenment, Illumination — the same and called by various names by the seers — is the singular coin of this most subtle realm, and only it can pave the way to admission into another's being in order to sow seeds of Truth there, and bring about the ultimate state of well-being that is native and natural to the Soul.

This lesson will focus only on this one sutra, so that the functions of the five pranas that occur in the next set of sutras can be taken in a group for study and consideration.

## Lesson Eighty-two, 9/20/13
### Pada III, Sutras 40 & 41

The subject of the prana naturally arises in this installment of our on-line Yoga classes. As most of you know, I have called this subject a missing link in the West's understanding of the total makeup of the universes in space and time, not merely the physical makeup alone. Prana is also the potential meeting place for western science, psychology, and religion, informing them all of subtle, unseen dynamics that will solve many of the arguments and riddles of the peoples of present times. As we approach this set of sutras on prana, the questions of the students of authentic Yoga are to be considered, settling in their own way the often hidden issues and concerns of spiritual practice:

**Questions and Answers for Lesson 82**
R.O. from Hawaii writes:
QUESTION: "Thank you for your detailed reply in RY#81 to my question. However, I cannot understand when you say 'soul's original desire to embody apart from or devoid of the knowledge of Brahman...(causes) the soul's exit from Formless Reality.' Since soul is dwelling in Brahman, where does this desire (or original karma?) come from? That desire cannot come from Brahman; and how can it enter Brahman from outside?"
ANSWER: You must remember, that when we use the word "soul" in Vedanta, it means a transmigrating complex, not the Ultimate Reality. That is why we lower case the word. If we were to upper case it, or call it Atman, then it is the Supreme Soul which is all-pervasive, indwelling in everything, and thus stable and motionless — like Brahman. The difference between the two — Soul and soul — is revealed via the mistake of embodying devoid of higher wisdom, which is also gained in previous lifetimes, and which will later stop the soul from reincarnating in ignorance. As Sri Ramakrishna has stated, *"The soul bound is man; that same soul freed is God."* And so, and playing with Shakespearean language here, "To be Aware, or not be Aware — that is the question. It is far, far better never to have embodied, than to have embodied in ignorance.

To add to that, there is no "soul" in Brahman. One cannot "dwell" in It. You are That. The mental complex, even all forms — subtle and causal dissolve There.

And so my answer, and the specific sentence you culled out from it above, is coming from the standpoint of the soul (mind complex) who wants to embody. And the reason the soul has this desire is due to past karma of its own, since Brahman is karmaless. That is the purpose of the causal and subtle bodies of mankind, for in-between deaths and rebirths it will store the karma-prone, desire-prone, mental complex (antahkarana) in one of those bodies. That is where the reincarnated soul comes from, as a soon to be reembodied complex holding unresolved karma and desires.

QUESTION #2: "I have more questions, and they concern reincarnation. You speak many times as though the reincarnation process is automatic. For example you've said a person dies and then, 'waa,' he's in a baby's body again. Can you go through the steps? By that I mean, does he go into an unconscious limbo state and then suddenly wake up in a body?"

ANSWER: It is intricate, as most things in the apparent evolutionary process are. I say "apparent," because we must always start off declaring the Truth — that transformation takes place only in show, never in actuality. Nontransformation, called Aparinama by the knowers of Truth, is the stable and underlying foundation of all this apparent change. It is the reality behind deep sleep, death, nondual meditation, and Samadhi — all forms of formlessness.

With that emphasized first, we can then look into the transmigration of the soul or, as Indian darshanas would state, the dream movement of the mind-complex at the behest of the desirous ego. There, we must understand initially that souls operate under different sets of veils, all with different content and densities. These veils hide and distort the Truth of the unmoving, undying Consciousness. They consist of karmas from present and past lifetimes, mental impressions (samskaras) that are formulations of unresolved karmas, doings, and desires, and upbringing amidst hypocritical pseudo-religion and other social conventions observed by beings who care for little else than wealth and the pleasures it affords. Added to that is the absence of a strong and resilient philosophical and spiritual base which is the only thing that can shrink these veils, or better yet, rend them apart.

And this is an essential part of "the steps" that you ask for herein. The first would be recognition of one's plight in the embodied position. Even this mere step has so much railing against it. Contentment with matter is one, apathy about higher learning is another, and disbelief in Divine Reality due to all that is listed above must be included as well. After some recognition has dawned, however, usually attended by suffering or discontentment with life, the step of seeking occurs, and of finding an illumined soul to guide one, and to provide inspiration — like from the scriptures — to compel one along the true path.

All of these steps happen in life. I realize that you are asking mainly about the steps of reincarnation after death and prior to rebirth. But that is a part of my point. All of this process does not happen by coincidence, or via chance. It is all dependent on what the tradition calls "conditioning," and this enforces the teachings in the science of samskaras.

And to continue, I wait for your next question, below.

QUESTION #3: "Or perhaps the individual goes to a 'heaven' of the afterlife, or the 'realm of the ancestors.' There he might meet with guides who can help him choose a new birth: parents, body, and sex? And might there be many choices, including some highly desirable births that are in demand and have a 'waiting list?' Not all desirable births would be available, and they might have certain required qualifications."

ANSWER: Yes, you have the right ideas here. And actually, it is not that much different than what happens here on earth, that certain positions are to be gained or lost depending on qualification or lack thereof, prevailing conditions, right timing, the good graces of others (and the bad graces as well), etc. One is still in a form in the ancestor realm (lower and higher heavens), so certain conditions and criteria will be present, and will need to be satisfied. The fundamentalist idea of heaven being a place that is full of happiness is shallow and one-sided. Physical suffering may be absent there, but the cause of such suffering here on earth is the mind and its choices. Would it be any different in other realms? In other words, the mind is still there and, in fact, it is that very transmigrating soul. What else moves like it? As Holy Mother said, *"The mind is everything my child. One must keep it in fine shape. For, you will have to take it with you all the way to Brahman."*

Heaven is also replete with some very masterful souls. Most of them are only masters of earth, it is true, not of the higher Jnana realms, and these are headed back to earth for more masquerade, more sportive play. But again, just like here on earth, there are guides in the heavenly lokas for those who want to transcend form and its limitations — for those who are seeking Freedom and its incomparable exhilaration. Read Swamiji if you want to catch fire with That.

QUESTION #4: "Can the individual track and see future parents? For example: I believe it's said that the Dalai Lama predicted his parents and birthplace?"

ANSWER: As far as the art of conscious rebirth is concerned, this is a main point. The Tibetans did not spend 14 centuries meditating upon the teachings of Yoga, Tantra, and Buddhism just to find that singular Freedom that the Buddha attained. They also noted down everything that had to do with reincarnation as the Buddha saw it as they lived their dedicated lives, and turned it into a prime method for seeking souls. In other words, there is Freedom, no doubt; but there must also be the means to Freedom so long as so many beings get caught in Samsara/Maya — maybe for lifetimes — while they are engaged in sportive play on earth.

Of greatest import, then, is the living of one's first conscious lifetime, a lifetime in which one will receive the dharma and its teachings from an illumined soul, take it within to cogitate it, and come forth with the Light of Self-Realization that, whatever one might call it, is the essence of every religious tradition. This is the prime directive, then, for embodied souls seeking spiritual liberation, what Patanjali calls Kaivalya.

QUESTION #5: "Regarding karma, would the individual be partaking of the parent's karma and the country's karma that he or she is born in? Some countries have done horrible atrocities in the past."

ANSWER: Karmas of all kinds attend, permeate, condition, and fester at the very hub of the reincarnation process. They are, easily described, individual, collective, and cosmic. The only thing the soul can do about the latter, what is of cosmic design, is to perceive it, study it, meditate upon it, and transcend it, like the Buddha did. Regarding the first, the individual karmas — called sanchita, prarabdha, and agami (past, present, and future), the soul has to acquire the desire for Freedom and engage in sadhana, spiritual practices. The veils I spoke of in your first question come up here again, for many other desires lie in wait amidst one's unresolved karmas, and will naturally rise up when one begins to seek. These may waylay, or even spoil, the soul's bid for Freedom in that particular life. Even those things which society and people call "good," are often only sidetracks away from the true path, though these have the chance to turn more positive and help the aspiring soul. It really all depends on the quality of that soul during the time the desire for Freedom comes upon him/her. The most painful thing for a spiritual teacher to see is the turning away from the path on the part of a seeker due to the petty distractions and the paltry attainments of the world.

But it is the second type of karma that you bring up in this question, that of the collective kind. Yes, we all take it on, so long as we embody in this realm. And many of us, since we still sport individual karmas, also contribute to the collective karma store in each of our lifetimes. That is why it is of utmost importance that beings begin to seek and find answers for their problems and issues in relativity. But one must not get caught in this process, else the soul only begins to wallow in the general realization that "everyone is lost here" and "all is empty here." The answers we seek and find must be spiritual ones, ones that lead us up and out, not down and deeper into the morass of karmas that are always festering in the human mind. For, the collective mind might as well be another name for universal suffering. I mean, the Cosmic Mind is balanced and peaceful; individual mind is mainly a matter of one's own choice and predilection. It is the collective mind that both throws up the most dangerous risks and offers the greatest challenges, depending on how one views it.

When you bring in the subjects of family and nations, then collective karma begins to reveal the immensity of its real issue and nature. For instance, *"Who did sin, the child or his parents, that the man was born blind?"* was the question of one of Christ's followers. Was it the fault of the parents or the fault of the incarnating soul itself? Well, the fact that this question came up in Christ's time reveals that karma, i.e., reaping and sowing, was on the minds of living beings even then. For how could there be no such thing as reincarnation if one is asking a question about the passing on of the effects of good and bad deeds from parents to newly born children? Where did the parents get their karma, and how is the newborn connected to it, and to them? A one lifetime scenario will hardly satisfy the query, what to speak of the situation.

But the answer that Jesus gave to this question is the stuff of pure realization around the inexorable laws of karma. *"Neither hath this one sinned, nor his parents,"* came the answer. The parents? What was their fault? Heredity cannot explain it. And if one subscribes to the theory of predestination of the Theologians, God becomes a partial and unjust party in the matter, and rational beings will not accept that. What was meant was that the man was born blind due to actions he did in a previous lifetime; that is all. The parents, then, have to bear and raise a child who has negative karma, and this is their connection, among others, to collective karma.

Embodied beings all share in the collective karma. But it is a mental phenomenon, not a spiritual one. The seeker of Truth seeks to 1) refrain from being a part of the problem by neutralizing his/her individual karmas via spiritual practice that purifies the mind and, 2) transcend all karmas, including the Cosmic variety (origins, creation, desire for lordship, etc.) in order to attain Witness Consciousness and be able to truly assist aspiring beings along the path to ultimate Freedom.

Recognition of one's state of bondage, cultivation of the desire to be free, finding an illumined guide and receiving pertinent instructions, striving for spiritual advancement and attainment, and realizing the inherent Perfection of the All-abiding Soul — these are the steps in working one's way out of the three fields of karma.

QUESTION #6: "Lastly, might there even be several souls taking birth in the same body (so called 'multiple personalities')? Might there even be the 'stealing' of a birth by an entity?"

ANSWER: No, not in that sense. "Multiple personalities" is an expression in Western Psychology, and ought to be left there. If a Western psychologist had met Sri Ramakrishna Paramahamsa, they would have concluded that He had multiple personalities. The fact was that He had both Himself and Mother Kali within Him, and the therapist could never have understood that truth within the context of the conventional conditioning that his other profession had marked him with.

There is, however, a teaching in the tradition that cites how an illumined soul creates "mind-born children" from his disciples. After the yogi passes, he will get into the mind and body of such a fortunate soul and work through him and assist him in furthering the work of the dharma and his lineage/tradition. It is also probable that several great souls will work through such a personage, visiting and influencing as the time and situation dictates.

J.M. from Oregon writes:
QUESTION: "I've begun to inspect my thoughts through witness consciousness. It has been helpful to know I can discard the bad ones and other garbage that gets into my mind. What I would like to know is, how do I begin to trace them back to their origin, so that I may destroy the source of the bad thoughts? I think the source of many of these thoughts are samskaras from the past."
ANSWER: "Destroying" thoughts is not really possible. Rather, one returns them to the curtain of cosmic ignorance from which they sprang. Mind, at all three levels, consists of thoughts and their power, called Chitta. And "Chit hap-

pens," as we say. A perfectly still mind, well, how many have attained that? But to start, one can practice controlling thoughts so that they do not rise up when they are not wanted, and insinuate themselves on life situations -- especially at the most undesirable times. Or, to put it in a more positive way, that thoughts only come to you when you want them, to assist you, inspire you, etc.

Therefore, knowing this fact first (so that one does not try and proceed under the false assumption that thoughts can be destroyed), the subject of tracing origins comes up. And it is precisely the exercise of tracing origins that helps one to realize that nothing is ever destroyed, for when one finds the origin — of matter, of worlds, of thoughts, of intelligence -- one finds that an actual creation is a myth, an impossibility. Simply put, everything exists at all times. It is just a matter of whether it is in a manifested or unmanifested state in any given period. To actually bring anything — like objects, worlds, bodies, intelligence — especially a soul, The Soul, into being from nothingness, is absurd, is the thinking of addled brains.

Speaking of origins, where did such odd misconceptions such as that come from? Why is it that so few have discovered the simple truth that everything is a projection of the mind? As the Prajnaparamita Sutra states it, *"The Sutra of the Diamond Cutter of Supreme Wisdom declares that all phenomena are projections of one's own mind. The work of cutting away all mental conceptualization brings one to the furthest shore of Enlightenment."* In the Mahamudra teaching of Tibet, it gets expressed in this way: *"All manifestation, the Universe itself, is contained in the mind, and the true nature of mind is the realm of illumination, shining with radiance that can neither be conceived nor touched."*

Here is what you are on the trail of, which we are calling "inspecting one's own consciousness." Did you think that the purpose is only to rid oneself of negative thoughts? They never should have been there in the first place! It is ignoble for anyone to entertain them. It is most unfortunate that a spiritually realized soul, who has spent a dedicated series of lifetimes realizing the Highest Truth, has to come to earth and take so much time helping people rid their minds of contents that have no place there — and all that effort before the luminary can introduce to them precepts like Projectionism over Creationism. As one poet wrote, *"Grasping matter, losing Grace — strange indeed this human race."*

Watching, in order, with a single eye, Intelligence emanating off of The Word, thoughts radiating from Intelligence, gradated worlds formulating from the collective thoughts of the multitudes (deities, celestials, human beings, etc), and finally, objects congealing due to the (solidifying, liquifying) power residing in the mind and senses, the newborn seer's previously held beliefs around creation theories and evolution get replaced by the higher wisdom that everything is a projection, not a creation. And mind is the projector; matter does not have any intelligence to do it with. All matter can do is congeal and dissolve at the behest of the power of intelligence.

Certainly, this is a much deeper answer to your simple question than you expected, but imagine the fate of negative thoughts under the power of such a revelation! Would they dare even rise up anymore, once such profundity had visited the mind? Conventional persons talk glibly about the power of positive thinking, but what about the power of higher thinking leading to no thinking at all? This is uncharted territory for most beings. The seer can rid himself of all thoughts — positive, negative, mixed, superficial — anytime he wants to, and then enjoy pure, conscious Awareness. There is no mind There to bother one; only the mind's Nondual Origin. It is Samadhi. Personality may be gone, or placed in abeyance for a time, but that does not result in an empty void as some suspect and fear, like an "emptiness" — not unless one defines "emptiness" as empty of problems, empty of brooding, empty of suffering, empty of impeding forms, empty of troublesome ego and its hosts of names and desires — and particularly, empty of binding concepts.

In short, tracing origins leads the soul to That which is beyond all origins — Brahman, Allah, All-Mighty Father. That is an Ocean of Existence, Knowledge, and Bliss Absolute. Glimpsing That, the human soul will no longer think of anything else but That. What happens to thoughts then?

QUESTION #2: "How do I begin to master the prana?"

ANSWER: Usually this beginning involves breathing exercises. Too bad that most aspirants — if they can even be called such — leave it there. They seem to think that breathing in and out and watching that happen will bring Enlightenment. It is hardly even a start. Thus, Shankara states in the Vivekachudamani, *"Not by hundreds of asanas or a thousand pranayams can the Self be realized."* And so many so-called teachers, particularly of the hatha bent, know no better and see nothing higher than to let students stop there.

The real essence of watching the breath is to actually become aware of the prana and begin to utilize it to concentrate and help illumine the thoughts. The fact that we breathe is no great secret. It is what causes breath that is to be looked into deeply, just as you are looking into your thoughts for secrets. Prana has many important functions — not just in outer life, but in inner life as well. Oh, they go on teaching, ad nauseam, about the five pranas and how they evacuate waste, distribute nutrients to the bloodstream, and so forth. It is all physical. They may as well be materialists like the rest of the world. As Swami Vivekananda states, only the Yogis know about prana and its psychic element, and how it carries thoughts heavenwards, and souls to other realms, and incarnating beings into the womb at the time of rebirth.

So here, to inspect the breath, like inspecting the mind, is really to seek for keys to spiritual life. That is real origins. One must use meditation, guided by an illumined soul, coupled with taking the teachings of the dharma, to come upon and seize the upward, inward moving prana. You will know when you have it when depression, brooding, boredom, and things of that ilk leave you and do not return, and further, when thoughts of Higher Wisdom and Divine Reality take their place. Prana is the divine vehicle, the Great Garuda Bird, and it will carry the inwardly ascending soul to the kingdoms of heaven within. Pray that you never leave it in a role of a healthy life and sattvic pleasure alone, but master it for all time.

QUESTION #3: "I have noticed over the last two weekends at the ashram that there has been much pain in the body, and some digestive issues. I think it may be because I'm not used to sitting and having good posture, or eating certain pure foods. Could it also be that hearing the teachings will produce a physiological effect in the body?"

ANSWER: Yes, but it is all connected, and happening spontaneously as you find yourself in different mental altitudes. What is really occurring is that your nervous system, both gross and subtle, is being purified, thus remade. This "cut in the image" process is natural to one who is detoxing from worldly living, and trying to sustain spiritual life and practice. If there is not enough strength and substance yet due to the mind's aversion to giving up what is non-beneficial (the unreal), then the aspirant can fall. Sri Ramakrishna cites that this is like trying to take a worm from filth and placing it in white rice. It will simply die there. Thus, a gradual stage by stage advancement is good for physical and vital growth, but not always so yet for giving up the unreal.

QUESTION #4: "Can one bless the food of others, or even food for pets, and there be positive benefit? I've been blessing my cat's and dog's food in the morning, everyday, to send them good energy, love, and devotion."

ANSWER: Blessing food for an animal will not do it any spiritual good, since it cannot understand spirituality, teachings, etc, in its present body. It is enough if the practitioner blesses his or her own food, and then a natural vibration of sattva will transfer through all that he or she does to all beings around him/her – even to the pets one feeds and the plants one waters.

Blessing food for other human beings is another matter. If they are open to it, and also willing to undergo spiritual practices that take the prana from food and lift it up the spine to higher centers, then much overall good can be accomplished. The main thing is to purify food with the mantra, for *"food taken without such a blessing turns to poison in the bloodstream."*

QUESTION #5: "Great Souls have informed us that we will only achieve liberation through the grace of God. It has also been stated by Swamiji that the goal of Yoga is to shorten the time to enlightenment through a sequence of self-efforts. Given this, and the applicable teachings about unresolved karma, desires, and samskaras, can you explain whether or not free will exists for the sincere spiritual practitioner?"

ANSWER: Absolute free will is a misnomer; as Ramana Maharshi tells us, there is no such thing. For the devotee, this is not a problem. He loves the idea of the Supreme Will, and wants to give everything into That. In the meantime, and in order to be able to make such an offering, he must neutralize his karmas, fulfill his desires in the dharma, and transform his samskaras into one's of higher wisdom and samadhi. This he does via Yoga.

And as far as grace is concerned, the wise have also called it "auspicious timing." To know when to strive and when to prepare via qualification, for instance, that is real grace. Further, to know when to stop seeking God and just start seeing God, that is grace. The grace that the lazy person is looking for, that is hope, often just procrastination. As my guru used to tell us again and again, *"Grace and self-effort must go hand in hand. They are the two wings of a bird. A bird cannot fly with only one wing."*

Therefore, we are to come to know that all of the above are to be combined in a mature synthesis, a "Purna Yoga." The will to do practice to attain it is Grace, and you, the Lord, the Atman, granted it unto yourself. Now, to make the most of it.

G.S. from Oregon writes:
QUESTION: "You wrote in the recent lesson that the yogi can attach and detach at will, and that this makes him unique among luminaries. I don't understand this. What does he attach and detach from?"
ANSWER: The yogi or yogini detaches from all that is unreal, illusory, and changing. After this considerable feat is accomplished (very difficult, and that is why no one is doing it), they attach to such Principles as Brahman, Truth, Ishvara, The Lotus Feet of the Lord, etc., i.e., all that is Real. Once their detachment is mature, they are then free to *"attach and detach at will,"* as my guru often said. This applies to all things, such as food, relations, the world, even spiritual practices. Finally, it is the body, and embodiment, that applies as well. A yogi can attach to a body, then give it up, as easy as *"a child dons and outgrows sets of clothes as he or she grows up."* So, this is a unique soul, yes?
QUESTION #2: "You say that working in the world purifies a person. What kind of activity is there that will help?"
ANSWER: All activity will help, so long as one does not get attached to it alone, or to its fruits. Otherwise, every activity and all activities will bind one fast to work in the world and its outcomes, producing karmas along the way. As Vivekananda has stated, do all work as worship of God in mankind. For, work has no other facility than for purification of mind in order to make the soul fit and ready for real knowledge. It all depends, then, on how one approaches work, or in what mindset one takes it on and accomplishes it.
QUESTION #3: "I do not understand the statement, 'Those who, when they act, know that they act not, are the best of all agents — are really nonagents.'"
ANSWER: One of the subtlest of all teachings is this. These words infer the state of mind of a yogi who can engage in action without accruing binding repercussions from it. The key here is to make sure the human ego is taken as far out of the quotient as possible. For, work engaged in while sporting a sense of agency, i.e., as in the feeling that "I am the doer," will always acquire the stain of personality and its wants and desires, along with its pride and often desperate need for credit and attention.

One of the practices that a spiritual aspirant will attempt, then, is to remove the sense of agency from the mind, or at least diminish it substantially. Watching the ego as one works and lives in daily life, one can gradually begin to see its negative insinuations and, by observing this under the mantle of aversion to such influences, do away with ego for good. This is called a ripe ego, which does no harm.

These are a few of the hidden secrets and dynamics behind the subtle teaching of what the gurus and acharyas call the "sense of agency."

Anurag from Oregon writes:
QUESTION: "Thanks for the brief but potent commentary on Sloka III:39. You write: 'You must know thyself before you can know another, and you must fully trust in the Self as well.' Could you please go into a little more detail regarding this trust in the Self. I sense that it goes well beyond shraddha (faith) in the general sense, and touches upon an all-pervasive calm and peace that must by necessity accompany the experiential investigation into the hidden network of subtle nerves and prana. You addressed this somewhat in your reply to Akshaya Bhakti around the question of fear: 'Meditation, anyone?'"

ANSWER: As subtle nerves (nadis) and prana are the subject of this lesson's two sutras, and many of those that follow as well, this question is timely. Besides teachings like the Six Proofs of Purusha, and the many axioms of Advaita and inherent qualities of the Paramatman that have been revealed and put forth, additional "proof" exists in the revealed scriptures for the existence and pervasive quality of the Atman. This proof is needed for convincing the ego/mind complex of the aspirant after Truth, and will increase the faith of the devotee in all that is true by removing the false belief in all that is untrue. Thus, as you often hear me saying, Know thy Self by first knowing the nonself. Knowing thy Self is a matter of sadhana coupled with right timing (grace). Knowing the nonself is a matter of viveka and vairagya, in all its many forms and inclusive of all its concomitants.

In the *Srimad Devi Bhagavatam*, the Divine Mother Herself states: *"The wise state that there are seven modes of proof of the Atman — perception, inference, verbal testimony, implication, witness consciousness, and hearsay* (even rumor is sometimes added as an eighth). *Now, the Vedanta Shastras say that the Supreme Being, Parambrahma, cannot be comprehended by these seven proofs. Therefore, at the outset, adopt reason leading to sure belief via the intellect according to the words of the Vedanta, and discriminate and discuss over and over again. Then use this matured inference to draw your wise conclusion about Brahman. Further, the intelligent person should adopt what is seen by perception as self-evident, and what is inferred through witness of good conduct in the wise. The wise say, as is mentioned in the Puranas, that the Prime Force is present in Brahman — is present in Lord Brahma as the creative force, is present in Lord Hari as the preserving force, is present in Lord Hara as the dissolving force — all like burning power is present in fire. In short, stripped of force, none, no one, not even the Trinity, can even move. Therefore, the proof of the Atman is found in It's Force. None can deny Her existence, even if only the presence of intelligence is admitted."*

To conclude, then, there is our mind and its comprehension, and then there is our heart and its faith. Divine Mother advises utilizing the seven proofs for the former, and the evident presence of the Divine Activity all around us for the latter. The seven proofs are what we have been using for some twenty years now in SRV and its classes/retreats/satsangs, and celebrating the Divine Energy all around and within us is what we have been doing in our worship of the Divine Mother for just as long. What more can I say but *"Go Forward!"* with these two, until the definitive moment of realization dawns clearly and completely on the fully awakened ego/mind complex.

**Pada III, Sutra 40**
*udana jayat jala panka kantaka adishu asangah utkrantih cha* (*udana*, prana of ascension; *jayat*, victory/mastery; *jala*, flowing; *panka*, earth; *kantaka*, thorns; *adishu*, along with others; *asangah*, transcend contact; *utkrantih*, ascension; *cha*, and)

"*Gaining victory over the prana of ascension, the yogi can transcend all contact with earth, water, fire, and the sharp thorns of other pain-bearing elements.*"

The udana, the upward moving life force, and prana, with its all-pervasive and inward/outward moving breathing processes, are in need of mastery in worldly minded souls. The yogis have concentrated early on in these primal areas in order to gain victory there. The results are seen in them as spreading out in both directions — from life force on out to the senses and the elements, and from life force on inwards to the mind, its thoughts, and intelligence. All levels of the being, then, are balanced while in Meditation and inaction, and operating and flowing properly while the yogi or yogini is engaged in Divine Action.

To freshen one's knowledge of what Swami Vivekananda cites as the "....one prana in its five forms," the student can look back on lesson #75. Prana is in everything, from high to low, from gross to subtle. Even when Consciousness assumes the loftiest of manifest conditions, such as Intelligence, Mahat, and The Word, prana only neatly and imperceptibly merges into Shakti, and into the Mahashakti Herself.

Those who have spent quality time in the main aims and ends of spiritual life as taken up and disseminated by the SRV Associations and its works, have heard there that 1) the comprehension of prana is a missing link in present day understanding, particularly in the West, and 2) that many commentators of the Yoga system (Patanjala, the Eight-limbed Yoga) leave the subject on the physical level only, failing to bring out its deeper implications which rest in levels that are vital, mental, intellectual, and finally and most importantly, spiritual.

Awakening spiritually means that beings are to study and ascertain that there is more to life than the body. Yoga has eight limbs, not just two (asana and pranayam); Vedanta teaches five sheaths, not just one (the annamayakosha); Sankhya lists subtle senses and elements, not just gross ones (like procreation and excretion). Even in Tantra, some fifty-two sadhana exercises for realization are taught, not just two (sexuality and intoxicants). Unfortunately, then, and as it has been seen so far to date, if a materialistic culture were to begin to explore such powerful philosophies as Vedanta, Yoga,

Tantra, and others, they would only gravitate early on to those elements in them that seemed attracting and pleasurable, and would steer clear of those that demanded austerity, detachment, study, and strong self-effort. Beings with a deep desire for freedom, and with some yogic abilities already under their belts, will undergo further purification.

Speaking from the arena of direct spiritual experience, gotten after the necessary disciplines have been undertaken and undergone, the upward moving prana is invaluable for spiritual well-being. As a part of the breathing process, it conduces to physical health, to be sure, and at the intermediate stages of practice it helps to focus the mind of the practitioner so that vital restlessness *(shvasaprashvasah)* and unsteadiness of limbs *(angamejatva)* are overcome. But let us not leave the benefits of the prana there, with body, lungs, and breathing only. There is also the steadiness of mind to be considered as an attainment, and, the fact is, that if the mind had have been steady in the first place, i.e., before incarnating in the body, then the breath and the limbs would not have posed problems at all.

Here, we see the real order of things — that Consciousness is King, and that its prime evolutes such as Cosmic Mind, Intelligence, etc., are anterior to energy, senses, and body — just as the Sankhya Yoga enumerates them. This knowledge hinges on the Advaita, which is another great insight that should have been learned at the outset, before practice was undertaken. In other words, and pertinent to the subject at hand, Yoga is Samadhi. Its title, "yoga," means union — a union that is always at hand, as Shankara states, not something to be attained.

The past master, then, has the upwards moving prana as his constant companion, and enters the worlds of name and form with it in tow. For the practitioner, udana, when perceived and gained control of, will put an end to such problems as depression *(daurmanasya)*, sorrow *(dukha)*, and the brooding that always accompanies them. Even disease *(vyadhi)* will either fail to manifest, or will die away swiftly in the presence of that yogi who can, via usage of the inward/upwards moving prana, lift the mind off of the body and place it on Atman.

In brief, then, if Yoga is Samadhi, why should the practitioner think of anything else? If impediments such as complacency *(styana)*, doubt *(samshaya)*, negligence *(pramada)*, idleness *(alasya)*, sensuality *(avirati)*, confusion *(bhrantidarshana)*, inability *(alabdhabhumikatva)*, and backsliding *(anavasthitatvani)*, are all due to the mind's focus on every little thing other than Yoga, than Brahman, why should he demur any longer? As Swami Vivekananda puts it, *"If you have known Atman as the one Existence and that nothing else exists, for whom, for what desire do you trouble yourself?"*

Indeed, then, in the light of all this, the meaning of this sutra duly dances to the foreground. The mind's dalliance with mud *(panka)*, with water *(jala)*, with thorns *(adishu)* as the sutra suggests, of what benefit is this? The yogi transcends, i.e., gives up the company *(asangha)* of such gross things, and places the thinking process on the Eternal Union of mankind with God. That is his secret, the secret to his health, his longevity, his ever-flowing and inexhaustible energy, his ingenuity, and his expansive mind.

The student is asked to take another deep and long look at the chart in Volume 1, page 310, entitled "States of Dissolution of the Mind in Yoga." From top to bottom as the past master would see it, or moving from the bottom to the top as the practitioner must encounter it, all that is really essential to the yogic process is contained therein. The five states of the awakening mind and the three stages of transformation of consciousness, as sidebars, are also affixed appropriately. For, what is Yoga, Union, if it is not the stripping away of all that is covering the Truth. As Ramprasad Sen sings about it: *"O Mother of the Universe, my entire being is breaking apart. There is nothing left but Thee!"*

## Pada III, Sutra 41

*samana jayat jvalanam (samana,* force of digestion/comprehension*; jayat,* victory; *jvalanam,* radiance*)*

"*Gaining victory over the digestive prana that grants comprehensive abilities, an atmosphere of radiance surrounds the yogi.*"

Obviously, here, in this short but pregnant sutra, it is much more than the digestion of food that is implied. As we have often heard from our Vedanta preceptors, there are other types of sustenance than physical matter. The mind of the yogic practitioner consumes enormous amounts of knowledge from the scriptures, from the guru, and from his own spiritual experience. With a diet such as this, which is what the energy from food is best suited for (*"Man does not live by bread alone"*), the entire human constitution, from body to Spirit, enjoys prime health. It is only then that beneficial works and authentic sacrifices can be accomplished.

Samana, then, is an important form of prana. Leaving it to merely digest the food in the belly, and distribute nutrients to the organs, is an incomplete definition for it, at best. A healthy body fitted for supporting the task of yogic practice is important, no doubt, but all should note that the body exists by prana, not the other way around. *"Man eats to live, he should not live to eat."*

In other words, so many eat and eat endlessly, mostly for pleasure, or even survival. But who eats in order to digest food so that subtle energy can be generated in order to invigorate the mind? Healthy, happy, eaters never realize God, their focus being food and senses alone. Yogic practitioners forgo pleasure and survival on the bodily level only, so as to attain cognition of That which is independent of matter.

There is infernal life, then there is Eternal Life. There is ordinary mind, then there is Original Mind. The spiritual aspirant who has rightly determined these essential distinctions plunges the mind into the realm of Awareness. As he does so, the samana prana that was helpful in maintaining his body in a healthy condition, transforms into a subtler form of itself and begins to assist him in digesting that "food for thought" gleaned from the scriptures. That very form of subtle samana is present in the practitioner who sits in front of the spiritual preceptor, striving hard to comprehend all that falls from those divine lips and mind. Even later, even further along the path to Enlightenment, this "digestive" force is responsible for taking the teachings of the dharma heard earlier, and transmuting them into actual insight and cognition. Digestion of higher wisdom, then, is tantamount to the realization of Truth. Prana, there, is the Mahashakti Herself — The Mother of Wisdom.

Since several types of victories have been mentioned in this lesson, the reader is asked to look at and memorize "The Seven Qualifications and the Seven Victories of Tantra," In it the avid student of philosophy and spirituality, combined, will find the need for mastery over the elements, the senses, the primal life force, and others. All systems, called *darshanas* (paths of clear seeing) in India, include the attainment of such especial accomplishments in their astute ideologies around Self-Realization. Taking them into study and practice, the consummate yogi and yogini reach the goal of human existence in this very lifetime.

In forthcoming lessons, sutras involving more teachings on samyama will appear. Thus, please eat well, digest well, exercise well — using the life force in all of its many functions, and for ends that are conducive for understanding it on its deeper levels as well.

## Lesson Eighty-three, 11/10/13
### Pada III, Sutras 42 & 43

After a break of over a month, we pick up the trail of Patanjali's Raja Yoga system after pondering the sutras of the last lesson. The questions below fall in accordance with those, along with the naturally arising queries that come about via in-depth inspection of Reality — Atma Vichara.

**Questions and Answers for Lesson 83**
Avinashi from Pennsylvania writes:
QUESTION: "Is it necessary to be fully enlightened in order to break the bondage to the realms of the ancestors? If it's not necessary, what is? What are the minimum realizations, achievements, or whatever are needed so one does not have to again get hung up by the heels and have the mantra 'Wah!' elicited with a slap?"
ANSWER: To avoid being born again, particularly in ignorance (avidya) of one's true nature, and so as to live a divine life of dedication rather than a regretful life of compromise, is indeed an important consideration. First, one would have to define "enlightenment," or being "fully enlightened." Shankara states in his Vivekachudamani, *vedanta siddhanta niruktir esa brahmaiva jivaham sakalam jagad cha akandha rupa stithir eva moksho brahmadvitiye shrutayah pramanam,* which means that enlightenment is living constantly in a state that recognizes that time, space, living beings, and the worlds are all Brahman. This pregnant statement affords a prime opportunity for lazy compromisers, comfort zone dwellers, and pseudo spiritualists to look upon the world as their

oyster. They can pretend, then, that the world is real, that objects can be enjoyed, and thus conveniently avoid the daily spiritual practice so necessary for maintaining peace of mind in the world, and spiritual growth, both. The world is not real; that is not what he meant. It is as hollow as bamboo, as erratic as a rattlesnake on fire, as empty as a lone bean in a boxcar, as unreal as the son of a barren woman, and as evanescent as bubbles rising from a newly opened bottle of "spirits." One should never attach to it, and should transcend it as soon as one perceives it.

What lies at its foundation — that is Real, and the only Reality. Beings coming into form act as if they are produced; but they are really unoriginated (see Gaudapada's karika). Coming to believe in their fictitiously produced state, called embodiment, they soon fall victim to false superimposition (vivarta) and begin to participate naively in worldly life (vyavaharika). They enjoy the world, and thus create deep mental impressions (samskaras) of enjoyment after life is over as well. This is called heavenly existence; it involves frequenting both the subtle realms of one's ancestors, and those bound souls that abide there in cycles — they who are disinterested in Freedom. Rebirth gives them opportunities, over and over again, to go beyond this wheel (kalachakra) of constant returns, but they only squander them repeatedly. Such souls are in the cosmic dream for yugas, and never taste the inherent Freedom of their Eternal Soul — Atman.

What is required for such singular emancipation, and what also defines the word "enlightenment," is the death of ignorance. As soon as the embodied being knows, even suspects, that he/she is not the body/mind mechanism, then Freedom is at hand. Only a little effort and some mental adjustment will need to happen. In other words, the transmigrating soul (which is essentially ever free) sees the (authentic) Guru, hears the Truth, receives the mantra, reads the scriptures, increases devotion, and all the rest (sadhana/spiritual life) of the coverings of ignorance are already falling away fast. "Fast," here, means one lifetime, especially if we are talking about a thoroughly materialistic culture like America whose masses do not have the foggiest notion of what or who God is. Most do not want to wake up. Of those who do, most fall back asleep far too easily. A few among these latter struggle a little and fail, then give up.

But as Vivekananda stated once, *"As soon as human beings perceive the glory of the Vedanta, all abracadabras fall off of themselves. This has been my uniform experience. Whenever mankind attains a higher vision, the lower vision disappears of itself."* This is good news for the sincere Truth seeker. However, lack of sincerity is the problem — along with the root desire for "Mammon" over God. As he stated elsewhere, *"Formerly the characteristic of a noble-minded man was 'to please the whole universe by one's numerous acts of service,' but now it is 'I am pure and the whole world is impure. Go and get money and set it at my feet."*

So, "full enlightenment," whatever that may constitute, will accomplish transcendence and other wonders, but that enlightenment that is accompanied by the demise of ignorance will be enough to cause one to see through the ruse of heaven and its enjoyments, and pierce through the curtain of nescience to go beyond the realm of rebirth with the ancestors. As Sri Krishna states in the Gita: *"The worshippers of the bhutas (worldly beings) go to the bhutas. The worshippers of the pitris (ancestors/heaven bound souls) go to the pitris. But My worshippers come to Me."*

QUESTION #2: "A person is advised, on one hand, to face his or her sufferings — to 'face the brutes!' as was shouted to Swamiji when he was being chased by fierce monkeys. On the other hand, one is advised to avoid brooding. What is the difference? How can one tell when one has crossed the line from brooding to intelligent reflection on inner experience?"

ANSWER: In the moment, it is certainly not hard to tell the difference. Brooding is weighty, futile, and leads nowhere. Inner reflection grants the light of intelligence and deeper understanding. The former leads to tamas and rajas; the latter, to sattva. Use the gunas to determine it. As far as long range knowing, brooding will go away forever if the mind develops the habit to rest naturally in peace, in study, in dharma (teachings), or in meditation. One morning, the aspirant will wake up and brooding will be *"Gone! Gone! Utterly gone!"* as Ramprasad sings in his wisdom songs.

QUESTION #3: "When I started to meditate a few years ago, I tried to hold the image that I visualized in the heart to one, steady, unchanging form. As time went by, though, this started seeming more and more hopeless, for, like everything phenomenal, the image in the heart also changed, sometimes dramatically, sometimes subtly. My response to this was to begin going with it, and for awhile this led to chaos. But now the situation has stabilized. Now, each time I sit down to meditate, I survey my inner state, and choose a starting point based on my growing mass of experience concerning what works for me; sometimes there will be inspiration, and I'll consider that to decide if it seems sound and helpful. I'm not saying that each morning's point of departure for meditation is just willy-nilly; there's always the Ishtam and the mantra. But I am saying that I've adopted a fluid adaptability regarding my starting points, and I wonder how this compares with your experience and with the experience of your students through the years? I also wonder what advice you can offer."

ANSWER: Meditation is very subtle, and differs widely from person to person. Over all, what you write here seems to point towards a willingness to be flexible, even forbear temporary "chaos" in the mind in order to arrive at an ever fresh and forward moving spiritual growth in Raja Yoga. In other words, or put obversely, stagnation in meditation and practice is to be avoided. It can even masquerade as routine sitting daily, causing the meditator to simply say "I have done my practice for the day," now on with life, and all the while overlooking the fact that, as Holy Mother states it, *"Does God exist only when eyes are closed, and cease to exist when eyes are open?"*

As far as further advice is concerned, and given the sensitivity of the subject, I like the Tibetan teaching that states — and I never mind repeating it:

*When focusing occurs, focus without objective.*
*When stabilizing occurs, stabilize without distraction.*

*When shifting occurs, shift without grasping.*
*When manifestations occur, experience them as Reality.*
*When liberation occurs, allow it to occur naturally.*

This pretty much covers the gamut of what to watch for in a deep meditation practice. The result of this more comprehensive observation is: freedom from the duality of liberation and the agent of liberation; freedom from intellection and conceptualization; freedom from false identities and projections; and freedom from hopes and fears.

D.G. from Belgium writes:
QUESTION: "I have a question regarding prana. There are different vibratory levels of prana corresponding with the different akashas, like bhutakasha, etc. My question is: does one need to have the experience of all these higher pranic frequencies in order to come to Atma Vidya? Are these experiences necessary stations on the path?"
ANSWER: Most beings are actually experiencing these levels of vibration all the time (except for the deepest and subtlest ones, called samadhis). The problem is that heavy mental gravity that causes the mind to sink and fail to rise again. Sri Ramakrishna likened this weight to *"rainwater that seeks the lowest level to collect in."* What is wanted, rather, is to turn one's mind and thought process into a *"hot air balloon"* and experience buoyancy.

For Atma Vidya, the supreme knowledge of the Self, that will require that one not only experience these levels of vibration consciously, but also master them. That is accomplished by adjusting to them over time as they occur to the mind in meditation, and through life experiences as well. Dealing with obstacles can clear the mind suddenly, posing a strong contrast to the mind that is freeing and welcome. So, all of this begs for constancy in daily practice until the ponderous weights of life and mind become transparent, and one does not feel them anymore. This is called sattva, and when it is made pure — shuddha sattva — Atma Vidya begins to occur to the mind quite naturally.

J.M. from Oregon writes:
QUESTION: "Can the aspirant obtain the four treasures and six jewels without fully comprehending or obtaining the 8 limbs of yoga?"
ANSWER: Of course, you are blending two systems — Yoga and Vedanta — which are seen as complementary, no doubt. The former is practice that incorporates body, energy (prana), mind and intellect. The latter is all Mind, i.e., Consciousness. For most, then, the Eight Limbs of Yoga are to be approached and mastered, and Consciousness awaits. The Sadhanachatushtaya, Four Treasures and Six Jewels, is more of an accounting of what already exists in the focused and concentrated mind, and is thus less of a practice. The Limbs of Yoga get applied *to* the seeker, but the Four Treasures and Six Jewels are applied *by* the seeker.

A greater percentage of practitioners, then, will need to acquire a practice, and Yoga is as good as any, better than most. When fundamentals are mastered, and attainment has been acquired, Vedantic jewels like inner peace and self-control come forth and burgeon. Both systems, if they can be called such, lead to meditation and samadhi. It is temperament, karma, and other factors that formulate the tact that any given soul will take with regard to them. Probably, Vedanta does not run the risk of getting caught in hatha and pranayama as yoga does, what to speak of occult powers. Still, getting exposed to these potential dangers is one way of transcending them — if the soul needs such exposure. In Vedanta, the physical, the prana, and the psychic prana all get subjected to Viveka at the outset, and are exposed and thereby transcended by Vairagya. The first two Treasures, then, should do most of the initial work for the advanced practitioner.

QUESTION #2: "Why does mastery over the prana help reduce cycles of tamas and rajas and help one get beyond the gunas?"

ANSWER: If one's energy (prana) is erratic (rajas), one's life reflects the same. If energy is lethargic, life drags and mind suffers. Karma accrues in both cases. When one's energy is balanced (sattva), there is both contentment and peace, and much less of karmic effects to forebear. Really, everyone is dealing with the gunas, trying to maintain a balance in life. Most do not trace such equilibrium and its loss back to the mind, however, and rather just let moods come and go while engaging in activities despite the mental condition of any given hour or day. Like most other concerns, bringing consciousness to bear in life and mind is the solution. The real task, then, is becoming ever conscious of Consciousness, aware of Awareness. What is inherent in mind and mankind is higher Intelligence; on earth, only mankind has it. Thus, examining the contents of mind, the inward moving yogi and yogini come upon the gunas and note their behavior. Since the movements of all other entities are based on the prana and its varying conditions, so too must the gunas — the very mind itself — also be. But first, the prana in the body, in food, in the senses has to be mastered. The gunas are an extremely subtle matter, to be discovered early on and measured, but taken up for mastery at a later stage.

QUESTION #3: "Are there any non-obvious petty distractions that impede sadhana that new students need to aware of outside the usual ones mentioned, such as conventional life, and lack of moderation of appetites?"

ANSWER: Most everything that occurs in the life of a person under the influence of mundane human convention is a distraction. These are not "obvious" to such a person because they seem like normal occupations, and everyone around them in contemporary societies are also involved in them. No one questions this filmy curtain of lifeless methodical plodding accompanied by an overlying pall of mental haze. Their own deviation from this humdrum course is when some fresh wave of excitement surfaces in secular, scientific, and intellectual realms, like the ongoing antics of politicians who are only manipulating the lives of others under the selfish regime of personal power and accolades — what Tantra calls *Mada,* vainglory.

Dharmic life is at least the alternative, if not the answer. Here, the seeker gets the world behind him and focuses, once again, on what is essential. That is why Viveka, discrimination between the essential and the nonessential, is the first quality in Vedanta. And it was important in the days that Jesus spent on earth as well, as He often advised *"separating the wheat from the chaff."* Sri Ramakrishna and Jesus are one and the same, the same soul manifesting two thousand years apart. By this we do not mean the same personality. Does the personality even persist? It is a part of the domain of the ego, which inflates and deflates lifetime to lifetime. They are the same Consciousness.

And it is this search for one's own Consciousness that defines the Eastern spiritual pathways from the Western march for lands and material objects under the umbrella of vainglory. Really then, the entire occupation of nations today is a distraction from what is, or, if one has fallen so low, from what ought to be. Come to realize that we have been born into a world that is populated with beings who are mad with greed for personal gain, and will not stop at killing others to get it. Is distraction a small thing then? We must *"grant unto Caesar what is Caesar's,"* then, and start *"storing up our treasure in Heaven."* Buddha called this *"collecting dharma drops in the bucket."*

QUESTION #4: "How does one stop the mind from brooding when it feels like its own inertia forces it to do so at the slightest stimulus from daily life?"

ANSWER: As Sri Krishna stated to Arjuna on the battlefield of Kurukshetra, the mind is difficult to control, but it can be controlled by Abhyasa Yoga. He means the Yoga of constant practice. In the Upanisads, one sloka relates that the Eternal Soul of mankind *"is realized by moderation, continence, knowledge, and veracity — all constantly cultivated."* If one or any of these qualities was taken into practice, some small good would come of it. But not Self-realization. For That, all four must be applied, and for a long period of practice that leads to illumination. So many gem-like qualities are to be mined from the inner reaches of the human mind, and all for creating a rock-like stability that will, as Sri Krishna states again, *"not be shaken even by the heaviest of afflictions."* People speak glibly about Nirvikalpa Samadhi, Nirvana, Satori, etc., as if it is something that can be bartered for, *"like fish and greens in the marketplace,"* as Holy Mother said. Read His lips! It is the *"Pearl of Great Price."*

So thoughts like these, constantly cultivated, form the way out of brooding. This I say from my own direct spiritual experience. A focused mind is a peaceful mind. A brooding mind is a scattered mind. One needs to practice the art of the former for his or her own highest good.

QUESTION #5: "Why does pranayama eliminate depression and brooding?"

ANSWER: Pranayama itself cannot eliminate them. It is just an exercise for purification and expansion. The prana itself can heal though. The reason to perform pranayama is to make a strong connection to it that results in its mastery. The signs of such control are a healthy body, a clear voice, vital strength, control of the five senses, and natural moderation.

In order to gain actual mastery of the prana it will not do to simply turn the lungs into a set of bellows. Mind, intelligence, and consciousness must be brought into the picture. Connections of this sort are made by mind and its minions. Body, senses, and prana are not sentient, and certainly objects are not.

Prana becomes imbued with more force (shakti power) when mind is purified and turned towards the real yogic task of integrating all aspects of one's being.

QUESTION #6: "How can we discriminate between aversion and attachment, especially when fulfilling desires in the dharma?"

ANSWER: These two are easy to discriminate. I would have thought the question would be more like, "How do we discriminate between attachment and real love, or aversion and detachment?" But for more help with this question of fulfilling desires in the dharma, please see the chart called *The Two Forms of Desire*.

QUESTION #7: "How can one begin to perceive the udana?"

ANSWER: By watching one's thoughts, since that force takes them upwards (buoyancy) and inwards (to the kingdoms of heaven). The initial movement of the breath, the beginning part of a sneeze, etc., are operated by the udana. The hathis leave it there. But the jnanis get ahold of it and use it for aspiration and inspiration. In other words, "aspiration" is not only a part of the breathing process. Its higher meaning is tending towards realization of one's true nature, Atman.

So get ahold of that subtle upward current of mind that can been felt and perceived if one watches the mind and its thoughts in meditation. Rise with it when it occurs, and let it take you where the yogis, seers, and rishis go to abide. Is Devaloka a planet out in space? No. That is Bhutakasha out there, the loka of the bhutas. Inwards lies the space of pure thoughts. Propitiate the god of udana prana and make a reservation with him for your visit there soon.

Anurag from Oregon writes:

QUESTION: "Thanks for your reply to my question in Raja Yoga Lesson #81. I found particularly valuable your discussion of the udana prana, mastery of which conduces to physical well-being and, more importantly, steadiness of mind. The investigation of the udana prana continues nicely in this RY # 82, Sutra III:40, and the very interesting quote from Swamiji that you cite, *'If you have known the Atman as the one true Existence and that nothing else exists, for whom, for what desire do you trouble yourself?'* What a wonderful attainment! You have also mentioned at various classes and retreats to leave brooding behind, to pierce the Vishnu granthi and not allow one's awareness to drop below this station. From a practical point of view, I am often noticing a perceptual 'chicken and egg' phenomenon. Apparent problems appearing 'out there' are reconsidered as a projection of mind that may not be as they appear. Quite often, a reconsideration of the perception utilizing the udana prana will alter the apparent situation into something less distressful, or even transform into something positive. This is quite interesting. As Swamiji notes in the above quote, our spiritual standpoint has influence over our reactions. I am noticing that a spiritual standpoint even has the potential to alter apparent events themselves. As Holy Mother has noted, *'The world is mind made manifest.'* Can you speak a bit about the mind's influence on events via the mind's perception of these events?"

ANSWER: The interesting, and telling, phenomena of two physicists looking into an electron microscope at the same particle within the same hour, and coming back with different conclusions, is a metaphor for the mind's ability to make changes at all levels of our being. All matters under question and inspection, either intellectually or ineptly, can be explained by this ability of mind — the power of positive thinking in the minds of mentors, occult powers for the psychics, faith healing and miracles to the charismatics, etc. Changes are made by mind as it focuses on the materials (matter) that it has projected, and this holds both positive and negative ramifications. The positive means placing the direction of one's life in a better direction. The negative involves being attracted to and enchanted by manipulating matter with the mind — becoming a prakriti laya. Beyond both the positive and the negative lies the realization that every little thing is interconnected, that all phenomena are caused by mind at cosmic, collective, and individual levels — and taking steps to transcend such subtle binding causes to get free. Rare is that soul — Buddha, Christ, Shankara, Ramakrishna — who reaches Kaivalya, isolation from all forms of Prakriti. Who would ever want to, even think of, divorcing nature? Only those who have grown tired and wary of the limiting nature of such a marriage.

But going back to involvement in the world and freedom seeking, when the aspirant after Truth/God sees that *"Everything is just mind made manifest,"* that *"all objects are only thought concretized,"* an important connection is made as to the origin of all things. No longer does the seven day creation theory, or the theory of evolution, satisfy. One begins to see through the illusion of time, the projection of space, and the net of cause and effect. All types of cycles are seen to be binding, and the possibility of removing the soul from them (transmigration/rebirth) has arrived. The mind is also indispensable at this juncture, for it must attend upon the subtle processes of withdrawal from name and form, absorption into a nondual state, and immersion into the all-blissful Awareness. As Holy Mother has also stated, *"The mind is very important at this juncture, my child. Make sure that you keep it in fine shape all your life. You will need it in order to go to Brahman."*

Kanyakali from Hawaii writes:
QUESTION: "I get confused sometimes when I contemplate prana as Shakti. When I think of the prana contained in food, it seems very gross, so it is easy to relegate it to the realm of maya. But as prana gets refined, and especially as we start to know it as Shakti, it is harder for me to keep it in the category of maya. I turned to your Reclaiming Kundalini Yoga book for a refresher and found these quotes very helpful: 'This formless form called prana, as it moves inwardly to other internal worlds, is Kundalini Shakti; it is one of Her less refined forms which permeate existence at all levels.' And, 'If beings devoid of knowledge and faith look out through the senses connected to the mind they may see only maya – confusing, and beguiling, albeit insentient. But one who has awakened spiritually, beholds the workings of the Mahashakti in everything, everywhere.' I find myself wishing that I had the insight and vision to

fully know maya/prana and Mahamaya/Mahashakti but I guess what I'm wishing for is actually a very high state of awareness! Do you have any guidance for keeping all this straight?"

ANSWER: Beyond wishing is knowing. Today's imaginations must become tomorrow's visualizations. Then, tomorrow's visualizations transform into eternity's realizations. It is all a gradual inward ascension, provided by Her, revealed by Her, and led by Her via Her subtle energy.

For most, then, and as described in the book you mention here, and in the Yoga Kundalini Upanisad, the process is initiated by getting ahold of the prana and the psychic prana. One should not merely watch the breath; that is for beginners. The prana is not the breath, nor the lungs. It is the cause for both.

Using the visualization powers of the mind in meditation, the witness perceives the flow of subtle energy to the senses, then comes to know about the power of the eyes to see, the power of the ears to hear, etc. That one also sees the connection of the gross elements to the subtle elements — the tanmatras. Both prana and tanmatras are hidden facets, unknown to most, and that is why so many are bound to the body, senses, and matter alone. But the power inherent in the senses connects one to the subtle senses (like in the dream state) and to their witness — which is the same witness that is looking inward upon this entire process. With this connection made, the self becomes one with the Self. As Lord Buddha stated: *"The Self is master of the self. Who else would the master be?"* Some other inner dynamics then take place in order to facilitate "a very high state of awareness" that you mention here, but by this time all is assured. It would be more possible that the sun not rise tomorrow than it would be for a sincere soul who is aware of the prana to fail reaching enlightenment. But then, you see, the Divine Mother of the Universe has Her own timing for all this.

## Pada III, Sutra 42

*shrotra akashayoh sambandha samyamat divyam shrotram (shrotra,* power of hearing; *akashayoh,* ether; *sambandha,* interrelation; *samyama,* the power of concentration, meditation, and samadhi; *divyam,* divine; *shrotram,* the ear)

*"The yogi applies samyama on the interrelation between the element of ether and the power of hearing and attains the realm of divine sound."*

As spoken of so many times in SRV classes, inward moving consciousness must sometimes go back and undergo the process of connecting the five senses with the five elements. This sutra explains the fruit of such meditation in relation to the subtlest pair of these ten — hearing and ether. We must remember that the ear is not just a fleshy flap of skin on the side of the head. It is so much more. The very presence of the power of the ear to hear indicates subtle secrets to be uncovered by the yogi and yogini, such as the presence of prana, tanmatras, deeper intelligence, and Awareness. Losing the sensitivity for recognizing the inner power that the senses possess is thus inadvisable.

The essence of inner worlds is attained by mastering subtle vibration, just like the properties of the outer world are gained by listening intently to gross vibration. Both inner and outer vibration have their ultimate origins in The Word, which is the Eternally Still Vibration — the Unstruck Sound lying in the Holy Hands of the Wisdom Mother. It is all the grand realm of mantra, really. As Ramprasad, the poet saint of Bengal sings, ecstatically: *"All sounds you hear are Her sacred mantras, echoing spontaneously, as the entire world worships Her."*

But ordinary souls never experience this, having either failed to connect the outer world with the inner worlds, or having lost the ability for that internal art for lifetimes. Birth in ignorance of one's true nature is due largely to this. Yet, all beings are also drawn inward by sound, by music, discourses, speeches, the sounds of nature via birds and elements, etc.. Even the nearby sound of thunder brings them up in awe. All of these really are outer indications of the imminent presence of God.

The ear as a sense organ is called jnanendriya, an organ of knowledge. Indra is the name for the God of all the gods. The reference in this sutra, then, has to do with assigning the power of the ear to hear to the inner existence of a minor god. As the psychological science of Yoga urges, the aspirant is to connect the five elements to the five senses, meditate upon the results of that coalescence as a finer form of wisdom, then store up the power from that culminative experience. With that force in possession he/she can begin to penetrate all forms of Maya, all veils, all overlays, and gain the secrets of spiritual life in inwardly ascending fashion.

Of course, this cannot be most effectively accomplished until the ability for applying samyama is gained. This will demand that the sixth (dharana), seventh (dhyana), and eighth (samadhi) limbs of Yoga are mastered, and that feat will in turn require that the first five limbs of Yoga have been practiced and understood. In the meantime, the joining back together (they became apparently dispersed at the time of physical embodiment) of the five gross senses with the five gross elements will help bring about its own special fruits. An easy abidance with nature is one of these or, in other words, the enjoyment of a natural harmony on earth and in the body amidst the elements and objects formed by nature.

There will be later and greater attainments, to be sure, like the dawning of higher wisdom that reveals that the physical universe has emerged from the thought processes of the mind at individual, collective, and cosmic levels. But these marvels will unfold naturally once the early steps are undertaken, especially under the adept guidance of an illumined guru and the revealed scriptures — like the one we are presently studying in depth here, over years.

## Pada III, Sutra 43
*kaya akashayoh sambandha samyamat laghu tula samatatti cha* (*kaya,* the body; *akashayoh,* ether; *sambandha,* interrelation; *samyamat,* power of concentration, meditation, and samadhi; *laghu,* minimized; *tula,* cotton; *samatatti,* gains union; *cha,* and*)*

*"Like air passing through cotton cloth, the yogi's samyama on the interrelation between his purified body and the element of ether produces swift penetration of all atmospheres, and ultimate Union."*

As Swami Vivekananda has stated, the physical body of the yogi is just ether/akasha in another of its forms. There is no reason, then, that the luminary, once he/she has gained transcendental abilities, cannot abandon it and take on subtler and subtler versions of it, thereby accomplishing inward ascension swiftly and with ease. This is movement of the most refined variety, and is actually a way of leaving behind the physical and taking up the subtle, then dropping that subtle body and arriving at the causal body.

As this process goes forth and deepens, the yogi can leave his gross body where it sits or lies, and return to it once the inner sojourn is accomplished. This is one good reason why the aspirant practices meditation every day, for the same process, ideally, is occurring there as well. This does not leave life out of the picture either, since moving from waking (jagrat) to dreaming (svapna) to deep sleep (sushupti) every twenty-four hour period is also a version of this spiritual journey. It is all a matter, then, of whether this inward ascension is managed consciously, engaged in semi-consciously, or done merely through unconscious movements that are dictated by the forces of nature alone, leaving mind and soul out of the picture. Doing all in full awareness is the route advised by the luminaries.

Whatever the case may be, the idea in Yoga is to get ahold of the prana and bring it into the life-process so that the soul becomes adept and facile in these inner abilities, for Yoga, Union with Divine Reality, awaits at the culmination point.

## Lesson Eighty-four, 12/5/13
### Pada III, Sutras 44, 45, 46, & 47

Lesson #84 will take a large step forward in the study of the sutras, not only in terms of subject matter, but also in terms of quantity. We will take four sutras in this lesson, 44 through 47, and head towards the end of the third pada which has 56 sutras in total. The subject matter is still concerned with that power of refined and mature Yoga called samyama that, once attained, allows the yogi/yogini to place the pure and focused mind on any object, subject, principle, or being, and come forth with the desired essential answer or quality of that concentration. Aspiring beings, then, are all ears around this kind of information — as is instanced in the inquiry that some of the students are making via their astute questions, below:

**Questions and Answers for Lesson 84**
R.O. from Hawaii writes:
QUESTION: "I see here in RJ#83 that the question of ancestors came up. I recall that we had a brief discussion at one of your talks regarding the effect of

enlightenment on one's ancestors. I believe you said that 7 generations back and 7 forward gain freedom if one person in the family line reaches enlightenment? The enlightened soul would then be a means of release, or a role model, teacher, guide? Can you clarify? Is this a generation of 30 years? Therefore 210 years in the past & 210 years in the future? Are we looking at just the blood line, i.e., parents and children, or also friends, spouses, other karmic relations?"
ANSWER: The idea here is to inform living beings as to the great power and efficacy that *moksha,* Enlightenment, confers upon the soul, upon all souls, really. Why should we restrict it to just a few generations? — although the ancient rishis of India are certainly good examples of how higher wisdom got passed along from generation to generation, and how that especial bequeathal resulted in thousands of years of spiritual growth and attainment of perfection, what to speak of 210 years!

And yes, a great, or even competent, teacher/guru must be born into a group of reincarnating souls in order to help free them. This freedom is not only from suffering, which is noted and spoken of at length with regard to this world, but also entails the acquisition of dharmic qualities and, even above and beyond those, of innate bliss: the luminaries have Bliss *(Ananda).* How would we know this after such a lengthy passage of time — like centuries, even ages — without seeing Sri Ramakrishna Paramahamsa come amongst us in recent times to reveal such intense Bliss in life and mind. His life was not marked by riches, pleasures, lands, etc. Quite the opposite; it had much of difficult circumstances in it. These were all around Him, but not in Him. Thus, a luminary shows humanity much more than how to transcend suffering, which is there in every shred of relativity, i.e., Lord Buddha's first Noble Truth, "Suffering Is." He/She beckons all towards Infinity — Infinite Love, Infinite Grace, Infinite Freedom.

As to the effects of this gaining of the Pearl of Great Price called *moksha, mukti, kaivalya, nirvana, samadhi,* as I said above, it is not limited in its scope or periphery. When an Avatar comes, liberation spreads "across the board." and the entire field of collective mind vibrates in harmony with the principle of spiritual emancipation. As Holy Mother said about Sri Ramakrishna: *"Is it ever possible for a man to free himself unaided from the clutches of Maya? It was for this that the Master performed austerities to the utmost extent and gave the results thereof for the redemption of mankind. Well, this is the Master's kingdom! No rules and regulations are valid here. Here the door is open to all. Whenever one gets the opportunity, one may call on Me."*

This divine descent, so veiled and impossible a presumption to the worldly, is the prime focus of freedom-loving souls who embody here on earth in such challenging, even threatening conditions. Being a rare thing to even see, what to speak of attain, the achievement of moksha is so imbued with force for good and beyond (transcendence) that it cannot help spreading to others. I am seeing this even in and amongst the circle of several hundred that attend upon SRV Association and its efforts for spiritual education of the masses. It happens slowly; that is all. Just yesterday it happened again, and a message came in that "my niece is interested in the teachings of India and the Deities." The Deities only show us the way to formlessness, and so represent a good start to a well-rounded spiritual life.

We must understand, however, that we are not looking for a sensational occurrence, or anything of a spectacular nature. Liberation, like Grace, flows like an underground river, nurturing everything on the surface without ever giving away its subtlemost Presence beneath. That is why Holy Mother asked one person, *"Why have you come to see me? Have I grown two horns?"* She meant that Her unique realization, moksha, did not change Her outwardly; such inward transformation is not on the surface to see.

And so we must be about searching for those illumined teachers who can transmit the singular desire for Freedom (mumukshutvam). Then we are to dedicate ourselves to that ultimate end that they exemplify, letting the salubrious vibratory flow that naturally emits from them do its work of transforming loved ones, friends, family — even our enemies. For as Holy Mother has stated, *"This time the Master has come to save all — the rich and the poor, the wise and the foolish. Now there is a special 'Malaya breeze' blowing. Just set your sail a little, take refuge in Him and you will be blessed."*

J.M. from Oregon writes:
QUESTION: "What does Swamiji mean by 'changing mind into will?' If he means will power, what deeper meaning does this have beyond everyday usage, like in the statement, 'I quit smoking by will power alone?'"
ANSWER: He means getting qualified for receiving the Divine Will. Man has no free will; his is all relative. Therefore, he seeks to control his mind and place it at the Fearless Feet of the Divine Mother of the Universe, and at the feet of Their noble sons and daughters (gurus/acharyas/preceptors) in the interim.

The problem here is that the ordinary mind is not given to seeking higher wisdom and Truth. It has to be changed so as to open up to these boons. This is called spiritual awakening. Thus *Jnana,* higher wisdom, is to be sought via *Iccha,* higher Will. These are two of the four main shakti powers of the Divine Mother. The other two are *Kriya,* spontaneous divine activity, and *Dravya,* production of abundance. Putting these four together, as in a four-armed goddess, the heretofore bound soul is able to free itself from the restrictions of all manner of bonds — karmas, samskaras, sufferings, and yes, even that horrible habit of smoking yourself uncontrollably into an early grave.

So, utilizing Wisdom (jnana), gain the power of Will (iccha). Then act in a free manner (kriya) and secure everything (dravya) that you need for living a divine life here on earth. You will thus be "armed" for Freedom.
QUESTION #2: "On page 60, Swamiji seems to allude to several paths or methods for awakening the Kundalini. What method does he recommend? Is it really a synthesis of several methods? In what ways does the recommended path differ from Patanjali?"
ANSWER: Yoga (Patanjala) and Kundalini Yoga complement each other and, in fact, there is probably no India darshana that does not borrow from and

depend upon the Kundalini system of spiritual awakening and mastery. There is even an Upanisad called the *Yoga Kundalini Upanisad*, showing how intertwined the Kundalini system is with Vedanta. Sri Ramakrishna has stated that *"....there can be no substantial spiritual progress without the awakening of Kundalini Shakti.'* So, whatever one calls it, and by whichever method one chooses or prefers to utilize, that Divine Mother power is in everything and needs to be both acknowledged and encountered in order for an authentic spiritual life to proceed. In Patanjali's Yoga She is called *Chiti-shakti,* and therefore is the very power of our thoughts.

As in your first question above, then, our thoughts are imbued with the power of intelligence, the force of will, with right thinking and right activity. One might as well site the *Ashtangika Marga* along with the *Ashtanga Yoga* here, for many of these attributes are cited there in the Eightfold Path of the Buddha. And She is called *Prajnaparamita* by the Buddhists, the Mother of the Buddhas.

So, She is to be supplicated and rendered very interested in moving up our subtle spine in order to cause the seven chakras to bloom. All else will happen automatically when that auspicious event takes place in us.

QUESTION #3: "Can it be said that the ignorant/dual mind thinks that wires (nerves) are needed to carry psychic prana, while the process of making the mind nondual or the mind's eye single is the method of discarding the wire and convincing the mind of its uselessness."

ANSWER: First we must say that the ignorant mind is not aware of the psychic prana, or any other prana for that matter. The existence of prana is one of the two major missing links in western knowledge. Not even the healers, shamans, and psychics know much about prana. If they did, those three cross sections of beings would have gained enlightenment long ago instead of dallying around with mere physical and psychic energy for the sake of anything other than Enlightenment.

The rare act of a conscious birth is preceded by attaining a conscious death prior to it. People talk glibly about pre-natal and post-natal experiences, but few know what it means to be trans-natal — to be aware of both the soul's passage to various *"kingdoms of heaven within"* after leaving the body, as well as of the Witness who looks on to this process — to all processes. Mastery of the prana enables these two feats of Consciousness. "Wires" *(nadis)* by the hundreds of thousands infuse the subtle and causal bodies of mankind, and are conduits by which the soul (if it still wishes to play the game of transmigration), enters and leaves the womb of the mother. These nadis are not useless, though, even to the realized soul who has attained the highest end — that of *Samadhi,* in which the "eye" becomes "single." The "discarding" of these "wires" is only desirable to those who are completely through with all forms of embodiment. Such a being is like a man who takes a canoe to a far off island and, after arriving there, burns it to ashes so that not even the slightest thought of returning will ever occur — and even if it does for some strange reason, there will be no choice in the matter. In the meantime, there are plenty of fully realized souls who make use of the subtle passageways in order to come out from inner lokas to places like earth in order to help striving and suffering souls. The atmic-ambulance will not run, will not be able to save those who have an emergency if the wiring in it has been stripped out or burned. Thus, the yogi takes good care of the nadis, for comprehensive Yoga would not be possible without them.

QUESTION #4: "Please explain how the Master's analogy, 'A palm frond easily drops from the tree when it turns brown, but if it is pulled off while it is still green, the tree gets damaged,' relates to desires. Are the palm fronds desires, and their dropping to ground their elimination? Then we are to understand that in spiritual life they will fall away naturally through sadhana, but if we try to do away with them prematurely there will be problems, as in plucking the palm frond while still green."

ANSWER: Yes, desire is exactly what is being referred to by these words. In the analogy, however, the distinction is made between desires that are forced away, and desires that fall away naturally in the fullness of time. The "fullness of time," here, does not refer to beings leading a sedentary spiritual life, or no spiritual life at all; desires will not drop away in such a drab and lifeless atmosphere. In other words, there is not enough strength in these types of beings to either mature the "fronds" of their desires, or pull them off the tree.

For both aims and ends, then, the analogy is meant for those two types of beings who are active in seeking spirituality leading to Freedom. The first type of aspirant may even be strong enough to tear off branches of desires, and though this act may leave some damage behind, the strength of such beings overrides it, and progress is made swiftly. In other words, there are some beings who, once achieving a vision of Reality, cannot bear to put up with their desires for objects and the impediments they represent any longer, and simply leave them behind in whatever way is required or necessary. Ascetics and monastics often go by this method.

But for most practitioners, the natural falling away of desires is recommended. Again, this will not happen unless spiritual life is being engaged in. One can watch desires and attachments vanish over time if scriptural study, worship, meditation, and selfless service are present, and all of these four should be subjected to Holy Company over an extended phase of sincere self-effort.

QUESTION #5: "It is stated that ether is the subtlest of the five gross elements and undergoes no modification. How then can ether take the form of a human body? Isn't it really that the body occupies ether?"

ANSWER: Being all-pervasive, ether, *akasha,* does not move, so it would not take or be taken. Even when the physical body is formed, whether that form be a human one or a celestial one (as in a planet or an "angel"), ether still persists in it, unmoved.

So yes, the physical body "occupies" ether, and ether also pervades all bodies, but the real import of this fact on the physical level should lead beings to question and investigate the presence of ether on subtler levels. If embodied beings realized that it is not just physical forms that occupy physical space, but that energy (prana) occupies a pranic ether *(pranakasha)*, and that thought occupies its own ether *(chittakasha)* as well, it would eventually lead to the knowledge that Consciousness occupies them all. This, the seers call *Prakasha* (the Light of Awareness) — the Supreme Space of pure Being — and its single Occupant, *Prakashaka* (the Revealer, the Illuminator).

**Pada III, Sutra 44**
*bahih akalpita vrittih maha-videha tatah prakasha avarana ksayah (bahih,* external; *akalpita,* inconceivable; *vrittih,* thought-vibration; *maha-videha,* transcendent Seer; *tatah,* with that; *prakasha,* light of higher intelligence; *avarana,* obscuration; *ksayah,* obliterated*)*

"*All gross obscurations of the external world and body get obliterated when the thought vibrations of the mind combine with that light of inner intelligence that produces a transcendent Seer.*"

There is hardly a better admixture for growth in the arena of spirituality than that of purified thought and natural intelligence. When the two work together in a sincere and self-surrendered aspirant, the hardships of sadhana, such as working with the limitations of the physical body and forbearing the world, fade to the background, and only mind remains. This heralds the opening of the doorway to transcendence and the formulation of one of those most marvelous of all phenomena, the illumined seer. Of course, a Soul is not created; that is a ridiculous idea. Words like "inception" do not apply to It, the Atman. It does not consist of matter, but of pure, conscious Awareness. It does not suffer beginnings, middles, and ends. The Svetasvataropanisad states: *"Matter is perishable; God is imperishable. That One, the only Reality, rules over perishable matter and individual souls."* And again: *"After setting the creation in motion and withdrawing from it, It unites the principle of Spirit with the principle of matter...."* After knowing this, the only thing left to do is strive for realization of Divine Reality and live in That for the duration of the body's cycle.

But most will not do this. They begin to believe in the body's cycle as real, as the only reality. Even short of this density of mind, they never stop to consider that the bodies of living beings have many cycles, since unawakened consciousness moves *"from birth to death and death to birth,"* devoid of higher wisdom that allows the soul to escape reincarnation if it so chooses. As Swami Vivekananda states in his commentary, the body-oriented mind and thought process limits itself to only *"one system of nerves."* The hundreds and thousands of subtle nerves that conduct everything from gross prana, to psychic prana, to streams of thought — all the way inward to the unique and singular flow of Kundalini Shakti Herself — and which moves from form to form, they remain unaware of. This is like blinding the soul to all of its infinite potential. As Ramprasad sings ecstatically, but pointedly, about these hosts of souls: *"They give themselves to the illusion of finitude."*

Freedom from embodiment of the soul after death is a subject that Yoga and Vedanta — and all the darshanas of India — take up for study and contemplation. However, disembodiment while the soul still inhabits the body is a rare type of study, and it points directly at practices such as meditation for its efficacy. Looking inwards towards what Jesus called *"....the Kingdom of heaven within,"* the embodied soul that is practicing Yoga begins to develop abilities that will allow for "out of the body experiences." "Out of the body" does not mean up in outer space, or hovering up on the ceiling of one's room looking down, or flights of fancy induced by drug experiences reported in the 60's, etc. In Yoga it means outside of the limitations of physical matter, occult projections, and the illusions conjured up by the desire-prone, intoxicated human brain. We must always remember that if we declare that Consciousness is birthless, deathless, and transcendent of the realm of forms produced by Nature, then it must also be true that Consciousness is both beyond and remains unaffected by the various substances found in Nature as well. For a quick look at what both the Fathers of Yoga (Patanjali) and Vedanta (Vedavyasa) conclude about such matters, please see the chart on page 241 of Volume 1 of this work *(Patanjali's Kriya Yoga)*, particularly the part of it that deals with the Five Types of Aspiring Yogis.

**Pada III, Sutra 45**
*sthula svarupa sukshma anvaya arthavatta samyamad bhuta-jayah (sthula,* gross; *svarupa,* essence; *sukshma,* subtle; *anvaya,* all-pervasiveness; *arthavatta,* real meaning; *samyama,* dharana/dhyana/samadhi; *bhuta,* element; *jayah,* victory*)*

"Implementing samyama with regards to the five elements, the yogi perceives their real meaning — like their essence as solidity, all-pervasiveness, etc. — and attains to victory through knowledge of the connection between mind and matter."

To become aware of one's own awareness, and then Awareness Itself, is all about realizing the stationary and all-pervasive *(anvaya)* Consciousness that, according to the Upanisads, *"....infills everything."* *"Svarupa"* means Essence. There is hardly another word in Sanskrit that is more indicative of true and substantial meaning — *arthavatta.* Consciousness is a most subtle *(sukshma)* principle.

On the other hand, the essence of an object does not have to remain a mystery to us. Objects are *sthula,* of gross quality. Even science has found their secret, which hides in vibrating particles; they have just failed to make the right conclusion about them (that they are illusory, therefore to be renounced). Therefore, the "real meaning" of the five elements of nature remains unknown to most embodied beings, which is passing strange, to be sure, since their very bodies and the physical universe are made up of them. To explain, then, what very often ends up as a conundrum in the human mind: there is the Actual, as in nature/five elements; there is the Nonactual, i.e., all that is falsely or ignorantly projected, imagined, etc.; and then there is what is Preternatural, such as the Invisible, Indivisible Soul of mankind. Ironically, this latter, called Consciousness, is as indeterminable to human beings as water is to fish, yet they live in It, subsist on It, and exist by It. Veils — especially over human consciousness — are to be penetrated, torn away, even shred apart. We were not born to live in darkness, not even the semi-benighted state of mere knowledge of matter and energy. The nature of Consciousness is Light, *Jyoti*. Its "essence" is Sound, *Shabda*. *"That illumines the Cosmos,"* as the scriptures declare.

For a very clear illustration of how the quintuplication process works in the wider cosmos (the "Three Worlds"), and what its inherent connections actually are, the reader is asked to look back on lesson #80 to see the chart, *Yogic Connections and Correlations in Meditation Practice*. There, and checking it against this particular Yoga sutra (III:45), both the statement of its fact, and the process of its practice will become more clear. The special yogic ability of samyama will also take on deeper ramifications, and being more appreciated, will cause the aspiring yogi and yogini to measure individual consciousness up to such a sterling power and principle in order to gain mastery and victory over mind and matter, Purusha and Prakriti.

## Pada III, Sutra 46

*tatah anima adi pradurbhavah kaya sampad tad dharma anabhighata cha (tatah,* that; *anima,* invisibility; *adi,* and more; *pradurbhavah,* expression; *kaya,* body; *sampad,* excellence; *tad,* those; *dharma,* right accordance; *anabhighata,* non-impedance; *cha,* and*)*

"Through such realization the yogi can gain mastery over subtle powers like invisibility and more, and express them in right accordance, free of impedance."

In lessons past, and on record from luminaries ranging from Sri Krishna on through to Sri Ramakrishna, the advent of occult powers such as anima (power of invisibility) in the aspirant's spiritual life are to be closely guarded against. True, all eight of these powers may come to some practitioners as a natural result of their intense practices and attainments, but the authentic seers frown upon their usage.

For a full-blown Yogi, the unwanted acquisition of these powers *(astabala siddhas)* is merely a matter of storage. They will hold them inside and seldom call them forth. It is as if the mere possession of them is enough, rather like the case of a highly advanced researcher gaining access to areas that are "off limits" to others simply due to a special identification card pinned on his chest.

Further than this, and much more to the point, unknown to most beings, even seekers of Truth, a much more advanced and wondrous power than *anima* and *lagima,* etc., exists in the mantri guru's ability to initiate the soul into spiritual life, or the shakta guru's power of transmitting the freeing wisdom of the *dharma* to sincere students. This sutra, given by the Father of Yoga himself, speaks of utilizing all powers in "right accord" in order to put an end to impediments along the path towards Enlightenment. We must remember in this regard that Sri Ramakrishna has drawn our attention away from "supernatural" powers in this age, and placed it towards powers that are very natural indeed, called the *Six Divine Powers of God.* To recount them for you, they are: 1) the Living Being; 2) the Universe; 3) Mind; 4) Intelligence; 5) Love; and 6) Knowledge. Any and all of these are marvels. Please meditate on each one of these in turn, find them within yourself, and then realize what true power truly is, and how the Mother of the Universe has invested you with it! All other lesser powers will then become like *"crow droppings by the side of the road,"* to quote Sri Ramakrishna Paramahamsa.

**Pada III, Sutra 47**
*rupa lavanya bala vajra samhanana kaya-sampat (rupa,* form; *lavanya,* beauty; *bala,* strength; *vajra,* firm resolve; *samhanana,* forbearance of troubles; *kaya-sampat,* balanced body*)*
    *"This well-rounded body possesses beauty, strength, firmness in thought and activity, and is able to forbear all troubles that may afflict it."*
    Along with the subject of power, the previous sutra also inferred the special body of a yogi *(kaya)* that is indestructible. In this sutra a short list of special qualities of that pure body are given, attributes such as beauty, strength, and importantly, steadiness and evenness of mind. Implying more than the idea of immortality in the body, the hidden facet of this teaching relates to a fusion of three bodies — gross, subtle, and causal — and how eternal Consciousness utilizes these casings to confer real and highest good upon humanity. As Swami Vivekananda states in his commentary, *"Breaking the rod of time he lives in this universe with this body,"* and *".....there is no more disease, death, or pain"* for him.
    Looking back on the subject of powers, clues like this from an illumined soul indicate the supremacy of divine powers over occult powers. Those beings dubiously invested with and misguidedly enamored of powers like invisibility *(anima),* levitation *(lagima),* and domination *(ishitva),* to name a few, are obviously mostly concerned with personal lordship and dominion over others and over nature. This bespeaks of the desire for longevity of life and pleasures — two of the main traps of the hatha yogi.
    This certainly does not reflect "right accord," *dharma.* The above sutra speaks about "forbearance of all ills" *samhanana,* as a quality of the yogi's attainment of such a body. Also, *vajra* — "firm resolve." Qualities such as these come from intense sadhana that pierces through all such lower temptations to attain the highest. As Swami Vivekananda states, quoting Patanjali: *"Herein lies the secret. Says Patanjali, the father of Yoga: 'When a man rejects all the superhuman powers, then he attains the raincloud of virtues.' He sees God. He becomes God, and helps others become the same."*
    To quote Patanjali himself on wayward and misguided beings: *"These beings suffer via bondage to pleasure due to performing actions because of attraction and aversion to matters they have assumed to be accurate based upon unstable vrittis of the mind."* Such a statement points strongly to the wisdom of achieving qualities such as *kaya-sampat,* a stable body/mind mecha-

nism, does it not? And more to the ultimate point of the sutra, and taking a cue from Kapila, Patanjali states: *"To overcome the impediments to Yoga and other distractions, recourse to the one-pointed practice of a single method is enjoined. As concentration occurs, knowledge of all things, from gross to subtle, is gained, and samapatti, mastery over the mind-field, is attained."*

Most beings, in their sojourn in this life, come to know the difference between outer and inner beauty. The yogi/yogini has both. There is no more exalted and comprehensive being in the three worlds than the one who is possessed of yogic lifestyle and yogic realization. As Sri Krishna advises His devotees: *"Be thou a Yogi....."*

## Lesson Eighty-five, 1/14/14
### Pada III, Sutras 48 & 49

As 2013 begins to fall behind us, so does our in-depth study of these final sutras of pada three of Patanjali's Yoga Sutras. It is a fitting ending for this phase, these fine sutras on the refined spiritual art of *Samyama,* that reveal consummate awareness that is scarcely known by most of the beings of this age. Our knowledge and our practice of Yoga is extremely enriched by even knowing a bit about such lofty and inward spiritual dynamics. After the presentation of questions below, then, we shall proceed to some penultimate sutras of the third pada of the Eight-limbed Yoga, which has brought us to the uppermost branches of this incomparable and timeless tree of God-realization.

**Questions and Answers for Lesson 85**
Akshaya Bhakti from New England writes:
Comments: "Lesson 84 was especially meaningful to me as I am just recovering from 5 weeks of illness that started with the flu, and am inspired to learn how to transcend suffering! Not only was my body debilitated, but also my mind. I am very drawn to meditating on The Six Divine Powers, especially that of Love, as enjoined by the guru in Sutra 46. Although I could not seem to draw the power of light to me, the comfort of love permeated me at all levels and also, a keen sense of longing to send love to all other creatures who are suffering. Whenever I have gone through such bouts of suffering, I can't help think, perhaps wishfully, that it is the work of concentrated Prarabdha Karma that ultimately will have a positive result of winding down the spool and also, giving me a needed sense of urgency to re-establish and then deepen my practice permanently. This time I felt it more than ever since this event punctuated a whole year of sadness and suffering. As I was researching the term 'Prarabdha' to make sure that was the "arrow" that has already been shot into the air, I came across a quotation from Swami Sivananda that referred to exactly what I had been trying to express and validate for a long time: *'Do not murmur when you get difficulties, troubles, diseases. Many old karmas have to be purged out quickly. Mother Prakriti wishes you to unite with the Lord quickly. Therefore,*

*only the thirsting aspirant will get more pain and trouble, but the all merciful Lord will at the same time give you wonderful power of endurance to tide over the crisis. Only then will real spiritual life begin.'"*

QUESTION: "Could you further elucidate this revelation, dear teacher? Is there any way to tell that a particularly stressful event in our life was beyond recall, that it was already Prarabdha Karma, and as Swami suggests, that it may be of particular help in our spiritual progress? Can 'dis-ease' ever have a purpose in our lives as we strive to discover our true Self again?"

ANSWER: Ultimately, the yogi/yogini wants to surmount all diseases, all pain. But there are the six transformations of birth, growth, disease, old age, decay, and death that come to all embodied beings. So, we must first deal with the unnecessary suffering that is upon us. Much of that is mental. Of course, the mind is the inner cause of everything we experience, so the yogi works on the mind. There are powers of transcendence, of rising above, in the mind. They are gained by developing strength. Vedanta calls this *titiksha,* or forbearance. The Gita refers to it as rising above *dvandva mohena,* the deluding pairs of opposites. Sankhya Yoga puts it in terms of mastering the *gunas* and remaining in *sattva* as much as possible. In Yoga, as you mention, Patanjali advises that we not react to diseases, or to unpleasant experiences, when they are upon us. All, any, or a combination of these are helpful to us when seeking balance.

As to the other element in your question, there is really nothing here on the earth plane but karma. Karma is the god of this physical universe. Its retribution is unavoidable, and comes in its own time. Past, present, and future karma play on the field. Much of what transpires there is the taking up of past karma and bringing it forward to the present. Future karma is less applicable, as it can be offset if the aspirant maintains spiritual practices such as mantra, constant study of scripture, and meditation. Serving others is also a good way of cutting karma down.

There are, unfortunately, *samskaras,* which are mental impressions that lie in the mind, mostly unnoticed, until they suddenly fructify. Let us not forget good karmas and samskaras, of course. But when the subject is pain and its onslaught, the cause is usually of a mixed or a negative nature.

It is hard for the Westerner to look at karma and its repercussions and not overlay the entire affair with misguided thoughts bringing in immorality, sin, a big judge of a god looking on to reward or punish, a horned devil chasing to scare and torture, and mental oddities of that ilk. Quite often you have madcaps such as the "fire-darting reformers" who think that the calamities of nature that occur to humanity are somehow visited upon them by a wrathful god or a vengeful devil. All this is superstition. One might expect to find such nonsense among the spiritually uneducated and beings that dabble in the occult, but it should not be allowed in true religion.

Karma has more to do with time and space. You have heard the definition for Maya, i.e., name, form, time, space, and causality. When a soul takes on name and form and enters the field of karma, it does so at a particular time and in association with a certain area or areas. Then it moves around in the body, visiting locations and performing actions. Its own actions and their effects begin to direct it here and there in space, under the auspice of its own timing. So, if it comes into a particular location where a calamity is about to occur in time, all due to the soul's own acts (karma), is that the fault of god, devil, or nature? Of course not. And neither is it luck or serendipity that brings the soul in contact with good or wonderful occurrences; that is its karma too. Even if one were to believe in positive and negative forces that dictate destiny, the soul needs only to keep its actions non-karma bearing *(aklishta)* in order to avoid running afoul of negativity. *"One reaps what one sows"* is the simple way of putting this.

Besides, when karma fructifies it is a good time for growth. Lamenting it misses this opportunity. Quite often, the body merely needs cleansing, and disease is there to effect that. This is personal karma having to do with nature and the body; nothing else. One should not project the involvement of independent outer forces on these situations. If time brought it to bear, it will take time for it to work itself out; that is all. Sri Ramakrishna once said, *"A man had a serious illness. His relatives took him to visit a healer, and he suddenly got better. Though no one knew it, nature had already cured him on the day of his visit."* Appearances can be deceiving, then. Much more can be said about this inscrutable subject.

QUESTION #2: "I appreciate the chart you have created of *The Seven Qualifications & Seven Victories of a Tantrik Aspirant,* and especially the bottom part where the Seven Victories of Involution are listed, because as far back as sutra 16 I have found the process of regressing the 24 Cosmic Principles particularly insightful. Concerning *Pradhana Jaya,* control of the primal principle, does that refer to Sankalpa /Projection?"

ANSWER: Pradhana is a Sankhya term for Prakriti, insentient matter. It really refers to nature in its unmanifested form, before solid worlds are formed. Thus, it is the root of all elements and is the material cause of the worlds. That would infer that it is the primal cause of matter, occurring very far back and deep within the entire evolutionary process. Gaining control over it is tantamount to gaining mastery over the modes of nature (gunas).

But nature, Pradhana, is only involved in Sankalpa; it is not responsible for sankalpa. Sankalpa is the work of Mind at cosmic, collective, and individual levels of mentation. Mind may be both imbued and accompanied by nature, but it is also attended by intelligence, and thus, is a temporary home for consciousness. This makes mind far more than matter, and the holder of a certain kind of sentience that Pradhana can never know.

Avinashi from Pennsylvania writes:
QUESTION: "How is it possible for everything to be knowledge when there's so much ignorance in the world, and when so much of the human world seems to manifest from ignorance? Maybe the answer to this question depends partly on what kind of knowledge you're speaking about. Is this a kind of knowledge that can somehow include ignorance?...or maybe ignorance is seen as just par-

tial knowledge... and therefore knowledge indeed, but incomplete?" This question comes to mind when you mention the samadhi wherein everything is seen as knowledge. How is it possible for everything to be seen as knowledge when so much seems to clearly spring from nescience?"

ANSWER: Wisdom samadhi takes one to another world, as it were. People see dullness, illness, depression, death, duality, and the like simply because they leave their minds in that selfsame state of ignorance that you mention above. Put obversely, they will not work to raise the mind out of illusion and delusion, so they simply see these everywhere.

Whatever the case, Brahman does not change, whether or not the mind changes from low vibration to high vibration. The statement "All is Wisdom" is true, whether or not knowledge or ignorance presides in the mind from time to time, phase to phase, cycle by cycle. Beings who strive to keep a balanced mind, called *sattva,* are less susceptible to the covering of ignorance; that is all. But even they seldom have wisdom samadhi, thereby actually perceiving, as Holy Mother taught us, that *"Objects are mind made manifest."* Another time She put it, *"Matter is thought concretized."* This is not an ordinary vision, nor an average state of mind. We do not call it Samadhi — *sama,* equality, *adhi,* original — for nothing.

QUESTION #2: "Will you explain what tantrikas mean when they speak about the ripening of impurities? They surely can't mean that karmas, good or bad, simply come to fruition? They can't mean, for example, that a person who feels a fascination with murder finally murders, or a person who's fascinated with money finally amasses a fortune. Well, maybe they do mean that, but I doubt it. I get the feeling that the ripening of impurities somehow involves the emergence of wisdom, since it seems to be related to liberation rather than the deepening of bondage. But beyond this I have no clue as to what the ripening of impurities really means, so maybe you will clarify this?"

ANSWER: I would be glad to. *Malas,* or imperfections in the mind, are legion; most all embodied beings suffer them. Some malas are done away with via moral and ethical life and living. Others get destroyed by sadhana. Some subtle ones get transcended by successful meditation. The ones that "ripen" are singular, though, in that they were consciously taken on prior to birth. These are of the type that veil at first, only to suddenly mature along the path of life and reveal insights at the right time. Beings of a tantric nature love this kind of spiritual progress, as it puts them nearer and nearer to God through several lifetimes, and ensures that they be close to God in every embodiment until pure intimacy or absolute unity occurs — as in *"I and my Father are One."*

So you are right to distinguish them from negative acts and from bad karmas. Really, they are the result of past good karmas. This is precisely why man should never think of himself as a sinner, or call another a sinner. As Vivekananda has stated, *"Liable of liables, it is the greatest sin to call another a sinner."* Our imperfections are actually quite precious, then, and for several reasons. Malas, tantrically defined, are self-imposed veils of bondage that reveal, but over cycles of maturation in time, and when they do mature they leave the soul close to its Ishtam. They have been described as being like an unripe apple that is not fit to eat yet, but soon will be. And so, the entire matter also has to do with auspicious timing.

QUESTION #3: "When it comes to the mumukshutvam of jnana-yoga, how is one to wield this desire for liberation in a way that in fact leads to liberation, seeing that the desire — even to the brink of moksha — must be for a form of personal enjoyment? I've heard it said that an ordinary man's desire to enjoy relations with a woman is as nothing compared with the super-desire of a yogi who wants to enjoy eternal bliss in freedom. Isn't there a lot of truth to this? And if there is, then what is the way out of what seems to me this paradoxical, circular trap? The desire for liberation, described as being so important to the realization of liberation itself, would seem, at the same time, to block our entrance; or maybe not. I am, of course, aware of Buddhism's bodhisattva teachings and wonder if something of this sort is absolutely necessary for moksha? Or perhaps the desire for liberation can be purified in another way? Will you shed light on this, and maybe also share some teachings relevant to it?"

ANSWER: By the time the aspiring soul reaches such elevated areas as the desire for moksha, the personal desires have already died away. This simple answer will clarify the entire matter for you. Higher stations of Consciousness — since they have not been experienced yet — the as yet uninformed soul can only measure by standards of desire that are common. The same is true in the estimation of a worldly person, or any unenlightened soul, of seers and sages. It is just not possible yet to be accurate in such an assessment. The saying of Sri Ramakrishna, *"It takes a jeweler to assess the value of a diamond,"* applies here. We must all become jewelers before we can comprehend both the illumined souls who come to teach us higher Truth, and the experiences that proceed from such in-depth teachings.

QUESTION #4 "I'm unclear on the difference between vyavaharika and pratibhasika. I understand vyavaharika as essentially being a perception that can be shared by many. On the other hand, I understand pratibhasika as being private, in the nature of a hallucination. But what kind of reality is it when one person's hallucination becomes the shared perception of many? An example might be the fear of witches in old Salem, which started with one person and swept over almost the whole town. Would this be vyavaharika or pratibhasika? Its also said that an attribute of vyavaharika is that it is "pragmatic," but I have no idea as to what that really means. And finally, will you critique my usage of these terms? I don't know which forms are nouns and which are adjectives, and when to use the one or the other."

ANSWER: I have removed a few words from your question here to make it copesetic with your intended meaning.

As far as the distinctions you seek to know, *Pratibhasikasatta* pertains to what is outright illusory, and what therefore, when accepted by the ignorant human mind, brings miseries untold. *Vyavaharika* has more to do with what is empirical, or what is a matter of practical everyday living. This everyday living, as many of us are finding out, is seldom conducive to spiritual growth, nor ultimately fulfilling, so it has a somewhat illusory element in it as well.

Philosophically speaking, Vyavaharika, empirical existence, is used in contrast with *Paramartika,* Absolute Existence. In the case of Pratibhasikasatta, its polar opposite is *Pratibhandikabhava,* which is the power of piercing through and destroying illusions in the mind.

QUESTION #5 "Do you consider that the realization of Ishvara is contained in or follows from the path of jnana-yoga as you teach it? And do you consider the path of bhakti to be essentially a diversion, except maybe for beginners or weakling souls, as it were? I'm not referring to the attitude of bhakti, but to the path as taught by Narada. That, of course includes austerities and study of the scriptures. I'm definitely not referring to recreational bhakti."

ANSWER: I teach what the tradition teaches, and Vivekananda, and how Aseshananda taught me. Of course, there is my own contribution to it all. It is not only Jnana Yoga, but all four yogas, as you know from studying (and being very inspired at times) with the Raja Yoga course. Mainly, the way in which I go about transmitting is also the way our founder, Lex Hixon, approached it (another influence of mine). I have had some four decades of teaching experience by now, and have seen a good cross section of today's people, Eastern and Western. What I have seen in the West is that those few who actually get attracted to perennial wisdom are not able to go very far in it, or give it up completely too soon due to weakness and ignorance. Since they have little or no grounding in Yoga, their karma (work) is skewed, their meditation is either misguided or absent, and their bhakti is surface. With novices like these, and as Vivekananda has said, they need to go to the studies in order to ground themselves first, then qualify themselves next. Westerners are at least good at study, generally speaking.

*Ishvara* gets the go around here in the West. Christianity (and a behind the scenes conventional Judaism) has spoiled the European and American for any kind of worship of God with form. Christ is misrepresented, and it is a boon indeed if even a few of us retain our love of Him. Then, there is the aversion of the Westerner to any Eastern form of God as well. This being the case, money will then become their first God, followed by Science — which is steeped up to its nose in materialism, along with the pipe dream of trying to create a utopian society.

Wisdom! That is the way out of this predicament for the sincere seeker. Sri Ramakrishna's statement that *"Bhakti is the path of the age"* was given for and amidst Hindus. He never set foot out of His country. But Swamiji did. He saw it first hand in 1893 in all the big American cities, and in London too. He saw we were ready for higher intelligence, having exceeded in the lower type.

I have been trying for three decades to interest the Americans in bhajans, pujas, Ishvara, and fealty to the Lord and Mother of the Universe, and most are not having it. Even among my own SRV students and disciples, they do not show up for puja; they show up for classes — even though I put equal emphasis and import on them both, early on. We are only fortunate that we have Sri Ramakrishna — a human form rather than a god or goddess — as our

Ishtam. That, the Americans are beginning to understand. But then again, to accept that God appears in the human being, any human being, is a hard thing for them. The yen for materiality and physical science is too strong in them. The occult, i.e., forms of magic, fascinate them too. And conventional religion, with its harping on sin, keeps them from entertaining thoughts about their divine nature — what to speak about seeking It and finding It.

QUESTION #6: "I've heard you often say that 'God is just a thought.' I personally understand this idea to be an expression of truth from the Absolute, nondual platform. But from the position of the relative universe, can it be said that God is 'just' a thought? Sri Ramakrishna, through the course of his theistic and tantric sadhanas, had many experiences of Ishvara that were of undeniable depth and richness. Of what nature was the God he experienced in these sadhanas? From the Absolute position, the idea that God is just a thought makes perfect sense to me; but from the relative position it seems to me that God — as Ishvara or Saguna Brahman — is poised in that station where all things are seen to rise and fall in concord with the One whose very being all these things are. So will you clarify, in all-round, 360 degree manner, your statement."

ANSWER: It comes from Swami Vivekananda's statement that Ishvara is a concept, though It is the highest concept that the human mind can comprehend. Since most of mankind cannot understand God in Its Essence, as Formless Reality, then Ishvara is the main takeaway concession. As he used to say, if two monkeys have a disagreement, they go to the king of the monkeys to settle it. This is because they cannot conceive of a higher authority than that.

Of course, all of this seems to belittle Ishvara. That is not the intention. It is the highest authority inside of the realms of name and form. One *"....gets to the Father through the Son."* Souls either go to It or go through It. Those who go to It prefer God with form; those who go through It use It as a doorway into Formless Samadhi. These latter also use It as a doorway back into form. This explains the crucial importance of Ishvara, I should think. It can also be said that Ishvara's main function is to act as such an open gateway so that aspiring souls can experience *Nirvikalpa Samadhi* — a rare state. Even those who love to sport with God in form will at sometime wonder at Its essential secret, at Its homogenous Nature.

And so you ask, "But from the position of the relative universe, can it be said that God is 'just' a thought?" The answer is, that it is particularly from the standpoint of relativity that It is. When the soul dissolves into Essence, all thoughts will dissolve with it. That is the Absolute. No thought takes place there, and certainly no desiring (vikalpa), mental projection (sankalpa) dreaming (svapna), or playing/sporting (lila). My God, there has to be one State wherein no form intrudes, one Being that nature cannot formulate. Let's have That, amidst all other expressions, and leave It untouched.

QUESTION 7: "May I have teachings on sahaja samadhi? When I think about this subject, the following questions and reflections arise: I wonder what its basic characteristics are; I wonder what prior states, stages, attainments, or other samadhis are necessary for its realization; I wonder what forms of wisdom come to dominance with its arising, and I wonder how one sees the universe, God, and self from within it."

ANSWER: If one could somehow describe the state of Nirvikalpa Samadhi, then there would be a definition for *Sahaja Samadhi*. The phrase, *Sahajanirvikalpasamadhi* is in Sanskrit dictionaries. I would venture to say that among the few rare beings that receive Nirvikalpa Samadhi, most of them leave the embodied state forever. Only a rare and specific few return, and these live in *Sahajanirvikalpasamadhi*. It is a state of Nondual Samadhi wherein consciousness of Brahman has become natural, i.e., "sahaja."

On a lower level of awareness, there exists *Sahajakumbhaka* (the natural retention of the breath), and *Sahajananda*, wherein blissful abidance has become natural. So, you see, about anything that one is wholly and irretrievably established in can be described with the word "sahaja."

R.O. from Hawaii writes:
QUESTION: "A question that often comes up in western philosophical systems, and which draws a multitude of commentaries, is, 'How do we know that we know?' In the context of the Raja Yoga system that is being taught now, can you answer this?"

ANSWER: Yes. An already established conclusion, called a *siddhanta*, is and has been arrived at and agreed upon in India by the many darshanas (paths of seeking Truth) based upon the testament of the various seers and sages of such philosophical systems. This unanimous conclusion could never have been possible if the age old argument about whether God exists or not had persisted. In other words, the seers and pathways of India have all come into agreement that God Is Existence or, Existence is God, and proves God.

By giving up kicking the dead horse of whether God exists or not, of the dead end of belief or nonbelief, simple and profound agreement can be reached. Then, real religious, philosophical, and spiritual progress can be made. India has made that. We, in the West, are still in the dark ages, arguing futilely and in cycles of circular reasoning about nonessential matters better put behind us so that we can actually seek, find, realize, and express Truth in our lives.

The problem in the West is that we do not have any sages and seers. There are just a host of intellectuals, plying the trade of "occupations" like science and philosophy for a paycheck and some hoped for notoriety. Intellectuals and professionals do not combine actual practice with their philosophy. Real Philosophy starts with reasoning and intellectual inspection, no doubt, but they must agree with us (the practitioners) that it ends in spiritual experience, and with various insights gained along the way. Proof of Truth, then, is based upon direct experience of God, and this is approached by combining knowledge, knower, and that which is to be known, in one final realization. As one mystic philosopher of India writes:

> *Mother of the Universe, why are You attempting to hide from my gaze?*
> *I have realized at last the true nature of prayer and meditation.*

*You may choose to veil Your sublime Existence by allowing good fortune
to pour into the lives of everyone except those who devotedly worship You,
but I can now evoke Your sparkling Energy
at the spiritual root of this human body.
You are no longer able to conceal Yourself or to appear distant from me.
My very breath and being have become bonded with Your potent mystery,
and I experience Your Liberation as my own inviolate strength.
I know, and I know that I know.
Freedom from the illusion of not-knowing has been attained only through You.
What more is there for You to give me or to withhold from me?
No one can remove this realization. Not even You.
I have bound You at the center of my being
with adamantine strands of energy.
This courageous poet is now waiting to see if Goddess Kali
can unravel my knots of pure Love.*

And so, you see, that practices like prayer and meditation figure in, that love is a part of the quotient, and liberation from bondage to the senses and limitations of the mind must be sought after. Moreover, Grace is courted, as in *"Freedom from the illusion of not knowing has been granted by Thee."* As Swami Vivekananda used to say, *"If not you, who? If not now, when?"* In other words, you yourself must rise up, destroy your ignorance with knowledge, seek and find the higher wisdom, and then make it all end in Truth.

This all may sound too simple to the intellectual Westerner. But it is not like India has skipped over the power of reasoning and speculation. To the contrary! They have refined it into a convincing art.

D.G. from Belgium writes:
QUESTION: "Why does Swamiji make a difference between psychic prana and prana."
ANSWER: There is a great need in modern man, especially in the Westerner, to become aware of the prana, even to any small degree. And where people of the world actually have connected with the word and principle of prana, as in the case of the hathis and shamans, they are leaving it in the physical region only, and not understanding it on the level of internal mind. That is why physically-based practices and people have not yet developed a spiritual life, and have barely begun to comprehend a dharmic life.

It is all well and good to become aware of and then activate the energy coursing through the body, aligning it with pure food, good health, and balanced breathing, but this is only where the *"one prana in five forms,"* as Swamiji called it, leaves off, and the psychic prana begins. To transform the mind's thinking process will entail inner work with the *manas* (dual mind), the *buddhi* (intellect), the *ahamkara* (unripe separate self), and the *chitta* (one's thoughts), and this is the domain of the psychic prana. Patanjali's Yoga provides all manner of teachings for this essential area of consciousness, which far outstrip and overshadow any mention of physical practices in the sutras. Purifying and utilizing the psychic prana helps purify the antahkarana, the fourfold mind, and reveal to it its special powers as well.

In today's spiritual circles — those ones that are leaning towards Yoga Psychology as the means — only the basement and the roof are being shown and emphasized; that is, hatha for the body and meditation for the mind, with nothing in between. All that has to do with purification of the mental apparatus — like study of scriptures, devotional worship, and finding an illumined teacher and adhering to his instructions for an intense period of time in sadhana — is being skirted. All the real work along with its essential transformations is thus missing.

But the soul cannot jump from asana to meditation without major gaps in attainment followed by serious repercussions. That is one of the reasons that Patanjali cites backsliding and the inability to make any spiritual progress *(alabdhabhumikattva & anavasthitattvani)* as the two spiritual impediments *(viparayas/antaryayas)* to Yoga. The ordinary yogic practitioner of the day carelessly skips over the *yamas* and *niyamas* — necessities such as study and memorization of scriptures *(svadhyaya),* increasing devotion to God *(ishvara-pranidhana),* and consciously undergoing mental austerities *(tapas)* — and just stretches and sits. A little physical prana gets stirred up in the body, but this will not help meditation, and in fact might hinder it, since the body is to be left behind in real meditation, certainly in samadhi. But whatever the case, no inner work whatsoever gets accomplished on the mental apparatus *(antahkarana)*, and the mind wanders blindly into meditation with all of its karmas and samskaras intact and ready to surface.

This is worse than it sounds. If you take an unclear mind and subject it to intensification, you run the risk of intensifying its imperfections as well, or mixing them in with the higher insights that may also rise in meditation practice. An immature spiritual outlook *(bhrantidarshana)* attended by undigested spiritual moods is the result, and also becomes ongoing in life.

Active, pure, and free-flowing prana, on all levels, is essential to Yoga. The psychic prana operates in the inner territories of mind and intellect, and the physical prana flows through the body, organs, and lungs. The former courses along subtle nadis, the latter along grosser ones. Gross prana carries blood, nutrients, breath, etc., while the psychic prana carries thoughts and intelligence. What is more, and an understatement, one's thoughts need purification as well, along with inspiration and direction. Helping the physical prana to flow will help the body/mind mechanism for a time, off and on, but mastering the psychic prana will take the mind towards transcendence of all that is problematic and limiting in the physical universe of matter.

Mind and matter; it is an ancient combination. They have their connection, but each has its own atmosphere, along with methods and practices that respectively assist each to function. It must be remembered, though, that body decays and returns to the elements of nature. Mind has the double distinction of taking the soul from state to state (a function of the psychic prana), and also

facilitating immersion into Brahman at the time of Samadhi. There is no comparison.
QUESTION #2: "Can one equate psychic prana with Kundalini Shakti?"
ANSWER: No, not equate, but connect. Kundalini Shakti is innately intelligent, supremely independent, and fully Aware. Prana, of all types, is insentient, dependent on other forces, and unaware of itself.

Kanyakali from Hawaii writes:
QUESTION: "Thank you very much for pointing out 'The Six Divine Powers of God,' and suggesting that we meditate on each one of them in turn. It has been very illuminating! When I meditated on the Universe, I recalled a depiction I saw recently of the Big Bang that showed a ball of intensely charged energy swirling around and getting ready to explode. It occurred to me that although the scientists theorize that all matter in the universe, including space, came from the Big Bang, they fail to explain what the source of the material is all around that swirling ball. We would call that matter Ether, but if it is Ether, and it existed before the Big Bang, what created it? Oops. Anyway, I just further proved to myself that science has some pretty major unknowns yet to solve while being stuck in belief in a material cause alone. From there I continued to explore causality as we know it, i.e. what caused Ether, the Mind, what caused Intelligence, etc. Whenever I can manage to restrain the mind-stuff from taking various forms for longer than a moment, I experience a formless meditation. The witness is still there, but the rest of the mind is emptiness. Now, do I explore that emptiness and wait, expectantly, for forms to appear again?"
ANSWER: It is the Great Three — form, formlessness, and Formlessness — also called in the Gita by Sri Krishna, manifest nature, unmanifested nature, and Supremely Unmanifested Nature. These are the three levels/worlds/states/principles that contain all else, from time and space on through to stations of consciousness like mind and intellect, all the worlds existing therein, and all pervaded by that One Soul appearing as many souls. When meditation renders it all clear, like a book, then Witness Consciousness becomes evident as the "Reader." As Vivekananda has said about a conscious life, and to paraphrase: "The Soul picks up the book of nature and reads it, page by page. Then it puts it down when it is finished. All the while, nothing happened; the Reader did not move. The Soul, or Reader, simply drank deep of its own wisdom, and all of nature that came from It." I could add, about closing the book (death), that it probably had a good cup of tea and went to bed for awhile. Other books were waiting to be read when it awoke.

So yes, when you are finally graced with a formless meditation in consciousness, watch that emptiness for what appears next. A sorrowless Ocean of Light, for instance, is quite a sight. If forms return to you, observe them without attraction or disappointment, and continue to breach the line of demarcation between form and formlessness every day in meditation practice.
J.M. from Oregon writes:
QUESTION: "There is one mention of Ishvara in the Yoga Sutras. Patanjali

lauds that being. I am wondering, what is the relationship between Ishvara, Prakriti, and Purusha? If Ishvara is the ruler of the universe, does that mean It performs action as well?"

ANSWER: Prakriti is insentient matter, Purusha the sentient soul, and Ishvara is the Oversoul. Ishvara, or Ishvari, oversee all functions that take place in the realms of time and space, as well as the affairs of human beings. If human beings keep a relationship with Ishvara (the personal God), then their lives remain dharmic and go along as should be; even the negative things are for the best. But if this relationship is forgotten, the soul has to fall back on its own auspice, called the ego, and things, as we have seen, do not go well much of the time — and even when they do there is always an insinuating sense of foreboding underlying all thoughts and acts.

As far as acts go, beings perform their own acts and reap the results. Ishvara is practically without acts, and rarely enters into the field (except as Avatar, occasionally). As I just said, She/He is not needed if beings simply keep up the dharma and the proper spiritual relationships in the world. A story by Sri Ramakrishna illustrates this nicely:

*"Once, Narayana and Narayani (Ishvara and Ishvari) were seated comfortably, talking about Truth. All of a sudden, Narayana got up and left. But He returned quickly. The Goddess asked Him where He went. He explained: 'A devotee of mine was going along the road, when he accidently trod over some washed clothes that were placed there to dry in the sun. The owners saw this and began to curse him. As their anger escalated, they begin to search for rocks to throw at him. I immediately sensed his danger as was going to help him, but then I found that he was picking up rocks himself to scare them away. Thus, my help was not needed.'"*

This is how God is not needed for the dharmic man or woman. They will not drag Him/Her into the affairs of everyday life. This is why the spiritual being does not pray for things. If he prays at all, it will be for spiritual treasures, spiritual advancement, wisdom, etc. — all that happens inwardly. And the really selfless ones pray for the enlightenment of all sentient beings.

QUESTION #2: "Can all acts that uphold the yamas and niyamas be deified and transformed into a yoga? I ask because the business opportunity has been a way for me to diminish tamasic cycles and break away from habits of overeating and brooding over the future. Other benefits have been to employ Witness consciousness while doing work, to see if I'm getting attached to the outcome. I also get to watch if I can keep a posture of fearlessness when acquiring new customers. It really has been a blessing in this life."

ANSWER: Yes, all thoughts and acts are to be deified. Care must be utilized, though, as one does, to inspect, over time, the intentions and results of such a way — the way of sublimation. Most necessary is knowing the fact that the world is unreal and passing. Thus, detachment is the constant companion of the wise. So, what I am saying to you is to not mix God and the world. Keep each in its own place. You ask about setting up a shrine, for instance; well, never do a worldly thing or have a worldly thought in there. Don't even bring a glass of water in there, or place a nonreligious book there. It is all God the moment one enters, and it remains so as one leaves and when one returns.

People have this romantic notion when they begin spiritual life that spirituality and work can coexist. They cannot. Sure, one can keep the mind high and pure, or try to, but the plain fact is that God retreats when activity approaches. And vice versa. God is Samadhi, Nonduality, Inaction — everything that the revealed scriptures say It is. It is beyond gender too. It must be kept sacrosanct in order for the mind to have a place to retreat that is free from actions taking place in the world, simply because all acts and their works are good, bad, and mixed, i.e., not transcendent of cause and effect.

So do business dharmically, but leave God free of action — like It is. And sattva — the pleasure and goodness that one gets in a balanced life — is not God either. It is a fine temporary resting place, and a balance point, but it will not produce enlightenment. Only mature transcendence can do that. So, keep an Ideal that is untainted. As the poet/saint sings:

*The Divine Troubadour alone can tune you with Her strong, skillful hands.*
*From Her alone the poet receives these lines:*
*Never allow the world's opinion to dim the ecstasy of your worship,*
*or draw you even slightly away from your Mother's sweet intimacy.*

## Pada III, Sutra 48

*grahana svarupa asmita anvaya arthavatta samyamad indriya jayah* (*grahana*, comprehension; *svarupa*, essence; *asmita*, sense of I-ness; *anvaya*, permeation; *arthavatta*, right determination; *samyamad*, concentration, meditation, and samadhi; *indriya*, senses; *jayah*, victory/mastery)

*"Mastery over the senses is gained by making samyama on refined components such as the power of mental comprehension, natural permeation, the refined sense of I-ness, and one's own pure Essence."*

Those of you who are familiar with and have studied the tantric teachings given in SRV over the years will begin to recognize some of the aspects of the Seven Victories of a Tantric Aspirant in these particular yoga sutras presently under study. Manojavittvam, for instance — the mastery of the mind and its thought — is a giant leap of attainment for the aspiring soul. If one knew the incredible speed with which the mind can move within, to penetrate the deepest levels of awareness, there would be practically no impediment that one could not overcome, even with relative ease. The only stage after that would be to slow down so much that all movement and thought stops completely. Immersion and absorption would then take place.

The five senses in man, left unmastered, uncontrolled, stand in the way to these special types of attainment. In Yoga, as instanced by the Sanskrit in this sutra, *anvaya-vyatireka* suggests that Atman is "mixed in," as it were, among the five sheaths. The process of affirmation and negation, both, will suffice to cause the necessary separation, leaving the yogi's vision of the Absolute free and unencumbered. This is a level of mastery that is crucial for realization of Yoga. Samyama will then be powerful and complete, and any veil can then be penetrated.

Among other things, this sutra tells us of the need to go beyond the usual attainments, and to not rest on one's laurels. This extra effort and result is provided to the yogi by the power of Samyama, which is really the full utilization of the yogi's subtle powers gleaned in the later stages of spiritual practice. A glimpse of Reality via a flash of samadhi does not a Yogi make. Lightning may illumine the landscape at night for a few seconds, but the darkness that follows is all the more obscuring. The consummate yogi wants to illumined the entire cosmos, thereby revealing the Source from which all of it emanated. Samyama is the power of constant Light, not a mere flash. Constant Light allows for constant examination, and this makes for the marked difference between a past master and an adept. The former is like a blazing midday sun that lights up the inside and outside of a house, while the latter is like a lamp that only illumines the inside of a room. Matured practice is all the difference. As Lord Buddha stated about this level of realization, *"Like a beautiful flower, devoid of color and devoid of aroma, fruitless are the fair words of one who does not practice them."*

## Pada III, Sutra 49

*tatah mano-javittvam vikarana-bhavah pradhana jayah (tatah,* utilization; *mano-javittvam,* speed of the mind; *vikarana-bhavah,* full cognition; *pradhana,* primal cause; *jayah,* mastery*)*

*"Mastery over the mental organ brings about cognition of the inconceivable speed of the mind and its higher thoughts, as well as perception of the primal cause out of which all manifestation arises."*

We have spoken in the last sutra's commentary about what the Tantracists have called *manojavittvam,* the inconceivable speed of thought. Another of the Seven Victories in Tantra also includes what Patanjali indicates here, which is the mastery of *Pradhana,* the Primal Cause of all. To define it more specifically, it is what Vedas and Vedanta call Unmanifested Prakriti. It is nature held in abeyance in a formless state before it is released to become the insentient material of the worlds of name and form in time and space. Thus, it is much like the Maya of Vedanta, except that maya is considered to be both unreal and dependent upon Brahman, whereas Pradhana is said to be real, and an independent reality all its own.

Whatever the case around such details, there is no denying the elevated position that the yogi attains when Pradhana is mastered. Among other abilities, the possibility of gaining Kaivalya, isolation from nature and its form-producing powers, is gained. The only impediment in the way at such exquisitely subtle levels of yogic mastery is the now insinuating presence of causal form. Gunas in their origin are there, for instance, and will have to be returned fully into their original state of equilibrium. The student can look back on lesson #82 for a clearer presentation of this in the chart titled, "Stages of Dissolution of the Mind in Yoga." In the seven levels of attainment listed therein, the sixth and penultimate one is the dissolution of the three gunas of Pradhana, or Prakriti. It indicates a very deep and advanced level of yogic mastery known to only a very few.

For good review, the reader can look back in Volume 1 of this work to study the chart entitled, "The Seeded Samadhis of Patanjala," on page 187. It tells of the basic order of attainment in the pursuit of Nirodha, wherein ordinary mind is made extinct forever. Towards the later stages of gaining Asamprajnata Samadhi, the singular "unseeded" samadhi, the gunas of Prakriti are drawn back into their origin (pradhana), and soon even the sattva guna submerges, causing an end to the desire for all types of subtle pleasures and desires. To review this process by visual, see the chart, "Stages of Dissolution of Mind in Yoga" on page 310 of Volume 1.

This lesson is being composed on the last day of the old year, and will come to you all in the new year. Early in the new year, the fourth and final pada of Patanjala will come up for study, and a six year process will continue to reach towards full fruition and masterful completion.

## Lesson Eighty-six, 3/6/14
### Pada III, Sutra 50

As we close in on the final sutras of the third pada, the inner atmosphere of Yoga gets deepened and further elucidated. At this juncture the student can claim that the philosophy of true Yoga in its eight-limbed form has now been gleaned. All that is left is to always "Go forward," as Sri Ramakrishna has advised, and spend time in yogic practice with this newly clarified mind. Application of the concentrated abilities of this singular and salutary discipline to life will then occur spontaneously.

The continual stream of questions and answers are also a natural result of this process of all processes. Please see below what other practitioners of all levels are considering and asking along the trajectory of well-guided spiritual life and practice:

**Questions and Answers for Lesson 86**
Akshaya Bhakti from New England writes:
QUESTION: "What exactly is the 'causal body,' anyway? What is its purpose as opposed to the subtle body, which seems to act like a holding station between lives? While I know that only more intense and sincere sadhana can truly resolve this, I must confess that I still find some fear of death in myself. Sometimes, I wonder whether my sense that I will always feel alive is just foolish clinging to this body — to the force of prana, ignoring its inevitable death — or whether that sense of 'being' or 'am'ness comes from a deeper knowing that is beyond the small ego. I am truly immortal, belonging to the One. Contemplation of the analogy about Consciousness, given in Lesson 84, Sutra III:45, that It is '... *as indeterminable to human beings as water to fish, yet they live in it, subsist on It, exist by It,*' certainly helps on a subtle level, and must be

remembered again and again, but I would like to roll your answer around in my mind too."

ANSWER: Basically, like the subtle body is, as you put it here, "a holding station between lives," the causal body is somewhat like a holding station for unmanifested Prakriti. All form eventually goes formless, and the causal state is the formless realm where it "rests in seed form."

But the soul only "moves" through such territories. It, Atman, is sentient; the subtle and causal bodies, being insentient, belong to It. And in fact, what little is known about the causal body *(karana sharira)* shows it up to be temporary as well. For instance, the causal body is:

- Undifferentiated
- Where the intellect ceases to vibrate
- Where the mind exists in a subtle state
- Where the three gunas rest in equilibrium
- The state of deep sleep
- The cause of the physical worlds
- The cause of both the subtle and physical bodies

All this is enough to know right now about the causal body in order to meditate upon it, and thereby draw final and lucid conclusions about it.

QUESTION #2: "I have been especially wondering about what happens after the udana prana assists the soul in leaving the body. If prana acts as a life force within the body, what aspect of it remains with us after death, as noted in charts of the subtle and causal bodies or the koshas? How does it function and by what name is it called then?"

ANSWER: Only wisps of the mukhya prana remain in the body after its demise. The signs of this are continued growth of hair and nails, etc. The rest of the prana persists and moves inward, carrying the mental complex (if it still remains in conglomerate form) to other realms of existence. This all happens along subtle *nadis*. For the illumined soul, there is no movement at all, either needed or necessary. It pervades, so does not transmigrate. Witness is its station. For the soul that still has work to do, desires to work out, or karmas to satisfy, the worlds of name and form will still be its habitat. For unfortunate souls that have no wisdom or inner capacity at the time of death, the lower realms throw open their gates and receive them. Thus, Absolute Reality is true, the higher lokas and life heavens are true, and the patalas (hell-realms) are also true. As Vivekananda stated, *"Maya is a statement of fact."* The koshas that the soul takes on at the time of death is dependent upon where it is projecting itself based upon its strengths and abilities. Quite often, the physical kosha re-forms, and the soul finds itself in the physical realm once again. Transcending this predicament is a main hurdle in spiritual life and practice, and one that seldomly gets jumped.

QUESTION #3: "When in the prayer, *'Om Na Tatra......,'* where it is translated, *'There within the individual self, the sun shines not.....much less this tiny mortal Flame'* — what is referred to? Is this 'flame' mistakenly taken as the prana (I used to even think it was the breath itself, until we were taught it is the prana that causes the breath), or is it reflected Consciousness, or even our small ego? While I understand that the true Light is Consciousness Itself, what is it that we are mistaking It for as expressed in this particular Vedic prayer?"

ANSWER: The portion of the chant that states, *"...much less this mortal flame"* is what you are referring to, I think. That is a reference to prana, for certain. And you have asked about the ego as well. Yes, the prana and ego form a complex of their own, especially when the thirst for embodied life is strong in the soul (mental complex). The ego must be trained, via truth teachings called the dharma, to let go of its penchant for clinging to life. It does not, then the prana will flow in directions that take the souls towards re-embodiment in the realms of name and form. One of these is the earth realm and, unfortunately for most beings, it is the hub of the three worlds. That is, souls have to pass through it often in their transmigratory process.

Even in Buddhist teachings, the links *(nidanas)* that chain the soul to the body, do so for three lifetime increments at a stretch. To explain, it will take most souls — those who have the good fortune to be awakening spiritually — one lifetime to recognize their heavy karma, another lifetime to work it out, and a third lifetime to attain enlightenment and be through with embodiment in ignorance. Now you can see why it is most lamentable for beings to take a teacher, begin a spiritual path, start to practice sadhana, then suddenly betray all three — all for the sake of retuning to the world to enjoy and suffer in turns. Much better to realize, right away, while the getting is good, *"that one Light shining that illumines all others, and through whose light all is made radiant,"* as that selfsame Vedic prayer concludes.

QUESTION #4: "Beyond working with pranayama and slowing down the breath, how do I begin to overcome fear of death, and in turn, attain separation from the world of name and form?"

ANSWER: It is true that the sense of mortality will accompany the soul, even late into its enlightenment process. One could say that it is somewhat natural. In *pratipakshabhavanam* fashion, one must concentrate on the flowers of the teachings of immortality, and leave aside brooding on the weeds of death. That one mental act will accomplish a lot. Then, as one studies, and hears from the guru's lips about the illusory nature of death — that nothing ever dies since all is really unborn — the final coffin nail, if you will, gets hammered into the whole mental issue, and death is placed in its own grave for all time. Then, the soul can live an eternal and divine life, and never even think of death. Further, when one sees or witnesses a person who is deathly afraid of death, then it becomes evident how unreasonable is this hold of death over the human soul. Fear of death, according to Vedavyasa — *abhinivesha* — is the lowest of all hells to fall into. Such is the opinion and conclusion of illumined souls around the subject.

QUESTION #5: "Could you please explain what the practice of Yoga Nidra is, and if that is something that might be undertaken even for someone who has not yet perfected the steps of Raja Yoga?"

ANSWER: Yoga Nidra is not really a practice. It is a state that occurs to the yogi or yogini along the line of his or her practice. Follow the Eight-limbed Yoga and it will occur naturally, over time. Its signs are a half-aware, half asleep state of consciousness. While not being wholly illuminating, it can nevertheless be helpful since it does foster the idea of Witness Consciousness in the striving and awakening soul. Of course, on the level of Cosmic Mind, Yoga Nidra is the state of deep sleep that Vishnu falls into at the end of a very long set of cycles. All goes into abeyance at that time.

Avinashi from Pennsylvania writes:
QUESTION: "A man goes to see his doctor. The doctor tells him he has cancer and that it's metastasized throughout his body; he's also told, through the course of the ensuing conversation, that if he wants to live, chemotherapy and multiple surgeries will be required. How should this man respond, inside himself primarily, when he perhaps starts to feel fear arising?"
ANSWER: It all depends upon what kind of man one is speaking of. If fear rises, then it is an ordinary soul that is being referred to, one who has never heard the dharma teachings from the lips of an illumined preceptor. I have heard many of my students tell me that after getting teachings on the Eternal Atman, and Its birthless, deathless state, they have gotten over their fear of death.

One would suppose, then, that the thought of a life-threatening disease would cause such an awakened soul to begin to plan for his/her life after death, much like a person going to sleep one night plans out his next day and morning before he falls asleep. Such calm is characteristic of the religious and spiritual soul. For the fearful soul, what other recourse to take than to find a good dharma teacher and spend the rest of his time in contemplation of the truth of Eternal Existence?

QUESTION #2 "I've been looking inside myself in moments when I feel pleasure, questioning whether the pleasure I feel has any relation to happiness at all. When I reflect, it seems that a certain degree of pleasure at least accompanies happiness, and that suffering or pain concomitantly accompanies unhappiness. But maya is an expert in hiding the truth... even more so in replacing truths with untruths... and so I find myself questioning about the ultimate value of pleasure. I'm wide open to hear what you have to say on this subject."
ANSWER: Pleasure has all relation to happiness. That is why happiness is not considered the goal in Vedanta and in Yoga, and its presence as well as its attainment are warned about. One could say, however, and so we do not become confused when we behold it, that a luminary is the happiest of people on the planet. His secret to the enjoyment he receives lies in his nonattachment to happiness, his purity and transcendence of the five senses, and his firm knowledge that contentment and peace of mind are far greater attainments than mere happy feelings.

Finally, and this is unusual among living beings, he welcomes his pains and sufferings, for they not only test him, but also teach him how to transmute the poison of relativity into the Nectar of Immortality. If this were not important, then he would remain only an "ordinary luminary," if the term can be used. Some there are, however, who expand in their capacity to convert such poisons — like of the collective mind rather than just the individual mind — and this is due to their "teething" themselves on the trials and challenges of their own lives early on.

And so, we see that the more enlightened soul takes pleasure and pain on an even keel, neither shunning the former or trying to escape the latter.

QUESTION #3 "Is distaste for worldly pleasures, though often a stage on the spiritual path, actually necessary for progress? It seems to me that simply losing interest in lesser attractions would be better, so that one is neither for nor against. Once again, I'm wide open to hear what you have to say."

ANSWER: Continuing on in the same vein as the final sentence of my answer just above, it all depends on one's personal destiny and karma. For some, it is easier to renounce outright, even utilizing or feeling a sort of distaste for the things of the world and the feelings of the flesh. Others see right away the impossibility of trying to "stuff" their feelings or renounce desires prematurely, and make moves to gradually replace them after satisfying basic enjoyments. Sri Ramakrishna illustrated this to the modern world, looking on, when he put on the silk robe that Mathur Babu brought Him one day, and sat to smoke a pipe that He was also given and enjoy a smoke. As they watched, He said aloud to Himself, *"O mind, this is what is called wearing fine clothing and smoking a pipe. Do you really want these things?"* Then, of a sudden, he jumped up, threw the pipe aside, tore off the expensive robe and dashed it to the ground, stamping it into the dirt. We can imagine Mathur's shock at seeing this occur to his expensive articles! But the entire show was a teaching to the people of the world, particularly the materialistic West. The Great Master's entire life was such a show, as is any Avatar's life on earth. We should never even imagine that He actually had even the slightest trace of such ordinary desires left in Him.

This question brings up the "Nine Ways of Satisfying Desires" chart that I placed at the end of lesson #63. Please look back and see that valuable teaching – one of the composer's favorite charts. Also, and to make it simpler, I place at the end of this lesson the old classic called "The Four Fruits of Life," so that we can see and remember what lies at the end of the devotee's experiences with wealth, pleasure, and particularly the dharmic teachings — mainly, Moksha, Liberation. The chart, The Two Forms of Desire, in lesson #83, is also worthy of reviewing.

QUESTION #4: "I've heard the common mind compared to a slipper full of spiders and scorpions, and that, if we wish the Master to put us on like a slipper, we'll have to clean ourselves out. But when I look inside, the task seems daunting, and often I wonder: if I were one of those who had been able to visit the Master at Dakshineswar, would he have suggested that I go have a look at the temples and gardens? But then I think, also, that he was, in a literal sense, on the stage of history at that time, pulling together those chosen few who would carry his message and mission on, and thus his time was at a premium. Now,

when his abode is in the hearts of his devotees, I think and hope that those old limitations may no longer pertain, so that my access to him might be more possible than when he was on Earth. I'd appreciate hearing your thoughts on this."
ANSWER: As a matter of encouragement, the Atman is equal in all beings, all things. We need only strive to realize That, and when we do, all these inconsistencies and imperfections that plague us here and now, in this physical realm, will disappear, and we will look back and see them as having been unreal. It is an extraordinary soul who can, much short of mere looking back, see the insubstantial nature of all impediments and transgressions while he lives, in the moment, like Swami Vivekananda. Therefore, we will be very glad to place the precious teachings and personage of Sri Ramakrishna Paramahamsa inside his capable heart and hands.

As far as access to Him in this lifetime, what with all our shortcomings, I know that the Master used to visit the homes of devotees who occupied all levels of society, even the poor and lowly ones. As long as we are devotees, then, we can at least look forward to a visit from Him now and again into the humble abodes of our body/mind mechanisms, despite the presence of a few "bugs."
QUESTION #5: "The 'dispassion of the graveyard' is, of course, the detachment that follows after the loss of material wealth, health, the demise of a loved one, and so on. Typically, after a certain period of time, the taste for mundane pleasure, for temporal allurements, returns. What factors, then, give rise to and sustain actual vairagya, real detachment?"
ANSWER: The answer is the nonreturn of attraction and attachment to pleasures of the world. For instance, to see old people looking for mates again in this life, after having had a married relationship for decades, is often distasteful. Even at old folks homes, here in the West, you see them courting one another. Two skeletons may as well be grinding jaw-bones on each other, two skulls scraping fleshless lips against one another. Is it not time to learn the lessons that life has taught up to that point, one being that lasting happiness can only be found in oneself, not in another, and certainly not in physical objects? Please refer to lesson #76, and the chart there titled "The Nine Levels of Detachment," for more information on how a soul gradually weans itself off of relativity and reaches Paravairagya — Supreme Detachment.
QUESTION #6: "Everyone who's not enlightened is subject to binding attachments. Do these attachments have, as it were, a kind of 'shelf life' — something like a minimum given period in which to continue functioning before they can be extinguished? To be clear, I'm not talking about karmas; I'm talking about the attachments that give rise to and sustain them. And although there's certainly a relation between the attachments and the karmas, at the same time the attachments seem to be more under conscious control than the karmic formations themselves. Yet, they also seem to have tremendous powers of entrenchment and self-regeneration. They seem, almost, to have their own life, and I'm wondering if it's realistic for most of us to fancy that, apart from some radical act of Divine Grace, they can be anything other than gradually whittled back through a long process of dedicated inner work. The waters here are very

murky, so clarification would be appreciated."

ANSWER: Really, attachments have, or can have, an unlimited shelf life. The problem is, the stuff inside the cans sitting on the shelves, in such cases, is already rotten, so it is not until one recognizes this fact that he/she will go about transferring them swiftly to the garbage. The reference here is to your statement suggesting that they get, "gradually whittled back through a long process of dedicated inner work."

There is nothing like sadhana for the sincere aspirant, and once he discovers it he will not wait on things such as Grace or a postmortem emancipation. There are several reasons why people do wait to enact such a regimen, the worst among them is pretending that one is already perfect due to hearing but not working to realize that the Atman within is flawless. This is like the man who walks around telling everyone that he has a clean bill of health from the doctor, but all the time disease rests within him, just waiting to manifest itself — usually at the most inopportune time.

And that brings karma into the picture, but you did not want to go there in this particular question. So, one teaching that may help is that the devotee can realize the difference between binding attachments and nonbinding attachments. Many beginning aspirants go around with thoughts of guilt in their minds caused by the lack of discrimination between attachments and desires that are unhealthy, and others that are either harmless or temporary, or both. Come to find later, along the path of spiritual growth, that he/she did not have to brood and worry about certain attachments at all. They were already "burnt ropes," present but unable to bind. They only appeared and seemed binding, but one did not consciously relegate them to that category.

So there are many tools, even tricks, in the toolbox of successful sadhana, and many of them are psychological. Refusing to be daunted is the validation for opening that beneficial chest, and finding there all that helps to affirm the fact of *"Ayamatma Brahma — This Self is Brahman."*

QUESTION #7: "Yesterday in my reading I came across the idea that there are four aspects to full enlightenment, namely love, unity, emptiness, and Tao (or harmony). The concept struck me as profound, though I felt inclined to rearrange those aspects to express what I saw as a necessary progression, with emptiness first so there can be preliminary release from the notion of egoic selfhood, then maybe followed by realization of unity, harmony, and love — or something like that. Now I'm bouncing all of this off you. In the Tantra-infused Vedanta so characteristic of SRV Associations and the Ramakrishna Order as a whole, can full enlightenment be thought of as having certain central aspects, and if it can be thought of this way, do they tend to be realized in any particular order?"

ANSWER: The method and its order you cite here is a good one, of course. The reason why we do not find an emphasis on order of teachings, practices, enlightenment, etc., is due to the seers who know that there are many different temperaments, thus many paths by which aspiring beings will proceed. For instance, there are many things that will have to go by and get realized long before emptiness dawns, and when and if it does (according to temperament), it may take some souls on sidetracks, even dead ends.

Sri Krishna states that to follow one's own destiny is far better and less dangerous than following another's. So, we need to find our own way. We take teachers for this, no doubt, but sometimes it is not meet that we follow the guru's path; it is more that we need to follow his teachings and apply them to our path. For instance, again, if western householders follow a guru who is a monk, and try to be like the monk by living his standard, what will happen to them, and to their families? Some rare few, whose destiny it is, may succeed marvelously (like Nag Mahashaya and his wife), but others may get disoriented and lose the way. The saying, "Do what I say, not what I do," if it applies at all, applies best here.

Take the dharma teachings, then, and apply them to your own life. The result will be best for you. It will teach others by its example, not by a one-size-fits-all enforcement. That is why Sri Krishna teaches in the Gita, *"That one who knows the Soul and Nature, in all their various modes, is never born in ignorance again, however that one may live."*

QUESTION #8: "Sometimes you assert what sounds to me like a course of heroic willing, that if God's grace is not forthcoming, then get to enlightenment yourself; don't wait for God's grace, and blast your own karma. At other times you point out that the limitations on free will are so extreme, that it's almost as if there is no such thing. This can leave me feeling like the figure in Hindu mythology named Trishanku, who hangs suspended between Heaven and Earth and can neither go up nor down. Will you please harmonize these two poles in your teaching?"

ANSWER: My guru always used to say that Grace and Self-effort must go hand in hand, like the two wings of the bird. Holy Mother taught him that without engaging in self-effort, God's Grace will remain far away due to the mind's still present and persisting veils. Sri Ramakrishna taught Her that the wind of grace is always blowing, but that the spiritual mariner has to raise their sails to catch it. What is not wanted in this seeming dichotomy, is for any type of stunned state to occur to the mind, causing it to seek neither just because both represent two possibilities. Using present day mantras again, "Just do it" applies here. Once one is launched into sadhana, God's grace will show up as inherent spirituality — *"which was incomprehensible earlier due to the limitations of their own intellects,"* to quote the *Svetasvataropanisad*. To put it simply, all limitations are removed by sadhana. Grace is the natural result.

R.C. from Canada writes:
QUESTION: "The most important question that has just surfaced is about Arjuna at the beginning of the Gita. I relate with his 'depression' yoga and his struggles with ordinary mind even though having gained higher knowledge on truth, since he must have had such teachings from his time with his guru prior to the battlefield. This battle that he finds the non-self in is relived in this tamasic mind even today. Not to face this battle, and rather to run and hide, is what

I have done all of this life in order to get to this point. I appear to be as I am today as a result of this way of being. There are no others who see as this mind does here in my so-called hometown. This mind must be faced in battle. You, beloved father, are my Krishna, and I, your Arjuna in depression yoga. Where is there to run in a dream, when all are dreaming and not awakening. It's going to have to be with holy company at satsang. The hound of heaven is after this mind, and coming closer to holy company is the only solution for this dreamer, stopping not till the goal is reached. All are lost here, and getting out of this place is all that there ever will be in the appearance of gaining realization of truth. Can you speak to this problem of depression and the continual skirting of the issues?"

ANSWER: Whereas it is true that we must evacuate this realm of maya, this battlefield with its constantly warring factions and its senseless violence, we must also face the reason why we are here, like Arjuna was at Kurukshetra. That is, to transform this realm of supposed maya into the Real Brahman — for only Brahman exists. Maya is our own overlay, the work of cosmic, collective, and individual mental projection. As long as we inhabit the body, then, we are to attempt to express the dharma here. And in order to do that, we have to expose ourselves to it and learn it. That comes from holy company with satsang, classes, puja, etc. So you are on the right track.

Never mind if all others are lost; you must find your way. Their time is not upon them yet, but yours is upon you. That is what is most important. So begin to let the hound of heaven catch up to you. He is friendly and will lick your hands and face of all the salt that has been deposited there by sweating in suffering and crying tears under the press of maya. Then you will be free and live free.

It is most likely that Arjuna never heard the Truth very succinctly until Krishna transmitted it to him on that battlefield — a very intense and unforgettable way to receive It. He had learned the Vedangas from his upagurus, but never the Vedanta from the Guru — especially not the Avatar! The time for that is when it is upon us; we must then be about realizing it. For there is just no telling when karmas, gunic cycles, and circumstances, will rise, like a shroud of fog, and obscure dharma, Truth, and our chance for Enlightenment — all three. Further, there is no telling when that fog might lift and reveal them again. So, now is the time.....

R.O. from Hawaii writes:
QUESTION: "In RY #85, you explained that Ishvara is the gateway to Brahman. Can you clarify who Ishvara is in relation to Brahman? Is Ishvara a creation of Brahman? How did Ishvara come to exist? Can Ishvara manifest in human Form? If Ishvara enters Brahman, the Formless, then does Ishvara cease to exist, since all is Brahman? Ishvara would need some residual karma to leave Brahman, right? Or is Ishvara co-eternal with Brahman, being the personal aspect of Brahman? But then Ishvara would not have any karma, correct? No beginning or end?"

ANSWER: The Absolute Reality, Brahman, does not engage in any act of creation. It remains, to quote Vivekananda *"acreate."* To borrow a useful English word, *Ishvara* could then be called a direct "emanation" off of Divine Reality.

But to put it more philosophically, everything in the worlds of name and form are thought-projections, with mind at its cosmic, collective, and individual levels doing the projecting. Since Ishvara is a form, It too must be a projection — though a very powerful one, indeed. To quote Vivekananda on the subject, in relation to the *Jiva, Ishvara,* and *Brahman*:

*"Ishvara is the sum total of individuals, yet He Himself is also an individual in the same way as the human body is a unit, of which each cell is an individual. Samashti, or the Collective, is God. Vyashti, or the component, is the soul or jiva. The existence of Ishvara, therefore, depends on that of jiva, as the body on the cell, and vice versa."*

*"Jiva and Ishvara are co-existent beings. As long as the one exists, the other must also."*

*"Again, since in all the higher spheres, except on our earth, the amount of good is vastly in excess of the amount of bad, the sum total, or Ishvara, may be said to be All-good, Almighty and Omniscient. These are obvious qualities, and need no argument to prove, from the very fact of totality."*

*"Brahman is beyond both Ishvara and the world, and is not a state. It is the only unit not composed of many units. It is the principle which runs through all, from a cell to God, and without which nothing can exist."*

To field other aspects of your question, we usually do not think of Ishvara as having any karma, at least not that It does not take on purposefully — like the collective karma of all beings, for instance. Regarding its presence in and out of Brahman, Ishvara's special attribute of "formless form" allows it to maintain its presence in seed form when everything else goes into dissolution at the time of *Mahapralaya* (the Great Dissolution). To understand this better, we can take a clue from Sri Ramakrishna when He said that most icebergs melt under the summer sun, but certain ones, huge and solid, as if like crystal, do not melt, but remain in the ocean when all others melt. That means that Ishvara-forms such as Krishna, Buddha, Jesus, and the like, will remain in the minds of beings forever, over countless cycles of time — even returning to the mind's memory at the time of the advent of a new major cycle after Mahapralaya is over.

J.M. from Oregon writes:
QUESTION: "What is meant by a consecrated partner for the dharmic householder?"
ANSWER: This usually means a husband or wife, at least where social conventions of this period are adhered to. Where such are not observed or followed, a chosen partner with which to follow the practices of divine relationship is meant, in order to bring about the union of the Siva/Shakti principle leading to union and Enlightenment. This quite often has to do with Tantric forms of wor-

ship and practice.

QUESTION #2: "How does the dharmic householder bring consciousness to bear in sexual life?"

ANSWER: With moderation. The expression of love between consecrated partners, and the procreation of children, are legitimate ways to express sexuality in a dharmic way. Then, as Sri Ramakrishna has stated, after the birth of one or two children, dharmic householders can turn their attentions to spiritual practices and the pursuit of liberation, and live like brother and sister in the interim.

QUESTION #3: "Even despite beginning the development of Witness Consciousness, the mind and ego tend to seek out sexual pleasure. What should be done to destroy these tendencies? This is very frustrating and easily creeps into the mind?

ANSWER: In the beginning period of increasing one's spiritual abilities, sexuality may persist. It is when the middle and advanced stages of increasing qualities like Witness Consciousness occur that the thought of sexuality will diminish and finally go away. In the meantime one must forbear and practice moderation rather than opting for premature renunciation.

QUESTION #4: "What is the key thing we should focus on if we are to take up brahmacharya as a mental posture?

ANSWER: The spiritual rather than the physical. Ennobling thoughts of the mind should be concentrated on, and worldly thoughts are to be avoided. Further, if one says or thinks, "I am practicing brahmacharya," the very thought of engaging in that brings up thoughts of the opposite sex. So it is best to keep the mind in the scriptures, worship, practices, and the arena of selfless works.

QUESTION #5: "You have explained with regard to work that the mind by its very nature will, in subtle ways, allow selfish desires and desires for the fruits of acts to creep in. Is it also true that the mind, by its nature, will go through cycles of brooding? If this is true, will the aspirant just need to be the Witness and renounce the mind's understanding that its perturbations are unreal and nothing to worry about?"

ANSWER: If people knew that the mind is at the root of everything in the worlds of name and form, all the way through the life heavens and further inwards to the apex of the Trinity's Great Mind, they would immediately abandon all other forms of work and effort and get down to the attainment of a pure mind — or would direct all work and action towards that single, salutary aim.

Pure mind will entail purification; what else? But what the seers mean by purification has less to do with giving up bad habits (which are a part of the mind along with its good habits, i.e, duality) or trying to obey moral laws and commandments, and much more to do with the feat of transcendence of mind. That is one great reason to engage the mind in meditation, so that it will begin to see beyond all that lies in it and impedes. With this higher view into Atman/Soul present, there can be no dependence upon mind anymore, which means no producing of bodies and karma where none are wanted.

With regard to brooding, I suppose one could say that there is a higher form of it, like the case of a luminary thinking about the problems of the world, as Swamiji was seen to do often. But there is a definitive and compassionate reason for such use of the mind, and that is what is missing in most people's ruminations.

QUESTION #6. "Is the fact that the mind is untrained the reason brooding seems inevitably to creep in? Do even the illumined brood from time to time?"
ANSWER: Yes, training is crucial; otherwise there is confusion, havoc, and scattered mind. When focus occurs, not only does brooding go away, it stays away based upon the mind's favored position of concentration, which is economical, practical, and engaging — all three. Depression never visits the mind that has the sixth limb of Yoga mastered. At that point, one's sights are set on the mastery of limbs 7 and 8, true meditation and samadhi. No one and nothing can disturb the mind, or call it out or away, from attaining that superlative end.

And as to brooding, specifically, just as there is *maya sankalpa* and *lila sankalpa* — the only main difference being the condition of the mind that engages them — so too is there heavy brooding and beneficial brooding. The former is known all too well among the people of the day. And, in fact, what makes the latter distinctive is the solving of all those selfsame problems that cause heavy brooding. When an enlightened soul descends out of the natural bliss that is his/hers, and takes up considering the sufferings of the world, that may be a type of brooding, admittedly, but it is of the type that moves mountains.

You see, seeing through the curtain of nescience, or the "cloud of unknowing," will require some preponderant thinking that necessarily takes on some sort of weight — the difference being that positive brooding, if it can be called such, subjects the heavier form of brooding (that is a huge waste of time) to the light of understanding so that some positive end can be achieved. The people of his time reported seeing Swami Vivekananda engaged in such brooding quite often, even in the presence of others, though totally in his own world. Part of the ability, and the marvel, of this, is being able to take the mind off of the self and place it on the good of others. This is another facet of successful Yoga and its bequeathal of qualities like samyama on the adept practitioner. Taking one's mind off of the world, the ego, and its dalliance with the senses and their objects is a rare thing, after all, and scarcely witnessed out and about in the conventional world. Thus, Yoga has other aims than just personal liberation.

Anurag from Oregon writes:
QUESTION: "We are entering truly subtle and sublime realms in these last two Raja Yoga Sutras III:48-49. Can you expand a bit, or a lot, on the mastery of Pradhana? Of all the seven victories of involution listed on the chart, *The Seven Qualifications of a Tantrik Aspirant,* Pradhana Jaya is the one that I find most difficult to imagine, let alone practice. I have trouble grasping what it is like to master and control the primal principle (as defined on that chart) and Unmanifested Prakriti, the phrase you have used in this lesson to help define Pradhana. I can understand and practice Kaivalya, but Pradhana seems to be an

extremely subtle level that I am either missing or am doing anyway in meditation without realizing that such a practice is even taking place."
ANSWER: Pradhana is just a Sanskrit word in the Sankhya darshana for undifferentiated matter, or the subtle material cause (not gross material cause) of the worlds in space and time. Mastering it consists of knowing that it exists, i.e., knowing about it, then meditating on the seed forms of objects in nature, and nature itself. You will find these seeds in your thoughts, and the source of your thoughts in the Cosmic Mind — finally in AUM. In other words, as the practitioner practices the "Dissolution of the Mindstream" meditation, with alambanas as the subject matter, one by one, in reverse order of transition, one is really already gaining mastery over Pradhana. It is just that the greater whole gets lost in the consideration process of its composite parts.

And that is why the process must both graduate and culminate. Most beings never take it that far. And then there is Ishvara, which is rather a "jump to the chase" type of penultimate meditation. Taking full refuge in Him, or in Ishvari, "Her," will accomplish Pradhana Jaya. But there one gets attracted to the superlative Sentient Soul and is not that likely to find the mind going towards the insentient matter in seed form.

You see, that is why people forget to think consciously about "God." Even if they contemplate "The Six Treasures of God" (see chart, lesson #79) — *Jivatman, Jagad, Manas, Buddhi, Prema,* and *Jnana* (soul, universe, mind, intelligence, love, and wisdom) — they often overlook the One who contains all qualities for the qualities themselves. To quote Sri Ramakrishna about people's fascination for this world, *"This universe is God's glory. People see His glory and forget everything else. They do not seek God. This universe has emanated from the Supreme Brahman."*

## Pada III, Sutra 50
*sattva purusha anyatakhyati matrasya sarva-bhava adhisthatrittvam sarva-jnatritvam cha (sattva,* balance of mind; *purusha,* individual Soul; *anyata,* subtle distinctions; *khyati,* mental and intellectual clarity; *matrasya,* merely; *sarva-bhava,* all states of awareness; *adhisthatrittvam,* superior; *sarva-jnatritvam,* all-knowing; *cha,* and).

"All-knowingness, and the mastery of all states of Awarenesss, occurs when the distinction between a merely balanced mind and the Eternal Soul becomes clear, resulting in omniscience."

There is no underestimating the value of a balanced mind. What is more, one will need to attain even-mindedness in order to reach Enlightenment, what to speak of utilizing that superlative state for the highest good of others. As the Holy Mother, Sri Sarada Devi, stated: *"The mind is very important at this stage of the process (of embodiment). One will need to take the mind with one to Brahman."* This is also why She said, *"One needs Peace of mind first and foremost. Nothing can be gained without Peace of mind."* This is also what Sri Krishna intimates when He explains the modes of sattvic behavior in chapter 18 of the Bhagavad Gita, and what Patanjali means by executing all action in the sattvic mindset only, not in rajas or tamas (restlessness or slothfulness).

But even with all of this said and rightly considered, the enlightened ones have not failed to note that the mind is not nearly as valuable as the Soul, Atman, and that the two are distinct and different in their role and essence. The mind, manas, is dual by nature, bringing in all manner of disparities — from dualities such as good and bad, and pleasure and pain, on inwards to the projection processes of maya sankalpa and lila sankalpa. Notably, it is not inherently conscious in and of its own accord like the Atman is. It is more like a moon that borrows its glow from the sun, which is self-luminous, *svayamjyoti.*

Yet, even though these and other fine reasons are present to consider, living beings fail to make the distinction between these two principles; they fail to *"separate the wheat from the chaff,"* as has been noted by Jesus in his time. When the coconut is unripe, says Sri Ramakrishna Paramahamsa, it is one solid mass, having no distinctions in its makeup. But when it ripens it separates into five layers, and the kernel inside rattles around, independent of them all. He is noting that the unripe mind/soul erroneously thinks that the five koshas of body, senses, mind, intellect, and ego are all one thing, i.e., they are scarcely aware that there is any difference at all. What is more, people may even call this five-fold complex "the soul," and think of it terms of the only existence, leaving the real Soul out of the picture, or mistake the five layers for the Soul. But the Soul, Atman, is independent of them all; they all appear via It's Existence. Therefore, it is all a matter of living beings recognizing the difference between what is innately Sentient, and what is insentient by nature.

And so, Yoga concurs with the seers, and the darshanas of India's long and glorious philosophical past. In Patanjali's Yoga, as in Vedanta, the key distinctions to be made (by the force of viveka) occur in deep meditation, even as late as the initial appearance of the mind's ability for utilizing samyama. Whereas in Vedanta, this classic movement proceeds by the practitioner's due and timely engagement with the Four Treasures, called *Sadhanachatushtaya* (*viveka, vairagya, shatsampati,* and *mumukshutvam*), in classic Yoga, this process is well defined by what is known as the "Seven Steps to Kaivalya" (see chart at the end of this lesson). The mind gains higher wisdom, discernment, clarity, and purity along the singular trajectory of intensified practice, and this allows it access into the realm of its causal regions where the subtlest of impediments to Unity/Yoga lie waiting for discovery and purging.

It is in this process of neutralizing all karmas and samskaras that the revelation of the distinction between Soul and the mind/matter conglomerate occurs, cited as the difference between *Purusha* and *Prakriti* in Sankhya Yoga. This difference is not meant to be related in the atmosphere of duality, but rather to be taught in the light of practice and realization. For, when the Soul, Atman/Purusha, recognizes this key distinction, it also then perceives that all of nature, defined as name, form, time, space, and causation, has proceeded from It. Further, it knows this spilling forth of mental manufacture as a "projection" rather than a "creation."

These three main cosmological/philosophical facts, then, are to be well contemplated by all those beings who sincerely seek and desire ultimate Truth: 1) the Soul is different from and ever-free of nature; 2) all of nature has come out of the Soul, and as it does, no change or transformation occurs to the Soul whatsoever; 3) as nature emerges from the Soul, it does so as a projected emanation rather than as an "created" manifestation. A fourth fact, helpful of note, can be added here; 4) The Soul, Atman, has an eternal relationship with nature, Prakriti, and if It only associates with nature and remains free of identification with nature, It can sport freely and transcend all limitations as it does.

A secondary fifth fact can also be given: nature has a manifested and an unmanifested side to it. To know this is to be schooled, then set free, of the mind's narrowness of conception (as occurs in Physics, for example) around form and matter. In other words, to watch and witness all forms coming in and out of nature is to know that all manifestation gets stored in seed form upon its apparent annihilation, and that it will all come back, or "return," when cycles of nonmanifestation (as in "the void") end. This is explained in simplest fashion by the words of Sri Krishna in the Bhagavad Gita, when He states: *"What is born, dies, and what dies is born again; where is the grief in this?"* To place it in the words of Lord Kapila, the master Sankhyist's view: *"'Sancharah prati sancharah.' "There is a chain of transition from unmanifest or nonevolved prakriti to manifest prakriti and its evolutes, ending in the grossest evolute, earth. There is also a reverse transition of evolutes ending in dissolution into unmanifested prakriti."*

In relation to the first great fact listed above, the student is referred to the chart, "The Twenty-Four Cosmic Principles of Sankhya Yoga," shown at the end of this lesson. For assistance in understanding the second great fact above, please look back to the chart, "The Five Akashas of Vedanta Philosophy" included in lesson #64. For teachings on the third great fact listed above, please look back and study the chart, "Aparinama — The Principle of Nontransformation," in lesson #75. With regards to the fourth great fact listed above, please study the chart, "The Ten Fundamental Tenets of Sankhya Yoga," placed at the end of this lesson. And for help with the fifth and secondary fact listed above, refer back to the chart, "Manifested and Unmanifested Prakriti," also placed at the end of this rich and important lesson.

## Lesson Eighty-seven, 4/3/14
### Pada III, Sutras 51 & 52

In our Raja Yoga study, some several years long to date, we are presently reaching into the final sutras of the penultimate pada, pada three. Our deep inspection of authentic Yoga is taken up as much to make an informative distinction between true yoga and the current hatha craze in the West, as it is to raise up a few devout and serious practitioners of this powerful aspect of Indian dharma. Beings attached to their bodies and the world will come by the millions, but only a rare few will see through the exterior level and conventional practices of contemporary fads and fashions and go to the heart of the matter. Of these, there are those who question deeply about the nature of the Self, as well as the nature of the world around us. What is this appearance called maya?; what is nature?; who is Ishvara? God with form; and who am I? — all predicated upon finding the Essence called Brahman. Once found, there is Yoga, intrinsically pure, ever pristine, and blissfully unalterable. So keep those sapient questions coming in.....

**Questions and Answers for Lesson 87**
R.O. from Hawaii writes:
QUESTION: "In your answer to my question in Raja Yoga #86, you referred to Ishvari (Her). Is the Ishvara (Him) emanation (your words) proceeding from Brahman both male and female? Or is it neither (neutral), and the usage of male and female are really for convenience (sexual equality in today's words!). In other words, can that emanation be whatever we wish to call it? Strictly speaking, however, it seems to me that the use of the term "emanation" means a proceeding from or movement out of (Brahman), e.g., like when we say that light emanates from the sun. Could we then say that this implies maleness? Would there then be a corresponding return movement (femaleness) back into Brahman, or would the emanation proceed to infinity? Maybe this is just another way of saying Mother-Father God?"
ANSWER: Yes, we can look upon and visualize Ishvara/Ishvari as either male of female. A case in point is the masculine and feminine admixture of beings like Sri Ram and Sri Krishna when they are portrayed in artistic renderings and sacred icons. This is up to the devotee and worshipper, depending upon their own predilection and preference.

In the Indian way of thinking, however, dynamic activity has always been characterized as being feminine, while the masculine is seen as ever static. This is really more of a philosophical measure rather than a gender reference. If we really look at the nature of things here on earth, we find that it is the feminine side of us that accomplishes an infinite array of duties and services. This is to be looked at by knowing that many men have predominantly feminine qualities within them.

And in fact, it is by searching out and examining qualities such as service, empathy, compassion, love, faithfulness, and other attributes, that we may espy the divine feminine in and throughout everything. Even wisdom is seen as feminine in India. Thus follows the importance of realizing the Divine Mother of the Universe in this day and time, as Sri Ramakrishna has brought forward and made accessible for us in His recent incarnation.

Whatever the case may be, and however living beings want to look at it, the important thing is to know that Brahman is beyond gender, transcendent of all dualities and attributes. There is a Formless Essence, and That is the subtlemost of all, Who often escapes detection of even the most religious of souls.

Avinashi from Pennsylvania writes:

QUESTION: "The paths of devotion and knowledge, though of course related, are also different. How the world and God are seen, how they're responded to, what's valued and devalued at a fundamental level — all these and more tend to be different. If a shishya is suffering from, say, bereavement, a guru who leans toward jnana might say, 'Watch your thoughts and feelings,' while a guru who leans toward bhakti might advise more reliance on the Ishtam. Sri Ramakrishna points to a basic difference when he points out that in the path of knowledge everything is to be negated, but in the path of devotion everything is to be accepted. And sure, they converge at the end, but that's not what I want to ask about. I'm asking for ideas, for wisdom, on how bhakti and jnana can be intelligently co-utilized in a single sadhana. It occurs to me that if we mix them indiscriminately, there might be confusions and traps we could fall into. Maybe this is a little like the difference between the hodge-podge of eclecticism and the clarity of universalism. Sri Ramakrishna himself lived a universalist sadhana in so far as when he was, say, a Sufi, he was not also a Vaishnava. He kept things clean that way, and I'm wondering if we shouldn't somehow do the same in relation to jnana and bhakti? I personally seem to have no problem combining the paths — and maybe in bringing this up I'm acting a little like the millipede who walked well until he started wondering how all his legs could move so nicely together. But as this has been occurring to me, so I now bring it to you — I think just to make sure I'm not making some serious mistake, unwittingly."

ANSWER: No; no outright mistake. You have expressed the matter succinctly. My answer, which is similar to many answers to the various questions I entertain, is that it all depends upon the quality of consciousness in the individual. That is, with all things considered, as you have done here, then it falls upon each individual to carve out his own way amidst the various yogas. Some will integrate; some will specify. Others will combine according to their temperaments, or even shift their stances as spiritual progress is made and circumstances change. In my four decades of "teaching" I have met those souls who, for a long period of time, were confirmed bhaktas and later become focused in the wisdom path. One advanced soul I met was a fundamentalist Vaishnava for a time, and when seen later was a avowed Buddhist! The most remarkable thing about a cross section of these beings is that when they shifted, they did not leave either fidelity to their previous path behind, nor forget the advances that they made previously via their early pathways.

Personally, I feel that the paths of devotion and wisdom are perfect fits, i.e., one knows what one loves, and loves what one knows. I could not even imagine separating them, what to speak of considering them separate. But then, integration is a part of my nature. My path is really one of Peace, Shanti, and it is only in such an atmosphere that any true synthesis can take place. To put it in another way, it is only in restlessness that the constant search for something else or other takes place. Contentment with what is has its great value, so long as the ultimate Ideal (Enlightenment) does not get compromised.

QUESTION #2: "I'd be willing to bet that, in some circles, probably Buddhist, the study of sutras has been developed to the level of a fine art. So what I'm asking for here is advice on how to most effectively study a set of sutras?"
ANSWER: With an illumined guru, no doubt, for otherwise — even though such study does take place, and does help somewhat in the early stages — there is just too much that the evolving soul misses without taking recourse to what the Buddhists term the "Triple Gem" of guru (Buddha), dharma, and sangha.

     This email course, in which all these questions appear, is not, then, the best way to study scripture; it is a second best measure, provided for a busy world and people that are plagued by distractions at every juncture of life. It does, however, set the stage for meetings with one's guru and sangha. In some cases it even leads seekers to their path and guru. In other words, we will take what we can get, seeing that both illumined souls and authentic light shed upon the dharmic teachings are rare today. Better to have heard the truth, contemplated it, and failed to realize it, than to never have heard It before. Better, too, to have read the truth in scriptures if no enlightened preceptor was ever around to teach you in person. A start must be made in some lifetime, for it is when the aspirant sets foot upon the spiritual path, that all of the saints, seers, sages, and saviors rush towards him to help. Otherwise, not.

Kanyakali from Hawaii writes:
QUESTION: "In meditating on the key distinctions between Purusha and Prakriti, I am considering your statement that the difference between them "is not meant to be related in the atmosphere of duality, but rather to be taught in the light of practice and realization." My mind, which is dual by nature, projects a world that is full of opposites. Therefore, if something has an opposite, it belongs to Prakriti. Meanwhile, Purusha, which is not projected by mind, has no opposite. Nevertheless the mind attempts to describe Purusha with terms that do have opposites, such as infinite (vs. finite), changeless (vs. changing), all-pervasive (vs. limited), sentient (vs. insentient), etc. So, your statement is true, but it is difficult to convince my mind to be satisfied with knowing Prakriti alone. Purusha is unknowable. On to practice and realization, then?"
ANSWER: Yes, it is sadhana that is the defining step in an aspirant's life. But there are a few other things to consider about your conclusions here. Prakriti is also ultimately unknowable. It is impossible to know an object, simply because it *Is* an appearance — is not real. When we say that we come to know objects made up of the five elements by meditating on them, as in the dissolution of the twenty-four tattvas in deep meditation, what we come to know is the fact of their illusory nature. Their illusory nature is formless; so is their essence (like the bijam for an object in the causal world), formless.

     On the other hand, the Purusha is unknowable by the ordinary mind, to be sure, but not by the illumined mind — for illumined mind is Original Mind, and that is Purusha. In other words, one comes to know one's true nature when one gives up dallying with the ordinary mind, and takes up permanent residence in the Pure Mind. So, some things to contemplate here.

Tadrupa (earlier J.M. prior to SRV initiation) from Oregon writes:
QUESTION: "In the last lesson, much discussion is focused on the importance of a balanced mind. What is to be done when karmas arise that disturb the peace of the aspirant's mind? Obviously karmas must be dealt with in some practical way, especially when one's livelihood is threatened. How do we do this without creating more karma down the road, and without panicking and letting our peace be disturbed?"
ANSWER: Rather, it is that we must not panic or let our peace of mind be disturbed, by any means, and at any time. Turn the question of search into a statement of fact. If you can do this, then you might be able to do what is right and practical; otherwise, not, and more karma then floods into the picture. Stem all that potential karma, then, by not reacting to trials and challenges when they arise. The real trial is not the trial itself; it is how you conduct yourself during the trial. You should rather be ready to live on the street without house and food and money, than to react out of fear and weakness to your situation. After all, that is what the sannyasin does, and he is the greatest of all beings. Whether he loses house and home, or gives them up on purpose, he still has *"the skies for his roof, the grass for his bed, and food, what chance might bring...."* And so, this is the importance of a balanced mind, and its versatile facility as well.
QUESTION #2: "How can it be that the soul is carried along the nadis via prana, when nature is in the soul? How can the soul move when akasha is in the soul?"
ANSWER: The soul, with a small "s" rather than a capital "S," moves; the Atman, the real Soul, does not. That same soul, called the mind, as a complex of thought, intelligence, and ego, gets carried along nadis, subtle nerves, to whatever destination awaits it, according to its karmas. The main point of spiritual life and realization is to stop the soul's dream movements from occurring, and to thereby rest in the original static "position" which is Brahman. A being who can accomplish that is free of karmas, and will never create them again. Any embodiment such a Soul undertakes is on purpose, conscious, and for a great purpose, usually only known to Itself.

It is in this way that we understand the distinction between the mental complex called a transmigrating "soul," and a stable, static, and all-pervasive Entity termed the "Soul," i.e., Atman. Peace belongs to That, and to nothing else.....
Anurag from Oregon writes:
QUESTION: "A very interesting distinction is being made in Sutra III:50 between the balanced mind and the Eternal Soul. From the point of view of practice and realization, are we to take the view that all mental sankalpas are projections of the insentient mind, even if that mind be balanced? It makes one want to be very cautious in regards to one's thoughts, sensations, and experiences no matter how clear they appear to be. Is it a matter of degree of predominance of insentience to sentiency, as the veil between the mind and the Eternal Soul gets thinner, so to speak, and the steps to attainment of Kaivalya are real-

ized? Is it also accurate to view it as a shift from mayic to atmic sankalpa as the insentient mind gradually loses its power and identification with nature. Hmmm, sounds like dissolving of the mindstream. I suppose what I am getting at is how do we recognize the difference between what is sentient and what is insentient as we approach and ascend the steps to attainment of Kaivalya. Is this unexplainable and really a matter of 'I'll know it when I see it?'"

ANSWER: I take the perspective that the mind is not wholly insentient. When you talk about the gross elements and objects, there you can make a point for insentience. As soon as the five senses enter the picture, there is God, or god, looking on, is it not? By the time that mind enters the picture (moving from gross to subtle, that is), then sentience is both possible and probable. The only question here, or qualification, is whether that mind has awakened to its inherent spirituality of not. If it has, the case for sentiency, as far as I am concerned, is closed and finalized. The proof of that pudding is the presence of higher wisdom and intelligence, plus a refined and surrendered ego mechanism.

So yes, senses, mind, intellect, and ego are all mechanisms; are all parts and portions of the not-self, the anatman. But the Atman uses them to reflect its pure sentiency, does it not? Otherwise, what are we seeing when we behold an Avatar or a luminary?

Thus, what you are saying about the veils getting thinner and thinner is correct. But just as clouds do not stop the sun from shining, so too do veils fail to change or affect Consciousness in any way. And by the way, when the mind gets that close to its true Essence, all thoughts of what is sentient and insentient will most probably lose both their hold and their validity on/for the soul, which is now in an enraptured state, and beyond any possibility of falling back to such mediocre considerations anymore.

## Pada III, Sutra 51

*tad vairagya api dosa bija ksaya kaivalyam (tad,* that*; vairagya,* detachment*; api,* as well*; dosa,* impediment*; bija,* seed*; ksaya,* rejection*; kaivalyam,* freedom from form).

*"The yogi attains absolute freedom from form upon developing the quality of detachment from seed desires, as well as rejection of powers such as omniscience."*

Desire, at all levels of the game, is the abiding danger of existence. Those caught in desire get trapped and suffer; those who are free of desire live in a liberated condition and enjoy peace and bliss, even here in the body, even with all its problems.

This sutra deals with a type of desire that swiftly attends those aspiring beings who rise above entertaining the world of matter alone and begin to discover and utilize the subtle life-force energy called prana. Being the most addictive substance in relative existence, prana, which confers the *"thirst for life"* and embodiment on all the realms of name and form, is the common foundation for both humans and celestials — celestials meaning angels, demi-gods, gods, goddesses and any deity that presides over realms of subtle inner expression where countless beings are busy enjoying their own desires for heavenly existence. It is only those of yogic temperament who escape the allurements offered by such realms and their presiding deities.

But more on that when we come to the next sutra. For now, the emphasis ought to be placed upon the fine and saving grace of the quality called *vairagya,* or detachment. Again, when we occasionally come upon beings in this world who possess the natural ability to renounce objects and pleasures, or who have no real desire for them in the first place, we are standing near to souls who are spiritually advanced. Those are the ones we want to keep company with, not the vaunted rulers over heaven and earth. In Bhartrihari's *Vairagya Shatakam,* beloved by Swami Vivekananda, one of the verses exemplifies this idea more than any other:

You are a king, but we have served Gurus who are great in knowledge.
You are known by your wealth as a king, we, for our knowledge.
There is an infinite difference between us and you.
Therefore, we are not the persons to wait upon you, O Kings!

This was precisely the mindset of Lord Jesus when he stated that the devotees ought to *"Grant unto Caesar what is Caesar's, but take unto yourselves what is the Lord's."* And if one were to ask what this "infinite difference" between the worldly and the spiritual consists of, the answer would have to cite the presence of massive amounts of the possession of vairagyam in the latter — among the first of Sanskrit words of this sutra under study.

Please look back in Volume 1, page 243, to study once more the chart titled "Patanjali's Nine Levels of Awareness in Aspirants," citing their meek *(mrdu),* middling *(madhya),* and intense *(adhimatra)* gradations. In addition, I am placing on the next page the *Twelve Levels of Vairagya* chart for further elucidation on the attribute of detachment. For it is in the Tejabindu Upanisad that it is told: *"Sages reach the inaccessible, making it accessible, via the three gates of vairagyam, utsaha, and gurubhakti. Serving the guru and the spiritual cause with great enthusiasm they learn the meaning of dispassion and attain to supreme detachment (paravairagya)."*

### Pada III, Sutra 52
*sthani upanimantrane sangha smaya akaranam punuh anista prasangat (sthani,* lesser deities; *upanimantrane,* allurement; *sangha,* keeping company; *smaya,* prideful accomplishment; *akaranam,* without cause; *punuh,* recur; *anista,* unwanted; *prasangat,* get connected).

*"The yogi should avoid the company of lesser deities whose prideful accomplishments are used to attract others, resulting in binding and unwanted connections with them again and again, through lifetimes."*

When taking up the subject of the occult powers, and the allurements of lower realms within the collective human mind, it would be well to consult our main commentator and what he has to say about the topic. Here is what we read

# The Twelve Levels of Vairagya, Dispassion

*"Sages reach the inaccessible, making it accessible via the three gates of Vairagya, Utsaha, and Gurubhakti. Serving the guru and the spiritual cause with great enthusiasm, they learn the meaning of dispassion and attain supreme detachment."* — Tejabindu Upanisad

*8* **Vaishikara** — A more mature state of detachment, sometimes called "the highest state of lower dispassion."
⇧
*7* **Sthulavairagya** — The Fundamental or "gross" stage of authentic detachment, which is not yet fully matured.
⇧
*6* **Anashakti** — The beginning of actual detachment which represents the early stage of nonattachment.
⇧
*5* **Uparamavairagya** — Detachment which arises from satiety of desires and disenchantment with works.
⇧
*4* **Karanavairagya** — Detachment caused by the arising of various difficulties of life mixed with ever-interrupted pleasures.
⇧
*3* **Madhyavairagya** — Middling type of detachment, lacking in intensity, which nevertheless rises up sporadically at times with intensity, but soon dies away.
⇧
*2* **Mrduvairagya** — Mild detachment which is intermittent, vague, and weak, and which easily falls victim to compromise and distraction
⇧
*1* **Yatamana** — Initial detachment of a beginning aspirant who, having come to know that the body and senses require purification, attempts to bring them under control.

*12* **Paravairagya** — Absolute and supreme detachment which leaves the mind completely and permanently free of thoughts of worldly objects.
⇧
*11* **Tivravairagya** — The most intense form of detachment short of fully matured vairagya, where a very keen sense of natural abidance is felt.
⇧
*10* **Audasinya** — A very lofty state of detachment brought about by jnana which causes indifference to sense experiences and transcendence of all contrasting pairs of opposites.
⇧
*9* **Adhimatra** — A high state of detachment under the influence of which the pleasures of life seem insipid, even feel painful.

*"Those who want to help mankind must take their own pleasure and pain, name and fame, and all sorts of interests, and make a bundle of them and throw them into the sea, and then come to the Lord. This is what all the Masters said and did. The fact is that the Lord is in us, we are He, the Eternal Subject, the real ego, never to be objectified, and that all this objectifying process is mere waste of time and talent. When the soul becomes aware of this it gives up objectifying, detaches, and falls back more and more upon the subjective. Until we are ready to sacrifice everything else to one idea and to one alone, we never, never will see the Light. If you want to give up everything for your own salvation, it is nothing. But do you want to forego even your own salvation for the good of the world? If so, then stem the tide of degeneration at the sacrifice of name and fame, wealth and enjoyment, nay, of every hope for this or other worlds."*

Copyright 2017, Babaji Bob Kindler

in the book *Raja Yoga* by Swami Vivekananda around this particular sutra: *"The Yogi should not feel allured or flattered by the overtures of celestial beings, for fear of evil again. There are other dangers too; gods and other beings come to tempt the Yogi. They do not want anyone to be perfectly free. They are jealous, just as we are, and worse than we sometimes. They are very much afraid of losing their places. Those Yogis who do not reach perfection die and become gods; leaving the direct road, they go into one of the side streets and get these powers. Then, again, they have to be born; but he who is strong enough to withstand these temptations goes straight to the goal and becomes free."*

The occult powers are everywhere, really. Beings here on earth are using gross versions of them when they perpetuate such diverse acts ranging from putting on lipstick to attract others, to going to war to dominate over other nations. Those forms of the occult powers that are more inward, and which are being spoken of here in this sutra, have more serious ramifications for spiritual life, acting as impediments on the inward journey towards perfection after the body's death.

Nevertheless, by engaging in these gross versions of power-seeking while in the body here on earth, beings create mental impressions that lead them inexorably to realms of prana alone after death, and into the clutches of beings whose design for manipulation of them hem them in further to the mayic cosmological process — which all sincere, freedom-seeking yogis and yoginis want free of. Thus, continued rounds of birth and death with one's ancestors is not the only closed loop that consciousness (which by nature is unbound) can fall into; rounds of birth and death with asuras, celestials, demigods, gods and goddesses — in short, lesser deities — can also bind the freedom-loving soul. Other great souls, such as Vedavyasa, and Shankara, also warned against these temptations, and Sri Ramakrishna goes so far as to describe them via His own direct experience of, as listed in the *Gospel of Sri Ramakrishna*. Therein, as He ascended the lotuses in Kundalini practice, He saw that gods in realms along the way beckoned to Him to enter their realm. He declined, and merged in the Sahasrara.

The yogic practitioner studying these lessons might want to familiarize themselves again with the list of the eight occult powers called the *Asta-bala Siddhis*. This is to be able to recognize them, and avoid them.

## Lesson Eighty-eight, 4/26/14
### Pada III, Sutras 53, 54, 55, & 56

In this particular lesson we will complete the third pada of Patanjala by finishing up the four remaining sutras. It is a big bite. However, there is much similarity in this conclusion of Section 3, both in terms of atmosphere and content. Besides, the two elements here involve a final visit to the subject of samyama, so beloved by the yogis, as well as the evaluation of the difference between Purusha and Prakriti via discriminative wisdom. That is precious to Vedanta. Fine points around such wisdom are found in the answers to the varied questions that have come in since the presentation of lesson #87. The process is rewarding, perhaps at least or more so than undertaking a study of Patanjala on one's own. Kindly take up the several questions, below, and decide for yourself:

**Questions and Answers for Lesson 88**
Avinashi from Pennsylvania writes:
QUESTION: "I've been thinking very deeply about the yogas lately, and sometimes it seems to me that there are really only two yogas....bhakti and jnana, with karma and raja yogas merely serving their ends. What is the truth of this?"
ANSWER: As a general statement it has some validity, but for specific ends it risks leaving out a pathway for the habitually active beings, and for those rare inactive souls. Of course, one must first start off by separating the wheat from the chaff and make a distinction between the worldly and the spiritual. That is, the worldly (if they be at least moral) have only two yogas "and counting," called karma and bhakti. They do actions devoid of true knowledge and then ask forgiveness of the personal God when things go awry. If and when higher knowledge visits them, there comes a turning point towards salvation, and the age of jnana may be upon them. The spiritually minded, including the sincerely devout souls, have all four yogas "and less," i.e., they are rapidly beginning to transcend the need for action and may begin to "major" in Dhyanam, meditation. Because work done in higher wisdom does not accrue karma, any actions done are really inaction, or meditation in action.

And it is in this way that the yogas serve each other's ends, as you say. But real incorporation, called integration, is a mighty concept, and one that the devotee who has escaped the jaws of the world should try to implement into life — all lives, not just his own. For there is the tendency that when one's own problems are solved, and one's personal issues are neutralized, one merely goes on and forgets the suffering of others. This is the spiritual version of "....all of you can go to hell in a hand basket, but I have my own, so the devil take the hindmost." So we must change the potential scenario from "fair faces and false hearts" to radiant faces and realized minds. This is accomplished by aligning and applying each yoga to each temperament, then guiding humanity towards collective freedom. As the credo of SRV Associations states: *"Setting the feet of humanity solidly on the path of Universal Truth."*
QUESTION #2: "In the words 'yama' and 'niyama', the common word is 'yama'; isn't 'ni' a negating prefix? Does this (or can this) throw any light on the distinction between yamas and niyamas?"
ANSWER: The prefix "nir" is a "negating prefix," if you will, but not necessarily "ni." "Nir" either dissolves or transcends; "ni" can either restrict or enjoin. Take, for instance, the niyamas themselves. Study (svadhyaya), worship (ishvara-pranidhana), purity (saucha), and contentment (santosha) are definitely enjoining qualities. Tapas is restricting. In the case of the yamas, yama

means observance, but it also means death — death to all the bad habits that the aspirant observes within the mind.

And so, to quip 'ni'cely, may we nicely nip the nightmare of niggardliness in the bud, and nimbly recognize the nimbus shining nigh unto nirvana.

QUESTION #3: "How clear should the understanding of our personal, spiritual ideal be? And could an insistence upon too much clarity or too much constancy in this regard, constrict us?"

ANSWER: How clear? As clear as one can possibly make it, or, put another way, clear enough to help one see through the appearances of this life and world and not forget God — the Lord and Mother of the Universe — ever again. For forgetfulness, avidya, or ignorance, is the veil covering all that we are, and all that we seek. It matters little whether one "believes" in God or not. Remove ignorance by higher wisdom and whatever, whoever, God is, will then become clear. And that is clarity. The more clear it becomes, the more evident is the Truth of it.

In answer to the second part of your question, can there be too much clarity? We have it on record that Sri Ramakrishna Paramahamsa was so attached to the Truth that He had to finally ask the Divine Mother to lessen His preoccupation with it in order to live a more practical daily life in the world. But this was only around minor matters; it was not about compromise of the dharma in the least. As Swami Vivekananda has told us, and for our own good: *"One might sometimes have to compromise with the world, but one should never do so with the Truth."*

In the world, then, where any act can go awry and cause suffering, even a "good" act, performing all works in clarity *(khyati)* is essential for both peace of mind, and for the boon of walking a relatively unobstructed path leading to the Supreme Goal.

QUESTION #4: "The process or practice of contemplation as I understand it involves questioning, but without any active attempt to find the answers; instead there's an open and expectant waiting and intuition (as in-tuition or teaching from within) is relied upon to supply the answers by whatever avenue (for example, by bringing something in memory to the surface of awareness, or supplying a metaphor, or whatever). The effectiveness of the process depends mainly upon how well formed the question is, and how strongly the questioner refrains from actively seeking an answer. My understanding of this is derived from Christian sources, but I've found it generally useful. I'd also like to add, lest it become a distracting issue, that I don't consider intuition infallible or beyond question. I also see that the more I practice this, the more rapid the appearance of answers are. Naturally, this has led me to wonder if there is any similarity between contemplation as I've described it here, and samyama as taught in Patanjala Yoga. There's the focus, the inward openness, the lack of grasping, and so on, which overall might be described as dharana, dhyana, and samadhi. So, are these two practices of contemplation and samyama similar? If they aren't, can the distinctions between them throw any light on the nature of samyama?"

ANSWER: Yes, contemplation is a rather passive tool wherein the contemplation and the contemplator rest in a combined atmosphere of observance and patience. It has as its fruit more of the style of revelation than of penetration, of observation than of uncovering.

But where contemplation really falls back is where it begs intensity. One can contemplate the impermanent and suffering-ridden nature of relativity, and contemplation may even play a part in helping one rise above all that, but it cannot effect an overall solution on the collective mind of mankind. For that one needs a powerful element such as samyama. Because it fuses the penetrating power of the final three limbs of Yoga, samyama can transform matters, situations, impediments, and the minds of human beings, like nothing else. That, the seers agree on, is the greatest of all miracles — the transformation of a single individual's mind resulting, in domino-like fashion, the many minds to follow. Just look at the amazing and unparalleled feat of Swami Vivekananda in this very time, when he turned thousands of human minds (young minds, at that) towards the twin ideal of renunciation of the world and service of God in mankind. Could such a wonder have been accomplished by contemplation alone? Contemplation is an avenue, while samyama is the destination. That is why Patanjali accents it so much in this collection of sutras.

QUESTION #5: "I've recently read that there was a difference in nature between the Vedic and Upanisadic rishis, and that the Vedic Rishis tended more to be composers of songs and hymns, while the Upanisadic Rishis were more explicitly seers of Unity. Any truth in this?"

ANSWER: I do not accept it. It is more that the ancient rishis did not want to write down their realizations, for they knew that this both limited them and might eventually lead to misunderstanding by immature minds, what to speak of the ills of interpolation and text torturing, over time. Further, songs and hymns are effective ways of transmitting truths to aspirants, and are often more able to convey the needed admixture of jnana and bhakti to the seeker.

There is another point to be made in favor of the ancient rishis. They were far more forgiving of the problems of name and form, and probably better versed in the art of deification than the more modern seers were. God with form was really the best and only thing to talk about for them, simply because the Formless Reality was inexpressible and inexplicable. The Lord with form, and the Divine Mother of the Universe, were looked upon as the compassionate benefactors of spiritual life in the world, because that is who They really are. Nothing will change that. We go to Brahman for final release, but we go to Ishvara/Ishvari for assistance with all the problems and impediments leading up to that glorious Union. Simply put, all embodied beings "need friends in high places," and the formless Brahman is beyond "high." *One comes unto to the Father through the Son."*

To give all their due, though, the more recent rishis and seers laid accent on espying maya and transcending and renouncing the world, simply due to the advancing density of the present age. All is destined to fall apart (you might have been noticing lately) at the end of long cycles of time, so it will help aspiring beings immensely to be able to withdraw from objects, transcend nature, dissolve projections, and merge into formlessness — attainments of that rare order — as the need for them approaches at the end of an age (or a lifetime).

I pay my obeisances to all illumined souls — from Brgu to Buddha, from Gotama to Gaudapada, from Vasishtha to Vivekananda, from Ram and Krishna to Ramakrishna; They were, and continue to be, the Prime Exemplars and the Eternal Overseers of the expanding and advancing spiritual lives of all aspiring souls. Victory unto Them!

QUESTION #6: "In Swami Bhajanananda's book, *The Light of the Modern World*, on the Universal Significance of Sri Ramakrishna's Avatarhood and Message, the Swami writes: '*Sri Ramakrishna's concept of Vijnana is sometimes mistaken for Ramanuja's Visishtadvaita. But the two are quite different concepts. Ramanuja regards Advaita as a lower kind of experience. But Sri Ramakrishna considers Advaita to be the highest pinnacle of spiritual experience. Vijnana comes after the Advaitic experience; it is a more advanced, holistic, integral experience that allows a fuller experience of the immanence of Brahman in creation.*' As I consider this, however, clear understanding in regard to the difference in these modes of experience eludes me. There seem more similarities than differences, and I, in fact, can't see where the differences are. Both Visishadvaita and the experience of Vijnana involve the comprehension that there is nothing in existence but Brahman; and both of them embrace Spirit in both its transcendent and immanent dimensions. So where's the difference, in experience, between the Visishtadvaitin and the Vijnani? The question interests me because traditional bhaktas continually insist that realization of Saguna Brahman brings the realization of the Nirguna with it automatically, without any need for other effort. I, however, take issue with this notion, both on rational grounds, and on the grounds that it's not what our Master teaches. Hence my question."

ANSWER: We should seriously read and consider Swami Bhajanananda's words on this crucial subject. He is a very realized soul, and one of our Order's prime teachers of the day. What I can add here is that there is quite a difference between having spiritual experiences prior to the attainment of nondual Samadhi, and after having It. It is similar to the difference between reading the scriptures the first time around, when young, and reading them later after much study and exposure to the guru's long-standing instructions. There is really no comparison. One gets worlds more of insight after such hallmarks of practice.

Part of the problem, here, is the nature of the word "Vijnana" itself. It has different shades of meanings in various religious circles. It is not a very high principle in Buddhism, for instance, being listed as one of the "nidanas," or links, associated with relative consciousness, leading the soul into rebirth. So, one has to be careful to understand it inside the religious locale and context in which it is intended.

Having said that, it can be declared that Sri Ramakrishna makes a wide distinction between jnana and vijnana. Jnana is potent enough, and we wish more souls would begin the real spiritual journey and take to it, using it to destroy their ajnana, ignorance. Vijnana is more on the level of what Lord Vasishtha speaks of as Atmajnana, the singular Wisdom that pertains to the Indivisible Self alone. And, whereas jnana can and will dawn when the aspirant studies the scriptures and begins to meditate, Atmajnana will only dawn after the superlative state of non-duality has swept the qualified and advanced soul into the unparalleled realm of Advaita. The profundity of the Buddha's teachings, for instance, after His experience of Nirvana, as opposed to what he knew prior to It, is a prime example of the sublime effect of nonduality on an illumined soul. Christ's teachings before going to India, and after He returned, is another example — though a bit more speculative. One thing is for certain: Advaita is not a "lower" experience; perish the thought! It is superlative, and the most blessed state one can attain.

QUESTION #7: "Prana, as it directs the movements of the physical body, is behind the movements of that physical body, and I would imagine that it is moved by impulses of desire, imagination, and emotion. When it comes to the psychic prana, this must be behind the movement of the mental (rather than physical) apparatus. But what moves the psychic prana?"

ANSWER: Desire, imagination, and emotion are not elements of the physical body, but of the mental body, so they are really under the auspice of psychic prana. The physical prana moves blood through nerves, breath in sets of lungs, and food and excrement through fleshy tubes, etc. Its terrain involves physical and vital health. For mental health that includes freedom from sets of dualities, the attainment of higher thoughts, a honed intelligence, and a ripened ego, the aspirant must transcend the physical sheath (stula sharira) and begin working with the subtle body (sukshma sharira).

Ultimately, the Mahashakti — Whom Patanjali calls *Chiti-shakti* — is the mover of prana, at all levels. But since She is really an "Unmoved Mover," only unveiled a bit by much deeper forces than prana, life force may as well be left to move itself. If this were not the case, then we would not have to exert in order to control its varied and often erratic movements. The yogi (the aspirant, not the adept), strives to get the grossly moving and raw prana under his control first, for all else — body, senses, breathing, heart rate, etc. — will settle down as a result. Then he can begin to enjoy freedom from disease, strife, lassitude, and the rest.

QUESTION #8: "In Nirvikalpa Samadhi, the meditator, meditation, and the object of meditation become one. Doesn't that mean that they simply disappear? If that's what it means, why not just say that somehow? Maybe the idea is saying something about how or by what process or principles they disappear. I've never understood this. Please shine light on it."

ANSWER: To understand such subtleties, even intellectually and philosophically, is to graduate to a more refined level of insight. One of the hallmarks of such special comprehension is coming to know that nothing ever disappears for good. The Father of Yoga is very clear about that. Even such problematic things as the five kleshas are never destroyed outright. And why is that? Because, for one reason, the fully attained and versatile luminary will require the usage of every element in the previously transcended "creation" when he decides to *"gather the mind back from formless meditation"* and re-embody, like an Avatar or a Buddha. Read on for more on this.

QUESTION #9: "In analyzing the tattvas of Sankhya Yoga, aren't we analyzing principles that ultimately have no existence outside of perception and conception?"

ANSWER: The words and idea behind the saying, "have no existence," have to be examined, and the correct conclusion drawn thereafter. Ultimate realization states that "Everything Is" *(sarvosmi)*, that nothing is not. With regard to the tattvas, they are eternal principles that return again and again in and outside of ongoing cosmic cycles. For instance, the Five Elements are titled *Panchamahabhutas* in Sankhya, the Five "Great" Elements. They are not referred to as the "small insignificant" Elements, or the "nonexistent" Elements. There are even gods that both dwell in them and preside over their functions. The paths of Deity Yoga, Ritualistic Worship, Bhakti Yoga, etc., demand that we honor these beings and their manifestations, and acknowledge their existence. May they remain benign so as to help us in future existences.

When we talk in terms of nonexistence, and thus shift the mind's awareness to another, and more transcendent mode, we are beginning to speak of the difference between Purusha and Prakriti, Brahman and its Maya, or to put it in more easily communicable terms, Sentiency and Insentiency. In objects and tattvas, it is their sentiency that is nonexistent, i.e., they do not have any. As insentient objects, though, they have existence. It is not just the armchair philosopher who does not understand this, but also the general sweep of human beings who are busy thinking that objects/nature/cosmic principles exist independent of mind and Reality, or that they possess some magical power of their own. And it is in the false belief in this presumed power that people allow objects to gain power over them.

Objects, their power of influence, and the human being's attachment to them, all exist in the mind, and therefore become projections of the mind. If the mind is cleared of its misconceptions and gains clarity, it then perceives its own part in creating appearances, and can also do away with them in realization. As the Avadhuta Gita states, *"Ignorance is unreal. Then how can it cause any real doubt? Therefore, what should the yogi do upon being endowed with a mind and its projections? He should allow them to rise, naturally, then do away with them one by one, like bubbles in water."*

So, what is really nonexistent, or unreal as the Vedanta states, is the mind's imaginings and projections — its *sankalpa/vikalpa* process. Come to find, upon further examination, that the mind itself does not possess any lasting sentiency; it is a moon that shines by the borrowed light of the sun of Atman.

This entire subject is put simply by Sri Ramakrishna's telling of the Bel Fruit metaphor. If you want the full weight of the fruit, you see, you must weigh rind, seeds, flesh, stem, and peelings, all together. The merchant may weigh and sell just the flesh, but he runs the risk of overlooking both the real existence of and the use for what he discards so easily out of hand. I mean, the cows are standing out back of his stall. Holy Mother said that these "as if nonexistent" leavings ought to be placed near their mouths so that they can eat and benefit by them. Likewise, there are beings to whom everything from the five elements of nature, on up to the higher cosmic principles, will be of immense value at their stage of growth and understanding.

All is real, all exists. This great fact is the result of fusing mature bhakti with nondual jnanam in the atmosphere of reverent worship of God existing in everything seen via nondual meditation. For the advanced sadhika, it is really only a matter of how much of that God is present from tattva to tattva, from object to mind to intelligence. As my guru used to tell us, *"Light reflects better on a leaf than a rock, reflects on a lake better than on a leaf, but reflects best of all on a mirror.* The halcyon Light of Conscious Awareness is present everywhere, and in everything. "Rocks" are like objects, "leaves" are senses, "lakes" are minds, and "mirrors" are pure minds — or "No Mind." May we strive and generate pure minds so that we can comprehend the Consciousness-filled principle of Pure Existence that is transcendent of mind.

QUESTION #10: "Through the course of reading your newest book, *Dissolving the Mindstream,* it became clear to me that, just as there is an appearance tree and a particle tree, (and also, the Atman or Buddha nature tree, though that doesn't seem relevant to this question), so too, regarding my physical organism, there is an appearance body and a particle body. Taking this into contemplation, my own experience of my body began to shimmer the way a mirage in a desert does, and I realized that my common experience of my body is indeed just an image created by the senses. Going more deeply in, I wondered if I could break identification with this mere image. Yet, no matter how clearly its illusory nature became, the identification remained. What's holding it in place?"

ANSWER: The ego structure, mainly. For the embodied being, distance from the body's overall influence is gained by diminishing the ego, or ripening it. It is natural that some attention is paid to the body, as it is a "vehicle" through which to move along the path towards freedom, and a "vessel," in which the Lord may reside.

As far as divine bodies are concerned, the physical form itself can "shimmer" after purification of body, senses, and mind have been attained via sadhana. Such a body is a positive boon on others, and also acts as an example of how to live a divine or dharmic life on earth amidst the preponderant weights of maya and matter. So long as one has been given the teaching of seeing through appearances, i.e., through the outer to the inner and on to the transcendent, then the body can move along the path under the guidance and direction of the pure mind and free soul. Then, as Sri Ramakrishna often said while pointing at His body, *"Just a pillowcase."* Or, as the Holy Mother quite often said, *"What is all this fuss over the body. It is just a few pounds of ash in the end."*

Tadrupa from Oregon writes:
QUESTION: "Beyond moderation and control of the senses, what is the best

way to increase our detachment from the finite?"

ANSWER: By realizing that all this *is* finite. When one senses, intuits, or divines the existence of the Infinite, then all other allurements and fascinations come to an end. That is why Swami Vivekananda stated, adamantly: *"Although I am in full sympathy with the various branches of religious and social work, I find specialization of work absolutely necessary. Our special branch is to preach Vedanta. Helping in other work should be subservient to that one ideal. As soon as human beings perceive the glory of the Vedanta, all abracadabras fall off of themselves. This has been my uniform experience. Whenever mankind attains a higher vision, the lower vision disappears of itself."* Nothing ends the romance and sentiment of dalliance with nature and form as swiftly as the insight that *"....all this is Maya,"* for what sensible person wants to remain a fool? When metal objects cease to shine, one turns the gaze elsewhere. In the same way, when the shine of excitement and expectation for fulfillment in this realm of disease and decay diminishes, the soul looks elsewhere to seek for that one Reality that remains unchanged and untarnished.

Moderation and control of the senses, well learned and applied, both lead to this level of realization of the finite nature of all things material, of the ebb and flow of all types of energies, of the changing nature of the thoughts of the mind, in repetitive cycles. Matter, energy, and thought are not the Atman. The immutable and ever-blissful nature of the Self is singular; It is the only Light that shines Eternally, and which is self-luminous. A positive approach towards the Self within will speed up the phases of time required to realize It, along with one's wise consultation of the guru and the sincere aspirant's intensified sadhana.

QUESTION #2: "What is the difference in mental attitude between those who have reached level 4, and those at level 5 of detachment?"

ANSWER: You are writing and asking about the Twelve Levels of Vairagya that are shown on the chart in lesson #87. Level four, called *Karanavairgya*, and level 5, *Uparamavairagya*, demonstrate a subtle shift, as they are both associated with work in the world. Surprisingly enough, one can shift from infatuation with work, to sudden disenchantment with work, and finally to detachment from work — all the while maintaining one's duties and responsibilities. The mental attitude you speak of here says it all, that is, that it is all dependent on the mind and its condition. As Ramprasad sings in one of his wisdom songs, *"Misery and misfortune will come if you do not chant the Name of Kali, but even if misery comes, oh mind, always remember the Mother. Whatever happens, know it to be Her Will and surrender yourself completely."*

Taking the teachings of this wisdom song as our foundation, we then see that constancy of mind, steadiness of mind, equilibrium of mind, mental balance, whatever name you don upon it, is accomplished due to the mind's forbearance and steadiness. Most beings buckle under unfavorable changes, sometimes right at the very first sign of them. But the determined aspirant remains impervious to external changes, as also to internal ones. What starts off as imperviousness to the world eventually matures into natural abidance in the Self — into the more developed stages of vairagya that are shown in the higher steps of the chart under discussion.

People often look for solutions, opinions, tools, and advice; it is natural. But nothing beats steadiness of mind, determination of mind, resolution of mind. That itself, if it can be attained and held, outstrips all other mental moves. In the *Bhagavad Gita,* Sri Krishna holds it up to Arjuna some five or six times, calling it *stithi prajnasya.* Those devoid of it continually suffer the hellish storms of problems like *shobha,* emotionalism. But *akshobha,* freedom from emotions, is the salubrious zone of inner peace, and thus the proper mental attitude to strive for and adopt.

QUESTION #3: "If one analyzes certain mundane conventions, like family and professional life (using the teachings of maya and jnana yoga), and proceeds to detach from them at least mentally and based on their transitory nature, would this be considered a sincere and mature form of detachment?"

ANSWER: Yes, but this way is not necessarily for everyone — probably not even for most. For the masses, these modes (recognition of maya and discrimination) are used in bits and increments; only the strong of mind can use them more broadly, and apply them like a healing salve to the vagaries and vicissitudes of life. The masses would thus be well advised to increase their devotion for God and move forward by faith. Whatever the case may be, however, from individual to individual, from soul to soul, if you speak of maturity in spiritual life and practice, then the workplace and the family atmosphere are both fine opportunities to practice a combination of detachment from the unreal and acknowledgement of the presence of God in everything. For instance, we think of Swami Vivekananda as a grand renunciate. But one of his main disciples, Sister Nivedita, gleaned this special attitude towards life from him:

*"As mankind is divinity itself, and as the many and the One are the same Reality, it is not one particular form, mode, or medium alone, but equally all forms, modes, and media which are paths to Self-realization. There can be no distinction between 'sacred' and 'secular,' nor any difference between the service of God in man and the worship of God in a temple.*

*"To labor is to pray. To conquer is to renounce. To have and to hold is as stern a trust as to quit and to avoid. Life itself is religion. The farmyard and the field, the workshop, study, the studio are as true and fit scenes for the meeting of God with man as the cell of a monk or the door of a temple. Art, science, and religion are but three different ways of expressing a single truth."*

This message, framed in large letters, has graced the entrance way to my private residences in Hawaii for decades. Those few who make it to my door see it first, and I hope they read it and take it in. To understand this message is to select and implement the best of both the householder and monastic pathways, and to know, as well, the combined secrets of mature detachment of all that is not, and universal acceptance of what always is.

QUESTION #4: "Will the mantra stimulate and awaken our detachment through the bringing forth of karmas and 'trials' in life? Is it sometimes the case that Divine Mother will 'rip' things out of this life to increase our detachment and renunciation, often in ways our limited minds cannot understand in the moment, or even over a period of years?"

ANSWER: Though this bringing up of karmas due to the early practice of mantra recitation is true enough, we must neither hide behind it nor allow it to frighten us away from the Goal. In my experience it is far more likely that the mantra is given by the guru at the perfect time in life (and in a succession of lives), and its newfound presence will either stymie or reduce karmas that are already headed one's way.

You see, karmas already held *(prarabdha)* will have to be lived through; there is no solution for them other than *"staying close to Brahman"* all one's life. Those karmas which the mantra brings forward will only come up anyway eventually, so the fact that they come up after the guru has been encountered and the mantra given — or in other words, in the presence of holy company rather than in worldly company — is a boon. I have had the experience many times over of devotees coming forth years after having taken initiation to tell me that if they had not received the mantra when they did, they would have never been able to handle what was in store for them, i.e., the fructifying negative karmas of their recent past.

And so, let us not rue or shy away from mantra due to its power to purify; we ought to celebrate that and, in yogic fashion, face off with our demons and get free. Moreover, and to repeat, mantra protects against what is coming. That is more important than the working out the few minor karmas that might be hiding in sincere devotees, because, oncoming karmas can spoil one's hard gained and precious forward spiritual progress. Speaking by way of analogy, dealing with a few boils and warts rising up on the skin is a simple matter compared to shutting down all endeavors in order to fight a debilitating disease that threatens to undermine life itself.

So let the mantra do its salubrious work, but know that its work is multidimensional, not one-dimensional. All three types of karma — past, present, and future — are part of its territories, and it acts as a clarifying agent on all of them, each in their own way.

QUESTION #5: "Is the recognition that spiritual life is all that really matters, and then acting upon this conclusion, a sign of sincere detachment?"

ANSWER: Yes, and of advanced detachment as well. Many enter spiritual life half-heartedly and part-mindlessly. They recognize that God is most important, but they can muster no follow up, therefore no progress. The level of their exertion for the All-Important does not match the profundity of their insight about the same. That is why Swamiji spoke out on the weakness of the mind, and on mankind's selfish clinging to the world of matter and objects: *"The only knowledge that is of any value is to know that all this is humbug. But few, very few, will ever know this. Know the Atman alone, and give up all other vain words. This is the only knowledge we gain from all this knocking about the universe."*

This clinging to petty individual concerns, this prevaricating abidance with mundane human convention, renders the soul helpless to proceed, despite its inner knowing about the existence of God and the special wisdom *(atmajnan)* that leads to the realization of That which is most important. God even comes to earth as the guru to help with this and other impediments, but they turn away or run away from such benign assistance — often for a few petty concerns of the ego. Swami Vivekananda stated about this strange dichotomy, *"You may go and knock your head against the four corners of the world, seek in the Himalayas, the Alps, the Caucasas, the desert of Gobi or Sahara, or the bottom of the sea, but perfection will not come until you find a Teacher."* As one contemporary poet wrote, *"Grasping matter, losing Grace; strange indeed this human race...."*

R.O. from Hawaii writes:
QUESTION: "What or who is the origin of Maya?"
ANSWER: It is originless, like everything else — Brahman, the soul, nature — but that is the Advaitic, or nondual, assertion, and it needs some deep retreats, series of classes, and personal contemplation in order to come home to the mind. The qualified position, and what you want to hear, can be answered by taking up your following questions.
QUESTION #2: "How did Maya get started in the first place (In the very beginning, if there is such a thing as beginning."
ANSWER: The seers tell us that Maya has no beginning, but it does have an end. That end is in Enlightenment, called Moksha or Mukti. This is actually a welcome teaching, for certain questions as diverse and different as "Where do souls come from," "What is the origin of the Universe," and "Why is there suffering," etc., get answered when it is entertained by the mind. Sankhya Yoga, as well as the Tantric teachers, explain the inexplicable Maya by citing its characteristics that they have gleaned from it by examining it from a distance. For, no one in their right mind would go close to it, or enter into it This is an explanation for the fact that most of humanity is not in their right mind — at least as long as they remain in the clutches of the world-bewitching Maya.

    Those characteristics of Maya just mentioned make a good study for all who want free of it. They are: *It is eternal; It is illusory; It is insentient; It transforms and changes; It is the seed of creation; It is the cause of manifestation; It is has no beginning or end; It has evolutes similar to it; It supports karma; It can be recognized.*

    It *"has no end"* in the sense that, whereas certain individual souls *(jivamuktas)* will get free of it, so many countless others will cling to it for ages. The reincarnation principle finds much of its validity in the teaching of Maya, then. *"It can be recognized"* is a boon and blessing of a teaching. When I was a teenager, and very dissatisfied with everything around me, it was a revelation to find that the ancient seers of India had both recognized Maya and given it a name. That it is hard to recognize can be proven and seen by the fact that most all beings, even the intelligent, are completely hypnotized by it. That *"It is the seed of creation"* and *"the cause of manifestation"* shows how much influence it has over all beings who manifest a body/mind mechanism within the creation.

For more teachings on Maya come on retreat, attend classes, participate in satsangs, and in all other spiritual opportunities and involvement that can be taken.

QUESTION #3: "Since Brahman is Formless and does not create, is the origin of Maya outside of Brahman? And if so, how can anything be outside of Brahman?"

ANSWER: Exactly right! Your train of questioning is following the rational course. Simply and easily spoken, Sri Ramakrishna stated that Maya is in Brahman like poison is in a snake. That is, just as the poison in a snake will not harm or effect the snake, in the same way, all of the negativities conjured up by the mind in maya will never affect Brahman. As He often said, *"Good and bad smells may pass on the air, but the air only carries them temporarily."* Will this kind of a teaching only give rise to people thinking that nothing that they do matters, virtuous or sinful? No, because there is karma to consider. As Sri Ramakrishna went on to say, the poison in the snake may not cause harm to it, but it will harm you if you get bitten. Such "harm" is formulated, assigned, and suffered in and through the laws of karma. As Holy Mother said, *"The laws of karma are inexorable, and must be paid to the last penny."* So, yes, all occurs in Brahman, but Brahman Itself remains unaffected and changeless; also inactive and stationary.

QUESTION #4: "Lastly, since many times you have said the world is all Maya, where would we be without Maya? In other words, if all Maya were eliminated, would we wind up with nothing? For example, if physical hunger is Maya, and it becomes satisfied by food Maya, if we realize this, do we no longer have to eat? One Hindu(?) myth I recall reading is that the Lord Brahma dreams, and His dream is the world (Maya) This would imply creation of Maya by Brahma."

ANSWER: Like green scum that forms on the waters of an otherwise clear lake, and is present inherently in the lake before it forms, Maya makes its appearance unseen and unbeknownst to all beings, as if from nowhere. Like all other things, it arises from seeming nothingness, and into seeming nothingness it returns, which is the case with all forms. If it were possible to actually create something, anything, then that thing or things would not have existed before. The seers state that all is unproduced, all is uncreated, in essence. Everything exists at all times; it is only that sometimes it disappears from view, while other times it appears.

For embodied beings, in all realms, Maya is the provider of substances, from flesh and bone bodies to all of nature and the five elements. As mentioned above, *"it is the cause of all manifestation."* This is with regard to insentient materials. As for the sentient Soul, It remains unmanifested. Only projected parts of it — ego, intellect, mind, senses, body — reside in Maya, in Nature. This is the validation of the teaching that the Soul of mankind is unborn, and deathless.

As for the question, "Where would we be without Maya?" and "Would we wind up with nothing?" that rather pinpoints the issue. In the

*Vivekachudamani,* a scripture by Shankara, after listening to the guru speak at length about dissolving all principles and phenomena into Formlessness, the students asks: *"I do not understand. You ask me to do away with all these elements of my being, but when I do I see nothing but the void. Tell me, then, what is to be seen there?"* The answer comes, *"Want of change, that is the Atman. You are the witness of what you see. But where nothing is seen, the idea of a witness becomes irrelevant. You must realize that the Atman is witness of Itself. Therefore, what you are seeing as form and formlessness is that Atman. It manifests as the three seemingly separate states of consciousness — waking, dreaming, and deep sleep — but never forgets that It is essentially uniform."*

Human beings have become so conditioned to being in form over many lifetimes that they have forgotten their formless Essence. When, through intense sadhana, like meditation, they catch their first glimpse of formlessness after such a long time, i.e., when Maya disappears on the horizon of purified mind, they balk and think, "There is nothing there." But like a man entering a dark room from a sunlit day, and seeing nothing after the door closes, then gradually becoming aware of shapes in the darkness, likewise, will the meditator see nothing but voidness in early meditative experiences. He must persist in order to see the Seer that is looking on, then merge that sense of Witness, once known, into Higher Awareness. This is the famous moment where the Seer, the act of seeing, and what is seen, all merge into Oneness. Living beings do not know of this, or believe in it, simply because they have never tried to attain it. But as the Upanisad states about those who do, *"To them belong Peace, and to none else."*

So, where would we be without Maya? We would be enlightened, in our own original state. That state is free of suffering because it is devoid of names and forms and worlds. All and everyone, from the ignorant to the illumined, take on Maya when they enter the realms of form. It is all a matter, then, of whether they take it on not knowing its nature and influence, or take it on in full knowledge of its covering, distorting, and revelatory powers. The ten characteristics of Maya listed above, if studied, will help beings know what happened to them when they fell into the realms of Maya at birth, or many births ago, and also help them get free of its influence.

Akshaya-Bhakti from New England writes:
COMMENTS: "As I studied Lesson 86 and reviewed my questions, I realized that it wasn't so much a fear of death I had been experiencing as a lack of clarity, which was greatly alleviated by the guru's responses, especially about how the causal body is like a holding station for unmanifested Prakriti. The chart of the 'Tip and Mass of the Iceberg' was a powerful visualization tool and metaphor for all the various explanations of the One. How can I really practice involution until I am willing to submerge below the surface of my everyday life. The poem by Kabir to 'Dive deep....' which is embedded within it, automatically triggers surrender within me. In hearing how the prana can persist and carry the mental complex to other realms of existence and, especially how

the links (nidanas) that chain the soul come in 3's, helps me to finally come to terms with the idea that this might not be my last life. The thought of reincarnating again has felt oppressive, but now I begin to see it as an opportunity to complete my journey in the Light. It is so instructive to see Chapter III as a whole, the sense of 'being focused yet maintaining the wider context, like a laser,' as we were enjoined to do when the Raja Yoga lessons first began. I had seen the revelation of the yogic powers as just a precautionary tale, not sure how to incorporate understanding of them into my study, let alone my practice. But it was revealed to Anurag that '....mastering Pradhana, undifferentiated matter, consists of knowing that it exists, i.e., knowing about it, then meditating on the seed forms of objects in nature.' And now, Swamiji begins to review his elucidations on how to proceed from this gross form to the subtle, as in Sutra 43. So many of the precious teachings, such as Discrimination (Sutra 53) and the art of Samyama, have been renewed here, and it is very em-'POWER'ing.

QUESTION: Going back to Sutra #21 to try to further understand the levels of form, 'He does not really vanish, but the form and the body are separate — form and the thing formed have been separated.' Could you please explain further, dear teacher, what is meant by "form" in this sense?

ANSWER: As has been taught in the tradition, the seeker should know that he/she has three bodies. All three of these fall in the realm of form. And anywhere that form appears, Maya is at work. The mind (subtle body) is form due to its thoughts. The causal body (like in deep sleep) is also a type of form due to its seeds. The causal body is connected to the realms of form and the other two bodies inextricably, because it provides them with their materials. It is much like the thought of a tree in the mind of a man, the seed of a tree, and the actual tree itself. The thought precedes both the deed (act of formation) and the result (the form). When we meditate, we try to stop all form, and do this, usually, by quelling the thoughts of the mind. That is the early door to formlessness, and thereby to Samadhi.

QUESTION #2: "I have noticed with great happiness that J. must have recently taken initiation. Could you please tell us what his new name, Tadrupa, means?"

ANSWER: Yes, we have two new initiates to receive and celebrate. One is here in Hawaii and took his mantra-diksha recently on Ram Navami. He received the name Vibodha, meaning Awakened Intelligence.

Tadrupa, formerly J.M. in Oregon, was bestowed with the name Tadrupa, which means "The very form of That." "That," here, and to the Vedantist, is a very profound name or indicator of Brahman. So there is a lot to live up to for both these aspiring souls.

## Pada III, Sutra 53

*ksana tat kramayoh samyamat viveka-jan jnanam (ksana,* moments; *tat,* that; *karmayoh,* phase; *samyamat,* concentration/meditation/samadhi; *vivekajan,* born of discrimination; *jnana,* wisdom).

"*By concentrating, meditating, and having samadhi upon phases of time, the right wisdom is born via proper discrimination.*"

The mastery and transcendence of time is not an uncommon topic and ideal in all of the Indian Darshanas, whether orthodox or unorthodox. In Tantra, particularly in Shaivism, the principle of time occupies a very deep and inward tattvic position, and level of potential mastery. Both kala, time as a whole, and kalas, phases of time, are accounted for, and represent vibrational spheres called spandas where reside beings of exceptional attainment. Utilizing the ancient Sankhya Yoga system (as everyone from Sri Ram to Lord Buddha to Patanjali to Shankara did), Shaivism added to the twenty-four tattvas transcendent of the Purusha with a set of a dozen subtler vibrational atmospheres wherein are found kala and kalas. This gave time a new footing, and lent it a deeper area for study as well. It also defined it as a member of the "impure" order of things. The word, "impure" does not mean corrupt of unwholesome, but indicates its far-flung position from the Source — in this case, called Paramasiva.

"Impure" also suggests lacking in sentiency, and the student can see Shaivism's estimation of what principles are more endowed with sentience by looking at the "pure" order that transcends it. Pure knowledge *(Shuddha Vidya)*, God with Form *(Ishvara)*, and the Lord's own Intelligence *(Sadasiva)*, are infilled with Light. There is nothing less than peaceful abidance in these, having nothing of the mixed variety that is found in the impure tattvas.

All of this connects well to sutra 53, because only a lofty attainment like samyama can make real sense out of the perplexing and far-reaching principle of time. For the aspirant, contemplating time may become less of an occupation and requirement, than finding the proper usage of it. In today's swift-paced world, spiritual practice is left unvalued, even abandoned, its ultimate solutions unwisely traded away for conventional means that are both ineffective and unequal to the task of gaining freedom. Until observance of time as a spiritual tool is gained, time as a cosmic principle will remain untouched by the mind, its secrets veiled behind mundane preoccupations that are really only temporarily effective at best.

The yogis forego conventional means early on in the process, and begin developing special yogic powers at a young age (having courted them in previous existences). As Lord Vasishtha told the teen-age Ramachandra, who was the Avatar of the Age — a fact known only to twelve rishis at that period: *"Those virtuous ones alone gain moksha who, from their early childhood, train themselves in Atmajnan scriptures in the company of holy beings. Therefore know, oh sedulous seeker, that the state of Brahman is attained via the combination of the illumined preceptor, the jnana-shastras, and the sincere disciple."*

This focus on time as a tool for gaining spiritual merit, combined with a ready and easy disavowal of all that stands in the way of progress — even conventional means taken up by hosts of ordinary souls — is an attribute found only in those who are bound and determined to use this present existence and body for the purpose of attaining moksha. Mastery of time, then, is a sublime quality that rather determines, earmarks, and separates the yogi/yogini from other beings following variegated pathways, many to who knows where. The proof of validity for this is found in the present life. What a soul has been doing prior to its present incarnation, what a soul manifests due to its earlier practices and attainments, and what forward progress it is mustering in the present lifetime, are all signs of the advanced spiritual practitioner, as well as the presence of God in the human form. As Sri Ramakrishna has stated, *"....if a man eats radish, he belches radish."* That may be true, but if he consumes nectar, he becomes nectar, and doles out that selfsame ambrosia to others.

### Pada III, Sutra 54
*jati lakshana desha anyata anavachchhedat tulyayoh tatah pratipattih (jati*, species; *lakshana*, markings; *desha*, space; *anyata*, distinction; *anavacchchedat*, indistinguishable; *tulayoh*, similarities; *tatah*, from that; *pratipattih*, right knowledge).

"*Anything that is indistinguishable with regard to species, markings, space, time, etc., can be rightly known through this process of samyama.*"

Following along in the vein of the previous sutra, the point is brought home that discriminating wisdom leading to the attainment of the power of samyama will unveil everything in the universe, in both the gross and subtle realms as well. Nothing in the Three Worlds can remain hidden for long from the yogi who has gained this singular, penetrating power of samyama that is accompanied by the most exacting and perfect form of discernment, wholly spiritual in nature.

One of the main areas of impasse that comes up in regard to this set of sutras concerns those problematic inner realms where occult powers are brandished, bargained for, and gained. Discrimination — if it is not finely tuned and well honed via study of scriptures, holy company with the guru, and sincerity on the part of the truth-seeking soul — will not take one safely beyond such menial considerations, and the risks of getting caught at the arcane and occult levels of awareness are as destructive to spiritual progress as becoming trapped in the realm of the ancestors. It all involves the prime addiction to life force, or prana, on the part of transmigrating souls. An addiction to rebirth and cyclic life for the sake of utilizing and enjoying menial powers that bring lands, wealth, objects and pleasures, is the curse of weak souls, and eventually opens up the darksome path leading to the urge to dominate and control others. The gods in the higher heaven lokas have this addiction to domination (ishitva), whereas the small minded but powerful ancestors prefer celestial pleasures (kama-vasayita) in the lower heavens. Both are limiting, to say the least, and far from freedom.

Yogic masters, Buddhist dharma teachers, and even Tantric masters, dispense teachings on the dangers of coveting the occult powers. In the Bhagavad Gita, Sri Krishna warns his beloved disciple, Arjuna, away from these powers, stating: "*If you covet even one of the eight occult powers, Arjuna, you will not be able to realize God.*" In present times, Sri Ramakrishna Paramahamsa called these eight occult powers "*Crow droppings by the side of the road,*" indicating something filthy that should not even be looked at, what to speak of being sought out and coveted. Finally, Lord Kapila, author of the early Sankhya system, put this risk forward in earliest times to ensure that practitioners not get waylaid by the allurements of psychic powers, nor bound into the lower life-heavens in which they operate.

Along with proper discrimination around the risks and dangers of inward contemplation and attainment, the sutra under study also declares that anything of a confused or convoluted nature can be clarified using the power of samyama. Time stands forth, again, as an area where special knowledge can be gained. Looking inward, and into the past, or the future, becomes possible for the yogi, who will use the facts gained there for the highest good of sincerely aspiring beings. The presence of the sheer force of samyama acts as a natural shield for the yogi, and this shield also guards the secrets of time, space, and cause and effect (to name a few) from those who covet occult powers, and would use such secrets for their own personal and selfish purposes. In other words, samyama is one of the great boons and privileges that the yogi and yogini gain from the Chiti-shakti, the Divine Mother of the Universe. The natural order of things is thus well-guarded, and in the hands of beings whose fine integrity is unimpeachable and unquestionable.

**Pada III, Sutra 55**
*tarakam sarva visayam sarvatha visayam akramam cha iti viveka jan jnanam (tarakam,* higher knowing; *sarva,* all; *visayam,* means and ends; *sarvatha,* by any and all means; *visayam,* means and ends; *akraman,* beyond relative order; *cha,* and; *iti,* this; *viveka,* discrimination; *jan,* born; *jnanam,* wisdom).

*"This higher knowing, brought about by discriminative wisdom, is the means and end of all means and ends, and transcends conventional sequence and order, naturally."*

The all-important aspect suggested in this set of sutras under study is that of the possession of a most elevated type of viveka, discrimination, that helps the aspiring but still transmigrating soul to mature and finalize the distinction between Purusha and Prakriti, the Soul and Nature. Patanjali calls this attainment by the word, *Kaivalya,* which implies a special ability in the advanced soul to separate itself from name and form caused by its relationship with Nature. Swami Vivekananda's commentary on this sutra is worth listing here. He states: *"The highest philosophy of the Yogi is based upon this fact, that the Purusha is pure and perfect, and is the only 'simple' that exists in this universe. The body and mind are compounds, and yet we are ever identifying ourselves with them. That is the great mistake, that the distinction has been lost. When this power of discrimination has been attained, man sees that everything in this world, mental and physical, is a compound, and, as such, cannot be the Purusha."*

This earmarks the Purusha as a spark of pure, conscious Awareness, existing, at least apparently, within the realms of name and form in time and space. What a marvel! Is there such a thing as a lost Purusha? Of course. The previous sutras have already declared that everything from susceptibility to confusion and deception, as well as being tempted by the presence of the eight occult powers, is awaiting it. But that aside for the moment, the wonder of enlightened souls returning to the embodied condition, thereby to the earth plane to awaken sleeping souls and clarify confused minds, is highly worthy of consideration and gratitude. Patanjali's own rebirth, or several of late — one, as the student of Gaudapada and the guru of Shankara, and, prior to that, as the Father of the Ashtanga Yoga system — is a prime case in point. Who can fathom such compassion, what to speak of his very real power? Like the two commentators we are consulting here regarding his Raja Yoga system, Vedavyasa and Vivekananda, he is highly blessed by the Divine Mother of the Universe.

When Patanjali states in this sutra that the special ability of samyama transcends conventional sequences and sets of orders, he is pointing out that it goes beyond not only human convention and the physical order of things, but even transcends the cosmic order as well. As Vivekananda states, *"The whole of Prakriti in all its states, subtle and gross, is within the grasp of this knowledge. There is no succession in perfection by this knowledge: it takes in all things simultaneously, at a glance."* The following sutra gives even more depth and understanding to the power of samyama, and the excellences that it bestows on the adept yogi.

### Pada III, Sutra 56
*sattva purusayoh suddhi samye kaivalyam iti (sattva,* balance; *purusayoh,* conscious indweller; *suddhi,* pure; *samye,* equal; *kaivalyam,* separation from nature and form; *iti, this/final).*

*"Revelation of the equality between the balanced state and the conscious indweller brings about separation from form, and final freedom."*

The realization of the similarity between the conscious Soul, Purusha, and the pure sattvic state of mind, ends all doubts, and brings an end to the false projection, however subtle it might be at this stage, of differences and separations. The result is the final release called *Kaivalya,* or conscious isolation from all conceptualization — names, karmas, samskaras, etc., but predominately, all form. Nature, Prakriti, is a form-producing machine; but what is produced in Nature has its origin in the mind as thought. This primal connection, once realized, brings higher wisdom to bear once again, followed by the mind's revelation that it can divorce itself from Prakriti to gain the bliss of the Purusha at any time if it so chooses.

What happens to form and nature then? Are they destroyed? No. They and all their concomitants are reduced to their essential seed forms, to be brought back again in a fresh cosmic cycle. They are effectively put away, then, like freshly-ironed clothes folded and tucked away into a cosmic chest of drawers, and stored there for all time, never to impede or presume upon the pure Soul again. As Vivekananda states, *"When the soul realizes that it depends on nothing in the universe, from gods to the lowest atom, that is called Kaivalya (isolation) and perfection."*

# Pada Four
## Lesson Eighty-nine, 6/12/14
### Pada IV, Sutras 1 & 2

We begin the fourth and final pada of Patanjali's Yoga Sutras. We have taken 88 lessons to get to this point, showing what depths can be plumbed in a study of a noble Indian philosophical system such as Yoga. Our longevity to date is a testament to the tenacity of the students who have remained constant in both their concentration and their line of questioning. Pertaining to the initial sutras, before the ultimate secrets of Yoga can be laid out, the stumbling block of occult powers is taken up again, ushering in the fourth pada. Questions from the end of the third pada are listed below, with their respective answers.

**Questions and Answers for Lesson 89**
Avinashi from Pennsylvania writes:
QUESTION: "Devotees of different avataras, sages, and prophets, serve their masters in different ways, according to their master's teachings. But what does it mean to serve Sri Ramakrishna? I'm asking this question from a perspective which includes all the major dimensions of human beingness as represented by the four yogas. As a jnani, a bhakta, a raja yogin and of course a karma yogin, what does it mean to serve Sri Ramakrishna on planet Earth in the 21st century? Of course, to understand and engage all the yogas as one yoga is definitely a part of this service, but I'm looking for a breakdown that will allow me to better understand the whole by better understanding the parts."
ANSWER: As Sri Sarada Devi told us, *"Since Thakur Sri Ramakrishna was an advaitin, you, too, are all advaitins."* The disciples and devotees of Sri Ramakrishna Paramahamsa are thus universally minded, which means that they will accept the teachings of all religions and their founders so long as they tally with this new incarnation's declarations and experiences. Thus, all that is outmoded, outdated, and outrageous in aging or antiquated religious perspectives will easily get rejected, and what is healthy and not contrary to universal dharmic principles will get upheld. Now, all that is left to do is to implement those elements of dharma that He exemplified in life, put them into practice for oneself, and use them for service of the one God residing in the multitudes of human beings. If this sounds too general, then it is to be seen that the four yogas that Swami Vivekananda championed are what is specific.

The four yogas, all understood and duly exercised on the world scene in the atmosphere of nonduality, form the path and the way, with He, the Great Master, being the focus of worship. Worship of Him is now being undertaken not only by the vast numbers of monks and monasteries that have come into existence in a short time since His advent, but by some five million devotees and more across the face of this earth.

And unlike other gurus with large followings, the Great Master's noble fold is not a flash in the pan type of expression. It will have a "shelf life" of millennia, while those others will fade after a short time — most of them suffering death by compromise, scandal, wealth, or other means. It is right there, that the path of an authentic Avatar is perceived and revealed due to its integrity and longevity. *"The many change and pass, while the One remains the same."* The one Avatar coming in many forms (Krishna, Buddha, Christ, etc.) has recently come among us as Sri Ramakrishna. One has only to look at 1) the host of luminaries that accompanied Him to earth, and 2) the high quality and vastness of His following in just a short time after His appearance here.

QUESTION #2: "When you say, 'Avoid the void," my inclination is to applaud. But what void, specifically, are you counseling us to avoid?"

ANSWER: That void that is empty of real substance, that is devoid of Consciousness, Awareness, Buddha Nature, Atman. Avoid that void. It is the void that is reverted to by materialists, by secularists, by the Godless, all who are themselves void of any real intelligence (another void that one should avoid). That Grand Void wherein name, form, time, space, and causation all merge, along with all sufferings and miseries as well, wherein is found only the Bliss of pure, Conscious Awareness, that Void that is stripped of dualities, one can embrace with all assurance, for that is one's true nature — empty of maya but full of Divine Essence. One will recognize It and know It by the permanent Peace that it leaves behind as its calling card. As Vivekananda so aptly put it, *"....where rolls the stream of knowledge, Truth, and the Bliss that follows both....,"* Where eternal qualities such as these are present, and all limitations are happily absent, then one has found Brahman.

Those beings who fall short of realizing That, or who decry It due to their fear of It, along with their attachment to all that sports form, let them "cling to life," as the Father of Yoga states. Their true nature awaits them, nevertheless. Where else would It await? In the changing realms of pain and pleasure? It never visits those empty realms.

Tadrupa from Oregon writes:
QUESTION: "At the recent retreat, I seem to recall it being mentioned that ether is not present in the dream state. Is this also true of time? Is it absent, or just the ability to perceive it greatly diminished?"

ANSWER: You did not hear arightly. The five elements have their five subtle concomitants, called tanmatras; they are all present in the dream state. The people of the present times do not know about prana and the tanmatras, and therefore do not know how to access the *"Kingdom of heaven within,"* or the *"many chambers of my Father's Mansion."* And so, the five elements in the waking state simply give way to the five elements in dream when consciousness shifts from the external world to the internal worlds. Space, called ether, is there, as well as here. Its nature "there," however, is a backdrop for thought projections rather than for objects — the former being the source of the latter.

In the Taittiriya Upanisad, it is said that, *"The ancient seers of India who revealed the Truth have grouped the various objects and their appearances based on sets of fivefold principles, and declared that one set of fives preserves the next."* This all-important clue to orderly divine manifestation, known as the

*Panchakarana* process, is what SRV members have been designating of late by the phrase, "Can you say five?" Then, after saying it, we must acknowledge it. Then, meditate upon it. This Upanisad (Ch.1, sl. 8) goes on to say that the aspirant is to *"....meditate on the elements that compose nature, namely the earth, the intermediate space between earth and heaven, the sky, major and minor points of the compass, fire, air, sun, moon, stars, water, herbs, plants, ether, and one's body. After that, one is to meditate on oneself while reflecting on the five pranas, along with skin, flesh, muscle, bone, marrow, the organs of sight, hearing, thinking, speech, and touch."* Notice that "ether" is a part of the list. Further, when mentioning the five pranas, a subtler ether is inferred.

Such an extensive list, and the trouble taken to gather it into a cogent system, indicates how crucial it is to both have a cosmology and to reflect on it. From ancient texts like these, Patanjali, the Father of Yoga, drew from and based many of his sutras — sutras that we are presently studying in depth.

Regarding time, it is still present in dream but gets expanded and contracted in turns, and finally goes away for a time in deep sleep. This fact is another clue to examining the inner states of the human mind. And that is why the succeeding sloka of this Upanisad brings in the Eternal Word, AUM, for its further elucidation, for in The Word all things find their source of origin and their dissolution.

QUESTION #2: "What is the practical importance of 'mastery of time,' especially for the new student of Yoga such as myself?"

ANSWER: For one thing, efficiency in action and work is important. When time has been brought under one's control, all manner of work can be dispatched, and all with very little effort or angst. What is more, work accomplished under the power of control of time not only brings all fine things to fruition, but also restrains karma from cropping up as the result of actions. Old karmas get destroyed swiftly as well.

And so, if practicality is the focal point, one can cite no better accomplishment than the mastery of time. Siva, Himself, is the *Trikaladarshi* — the "Overseer of the Three Phases of Time" — and He seems to get all accomplished to His satisfaction.

QUESTION #3: "Is the discrimination spoken of in Sutra III:53 simply between the real and the unreal, or is there some different meaning here?"

ANSWER: No difference, really, but only a matter of specific area. The particular phase of discrimination there is around coming to know the difference between the occult powers of heavenly beings, and one's own innate soul-power. We must not sacrifice the latter, and its magnificent opportunity to realize Itself, for the paltry enjoyments of heaven. When Swamiji writes or speaks of higher and lower powers, he is careful to draw out the distinction between those who take to the "Eternal Body," pathway, and those who opt instead for the "Samadhi" pathway. The former pursue births in the realms of names and forms, while the latter know that only through Samadhi can one be truly free.

This subtle discrimination is what is at the root of Patanjali's sutra cited by you here. In other words, "time" here, to Patanjali, has to do with falling victim to its illusion again and again. Dualists run this risk all the time. The example of Sri Ramakrishna is a good one for this subject, since He was based in Nondual Samadhi, but still engaged masterfully in Divine Sport like none other. And, in fact, the next question broaches this subject.

R.O. from Hawaii writes:
QUESTION: "I have been rereading your answer to my questions on maya in RY #88. Since all is maya, perhaps the best way to look at maya is from the point of view of the realized individual, eg., Ramakrishna. He certainly lived in the world (maya) but was evidently free of it. — '...to be in the world but not of it.' How do you explain this? Some of the common statements are: "the world is illusion," or 'unreal.' These need to be clarified. He ate food, drank water, used transportation, lived in a temple; all maya? So in that sense maya is real. Is not maya all of creation?"
ANSWER: Clarification comes when we define the world "unreal." Vedanta does not mean the world is unreal as in the cases of "water in a mirage," or "the son of a barren woman." These are metaphors *(abhayapadarthas)* used as examples for impossible things. Unreal in Vedanta means changing, thus *ultimately* unreal. That is, when the world goes away (like in deep sleep, death, a good meditation, and nondual samadhi) Reality, Brahman, remains. *"The one remains the same; the many change and pass."* Otherwise, nothing and no one — including maya — would come back. Something, such as yourself and nature, cannot be produced out of nothing. The eternal backdrop is always present, though never seen. Maya goes away with Liberation, but Brahman is the very nature of liberation.

As was just written above, Sri Ramakrishna — the real Paramahamsa, free of impurities — demonstrated how to live in the world but not be of it. *"The mud fish lives in the mud at the bottom of the lake, but its scales still shine." "The turtle swims in the boundless ocean joyfully, but its attentions lie on its eggs buried in the sand on the beach." "The duck gets into the water, but the water never gets into the duck." "The maidservant employed in the city takes care of the Master's children as if they were her own, but her mind dwells on her own children back at her home in the countryside." "Keep the boat in the water, but do not let water in the boat."* In so many simple but direct ways did the Great Master tell the people of the world about the risks and dangers of worldly life, while also informing them of a higher way to both deal with them and transform them.
QUESTION #2: "Since the void that you refer to contains all potential, or is the "suchness" that Buddhism speaks of — two sides of the same coin, so to speak — is not creation just the manifestation of that potential, or maya? Do we need to differentiate between maya & the poison? Might not the maya poison existing in Brahman that you speak of be simply the undue desire or attachment to maya?"
ANSWER: Yes, it is attachment to money, wealth, fame, and the like that is the real problem. Maya is insentient, i.e., is not an incarnate devil out to get you,

as is the case in some religious ideologies.

When you speak of Buddhism (as well one should) especially Zen, one finds the evolution of the idea that maya, or samsara, is ultimately not different than Enlightenment. The Diamond Sutra's famous statement is that *"samsara is nirvana, and nirvana is samsara."* Tibetan Buddhism puts it that *"There is no samsara here to renounce, and no nirvana there to attain."* This is a radical way of putting it, and, again, needs to be understood so that premature conclusions by ignorant minds do not lead to undue (or due) suffering. It is obvious to intelligent people that a man caught in maya lives in a completely different mode than a man availed of Freedom. Simply put, one is bound, the other is free. One suffers like an animal, while the other suffers conscious of the fact that the world is "unreal" — a fact that brings him bliss.

It is the ultimate unreality of suffering, however, and the knowledge of the inability of worlds, nature, and maya to change the Soul even one iota, that forms the difference in comprehension between the two. For, who would attach to something that is known to cause suffering, what to speak of being unreal?

Still, until we know without a doubt that all phenomena are passing and changing, and that attachment is gone from the mind, we will need to discern between the world and its poisons, and the singular state of God and Enlightenment. One cannot pretend the latter away so long as the presence of the pretender still persists. Maya is insidious, like the covering power in water even before it forms itself into scum on the surface to cover the view. Otherwise, the seers would not warn about it, and steer souls, as the Upanisads say, towards *"....the farthest shore beyond all darkness."*

QUESTION #3: "Then the final question arises: what is the ultimate origin of that desire or attachment?"

ANSWER: The final answer, according to the radical nondual school of Advaita, is that everything is originless. Good or bad, higher or lower, there is no beginning, middle, or end to any of it. God, Nature, Human Beings, and Maya are all free of origin. By settling this question first, then one can look into the relative and apparent origins of things. It would help to be able to "count to five" for that search, because every set of fives (like the five elements) rolls out of another set of fives. But that is a subject for another set of questions. To focus on Ajativada, nonorigination, will clear that wash of conflicting questions around relativity from the mind, and leave all that is cosmological and philosophical by nature free to reveal itself. Then, "Ah, come sweet khyati (clarity), come....."

Akshaya-Bhakti from New England writes:
QUESTION: "Regarding the Twelve Higher Spandas, and #11, raga, adhesion, is it just a more intense form of attachment, or is there a subtler difference?"
ANSWER: In defining of the tattva of *Raga,* I have given the student a choice of words that all mean roughly the same thing — attraction, adhesion, attachment, involvement — with only shades of difference present in each. The idea is to convey the difference between a physical law, and a cosmic law. The

word, "attraction," is given first, as that is the usual English word selected by most commentators to describe Raga. Raga can manifest in the universe as the love of a mother for her child, and vice versa, but can do the same on the cosmic level as the power that attracts souls to *Ishvara* — which is a higher tattva on this same list. Its placement in the list is directly above the Soul, *Purusha*, showing it up to be a level of awareness that is transcendent of ignorance and forgetfulness (i,e., the ego, *ahamkara*, falls just before Purusha).

So, the Soul, Purusha, gets "attracted" towards Ishvara (God with subtle form,), "adheres" to it as the goal, "attaches" there for its highest good, then "involves" itself with that in order to get to That — *Paramasiva.*

QUESTION #2: "Could you please discuss niyati, the cosmic laws & their natural order?"

ANSWER: The great Indian rishi, Abhinavagupta, cites *niyati* as the power that determines all cause and effect relationships. As a cosmic power of high order, its presence removes inhibitions that may otherwise impede proper order — which is often absent, for instance, in the lower order of things on earth, i.e., cause and effect manifestations coming from such errors as violence, war, and other confusions of exacerbated karma. One could say, then, that niyati acts rather like predestination, and its contemplation as such will clear up the mind that is confused due to seeing and experiencing obvious injustices of the world and errors of its living beings.

But we cannot enclose niyati's functions inside of this level alone. Niyati acts as a limiting power as well. Fire burns due to niyati's overseership. Cloth comes from thread due to niyati. The supreme Paramasiva, Itself, gets limited — apparently so — by its own power of niyati. In other words, what is really all pervasive becomes, as it were, restricted to a level of space, which is also why this cosmic law is so close in order on Shaivism's list of spandas with *kala* and *kalas,* time and its various phases.

QUESTION #3: "In the text, regarding Sutra 54, Swamiji says, *'When objects are so mixed up that even these differentiae (species, sign, and place) will not help us, the power of discrimination acquired by the above mentioned practice will give us the ability to distinguish them.'* How or why would one want to differentiate that which is not distinguishable. Wouldn't one be at the ultimate goal of seeing the One at that point? Could you please give another example, besides the cow, which might demonstrate how this discrimination would be a higher 'power'? Deepest gratitude as always."

ANSWER: Swamiji is speaking here of states of mind that occur in people prior to seeing the "One." We can call it confusion for now, or lack of clarity, and just say about it that when things become so convoluted that ordinary means fail to see through them and perceive the root cause of them, this special type of discrimination is required and will succeed.

So, "not distinguishable by ordinary means" ought to be looked at here, for that problem of non-seeing, or lack of seership, occurs there. Just look at even the intelligent beings of this day, and how blind they are to higher Reality. With them, it is all about relativity; that is Reality to them, and they know of nothing higher. For an example of the power of samyama, Sri Ramakrishna has given an excellent one. There is a substance called alum that is a clarifying agent. When a painter drops a piece of alum into a jar of water that he uses to clean his paintbrush, that is mixed with all the colors of paint he has been using, the water quickly clears up. This is analogous to adding a bit of this precious type of higher concentration blended with meditation and samadhi, called samyama. The mind then gains crystal clarity, and everything — even indistinguishable matters — get revealed for what they contain and where they originate from, i.e., their interrelation with everything else. In the Svetashvataropanisad, the sloka reads: *"Via special meditation, the rishis of India espied that Divine Being in everything, existing everywhere, Who had been indistinguishable earlier due to the limitations of their own intellects."*

Kanyakali from Hawaii writes:
QUESTION: "Regarding the mastery of time in sutra 53, I have contemplated time enough to know that it is a useful human construct that allows us to differentiate between 'now' and 'then.' However, it came out of my mind, so it is therefore to be mastered and transcended. When I stop and remind myself that only the Eternal Moment exists, and that all is happening inside this Eternal Moment, (while nothing is actually 'happening'), then I relax, and the gunas become more balanced. I also find it helpful to think of Swami Vivekananda saying, *'When would the Self go, when all time is in the Self?'* The power that time usually has over me then starts to lessen. But to really master time and learn how to use it as a spiritual tool, there must be much more to contemplate. I was intrigued by mention of the Twelve Higher Spandas of Shaivism. I would like to learn more about the Spandas. I see that while going from 'impure' to 'pure,' Kala (the concept of time and infinity) and Maya (the deluding power), are right next to each other. That must mean that as I go inward and master each of these principles, once I master time, Maya will be next! So time is very far inward indeed! Would you please give me some more guidance on what I should contemplate in order to make the progression of the Spandas more clear?"
ANSWER: It is not so much *what* you must contemplate, but *that* you must contemplate. You are on the right track, indeed, when you look deeper at the order of these spandas as gifted to us by Tantric adepts (Pratyabhijna System, Kashmiri Shaivism, etc). All will reveal itself as one contemplates over time. You have taken teachings on the various pancha processes (quintuplication), and have come to know that everything evolves outwardly by sets of fives, and therefore one should become aware of these sets, contemplate them, and then roll them up into one another in turn in meditation. That is involution of all tattvas/principles.

Interestingly enough, the spandas/tattvas ranging from raga on inward to kala, form another well-known and documented set of five. Maya is exempted from this set, because it is of a purer order. Maya is the Lord's own power, the Mother's own vehicle. Through it, the subtle concept of time (kala) and its burgeoning stages (kalas) come into manifestation. Since maya is closer to Her, it is aligned more with the intelligence side of the tattvas, while these other five spandas aforementioned fall in accord with the insentient side.

**Pada IV, Sutra 1**
*janma ausadhi mantra tapah samadhi jah siddhyayah (janma,* birth; *ausadhi,* elixers; *mantra, sacred* words; *tapah,* austerities; *samadhi,* nondual experience; *jah,* born; *siddyayah,* psychic abilities).

*"The five ways the yogis use to attempt perfection are: utilizing abilities from previous births, ingesting herbs and elixers, practice of the mantra, performing austerities, and gaining samadhi."*

This teaching of Patanjali should be brought forward and exposed to more people in this day and age, because the ills of complacency — especially the spiritual variety — could be avoided, and real progress achieved, if it were. For one thing, the huge issue of imbibing intoxicants *(ausadhi)* would finally find its solution and its champion, one that would destroy the foggy notion that spirituality has anything to do whatsoever with ingesting substances from nature. Spirituality is not in nature; it is in Brahman, where else? Something relative in nature cannot bring about realization of Reality. As my guru used to say, *"One cannot realize the Infinite through the finite."* He also used to say, *"Do not idealize the Real, realize the Ideal."* Reality is beyond ideas, then. Only That can give That. In the Upanisads it is stated, *"It is the Atman that grants Its vision, and only to those whom It chooses."*

To broaden out the scope of the teaching in this sutra, then, we must cite the five ways in which seeking beings try to attain the Absolute, three of them ineffective, but the other two infallible. The student of this course and commentary can look back at Volume I, page 241, for a review of these five. — a "quintuplication" of a rather mixed nature.

At the bottom of the chart in that lesson, entitled *Patanjali's Kriya Yoga,* can be seen The Five Types of Yogis. For beings who are practitioners born in the West, this eye-opening teaching is a full validation for all the wise reasons that they, as sincere seekers, avoided the inferior means that were generally accepted and embraced by the greater percentage of beginning seekers. You see, and to cut to the chase, without mastery over yamas such as *aparigraha*/nonreceiving (like seeking after intoxicants that give enjoyment) and *ahimsa*/nonviolence (like doing harm to the mind and body by introducing foreign substances into them, etc.), and niyamas such as *saucha* (purity of mind) and *santosha* (being content with original mind), authentic Yoga is not even in the picture. What the neophyte is doing, rather, wreaking by taking intoxicants, is an unhealthy amalgam of desire and egotism that spoils the ground for any future progress in Yoga.

And all of this is in reference to only the second type of yogic beginner, called *ausadhi* — the imbibing of intoxicants, like herbs and elixers. In the case of category one, named *jati* or *janma,* the risks are as equal, and failure to reach the Goal practically a given. This is due to the fact that many upon many are born with the desire to be free (janma), in some way, shape, or form, but purifying and realizing that desire amidst the many impurities (the six passions seated in the mind), the negative influences of society (like preoccupation with wealth and war), and their own individual karmas and samskaras from past births, — to name a few — is going to be difficult indeed. Only if these beings take swift recourse to a guru, path, and dharma teachings early on, will they destroy these influences and achieve growth towards freedom.

And how many will do so? Perhaps that is why Sri Krishna states in the *Bhagavad Gita, "Among millions of beings only one seeks Me in truth, and among thousands of those, occasionally one attains to Me."* He then goes on to declare that, short of rare grace, only by *Abhyasa Yoga,* the Yoga of constant practice, will they gain Enlightenment. Such is the fate of what we refer to as "good intentions" in this day and age. As Lord Kapila noticed (which is yet another quintuplication), even early on in India's spiritual history: *"The sattvic ego/mind complex is inclined to do good actions; the rajasic ego/mind leans towards evil actions; the tamasic ego/mind is bound into performing acts of stupefaction. Other than these there are two other types of minds, and they do acts of good stupefaction, and acts of bad stupefaction."* We can see by this teaching that the path is indeed full of twists and turns, and that we need clear guidance in order to navigate its subtleties, as well as its apparencies.

The third type of beginning aspirant in Yoga is called *mantra,* or *mantri.* What Patanjali means by this refers to those who do the mantra devoid of both enthusiasm for the practice and devotion to Ishvara, not for those who seek and strive by right means. With this said, it is fairly easy to comprehend that dull and parrot-like repetition of the mantra is not going to amount to much in the way of spiritual growth. Mantra is mainly for the purification of the mind. It is not able to fully Enlighten on its own.

But purification is tantamount to Enlightenment, so the import of mantra practice is confirmed. Patanjali himself has a sutra or two on it, and on Ishvara as well. Still, and as Holy Mother, Sri Sarada Devi — perfect in the practice of mantra — stated, *"At first, the practice of mantra feels like digging the dry earth with a spade."* Therefore, one can see how practitioners might run afoul of the right means of fulfilling japa, and lose faith in the mantra, in its deity, and in its long-range and ultimate effectivity. Study of scripture, the niyama of svadhyaya, is the solution for this danger. Add to this, that the practitioner of the day is overlooking the crucial import of securing an authentic mantra from that divine source who has practiced and realized it — called, the guru. This glaring oversight, along with the problem of the many quotidian, even spurious, gurus on the scene today, makes the teaching of the failure of this third type of aspirant all the more evident and understandable.

But when one arrives at the level of *tapas,* authentic and properly-oriented austerity, there is little likelihood of falling again. This is because real austerity will effect real growth. This is great, indeed, for actual spiritual growth is really rare among aspirants, and valid spiritual experiences verily uncommon. And it is even possible that this fourth type of yogi may fall from attaining the Highest, for austerity, tapas, is subject to both the human ego and to reliance on sadhana. The fact that tapas may not always be enough to secure the highest Enlightenment is evidenced in Swamiji's commentary on sutra 4:1. He states: *"....concentration is Samadhi, and that is Yoga proper; that is the principle theme of this science, and it is the highest means. The preceding four are only secondary, and we cannot attain to the highest through them. Samadhi is the means through which we can gain anything and everything, mental, moral, or spiritual."*

A close look at Samadhi, then, is to be had, and that has already been taken herein via studying all the recent sutras on samyama in pada three, which is a fine combination of dharana, dhyana, and samadhi. To cite anything further is to finally bring forth Patanjali's comment on it, as he declares that this singular and unique samyamic ability must be "profound," and can be utilized effectively only after a complete purification of mind has been effected.

**Pada IV, Sutra 2**
*jatyantara parinamah prakriti apurat (jatyantara,* change of body/species; *parinamah,* transformation; *prakriti,* nature; *apurat,* completing).

*"In order to complete all processes and realize their true nature, they move from one form to another."*

A clear understanding of the word, "form," here, will usher us into the proper meaning of this sutra. We are back to considering the subject of higher and lower powers that come to the yogic practitioner. Mention of the form refers to the passage from one vehicle or tattva to another, over time, in order to realize a perfection that is already within them, but that is naturally veiled by everything that partakes of form. This is one of the subtlest of contradictions, really.

Whatever the case may be, the commentators describe this process as an "infilling" that results in the emergence of our true nature, much like the Upanisads point to at times. One commentators has it that *"....we start with a blueprint in the causal level of our being, from which we then "fill in" with the subtlest material (prakriti) so as to become a complete, whole person. Trace your way backwards for enlightenment: The significance of this filling in process is in understanding that enlightenment comes by awareness tracing its way back, in reverse order."*

Those of you who have studied in SRV for several decades will recognize this teaching, and its close connection to the *Panchakarana* process that seeks to "connect the dots" between what the tradition describes as our Three Bodies and the Three Worlds. This "tracking of the bread crumbs" of our embodiment process is pure, early Indian Cosmology (Sankhya), and without it no complete comprehension of either our series of incarnations, or the source of our origin, will be found — how much less, then, India's supreme secret — the originless nature of all things, of all beings.

In the forthcoming sutra (IV:3) we will find out how this process of taking form and filling in takes place. In the meantime, please study these sutras well, and come forth with queries from that healthy process and submit them in a timely fashion.

## Lesson Ninety 8/20/14
### Pada IV, Sutras 3 & 4

After our initial thrust into the fourth pada of Patanjali's sutras via the last lesson, we will now take up some salient sutras on the mental complex, known in Hindu Philosophy as the *antahkarana*. This fourfold conglomerate, consisting of subtle and inward mechanisms, is seen as the source of all projection, thus the "inner cause" of all outer manifestations. It is by working to purify this overall unit that mankind makes any appreciable progress in the spiritual realm, straightening out and rendering pure all other realms as she/he does so. Though one may start from the outside and purify elements, body, and senses by various and more or less popular methods (cleansing of body, asana, fasting, etc.), little actual spiritual gain is ever acquired until the mental organism, the antahkarana, is taken up and subjected to purificatory exercises, i.e., study of scripture, devotional practices, inner austerities (such as withdrawing the senses from their objects), and meditation. All of life, for the sincere practitioner, is both fair game and a fitting field for this salutary accomplishment.

The questions that come in from yoga practitioners reflect attempts at accomplishing this singular type of purification, the most recent listed below:

**Questions and Answers for Lesson 90**
D.G. from Europe writes:
QUESTION: "I have a general question. When the seers divided up Reality in so many categories, are these just a very refined and sophisticated tool for the mind to cope with reality, or do they also exist apart from the mind who sees these categories? So do we (or better, the sages) impose those categories on reality (to help us to become clear and to give us a map), or are these categories intrinsic to Nature."
ANSWER: If you are speaking about categories such as Yoga, Vedanta, Buddhism, etc., these darshanas are eternal. They return to the realms of outer expression again and again. They are rendered accessible to us by the human mind, but the general human mind alone has not the power to conceive of such inward truths. But it can develop the wherewithal to plumb them. Moving towards a nondual state, the mind that seeks inwardly and meditates constantly passes through the realm of subtle truths and becomes devoted to the dharma — a body of teachings that are crafted out of Truth by the luminaries throughout the ages.

With such powerful tools available to it, the soul does not have to "cope" with Reality, but can actually realize It — which is the Goal of human existence. And as far as 'impositions' are concerned, there are plenty of these to be dealt with in relativity — cosmic, collective, and individual — but true philosophy is not one of them. Rather, it is the main means with which to remove and do away with such coverings so that Truth can be realized.

In further answer, a point can be made that 'nature,' being insentient, and though it teaches the soul "lessons," cannot host wisdom teachings The Great Mind *(Mahat)* with its vast intellect *(buddhi)* does that. Memory *(smriti)* is the key to this. However, in Indian dharma this memory is not a surface one only, like in the West. Instead, it holds a connection for the embodied soul to past lifetimes and inner realms where powerful deities are resting at the foundation of it and informing it. And this is also one of the secrets of eternal existence of dharma. Truth, dharma, darshanas, philosophy, and religion — when properly utilized — are the eternal basis for everything, as in, *"Thou shalt know the Truth, and the Truth shall set you free."*

On the other hand, if by "categories" you are asking about the 24 Cosmic Principles of Sankhya Yoga, called *Tattvas,* this system is meant to be a map of all the existing stations of existence that will help the inward moving soul to see clearly the makeup of the Mind's many projections. The totality of it is termed Nature in its manifested and unmanifested forms. Western philosophy does not really account for unmanifested prakriti, and so has not idea of where all manifestations come from — from subtle seed form in the Cosmic Mind of God.

Avinashi from Pennsylvania writes:
QUESTION: "As you said to me in reply to a query a few weeks ago, the body has some prana, as evidenced by how the hair and nails continue to grow after death. But in the absence of the antahkaranic soul, the organs cannot carry out the higher, biological functions by which waste is cast out from the body, and the part that goes to sustain the body which is integrated into the organism's tissues. These are clearly evidences of the antahkarana's higher, integrating, and purpose-driven functioning, since without that the material body becomes incapable of the sophisticated functional symphony that contemporary science marvels at, wrongly placing the ability for such functioning in the body itself. Hair-splitting aside, what the ancient sages said indeed appears to be true, then: the body has no life in itself, at least if we're talking about higher, more complex functions. For me, to see this clearly is a basic aspect of spiritual life called discrimination, (viveka). But in order to completely break identification with the physical body, I need to be able to lucidly grasp the fact that it doesn't even extract or produce, from food, the bio-energy so necessary to its own livingness. The dynamisms of the antahkarana are needed to extract the raw prana from food and — using the material organism as a tool no doubt — turn that basic prana into nerve energy, and also into the still finer vital energy which replenishes the pranamayakosha. The body, by itself, doesn't and can't do any of this. So what I'd like to clearly understand is how the prana in food is transformed into the higher, finer forms of life-energy alluded to just above. Are chakras somehow involved in the transformation of the mukhya-prana in food into forms of energy important to the physical sheath and the pranamayakosha?

If this is so, what can be said, if anything, about the way the chakras do this? I understand the importance of offering food and that, without offering it, most of the raw prana in food is likely to remain unextracted and untransformed; but my question does not revolve around this. I want to understand how processes of the antahkarana and chakras function to transform the mukhya-prana into forms of life-energy utilizable by the nerves and the pranamayakosha."

ANSWER: I have left both the content of your question(s), and the length, intact, as both the subject, as well as your own knowledge expressed, are worthy of study and response.

First of all, I would offer that the chakras are not so much centers of transformation or refinement, but are more certainly realms of Consciousness in their own right. What you are seeking, I assume, is what takes place before they are reached by the inward ascending soul, and what occurs in the interim of arrival there. The mention of both prana and psychic prana by Swami Vivekananda in his book on Raja Yoga infer that there is a shift of quality that energy undergoes as it moves inwards towards higher centers, or "lotuses." But just as science and biology cannot really visually detect or actually see the conversion of food matter into energy, and only assume it based upon the physical organism's overall health or lack thereof, in the same way it is even more difficult to perceive prana and its subsequent shift and refinement into mukhya prana, what to speak of into psychic prana. Some things we need to merely accept and let happen. For instance, it is probably the case that we should have left the physical atom untampered with, just allowed to do its work naturally, and refrained from splitting it — at least until the atoms of our Consciousness, called *jnana matras*, which are particles and flows of Intelligence (buddhi/buddha/awakened), were gathered and rendered effectively operative in life.

What would come into focus and clarity, then, in terms of knowledge of subtle energy, is that first, it exists, and second, that it can be gathered, centered, and utilized to live a divine life. A divine life would not be nearly as possible without good health. There are already so many things that impede dharmic life and living; ill health is not needed on top of all of those. It will be quite enough to know that once health is mastered — like the yogis have done — that mukhya prana is then upon them, and they can begin the refinement process called sublimation of energy that results in the emergence and control of the psychic prana. In short, it is much like saying "Atman exists," even though we do not see It. Just so, energy exists — physical prana, mukhya prana, and psychic prana — but it will not be of much help to us to know this until we subject each level of it to refinement and feel its effects — on our bodies, our senses, our minds, and especially, in our dharmically-based lives.

Further of note, and next in line, is that sadhana, rare and specialized spiritual exercises, do the refining; they are the powers of sublimation. The effects of such subtle inward exposure show on the features of the yogi, make themselves known in the words of the yogi, and even emanate off of the very body and being of the yogi. Ask him how this happens and he will say, "through long and dedicated practice."

Recently, at the SRV ashramas on the West Coast, we revisited Holy Mother's story about the rancher who once carried a newborn calf from the barn to the field so that it could graze. The two came to love one another, so the man continued to carry the calf to and fro, even after it had developed strong legs of its own. A few years later, a visitor to the ranch was amazed to see a man carrying a 500 pound bull to the nearby field. Approaching the rancher, he asked, 'How is this possible? How did you come to be able to lift such a weight? The rancher answered, 'A little at a time.' Just so, the yogi accomplishes seemingly impossible feats, both inner and outer, via mastering all levels of prana over time. But he is not as interested in how the process works as much as in accomplishing it and putting it to work for the highest aims and ends.

I realize that what is offered here may not be entirely satisfying. Light may be shed in this manner, but the entire realm will not get entirely lit up. Such is the nature of inward principles. It is only once they are realized within us that we understand more fully. We do not get to actually see the growth of that bull that we are carrying; we only know that it can be lifted and transported here and there. The workings of the secrets of prana are just that — secrets. What can be gathered and communicated about it has been done, no doubt, spread among the seekers of esoteric wisdom, but precious little of it finds it way to the masses or to beginning seekers, even in the scriptures. It is no wonder that the West is almost entirely ignorant of both the presence of prana and its workings.

Filling in the gaps in our awareness around this most important subject of prana will lead to that singular phenomena of its actual appearance and experience. In the interim, who knows, but that the actual dynamics of the process, with all its many subtleties, may become revealed to us — all by the Grace of the Divine Mother of the Universe whose existence and energy all forms of prana belongs to.

Tadrupa from Oregon writes:
QUESTION: "How can one tell when pratyahara is obtained?"
ANSWER: A two part answer can be given, though there are other signs as well. First, the mind will not, does not, want to drift back to its old ways of thinking and acting. It is not a matter of trying to keep the mind away from objects, at that point, but rather a natural ease with the precepts of not owning, not having, not coveting, not desiring, and even thinking of nothing. That "nothing" is God, Brahman, and that is the second sign — that the soul does not seek after nor crave for forms anymore, but looks ahead to the vision of the Divine Beloved whose Presence causes every other thing in the world to pale to insignificance in comparison. As one beautiful bhajan in India puts it, *"Beholding That, man is bewitched for evermore; No other form can he enjoy."*

Pratyahara, successfully withdrawing the mind from objects, both external and internal, is the fifth limb of Yoga. It is attempted after the prana is controlled, and is mastered prior to full concentration. It is positioned there as if to test the soul's strength and resolve around renouncing the world of maya.

On one hand, its attainment vaults the practitioner into Yoga proper, but on the other, it is a stumbling block for most beings — mainly among the rare few who attempt navigating the superlative path towards Enlightenment. As the Upanisads state, *"Sharp as a razor's edge is the spiritual path, and difficult to tread. So say the wise...."*

QUESTION #2: "You have said in a conversation over a meal that japa alone is enough to obtain realization of the Personal God. Can you explain what is missing from this experience that makes someone fully realized? Would such a partially realized soul be fearless and have mature renunciation?"

ANSWER: Holy Mother, Sri Sarada Devi, also called *"Japa Siddhini"* — She who is perfect in the art of mantra and japa — has told us: *"Japa, being a practice, will not bring about full realization. It is a means to an end, and is one of the best means available to us."* "Full realization," here, means the nondual state of samadhi, specifically, Nirvikalpa, also termed Nirvana. The practice of japa brings the soul to a one-pointed state of mind, similar to what Yoga calls *"Ekagra."* It has been described as a way to take all the waves *(vrittis)* of the mind and to collect and render them into one mighty wave. That massive mind-wave is *Ishvara,* one's chosen Ideal in form. Thus, japa's aim and end is to settle the mind and help it gain the vision of the Cosmic Form. For entering into Formless Reality, however, *Brahman,* and its state called *Nirvikalpa — Asamprajnata* in Yoga — one will need to take that one-pointed mind attained through japa practice and enter into transcendence, what Advaita Vedanta refers to as *Turiya,* or what Yoga calls the *Niruddha* state of mind (or "no mind").

The reader may kindly look at the chart on the facing page entitled, "The Five States of the Mind-Field in Yoga," for a more complete rendering of this teaching by Lord Patanjali. Sri Krishna's "mini-manual for mind-control" can also be studied there.

Taking up your final question above, total fearlessness will not be available to a soul who has not gotten the upper four limbs of Yoga mastered. Some degree of boldness and courage may be present, however, and with that the soul can make its way to finally claim outright fearlessness — *abhayam.* Thus, the absence of fear that makes mature renunciation possible is itself made possible of attainment via following the yogic course of sadhana, step by step, limb by limb. As Sri Ramchandra has put it, *"Enlightenment dawns on the mind by stages."*

QUESTION #3: "In sutra 4:1, does 'utilizing abilities from past lives' mean sadhana learned in a previous life?"

ANSWER: Yes; the two equate. You see, previously, a positive samskara got formed in a past lifetime around spiritual abilities due to practice of sadhana. That is why some are born with these abilities, to greater or lesser degree, and others still need to enter a religious and spiritual path and pursue them in the present life. It is the same with all abilities, not just spiritual ones.

But higher Wisdom *(paravidya)* is rare, while lower or relative knowledge *(aparavidya)* is somewhat common. There are very few seers and sages around, but quite a few intellectuals. Unfortunately, there are hosts of human

# The Five States of the Mind-Field In Yoga

*"Like seeds fallen even briefly into the fire, thus losing their generative power, the first three states of the mind-field are worthless for gaining samadhi. They are scarcely worthy of detailed mention and are not fit to be included in the category of Yoga, since Yoga is Samadhi."*   Vyasa

| | | |
|---|---|---|
| I.   Kshipta – Disturbed | Continually agitated<br>Completely unsteady<br>Dominated by rajas | Lost among objects<br>Average waking state<br>of a normal person |
| II.  Mudha – Lethargic | State of dull stupor<br>Steeped in stagnation<br>Dominated by tamas | As in states such as<br>comatose, inebriation,<br>drug-affliction, etc. |
| III. Vikshipta – Distracted | Experiences balance<br>Stripped of balance<br>Drawn away by habit | Gives rise to the 9<br>vikshepas such as<br>disease, doubt, etc. |
| IV.  Ekagra – One-Pointed | Samprajnata state<br>Illumines all wisdom<br>Removes impurities | Loosens karma's hold<br>Leads to full control<br>Gives pure perception |
| V.   Niruddha – Absorbed | Asamprajnata state<br>Full control of vrittis<br>Karmas nullified | Confers paravairagya<br>Only samskaras of<br>samadhi persist |

## Bhagavad Gita's Mini-Manual for Mind Control

*"Constantly engaging in resolute practice, the yogi who has fully calmed the mind and purified the senses attains with ease the infinite bliss of intimate contact with Brahman."*   Sri Krishna

*Sankalpa prabhavan kamams tyaktva sarvan asheshatah*
"Abandon, without reserve, all desires born of sankalpa."

*Manasai've'ndriya gramam viniyamya samantatah*
"Utilize the mind to curb and control the senses."

*Shamaih-shanair uparamed buddhya dhrtigrhitaya*
"Settling the intellect, strive to attain peace by degrees."

*Atmasamstham manah krtva na kimchid api chintayet*
"Thinking of nothing else, focus the mind on the Self."

*Yato-yato nischarati manash chanchalam asthiram
   tatas-tato niyamyai'tad atmany eva vasham nayet*
"By whatever reason or means the fluctuating mind may wander,
   call it back and fix it solely on Self."

beings that possess and utilize neither calling yet, and so the quest for learning goes on. As Sri Krishna states in the Bhagavad Gita, *"Knowledge is the best of all purifiers."*

R.O. from Hawaii writes:
QUESTION: "In your last talk at the Honoka'a Ashram you spoke extensively about the kundalini, and Swami Vivekananda's emphasis on it in his book, Raja Yoga. In Vivekananda's book, I seem to recall a statement that no spiritual progress can be made without it. Therefore, would you explain exactly what kundalini is? It seems to be a term that is used (or misused) quite freely with the assumption that everyone knows what it is. Its definition appears to vary with the person or group using it. For example, in our western popular culture, kundalini seems to be associated with the sexual energy."
ANSWER: The Kundalini Yoga system is one shared by all the darshanas of India in one way or another. In Tantra, it is prominent. In Vedanta, it is present. In Ashtanga Yoga it is rare of mention but crucial to the process. Suffice to say that It/She pervades all of them, and all of India.

    Kundalini is a major name for the Divine Mother of the Universe in Her most subtle and powerful form. "Who" She is must be explored by Her dedicated acolyte. But you ask "what" She is. If we take the impersonal approach, which is fine, we could call Her the "dynamic energy of Brahman." A snake sits still, coiled up, then it suddenly wriggles across the ground. Kundalini is likened to the wriggling motion of that Brahman snake. Yes, She accomplishes everything in the Three Worlds, but Her real power and secret lies in spiritual transformation. The mystics and yogis say that Her force lies dormant at the base of the "spine,' in the subtle *"chakra"* that is involved there. There are seven (six others) of these subtle centers in toto, popularly and metaphorically called "lotuses," and when the time is right, circumstances are ready, and karmas and other impediments have been neutralized, then She begins Her rise to these respectively subtler and subtler lotuses. The intoxicating effect of this inner movement brings profound peace, upsurges of bliss, the birth of higher wisdom, and the ability to merge, more and more, with the Atman/Brahman — called *Paramasiva* in Tantra. She is the *Chiti-shakti* in Yoga, mentioned by Patanjali. At the end of his life he was supposed to have been swallowed by a huge snake, symbolizing his merging into Kundalini.

    As far as Kundalini Shakti's relation with all manner of skewed, surface associations, and the ignorant overlays in this day and age, that is indeed the fault of insincere and sensationalist mystery-mongerers. The popular influence in the West with regard to the Divine Mother is not even a movement; the religious savant or tantric priest would be hard put to even grace it with the title of "cult." Tantra, for surface dabblers in the occult, consists of only two of some 48 esoteric practices. Those two they have prematurely settled on are 1) the taking of intoxicants, and 2) engaging in sexuality. Ironically, these two practices are precisely what Sri Ramakrishna, the consummate Tantric adept of this age, avoided in his tantric disciplines, sending a message to both sensationalists and sensualists that to court authentic shakti power and beckon Kundalini inwards to higher centers of Awareness is not accomplished by intoxicating the body/mind mechanism or engaging in pleasurable pastimes; far from it! Austerities demanding great strength and the building of character are prerequisites for Her Grace. As Ramprasad Sen sings in one of his tantric hymns of enlightenment, *"She does not accept cheap bribes...."*

For more on the Kundalini Yoga system, the recent book entitled *Reclaiming Kundalini Yoga,* by SRV Associations, is a good read, a swift study, and provides essentials about the pathway that allows for safe and deep practice and attainment of its tenets. Of course, a guru, or spiritual preceptor, is required for this, as for any authentic darshana, so as to avoid mistakes and misrepresentations — the kind described above, committed by those who have not qualified themselves by deep and long lasting study in the tradition, fortified by decades, even lifetimes, of deep meditation and devout worship.

## Pada IV, Sutra 3

*nimittam aprayojakan prakritinam varannabhedastu tatah kshetrikavat (nimittam,* cause; *aprayojakam,* not leading to action; *prakritinam,* subtle nature; *varana,* impediments; *bhedas,* overcoming; *tu,* instead; *tatah,* that; *kshetrikavat,* as a farmer).

*"Good acts do not remove the subtle causes found in nature, but do help overcome them — much like a farmer breaks down barriers to allow water into his field."*

The metaphor of the farmer was one of Sri Ramakrishna's favorite stories about sadhana, and the illusion of transformation. Whether this sutra inspired that story, or it was brought about through Patanjali by the Great Master's earlier incarnations, Ram and Krishna, makes for good contemplation. Nevertheless, the meaning of the sutra is obviously clear to all four of them.

But it probably is not at all clear to the bulk of humanity. The idea of doing good, and that it will make any real change in the world, persists in the minds of the unillumined. In truth, there is actually no such thing as real change, or *"real modification;"* there is only *"progressive manifestation by unreal superimposition,"* as Vivekananda stated. Declaring the existence of a "good world" is tantamount to saying "hot ice," he once quipped. *"Envolution and Involution take place only in show."* With the five koshas or upadhis covering them, and remaining confused by their ongoing cycles of change, mankind scarcely perceives the static and immovable, all-pervasive Self (Atman) that is independent of them. He clings to his individuality as if it were the only reality.

And this delusion of his is fortified further by the call to action that family, friends, society, and his own ego foist upon him (see forthcoming sutra and its commentary). It is neither good action *(karma),* nor bad action *(vikarma),* nor a combination of both, that has any actual effect — positive, negative, or mixed — on life and the world. Knowing this, the wise move surely and swiftly towards learning the art of inaction *(akarma)* as if it were the sole savior from all the vagaries and vicissitudes of the world and maya. Having attained to it (*"He who sees inaction in action, and action in inaction, he truly knows karma"*), they return to the world of activities and effect the only lasting and beneficial transformation that can be had here — the transformation of the mind towards transcendence. *"They act out of nonattachment, desirous of the higher guidance of the multitudes,"* states Sri Krishna.

And what does that nonattachment consist of? The knowledge that *"....the Lord does not create agency or action for the world and living beings, nor union with the fruits of good and bad actions; nature does all that."* Lack of knowledge and acceptance of this spiritual law causes *"vain hopes, vain actions, and vain knowledge,"* in most of humanity, and the *"inability to develop discrimination"* even over time — even over many lifetimes.

And so, with the help of Sri Krishna's teachings, light gets shed on sutra IV:3 of Patanjala. But Patanjali's way of teaching suits more the age he was living in, and the problems that were more evident all around him at that time (see the chart on the Nine *Antarayas/Vikshepas* on page 302 of Volume I). To him it is all a matter of practicality, of simply studying inwardly and meditating to perceive the natural laws of karma with regards to the universe, and then adjusting accordingly. There is no angry God or devious Devil looking on to judge. As one perceives, so one attains; as one envisions, so one realizes.

The real problem today, however — close to two millennia later — is that few are disposed to look within and find the cosmic laws that dictate outcomes in relativity, what to speak of even believing in interior worlds and subtler causes in the first place. Science, medicine, biology, archeology, and other modern modes of learning *(aparavidya)* focus upon and accept only the physical universe. It is doubtful whether even today's religion, overall, really takes subtle and causal realms to be literal, what with their penchant for and accent upon lands, money, domination, and occult leanings.

And in that regard, and for those who still do believe in a divine providence, good acts lead to heaven. But Jesus, Buddha, Krishna, and other perfect souls were not indicating heaven as the final resting place of man, but rather pointing to the transcendent Reality beyond all worlds of name and form, no matter how sublime they may be or seem. As Swami Vivekananda has revealed, good acts are a gold chain and bad acts are an iron chain. Both must be struck off in order that the *"Peace that passeth all understanding,"* along with That which is beyond all dualities, be attained. We must all become like farmers, then, at least as long as we sport upadhis and desire to play in the fields of the Lord. And it is in such play that the yogis take care and remain aware of the various facets and functions of the mental complex.

## Pada IV, Sutra 4
*nirmanna chittani asmita matrat (nirmanna,* mental projection; *chitta,* mind and its thought; *asmita,* ego; *matra,* unit).

*"From the ego springs mind and its thought, which produce all projected things."*

The *antahkarana,* the fourfold composite of dual mind, thought, intelligence, and ego, is the actual hub of what religion calls creationism, and what science thinks of as the evolutionary process. In other words, the physical universe — so coveted by the earthbound souls — has originated from a mass of profuse thought that has mind as its basis, intelligence as its power, and ego as its agent. This apparatus is both individual and collective. If the Cosmic Mind is counted, as it should be, this is a fivefold package, and thus follows by way of the famous quintuplication process (*panchakarana*).

This mental conglomerate holds another quintuplication, a fivefold impediment (kleshas) that rails against its freedom. Egoism (asmita) is a foremost member of these. Patanjali points to it in this sutra. The ego, situating itself in relativity based upon its own connate ignorance (avidya), will then swiftly bind itself with a host of attractions and aversions (ragadveshau). A deeper level of bondage then sets in over time due to the burgeoning of fear with regard to losing its attachments and facing its demise (abhinivesha). Thus, the five kleshas, already taken up earlier in the sutras, assumes its insinuating operations. The reader is asked to find and study the chart, "The Insinuation of the Five Kleshas on Spiritual Life," (Volume 1, page 143) again. In addition to teachings on the traditional five, a contemporary list of kleshas is also given at the bottom — a gift of the SRV sangha that was gathered at an Raja Yoga retreat in the recent past. For additional information on this potentially troublesome quintuplication, students can also look back at the chart, "Stages of Dissolution of the Mind in Yoga" (Volume I, page 310).

In sutras to be taken up in forthcoming lessons, Patanjali states that the Original Mind is the controller of all other ego-mind mechanisms. And of all the thoughts pumped out continuously by various ego-mind complexes, it is only the Original Mind that projects them free of desire. The mind and its control — or lack thereof — will be the emphasis of lesson #91, which is yet to come.

## Lesson Ninety-one 10/15/14
### Pada IV, Sutras 5 & 6

Sutras IV:5, and IV:6 continue on with the sweet affirmation of the truth that mind is the projector of all phenomena, and of itself as well. The one, Original Mind, or, "OM," as we like to refer to it, directs all other minds at play within this set of worlds and lokas — all of them being projections of Mind overall. When the yogi finds out that two principles are being manipulated all the time, namely, thought power and nature, he swiftly realizes that he is the manipulator and, with his mind already purified by yoga sadhana, becomes a rare boon of blessing on all beings in the Three Worlds.

In response to questions around this broad and diverse topic, and other specific subjects inside of authentic yogic practice, the questions below can be studied:

## Questions and Answers for Lesson 91

Tadrupa from Oregon writes:

QUESTION: "Is pranayama both an obtainment and a practice? Does it culminate in one becoming trigunatita?"

ANSWER: Obtaining control over the prana is a primary and initial directive of Yoga, but possession of the prana for personal gains or manipulation of forces is never the yogi's aim. He first wants freedom — from nature, maya, rebirth, from limitation in general — then he seeks the freedom of others. There are other elements which may figure into the quotient along the way, but these two form the essential aim and end.

Transcendence of the three gunas, trigunatita, will be one of the last and more difficult of attainments that fall within the scope of his rare and unconventional path. In the beginning, when he was scarcely aware of the prana (in the case of a newly awakened soul), his practice necessitated bringing it to the fore where it could be studied, like in meditation. As the prana became more and more under his control, it opened onto vistas that were transcendent of food energy, health, feelings, elation, and the like, and introduced him to the realm of the mind and its thoughts — not as an intellectual or a scientist might see them — but pointing instead toward the source of their origins, called utpatti.

And this is where the thinker falls behind the pace of the visionary, where the physicist trails far behind the abilities of the seer. Further, this is what really defines the difference between inner life and external existence., i.e., that discovery of an inward moving power that both unveils the subtle worlds within the soul, and confers wings with which to explore them as well.

Thus, prana is the Garuda, the mystical dragon bird of Indian mythology that carries the soul to places that are completely different than planets floating in a physical ether in outer space. What person in their right mind would want to travel out there, where life is reduced to some mere three elements instead of five? What about the subtle elements, called Tanmatras? One should transcend the need to drink and breathe and go inside to explore them.

And so, the connection between the prana and the tanmatras gets revealed, which according to Swami Vivekananda are the two important areas that remain completely undiscovered and unexplored to the Western mind, maybe even the contemporary human mind of this day and age in general.

QUESTION #2: "Other than awareness of the following: the cosmic significance of prana as described by Swamiji, the sublimation process of prana into shakti power, and informed control of the breath (important sets of threes), what is required of the aspirant for obtaining or practicing pranayama?"

ANSWER: The answer is, another set of threes, and one that is greatly missing today in spiritual circles, and in the hearts and minds of aspirants. First, a good teacher; second, unswerving devotion to the teacher; and third, unflagging commitment to the spiritual path. As Sri Sarada Devi told us, in and by Her own experience, that if the aspirant does not secure an illumined teacher, and then look upon that teacher as God, and follow the instructions of said teacher to the letter, then no appreciable progress along the spiritual path can ever be made.

So many souls are trying to navigate the spiritual path on their own. This is usually due to either arrogance or naivete. The Vedas state, *"Arise, awake, and stop not 'til the goal is reached. Approach the wise teachers and learn from them. For, sharp as a razor's edge is the spiritual path, and difficult to navigate. So say the wise."*

Then there is the case, which we see so often nowadays in the West, after several generations of gurus have come from the East. This is the case of good people following bad gurus. Many of these opportunists and spiritual marketeers have passed away, leaving some small followings here and there. Based on starts that were grounded in inferior principles such as hatha yoga, seeking occult powers, seeking fame, mere health, and prosperity devoid of knowledge of the dharmic teachings, etc., their students are trying to make progress. But one sees them falling into pathways that are, at best, only service oriented, and otherwise, desirous of power and money.

So any practice, pranayama included (and maybe most of all), must be subjected to the inspection of a spiritual master, not a pretender. How to find Them? Four criterion are given in the tradition for an authentic guru. The West needs to know them.

QUESTION #3: "How is dharana even possible if one practices the dual focus of heart center, and prana in the brain, during meditation, as given in the Gita? This seems like multi-tasking, not concentration."

ANSWER: The yogi is the "master multi-tasker," but, as they say, "Don't try this at home, kids." But that aside for now, when we refer to the teaching in the Gita that states, *"...all the gateways of the body closed, engaged in firm Yoga, having fixed the life-force in the heart, with the mind confined within the head, uttering the single syllabled OM, then think on Me alone,"* we have to consider that this advice is being given for advanced souls who, besides having decades, even lifetimes, of practice behind them, are also about to leave the body for the final time — *"the time the yogis depart, never to return again."* This practice, if it can even be called that at this stage, is all oneness. Such a soul has long since opened the necessary channels that the prana will course along to reach the heart center, and has meditated, as well, on the subtler passages, nadis, that allow refined shakti power to enter into the "head," the three inmost lotuses. So, dharana at the outset of practice, and dharana already commingled with meditation and samadhi, are two vastly different things.

QUESTION #4: "At the end of Raja Yoga #6, Annapurna commented that, 'Pratyahara, through the facility of dharana, concentration, is the disconnection – the withdrawal of the mind from the senses, as also the sense from their objects.' Is it then to be understood that pratyahara is only possible through dharana? If so, is the converse true as well, that is, dharana is only possible through pratyahara? Thus, these two limbs go together in parallel or as a co-dependant pair?"

ANSWER: This is a good way of thinking about it. Real spiritual advancement is seldom made by following the strictly orthodox way alone; there must always be originality and spontaneity mixed in. And, of course, it all depends on the soul who is taking up the practice of Yoga. For those masterful souls who have long ago abandoned the basic machinery of the eight limbs, and then need to don it again, like a suit of armor, for them, the limb of dharana tackles pratyahara and renders it subservient to all that is demanded by the yogi. Others, less proficient, have still to gain the mind's assent and ability to become one-pointed. For certain, however, is the fact that once the state of ekagra, one-pointedness, is gained, the soul will never again want to descend into that field of restlessness and chaos that once characterized its life and, at that time, and knowing nothing better, seemed the only way in which to live to it. So it is best — if one can adeptly mount the mental asana for it — to somehow start with the resistant mind and convince it of the desirability of freeing itself from habitual connections that are, as of yet, contrary to its highest good, i.e., connections and relationships with the as yet erratic senses and the insentient objects.

QUESTION #5: "How should the beginning sadhaka take up the practice of pratyahara?"

ANSWER: With a teacher who brought him/her into the practice of yoga by first mastering the yamas and the niyamas. Too many try to jump to higher limbs devoid of such mastery.

QUESTION #6: "What is the different between raja yoga and buddhi yoga?

ANSWER: Their aims are nondistinct. They both court Original Mind, OM. In the Bhagavad Gita, Sri Krishna teaches the four yogas in one of its earliest forms. There, the jnana yoga is called "buddhi yoga." In contemporary times, Holy Mother Sri Sarada Devi, taught us buddhi yoga too. This yoga, whatever one titles it, is mainly about control of the mind via discriminatory wisdom. It is used to destroy the ignorance-born darkness that enters the soul unasked, rendering it a victim of unnecessary sufferings and the many ignoble states of lower mind.

QUESTION #7: "In earlier commentary, the superconscious state is described via the quote from Yoga Vasishtha, '....a mind that is dissolved but simultaneously maintains its spiritual element.' It terms of the dissolution of the mindstream process, does this mean that all the tattvas have been dissolved up to the mind, with the atman shining through the pure intellect? So basically we have only atman, intellect, and mind remaining?"

ANSWER: Actually, up and "through" the mind, since the mind, too, gets dissolved. *"Pure Mind is God,"* as Sri Ramakrishna said, so it cannot be counted as a tattva, or as mind per se. The intelligence that remains, as well, is not the intellect, but particles of shining sentience that are the natural sheen off of the Atman. Ironically, then, when Ramprasad sings his famous song, the line of which goes, *"Oh Wisdom Mother, drive me completely out of my mind,"* he is indicating this all natural condition that is free of gross mind — at least as far as it is conventionally seen. The Upanisads get on board with this idea too, when they quote: *"....that which is beyond the mind, but by which the mind perceives...."*

Other than that, yes, all the tattvas are gone. "Gone" means they do not impede the soul any longer, being seen by the yogi as empty of real substance, as insentient, as projections of the dual mind, and thus being returned to the cosmic ignorance (the gunas) from which they sprang.

QUESTION #8: "What is the difference between ekagra and nirudha? What barriers are overcome in progressing from the former to the latter?"

ANSWER: That is a good question, and one that beggars description, as they say. The difference is very subtle, but perhaps can be described by citing the exquisite distinction between the seeded samadhis of bliss and ripe ego (*sasmita* and *sananda*), and the unseeded Samadhi called *Asamprajnata*. In other words, seeing superlative forms, or going beyond perception of all forms — that is the difference.

As far as the "barriers" that are encountered and overcome when this subtle shift transpires, they are tiny ones, to be sure. But sometimes the smallest things are the hardest to see, thus the most difficult to surmount. For the soul seeking absolute Union with Divine Reality, transcendence of form (at that blissful level) is a considerable challenge. In Kundalini speak, it would equate to moving from the *Ajna Chakra* to the *Sahasrara Chakra* at will. But there is a practically imperceptible veil, called *Rudra Granthi,* between them,. and that is seldom pierced through, even by spiritually adept souls.. In the end, it all goes to show again, that attachment to bliss, on any level, is a significant impediment to the main Goal of Yoga.

QUESTION #9: "Can one be in the natural functioning state of mind during the waking state? Is this state beyond words?"

ANSWER: The waking state and the "natural functioning state of mind" are one and the same to a luminary. You see, embodied beings have come to accept the unreal as being real, to quote from the Vedanta, so they are born thinking themselves to be the body/mind mechanism. The seer never accepted this, never fell into this misconception, on any level — cosmic, collective, or individual. The Witness Consciousness is always intact in the seer's case, and so he sees the ego, or transmigrating soul, moving from place to place as in a dream. His mantra has always been, *"From dreams awake, from bonds be free,"* and so he watches souls play in the fields of the Lord (*karmashaya,* or the mind-field), trying to help them when they are ready to awaken. It is they who have taken on the fourfold mind (*antahkarana,* the fourfold cause of relative existence) in earnest, not he. He lives in Original Mind — OM. And when he himself works through the antahkarana, the mind has already been made single, the thoughts are pure and motiveless, the intellect is honed, and the ego is ripe.

Admittedly, from the ordinary mind's state, where embodiment seems so real and life is The Thing, we could say that it is the purpose of one's spiritual life to attempt to render the dual mind singular in order that our waking state become illumined. For if the waking state, where all karmas are formed, gets lit up, then so will the dream state. If the dream state becomes translucent, then the curtain of nescience which veils the wonders of the deep sleep state from view will thin out, and the soul will begin to move more freely, having swift and open concourse with the real Self, our Soul, the Atman. In some spiritual circles this is described as usurping the ego and placing God/Self back on It's rightful throne.

QUESTION #10: "Would the types of insights that scientists and mathematicians get when completely absorbed and self-obsessed in their work be an example of the lowest type of wisdom samadhi?"

ANSWER: Yes, I would say so — as long as we define the term "self-obsessed" as concentration rather than as ego obsession with "name and fame and gain." Anyone who loses the sense of self in deep concentration is experiencing a rare state of mind, a samadhi, if you will. The difference between the intellectual man or woman's samadhi, and the samadhi of the luminaries, then, is that the luminary catches the mind going into that rare state and observes the marvelous shift, whereas all others get hypnotized by it and only observe what they are concentrating upon.

In short, it is not, say, the intricate atomic particle and its properties that is the most amazing thing; it is the Consciousness that looks on. For inside of that sublime Awareness, everything that amazes, attracts, reveals, and galvanizes the human mind, resides in full.


Akshaya Bhakti from New England writes:

COMMENTS: "I appreciate Pada IV a lot, along with the questions/answers that accompany it. I really like the reminder of the lesson/story about the cowboy and the bull, which is so encouraging. It says that we may not feel our spiritual growth at the moment, but it is happening nonetheless. Especially, I like going back to study the mind complex! I remember Swamiji discussing early on how 'the powers of the mind should be concentrated and turned back upon itself.' But when practicing involution of the 24 Cosmic Principles, or the Sequence of Causality, Origins, & Reincarnation, I still feel stymied when I reach the level of the mind."

QUESTION: "Any help as to how to best navigate this intricate terrain would be welcome. What steps of contemplation could be taken — such as we had received for the 5 elements — since it's been so long since we first studied the 4-fold mind.? Could you please review the distinctions of its four aspects, dear teacher? I do understand these divisions are in this case, 'a very refined & sophisticated tool for the mind to cope with reality,' if I may borrow Dirk's apt description in Lesson 90, when he was discussing other categories. Is there one of your intensive charts available just for the Antahkarana? That would be perfect!"

ANSWER: In lesson #61, page 64, in the chart titled, "The Process of Samprajnata and Asamprajnata Samadhi," the antahkarana is shown, according to Yoga.

As a general guide, to begin, we must take the mind apart and meditate upon its four aspects, namely, the dual mind itself, its thoughts, its intelligence, and the ego component that resides within it. Each of these, when well contemplated in silence, and after a divine atmosphere has been established, will offer up a huge amount of insight. Many would say, regarding this process: "I learned a lot about myself today;" but this is only the therapy perspective, used for healing, etc. On the other hand, the spiritual aspirant would aver that this type of inward study really reveals all that is the nonself. Do you see the difference — not just in definition, but in perspective? Human beings using conventional methods have already taken the mind to be real, even before they find that it is innately "unwell." In other words, the mind is not just full of complexes, as the psychologists and therapists would say, it *Is* a huge complex itself. It is the wily projector of illness, healing, and healer — all three. Knowing it to be so, the wise soul would begin to transcend it, part by part (the "fourfold" antahkarana). Thus, we engage in this inward act of dissembling the projector to find out how it works (karana/cause). So, look into the four portions of mind to see 1) how it operates; 2) where its origin is; 3) relatedly, to see if it is eternal or has an end. This is explained well in the chart, "Yogic Correlations and Connections in Meditation Practice," shown back on page 269. Besides the connections, one can see at the bottom of the chart all the modes the meditator is to utilize on each aspect under study.

As for another chart that would be helpful, and more towards the obstacles one may encounter in this deep, comprehensive, and exhaustive (but not exhausting!) search, I will place on the following page the chart, "Some Obstacles and Solutions in Spiritual Life" for your perusal and study.

QUESTION #2: "While 'inaction in action' has finally started to make more sense to me after suddenly connecting it with what the guru has always taught, how can my Real Self go anywhere, how can I be born or die? I am not the doer. So how to grasp the concept of action in inaction? Could you please explain that to us again? What is the definition of action here?"

ANSWER: In short, what is wanted is action free of selfish motive, free of any motive at all, really. Since 1) all action takes place in nature, and 2) no action can ever change our Divine Nature, and 3) millions of actions cannot add one iota to Brahman, nor take one iota away from Brahman, then "action in inaction" is offered to the Lord (dwelling in humanity), by the Lord (who is the supreme sacrificer, *Adhiyajna*), and for the Lord (since Brahman is all that is).

Add to all of this, that the Atman is stable and motionless, everywhere at once, then one begins to get the idea that It is only present in the world of action to convince us to give up all action that is karma-bearing. That is why Sri Krishna states in the *Bhagavad Gita* that the renouncer should "*....give up all works*" other than those that are "*....scripturally ordained.*" He also gives ignorant beings a clue when he reveals the obvious fact of "*....wretched are the result seekers,*" To learn to "*....do all work as worship,*" and to "*....offer one's labor as love,*' as Vivekananda has stated it, is the secret to living a divine life in the body here on earth. In other words, all of it makes no difference at all when the soul is merged in oneness, or in deep meditation, or has passed out of the body, etc., but while in the body and subject to the world of time and space, it is impossible to refrain from works. Therefore, the seers tell us how — which is my favorite way of working — is to "Do all work in Wisdom." Put obversely, that means never do any act in ignorance, i.e., in restlessness (*rajas*) or sloth-

# Some Obstacles & Solutions in Spiritual Life

*"Pratibhasika is the illusory reality, and Pratibha is the intelligence which is developed and honed to bring about the power (pratibandhakabhava) to destroy it, outright, along with all the impediments (pratibandhakas) in the mind which restrict the naturally enlightened state of pure, conscious Awareness."*
— Babaji Bob Kindler

## Pratibandhakas – Obstacles | Pratibandhakabhavas – Solutions

### The Main Impeding Mental Vrittis

1. **Vishada-vritti** – Dull vibrations which cause despondency and dejection → **Pranayama-manana** – Conscious breathing accompanied by contemplation of scripture

2. **Vitarka-vritti** – Thoughts containing demonic vibrations which foster violence → **Indriya-nigraha-nirodha** – Control of the senses and restraint of negative thoughts

3. **Shushna-vritti** – Mental vibrations beset by falsehood and deceit, leading to suffering → **Yama-niyama** – Practice of the moral exercises and daily observances of Raja Yoga

4. **Vijatiya-vritti** – Turbulent and contrary vibrations which confuse and fluster the mind → **Darshana** – Keeping holy company with the guru, sangha, and other enlightened beings

5. **Kashaya-vritti** – Vibrations rising from residual impressions due to enjoyment of pleasure → **Pratyahara** – Practice of withdrawing the mind from thoughts of sense objects

6. **Manorajya-vritti** – Ungrounded vibrations which cause the mind's awareness to drift → **Dharana** – Focusing inward on the immediate nature of mind and awareness

7. **Chanchala-vritti** – Intermittent and inconsistent vibrations which cause gaps in awareness → **Dhyan-samadhi** – Meditation, without breaks, in order to realize the continuity of Awareness

### The Two Powers of Avarana Shakti

1. **Asadavarana** – The power of obscuration which covers the truth of Brahman → **Bhavanas** – Hearing, contemplating, and realizing the truth, which destroys all doubt

2. **Abhanavarana** – The power of obscuration which distracts the mind from Brahman via the manifestation of lesser lights. → **Aparokshanubhuti** – Direct and immediate spiritual experience gained via sadhana, meditation, and samadhi

### The Two Processes of the Mind

1. **Vikalpa** – The mind's unbridled tendency towards superficial fantasy and imagination → **Siddhanavakyashravana** – Guided study and right conclusion with regard to the scriptures

2. **Sankalpa** – The ego's improved shift towards more controlled and self-willed thinking → **Samskara-vinasha** – The destruction of subtle impressions of the mind via samadhi

*"Using spiritual disciplines, the aspirant after perfection destroys all mental obstacles, snaps the chain of rebirth, and attains freedom from suffering."* — Sri Ramakrishna Paramahamsa

fulness (*tamas*). Then there is *Peace, Peace, Peace* throughout.

Kanyakali from Hawaii writes:
QUESTION: "A new connection was brought to light for me recently during the Gita class in Hawaii, and now again in this Raja Yoga lesson, that 'All karma happens in nature.' I don't know why I hadn't made this connection before. It seems obvious now that I think about it. The Atman is perfect, inactive, and separate from Nature, so obviously whatever is active and leading the Atman toward recognition of its perfection, must therefore be in Nature. I often feel like karma is something that I'm carrying with me, almost as if it's some sort of possession or innate characteristic of mine that's so hard to get rid of. But making the simple realization that it is part of nature, and not part of the Soul, makes it easier for me to drop it. By making the further connection that karma is the cause of the Atman to make more bodies with which to associate, I started to wonder about its relation to the causal body, and whether Karma is more closely associated with the mind or with the causal body. Specifically, when dissolving the mind stream, at which point would I dissolve all karma — when the mind is dissolved, or when the Cosmic Mind (causation) is dissolved?"
ANSWER: Complete dissolution of all karma will only occur with the complete dissolution of the mind. That is, there is still karma, albeit very sattvic karma, at the level of Cosmic Mind, which is precisely why there exist teachings for special advanced souls that will lead them beyond the *Mahat* and into Nonduality. We must remember, as well, that it is possible, and extremely desirable (there is no other option for the luminaries) to live in the body on earth while being free of karma. That is the inscrutable state of the *jivanmukta*, the living liberated soul. It represents the highest ideal up for attainment for many advanced souls here on earth.

Other than that, there is the path of attenuation of karma that the sadhikas of this world tread, which, according to some Buddhist schools, is a three lifetime scenario — one to form the karma, another to recognize it and work it out, and a final lifetime to live free (some say that the third lifetime is the working out of the final vestiges of karma). And along those lines, you are right that key bits of Wisdom gotten from the guru and the scriptures, heard enough times so that on one occasion it really registers, provides the impetus to begin the struggle for freedom in earnest. Perhaps, then, this is that selfsame third lifetime wherein some of us are working out the last traces of karma

Suffice to say, that knowing by the words of a supreme soul like Sri Krishna, through the wisdom melodies of His own *Song of the Lord,* that "....*all action really takes place in nature, not in the Atman,"* is more than just a comfort for the philosopher, or a fine teaching for the dharmic practitioner. It is Truth brought into tangible vibration on the earth plane, and the sincere devotee rushes to put it into practice and reap the many transformative benefits of it, in total.

**Pada IV, Sutra 5**

*pravritti bhede prayojakam chitta ekam anekesha (pravritti,* activities; *bhede,* difference; *prayojakam,* to direct; *chitta,* thoughts; *ekam,* one; *anekesha,* numerous).

"*Though minds and their different activities are numerous, the one, Original Mind directs them all.*"

As a line from a well-known bhajan of India relates, "*All work belongs to You, Divine Mother, others only call it their own.*" This Original Mind, then — call it *Ishvara, Ishvari, Mahat, Hiranyagarbha,* Lord *Brahma,* or others — directs all activities, but from a detached witness standpoint. In Sankhya Yoga, that puissant Presence is called *Kutasthanitya,* the "Cohesive Substratum." By It's mere proximity all activity gets efficiently and effectively coordinated. And since "thought is father to the deed," this divine but detached Director manages everything, at the level of mind first, then all that manifests outwardly into various activities. Beings who forget this opulent Overseer fall repeatedly into a pit of delusion filled with divisive and demented tendencies called "I do all," "I shall possess that," "It is my knowledge," and other misguided assumptions. This type of conditioned ego does not go away at the time of death, but returns, with all its unresolved "baggage," in a series of other equally unsavory lifetimes

On the opposite end of this downwards spiral are those who acknowledge the supremacy of what is indicated by the seers as The Unseen Seer, The Unmoved Mover, The Inactive Agent, and by many other enigmatic but all-attracting epithets. Unlike their ego-bound counterparts, they are content, peaceful, luminous, and blissful. Being obedient to and aware of the benign decrees that shower out upon the worlds of name and form from "On High," this enlightened contingent of souls live in pure sattva, in profound mental balance, or they will not live at all in the body.

And, in keeping with the import of Patanjali's sutra above, the activities of these embodied spirits are 1) selflessly enacted for the highest good of all, and 2) always offered back to the Source from which they emanated. In this way do they benefit the worlds of living beings, from plants, animals, and humans, all the way up and through the realm of the ancestors, while remaining free of karmas that always spring from various selfish activities — as the next sutra reveals

**Pada IV, Sutra 6**

*tatra dhyana jam anasayam (tatra,* among these; *dhyana,* meditation; *jam,* birth; *anasayam,* free of past life conditionings).

"*Among these diverse sets of minds, only that one that is born of meditation is free of conditionings from past lives.*"

It is here that we find out the reason why luminaries are both who they are, and why they are the way they are. It is because they have lived contemplative lives previously, in their past existences. The way of dharmic and divine life has thus either lessened or completely removed those problematic mental tendencies called *samskaras,* the presence of which plague other souls taking on bodies in relativity. As Swami Vivekananda's commentary reads, *"Among the various chittas, that which is attained by Samadhi is desireless. Among all the various minds that we see in various men, only that mind which has attained to Samadhi, perfect concentration, is the highest. A man who has attained certain powers through medicines, or through words, or through mortifications, still has desires, but that man who has attained to Samadhi through concentration is alone free from all desires."*

In this sutra, then, the teaching of being "born of meditation," *dhyan jam,* provides a huge hint for the seeker of Enlightenment, and even for those who are looking for any real and beneficial happiness. Parents of contemporary times who start their children on the path of meditation from an early age, though few and far between, are giving their young charges the best that life can offer. It should be the first objective of all souls that embody on the physical plane, to seek within for the causes of their appearance in form, and to detect what samskaras are suggesting themselves in the mind, insinuating themselves early on, and especially, lurking within, just waiting, as it were, to spoil the finer aims and ends of human life and embodiment.

All beings are to help one another in this important undertaking once it is perceived. Otherwise, if samskaras are left unseen and undetected, untreated by spiritual techniques such as meditation, they will both burrow themselves deeper in the mindstuff *(chitta),* and join together with other impressions in the subconscious and unconscious mind to form *samskara skandhas* — a collection of complexes that work in conjunction with one another.

This is actually what we are seeing in action when unfortunate manifestations like retarded minds, or "challenged" minds, appear. They are neither "accidents," "mistakes," or "abberations of nature," and are certainly not "intended by God." They cannot even be attributed to what are called genetic flaws, though genetics play a part in their production on the physical level. In short, these types of minds are the result of *samskaras-skandhas* that formed in previous existences, and which were left untreated and unhealed over time until they surfaced, unfortuitously, in the previous life. Warning signs of their dangerous presence surface in the present lifetime as the manifestation of habitually slothful and restless minds, along with, of course, the onslaught of problems such as addiction, scattered mind, and evil tendencies. Modern medicine and contemporary western psychology team up together to try and treat these already well-imbedded "diseases" with pills and medicines that commonly only dull the mind further.

Yoga Science and Psychology is not necessarily best served by being used as a platform upon which to discuss matters of this type, since the higher aims of meditation and Samadhi form its main subject. Nevertheless, when matters regarding the human mind's fall from yogic equipoise are brought up, the ancient art form of samskaras needs to be presented — both for the reasons of revealing the cause of such unwanted tendencies, and for the purpose of drawing a externally-oriented world and chemically-conditioned and dependent culture back to the salient and salubrious solutions that Yoga has to offer.

# Lesson Ninety-two 11/26/14
## Pada IV, Sutras 7 & 8

As we penetrate deeper into the opening sutras of the fourth and final section of the Raja Yoga scripture, the subjects of desire, and the karmas and lasting mental impressions called samskaras, are taken up by the Father of Yoga. That nagging and age-old question as to why some beings suffer painful repercussions in life while others seem to escape these ignoble backlashes, comes clearer – all in accordance with the three types of karma – good, bad, and mixed. This is a key teaching that is indigenous to the fertile soil of the Eight-limbed Yoga, and with its clarifying impetus comes the will to neutralize karma altogether and live a life of uninterrupted Freedom. The questions that precede the sutras and their commentaries reflect both the state of fructifying karmas in humanity in these times, and the deep yearning for spiritual emancipation as well.

**Questions and Answers for Lesson 92**
R.O. from Hawaii writes:
QUESTION: "My question is regarding the last page of the RY Lesson where you show the list of impediments to spiritual growth. Might not some of these, e.g., like reaching Cosmic Mind, or becoming formless matter, or even attaining a siddhi (or two!) simply be stepping stones on the path?"
ANSWER: The possibility of what you suggest depends upon the quality of consciousness in the aspirant, in each individual seeker. At this level of practice, i.e., in the matter of obstacles to spiritual advancement, so many have fallen – not only from the Goal, but from the very practice of Yoga – and have even fallen from any and all religious seeking as well.

If I were to take up each of the potential impediments you list here, I would venture that no one in their right mind would ever want to "become" matter, manifest or unmanifested. Nor is it advised by the seers that the inward moving yogi ever merely "reach" the Cosmic Mind and go no further. Cosmic Mind, Mahat, is a very high station, and as an *alambana* (a subject of meditation) it offers up many beneficial insights upon being pondered. But just as you and I are not our minds, so too, God is not "His" Mind. You, I, and Brahman, are essentially all pure Consciousness. That is our Essence. The wise concentrate on such realizations.

In another way of saying, all stations that the yogi reaches and passes through have imperfections and blockages in them. Take for instance the ego, *ahamkara*. It is the cause *(kara)* for the sense of separate "I-ness" *(aham)*. It is responsible not only for the sense of ownership and agency in a person, but also for the sense of separation from God – an idea that is false in its very inception. *"The Jiva is Siva!."* *"This Self is Brahman."* Meditating upon the individual ego certainly offers up some clues about the limited nature of the human being on several levels, but one will have to avoid the many stumbling blocks present in that complex, as well as the stored karmas and subtle tendencies associated with it. This subject actually segues well into your next question, about the "Curtain of Nescience."

QUESTION #2: "Would you explain 'the Cloud of Unknowing.' I was wondering if this is the same as a medieval Christian meditation text with the same title?"

ANSWER: The term, "Cloud of Unknowing," as you refer to it, indicates a text on prayer that the 14th century monastic Christians used in Europe. I am using the term in conjunction with the phrase, "Curtain of Nescience" instead, to denote the formless background of the human mind that, until it is seen, covers over the human being's innate wisdom of Reality. The difference (and it should be well-noted) is that in Christianity at the time, the "cloud" symbolizes a place of self-surrender that the acolyte offers himself into. In other words, this sect believed that God cannot be known, so self-surrender is the only and best way. This is usually the way or method of any faith-based tradition.

But in India, in wisdom-based traditions, and as taught, for instance, in the *Srimad Bhagavatam,* the seeker of Truth is impeded by this subtle, even causal, obstacle, and must shear through it with the scissors of higher knowledge and self-effort. This is best applied in meditation after study of nondual scripture has been engaged in. Both ways have merit, and actually represent two stages of spiritual progress. That is, the individual's store of knowledge of God, or what one conceives of as Divine Reality, is always limited and subject to the human ego and its influence. Thus, self-surrender – *sharanagata* – is a good tool for transcending that. But one transcends limited knowledge only to find higher Wisdom. It is like going from a regimen of ethics and morality, to the jnana-infused realm of dharma.

And in fact, this is why most beings do not take to the dharma, the Truth, when they first hear it; so many are attracted, then fall away, blaming other reasons such as intellectualism, choosing a wrong path, the guru, non-preparedness. The final reason is usually the real cause. If the aspirant prepared him or herself in the vein of self-surrender, then, when next hearing the dharma teachings, they would snap to them instantly and make headway.

Whatever the case may be, this Cloud/Curtain is documented in various ways. It is that backdrop emptiness of nonfulfillment that one feels in life and its pursuits; it is that weight one feels in the mind that stymies any appreciable progress; it is the hindrance that upsets that flow and balance that is enjoyed because spontaneity cannot be initiated anymore; and it is that space the meditator drifts into when on the verge of deep concentration and insight. Finally, and importantly, it is that state of nonknowing and nonbeing that all beings fall into when taken over by deep sleep. This last facet prompts the seeker to study deep sleep after illuminating the dreaming and waking states, and attempt to penetrate through it to unite the three matras of the Word and attain *Turiya.*

QUESTION #3: "My final question is about the 'Rainbow Body,' which is a concept in Buddhism that an enlightened master or teacher can pass into at the time of physical death. Can you elucidate more on this?"

ANSWER: Of course, books and articles have been written about the "Rainbow

Body,' but one will have to check sources as wide and varied in meaning as Christianity, Taoism, lineages of Tibetan Buddhism, Dzogchen, Vipasana, and more, to gather information about it. Perhaps it is Tibetan Buddhism that has done the deepest exploration into this "phenomenon," and has the most current wisdom to add to it. As outer expression, and in some meditation masters, the Rainbow Body can actually be seen, like an aura, around the adept and master – but after the body's death. Preoccupation with examining the physical traits of its appearance, measuring the growth and shrinking of the dead corpse while the Rainbow Body is manifest, and a host of other explorations have been conducted.

Taking this spectacle a step further inwards, there is speculation that it is a sign of abiding presence, or deathlessness, shown by the illumined soul that just passed from the body, thus gifted to his students and disciples, giving them hope and inspiration to stay the path. In this vein, the same has also been reported on the level of the sense of smell, where the deceased body emits pleasant aromas long after death. This all falls in the realm of the occult, of signs and miracles, etc.

More towards the truth of the matter, whether or not the departed soul is consciously showing signs of its passage and arrival elsewhere, or proof of it, such luminosity can be seen around luminaries when they are alive. Why wait until they die and then fawn over some post-mortem light show? Or rainbows forming in the sky? In Kundalini Yoga, when the chakras have been opened and the awakened soul is moving through them, the result is quite often what the yogis call *"tejas."* Tejas is a more highly developed *"ojas,"* ojas being the subtle spiritual energy that is gleaned and gathered from spiritual self-effort (sadhana) accomplished after the senses have been purified by observing practices such as taking pure food, praying, repeating the mantra, and so forth. The difference between tejas and the rainbow body is that if one were to enter the tejasic light emanating from an enlightened teacher, the teachings being transmitted in that light would take root in the mind of that aspirant, or, at the very least, would make such an impression as to transform the mind of the attendee for all time. And certain sensitive souls can see this Light shedding off of such souls, like they did in the cases of Lord Buddha and Jesus Christ.

So, "rainbow body" is subtle body *(sukshma sharira),* is causal body *(karana sharira),* is "wisdom body" manifesting outwardly. It is not the physical body. Preoccupation with it on that level is a form of mystery-mongering, and rather nonproductive for spiritual growth.

Tadrupa from Oregon writes:
QUESTION: "Why is peace in the three worlds important for successful meditation?"
ANSWER: Peace of mind is crucial for meditation in any world, and at all times. Simply put, there is no spiritual progress to be had via the lazy or restless mind. Though obviously apparent when spoken or written out like this, it is surprising how many beings go ahead and try to attain higher things – wisdom,

worship, meditation, service – despite the presence of a restless mind. They need to work out their erratic tendencies first, then strive for the overall equanimity that is conducive to unbroken peace of mind. They also need a teacher to instruct them is this endeavor, but most will not take one. They try out conventional methods instead, attempting to use these as tools to achieve the higher ends of spiritual life. It will not work. As my teacher once said, *"The guru is not popular here in the West, and that is because the church has taken his place."* And what has the church ever done for spirituality other than to try and stamp it out.

Even a peaceful mind does not guarantee spiritual growth right away. Those three elements that Holy Mother has cited, i.e., patience, purity, and perseverance, must also play into the greater picture. This is due to the many subtle impressions that the mind holds, carelessly gathered and stored in previous lifetimes, that were not neutralized before the time of one's passing. Now, here they are again, springing up in this lifetime to spoil one's bid for said peace of mind.

Successful meditation? That is like saying "hot ice" nowadays, especially for this culture. Meditation, *Dhyanam,* is practically the highest limb. Limbs five and six of Yoga will have to be mastered first, they being *pratyahara* and *dharana* – renunciation of objects, both internally and externally, and one-pointed concentration on Divine Reality. Is it too difficult? Impractical? Not if the steps and stages are managed one at a time under the close tutelage of guru and scriptures. But everyone thinks themselves to be an expert, you see. They think they can get it, i.e., the Pearl of Great Price – on their own. As Lord Vasishtha states, *"To try and attain perfection in spiritual life without the guidance of the guru and the revealed scriptures is like trying to grow crops only at night."* So, we take one well-guided step at a time. And, as Holy Mother has told us, *"You need peace of mind first and foremost...."*

QUESTION #2: "Are the ancestors, celestials, gods, and goddesses nothing more than anthropomorphic thought projections of the ego stemming from the selfish desires of the collective mass of ignorant souls? If this is true, can it be, then, that a being such as Hitler is simply a collective thought-karma manifesting as a powerful being here on earth?"

ANSWER: Your description of the higher beings here seems a bit callous, and somewhat presumptive as well. If you are trying to come to a swift and overall conclusion concerning the powers of the collective mind, then yes, thought projection is responsible for the appearance of all things. But as Vedantists, whereas we strive to see through the appearances of name and form in time and space in order to perceive Divine Reality, we always affirm the Consciousness that dwells in all beings. And whereas it is true that the collective mind can pose a huge problem to those who are seeking nondual transcendence, it is also true that consummate realizations come when both the Real and the relative have been considered and properly understood. As Sri Krishna has said, *"The unreal never is; the Real never ceases to be. The truth of both of these has been realized by the seers."*

As to beings like Hitler, and the massive amount of negativity caused by his skewed mind and intellect, the quick answer to your question here is that he is a manifestation of thought coming from beings in the collective consciousness who are similar to him and who share his ideas. Thankfully, that constitutes only a small percentage of the collective mind. The balance of the collective mind turns away from such a being, wisely looking elsewhere for ideation that leads towards freedom for all, and away from suffering for anyone.

QUESTION #3: "How can we increase our devotion and faith in the guru?"

ANSWER: By all and any means possible, I would say. In my own case it was easy, as my guru was an illumined soul. When in the company of such a being, Reality fairly stands out for the taking, and the old tendencies that covered It die away rather easily.

But the bulk of the responsibility for one's freedom still rests on one's own shoulders. One can have the greatest and best guru in the three worlds, but if one's self-effort is lagging, and one's ability to carry the guru's instruction to fruition is missing, how then can one expect positive results? On the other hand, one can have a simple and sincere preceptor, one who gives the teachings out honestly and in a straightforward manner, yet if one's inspiration flows and the timing is auspicious, Enlightenment can be had readily, in this lifetime.

All told, it is the facet of holy company that is indispensable. Being away from guru, dharma, and sangha is not an option for any truth-seeker – at least not until one learns to keep the torch of spiritual practice burning of their own will and incentive.

QUESTION #4: "Is it possible for one to recover prana wasted on hedonism from earlier stages of life?"

ANSWER: I would say that such spent energy is like an arrow already shot from the bow. Who could call it back? If karma were not the god of this universe, then it might be otherwise; but this is not the case. One reaps what one sows. Sri Ramakrishna used to relate the analogy of a honeycomb placed on the ground. The sweet liquid slowly drains from the comb and seeps into the ground, lost. But if the comb is placed in a large jar, the honey gets contained and can be savored later. Of course, he is talking about a man's vital energy. Wasting it on sensual pursuits early on, he only fritters away his "God-given" abilities, turns old before his time, and cannot attain and enjoy the higher and better qualities and attributes later in life – even if and when he perceives them after sensual life proves unsatisfying. It is a sad and oft repeated tale.

But then again, it is of no use crying over spilt milk, or lost honey. One can start today, gathering and storing vital energy gotten from food, purifying it with mantra practice, and offering its redeeming subtle essences to the powers that be, within. Create your life anew. Begin the spiritual journey. Late is better than never. I have seen and met elder pilgrims hiking on the trail to the source of the Ganges at Gomukh. Some of them can barely navigate the path, and have to do it all slowly. But they are there, nevertheless, making that trek once in their lifetime. Great merit will accrue to them if and because they do.

The same is true of the inner journey. A start must be made, and if one looks back and rues one's mistakes, then this is evidently the lifetime to make it.

QUESTION #5: "Does Patanjali at some point recommend nondual manasana to scale the limbs of Yoga, especially those higher than the first four?"

ANSWER: "Manasana" is not his particular wording, but every authentic seer of India knows that everything from a positive mind, to buoyant thoughts, to repetition of mantras, to bold affirmations, and finally to nondual Mahavakyas, are a major part of higher realization.

It has been said, and not without good reason and credence, that the first four limbs of Yoga are all about strong self-effort, while the upper four are more about relaxing inwardly, letting go, and following a course of least resistance. In other words, there must be perspiration in the early stages, then inspiration will take over in the later ones. For, exertion of the will of the individual ego, though necessary in the early phases, can form an obstacle later on, since the ego is used to getting what it wants. It is not geared to either seek nor fathom the unfigurable element of Grace on its own. Only a ripe ego can attempt that.

So, when the practitioner, equipped with the first five or six limbs of Yoga, reaches the puzzle of meditation – especially nondual meditation – the ability to become transparent will be extremely effective in making headway there. And of course, nondual *manasana,* as you say, will help immensely as well. What is more, it can be assumed even earlier on than facets such as ego-invisibility, i.e., *asamvedana.*

QUESTION #6: "Can you please review how we are to meditate on a given teaching, such as if we are to meditate on water or on the phases of prana? What connections should we seek to make during meditation?"

ANSWER: First of all, please look back to lesson #80 to find the chart entitled, "Yogic Connections and Correlations in Meditation Practice." At the bottom of that offering you will see a standard list to focus on with regards to the direction that both Patanjali and Vedavyasa ask you to follow in meditation. You will also note all the sets of fives, moving inwards, and these are the alambanic quintuplications, or cosmic principles. You are to take those, one by one, and spend time with them in meditation.

In case you have forgotten how to do this, how to use the mind and its intelligence in this way, the guidance is given to concentrate on origins, qualities, attributes, characteristics, consistency, contents, etc. Then, take the same method inwardly and find their corresponding aspects in waking and dream states by noticing the changes and transformations of these (earth, water, fire, flavor, thoughts, etc.) then the power they hold over you and the influences they exert on you, and finally, how all of it disappears in deep sleep. By the time you have taken such a journey it will probably become evident to you that the mind should not be left to lolly-gag around on the surface of existence anymore, when it can be used to plumb the very depths of Awareness. Welcome to the world of discovery, then, of invention, of genius, of revelation, and – beyond and much better than all these – Seership.

I can give another clue or direction in this regard too. Got *svadhyaya*? *Svadhyaya* is study and memorization of scriptural slokas, sutras, etc. Scriptures, their slokas, the lines of slokas, the separate words of slokas, and the letters of each word, are all fair game for the meditating mind to take up. As I have said before by way of analogy, one can split an atom with an electron microscope to see the secrets of matter, but the meditator must split the atom of wisdom that lies buried in a word in order to see the Truth of Divine Reality.

Take for instance, a line from a wisdom song by Ramprasad Sen that goes, *"O Meditator, kindly leave the pleasant shoreline of mundane existence and plunge into the silent and serene deeps of Mother Kali's oceanic Mystery."* Let us say that, when I hear that line, and although it gives me an overall blissful feeling to contemplate its entirety, I nonetheless want to penetrate deeper. To do this I recognize that the word, "serene," is calling to me, that this word conveys an extra special quality and profundity to me. And that becomes the doorway to my inner journey in this mode of practice, as I take apart that word and extract its full meaning in terms of the blissful awareness of its source and essence. And there are endless words of this nature to which my mind has an inner connection. Some will even lead me to reasons why I am so enthralled with these sounds; also, why I am not interested, even put off, by other words.

Of course, the opposite tact is also available to me, i.e., that I come upon words that bother me, agitate the mind, put me off, etc., and I have to contemplate them to find out why this is so. If, *"In the beginning was the Word....,"* then there must be a very long-time relationship going on between words and myself, on all levels of consciousness. Thoughts are just unspoken words, and I have access to millions of them. In Tantra, this method of utilizing words to uncover Reality is classed among "The Six Ways of Attaining Brahmajnana," which is the name of a chart I have composed. But I can hardly show it here, it being far too complex – a teaching to be taken apart in a several week's retreat, really.

QUESTION #7: "How is it possible for aspirants to know their teacher is a knower of Brahman when they (the student) are not a knower of Brahman themselves?"

ANSWER: The same way it is possible to love your mother as a child before you even get to know who she really is. One simply ventures forth, familiarizes oneself, gathers knowledge, and learns the lessons. Besides, the mainstays of spiritual life are well-established and well-documented. A discerning soul should have no trouble locating directions that will open up this pathway.

Sri Ramakrishna had a story for this. He used the example of a man noticing a particular rooftop in his neighborhood, and who had a sudden desire to climb atop it and see the view from there. This task is easy to imagine, but very hard to carry off. After all, the owner would not like him clamoring up on his roof, and even if he could get permission to do so from the owner, he would still need a ladder, some ropes, and other equipment to keep him from falling off. Some instructions for undertaking the task would also be very helpful, if only one could locate a professional and schedule a meeting with him.

The meaning is, that to see a great soul is not all that hard. Even today there walk among us some authentic and confirmed luminaries from different religious traditions. But are they "knowers of Brahman?" We will never know until we approach them. Case in point, Swami Vivekananda did just that early on in life, walking all over Kolkata to talk to beings who were supposed to know God. That is how he found Sri Ramakrishna Paramahamsa.

QUESTION #8: "Are samskaras the main catalyst for the chitta taking vrittis automatically? Will one get into union with God when all samskaras are destroyed?"

ANSWER: The desire for form, *sankalpa,* is the main catalyst. Samskaras are the result. Later on, after they are formed, samskaras seem to dictate the process. This is why we must study, then detach, then transcend nature, *Prakriti.* In Yoga this is called *Kaivalya,* isolation from the cause of form. Taking birth in nature is okay....once. The soul gets the experience of limitation, and learns from this that it craves freedom much more. It then gets free in no time, i.e., one lifetime. But if the transmigrating soul comes to like his/her place in nature, like the crab loves its hole in the sand, samskaras of desire for form are already coagulating in the mind. The result is a series of lifetimes lived in limitation.

What is this desire for individual life? and for heavenly existence? Did not Jesus tell us that *"Birds have nests, and foxes have holes, but the son of man hath no place to lay his head here?"* It seems that Indian darshanas and their offshoots are the only methods that cite both the need for freedom from nature, and the inherent perfection of the Soul, Atman. *"Separating the wheat from the chaff"* is all about knowing of this main distinction, and developing the root discrimination that makes it possible. But remember, this need is only for those who have fallen earlier into attachment to nature. Those who see through its charm live once and are "gone." They are called *Videhamuktas* in our tradition – *mukti,* freedom; *deha,* from all bodies. They shine light upon the potentially dangerous admixture of mind and matter. Take care, all who would enter there.

In answer to part B of your question here about union with Brahman, from the standpoint of the *Videhamukta,* and the *Jivanmukta,* it is always and ever accomplished. Again, it is only those who have gotten themselves caught in form, trapped in nature, attached to the sense objects, who must eventually have to think in terms of getting back into union. For this, the seers have provided for us the various pathways leading to the Source. There is a saying that goes, "All roads lead to Rome." That may be the case for some, but for the followers of Vedic dharma, all pathways both lead to and are eternally united with formless Reality. Union, Freedom, is a principle always and ever at hand.

QUESTION #9: "Is the main difference between seeded and unseeded samadhis that in the former the ego is present, while in the latter it is dissolved?"

ANSWER: Yes, that is it in a nutshell, though other factors also play into this. Of the four seeded samadhis, *Sasmita,* "with ego," – albeit the ripe ego – is the final one, occurring, as it were, before the singular unseeded Samadhi appears. That subtle line of demarcation drawn between the end of matter/energy/

thought, and the beginning of Spirit, is traced by none other than your own ego. What does that tell you?

QUESTION #10: "Does Vedanta agree with Buddhism, that it will take three lifetimes to work out all karma? Can't Grace make exceptions to this rule?"

ANSWER: Grace can do anything it wants, can even *"....erase what it wrote previously in the book of destiny,"* as Holy Mother once said. As to how many lifetimes it will take to reach Enlightenment, and putting aside for the moment the Advaitic pronouncement that you are always and ever Enlightened, even different Buddhist schools evince differences of opinion in their understanding of that pivotal feat. It is a good determination, however, and if one follows it to the letter, substantial headway can be made in dissolving impediments in this lifetime.

QUESTION #11: "Does aparigraha also include nonhoarding? What really defines hoarding according to Yoga?"

ANSWER: Yes, I would say that nonhoarding is suggested, or inferred, in the term, aparigraha. However, *asteya* is also one of the yamas of Yoga, and that observance fits the definition of nonhoarding ever better. "Selfish grasping" is a term often used in both Vedanta and Buddhism to pinpoint and recognize the problem. *"Storing up for the future,"* was how Sri Ramakrishna used to indicate it. Whatever the terminology used, it is a gross preoccupation and carries stark karmic repercussions, the likes of which often do not even manifest in the lifetime it is practiced. That is why so many wealthy beings never come to recognize their hoarding as overt attachment, and always depart the body in a dissatisfied state of mind.

QUESTION #12: "How does the aspiring yogi stop backsliding and being complacent for good? How do we make our vows to study and control the senses stick, never to go back on them again?"

ANSWER: Backsliding, called in Sanskrit, *Anavasthitatvani,* is a spiritual problem according to Patanjali. It is the ninth and final *antaraya,* or *vikshepa* – impediment to Yoga. Take a look back at the chart entitled, "The Nine Obstacles to Yoga," located in Volume 1. There one can see the preceding eight impediments, and this will convey some idea of what the aspiring yogi is up against when attempting to attain the vows and stability you mention here. Notice, for instance, the presence of unwanted influences in body, vital energy, mind, and thought, that must be ousted from human consciousness, negative qualities such as laziness, heaviness – both of body and of mind – doubt, inadvertence, restlessness, (also both of body and of mind), stubbornness, immoderation, reliance on the senses for happiness, philosophical misconception, the habit of failure, all of them vying for supremacy in the human being from day to day. Peace of mind, anyone?

I could say, by way of simple solutions, that one must attain equanimity and keep it, but would that help? Perhaps make your own list, like Patanjali has offered us here, and begin to eliminate everything on that list, one at a time, until you can maintain said equanimity. As Holy Mother said, and we repeat it often in SRV Associations, *"You need Peace of Mind first and foremost."*

Finally, I can offer this from my own experience. Try to generate authentic interest in the dharma, and also a real and lasting enthusiasm for sadhana, spiritual discipline. After a time, compare any real interest you have gleaned from those to how you feel about the things of the world, like matters of economy, the responsibilities of family life, relationships with objects, and enjoyment of pleasure. If you do not then appreciate the salutary and sterling attributes of the dharma, then you are probably not ready for spiritual life. The only course to take at this time is to try to satisfy all your desires in a nonviolent fashion, and in the spirit of good-will to all beings, i.e., just try to be a good person. Desire for a nobler life will come later.

QUESTION #13: "Is nondual manasana the only mental posture needed for the raja yogi?"

ANSWER: As I said above, the term, "manasana," is not the language of Patanjali, or of Raja Yoga. though Patanjali certainly knew about and practiced it. Further, we must come to know that Yoga is a discipline, while Vedanta is a declaration of Nondual Truth. The two go together nicely – one of ongoing practice, the other of eternal perfection – but they occupy two separate (though intrinsically connected) philosophical realms. The reasoning around this is obvious. As long as a man practices, he is not fully aware of his Divine Nature, the *Atman.* Otherwise he would not need to practice. As my guru once said, *"If we all knew who we are, we would not need to do sadhana."*

But this is a radical teaching, not to be given out to, say, people of a materialistic and opulent culture who are used to coming by all that they want easily. Otherwise, and as we see among the pretenders and posturers of the pseudo-spiritual intelligentsia in the West, all will be declaring themselves to be illumined, even before they exert an ounce of self-effort or attain to the tiniest modicum of authentic inner merit. Then, beings who are really just businessmen and women will be making impossible claims in their office brochures that they have had Unseeded Samadhi, of all things. And on the very day that such words come out of their mouths, they have just betrayed the guru and transgressed the dharma.

Spiritual qualification is both necessary and extremely rare today, which makes Self-realization even more scarce. Some things cannot be pretended, and cannot be gotten so easily. In Yoga, as well as in Vedanta, we maintain the standard for Enlightenment at the highest level, then attempt to measure ourselves up to it gradually. There can be no pretending, no second-guessing, no compromise, and no jumping of steps. And in this measurement we are downright exacting in the handing out of even the slightest personal credit, or of any admittance of actual spiritual growth and merit. That is how we reach *"sasmita"* samadhi with a ripe ego that is ready and willing to offer the very last shreds of its separate self into Brahman so as to experience Yoga.

B.H. from Oregon writes:

QUESTION: "I don't mean to quibble or get into a semantic argument, but would like to offer some of how I am seeing things and solicit your comment or critique of my perspective. Swami Vivekananda states '.......*but that man who has attained to Samadhi through concentration is alone free from all desires.*' Often, the second Noble Truth espoused by Lord Buddha is interpreted as 'The cause of suffering is desire.' Other interpretations use the word 'grasping' or 'attachment,' etc. It seems to me that desire generally implies want, but we all know in this context is included that which we 'don't want,' attraction/repulsion, good/bad, etc., or all pairs of opposites.

The truth of suffering (dukha)
The truth of the cause of suffering (samudaya) (aggregate)
The truth of the end of suffering (nirodha) (cessation)
The truth of the path that frees us from suffering (magga) (path)

Using the word 'desire' as the cause of suffering seems one interpretation, but if Samudaya translates as 'aggregate,' then it implies 'dependent origination,' or that all things arise dependent on causes and conditions. The cause of Dukha is therefore ignorance, or not seeing things for what they are. The cessation of suffering (nirodha) is realized by 'seeing' that phenomena is ever-changing and dependent, hence 'not real,' not absolute or able to stand alone. To me, Magga, or the path, implies the process of unraveling the ignorance via experience once the principle of Nirodha has been realized and the discriminatory faculties assist in developing the witness position while playing out one's prarabdha karma. 'First there is a mountain, then there is no mountain, then there is,' as Donovan's lyrics popularized the Chinese Chan teaching. When referring to Samadhi, I think of an internal, subjective state of Consciousness. A being can be in temporary absorption and experience that state of Consciousness, it may illumine their vision, but life goes on and desires rise and fall as part of the human experience. It seems a bit idealistic to presume that all desires just fall away. Besides, desires are not evil or bad or immoral in and of themselves. The same could be said of the Sutra highlighted in this lesson: *'Among these diverse sets of minds, only that one that is born of meditation is free of conditionings from past lives.'* This seems true in an idealistic way, but not the reality that human beings, even dharmic beings, face day to day. Now one could point to the word 'born' of meditation, but we are not speaking of the virgin birth here. A mind born of meditation is a mind with a human body born of human parents, dharmic or otherwise. I guess it boils down to the nexus of idealism and realism for lack of a better comparison. Thank you!"

ANSWER: Far from exposing your ignorance, what you have written in accord with a concise composite explanation of the Four Noble Truths is both accurate and well-expressed. Therefore we have nothing to "quibble" about. Vedanta and Buddhism agree overall. They are essentially the same, after all. With that said, I will get to the root of the question, and its answer. And please be patient with the fact that this, my answer, gets into the realm of personal experience a bit.

Most beings have never seen an illumined soul, what to speak of approaching, committing, apprenticing, and following the regimen advised by such a being. In my life I have been fortunate enough not only to see several of these unique souls and meet them, but was also so taken by their unburdened lifestyle and their overall free state of mind that I entered and accomplished all four of the avenues cited just above. To get to the real point, however, I studied, and studied with, a few souls who were free of desire. Their lives were not like others. Far from merely expressing idealism, or assuming an idealistic pose, they adhered to and became exemplars of The Ideal. They realized their personal freedom, then *(jivanmukti),* and they made this freedom look easy, as if it were "everyday life," as you write here. Really, for instance, Zen is much about this everyday Enlightenment that these rare souls are living. And the two or three Zen Roshis I met in my life were not living ordinary lives that were encumbered by desires.

What I am expressing here is that there is worldly life, there is dharmic life, and then there is Divine Life. We, here on this earth, in this age, and particularly in the West, have scarcely seen beings living a Divine Life, and have certainly not lived one ourselves. It takes 100% commitment to the Chosen Ideal, 100% renunciation of the world, and 100% dedication to one's ongoing practice – and to attaining the Goal that Lord Buddha spoke of when he uttered, *"....gatam, gatam, Paragatam."* That is, there are 1) worldly goals (material) 2) earthly goals (practical), 3) religious goals (morality/ethics), etc., but all these are still attended by desires at different levels – like the goal for heavenly existence that the Indian rishis warn against. Just look and think about it; all around us in this day and age we see people – from parents to friends to associates to ancestors – all bound in these three modes of mundane life.

How can anyone expect to transcend mere idealism and actually attain The Ideal that Buddha, Christ, and Vivekananda have all exemplified if they cannot fully give their time, energy, heart, and mind to Divine Reality? Personally, I can not see how it is possible in the least. As Holy Mother has said, *"Is realization of Brahman a subject to be bantered about, like the bartering of fish and vegetables at the marketplace?"* That people are trying to gain Enlightenment while believing in the worlds of name and form, armed with only the barest of idea of what is entailed in both the pursuit and the realization of Enlightenment, is the height of folly, the very stuff of unrealistic expectations.

About desires, it is all a refinement process. Worldly people are swimming in theirs. Struggling people are analyzing and trying to heal theirs. Dharmic people are busy transforming theirs. Yogic practitioners are sublimating theirs. But what we have not seen, or seldom seen, is a marvelous soul, like Swami Vivekananda, who has transcended them. Aggregates, attachments, selfish grasping, and the like: Vivekananda once said, *"I can not remember one thing that I have ever done for the sake of myself. Everything I have done has been for others."* In souls like him we not only see the Ideal realized, but the Ideal held up for all to see in life. We should not imagine that just because we ourselves are struggling daily in the difficult path of action *(Karma Yoga),* or that we notice some spurious guru, some pseudo-dharma teacher, or some self-proclaimed "supreme philosopher of the West," fall off of his or her pedestal in front of everyone, that real authentic luminaries do not exist, and further, that they live lives of mundanity, restlessness, confusion, and uncontrolled karma. I never witnessed any of this in my guru, or in these few realized souls I came across in my spiritual life.

Primarily, we can realize that there are desires that are natural attendees on the ordinary plane of existence, i,e, eating, drinking, moving about, solving the riddles of life, etc. This question has been asked before by people with the same curiosity as you. In the *Uddhava Gita,* the devotee asks Sri Krishna how a holy person sits, how he sleeps, how he eats, how he moves about, and all the rest. The answer, basically, is *"....just like everyone else, but free of desire."* So you could define this to read "without undue desire' if you like, but the real point is that no karma is being created or borne in these rare cases. And because this is the case, no samskaras, mental impressions, are being formed in the mind either. So now, with this in place, think upon that sutra wherein it is stated that *"Among these diverse sets of minds, only that one that is born of meditation is free of conditionings from past lives."*

Along with the point made above, we have these facts to consider – also virtually unknown and unpondered in the West – that there are 1) many lifetimes in which to perfect the mind, and, 2) beings who fail to do so over hosts of lifetimes, and, 3) beings who are past masters of the embodiment process who can return to earth unhampered by mental, philosophical, and spiritual weights (again, please look back and see the chart entitled, "The Nine Obstacles to Yoga" in Lesson #71) that others are suffering due to their karmas.

Third, there is the teaching of various Samadhis. Some of these, when experienced, leave a trace of God-intoxication after they subside. In this case the experiencer remembers some of what was seen therein. Other samadhis leave no trace of the experiences had therein, so the individual returns to a rather "ordinary" state afterwards. Even our deep insights and dream visions fall into this category, i.e., amazing at first, but swiftly dwindling away to the background of our memory shortly thereafter. But the singular "nondual" Samadhi transforms the mind for all time. There are great souls we admire, no doubt, but we can hardly fathom the ones who have merged in the nondual Brahman. They and their understanding, if it can be called such anymore, are purely and simply beyond us. And perhaps this is the purpose of the many samadhis, and the reason why the Divine Mother places beings in them – so that those trying to fathom pure, conscious Awareness and those rare beings who live in It can begin to comprehend It.

All of this is in answer to your citing, "A being can be in temporary absorption and experience that state of Consciousness, it may illumine their vision, but life goes on and desires rise and fall as part of the human experience." Yes, but temporary absorption can turn into full immersion and full absorption. That is the import of *Nirvikalpa*. It is also the *Mahanirvana* state. Beings having That either return no more to embodied existence, or return with their karmas, samskaras, and certainly the desires that caused them, rendered extinct. And others, who have not had Nirvikalpa Samadhi, but who experience

Savikalpa Samadhi, do away with mundane desires as well. Certainly, base desires were purged before the aspirant ever got into spiritual life, and if not, there is always hell to pay along the way. We see these hell states being enacted all around us in unguided, misguided, Western practitioners all the time, depending on how one defines the word, "practitioner." I like to keep the word pure and uncompromised, assigning it only to those who are sincere and accomplished.

Akshaya Bhakti from New England writes:
COMMENTS: "As I have begun to make more sudden and unexpected connections myself (such as the realization that not only am I not the body, but that the body isn't even real – double whammy), I could really relate to Kanya's similar experiences expressed in Lesson 91, and the guru's explanation that    '....key bits of Wisdom gotten from the guru and the scriptures, heard enough times so that on one occasion, they really register, provides the impetus to begin the struggle for freedom in earnest.' It is so helpful to understand more about the process of spiritual growth. I am very intrigued by the way that Swamiji explains Sutra IV: 4 and 5, in that he states how the Yogis can work out their karmas through groups of bodies and minds that they create for them. I am not sure how this would work on this dimension. It seems very mysterious to me, and even confusing, when I am to understand that God is the only Doer, as well as in the current context that, 'Though minds and different activities are numerous, the one Original mind directs them all.'"
QUESTION: "Could you please elucidate Swamiji's comments in the text, especially, concerning 'Kaya-vyuha,' dear teacher, and help us to understand this "phenomenon."
ANSWER: Before answering your question, let me try to shed some light on mentions in your comments, above.

Concerning the way that yogis get their work done through various bodies, it is much like the Lord and the Mother doing the same. Beings seldom see such subtle work in action, or, they see it but cannot comprehend it, as you have said. They only see the effects, later, we hope. The human being is such a contradiction. It will notice the negative effects of work and actions done, and lament them, but most often overlooks the positive ones and will not study the way they came about so as to learn the process and master it.

And so, the yogis work around the veils in people's minds, bringing about connections that are, for the most part, unseen. And how this creating of bodies happens on this plane is, like on other planes, via the mind. In subtler realms one can actually be "born of the mind," or a "mind born child" – like Lord Vasishtha of Lord Brahma. But on earth, everything is about, and everyone thinks, in terms of seed born, womb born, egg born, moisture born, etc; no other consideration is even posed. But among gurus, disciples, teachers, practitioners, devotees, dharma families/sanghas, and the like, a realized soul looks, measures, then selects certain souls that are ready to receive what we in spiritual life call a "transmission." This happens mind to mind, unnoticed, and free of dependence on the physical. Thus, a yogi, while living, can "create" dozens of such souls as his sons and daughters, sending them out to manifest their especial gifts for the highest good of humanity.

This is not difficult to comprehend when we come to know that, in all Indian darshanas, it is the mind that projects everything anyway. Therefore, it can easily project its wisdom into another vehicle if it has the power to do so, and wills it. What people call "influences" in their lives, for instance, is this very principle in action, though not usually on such a refined level. And there is the case of "bad influences" as well. Wouldn't it be wonderful if we all went about turning others into luminaries instead of turning them into fools or enemies? This, the yogi is attempting to do.

*Kaya-vyuha* is a term of interest, and with much cosmology attached to it. *Kaya* means "body," and *vyuha* means "a special form." In this respect, the Lord, *Bhagavan,* takes three forms. As *Sankarasana* He appears in order to dissolve everything. When he takes the *Pradyumna vyuha* form He is there to create, i.e., project everything. And when he appears as *Aniruddham* He sustains it all.

Relative to the many worlds, outer and inner, He presides in some five delineated modes. In the highest of lokas, called Para, He is known as *Vasudeva.* When He descends into intermediate realms, He appears as an *Avatar,* or a major *Deva* (a powerful God); these are the vyuha forms, per se. Other modes of His are humans, animals, and objects, these latter called "archa," or symbols. Thus, and helpful for the earth-dwellers to know, objects are not really matter. They are representations of God's existence in everything. Further, and there is more, He appears as *Antaryami,* the "All-pervading One," the Indweller in all hearts, known only to beings who have the refined intelligence to perceive Him in meditation.

These subtle forms, even causal ones, represent the Ishvara form of Divine Reality, and make up what we call "Deity Yoga" nowadays.

S.Z. from Canada writes:
QUESTION: "If this question applies, I have been wondering what is the difference between prana, shakti, Kundalini, and life force (sexual energy). Thank you for your consideration. Please ignore this question if it does not fit the topic under discussion."
ANSWER: Of course, anything that has to do with prana involves the Yoga darshana. Shakti is big in both Vedanta and Tantra. And Kundalini is its own system, related to them all. Sri Ramakrishna used to say that there is no spiritual progress to be had without the awakening of Kundalini Shakti. Thus, we see the import of all three of these mentions here.

The difference between the three above principles of our tradition is one of grade rather than of essence. To put it simply at first, prana is gross, shakti is subtle and causal, and Kundalini is transcendent. Still, all three of these can be all four of these, if you see my meaning. For example, prana is gross on the physical plane, associated with matter, the elements, and food. But it begins to become subtler when its "vital" element is discovered and purposefully brought out, as in taking the prana that is in food and sublimating it via mantra and method. At the conclusion of this more inward trajectory we see prana has literally "become" subtle, and shows up, for instance, as the power that animates thought.

And it is at this juncture that we see subtle and causal prana, actually Shakti Power. This is what the saints and seers of different religious traditions call variously by the name, "Mother." Patanjali calls Her *Chiti-Shakti.* She is the Mother and Overseeress of everything that has to do with the mind and its thinking process, particularly of higher mind. So, in actuality, and as related in the Upanisads, prana is actually Her web. This is the key to knowing about Her omniscience, omnipotence, and omnipresence, all three.

But shakti is power nonetheless, subtle or otherwise, so it "moves." It "acts." It fosters and it transforms – rather like prana, yes? So there must be a source for it, and that Source is Kundalini. That is Mother per se, the authentic and original, the *"Adhyashakti."* She is pure transcendence. If you think She moves, i.e., like "up the spine," it is really only your thinking consciousness that is moving. Meditate upon Her as occupying all seven chakras at all time, while you only need to find Her there. She does not awaken in you; you awaken to Her.

**Pada IV, Sutra 7**
*karma ashukla akrishnam yoginah trividham itaresham (karma,* samskaric actions; *ashukla,* not white; *akrishnam,* not black; *yoginah,* for the yogi; *trividham,* threefold; *itaresham,* for others/nonyogis.

*"Acts springing from the mind of the yogi are colorless, while nonyogis suffer the threefold results called good, bad, and mixed."*

We have had this teaching before, especially in studies involving the *Bhagavad Gita,* and Sri Krishna's explanations of karma. To summate, there are four kinds of karmas. The first three are well known to beings, since they conceive of, perform, and experience the consequences of their actions all the time – with good, bad and mixed outcomes. The problem is, that they do not really think in terms of karma, but rather in terms of things such as luck, good fortune, serendipity, coincidence, randomness, and the like. Or, they do not pay attention to cause and effect at all. Higher ways of thinking involve destiny, predestination, auspicious timing, and grace. Of all these, karma is the best for explaining why beings suffer, and why they take certain pathways in life, and thereafter.

Before commenting on the fourth and most transparent of this karma collection, namely "colorless," the karma called "mixed" can be brought up for inspection. Mixed karma is the most confusing type. Its results often come back with unexpected repercussions. One example given is of the family man who dams up the stream running through his back yard so that his children can have a swimming pool, but as a result, downstream, people are dying of thirst. In an opposite direction, though still of mixed proportions, an old and selfish man tries to sign his name to a forged check one night, but in the darkness of his room he mistakenly signs over the deed of ownership of his land to his neglected children instead. As Swami Vivekananda has put it, *"....good good, bad, bad, and none escape the law."* But good often brings bad, and bad brings good, and this is confusing and frustrating to the one attempting to make sense out of life and action.

Whatever the case may be, mixed karma is of the type that causes uncertainty in the minds of living beings. It has been recognized in modern times by the saying, "bad things happen to good people." So, when negative acts bring negative results, and good acts bring positive results, and mixed actions can go either way, the only routes left open to the seeker of Peace and Wisdom are either an unbroken regimen of good acts, or taking a deep and long look at the "nonacts" of the yogis. However, good acts have often been described in this tradition as gold chains, negative actions as iron chains. Further, good acts are for the *"heaven aspiring senses,"* as the Upanisads declare. Beings seeking transcendent Reality, or God/Brahman, must take a different pathway.

In turn, the colorless karma of the yogis has been described by sayings such as,*"The bird flies through the air but leaves no trace of itself behind."* Again, *"The martial arts master walks over rice paper without leaving a wrinkle on it."* These apt metaphors begin to clarify the principle of colorless karma. Since it is rather invisible in its workings (i.e., it really has none), it is rarely encountered or seen. To see its unseen workings, so to speak, could only occur by watching and/or attending upon a perfected soul over a period of time. Aspiring beings have only come to know of it by apprenticing a guru or spiritual preceptor. Then they may see, or catch glimpses, of how to act while not accruing any karma whatsoever.

Another way of clarifying this is to bring out the facet of "the sense of agency" as a teaching. If a man has the idea is his mind that "I am acting" or "I am doing" while engaged in work, then the work itself gets infused with erratic energy. This is rather akin to throwing a marble into a spinning bowl, or throwing a heavy object against a rubber wall. The returns may be painful. But colorless karma is more like throwing a marble into a spinning bowl that has no bottom, or throwing a feather against a rubber wall. There are just no returns, happy or otherwise.

Along with the absence of the sense of agency, colorless karma is also free of the element of desired results. If the act or work is simply done to the best of one's ability, but with no anticipation or expectation for results or undue desire for the"fruits of actions," as they sometimes say, then repercussions simply will not occur. In this regard, yogis/yoginis, or luminaries, can work both constantly and efficiently, free from any backlash whatsoever. This they can do because they have no desires for personal gain, or even for the "good" or welfare of others.

The "highest" good of others, however, is a very different thing. It has been called *Loka Sangraha* in the *Bhagavad Gita* by Sri Krishna. To maintain a world or universal balance, and to cater not just to the "common welfare of the people" on the material level, but also to their highest aspirations for Truth and Freedom, that is beyond pleasure, beyond good, beyond contentment, beyond *sattva*.

**Pada IV, Sutra 8**
*tatas tad vipaka anugunanam eva abhivyaktih vasananam (tatas,* therefore*; tad,* that*; vipaka,* ripening*; anugunanam,* in accordance*; eva,* each one specifically*; abhivyaktih,* expressed*; vasananam,* potential desire-based impressions).

*"This triple designation forms subtle desires and impressions that will express themselves later in accordance with each one specifically."*

Karma that is latent will work itself to the surface, i.e., into everyday life, at the predesignated time for its expression. This is much like the tip of a screw working itself through the top of a wooden board due to constant vibrations beneath and around it. Often times, this past karma interrupts other important processes that the soul is working out, which are not just spiritual in nature, but mental, intellectual, and even physical, as well. These interruptions stymy spiritual progress, and place every day of an aspirant's life in potential jeopardy.

This is where the link between the "three designations" of karma is to be studied. In brief, matters such as works and life actions that all are engaged in today are usually manifesting in our lives due to them being drawn from karmas of a previous existence. *Prarabdha* karma is karma manifesting in the present life. Much of it is springing from and connected to *Sanchita* karma, which is karma from a past lifetime or lifetimes. *Agami* karma is future karma, or karma being stored up now that will express itself in a forthcoming life and body if not attenuated. All three of these are formed of and driven by *"....desires and impressions that will express themselves later in accordance with each one specifically."*

The principle of karma, like reincarnation, is a relative one. That is, the Atman, the Divine Self of mankind, is not subject to either of them. Still, everything this side of formlessness operates by karma, so to know of it and a bit about it will help the soul immensely while it is grappling with the processes of embodiment and disembodiment. This is why the seers have meditated and left behind teachings pertinent to this subject, the four types of karma being one of them. Sometimes this teaching is correlated to the four shades of karma.

## Lesson Ninety-three 1/24/15
### Pada IV, Sutras 9 & 10

The mind and its impressions, based in the desire for embodied existence, forms the content of many of the sutras in pada four. Thirst for life, clinging to life, fear of death, attachment to relative existence — even the fear of formlessness, are ways of describing this potentially painful predicament.

But the "Father of Yoga" is on hand to provide sincere seekers with all the protection that they need. All one needs do is to question deeply in order to find all the answers for the problems of embodiment in the realm of Maya — as the following queries demonstrate:

**Questions and Answers for Lesson 93**
R.O. from Hawaii writes:
QUESTION: "Could you review and comment on some of the Samadhi states, from the lowest to the highest, in Yoga. For example, you once spoke of the Samadhi where the self, or the witness 'I,' disappears."
ANSWER: Chart wise, you are going to want to look back for visual renderings of the gradated samadhis of Patanjala. The charts, "The Seeded Samadhis of Patanjala," (page 187 of volume 1) and, "The Process of Samprajnata to Asamprajnata," (page 61 of this volume) can be seen and studied for further clarification of this otherwise abstruse subject. The chart entitled, "The Seven Steps to Attainment of Kaivalya," (page 583 of volume 1) is also helpful.

As for a list, from lowest to highest, and in a yogic nutshell, they look like this. I have given a little commentary or synopsis on each, below, as well:

The Four Levels of **Samprajnata,** or "seeded" Samadhi

1) *Savitarka* — This early knowledge samadhi proceeds with vitarkas, meaning gross thoughts placed on gross objects (*alambanas*) in meditation. As one commentator states, *"It is important to note that this concentration on the material principles is not on the objective world with its external forms, but relates to vrittis to be controlled which exist in the sentient personality. They are mastered within the mind."* In order to clarify what is to be meditated upon, the list is as follows and constitutes "The Fourfold States of Matter," from gross to subtle to causal:
- Sixteen *visheshas* — 5 elements, 5 active senses, 5 cognitive senses, and mind
- Six *avisheshas* — five subtle elements and ego (asmita)
- *Linga matra* — Universal buddhi or Mahat that gives rise to asmita
- *Alinga* — unmanifest Prakriti (in the state of equilibrium)

Further, these four connect in the following three fields:
*Grahyas,* the objects apprehended (visheshas and avisheshas)
*Grahana,* the instrument of apprehension (ahamkara/asmita)
*Grahitr,* the one who apprehends (Buddhi or Mahat)

Grahyas are the field of concentration in vitarka and vichara samadhi
Grahana is the field of concentration in ananda-accompanied samadhi
Grahitr is the field of concentration in asmita-accompanied samadhi

The yogi concentrates first on the alambanas, including *Virat* (the universe as the outer body of God) and the visheshas. This concentration is on their entirety such as, a) their parts, b) past, present, and future manifestations, c) nearness to oneself, d) distance from oneself, e) desirable or undesirable qualities, and f) even its unheard of manifestations. These concentrations include: a) examining all order of sequences, b) cultivating the full grasp of words, names, their meanings, and objects, and c) the knowledge consisting of the relationship between word and meaning. By following this contemplation the hidden nature of each alambana is revealed. This causes the object, the sense of perception, and the mind, to become united.

We can see by this thorough method of inspection both the crucial base of samadhi that is needed to begin, as well as the extent to which the meditator must lend his or her awareness in order to achieve Yoga, Union. This is, as I have said in past lessons, the way to see nature as it truly is, then see it as having come from within (the mind/Mind), followed by its complete and utter transcendence in Kaivalya. This leads one to *Asamprajnata Samadhi,* the "seedless" state. But first.......:

2) <u>*Savichara*</u> — This deeper knowledge samadhi proceeds with *vichara,* meaning subtle thought placed on subtle objects. Vichara is really just vitarka in a refined form. Having seen the imperfections latent in gross objects during Savitarka Samadhi, the yogi inspects the subtler elements, like the six avisheshas (see above). In short, the mind then assumes the form of concentration, or the expansion of the chitta (thoughts), towards the finer alambanas, and this begins to awaken true wisdom. Beings seeking outer (conventional) knowledge never perceive or come to know of the worlds within them, but for the yogi, at this level, the nature of outer objects becomes fully known due to observing the existence of inner objects which are their source. Here, the practitioner also perceives the immediate cause of the *tanmatras* (subtle elements), that being the ego, and with this perception comes the ability to bring this restless rascal under control.

<u>Sananda</u> — The third seeded samadhi is accompanied with the dawning of *ananda,* or bliss. I say "dawning" because this is not the full-blown *Ananda of Brahman,* but rather that happiness and contentment gotten via the *sattva guna* by the ego. This reveals for understanding why the ego is both attached to pleasure, and also unable to maintain balance. The objects, both inner and outer, bring it pleasure (and pain). It is only the arrival of this precursor of limited ananda that the ego has a chance to look deeper for the source of higher Bliss.

So, that pleasure tasted in the lower two samadhis has its fount here, in sananda. Adherents of the Yoga darshana, and even mystics and practitioners, have mistaken the bliss that lies here for the Bliss of Brahman. If we look at the order of alambanas on the previous page, we will see that though the ego has been brooked, both intelligence and Mahat still remain left to fathom. Mahat's bliss leaks into this samadhi, as it were, and that makes many aspirants stop here and not move on to the sasmita stage — what to speak of the highest Samadhi of *Asamprajnata.* This is also where, stopping to enjoy, semi-advanced beings see what is around them in this state, and get attached to occult powers, sensationalism, and the like. Even popular gurus are restricted from true greatness at this stage of samadhi, and instead of attaining Asamprajnata or *Nirvikalpa,* only place their occult mastery on display, or gather huge followings, or write popular autobiographies on themselves, and so forth.

But such as these have only mastered the body up to ahamkara, and no further. The pleasure of Sananda must be seen in its parts, and as a whole, as well. Ahamkara and asmita must be overcome and transcended, for only then can the ego perceive the state of sasmita.

<u>Sasmita</u> — The highest of the secondary samadhis, it is still accompanied by the sense of "I am-ness." Nevertheless, with the limitations of sananda samadhi transcended, the yogi gets a more mature dispassion towards pleasure, more distance from the desire to manipulate the siddhis, and thus moves further inwards. Here, the ego, *ahamkara,* dissolves into *Mahat,* which is the very first evolute of *Prakriti.* Mahat is termed, linga matra, "with subtle markings," and has no other object to contemplate than Itself. Here, *Purusha* and *Prakriti* really meet. The buddhi is also here, however, and it receives the reflection of Prakriti, while Purusha remains unaffected. The buddhi thinks to itself, "I am the composite of spirit and matter." This is the stark and straightforward definition of sasmita, with its still subtle limitation.

When the buddhi realizes the limited nature of asmita, this blissful "I am-ness," then it divorces itself from matter, makes a final break from *tamas* and *rajas,* and settles itself into pure *sattva.* In this pure sattva, Mahat turns away from the ego. The will to produce the ego, which in turn produces mind, senses, and objects, then ceases. The luminaries say that it is here that the *Chiti-Shakti* appears and takes over, dissolving even pure sattva in Her wake. The meditator feels "at-onement" with Her, i.e., as Patanjali states: *"Shakti-shakti-mayor abhedah,"* There is no distinction between shakti power and its possessor." Worthy of mention here, is that if one studies this inward process of gradated samadhis, the paths and minds of illumined souls get revealed. One can actually determine, for instance, how a being like Sri Ramakrishna traveled inwardly to samadhi, and how seers and illumined souls live in higher realization, all the time.

Though a very deep and refined samadhi, this 4th state is still dependent on supportive factors — being Mahat or Universal Buddhi. The Atman, the true Self of mankind, can only be fully cognized in Asamprajnata Samadhi. Still, at this fourth level, Unmanifested Prakriti, called alinga — free of markings — is perceived. Thereafter, aspects and attainments such as *Dharma-megha samadhi* (raincloud of virtues), *Kaivalya* (final release from nature/form), and Chiti-shakti, are all available.

These four samadhis, listed here at your request, are termed *sabija,* "seeded," while Asamprajnata is *nirbija,* "unseeded." The unseeded state is synonymous with the Nirvikalpa of Vedanta, with the Satori of Zen, etc. If I were to summate the main result of this entire soul-movement in a few poetic lines, it would read:
*Herein there lies a hidden truth, known only to the few,*
*You do not come from Nature, nature comes from You......*

B.C. from Texas writes:
QUESTION: "References to consistency and contentment in the Raja Yoga

lessons further refines my approach to practice while in a Western social environment, discerning that which we naturally are, and are not, in the gross, subtle, and causal realms. Would this be a proper way of sensing chittis and vrittis thru the various 'levels,' from all five-fold principles in to out, and out to in?"

ANSWER: Yes, if I understand your first query here, *chittis* and *vrittis* are formed from the processes that nature passes through, and the changes that the mind experiences in the interim, i.e., *"the senses coming in contact with their objects."* Ironically, most beings do not know that nature, objects, and senses all originate from the mental complex, it being the intermediary matrix that fashions them accordingly. It is ego that reacts to them, however. What is more, intelligence can balance all this if it is duly informed. But *"the seer must not become identified with the seen,"* or fall under the influence of what is insentient. The seer, Atman, should always be master of all processes, and it remains so by its power of discrimination, detachment, and transcendence (if it has developed them) or, speaking in another way, had never lost them throughout a series of lifetimes in the first place, therefore resulting in the descent of *avidya,* ignorance.

Tadrupa from Wyoming writes:
QUESTION: "How can the aspirant discriminate between chitta arising from the collective mind and individual mind? How can the yogis protect their own mind on the subtle level from the destructive thoughts (such as those pertaining to lust, greed and violence) arising from the collective mind? Does the yogi simply dismiss these thoughts as nonsense?"

ANSWER: Yes and no. They are "nonsense" if they are believed to be ultimately real, or actual. But if they are known to be mental projections occurring only in the three worlds (and not in the Soul) — gross, subtle, and causal — or as you infer here, appearing at the individual, collective, and cosmic levels of awareness (but not in nondual Awareness), then there is no danger. Danger, Maya, only threatens when ignorance, or forgetfulness of essence, happens, and even that is nonactual. One only needs to wake up and remember. Sri Ramakrishna tells the story of the man who dreamed a tiger was attacking him (which happens more often in India then here in the West, no doubt). He awoke to realize that it was all a dream, but his heart continued to pound for a while nevertheless. Awakening from the nightmare of Maya is like that, for even after we have awakened to the overall illusion of it, the "cosmic chimera," there is still a bit of trepidation present in the mind due to other influences around us, like collective avidya.

And that is why discrimination is important, implemented every day. There is constant vigil to be undertaken while the soul still remains in the body, and attached to it. In order to escape falling into the natural trap set by the collective mind in Maya (which is much like saying the trap of rebirth set by your ancestors), there needs to be discernment applied at all times and junctures. If, for instance, one can tell the difference between the karma that is returning due to the host of unseemly acts perpetrated in past lifetimes, and the karma that recurs upon oneself due to one's present actions, there can be spiritual progress. There can also dawn over time an ability to separate oneself out from collective consciousness, i.e., the benighted thoughts and doings of the worldly population and the intentions of the ancestors upon you. As Vivekananda once quipped, *"May God save them all, and save me from them!"*

You see, the luminary goes a different way than worldly souls. He/She has compassion for them, for sure, but involvement in their delusion (that lust, greed, and violence you speak about above) is neither acceptable to them, nor a good example of how to get free and live free. Instead, that refined and well-maintained discrimination that was gleaned long ago by the luminary is now on display for others to notice and partake of. Utilizing it, the aspirant can tell the difference between *"....what to do and what not to do,"* as Sri Krishna puts it in the Gita. It is not that hard, after all. All that is needed is to break old habits and create new ones, or return to the already attained but forgotten qualities and attributes of the soul.

QUESTION #2: "Is it possible to transcend or disconnect one's consciousness from the collective mind and still retain a trace of the ego?"

ANSWER: As you have already read in the outlay of yoga samadhis I placed at the beginning of this lesson, the sense of "I-am-ness" remains even into the fourth stage of seeded samadhi. Another way of saying this, is that by the time the more mature seeded samadhis are well under way, the advanced aspirant who is experiencing them has already seen the limited nature of the lower heavenly realms that are those of the ancestors, and where many of the presently embodied souls are heading for, even now. Human beings, ancestors, celestials, demigods, in total — these all form the collective mind. I suppose one could include the gods, Devas/Devis, but they bridge a higher awareness that is more related to the cosmic level.

But whatever the case, that trace of ego that you ask about is present in subtle form late into the individual, collective, and cosmic game. Its transcendence is all the point.

QUESTION #3: "Do the individual, collective, and cosmic minds, run along a discreet hierarchy, or can they be considered to run along a continuum, all mixed together— at least for the untrained mind?"

ANSWER: Both are true, often in spontaneous fashion. The mistake most beginners make when hearing and considering Indian Philosophy, with its remarkable emphasis and abundant wisdom around Nonduality, is to mix everything indiscriminately into overall consciousness. These various divisions that are cited, and those grand hierarchical and gradated levels that are present, are part and parcel of the makeup of relativity, in all its full sweep. In the West, only the physical is included, while the vastness of inner space is overlooked or unseen due to the spectacle of outer space and preoccupation with physical forms.

But when the seeker becomes a seeker per se, he/she will have to find a cosmology that explains, adequately, the many-tiered realms of existence —

what Jesus referred to as *"....the Kingdom of Heaven within." "Heaven,"* here, could mean nondual Reality rather than all the "life-heavens cited in Hinduism and Tibetan Buddhism," but nonduality is seldom proposed or taken up in Christianity. The declaration, *"My Father's Mansion has many chambers,"* however, speaks more directly to these vast realms within us. Unfortunately, and due to the West's penchant for matter alone, people think of and look to the skies above when they hear this statement. Thus, the inner cosmology gets the go by, and being forgotten over long spans of time, begins to look more and more like a myth to people rather than a space in consciousness where their ancestors went, and where gods and other deities reside. This provides ample cause for regret.

QUESTION #4: "Does backsliding according to Lord Patanjali simply mean inability of the yogic aspirant to practice hard with constancy in the ekagra state? If one is following the yamas and niyamas, controlling the senses, practicing hard twice a day, studying and questioning the teacher, and staying clear of harmful societal conventions and distractions, what else is there to ex out of the equation so that backsliding is not present?"

ANSWER: I read you clearly. The fuller answer is, that it all depends on the character of the aspirant and the quality of consciousness present at any given stage of progress. Hard discipline is best at the beginning or outset of sadhana. Later, a certain general ease should set in so that the natural state of mankind's awareness, i.e., the Atman, can be perceived.

Finally, one just feels God always, and at all times, until that special intuition transforms into *"I am Brahman."* Sri Ramakrishna Paramahamsa slid in and out of dual, qualified nondual, and nondual states of mind and consciousness all the time, easily and spontaneously. We should keep this in mind as we strive spiritually, for spiritual practice is not like filling a shopping list. It should be more about how much heart I can bring to bear in my daily practice, and how much of real love I can muster. An undistracted mind in full concentration *(ekagra)* can make a huge amount out of such congealed love and devotion. On the other hand, a strict regimen of separate practices enacted for purposes of gaining a post-mortem emancipation might not go that far at all. So again, depth of character and quality of consciousness — do you have these? Further, Got Love?

QUESTION #5: "For the yoga student who practices hard and with constancy (i.e. is not backsliding), what is the method for overcoming the three lower states of mind, and also the three gunas? I'm having trouble with that idea that inviting sattva when rajas or tamas are dominate is a pitfall in sadhana. How does the raja yoga student get into ekagra state without dependence on sattva?"

ANSWER: Actually, I do advise inviting sattva to visit when rajas and tamas are predominate. "There is no other way out but through," as they say. "Calling all sattva! Calling all sattva!" Putting out this clarion call brings about opportunities. The problem with sattva is not so much the pleasure and happiness it brings; for what is all that to an advanced aspirant? He has already spit them out in trade for higher attainments. The problem with sattva is not using it correctly when it arrives. The intermediate practitioner is lulled into complacency again and again when things balance out, i.e., sattvic mind. Then he thinks, "All is right with the world."

But it never is. People sit daily in meditation and complain that the mind never settles down. But it eventually does so naturally as the gunas circulate in the mind and swap positions. So watch for sattva to show up, then sit for meditation. Restlessness and laziness will disappear swiftly. Of course, just because your mind is not settled for every meditation, it does not mean that you should not meditate at the assigned time every day, without fail. By sitting anyway you develop subtle muscles that can dispatch rajas and tamas right away, upon taking your seat. That balanced mind can become a habit (replacing klistha vrittis with aklistha vrittis), settling one into a long and potentially blissful stream of fine meditations. Studying the dharma and reading spiritual books also fans this inner mounting flame of meditation. Where is backsliding and failure to make spiritual progress *(anavasthitatvani & alabdhabhumikatva)* when this refined practice is understood and implemented?

QUESTION #6: "At what limb of yoga will the practitioner have direct perception of the Chiti-shakti?"

ANSWER: It may not be so cut and dried as this, that we can select a limb, or a samadhi, or a chakra, and determine arrival there based upon hoping for Her vision, or gaining anything permanently. That is because She is so free and spontaneous; and so is our true nature. So should your mind be as well, in order to set up such growth in yoga practice. You see, great spiritual experiences have been had by mere beginners, even children, while advanced practitioners, struggling hard every day, searching deep within themselves, may get nothing for a time! In this way, She is like that child in the story of Sri Ramakrishna's who may deny a tiny piece of candy to a rich relative, but give away an expensive blanket to a stranger without thinking twice. As Ramprasad sings, *"Who can fathom the decrees handed down by the Mother of the Universe?"*

At any rate, Patanjali's Yoga is not the place to learn about Divine Mother. He has other aims for his teaching method, and only mentions *Chiti-shakti* several times. The mentions of Her in the Yoga Sutras can be summated thusly: First, is the statement I quoted earlier in this lesson, that being *"There is no distinction between shakti and its possessor."* Then, there is some definition of Her name that he uses, mainly that *shakti* is conscious force, *chit* is consciousness, and so *Chiti-shakti* would translate as the Consciousness Principle. She is also called *Drk-shakti,* the very power of perception. All these are good to meditate upon, just as one would have done earlier on the *alambanas (visheshas, avisheshas,* etc).

Finally, Patanjali gives the fine teaching that if the mind is involved in the outer world, then *Chiti-shakti* does not appear or present Herself. And even if She does present Herself in various ways, She seems impure, even though She is ever-pure. Thus, the commentators like Vedavyasa point out with regard to Her: *"The appearance of corruptibility is misleading, like silver in a seashell."*

QUESTION #7: "Does acquiring Chiti-Shakti mean that Kundalini has reached at least the fourth Chakra?"
ANSWER: As the answer to the first question of this lesson reveals, the actual acquisition of *Chiti-shakti* occurs in Yoga at the *sasmita samadhi* level, after the ego has surrendered to the *Mahat* and the subtle pleasures desired by the mind/ego complex fall away. In other words, the ego must die before She will take over the field. This is Her stipulation, and the aspirant must then choose what he/she wants — is it more mixing of spirit with matter, of Purusha with Prakriti, or just Purusha alone, i.e., Enlightenment?

As to chakras, or *Kundalini Yoga* rather than *Patanjala Yoga*, the heart chakra's opening is usually associated with detachment from the world and its concerns, increased devotion to God, perceiving AUM, and all that level of spiritual phenomena. At the sixth chakra, or "Third Eye," one is more apt to gain Her vision.

QUESTION #8: "In the stotram, *Vivekananda Pranjalih,* a verse states '....*whether sporting in the Divine Mother's lila, or immersed in serious study, you remain ever aware of the stainless Self.*' Is this referring to Swamiji's ability to remain in communion with Chiti-Shakti while acting?"
ANSWER: Yes, or Mother Kali, in his case. Same Deity, of course, but the name, *Chiti-shakti,* is particular to the Yoga darshana and can also be used in a less personal way — to indicate the Divine Energy that flows through all and everything. With that said, the point of the verse is to indicate and celebrate the spontaneous spirituality that was Vivekananda's, who, in addition to his divine Guru, Sri Ramakrishna, was one of those incomparable and thoroughly unique souls. The Great Master used to say that Narendra (Swamiji) was a *Nityasiddha,* a perfect soul.

QUESTION #9: "Is the Chiti--Shakti the power that allows one to perform action through inaction?"
ANSWER: Yes, when the soul is ready for such ultimate and extreme achievements. It can be put in another way too, that if the *Chiti-shakti* is not awake and operating in and through the precious human form, then such marvels as action in inaction cannot be possible.

QUESTION #10: "Does identification as a seer *(drashtuh),* regardless of whether a trace of ego remains, imply one is in communion with the Divine Mother?"
ANSWER: Yes, the seer will perceive Her, if that is what you mean. We have to remember, however, that the Divine Mother is not necessarily the Chosen Ideal *(Ishtam)* of all struggling, aspiring, and illumined souls. Lord Siva and Lord Vishnu are that for the Shaivites and Vaishnavas, for instance. But when the subject of *Kundalini Shakti* comes up, since She transcends gender and form, one would have to acknowledge Her as the primal spiritual power coursing through all awakening souls. As Sri Ramakrishna has said, *"There can be no spiritual progress without the awakening of Kundalini Shakti."*

QUESTION #11: "If the adept yogi can work on the relative plane while in awareness of and in communion with Chiti-shakti, does this mean that nirodha is possible even while directing the body, mind, and senses? Is this also, then, the *'rendering of the external and internal states into one indivisible state,'* as Shankara states in the *Vivekachudamani?*"

ANSWER: The seer, or illumined soul, can work wonders on earth, no doubt. One thing he cannot do is operate the human body/mind mechanism while he remains in the highest samadhi. All these systems simply shut down. Otherwise it would not amount to a "nondual" state. Words such as *Asamprajnata Samadhi* in Yoga, *Nirvikalpa Samadhi* in Vedanta, and what you mention here, *Nirodha,* bespeak of a conditionless condition or a stateless state wherein not only body, senses, and mind, have been abandoned outright, but the prana has also been fully arrested and the human ego has been transcended. One has even gone beyond the *Mahat* and the *Ishtam!*

It is in coming back to the body after having such an experience — which is rare enough in itself — that the yogi sets to work to implement divine assistance into the world and its living beings. In Yoga, as we have been reading lately, there is what is called *samyama,* which is the successful integration of the 6th, 7th, and 8th limbs. The special abilities which come from that divine amalgam benefit beings immensely, often without them even being aware of it. This is how, for instance, the guru assists the disciple in overcoming subtle barriers that otherwise would merely remain in place. The disciple feels only the release, and the feeling of freedom after the fact, but does not see how the internal feat that removed the subtle blockages was accomplished.

And this is another boon that springs from the seeded samadhis. The entire affair is not necessarily about rushing towards enlightenment. Remaining at the lower samadhis, seers and yogis get all manner of works accomplished, works that they otherwise would not have been able to carry out due to "being out of the body," being "free of the senses," and losing contact with the sense of individuality, or ego. Swami Vivekananda used to inspire and direct aspirants by telling them that they can get Mukti later. For now they should just give one lifetime in service to the suffering masses.

QUESTION #12: "In Raja Yoga #10, it is explained how if the ego identifies with objects and sensations, the buddhi becomes misinformed and ultimately this causes the lower self to preempt the Self. Is there a lower buddhi or other type of determinative faculty that is controlled by the lower self?"

ANSWER: Yes, there is the lower buddhi, or the average intelligence of living beings. There is also a dwarfed intelligence in many humans, and a mean one too. But there is also a cosmic intelligence and a universal intelligence. These are higher forms, and are open to knowledge at all levels of its manifestation and expression. Tapping into these opens the mind to pure sattva, and then to transcendent experiences. A balanced mind, a refined ego, buoyant thoughts — all well and good. But there is hardly any better element than the honed intellect, whose presence allows all of these to function correctly and efficiently.

QUESTION #13: "Is maya coupled with vivarta the main offender that causes the ego to identify with the objects and sensations?"

ANSWER: It is hard to even use these two words separately. One might aver that *maya* is more of a tantric term, while vivarta is a Vedantic one, but the thing is, that maya is known for covering, or veiling, and that is pretty much the meaning of *vivarta* as well. Via connotation, vivarta smacks of insinuation of all that is not really real, and as an act that the mind accepts and believes. Maya is the same, but is more associated with a direct *"statement of fact,"* as Swamiji has said — a very matter-of-fact occurrence. It would seem, then, that vivarta is more easily disallowed, while maya just happens. All of this is playing with the two terms and their finer points.

QUESTION #14: "Is the mind involved in the ego's identification with objects and sensations?"

ANSWER: In the *Vivekachudamani*, Shankara states: *"The inner organ is listed as manas, buddhi, ahamkara, and chitta. Manas considers the pros and cons of things; buddhi determines the truth of objects; ego identifies the body as the self; chitta remembers things of interest."* So, involvement, yes, but empowerment, not so much. Otherwise, the mind would not transform so easily and move away from bondage to the objects of the senses when the ego gets subjected to purification in sadhana. The dual mind's judging of pro and con is its limited field. The other elements of the *antahkarana* (fourfold mind), especially the ego and the buddhi, have much more to do with the major operations of mind overall. The ego, in particular, loves to involve itself with objects and sensations through the senses. The ego uses the mind for all this, and mind follows along, blindly. Thus, when we use the term, "enlightened mind," we are not referring to *manas,* or dual mind, alone; we are speaking of a fourfold package whose contents have all been brought to their highest level of purity and operation, resulting in an inner organ of great power and purpose.

QUESTION #15: "This question/comment is regarding the first paragraph of commentary from lesson 10 about sloka 4, which discusses Sankhya philosophy and the statement that *'there is an eternal relationship (between Purusha and Prakriti) where only oneness exists.'* Are Purusha and Brahman identical? Or is it that Purusha's true nature is Brahman? If Brahman and Purusha are identical, then how can it have a relationship with Prakriti? Are these points rectified in the Advaita when we state that it is merely by assumption, association, or appearance only, and is nonactual? Is then the need to discuss the relationship between Purusha and Prakriti used as an avasta for the Vedanta and Yoga aspirant to develop viveka?"

ANSWER: You have three words you are mixing in — *Brahman, Purusha,* and *Prakriti.* Purusha and Prakriti go together, and those are terms in *Sankhya* for the Soul and Nature. The equivalent in Vedanta would be Brahman and Maya.

Now, as far as sameness goes, Purusha in Sankhya is more like the true individual soul, while Brahman in Vedanta is the Impersonal formless Reality. In other words, there is no sense of individuation in Brahman. It might be better to place Purusha and *Atman* side by side in order to make a more valid and close comparison, for Atman, though one with Brahman essentially, has the distinction of associating with the five sheaths.

As for Prakriti, that is nature — both manifest and unmanifest , as we like to point out (for the concept of unmanifested nature is fairly much missing in both Western Science and Western Religion). If your question is, then, "Are Purusha and Prakriti one?, the answer is no — not from the standpoint of Sankhya; the former is sentient, the latter is not. However, there is the point to be made that all of nature, all of form, springs from the formless, i.e., *"....from the Infinite the finite has come."* It is in that way that Purusha and Prakriti are one, much like the moon and its reflection are one, or, cannot really be two.

In Vedanta, as well, where can Maya come from if not from Brahman? It is, as Sri Ramakrishna has stated, like the poison in the snake. The snake does not suffer because of its own poison, but just carries it, like in some secret duct in its body.

And if I understand you in the latter part of your question, yes, words such as apparent, nonactual, assumption, etc., are the best way to understand such mysteries, such conundrums, like how can Reality be two and one at the same time, or always one but appearing as two and many. And you are correct, further, when you bring in the need to discuss such philosophical underpinnings in order that the seeker's ability for *viveka,* discrimination, be honed and matured.

QUESTION #16: "Sri Ramakrishna has stated that, at a certain point, the mind becomes one's own guru. Since Purusha's inherent and eternally pure jnana reflects in the buddhi, can the following Raja Yoga explanation be applied to flesh out this statement? That is, 'Upon purification of the buddhi via development and ripening of the ego (i.e getting it to identify with the Self), and elimination of samskaras rooted in ignorance, all knowledge will become available via Purusha's jnana reflecting in the buddhi.' If this explanation is correct, does this provide the main reason as to why illumined beings can be quite illiterate, but extract Pure Wisdom from the scriptures with little difficulty — and also why a great scholar of lower knowledge cannot? So realized souls are getting knowledge from Themselves via the pure buddhi and a focused mind."

ANSWER: In a word, yes. It is a wonderful ability, but only those who know of the inner realms and the internal mechanisms there — *Buddhi, Mahat,* etc. — will be able to access it.

Anurag from Oregon writes:
QUESTION: "In response to a student's question in the last lesson, you suggested a look at the chart, *The Nine Obstacles to Yoga.* I was struck by the quote from Patanjali at the bottom of the chart, wherein he states, in regard to these obstacles: *'Adherence to a single spiritual discipline such as japa and practicing the presence of God, removes them.'* This is quite an extraordinary testament to the efficacy of these spiritual disciplines to remove such obstacles, implying the power to attenuate negative karma (and facilitate fruition of good karma), eradicate negative samskaras, and attain mastery over the power of sankalpa. Of course, one's effort in these practices must be extraordinary as well. Could you please offer some reflections on this quote, as well as practical considerations and advice to actually use these disciplines to reach that *'farthest shore beyond all darkness.'"*

ANSWER: The well-known teaching of *Ishta-nistha* in our tradition, which is one-pointed dedication and devotion to one's Chosen Ideal, is being implied here. Lord Vasishtha also has several beautiful quotes about the need to select and settle on a single discipline, focus in on it, hone it, apply it in practice, and emerge from the entire process in possession of the Goal. Why even start into spiritual life if you are just going to dabble, or fizzle out part of the way through, or fail to reach the definitive end?

Other traditions agree as well. In Zen Buddhism, for instance, there are the several types of "Zen sickness" that are helpful to look at:

* *Zembyo* - "Zen sickness," which make up the host of distracting thoughts, feelings, emotions, sensations, appearances, and broodings that arise during the course of a student's practice of Zen.
* *Katto* - "Thicket of creeping vines" meaning falling victim to hearing too many words while failing to take the essence from them.
* *Bonno* - Worldliness, sensuality, passions, longings, suffering, and misery, all rising from a false view of the world.
* *Makyo* - "Diabolical phenomena," like the negative circumstances of the ordinary world, which the practitioner should not entertain in the mind, letting them turn into mental hallucinations.
* *Goseki* - "Trace of Enlightenment," sticking to those practitioners who cling to their initial insight experiences instead of living as if oblivious to their own enlightenment — in a natural way.
* *Hasan* - Interruption of Zen practice by an enlightenment experience — celebrated but not stressed — that keeps the aspirant from gaining many more and higher profound experiences.

In addition there is *Yako Zen,* wherein the practitioner pretends to be enlightened but really only mouths the teachings, having no deep or true realization of the dharma at all. Then there is *Buji Zen,* which is a light and immature attitude towards the teachings, wherein practitioners think that since they are already Buddha Nature *(Atman),* they do not have to practice or seek enlightenment. Finally, there is that all too familiar one, similar indeed to those who are caught by the hatha yoga craze in Hinduism, called *Bonpo Zen,* wherein unenlightened persons get into Zen, only for the purposes of bodily health and sensual/emotional stimulation

Citations from both sides of the picture, i.e., pro discipline and con discipline, arise in spiritual atmospheres. Thank you for being one of those who sees the crucial need for sadhana. As for disciplines inside of The Discipline, the tree of sadhana is replete with many fruits. Common to all traditions (though in Christianity and Judaism it is replaced almost completely by prayer) is meditation. A contemplative nature is good to have before setting foot on the spiritual path. A seeker with an overactive temperament may find it hard to fit in anywhere other than via the avenue of service, *Karma Yoga.* Still, when performed selflessly according to the scriptures and the gurus, this deceptively difficult and beneficial Yoga is a very exacting and purifying pathway.

Jnanam and bhakti — wisdom and devotion — are disciplines of incomparable stature and unending benefit. An aspirant can go far along the path with these alone. On the other hand, their lack is telling among seekers, who fall down and quit prematurely without them.

**Pada IV, Sutra 9**
*jati desha kala vyavahitanam api anantaryam smriti samskarayoh eka rupatvat*
(*jati*, species; actions; *desha*, space; *kala*, time; *vyavahitanam*, differences; *api*, as well as; *anantaryam*, connected; *smriti*, memory; *samskarayoh*, mental impressions; *ekarupatvat*, equality.

*"Though differences may occur due to effects in time, space, and the march of species, there is a deep connection in them based upon memory and mental impressions of past lifetimes."*

Delving deeper into the impressions left from past lifetimes, Patanjali points out that experiences shape samskaras by leaving their traces in the subtle memory of the mind. This is outlined well in the system called The Twelve Links, or *Nidanas,* in Buddhism. As Vivekananda points out in his commentary, these experiences remain constant inside of any given species. It is like noticing that cows are always involved in the act of grazing, and that this experience shapes a samskara for grass-eating in the simple cow psyche. As Sri Ramakrishna said, camels who always eat thorny bushes develop a strong desire for that taste, even though it is mixed with blood from their own lacerated gums. When the camel dies, its brain's memory (which is more like instinct than like the subtle body *((sukshma sarira))* of a human being, ridden with the desire for the taste of thorny bushes, carries this memory with its passing, and that memory shapes the outcome of its embodiment as another camel — which is the same in the cases of all (camel) members of that species.

Thus, karma (repetitive acts), and samskaras (impressions in the mind-stuff deposited there, in part, from these acts), are the real motivators/causes for the appearance of consciousness in forms. Living beings are naive to think "God" gave us our lives. God, Brahman, is Formless, is Essence, and has nothing to do with form, its various transformations, and its sufferings. And by the way, this is precisely the answer for that ongoing question in ignorant minds that asks, "How could God allow such atrocities to happen," or, "How could God take my loved one away," etc. God does not "allow" any of this, of course, being truly beyond such painful dreams. It is all happening in the realm of karma, and nature, not in Pure Consciousness — which is always and ever Transcendent. One's habits, one's desires, brought one into this field. Brahman has no desires, is beyond habit and other cause and effect sequences — is the infinite Field of timeless, deathless Awareness. That is why Sri Krishna explains in the Gita, *"Brahman does not create the realm of action, nor connect it with its various fruits, good and bad. Nature (Prakriti) does all that"* (if we check our list of cosmic principles, we will find that mind, manas, is a part of prakriti/nature). In another sloka, He explains, *"The Omnipresent One does not take note of the merits and demerits of anyone. Knowledge is merely veiled by ignorance; mortals get deluded thereby.*" And with regard to the role of desire in this insidious mayic process, He says: *"As fire is enveloped by smoke, as a mirror is covered by dust, as an embryo in hidden by the womb, so too is higher knowledge covered by desire."*

And we cannot revert to the stupidity of randomness theories either. First you write books citing endless examples of cause and effect in physics, then you totally discount or overlook their connection to acts perpetrated in relativity and thoughts forming and reforming in the mind? How is that? The lack of knowledge of *samskaras* in the West, then, and of the causal memory present in the mind, renders its science, its psychology, and its religion, devoid of the key and explanatory element of reincarnation and unawares of the essential role of the underlying nondual Awareness that is all-abiding — which also grants each one of these aspects of relative knowledge their "day in the sun."

If we take these aforementioned examples of animal rebirths, cited above, into the realm of the more complex human brain, which is an aspect of what we call the Mind (which animals do not develop or have access to), we find all manner of human beings coming forth based upon a host of mental impressions from the past. For instance, a lawyer or doctor carrying the impressions of those occupations with them into the bardo state after death, most often return in kind to those selfsame professions in the next lifetime. That is why Ramprasad, the poet saint of India, sings: *"To hope for help from family and relatives proves no profound solution. Don't you know that all are lost here? Everyone lives in pallid imitation of everyone else."* It is only the facile soul that gathers experience and moves on, refusing to get caught in mundane repetition of the past, and of past lives.

Taking another example, in the case of a drug addicted human being, that soul will depart the body in a state of extreme attachment to intoxicating substances, and will likely be forced to go looking for parents who are also addicted, and who can thereby supply that unfortunate soul with the mead of its base desires. It is that old "like attracts like" law in operation. But since there is no belief in reincarnation, nor cogent understanding and conscious application of its inner mechanics, the internal dynamics otherwise left clear by natural processes get muddled up in the mind by ideas such as a heartless, soul-less void, or an original sin — i.e., nothing really matters, or the judgement of an angry God followed by the devil's revenge and retribution in hell — or belief that Consciousness comes from matter instead of preceeding it. It is a main role of true philosophy to do away with such untenable and unacceptable superstitions.

Really, it is the law of karma or *"....you reap what you sow,"* that is operating everything, not the universe, God, or devil. In order to break the bonds of karma one will have to locate the *samskaras* in the mind via deep introspection, then use the tools of sadhana one has developed in order to dissipate them. Souls who are, by way of order, happy, joyful, content, peaceful, blissful, and highest of all, Free, are souls who have accomplished this spiritual feat to one degree or another. Some have already perfected themselves in their previous existences; they are called "past masters." Others are working on this high and rare accomplishment in this very lifetime, while many of those who are suffering inordinately are unable to work their way out of base attachments and deep-seated desires to the cool and revivifying plateaus of self-discipline and holy company.

When the West looks seriously into such ancient wisdom of Mother India, there will come a fuller understanding of the birth, death, and rebirth process — what to speak of the principles of dharmic life, divine life, and Eternal Life. Untenable concepts such as original sin and eternal damnation will also get shorn away from the mind's thinking process, leaving it free to attain to wisdom and Truth — to realizing the full identity of the Soul *(Atman)* of mankind with God. Other subtle laws and secrets like these come forth in the explication of the next sutra.

**Pada IV, Sutra 10**
*tasam anaditvam cha ashisah nityatvat (tasam,* all these*; anaditvam,* without origin*; cha,* and; *ashisah,* desire for life; *nityatvat,* unending.

*"All these impressions are without origin, and unending, because of the strong desire for life in the body."*

In reasoning about such subtle spiritual laws as *karma, samskaras,* and reincarnation, the soul is bound to come up with the question concerning their beginnings. Swami Vivekananda states, *"All experience is preceded by desire for becoming happy. There was no beginning of experience, then, as each fresh experience is built upon the tendency generated by past experience; therefore desire is without beginning."* This simple but complete explanation rather puts an end to such a question. It also applies well to principles such as life, space, and time. In terms of the latter, for instance, we labor in the West over the subject. Time is a good topic for meditation, but such meditations ought to eventually lead us to the conclusion *(siddhanta)* that in the end, or ultimately, time is a fabrication of the mind, a construct of thought, an illusion proceeding from mental projection. After all, it either speeds by or drags along in the waking state, depending on the mind's mood, or it stretches and appears and disappears in the dream state. Finally, it goes away completely in the deep sleep state. If one were to indicate the passing nature of all three of these states, or determine that the waking state is the only real measure of time, then there is the consideration of the end of time at death — or apparently so. Only the confirmation of an "afterlife" might disprove this.

In Western sciences, time gets linked to evolution. Also, to the rotation of planets around suns, and the movement of whole solar systems in space. Thus, an estimated amount of time, like 4,320,000,000 years, is posited from the beginning to the end. In Indian philosophy and astronomy, the seers of time have broken through such limited speculations and stated that time, in relativity (because time ceases in Reality/Brahman/pure Consciousness), is endless. The concept of time in Vedic cosmology shows the idea of the appearance of time in endless cycles, these cycles broken occasionally by a *"pralaya,"* a dissolution of all matter back into its source — Unmanifested Nature *(Prakriti).* 320 years of human time equals one celestial year, or a year in "heaven" ("heaven," here is within, not out in space, and is not a very high realm to attend, upon, either). Then, if you take 1200 of these celestial years you will have what is termed a *"Manvantara,"* which equals 71 *Mahayugas.* Time expands like this, infinitely, until *Mahapralaya* (Great Void) brings all manifestation to an end. After an extended period of "voidness," the entire process begins again. Therefore, time is cyclic, elastic, thus ultimately free of beginnings, middles, and ends. This is what Lord Buddha taught in His powerful few words, *"Like the river, everything returns."*

The purpose for this explanation is to show how relative principles like time and space are flowing specifically for the utilization of consciousness. *Sankhya Yoga,* one of the earliest of all human cosmological systems, states that *"Compounded substances (objects) exist to serve a sentient being, an Eternal Subject."* In other words, nature is insentient, so there must be an intelligent agent present to experience its functionings. What is more, not only are the cosmological principles held together by inalienable laws, but the experiences of living beings in the cosmos (inner and outer) are all occurring simultaneously, which indicates the presence of a subtle Coordinator at all levels of existence. As the *Mundakopanisad* states it, *"Anterior to life and mind is Consciousness."*

More importantly, and more interesting than the workings of the physical universe (as multivaried ((and distracting)) as they are) are the operations of Mind. And among the many aspects of Mind, human awareness heads the list. Whether it is how humanity gets itself born and bound into forms, or how they find their way out of them to freedom, the subject of Psychology is of utmost import. Eastern Psychology, called *Yoga,* is supreme in both its explanations and its methods pertaining to both of these eventualities. That is, when Patanjali brings out the fifth and final *klesha* (impediment to Yoga/Union) called *abhinivesha* — clinging to life — and reveals it to be based in human desire, both the intricacies of karma and the field upon which it either gets played out upon or compounded become a little less complicated.

As long as human beings long for life in form, so long will nature continue to produce all manner of material combinations at the behest of the Mind. And beings will long and pine for fulfillment in form as long as they engage in actions that produce only base desires which lend themselves to the formation of negative and mixed mental impressions *(samskaras)* in the mind. This is why great luminaries such as Patanjali return to embodiment as well, and move to gather and transmit sublime and effective methods (like Yoga) for both the destruction of negative thoughts, and the building of samskaras based in positivity and neutrality — all the way up to samskaras of Samadhi that are connected to the profound and lofty awareness of mankind's essentially perfect Nature — the Atman.

To end this running commentary for now, Sri Ramakrishna has given a perfect story that illustrates the problem and nature of mental impressions caused by countless repetitive acts. He pointed out that cows go back and forth several times daily from the barn to the field, always plodding along the same path. Soon this path becomes so worn that it transforms into a deep groove cut into the ground by the constant fall of hoofs. Before long the cows are ankle deep in this groove, then deeper. Soon, they cannot move out of this deep slough, even if danger comes at them from other directions. The mental samskaras of human beings are like this deep groove, only cut into the subtle fabric of the mind. They cause a sort of paralysis that disallows any and all movement towards freedom. According to Yoga, these mental impressions are to be filled in and replaced with positive samskaras, ones concerning spiritual practices such as scriptural study, worship, and meditation. By this trading in of "new lamps for old," a more ideal position can be reached where the soul can take advantage of all the boons and blessings that life should and does provide for all those who seek ultimate Freedom first and foremost.

## Lesson Ninety-four 3/17/15
### Pada IV, Sutras 11 & 12

With a host of intelligent questions on the intricacies of authentic Yoga and its well-guided execution, our present group of contemporary practitioners continues on offering question about the fourth pada of Patanjali's spiritual masterpiece.

**Questions and Answers for Lesson 94**
R.O. from Hawaii writes:
QUESTION: "You spoke and wrote about the siddhi powers earlier, and not to pursue them, as also Ramakrishna cautioned against them. My question is regarding spiritual healing. Is this a siddhi also? It seems like a wonderful thing to eliminate illness, and in fact we are all pursuing modern medical treatment anyway. Is spiritual healing cautioned against by Ramakrishna? What are the pros & cons for the healer and the patient. The healer usually always says it is not he but the spirit that does the healing. In fact, when Christ healed the man with the withered arm he said, 'Thy faith has saved thee.' Are the siddhi powers a gift of Divine Grace, or a natural development of the individual?"
ANSWER: In the hands of a Christ or similarly illumined soul, healing powers are a gift, a grace bestowed upon other beings by such deep abilities, and by compassion for suffering. In the hand of others, however, they are a mixed bag, for many may declare that these healing powers comes from a higher place, but few really think about or know that higher place. How can one assign their healing powers to a higher presence, or authority, when the healer himself, or herself, has not practiced sadhana in order to realize this higher Being? Such statements then end up as mere hearsay.

No doubt, that healing is of the occult level. Thus, it is not prescribed as an avenue to take for those who seek Enlightenment, for one's attention will be then be drawn to things like suffering, which is ultimately unreal, and to illness, which is a transformation (when Reality is transformationless), and to perfect health, which is a contradiction in terms since illness, decay, and death come to everyone.

Now, if we are serious about the term "spiritual healing," as contrasted to physical healing (like that of a withered arm), then the case must be made that the "healer" in that case is working with the mind and not the body. Therefore, it is modern psychology, or Yoga psychology, that is at work there, the latter being superior by far. Western psychology does not have the advantage of knowing anything about karma, samskaras, and past lifetimes, so can only work in the realm of matters concerning upbringing, instincts, heredity, and the results of negative actions in the present lifetime alone. Some headway may be made temporality in this case, but no ultimate solutions such as permanent neutrality of mind and freedom from thought (good and bad) will be forthcoming.

Now, back to the occult powers, they are neither physical nor mental in constitution, but are more a matter of prana, of the "tricks of prana" as Sri Ramakrishna said of them. Using them for healing can and often does backfire on both the "patient" and the "healer" since, again, the workings of karmas that are in operation at that time are totally disregarded, and thus get meddled with in an untimely fashion.

To conclude, here are three laws that apply to each of the aforementioned levels of human existence: in the case of the body and its illnesses, they are to be forborne; in the case of occult powers, they are to be eschewed and transcended; in the case of the mind, it is to be purified and infused with higher knowledge. Real Health begins with knowledge of Reality, Brahman, and if this is in place, all other levels of existence will be or become naturally healthy. In the case of a fall into ill health, or "dis-ease," on any of the human levels, utilizing occult powers as a solution would be both ill-considered and fraught with potentially negative repercussions — for those who use them, and those who they are used upon.

QUESTION #2: "My second question is regarding the possibility that siddhi powers are already being used in the world. Some people have extraordinary abilities for power, money, or levitation disguised as magic, where they can levitate high above buildings, or even teleport the self and pass through solid matter. Are these things scientifically unexplainable?"

ANSWER: Yes, occult powers are on display in human life, though not the kind that you mention in the latter part of your question above. When was the last time you saw a person leap a building? I never have. Can you show that act to me, other than superman doing it in a fictional movie with "special effects?" Physical laws cannot be broken here on the physical plane. If consciousness shifts to another level of consciousness, like prana or inner intelligence, then these laws might be transcended – but that is not being accomplished on the physical plane anymore, only on another. Dreaming is another level of consciousness according to the seers, and we all break the physical laws in that realm, for instance.

But what you mention in the first part of your question above is a different matter, i.e., that of money and power. These are occult powers of a very real variety, for they can help accomplish some of the original occult powers mentioned by the ancients, like prakamya (the power to fulfill all one's desires), and mahima (the power to seem great before others.) Domination over races and nations is also of the occult variety of power, and is rampant here on earth, as well as in the lower life heavens.

And so, with this one distinction made, I concur. To live a purely dharmic life one will have to avoid the occult powers and place the mind on Reality alone, i.e., like the Upanisads state, *"Sharpen the arrow of mind by thoughts of Reality alone, then place it in the mighty bow of the nondual scriptures, take aim, and release and penetrate that mark — the Imperishable Brahman."*

B.C. from Texas writes:
COMMENTS: "I have thoroughly read/reviewed the lesson and chapters. My questions were answered through these other inquiries of the group. I am thankful for what is already naturally understood and being confirmed, as well as for any redirection. I feel as though I am in a period of devotional practice which is bringing up the subtlest of subtleties, while recognizing the coarse/fine states of in to out, out to in, yet so as not to stumble in any experiential state in full understanding. The amount of major epiphanies have become more sporadic, which I am grateful for. I have a thankful 'thumbs up' moment when it happens and continue forward. Otherwise, I have few words as of late, and am concentrating worldly renouncement, senses, and elements, transformed into discernment and divine knowledge. Just eager to continue. However — "
QUESTION: "In what method(s) or practice(s) can one properly discern and integrate aparigraha, if not done so already? I surely appreciate and welcome your insightful teaching and redirection for refinement concerning the above."
ANSWER: The yama of aparigraha is practical in that it takes the mind off of worldly commerce and places it on internal inspection. "Giving of gifts," as it is usually translated, conveys a wider message, and problem, to the insight-oriented seeker. It is not only the "strings-attached" issue that enters here, where pleasing or disappointing the ego is at stake. One's entire past is sacrificed, including all the knowledge one gleaned from past lifetimes, and other bits of awareness that need to be brought forward and applied in order to retain peace of mind and the power for forward progress in spiritual life — all due to surface focus of material objects. No wonder that the ancient rishis eschewed the this tendency. Sri Krishna reads the riot act on it in the latter chapters of the Bhagavad Gita, citing both the problems with rajasic and tamasic gifts, as well as advice for taking such considerations as right timing, circumstance, individual temperament, and sattvic atmosphere into the equation.

I was witness to true aparigraha while living in the same dwelling as my guru, off and on, over several years. He was a monk, so nonownership was natural to him. Nevertheless, the Westerners who were his students often thought to give him gifts, thinking to please him, or something. Walking past his room one day, when the door was open for a few seconds, I noticed that all the gifts that he had received were simply tossed unceremoniously into the unused fireplace, unopened. I did notice, however, that a few of them had been opened partway before they were hurled to their fate. I believe that he wanted to see what certain individuals had given him so that he could determine the contents of their mind and thus guide them accordingly. Others, whose gifts were unopened, were probably known all too well to him by that time. But the real teaching was aparigraha in action. To see and know a man who had absolutely no regard whatsoever for material goods was wonderful for me, especially in the face of the present day glut and attachment that attends upon the lives of most beings.

QUESTION #2: "In approaching, detaching, and transcending the fourfold mind (five, you say, if psychic prana is added?) the five Akashas, the five sheaths, perceptible objects, and physical Maya, I had a question. I gain, see, or interpret just as much in meditation as I do in my waking and dream states, as if it is one breath. Do I need to continue deeper into these limbs of Yoga, mental mantrams, svadhyaya, and the steps in Raja Yoga and approach from all directions as I naturally do while continuing through each moment?"

ANSWER: Any practice one takes up is to be followed to its consummate end. It was actually the Father of Yoga, Patanjali, who gave out that advice. He was inferring that students avoid mixing many methods, and that they also avoid coming in of one and out of another before the initial practice given by the guru is complete.

Part of the practice of Yoga is study and memorization of scriptures. Please note the spelling to be *svadhyaya*. Also, the mind can be said to be fivefold if one adds in the Cosmic Mind, called Mahat in Sankhya Yoga, not "psychic prana" as you wrote above. In this regard there is a quote from the nondual scriptures which states, *"One attains to the Supreme Goal who dissolves mind, intellect, the gross and subtle bodies, the gross and subtle elements, and the five senses, along with the ego, into the Atman, the indivisible Self of mankind."* This "Dissolution of the Mindstream," as it is sometimes called, really happens naturally in authentic spiritual pathways, but is also the focus of its own form of meditation. SRV Associations has published a book with that title in order to help seekers implement this cosmic process. Being the author of this book, it is my observation that some fifty years of attempted meditation by Westerners has turned out incomplete and unsuccessful due to lack of knowledge of the inner tattvas, or cosmic principles, that form the internal worlds. Trying to jump in meditation from the body/brain platform to transcendental Awareness devoid of knowing all the "kingdoms of heaven within" is both unwise and impossible except for past masters of Consciousness. As Sri Ramakrishna said, *"If one jumps from the lowest step of a staircase to the highest, he will then know that they are both made of the same materials, i.e., brick, lime dust, etc., but he will always have some doubt whether the middle steps consist of the same materials."* These middle steps in spiritual life are called *Tattvas*, and need to be mastered so that the soul can move *"....up and done the amber steps of birth and death"* at will.

Tadrupa from Wyoming writes:
QUESTION: "Is transcendence of the klista/aklista duality considered to be a high level of achievement in Yoga? Considering the teachings of original mind and its relation to God realization, is it a yogic parallel of the transcendence of form and formlessness one achieves just before complete absorption into Brahman?"
ANSWER: No. The transcendence of the base dualities is not a high achievement in Yoga. This is because since it is not even a directive for ordinary souls who get no dharma teachings in life, few beings consider doing it. They merely suffer dualities like pleasure and pain and never think that they can and should be overcome. Once sadhana is entered into, and there is movement towards evenness of mind, then only does the oppression of pairs of opposites suggest or insinuate themselves to the mind.

In other words, and citing an earlier age where this simple fact was more obvious, preoccupation with dualities should never have entered the mind and its thoughts in the first place; one should always be thinking in a nondual way, and retaining awareness of Reality. This is really the only way that subtler dualities such as birth and death and form and formlessness can be considered, and their respective problems overcome.

This teaching is clear due to Patanjali's teaching of the five states of mind — *mudha, kshipta, vikshipta, ekagra,* and *nirudha.* The first three types of mind cannot be taught the universal Yoga due to the prominence of dull, restless, and erratic waves *(klistha-vrittis)* present there. The fifth state of mind does not need the teaching. Only when the mind's waves are evened out can there be inner growth leading to transcendence. Thus, klistha vrittis must go, then, due to the rise of aklisha vrittis, and both must go and leave the mind in "Peace, Peace, Peace."

QUESTION #2: "Does Lord Patanjali ever discuss the importance of karma yoga as an avastha in the Raja Yoga path?"
ANSWER: As in all forms of practice, Karma Yoga is always being inferred. But Raja Yoga is concentrated on gaining Samadhi and in listing both the practices and the obstacles to that superlative state of mind, and to "no mind." Since it is mainly a mental practice, there is not a lot of physical energy or movement needed or exuded. Even at the early stages, and unknown to most, asana and pranayama are both simple and easy to apply, the result being the practice of a few practices of breathing for a short time until the prana comes back under control, and a few asanas, again, for a brief period, until ekasana (the single meditation posture) settles in. Laboring the process of asana formulates a desire for physical movement in the mind *(asana-vasana)* and practicing too much breathing exercise tends to imbalance the mind. It is more important to reach the fifth limb of *pratyahara,* freeing the mind from objects, both outer and inner, so as to move on to *dharana* — concentration. It is at that sixth limb

that Yoga really becomes possible.

But Karma Yoga, synthesized with the other three main Yogas, is always important. It tends to bring everything back in a full circle so as to help the many who are struggling for understanding — as your next question evinces.

QUESTION #3: "Can you explain the psychological underpinnings of sloka 5:6 from the Gita where Lord Krishna states, 'Sannyasa, O mighty-armed, is hard to attain to without karma yoga; the man of meditation, purified by karma yoga quickly goes to Brahman.' Why/how does karma yoga help one to meditate and obtain nirodha (control)?"

ANSWER: The Four Yogas of Jnana, Bhakti, Karma, and Raja can easily be divided into two pairs. This particular division is revealing, since it places wisdom and devotion, and action and inaction, in interesting juxtapositions. The conventional way of thinking has it that wisdom and devotion cannot mix readily, and that action and inaction are diametrically opposed to one another. In the spiritual field, however, these paths appear to the seeker as a way to expand the mind, making it ready for the highest of conscious experience.

In the Indian tradition they say that the Wisdom Mother takes such seemingly contrasting pairs of opposites and fuses them together to bring about results that transcend the usual rounds of thinking and attaining. In the case of action and inaction, this is particularly applicable, and Sri Krishna makes that point in the sloka you have indicated. The idea is that mankind is active, busy, even restless and anxious; Brahman is pure, peaceful, stable, and motionless. To attain to the beatitude of Brahman, a human soul will have to somehow rid him/herself of the overactive tendencies of both mind and body. The best way of tempering them is either through knowledge or through devotion, but most beings do not have the aptitude for the former nor the feeling for the latter. Thus, it is the path of action in the workaday world that both appeals to them and provides them with a chance to calm themselves.

However, as most of us have seen, work has a tendency to mount up. If karma is left as mere work, and never turned into Karma Yoga (service of God in mankind), then the result is just what the word "karma" means — a mass of initial causes leading to an equal mass of unresolved (and often unwanted) effects. What Sri Krishna is advising, then, is that to attain the supreme state of peace and bliss that is the Soul's actual content, work must be turned into worship, into wisdom or, failing that, into a means to annul adverse repercussions. The karma yogi must also learn to transcend karmas around pleasure, worldliness, happiness, and all other so-called good effects of work and life.

And so, by quelling passion for work and work alone, the mind gradually finds peace. Before peace, must come contentment with what proceeds from a measured and balanced regimen of work each day. Along the way, the soul begins to aspire for freedom from all work, and finds that there is a state called inaction, or meditation, in which all desires are quelled and many unseen virtues are suddenly present and accessible. Swami Vivekananda really puts the finishing polish on Sri Krishna's intention here: *"The dwelling place of the jivatman, this body, is a veritable means of work; he who converts it into an infernal den is guilty, and he who neglects it is also to blame. Those who are working for their own salvation will neither have their own nor that of others. So if you are to work, let the commotion that you make be as such as to resound to the world's end."* On another occasion, he said about right action: *"In your lips and hands the Goddess of Learning will make Her seat; the Lord of infinite power will sit on your chest to do works that strike the world with wonder."*

QUESTION #4: "If avidya is the primal klesha, does this imply then that constant viveka is the sword that will cut through all kleshas in one stroke? So can we, by our own will power, eliminate the kleshas from our consciousness by witnessing the vrittis and asserting the Nondual Truth every time ignorant thoughts come? Can neti neti also be understood as a practice of purifying the chitta in relation to raja yoga?"

ANSWER: Applying *viveka,* discrimination between what is real and unreal, is the real beginning of spiritual practice and divine life. Put another way, nothing can be gained until one renounces the world. This is the real secret to life. Those who are running across the earth desperately trying to grasp at shadows will never find peace. Perhaps they do not want to. Whatever the case, it is a given that the seeker of Truth must have peace of mind first. Further, he/she will find that all other qualities and attributes will come to them along the way. So Jai Viveka! Jai Vivekananda!

As for a single sword stroke that will cut the five kleshas away completely, if viveka is strong and single-pointed, it can accomplish this. But if old habits, karmas, and samskaras are present, this wisdom sword may have to be swung several times, persistently, and in conjunction with guru-bhakti and meditation, to achieve this high station. For, Freedom of the spiritual kind, called *moksha* or *mukti,* is not easily won back from the hands of triple bondage (spouse, offspring, and wealth) and worse. For monks, the step of renunciation is already accomplished. For householders, the lesson or renunciation has to be learned and implemented, then followed by turning the family dharmic and the workplace into a temple of service. Eventually, one's whole world will be given up into love divine, where "All is Brahman."

Akshaya Bhakti from New England writes:
COMMENTS: "In the discussions of Lesson 93 and of Sutras IV: 9 & 10, there was a lot with which I could identify, especially the concept of time. When I was growing up I learned that the concept of time is necessary to every day living, since it gives an impetus to action, that if we think we have endless time, we may procrastinate and not accomplish anything. But in my retirement there is an even deeper appreciation of time. On the one hand there is so much personal freedom that time begins to seem limitless; a false sense that life in this body will continue on just as it has been. However, on another level, there is an undercurrent of fear, knowing that although I have always been on the road to death since birth, that physical end is coming rapidly closer. The loss of my dear mother has jolted me into more acceptance of this, but more to the point,

I know as a Vedantic aspirant, in the light of the immortality of the Self, such fear itself is not only unnecessary, but inappropriate, to say the least. There is no question I can formulate in regards to my own realization, wishing I could ask for a shortcut, knowing that the answer lies in sadhana and prayer. However, any comments to further the discussion of time would be deeply appreciated — as are the answers to my questions that follow, dear teacher."

QUESTION: "Is time in the Cosmic Mind a part of Mahat?"

ANSWER: (Dear student: my answer to this particular question is for you, and for others of our spiritual circle who are either considering or even facing the imminence of death at this time).

Actually, in Sankhya Yoga, and though not specified as such, time would be located in Unmanifested Prakriti. That is, the thought of time, prior to its flow, is held in abeyance as a seed concept before mind begins its projection process. This becomes clearer when we look at the *spandas* of the Kashmiri Shaivite system of Mother India. If one looks at them there are two principles called *Kala* and *Kalas*. These equate to the concept of time and the phases it will assume and break into. These and the ten other "vibratory spheres" (spandas) are quite inward, occurring or existing before the *Mahat,* the Cosmic Mind, begins its operations of projection, sustenance, and withdrawal.

We can conclude, then, that time has different phases, not just as a flow in increments as we understand it on Earth, but as levels of subtle potential that exist prior to its commencement and role in the realms of manifested Prakriti.

Now, this may all sound or read like high philosophy, as it is, but is it not true that by reading it, what to speak of studying it, one feels the profound sense of Eternity? And does this sense of the Infinite not destroy the erroneous idea of death in its marvelous sweep?

The seers of India, like none other, plumbed the depths of Consciousness and penetrated the veils there to uncover these interior vibrating spheres, and came back to the body and to earth to tell us about them so that we could place death in its own grave once and for all. Now, do not forget to validate and pay homage to their divine sacrificial efforts, and duly make this final move on the misconception of nonexistence. As you do, and as the Father of Yoga himself put it, you will come to that sublime space where occurs the "awareness of cessation." When the soul experiences that, it will see its Self as all that remains — as the One, Indivisible Existence beyond all beginnings, middles, and ends. Om Peace, Peace, Peace!

QUESTION #2: "Could you please explain the difference between '....all pervasiveness as related to ether' and 'homogeneity as related to air.' We must have covered this much earlier in the lessons in the chart of *Yogic Connections & Correlations,* but I couldn't remember the explanations."

ANSWER: The idea here is the appearance of the five elements prior to their taking subtle and gross form. At the causal level they are mere wisps of ideas in the Great Mind, but they soon take subtle shape as they work their way out through the internal ethers (*"the kingdoms of heaven within"*), and then turn into the solid elements we know here on the earth plane.

With regard to air as homogeneity, the idea there is that it is not as subtle in nature as ether is, since it can be displaced, for instance, while ether is immovable. Thus, the best English word to describe ether is "all-pervasive," as it permeates all objects. The precious secret, yet undiscovered by modern science, is that physical ether gives way, inwardly, to four other types of ether. One will not find these ethers by examining splinters of objects; that only takes one further outward into an already externalized form. They are stations in Consciousness. Thus, the real secret to existence will not be found in matter or nature. The real secret to existence is found in Awareness, in Consciousness.

QUESTION #3: "In the current review of the Four Levels of Samprajnata given to one student, I noted that 'The Yogi concentrates first on the alambanas, including Virat' (the universe as the outer body of God). Could you please explain more about the term, Virat, and how to use that specifically in our meditation on the 5 elements?"

ANSWER: Just as we human beings have three bodies, gross, subtle, and causal (*stula, sukshma,* and *karana/linga*), so too does God with form have three as well, called *Virat, Visvarupa,* and *Svarupa*. Virat is the outer form, and can be thought of as the "Macrocosm." It is God appearing as the manifested universe. Visvarupa is God appearing as the Cosmic Person. Svarupa is formless Essence. These three intersect each other, and no precise division can be seen in them, i.e., nondual Essence connects Visvarupa and Virat to It, irrevocably.

## Pada IV, Sutra 11

*hetu phala ashraya alambana samgrihitatvat esam abhave tad abhavah (hetu,* impetus; *phala,* fruits*; ashraya,* underlying foundation; *alambana,* objects of meditation; *samgrihitatvat,* cohesion; *esam,* combined; *abhava,* absence; *tad,* these; *abhavah,* disappearance.

"*Impetus, desire for fruits, objects, and their foundations, all combined, cohese these impressions together (4:10), and they disappear when they are absent.*"

To make the proper connection and carry the sense of continuity for this sutra, and for IV:12 as well, the student is asked to look back at sutras IV: 9 & 10 for review. There will be found the main set of topics for this series of sutras, all having to do with inner life consisting of samskaras, memory, time, space, and the human species with its strong desire for embodiment based in desire, and out of root ignorance of its formless Nature/Essence.

Paying all this cosmic information forward to the particular sutra under study, Patanjali makes the point that these impressions of the mind, with all their content, appear and disappear in cycles in time and space, from embodiment to disembodiment and back again, going forth and returning, interminably. As Swami Vivekananda says in his commentary: "*Being held together by cause, effect, support, and objects, in the absence of these is its absence. These desires are held together by cause and effect; if a desire has been raised it does not die without producing its effect. Then again, the mind-stuff is the great storehouse, the support of all past desires, reduced to Samskara form; until they have worked themselves out they will not die.*"

Both the makeup of a samskara and its breakup and destruction are contained in this statement. Desires are the constructing power of our births and rebirths. In their absence, the samskaras melt away and dissolve, and the soul is free again. The key to this is not just the will power of the individual, but deeper knowledge of the process of embroilment. When the soul finds out that it and only itself is responsible for its bondage, and for its resultant suffering — not God nor devil nor chance nor destiny, etc. — it will hastily reverse the process of piling on subtle layers, like wet blankets, and *"shed all karmas like a snake sloughs off its skin."*

A further look at Swami Vivekananda's commentary accomplishes a kind of shedding of its own in this connection: *"Moreover, so long as the senses receive the external objects, fresh desires will arise. If it be possible to get rid of these, then alone desires will vanish."* A look back, once more, at the seeded samadhis of Patanjala will help us here, as shown on the chart, "The Seeded Samadhis of Patanjala," As we can see, the early samadhis are of knowledge of objects — first external views of them, then internal perception of their origin. The outer gross objects come from the inner thought objects; that is the first key, followed by the lifting off of desire for them due to recognizing their ephemeral and potentially binding nature. This is how knowledge of the process combined with one's own will power does away with false superimpositions, and allows for freedom.

## Pada IV, Sutra 12

*atita anagatam svarupatah asti adhva bhedat dharmanam (atita,* in the past; *anagatam,* in the future; *svarupatah,* its real essence; *asti,* as existence; *adhva,* circumstances along the way; *bhedah,* differences; *dharmanam,* their characteristics.

*"Regarding the past and the future, they exist in their own essence, but change with characteristics and circumstances along the way."*

The problem of taking time and space to be real based upon memory of events and anticipation of more events occurring therein, is brought forward more clearly here. Right perspective is everything. If we start off a journey on the right footing, and in the right direction, there is a very good chance that we will reach our intended destination. Otherwise, many deadends and detours are bound to happen. It is the same with the desire for embodiment and the desires, habits, impressions, and the eventual obsessions that cause it. And soon, along the way, beings even forget the pathway along which they passed to get into the body and, incredibly, the Source of their "origin" and their very Being! It is the ever-changing circumstances of Maya that cause both enamorment with the relative process, and attachment to its characteristics. To put it another way, Alzheimer's disease is not just a mental disorder; it is a spiritual one as well.

Therefore, may each being transcend hypnotization by the three phases of time, i.e., past, present, and future, and come to live in the Eternal Moment which is within Consciousness Itself. Then they will give up trying to make a positive change in this illusory world, and instead protect themselves and others forever from change itself.

## Lesson Ninety-five 4/13/15
### Pada IV, Sutras 13 & 14

For lesson #95, a host of profound questions have come in, all inspired by the Yoga sutras of Patanjali, and by the commentaries of the illumined souls. Such depth of inquiry reveals the fact that there are dedicated and intelligent followers of Indian dharma in the West, and lends forward impetus to the quest for Enlightenment of both individuals and the collective mind. Read on to find out what subjects, teachings, issues — even problems — that select students are engaging with, which may echo and thereby help inform and heal some of our own.

**Questions and Answers for Lesson 95**
Avinashi from Pennsylvania writes:
QUESTION: "From the way I've heard you use the terms, awakening precedes enlightenment. What are the characteristics of awakening at the most initial level? In other words, what are the subtlemost indications of awakening that we might observe in a person who's just beginning to stir from their spiritual slumber?"
ANSWER: In the live-streaming discourses I am giving at present, there is a five class series on the topic of "Success and Failure in Spiritual Life." We all know the obstacles in the way, or should by now, but success in practice is usually attended by signs of progress, and those signs can be used to indicate the much sought after event of spiritual awakening. According to Shankara in the Vivekachudamani, they are hallmarks such as *"the tendency to do right action; the presence of natural discernment; increasing knowledge of divine Reality; the nonreliance of body, senses, morals, family, wealth, and society; and the will to perform spiritual practice."* Each one of these is a key linchpin and major player in the process of spiritual awakening, and each one could form the topic for a series of discourses, even a small book.
QUESTION #2: "To move from over-the-top bhakti one week or month, to what feels like deep jnana the next, and then back again, requires that one stretch oneself dramatically. When I'm deeply oriented toward bhakti, jnana seems impossibly dry and unattractive, and when I'm firmly ensconced in jnana, everything relating to the bhakta's path seems a distraction — as if one is simply wasting one's time while death approaches. When I am in either jnana or bhakti it seems very difficult to remember that the other path has anything to recommend it at all. It's difficult to look over the wall. You speak of combining bhakti and jnana. But it seems the two paths are differently 'aimed' at a fundamental level: jnana is inward, to Shuddha Chaitanya, intensely nivrittic; and bhakti operates in a world of objects, even if those objects be of divine character. Isn't this like trying to go East and West simultaneously? How does one combine these paths, seeing they're so intensely antipodal? Can they in fact be combined at the same time? Or only in a kind of sequential way? The Pranava describes an endlessly repeating ontological cycle which moves between the

extremes of manifestation and destruction, manifestation and destruction, on and on. It's often occurred to me as possible that the paths of bhakti and jnana can only be embraced when their seasons have come, as it were; that there's a place or time on the 'pranavic cycle' for jnana and the same for bhakti, and when the time has come for one to rise then the other must set. What do you think of this oft-repeating thought of mine? To find their union at the end of the path seems to me a different matter, since they both lead to the same end. But before that time has come, it seems as impossible to combine the paths, in their full sense, as it is to combine oil and water."

ANSWER: The analogy of futilely trying to combine oil and water works for Consciousness and Nature, but not for *Jnana* and *Bhakti*. These two Yogas are not only the two wings of the bird, as they are called by the seers, but they also go together like concentrated juice and water.

So, what you may be describing is more a matter of moods than of modes. And the answer for it is to flow with the moods but keep up the modes, i.e., check oneself every day in meditation to find out what the "flavor of the day" is within the mind, then after such assessment flow into the practice that suits it and helps it flourish. Life is a problem. Embodiment is a predicament. Anyone who has not seen this yet is still "faking it," has yet to live long enough in order to know that "Suffering Is." But once that first noble truth is accepted, then it all boils down to day to day practice and continual balancing. That balance (for those who have seen the nature of embodied existence and renounced it) is more of a practice of the mind, than of the body, health, and daily commerce. Remaining in peace of mind, or *sattva* at least, equates to spending one's time here on Earth beneficially.

Beyond this, and still getting at the question, I can say that an advanced spiritual aspirant integrates not only jnana and bhakti, but also *dhyana* and *karma*. If wisdom and devotion seem at odds to you, then what about meditation and work? inaction and action? Those two are certainly more opposite of one another than jnana and bhakti, yet as spiritual seekers we sit for meditation and go to work every day without questioning them or complaining (too much).

So, moods; watch them as an observer and follow suit with what the day or time demands. Remember too, that moods also means *gunas,* and that these gunas have cycles. I have been able to help so many seekers, again and again, out of periods of lull and mental suffering by reminding them of the natural cycles of the gunas. They suddenly wake up and say, "Yes! I am in a cycle," followed by, "Right! This will pass." Of course, practice is different from gunas; the yogas are both practices and paths. A flexible practitioner is what is wanted.

QUESTION #3: In what ways will one first be aware of a karma as it's emerging from the sanchita state, and moving into the agami? I ask because I've been deliberately observing inwardly to try to catch karmas at the very first moments of emergence since, at that stage, they can be returned to the sanchita state through dispassion and therefore need not be lived out, as prarabhda karmas must in most cases be lived out. What am I going to notice in the realms of the body, attention, imagination, emotion, intellect, or impulse as they initially appear, having just in that moment sprouted due to the influence of a catalyzing factor?"

ANSWER: First, it should be explained that any karma one is "catching" via introspection is already of the *prarabdha* kind, i.e, is *karma* already contained in the (present) mind. When it shows itself, by one type of expression or another, it then attends upon life. But it was in the mind as present karma already.

So what you are "going to notice," or should notice initially, is that everything that occurs via the "realms of the body, attention, imagination, emotion, intellect, or impulse," is present life karma already; the mind has already taken it all up to work out in this lifetime. It is prarabdha, it represents arrows already released from the bow. People are just not aware of it.

What is needed to "notice it," then, is that form of practice and introspection that brings all of it to the surface — like mantra, intense worship, holy company, study of the dharma, and the like. What usually happens in the case of embodied beings, however, is that they do not engage in these practices when they enter the body and thereby leave all of that already seeded karma lying hidden in the mind. Life, in and of the world, then brings it to the surface unasked, and attended by all its potential suffering. Spiritual practice would have neutralized it before it surfaced, but they did not have the tendency (samskara) for it. But that is another topic.

The real point here is that if one wants to get to *sanchita* karma, karmas from past lifetimes that are not yet brought forward into this life and present mind, one will have to look deep within and come to observe the chain of one's past lifetimes and the actions performed or perpetrated there. This is more a matter of deep meditation than of a mere looking at the mind and its emotions, or an inward glance at the intellect and its ego. The latter is a matter of healing and correcting, a kind of therapy if you will, but the former is spiritual practice per se.

In short, the discovery of present karmas is helpful for the soul, but the locating of past karmas that are still set to insinuate themselves on future lifetimes is freeing. Just make sure that you know the difference between them, and the specific practices that go with and annul them.

QUESTION #4: "Is the term 'vivarta' an exact synonym of the terms adhyasa and adhyaropa?"

ANSWER: Yes, generally speaking, they all refer to the principle of false superimposition, the appearance of one thing that covers another — specifically, of the names and forms of the world, or *Maya,* covering the nameless, formless Essence that is *Brahman.*

However, *vivarta* is also the name of the actual school of such thinking, the nondualistic philosophy called Vedanta. Additionally, *adhyaropa* not only points to the strange occurrence of the unreal covering the real, it is also a practice used (with apavada) to do away with the covering power of Maya *(avarana shakti).* It, all three, is advanced spirituality that can only be utilized properly and effectively by qualified spiritual aspirants and long-standing adepts.

QUESTION #5: "Are turiya and the sakshin the same? Or is, say, the sakshin a bridge to turiya or an expression of it? If there is any distinction or difference in nature between turiya and the sakshin, what is it?"

ANSWER: The main distinction here, is that *Turiya* is a nondual state, while (the) *Sakshin* is the one observing that state. If one refers to the phrase, *sakshi-bhutam,* for instance, then one is indicating the "witness of all phenomena" *(bhutas).* The sakshin is thus the *Atman* at one of Its most elevated levels of Awareness. There is only a slight distinction left, and that can be cited and explained as the presence of a witness and that which is being witnessed. That distinction will go away, however, in *Nirvikalpa* (Vedanta), or *Nirvana* (Buddhism), or *Asamprajnata* (Yoga), or in *Turiyatita* (Advaita).

QUESTION #6: "I'm beginning to suspect that I may have been coming at your teachings and the way you teach from a less than optimal angle and missing much of what you have to say as a result. You present many rarefied ideas and often I've felt like, 'Well, this is an interesting idea, an intriguing aspect of a larger, admittedly fascinating vision, but of what ultimate use are these ideas when so many of them seem so unconnected from any form of actual practice?' But recently, you again brought the concept of the jnana-matra to my attention in an email, and not long after that indirectly drew a corollary between the jnana-matra and the rays which, coming out of Atman, manifest the universe. At first the comparison was jarring, but then I saw that employing the image of the ray, (which in its very structure of increasing width along its length describes the process of emergence), lit up the truth that the jnana-matra describes not just something manifested, but also the process of manifestation itself, (like the ray). In seeing that, I saw that the image of the jnana-matra describes more than structural components of Reality; it also describes dynamisms of Being and the Path itself and, pondered deeply enough, even how to walk the Path. My question then, is, although every sage, seer, teacher or guru of the perennial truths teaches basically the same truths, still, each has his or her own angle of seeing, saying, and conveying those verities, and I believe I've been missing the angle that's best to see your teachings by. I, for one, did not understand that many of the concepts you convey, though seeming to be simply structural descriptions of certain aspects of Reality, also describe dynamisms of Reality and even offer instruction on how to walk the Way. What I'd like to hear from you are your views on why it is that people sometimes miss what you have to say, even when they're trying hard to understand? And what is it about the way you teach that people would do well to grasp if they want to understand your teachings more easily and clearly?"

ANSWER: *Guru Yoga* has its difficulties, no doubt. But the guru-disciple relationship is so precious, especially when the two parties are both sincere, and out to reach the highest goal and best outcome for one another. The process takes time. The student may think that he/she understands the gist of what is being taught, and most likely he does — on the intellectual level. That explains our Western way of learning which, in addition to the influence of the money-making tendency, overlooks both the presence of the living Word *(Vak)* and She who holds the Word *(Vakdevi)*. For instance, Holy Mother has said that it is best if the disciple lives very close to the guru, though not in the same dwelling, so that day to day proximity can gradually bear its otherwise unseen fruits — which ripen on a deeper level than just the intellectual plane.

To get to a more practical/less mystical answer, however, we might take up the Master's fine story about the master weaver and his apprentice who was not, at first, while looking at all the balls of yarn lying on the floor around his master, able to tell the difference between a 30 strand yarn and a 31 strand yarn. He thought, therefore, that he would never be a master weaver like his teacher. But a few months of day to day proximity in the shop brought that fine ability to him nevertheless, even though the master never gave him specific instructions on it. The same is true with dharma teachings given by the adept guru. They may seem out of reach to the beginning aspirant, but time and proximity changes all that. Thus, first must come the will to spend time in Holy Company, and next must come the resolve to penetrate the deeper meaning of the teachings. Then only can they be placed in practice to reap the benefits. It is related well in the Eightfold Path of Buddhism, for instance: first perfect view *(samyag-drsti)*, then right resolve *(samyag-sankalpa)*. Perfect effort *(samyag-vyayama)* proceeds from these.

Going deeper into the answer, it is the nature of the dharma to be profound and infinite. Those very wisdom particles you speak of here *(jnana-matras)* are to be seized by the concentrated mind and split apart in meditation. This process and its forward motion is what gives bliss to the smiling yogi and the exalted rishi, so unconcerned with the world, unlike all others. Here, transcending equals splitting. These powerful particles cannot be allowed to remain solidified so that they veil and confuse, nor can they be left fallow so that their potential never gets realized.

Most teachers of Eastern spirituality today are missing a deep understanding of the many *darshanas* of India and the ability to transmit the wisdom contained therein. Rarer still in any living teacher is the will to live a spiritual life. And beyond even that, there is the inability to help others live a spiritual life. These are four different but related things. However, most aspirants in the West will barely be able to begin to take up and satisfy the first (which is the work to be done in the West at the present time). Regarding the last two, few really want them. And only if they spend time close to an illumined soul will they actually see what it is to be spiritual and come to live "In the Spirit." In the case of those exceptional beings I learned from, I saw that they were never divorced from Reality. They lived fully committed lives. Come close to the fire and you get warmed, i.e., the numbness of ignorance will disappear.

Maybe I can sum this all up by stating that the death of ignorance happens so much faster due to close and constant "proximity" with the guru. This is the Great Master's teaching as well. He used to say, *"Just look at what happened to the dinosaurs by keeping close company with the Earth. They became earth; stone."* He always followed this story up by speaking on the subject of Holy Company. Later, Swami Vivekananda, speaking of His own time with his great Guru, said: *"Let me tell you a little personal experience. When my Master left the body, we were a dozen penniless, unknown young men. Against us were a host of powerful organizations, struggling hard to nip us in the bud. But Ramakrishna had given us one great gift, the desire, and the lifelong struggle, not to talk alone, but to live the life. And today all of India knows and reverences the Master. The truths He taught are spreading like wildfire."*

B.C. from Texas writes:
QUESTION: "I have no interest whatsoever in obtaining the occult powers, yet is a yogi/yogini to purposefully concentrate upon these powers of Yoga as a challenge of renunciation and devotion, as well as experience in itself to the fullest, to realize the Eternal within? Or do these present themselves, similar to vrittis or samskaras, from the one-pointedness upon Brahman in order to be discerned and countered as the ever-changing dream of Maya?"
ANSWER: If I am understanding the gist of your question arightly, I would confirm the latter — that the discriminating spiritual aspirant must use discernment to counter the urge for occult powers. It will not be so easy these days, for all eight are woven into the Western mind-set as if they were natural to it. For example, supporting violence in any way brings the occult power of domination *(ishitva)* over others into the picture. This is why living a spiritual life is so unique, so rare, and so special; such a life demands both the rejection of such powers (as was stated by the Father of Yoga, Patanjali), and the acquisition of their opposites as well — as in, *"....where there is hatred, let me sow Love,"* etc. By supporting any of the occult powers, Christians are actually going against both the will of Jesus and the words of their own scriptures.

You mention here a *yogi* and a *yogini*. In their case — more rarefied than a beginner or an intermediate practitioner of Yoga — the occult powers will have long ago died away; have been "left behind" (why leave people behind to their worldly fate, with clothes or not, when you can leave lust, anger, greed, violence, and other impurities behind). That is why Sri Ramakrishna came forth with His famous saying about the *Asta-bala siddhas,* and said: *"The eight occult powers are like crow-droppings alongside the road; no one in their right mind would stop and stoop to gather them up."*

And the fact that so many beings are gathering them up only shows that the masses of this world are simply not in their right mind. The word in Sanskrit is *bhranti,* or *moha;* they are deluded. Those in their right mind are referred to as *prasanna,* of clear thought, and do not entertain in the slightest degree any thought about possessing powers. As Sri Krishna has said about such base powers, *"Anyone who keeps even one of the eight occult powers near them will never be able to realize Brahman."*

To put further emphasis on this cautionary teaching, the Buddhist luminaries, who call these powers *"riddhis"* instead of *"siddhis,"* have also looked at, collected information about, and concluded on the avoidance of the following forms of occult power:

- *to manifest multiple forms of oneself*
- *to transform oneself into another shape*
- *to become invisible*
- *to pass through solid things*
- *to walk on water or float in air*
- *to touch the sun and moon* (woe to the wastage of the space program)
- *to scale the highest heaven*

Coveting such powers as these in Buddhism is 1) *"a violation of spiritual laws,"* and 2) *"grounds for being dismissed from the spiritual community."* So the seers advise to give them up, and give up their courtship. As Milarepa sings in one of his songs:

*When you meditate, remain in solitude; do not think of the occult powers*
*or the evils of Samsara.*
*When you take the teachings, do not strive to use them for profit or power.*
*When you attend meetings with your precious spiritual family,*
*do not try to head the row.*
*When you venture out to make your living,*
*do not use the dharma for gain or fame.*
*Follow Mila's instructions: abandon deceit and pretense*
*and you will find your way.*

QUESTION #2: "Does Kaivalya 'compare' to Moksha, in that it is the Sattvic mind reflecting solely on the Purusha (unqualified essence/qualities); compared to Saguna), whereas the latter is a realization of freedom within the non-quality of Purusha (Nirguna)? Yet, being that Purusha is separate from nature, and both of these attainments apply to Atman, may one state that they can both be realized/combined from the non-dual approach like the wings of a bird, such as Jnana and Bhakti?"

ANSWER: I was reading in a scripture of Mother India the other day. In it, the seer made a distinction between enlightened souls and liberated souls. To have *Kaivalya* would mean enlightenment, but to have *Moksha* would equate to absolute liberation. Metaphorically speaking, the former is like a spaceship that can visit any planet in the universe and never be restricted to any of them, while the latter transcends the entire universe itself.

Nevertheless, the difference in elevation is subtle, to be sure. In *Raja Yoga*, Kaivalya, separation from Nature/form, is penultimate to seedless *samadhi*. That means that until one completely frees oneself from the desire for bodies *(deh'anuvartanam)*, the desire for worlds *(lok'anuvartanam)*, and the desire for rituals and conventions *(shastr'anuvartanam)*, there can be no full liberation.

QUESTION #3: "First, I understand keeping the body in purity until realization is achieved in food, exercise, cleanliness, etc. Yet, how does a Westerner like myself, accustomed to athletic workouts/lifting, supplementation, etc., properly keep the body in line with its purpose without disturbing the nadis or falling from the path of refinement? Guidance on how to properly 'treat' the body would be more than welcome and greatly appreciated. Knowing the body is made of nature makes no difference in my choosing to workout or fast, shave my face, wear contacts or glasses, as long as the focus is on living as an instrument until liberation dawns. This has been a question since from the beginning of my involvement in athletics from the age of seven."

ANSWER: The body can be either a temple or a prison house of suffering, but it can also be a dressing room of vanity. The first of these alternatives is the best, of course. The scriptures advise, *"Give the body just its due, and nothing more."* This is a rule for monks, to be sure, but if it is taken mentally it applies to everyone who would want to avoid egoism, and egotism. Egoism is one of the five main impediments *(kleshas)* to Yoga according to Patanjali.

As for the finer pursuits and principles in Yoga, like the nadis that you mention, purity around food is the main one to observe. We know that physical nerves can be benefited by *asana* and *pranayam*. We also know that if these two are overdone, they can imbalance both the mind and one's practice. The finer *nadis* benefit from *mantra* practice, study of scriptures, and meditation. They shrink and recede, unable to hold the psychic *prana*, when selfishness, pride, lust, and other passions and fetters pollute the process. All can take a look at my chart called "The Four Clarities of Spiritual Life." It is a good study for a guidebook on how to treat the body/mind mechanism at the fundamental level of practice.

QUESTION #4: "How may I further refine concentration and 'follow the bread crumbs' in order to move through states of awareness into that one state of consciousness of AUM? Is this 'Hansel and Gretel'-ing also applied to tracing back samskaras to previous memories, or the dissolution of the 24 Cosmic Principles into AUM?"

ANSWER: "Following the trail of bread crumbs" is a practice of discovering anew an ancient cosmology that all beings are familiar with, but that most have forgotten. Since Americans have no cosmology to refer to, this method applies in the U.S. very strongly. If accomplished as a practice under the guidance of an illumined soul (guru), many gaps in consciousness will get filled in.

You are right in assuming that a part of this practice has to do with uncovering memories from past lifetimes. It also has to do with Sankhya's Twenty-four Cosmic Principles, or *Tattvas,* that must be studied and meditated upon in order that they can be recalled as tools and stations of awareness, as well as affording dissolution back to the highest Source. Even the process of recollection involved in such a practice will, of itself, begin to restore beneficial memory to its original state. Patanjali states that worldly commerce, i.e., the eternal money-making (gift-giving/aparigraha), takes away the time we should be using to remember all that has transpired before this lifetime, or put another way, all that the soul is and has to its credit.

*"Deja vu"* (what a laugh) is not even the tip of the iceberg here. The soul ought to be having copious flows of subtle streams of memory occur to it in meditation, as natural as recalling memorized slokas (which is part of the reason why to engage in this practice, *svadhyaya*). This free flow takes place through the subtle nadis, which is why they are to be opened and maintained,

just like one's memory. Thinking about occult powers, for instance, just like thinking about money all the time, will clog the nadis. The result will be, as Sri Ramakrishna has stated, *"The onslaught of the chronic disease of worldliness."* To unclog the nadis that never should have gotten blocked, then, we can use the Dissolution of the Mindstream method. In order to implement it one will first need to "follow the trail of bread crumbs," or "connect the dots."

Akshaya Bhakti from New England writes:
COMMENTS: "Revered Teacher: Lesson 94 seems to offer a special field of synthesis for me, as well as an exemplification of Sutra 8 that karmas can only fructify at appropriate times, in the right environment. It also seems to connect with your reply to Tadrupa, that the Sword of Knowledge may need to be swung several times when we have been enslaved by not only experiences, but especially habits. I was very touched by your response to my concerns about time. Your profound words have given me a personalized context in which to transcend the confines of the small ego in which I have entrenched myself, especially of late. These new insights, especially that of Kalas as a seed, will further my efforts at involution and serve as a template for the other objects of contemplation as well. You have also included the instruction to "concentrate on their (the visheshas, avisheshas, and even ahamkara and buddhi) appearances in time and mind," even back in the introduction to the principle of involution (Lesson 16), but it never really registered what that meant until now. The new chart *From Atomic Particles to Atmic Particles* gave me a context to your teaching of the 'Jnana Matra,' the subject of your latest text — which leaves one awestruck! The thought that we must learn to live in the Eternal Present is also something which has been previously discussed. I just came across your Nectar article (Winter 2003, p. 13-17)) entitled, *Patanjala as Revealed by Shankara,* which ties in so perfectly. You wrote there: *'Time, like all other mayic projections, is seemingly independent but actually interconnected. In its apparently free scope & movement, it extends, entices, embroils, ensnares. But when seen as the very breath of Brahman, it ennobles, enriches, enlightens, and enraptures. How exceedingly fruitful, indeed, would be the practice of Yoga and its comprehension when based upon such superlative understanding. For one, the goal-oriented, process-oriented mindset would be replaced by moving, acting, thinking, and living in Brahman. Time, effect, result, would assume no hold on the practitioner's thinking process as the illusion of a linear flow of time would dissolve into the one Eternal Moment.'"*
QUESTION: "When you mentioned the '4 kinds of ether' in your reply to me, and that they are 'stations of consciousness,' does this refer to the 4 states of being — waking, dreaming, deep sleep, and turiya?"
ANSWER: Yes, a direct correlation can be drawn between the *akashas* and mankind's four states of Awareness. There are actually five kinds of ether (if one counts the *Chidakasha*), and so one can add in the supreme of the supreme, called *Turiyatita,* to cover that as well.
QUESTION #2: "Regarding Sutra 10, that there is no beginning of experiences,

and yet there is past experience upon which the rest is built, seems contradictory. Should I be thinking about the fact that time is circular to explain this? Could you elucidate further, dear teacher?"

ANSWER: No contradiction here, and yes, the knowledge that everything moves in endless cycles can help one comprehend this. The *advaitic* law of non-origination states that there is no beginning to phenomena whatsoever. We cannot find a time when we were incepted, nor do we find a time when we ever ceased to exist. Put another way, a Soul cannot be created; It is pure conscious Awareness that exists always, and is beyond the inception of time. Time is actually a projection of the mind, and the Soul, Atman, as the Upanisads state, *"far outstrips the mind."*

QUESTION #3: "On the chart, *The Four States & the Vital Breath,* please explain how to understand the definition of 'Nadis' as being parts of the Vital Breath? Is this connected to the definition that they are a multitude of nerve centers, whereas here there are only four!"

ANSWER: About the subtle topic of nadis, unknown to the people of this day and time, we are to remember that *"inside of the gross nerves are thousands of subtle nerves, and inside of these are tens of thousands more."* But the word, "inside," here does not mean physically inside, but rather located in an internal dimension. Further, just like in the body (which mimics the subtle body), there are a few major spiritual arteries along which flow a strong current of finer energy, and these feed tinier arteries, much like veins in the physical body, nourishing the entire system.

In the particular area and level we are studying here, those four channels of fine energy connect souls to the states of waking, dreaming, deep sleep, and transcendence (turiya). How many beings would ever think, even imagine, that these very channels are being used by their souls (subtle bodies) every night to conduct their awareness into states of dream and deep sleep? They are also key to the soul's passage to inner worlds at the time of the body's passing.

So we should envision keeping these four main arteries open. To even know about them, and about this esoteric system of thinking, helps in this aim. Next we are to connect ourselves to these states of Awareness consciously, in meditation, and by doing so, clear the heretofore closed off avenues of passage that have been blocked by the ignorance of many God-less lifetimes, and freely flow along them into the Light of Brahman.

R.K. from South Carolina writes:

QUESTION: "In Yoga Vasishtha, and also in many of your classes, it is emphasized that God is acreate, that there is no creation, and that this universe is an appearance. If this universe has no substantial existence apart from Brahman, and is a projection of Mahat, how does the Cosmic mind arise? If Brahman is alone real, then what is Mahat; does it really exist? Is Mahat then a modification of the all-pervading pure conscious Awareness?"

ANSWER: Yes, the word, "modification," is a good one to use in this respect. It also helps us to understand the difference between the Source of Existence and It's evolutes — another good word in English. *Mahat* is Cosmic Mind, also called throughout Mother India's spiritual past as *Hiranyagarbha* (Cosmic Egg). The Trinity is also God's Mind, i.e., *Brahma, Vishnu,* and *Siva*, though this level contains not only three overseers to the process of projection, but also much deeper and more profound stations of Awareness — such as *Ishvara*.

And to answer the part of your question about the reality of Cosmic Mind, it is real in as much as it has such powerful presences' within and operating it; but of itself it is also a projection. By way of analogy, think of a world, then think of a satellite station on the way to that world. Mahat is like that, i.e., it is a mechanism; therefore it cannot be the Reality. The mode of *Tattva-jnana* teaches us about principles, but we must also study and meditate in the mode of *Upasana-dhyana,* which teaches us about the presence of God (deities) within these stations. In the same way that you are not your body and mind, but are nondual Awareness (Atman), in the same way, Brahman is not its body (the lokas) and Its mind (Mahat).

All things that partake of matter, energy, and thought, then, are projections from the Mahat. It gets them from The Word, *AUM,* and the Divine Mother who holds it within Herself. She knows the secret that all the universes in space and time are projected. They cannot be "created" — not in the usual sense of the word — for something that gets created has to have its content drawn from somewhere. This "somewhere" is its formless nature, called Unmanifested *Prakriti* in India. Every insentient thing (including our bodies) dissolve back into it when their time as forms come to a close. And all sentience associating with forms, meaning living beings as Consciousness, dissolve back into Formless Essence, Atman, Brahman. In between these two poles, the Sentient and the Insentient, is thought, or mind (the Cosmic Mind holds the greatest thought power). It takes primal matter from its formless state and projects it into forms such as worlds, bodies, manifested Nature, etc. This is not an act of "creation," per se, for that would be producing something from nothing, which is not possible. Death and destruction, then, are also infeasible, since what is unborn and acreate by nature, i.e., in essence, cannot be destroyed.

Thus, India's Doctrine of Cosmic Projection *(sankalpa),* far outstrips the untenable idea of creationism, that God is a Creator. It far overshadows the theory of evolution as well. God is not a form, nor is It a being separate from us. It is blissfully Formless, *"one without a second,"* and the Essence within all. You will not find Brahman creating a world of imperfection and suffering. It does not create at all. Why would It, being ever-perfect. Even the cosmic art of projection it leaves to other deities.

And as far as evolution goes, the forms that appear to us, which constitute what we call matter, energy, and thought, never evolve; they only appear to do so. It is that appearance (Maya) that the yogi, seer, rishi, etc., strive to pierce through in order to debunk the relative theories of men laboring with no hearts and small brains, devoid of deeper comprehension. To quote Vivekananda: *"There is but One, seen by the ignorant as matter, by the wise as God. And the history of civilization is the progressive reading of spirit into matter. The igno-*

*rant see the person in the nonperson. The sage sees the nonperson in the person. Through pain and pleasure, joy and sorrow, this is the one lesson we are learning...."* "*....A kind of scientific advaitism is spreading in Europe ever since the theory of the conservation of energy was discovered. But all that is Parinamavada, evolution by real modification as contrasted by Shankara's Vivartavada, progressive manifestation by unreal superimposition. Ramanuja's theory is that the bound soul, or jiva, has its perfections involved, entered into itself. When this perfection again evolves, it becomes free. The advaitan declares that both these take place only in show; there was neither involution nor evolution. Both processes were maya, or apparent only."*

Notice India's coverall thinking in Swamiji's mention of qualified dualism and nondualism above. *"Evolution by real modification"* is ultimately not feasible to the deeper thinker, because there is no transformation in Brahman *(aparinama),* and Brahman is all there is....is the only Reality. Thus, *"manifestation by unreal superimposition"* (vivarta) is the superior "go-to move" of wise beings here on Earth (assumedly), in the embodied condition (apparently). As he once said: *"There is no God; there is just the Great Self. Call that God if you will, but swiftly realize It."*

QUESTION #2: "In his *Raja Yoga* book, Swamiji talks about Prana and Akasha, of the universe being composed of these two. He also talks about the 'beginning of creation.' The first part of this question is: What is the cause that brought the prana and akasha into manifestation, and what is their essence? The second part is: If the universe is ultimately unreal in and of itself, why then talk about how it is composed and the material it is composed from? Third, as for the 'beginning of creation,' is it meant the beginning of 'projection' and not creation, as from the creationist theory point of view?"

ANSWER: To answer these three queries in reverse order (pardon my involution), yes, when the Vedantist uses the word "creation," it should be assumed that he/she is referring to the appearance of everything via the power of sankalpa, projection of the mind. It is also to be remembered that the mind has three levels: cosmic, collective, and individual. Projection goes forth on these three levels. The individual can benefit by this via knowing that everything he/she projected can also be withdrawn, i.e., bad thoughts, bad doings, etc. What is withdrawn, however, should also be subjected to the "Fire of Yoga," or spiritual practice, so that it will get thoroughly dissolved and not rise up again later as fructifying karma.

While creationists and evolutionists are busy arguing about god and nature, then, the spiritual aspirant who knows the secret of Cosmic Projection can trace everything back to the self, then to the Self, then to the Great Self — from ego to Atman, to Brahman. Call this spiritual involution if you want, but the initial advantage is that the soul will see its own part in what it has fashioned in the realms of name and form in time and space. It can then take responsibility for its part. No blame will be cast upon a creator God; no pushing of responsibility will be leveled at an incarnate devil. All will be clear. The soul will then, as the *Upanisads* state, *"roll up the sky like a deerskin"* and take refuge in its own perfect Being. That perfect Being is God. *"I and my Father are one,"* and *"Be thee perfect as thy God in Heaven."*

In answer to your second question, we speak on the Cosmos because beings have gotten lost in it — lost in what they themselves projected with their own minds. The task of discoursing on the unreal is undertaken by the sages and seers so as to clarify the processes through which the soul has lost its way, and to uncover certain elements in Nature and in Mind that will act as signposts pointing back to Reality. You see, the West does not know about *prana* and *akasha*. People here cannot even identify the energy in their food, or in their bodies, along with its role in health and well being, what to speak of the role it needs to take in discovering one's inner holiness.

And our wise-men of the day, namely scientists, are unaware that beyond the physical ether *(bhutakasha)* there are four other levels of space, the *akashas,* and that these are where beings presently abiding in form come from when they remanifest their bodies, as well as where the "dearly departed" have departed to.

Moreover, all these comings and goings are dreamlike, nonactual. There is a changeless Essence that has gone unrealized, been wholly forgotten. So, put in another way, if beings believe that the world is real, then the only way to convince them otherwise ( *"....birds have nests, foxes have holes, but the son of man hath no place to lay his head on Earth"*) is to talk to them about the manifestation process *(parinama* and *sankalpa)* and point out its contents and consistency *(tattvas* and consciousness,) its origins and its evolutes, its shifting sands, and its many vagaries and vicissitudes. Is it not? How else will they learn that it is all a Grand Facade and give it up?

Taking up the first of your questions last, in conjunction with what has been brought up above, you ask after the origin of prana and akasha. Prana, according to the *Taittiriya Upanisad, "....is born of the Atman. Like a shadow it spreads out on That. It comes into the body by an act of will of the mind."* This relates that, in its higher expressions, it is very close to Divine Reality. In some scriptures prana even seems to be equated with Brahman.

But akasha proceeds from Unmanifested Prakriti, and this shows its insentiency. The five elements here on Earth are distant expressions of subtler components in finer and finer akashas, or forms of space. Of course, there is the *Chidakasha,* but that is not space at all, per se; it is mentioned only to help the human mind register a vision of the spaceless Space of Divine Spirit in the aspiring mind.

Tadrupa from Wyoming writes:
QUESTION: "Does Lord Patanjali prescribe a specific method or practice for detecting and burning out the subtle seeds of desire that still cause the thoughts of sense pleasures to rise, despite the practitioner's ability to successfully resist or side step them? Are such vrittis really just burnt ropes?"
ANSWER: If you are saying here that the practitioner in question is able to resist or sidestep the desires of the mind and body when they arise, then it is

only a matter of time, and of holding out until even the seeds of said desires are burnt out, never to sprout troubles and karmas again. And by whatever method the aspirant has succeeded in raising such intense and austere fires that burn impurities — Yoga, Vedanta, Tantra, Buddhism, etc. — the effect is already upon him/her.

Specific to Yoga, then, the entire eight-limbed system is that method to follow that will expunge all undesirable elements from life and mind. Patanjali recommends no half measures. He wants the entire sweep of relative existence to be seen as it is, and thereafter transcended. Practicing an element here, and an element there — like hatha yoga, pranayama, passivism (immature ahimsa), ritualism (outer worship devoid of love of God/Ishvara-pranidhana), study of scriptural texts (svadhyaya to know only the letter of the law), etc., will not bring the sojourning soul to full Enlightenment. Comprehensive understanding of the problems of the human mind, the origin of the many karmas it has gotten itself embroiled in, and the salubrious solutions left behind by the realized seers of Mother India, constitute what it will take to burn not only these relatively tiny matters called human desires to ashes, but to eliminate even the subtlest of barriers lying in wait in the deepest reaches of aspiring human awareness.

Ultimately, Yoga is Union with God; it is not a method. That this great soul, Patanjali, gathered centuries of yogic wisdom, then systematized it all for the good of practitioners who sincerely desire union with Brahman, is a matter of great good fortune for humanity. Such all out sacrifice is seldom seen, even among the elite of the elite of illumined souls.

## Pada IV, Sutra 13

*te vyakta sukshmah guna atmanah (te,* these; *vyakta,* apparent; *sukshmah,* subtle; *guna,* attribute of Nature; *atmanah,* essence).

*"All these abiding attributes, whether apparent or subtle, are in their essence composed of the three gunas of Nature."*

Taking up the thread of our yoga studies from lesson #94, from the sutras that spoke to us about *samskaras*, memory, time, space, and the human species we thus course omwards. Patanjali makes the point and brings it to our attention that the *Gunas* of *Prakriti* are at the foundation of all of them. Swami Vivekananda explains that *"They are all manifested or fine, being of the nature of the Gunas. The Gunas are the three substances, Sattva, Rajas, and Tamas, whose gross state is the sensible universe. Past and future arise from the different modes of manifestation of these Gunas.*

The three gunas, an important *triputi* teaching particular to the Vedanta, are unknown and go unseen to people overall. They only see their outer form, the "sensible universe," and when they see even that they overlook the underlying modes of Nature due to Nature's outer spectacle. As Sri Ramakrishna said, *"Everyone here is hypnotized by the garden, and never see or go looking for the gardener."*

The three gunas work in Nature, to be sure, and they infill human action as well, but more relevant to the spiritual quest of the yogi and yogini, they are also found operating in the human mind. If they can be seen there, the various moods that living beings are subject to, get attached to, and suffer by, can be controlled. And with such control comes the dissolution of karmas. But first, there is the task of perceiving them as the insentient substrata of matter, activity, and thought. Transcending the three gunas of Prakriti is an achievement that occurs deep into the more advanced levels of yogic practice and attainment. This makes sense when the above sutra is contemplated upon to bring home the message of what underlies this universe in space and time.

**Pada IV, Sutra 14**
*parinama ekatvat vastu tattvam (parinama,* transformation; *ekatvat,* based in unity; *vastu,* substance; *tattvam,* are real).

"*Though objects appear to transform, their substance is based in unity, all coordinated by the gunas.*"

As Swami Vivekananda states, "*The unity in things is from the unity in changes.*" To bring the point forward, the gunas are the cohesive power in various forms, like the glue of the manifest and unmanifested universes. Their presence is required for any form to coagulate. It stands to reason, then, that when they are retracted at the end of a cosmic cycle *(yuga),* all worlds and lokas disappear, returning to the formless nature from which they sprung.

But the aspiring soul who has seen through the ruse of name and form, this mayic sleight of hand called "false superimposition" *(vivarta/adhyasa),* does not want to wait for hundreds and thousands of years or lifetimes to gain freedom. As Kamalakanta states in one of his wisdom songs, "*Oh Lord and Mother of the Universe: How many more lifetimes of ignorance can I bear?*" The gunas are going to have to be encountered, mastered, and transcended, then, so that *Kaivalya* (freedom from nature) and nondual *Samadhi (asamprajnata)* can be reclaimed — ideally in this very lifetime!

It is one of the hidden advaitic facets of Patanjali's Yoga that the destruction of anything is not a possibility. This is not only true as a nondual law of Existence, i.e., that one cannot destroy what is never created, but is also true as a fact of relative existence as well. Phenomena itself can seemingly be stamped out by continual cycles of time, but it will always spring up again so long as there are souls who prefer playing with form and accruing karmas over merging in the Bliss of their formless Nature. Whatever the case may be, the point is that everything in the realm of duality, like right and wrong, good and evil, virtue and vice, and the six passions of lust, anger, etc., cannot be done away with. They will exist so long as the mind and its penchant for enjoyment of worlds and forms persists — even despite the suffering that inevitably attends upon such joys and pleasures.

Knowing this hidden truth, the spiritual practitioner moves to transcend rather than purge or destroy. This move works well with spiritual laws such as "resist not evil" — not only, again, because evil is not ultimately real, but because it is here to stay so long as the worlds of name and form persist — and that is a long, long time.

At present we are fairly deep into the fourth and final pada of Patanjali's Yoga Sutras. There are 33 sutras total in this fourth section. What to speak of looking ahead, however, a constant review of sutras past and studied is recommended, as this will bring a more ideal and consummate conclusion to the study of Patanjala overall.

## Lesson Ninety-six 6/3/15
### Pada IV, Sutras 15 & 16

Coursing on in the final pada of Patanjali's Yoga Sutras, we dive even deeper into the teachings around mind, its projection, and the practices of the path of Yoga, which can both alleviate many of the impurities in this on going manifestation process, and also lead the sincere aspirant up and out of bondage and delusion. The small collection of questions, below, demonstrate the depth and profundity of those who are contemplating well the teachings of the dharma of India, and benefitting substantially from that wise austerity the illumined seers call jnana-yajna.

**Questions and Answers for Lesson 96**
Anurag from Oregon writes:
QUESTION: "As one utilizes the tools and teachings that have been offered by Patanjali and expounded upon by you in this extraordinary Raja Yoga series, the presence and operation of the three gunas becomes ever more familiar and apparent. As one becomes more established in the sattva guna, we are warned of the danger of attachment to subtle bliss. Can you comment on how one maintains the sattva guna as a default level of consciousness, while remaining unattached to the bliss that the mind naturally wants to cling to. Sri Ramakrishna advises us to 'go further.' Is the next step Samadhi itself? How to maintain such a balance, wherein the vrittis become subdued, without clinging to that peace or becoming restless for 'more.'"
ANSWER: Since we are speaking of a spiritual principle, i.e., the three gunas, we may as well state that it is far better to "cling" to attributes such as peace, bliss, and balance, than to do so and attach to the world through restlessness. The best teaching in the scriptures, and on historical record, about the problem of attachment to bliss, is in the Vivekachudamani by Shankaracharya. He cites a fourth guna, as it were, called pure sattva. If one inspects it, the subtle shift away from happiness and refined pleasure to higher mind can be detected and won over. An aspirant under its influence is seen to possess purity, light, knowledge of the Atman, and a strong desire for total liberation. Prior to this more exalted state, the presence of spiritual disciplines in practice are noticed, wherein the devotee is still working to increase faith, devotion, and natural resolve.

Further, some selfishness is still seen in sattvic beings that is not present in the soul living in pure sattva. The sign of this is in works. The rare being of pure sattva is fully engaged in the service of God in mankind, and works tirelessly in and for that ideal. Others are still enjoying personal bliss — and this is where the clinging settles in. What is more, a being holding on to the benefits of sattva alone gets disturbed easily when his/her life and peace get disrupted, either by other beings, or by the recurrence of the other two gunas. Thus, and to answer your final question, a shoring up of one's balance is needed so that one can remain unruffled even in the most challenging of situations. This, again, is why the one with pure sattva excels, for he/she has tested personal balance in the hottest fires the world has to offer — the purifying conflagration of service to God in mankind.

Avinashi from Pennsylvania writes:
QUESTION: "Swami Swahananda writes in his commentary to Vidyaranya Swami's Panchadasi: 'In the process of evolution up to what is called the 'subtle stage' we are concerned with the diversification of 'chit' (consciousness) only — chit as the 'witness', chit as subjects, and chit as objects — due to maya or will, which is a mode, in the fact the first mode of chit. Even the tamas element from which matter in our sense is to come is more ideal than material.' For me, reading this passage over is like looking into the mysterious wellsprings of initial creation, and I find myself wondering why Swami Swahananda says that we're concerned with the diversification of 'chit only' in this 'subtle stage,' even though the subtle elements must be present for there to be subjects and objects. I'm interested to hear what you have to say about 'maya or will' being 'the first mode' of chit; and I also find myself wondering what the character of 'tamas' is in the subtle stage of creation. Of course, anything else you have to say would interest me as well. Thank you."
ANSWER: The subtle stage is inward, is the mind per se. The mind is fourfold, with chit, thought or mentation, as one of its four modes. As Holy Mother said, we need to treat the mind gently at this stage, for it will be the vehicle to get us to Brahman. If chit is being defined as thought, then, it is easy to see its import. Purify the thoughts, and the rest of the mind will follow suit. But if chit is being defined as "consciousness," then it is more general, i.e., we are talking about collective mind, and even Cosmic Mind. The latter is deeper in consciousness, both by way of locale and intensity/intelligence.

But it sounds as if Swami Swahananda (I knew him, and he was quite a paramahamsa type of soul) is on the track of origins, which is part and parcel of what the Panchadasi — a classic revealed scripture of the Advaita Vedanta fold — teaches. With the "mind only" schools of India, it is impossible to look anywhere, outside or in, and not see thought operating and manifesting itself. Thus, it is even in the objects, for they are, as Holy Mother told us, *"....just our thought concretized." "Objects are mind made manifest,"* She once said.

So if you want it put in "concrete," hands on terms, with heart, everything external is just a vast sky (akasha), and it is always and ever praying to itself, worshipping itself. Do not deny the inner sky that is made up of your thoughts, the chit-akasha. It is more like that ultimate and blissful Sky of

Awareness than anything out here. Out here we are all like rogue bees without a hive, thus devoid of our Queen, and we are flying about sipping nectar from various flowers for ourselves only, and with no where to deposit it. Selfish and random experiences lacking a Source amount to nothing in the end.

As for both maya and will, according to the tradition they are very high on the scale of cosmic tattvas. The swami is probably following the tracks of Vivekananda, who proclaimed that intelligence was the first compound of Consciousness. All of this is a great help in our pondering process which, after all, is all facilitated by chit — is it not?

QUESTION #2: "I know it is said that Maya is beyond description, but it seems to me that the only thing indescribable or indefinable about Maya is its ontological status — whether it's real or unreal in terms of the main criterion that Advaita employs to test Realness, and that is, permanence. Other than this, however, it seems eminently describable and understandable to me. For, don't the dynamics described in your talks on the evolutes of Maya describe it in regard to how it works? And isn't the same true in regard to the five kleshas, starting with ignorance (avidya), which is so integral to Maya? I know you proffer stiff warnings about putting too much intellectual energy into understanding Maya; but it seems to me that, apart from being clearly understandable in many ways, those understandings can be very useful to sadhana, (for example, comprehending the already mentioned evolutes of Maya and the kleshas could do nothing but smooth the walking of the Way); and apart from being dangerous, it even seems these understandings actually protect us from dangers. I'm not challenging you, and I'm certainly not looking for a face full of ice water in asking this question. I'm only looking for clarification: what is it exactly that we should be cautious about when it comes to the contemplation of Maya? Or perhaps it's some aspect of Maya itself we should be careful of? What is it about its contemplation that, as I read your warnings, could swallow us up as the whale swallowed Jonah? As always, thank you."

ANSWER: If great souls had not pondered maya and left behind teachings on it, the rest of us, especially in present times, would have gotten so enmeshed in it that we would not know up from down. And doesn't that sound like most of the souls on Earth here in the Kali Yuga? My first point is, that they pondered it so that we would not have to risk getting completely lost in it. I have seen that happen with all of you, all of my students, when the going has gotten rough in your lives. We should never take maya lightly, or say that we understand it. Narada did that on several occasions, and Vishnu finally showed him the world-bewitching maya. The result was total forgetfulness of who he was. Famous stories abound about this.

My second point is simple. My so called "stiff warnings" are given only from the standpoint of studying maya up close, like from within it — which is rather like trying to figure out the movements and directions of a fog bank when you are smack dab in the middle of it. From a distance you can ponder maya all you want, and note its evolutes in order to protect yourself for all time; time, which is in maya too. In fact, one of its characteristics is that it is eternal. It will only come to an apparent end when the soul has reached for and attained moksha.

QUESTION #3: "If I walk into a dimly lit room and imagine that a rope tossed into the corner is a snake, but at the same time, know it isn't, I might chuckle at the tendency of the mind to create such fancy; but I wouldn't be afraid. If I don't believe a rope is a snake; in other words, I won't feel fear simply because the illusion continues. In this example it's as if only half of adhyasa is operative — the illusory half. So it seems as if adhyasa, wholly speaking, has both an element of illusion (of false perception) and delusion (false belief), and that the delusive element is what is really binding. Is this 'half-adhyasa,' which I imagine to be necessary to Lila, (without it there would be only Nirguna Brahman), still adhyasa? Or is it something else? And how have the seers of India understood and described it?"

ANSWER: Adhyasa is the covering of Formless Reality by form. "Form," here, is everything from conceptualization, to energy, to matter. The snake in the rope analogy is just an analogy, and makes the covering and distorting process (avarana and vikshepa) and the necessary release from them seem simple. It is really not, as the world and its living beings shows us constantly. As Sri Ramakrishna used to say, avidya shakti is more powerful than vidya shakti, because so many people remain bound, maybe even prefer it, despite opportunities for freedom that arise. Whatever the case, half freedom is no freedom at all, and neither is half bondage. That is why apavada is present to stop adhyasa in its tracks.

QUESTION #4: "Can the calming of the mind through whatever processes, yogic or Vedantic, be properly conceived of as the end toward which sadhana moves? Or it just the means to the end?"

ANSWER: Calm mind is, in my estimation, a stage, or if you will, a means to an end. There are so many deeper shades of that word suggestible, even in English — peace and equanimity being two of the best. Besides, often times it is just not possible, even desirable, to maintain one's calm in the midst of sadhana; there are too many intensities to pass through — if it is done right.

But there is no doubt that in the beginning stages, "calming the mind's waves" is necessary. The aspirant must keep the mind still for long enough to catch a glimpse of what is beyond, what is underlying, what is purely transcendent. As Holy Mother has declared, and Sri Krishna as well, nothing can be accomplished via restless mind.

R.O. from Hawaii writes:
QUESTION: "It seems that there is much discussion about reincarnation, a soul coming back for another lifetime. Nothing is said about a brand new soul incarnating for the first time. Where does this soul come from, or we might ask how did it come into existence and why would It incarnate anyway, as It wouldn't have any karma?"

ANSWER: Advaitically speaking, there is only one Soul, the Paramatman, and it is eternal, i.e., beyond beginnings, middles, and endings, or birth, life, and death. All individualized souls are emanations of That. As for transmigrating souls, or what we would call ego/mind mechanisms, we can look at that soul's appearance as we would a bubble forming in an ocean. Its membrane is water, inside there is nothing but air, so water is water. To try to trace a beginning to that bubble is impossible, and far and away inconceivable. Billions of them form and burst all the time. Only the ocean is real, i.e., lasting.

The Buddhists have a way of explaining, as did Lord Vasishtha in olden times, about the first lifetime that is taken up. A tiny portion of Light separates itself out from the whole in order to inspect the realms of embodied existence. Usually, such a soul sees what is present in relativity and lives one life only, returning to its Source, satisfied. In the case of other souls, who become disoriented or attached, they create a karma in that first lifetime and must return to work it out. According to some schools of Buddhism, this equates to a three lifetime scenario: one to create the karma, one to perceive it and work it out, and a final lifetime to live and be free.

But it should be stated that a soul is never "created;" it cannot be made anew. It cannot be made at all. It is pure conscious Awareness that is eternal. And being One at all times, it is God. I is that selfsame God that seekers are always attempting to realize, throughout lifetimes.

Tadrupa from Wyoming writes:
QUESTION: "On page 116 from the Raja Yoga text by Swami Vivekananda, he says, 'From the infinite storehouse of force in nature, the instrument called Chitta takes hold of some, absorbs and sends it out as a thought.' In light of this, is it correct to say that the Chitta manipulates a portion of unmanifested prakriti and converts it into thoughts which we perceive through the senses? Thus, when we see or touch an object we are really just observing a thought-object. So does his statement really correlate well with that of the Holy Mother that objects are thoughts concretized."
ANSWER: Thoughts (chitta) per se are perceived by mind (manas), not senses. Aside from that, yes, the seeds for everything lie in unmanifested prakriti, awaiting animation by a more sentient force. The real answer lies in what level of force is doing the animating. Shakti force is the Great Animator, but She operates on a very lofty level. Mind and nature conduct connections such as mentioned here on a less refined level.
QUESTION #2: "On page 119 Swamiji says, 'Immediate salvation is impossible for a cow or the dog, although they have a mind, because their Chitta cannot as yet take that form which we call intellect.' Does the great Swami mean here that they are unable to rein in the senses from their objects and employ Witness Consciousness over the Chitta and its vrittis?"
ANSWER: He simply means that animals are verily devoid of intelligence, especially higher intelligence (and yes, this includes dolphins!). Animals do not have the slightest inkling of what is beyond the senses, and no inclination to find out. That inclination is called intelligence. I wish more people would understand this about animals, so that all the sentimentalism and fantasy going

on in conjunction with them would cease. Even if an animal displays any sense of intellect at all it is because a human being has invested it there, or projected it there. In this way, certain intelligence-invested animals could transmigrate into a human form in another life. That is why we see so many animalistic human beings here on Earth; their last lifetime probably was as an animal.

As for humans, they should spend more of their time trying to realize their own divine nature, and less time obsessing with animals as objects of pleasure. Taking care of the animal world is called bhuta-yajna in our tradition, and consists mainly of making sure that animals (and all sentient beings) do not suffer, as far as possible. This is where nonviolence and vegetarianism have their deep connection. Why help them, then eat them, for instance. The Jains, for example, find it abhorrent to tie an animal up, to put a ring through its nose, to pull out its feathers or strip it of its skin for monetary gain, or to make it carry more weight than is comfortable. All this is horrible behavior by the "more intelligent" of beings on earth, i.e., mankind.

QUESTION #3: "Can you please explain the philosophical utility of cognizing the word drashtuh (seer) as Chit-shakti as opposed to Atman? How does thinking of the seer as Chit-shakti benefit the yoga student? It would seem that Chit-shakti is rooted in dualism while Atman really is based in nondualism."

ANSWER: You are not understanding the supreme level of Chiti-Shakti as seen by Patanjali. It is Mother Intelligence. According to the Agamas, it is She who has placed and kept the Atman in human souls. Just because She animates all beings and all things does not make Her "dualisitc." She is aware of Her children caught in dualism and will help them work their way beyond it; that is all. This callous dismissal of Her just because She is here on the scene with us is poorly thought, and reminds me of people's low view of the Avatar just because He appears on earth and helps its living beings. There are many luminaries that appear here in the body, but due to their vaunted transcendence of body and detachment from humanity, are neverthelesss given a higher status than the Avatar. Ridiculous! It is as if mere association with those who suffer makes one open to criticism. The opposite is the case. There are beings who demonstrate compassion for the sufferings of others, but all of that is only "from a distance." They never go, roll up their sleeves, and get down with the suffering and actually help them. Such is the lasting difference between compassion and Love, between those who merely posture and pity, and those who serve.

QUESTION #4: "Please explain the difference between tamasic, rajasic, sattvic, and pure sattvic sleep. Is it merely a way of describing the gradation of consciousness one can bring into sleep?"

ANSWER: Just as there are tamasic, rajasic, and sattvic phases of mind in the waking state, just so are they present in the dreaming state. Dull dreams, lively dreams, and peaceful dreams is another way of explaining this. Blissful dreams would suggest a pure sattvic state bordering on deep sleep.

QUESTION #5: "Can samadhi be described as the natural or original samskara, since it is the state in which the vrittis naturally rest in an inactive state?"

ANSWER: It depends upon what kind of samadhi you are referring to.

Certainly not Nirvikalpa. Seeded samadhis, though, are described as being void of gross and worldly samskaras while still holding samskaras of samadhi. When the mind thinks of nothing other than Divine Reality most of the time, that is when ordinary samskaras have been replaced by samskaras of samadhi. Sananda samadhi, for instance, holds little other than bliss and remembrance of bliss. Spiritual intoxication — like the kind we saw in Sri Ramakrishna all the time — is the result of it.

**Pada IV, Sutra 15**
*vastu samye chitta bhedat tayoh vibhaktah panthah (vastu,* existing thing; *samye,* identical; *chitta,* thought; *bhedat,* variance; *tayoh,* multiple; *vibhaktah,* divided; *panthah,* pathways).

*"All existing things (such as objects) are identical to one another, but the mind's thought places them at variance, as if divided along multiple pathways."*

Patanjali continues on in his explication of the seer and the seen, in this case, the relative seer called mind and the self-projected objects it plays with. Each object considered by the mind, if it does not perceive them as projections of itself, become, as it were, a forest of multiple pathways. The mind follows them, often randomly. It seldom, if ever, comes to see them as having a unified transcendental basis (see sutra commentary IV:14 from last lesson). The ultimate result of this outward going mind and senses culminates in materialism, and from there in a fragmented mind with no firm foundation to stand on. One must not build their house on sand, as Jesus declared, meaning that physical objects, even by contemporary terms, are merely conglomerates of rapidly changing particles. As the Upanisads say, *"No sane being would covet them."*

It is in this way that the Father of Yoga reasons with the followers of Yoga about the projecting powers of the mind cited in the Gita by Sri Krishna using the word, Sankalpa. He tells Arjuna that it is a positive evil. Put in another way by a contemporary luminary, *"The power of doing will end nonproductively if the power of Being is not implemented first."* For aspirants living in modern times, in societies that are fully immersed in profitable commerce at any cost, the tendency of the mind to complacently fall back again and again on the false security and ephemeral pleasure that objects bring, must be deeply questioned, its methods and purpose purified.

Thus, it is not merely the philosophical fine points of sutras like this one that are important; it is understanding them and implementing them along the pathway of action — *"Being, then doing."* Ideally, it is witnessing manifestation from beyond the mind's station *(dhyanam),* then thinking astutely *(jnanam)* about how to enter into the mind-field *(chittam)* so as to steer clear of the karmic field *(karmashayam)* with its many potential ills.

**Pada IV, Sutra 16**
*na cha eka chitta tantram ched vastu tat apramanakam tada kim syat (na,* not; *cha,* and; *eka,* one; *chitta,* mind stuff/thought; *tantram,* proceed; *ched,* if; *vastu,*

existing thing; *tat*, that; *apramanakam*, not perceived; *tada*, before; *kim*, what; *syat*, becomes).

*"All relative things, perceived or not by the mind previously, proceed from and become existent due to its thoughts."*

As one thinks, so one becomes. But we should not place "Des Carte before the horse." It is not "I think, therefore I am"; it is, I am, therefore I think. Being precedes becoming. Intelligence is not a matter of evolution; it is a matter of revelation. In other words, there is an intelligence that thinks (manas/chitta), but there is also an Intelligence that knows (buddhi). The yogic practitioner needs to know the specific order of these, and also know that the universe in and of space and time, with its multifarious objects, has come out of the the lower intelligence. Therefore it is termed nivritti, *"...to be renounced."*

It is ironic that, when one is a youth, parents and society are trying their best to get him to think, to use the mind. Once the boy gets the idea, then he is off and running towards all the things the mind has to offer. When he runs afoul of this frenetic course and tries to find peaceful refuge, the spiritual teacher tells him to quit thinking. He was not trained to use the mental mechanism carefully early on, and never knew that the mind had projected all the worlds of name and form in time and space — internal as well as external. The cause of his erratic course in life are all the missing elements that are absent in upbringing and society. Study of nondual scriptures, dharmic teachings along the way, self discipline mated with austerity, the ideal of living a spiritual life, daily sadhana of the Four Yogas for a well-rounded existence — all of these are nowhere to be seen in most nations, cultures, societies, and the families of this Earth. Only a few individuals, properly oriented and well trained, carry on the most noble of all traditions called spirituality, or Truth. It is the collective chitta, the low and habitual thoughts and thinking process of manifested beings, that both keeps the present and detrimental conventional standards of worldly life in place and thereby loses track of the path of higher intelligence.

In this regard, and to end, I repeat our two sutras, under study in this lesson, for deeper and more radical consideration in the light of this commentary.

*"All existing things (such as objects) are identical to one another, but the mind's thought places them at variance, as if divided along multiple pathways."*

*"All relative things, perceived or not by the mind previously, proceed from and become existent due to its thoughts."*

(Repeated note: At present we are fairly deep into the fourth and final pada of Patanjali's Yoga Sutras. There are 33 sutras total in this fourth section. What to speak of looking ahead, however, a constant review of sutras past and already studied is recommended, as this will bring a more ideal and consummate conclusion to the study of Patanjala overall.)

# Lesson Ninety-seven 7/4/15
## Pada IV, Sutras 17 & 18

The subject of the two sutras taken up for study in this lesson are about, well, what else — the mind. *"The mind is everything, my child,"* sayeth the Holy Mother. She also told us that we were to keep it in good shape since it is what will take us to Brahman. In order that it do so, then, we turn to practice, or sadhana, the qualifying side of spiritual life, which is so obviously missing in this world, and particularly in the West. Sincere aspirants who are practicing the dharma ask questions in the sacred tradition of *Atma-Vichara* — inquiry into the nature of Reality. Here, and often lamentably, it is necessary to take up issues that arise in relativity, or in Maya as we call it. By the tone and tenor of the last lesson's questions, listed below, and their well-intended answers, we, as a spiritual society amidst worldly societies, can gauge how close, or how far away, we still are from the Ultimate Goal — what Patanjali calls Samadhi.

**Questions and Answers for Lesson 97**
R.O. from Hawaii writes:
QUESTION: "Thank you for your answer to my question in RJY #96. Could you elaborate more on the 3rd lifetime of the soul who is then living free? Specifically: 1) Is this individual totally realized or enlightened? 2) What kind of life/career would such a person have? Would this person be an Avatar? 3) What happens at the time of physical death to this person's body and soul?"
ANSWER: Answering your questions in the order they were proposed, first, the soul who gets realized in the third lifetime of this particular scenario (Buddhist view) is usually not "fully" realized. When the death of ignorance occurs to souls, rare as that is, there are choices open for what might be described as different kinds of freedom. For instance, there are the different kinds of muktis in Hinduism, i.e., kramamukti (gradual), jivanmukti (individual), videhamukti (no more taking of bodies, even celestial ones), etc. Back to the "third birth" soul, if they are returning to the world, then they may fit into society quietly, like living buddhas, either helping others to destroy their ignorance or further perfecting their own spiritual skills. Pertinent to this latter category, some will take up monastic life, and if they do, there are some ten stages, called "higher grounds" *(bhumis)*, spiritually speaking, that they can attempt to master. So, no "careers" there. Even the luminaries that remain in society are usually quite detached from it, and are not bound to a money-making, bread-winning occupation.

Touching on the subject of the Avatar, that is an extremely rare being — a Soul of souls. We should not be at all willing to hand out that moniker (Avatar) so easily, to be sure. They are a once-in-a-yuga type of visitation, called "past masters." In the Kali Yuga (at present) they come every five to eight hundred years or so. Certainly, there is no "career" for these beings, having given up the world long ago — if they ever saw it as real in the first place.

At the time of the death of an illumined soul, their bodies go the way of all bodies and return to the five elements. Since their minds are clear, they can attend upon higher worlds or merge themselves into Formlessness. The subtle body that travels inner worlds is rather permanent for these beings. These souls actually look like spirituality, like God. Worldly people look like their parents, like their father or mother. That's the common comment, yes? "Oh, he has his father's eyes," or "she has her mother's features." Too bad for them. It means ignorance is stamped onto their very appearance. For the devotees, they want no impress of worldly look or life on their features. They only have the look of the beyond. Like Sri Ramakrishna noted about Narendra (the young Vivekananda): *"His eyes are always gazing into the infinite; they have the look of a mother bird hatching her eggs."*

QUESTION #2: "My other question is about the 2nd lifetime. Since this individual is already working out his karma, can he/she do the work on the 'other side' (the heavenly realms or the world of the ancestors) rather than being reborn for the 3rd lifetime?"

ANSWER: It would be nice to think so, especially if one has the knowledge that life in the body is limited and prone to suffering and lack of fulfillment. But it is not the case if the soul still sports karmas. Karmas cannot be worked out in heaven; only on Earth. In the life heavens, pain and suffering is alleviated....temporarily. It is rather like a party here on this world in that souls forget themselves entirely and enjoy pleasures, albeit they are subtler ones. Such is the realm of the ancestors; not very lofty. And soon, their karma catches up with them and they have to submit to the evolutionary process once again, falling to earth. Even in the *Upanisads,* Yama, death himself, states it: *"To careless souls fooled by wealth and pleasure, the path of the hereafter never occurs. They think in their dull minds, 'This is the only world,' and conduct themselves accordingly. They fall into my dominion, under my control, again and again."*

And that is precisely why the teachers of the dharma, the sages, the seers, the yogis, the illumined preceptors, the Buddhas, the *Nitya-siddhas,* and the Avatars when they come here, urge us to practice sadhana, spiritual disciplines. Even a little study of the scriptures, a modicum of worship, or some occasional practice of meditation, will have the beneficial and gratifying effect of lifting the soul up out of its root ignorance, even if only for a time — even if only later in life, or after death. Yes, some light can visit the soul after death, and that is good karma. But its weighty karmas are already in it, and the future may hold another birth, or more, in its train.

QUESTION #3: "Lastly, I wonder how the soul who just takes a 'peek' via one human lifetime is able to do this (especially now in this age of distractions)? Is this individual in the god-realized state all the time, or born in that state (or attains it rapidly after birth; e.g. Shankaracharya wrote the 'Crest Jewel of Wisdom,' I believe, when He was 10 years old). Again, what kind of life/career would this person lead? Would this person be an Avatar?"

ANSWER: Certainly not an Avatar. The Avatar, as I have tried to emphasize, oversees even the Trinity that oversees all worlds and all souls at all levels. Let's leave Avatar out of the picture for now. The aspirant needs to meditate on such a being for lifetimes to even begin to understand Him/Her. That is a singular Soul, if the word "soul" could even be used to describe It.

But as for the videhamukta, who I think you are referring to here, i.e., one who takes a one-lifetime "peek" at the worlds of embodiment, that soul is perfected and fully realized. In fact, it is out of a select host of that type of light-filled souls that members of the Trinity will be chosen for overseership of the coming Mahayuga.

As to what type of life such a superlative soul might lead, that question has been asked throughout time, and noted down in various scriptures as well. Uddhava asked that question of Sri Krishna at one time, i.e., *"....how does such a soul act, how does he think, how does he eat, sleep; how does he come and go?"* To answer that question, aspirants strive to become devotees. Then they approach holy company, live in the sacred atmosphere created there, and realize the answer in the end or along the way — along the "path." As with any vocation, or occupation, one must dutifully apprentice an adept or a master to learn the trade. It is the same, but more so, in terms of learning the dharma and realizing the Self, Atman. As Vivekananda has stated, and I paraphrase: *"One does not get enlightenment from a book or a temple. One must get it from another soul....."*

R.K. from South Carolina writes:
QUESTION: "How is Pratyahara actually practiced?"
ANSWER: The fifth limb of Yoga is most important, and is where most practitioners of the day fall down in their practice of Yoga. Defined as detachment, more specifically it is drawing the five senses back from their desired objects using the burgeoning will of the mind. This has two forms: first, one has to do it on the physical plane by checking one's life and habits and seeing to what extent one is attached to and unable to go without certain objects and amenities. When one finds a thing or a pleasure that is overbearing or, in this day and age especially, distracting, then the soul must withdrawn from it for awhile -- until he/she can take or leave it at any and all times.

Secondly, once external detachment is achieved, one begins to examine the source of attachment — which lies in the mind. Pratyahara here is drawing back from thoughts that distract one from concentration (the sixth limb of Yoga) on teachings, *Ishtam,* and/or Brahman. When the mind settles easily and swiftly on what Patanjali calls the "desired sacred object," then is internal pratyahara mastered.

Notably, the objects of the world have come from the mind's ability to project unmanifested nature *(Prakriti)* into form. *"Objects are thought made concretized."* If this be true, the mind must also remember that it can dissolve what it solidified. Ironically, it does so every night in the dream and deep sleep states. Now all distractions and attachments can depart the mind, leaving it in a calm and blissful state which is its original condition, before embodiment.

We may question more on this limb of Yoga, but it should also be practiced in life (the external) and in meditation (the internal).

QUESTION #2: "Also, I started studying Patanjali's aphorisms. Can you please explain even more the meaning of chitta and vrittis, and how vrittis arise?"

ANSWER: These *vrittis*, thought vibrations, or *chitta*, are what the practitioner must master in the fifth limb that I just mentioned above. Think of an erratic flow of electricity and how it damages the component (like an appliance or a computer) through which it is flowing. Then think of how nervous energy flowing through nerves — both physical and psychic — will cause damage to the brain, and to the mind, if not evened out through effort and practice. The result is what people call "stress" nowadays. Vrittis can be dull (*tamasic,* and drag the mind down, or they can be frenetic *(rajasic)* and excite and confuse the mind. However, they can be evened out *(sattvic)* so as to both allow the mind to gain peace, and prepare it for higher states of awareness — called meditation and samadhi (the seventh and eighth limbs of Yoga).

Avinashi from Pennsylvania writes:

QUESTION: "It seems that there is no real inquiry going on anymore in society, in souls who seek refuge in shallow, pseudo-mystical acceptance, and in contemporary 'yogic' circles; and if there once was inquiry, it has stopped. Furthermore, there is complacency, so the soul is dead in the water in terms of growth, and is in a state of stagnation. I read your recent commentary on this problem, and I find it to be a good description of the New-Agey kind of 'accepting' that's floating about. This description, in its way, puts shallow acceptance in its proper place, and tears away the veneer, the illusion that it allows a state of perpetual unfoldment to commence. I love it! It is a clear understanding, if what I write here is what you meant. Can you comment further?"

ANSWER: Your feeling about the potential shallowness of mere acceptance is correct, probably in most cases. Of course we will leave aside the absolute equanimity of the seers and yogis in this assessment, as their acceptance was accomplished long ago via sadhana, and since then they have taken the initiative to move deeper into the essence of spiritual life and realization. In other words, clear and obvious, one does not see or feel any complacency at all in the luminaries. On the contrary, there is real verve there, and a strong desire to know more of Divine Reality — as one song of India puts it, *"...to become exceedingly wealthy with all the treasure in the Divine Mother's Kingdoms."* Sri Ramakrishna once heard a preacher say, *"God is Dry, so we must make him wet with our devotions."* The Master responded, *"This man has obviously never seen God. If he had, he would not say such things."*

This complacency about Divine Reality attends upon people who have gone just so far, but have not continued on to the Goal. You see, there is this strange conclusion drawn by pseudo-spiritually minded beings, that if one places the whole mind upon God, that this equates to extremism. They think that a balance needs to be struck, which is true, but their balance equals compromise. These beings usually cannot even find balance in their daily lives, so how are they going to do so in the case of the *"Peace that passes all under-*

*standing,"* or better yet, the Bliss that effaces all understanding? Once, a boy came into a gathering where the Master was present and made the statement, *"My uncle's cowshed has many horses in it."* The boy was obviously confused. People of the world are also confused about the nature of Divine Reality, and they are equally confused about the unreality of the world. Since they cannot give it up, they cling to it via modes such as naive acceptance.

Quite often, beings who feign acceptance, or have it only at a mundane level, have not even entered into the realm of uncovering Truth. Otherwise bliss would be present, along with peace. Further, this peace would be supported by several other factors, i.e., and in order of appearance — deception, reception, recollection, inspection, rejection, reflection, perception, and introspection. All this is followed, finally, by Perfection.

Deception has to occur first, knowing that we have deceived ourselves. The mind deceives us first with the projection of the universe in space and time, then all the distractions and imbalances come forward from society, upbringing, fundamentalist religion, etc.

After deception comes reception; another name for this could be acceptance. This means, that as a result of doubting the appearance of the world and what it offers, the human heart and mind opens to deeper inquiry. There is no stopping to dwell on the unreal world here, i.e., to "accept" it.

Along with such receptiveness comes the recollection under which surfaces both the memory of Divine Reality and a series of past lifetimes. Meanwhile, back with the soul who is enjoying "acceptance," only the present lifetime is real and all else has disappeared behind the multiple scenes that Maya projects.

And so, inspection must be taken up. Simply put, matter, energy *(prana),* and mind must all be examined to find out their mutable nature. Once this is confirmed, real transformation of mind is taking place. This is described in Zen as *"....an eskimo inspecting snow conditions daily."* One has to examine the mind all the time.

Then, after inspection has taken place, real rejection can begin. This is the state of emptiness, of "nothing whatsoever," and when the soul spends some time in it, what is Real begins to come forward. This brings about perception — perception of the Truth that underlies mind, energy, and matter.

Penultimately, true introspection can now take place, as the soul, purified of its dross, gazes inwardly, free of barriers over Brahman, the Reality. The exhilaration here belies completely any form of complacency. The difference between actual Introspection and complacency is like the difference between a lake that is always still and peaceful, and a lake that is often visited by high winds that always cause ripples on its surface.

Merging in this Supreme State does not cause indifference, nor mere acceptance. There is a serenity deep and vast, and so unencumbered by obstacles that it only seeks to dive deeper into its own Essence. This is how the seers would describe it, leaving no doubt about the relative ineffectiveness and undesirability of stopping at the beginning stage of mere acceptance.

Kanyakali from Hawaii writes:
QUESTION: "In this last chapter we are studying some very subtle points indeed! I am slowly starting to gain the understanding that the objects that block the realization of the Self are constructed through the interplay of the gunas (IV: 13-14). But considering the gunas as subtle elements is new to me because I haven't really examined them as such, for example, when dissolving the mind stream. In these verses we are not just talking about non-attachment of the grosser objects, but of the very finest forms of non-attachment and transcendence of the subtlest building blocks of the mind and reality. Is it true that to become free from identity with the three gunas will bring freedom from all of their manifestations?"
ANSWER: Yes, and it happens at a very lofty and subtle (causal) level of attainment and Consciousness, as you surmise. The Sanskrit word, *"guna,"* really means "born of nature." So, these *gunas* are born of nature at the unmanifested level, and come into play more obviously when forms begin to solidify at different phases of their manifestation. The worlds are thus *gunamaya,* full of qualities as gunas, and beings under their influence are called *gunashraya,* dependent upon the gunas in every way. Only the seers, or luminaries, are able to transcend their influence, so their awareness is referred to as *gunasamya* — in a state of gunic equilibrium. Where this occurs there is only Brahman. That is why Patanjali, here in our sutras on Yoga, places transcendence of the gunas at a penultimate level — about the same time as Kaivalya, separation from nature, kicks in.

If one follows the tract of reasoning and questioning that you are taking here to an even deeper level, one could see that attachments are given up in order that the soul might experience loftier climes of its own awareness. But really, viewing it from the top down, the primal attachments that form baser attachments later on in life begin with the onset of the three gunas at the inception of the personal ego complex. Welcome to the vast realm of the three gunas, then, as soon as one "becomes" an individual. As I say, "Give up the individual; instead, be Indivisible."

Anurag from Oregon writes:
QUESTION: "Reading the quote from Sutra IV:16 'All relative things, perceived or not by the mind previously, proceed from and become existent due to its thoughts,' reminds me of the line from Song of the Sannyasin, 'Thine only is the hand that holds the rope that drags thee on.' The ideas regarding the projecting powers of the mind in sutras 15 and 16 are profound. I have found the instruction regarding implementing the power of Being to begin to put a halt to such projections to be very effective. In those times when I catch the mind spinning sankalpas, I often take refuge in the mantra, dissolving thoughts into the Holy Name, and it often feels as if I am awakening from a dream. Is it inevitable that we cannot always identify with the projector and must get caught in the projection from time to time? Is it a matter of the sadhaka becoming more "savvy" about the projecting process so that the sankalpic dynamic

becomes more transparent and the dream a little less real — so that entry into the karmic field is less binding?"
ANSWER: Yes, well put. At first, and even into the middling stages of recognition or recollection of the power and perfection of one's own Consciousness *(pratyabhijna),* it is, as you say, inevitable, even somewhat natural, to identify with the projection and overlook the projector — the latter being one's own mind. That is why that famous bhajan states, *"Dreamer awake; you must! You are not the dream, but the dreamer."* The "savvy" spiritual voyager, however, is fast picking up both the tendency of the soul to fall out of awareness into hypnotism, as well as noting all the signs associated with this ultimately limited condition. He is becoming *pratyabhijnajnana,* that is, he knows that he knows, and is beyond mere recognition of the fact.

The real proof of the *purusha* pudding, though, comes in the form of startling experiences of being in two states at once. At first this combines waking and dreaming. Later, dreaming and deep sleep weave together as simultaneous experience. Finally, as described so well in Zen as "every man's consciousness," *samadhi* and life on Earth combine as the very same state of Awareness. Following this inner tract, again, one perceives how God can be seen in everything, and everywhere.

Tadrupa from Wyoming writes:
COMMENTS: "OM and namaste. Here are my Raja Yoga questions. The lessons on the five types of vrittis were great. I really like the part about controlling sleep by remaining in one state of consciousness, and the teachings about samskaras and memories. I still can't believe more people are not interested in these teachings, even those with worldly ambitions. If folks knew it was all in the mind all the time, they would not have so many lazy habits that are counter productive to achieving their goals. For the spiritual seeker it really cements the need to be close to the teacher and be in holy company to begin the process of overriding negative samskaras."
QUESTION: "In light of the teachings that Maya and vrittis are a projection off of Brahman, is it an immature sort of Nondualism to call the world unreal, meaning illusory like a mirage? Is it more mature to say that the world is unreal in the sense that the water that fills a whirl pool is temporary and will dry up and then be filled again after the water returns to the ocean or river?"
ANSWER: First of all, when you write that Maya and vrittis are "a projection off of Brahman," I should correct and say that they are projections off of the mind. Brahman has and gives off no projections. There is nothing of form in Brahman, not even seeds; there is only — to quote the *Hasta-Amalaka Stotram* — the *"pure Light of conscious Awareness, attributeless and free."*

With that clarified first, you ask, then, if it is an immature sort of nondualism to call the world unreal. No. It is a very advanced realization to have, to know that the world is unreal. It is just that there is a higher realization yet in store for those who follow the spiritual path to its culmination. That verity aside for now, it being nearly indescribable, few beings come to know the illusory nature of the world. When the soul begins to suspect it, that is when practices need to be applied in order to hone that understanding. In Buddhism this is the practice of *shunyata,* or "emptiness." It is so high, and so beautiful. In Vedanta we call that scarcely traveled route by the words *neti neti,* meaning "not this, not this." It means ridding the mind of all the overlays, i.e., the unreal superimpositions that it has gathered, sometimes over many lifetimes.

There is an explanation of why this great view is sometimes seen as immature by beginners. There are some rare beings who are so advanced, so far beyond the emptiness stage of realization, that they make it seem like a lower attainment. If the beginner hears about such beings, reads about them in books, or happens upon one of them in life, then hearing and seeing something higher, they form a premature lower estimation of the illusoriness of the world. This is a problem with the seeker, who then jumps stages before he is ready to do so. Seekers pretend this higher view that they have seen or heard about, but they have not even developed the emptiness view yet. One sees them talking big one moment, but the next sees them hugging the world and its comforts to their breast as if these were the only Reality. These are the very beings who run away from the guru, avoid going on retreats, skip reading the scriptures, and do everything possible to keep from doing the work that is required to renounce the unreal. The fruit of this avoidance is dallying with wealth, undue (and usually painful) involvement with family and children, and habitual rounds of mundane ritual that takes them nowhere. But the world is unreal. What makes them think that it will ever fulfill them?

QUESTION #2: "Does the Chit-Shakti preempt the antahkarana? Where does it fit with the 24 cosmic principles and projection process?"

ANSWER: Let us not say "....the *Chit Shakti."* You write as if She is a thing, an object, or a cosmic principle. She is pure Spirit, the very refined force and carrier of Higher Intelligence. She does not need to preempt anything, for everything is Hers to do with as She pleases. If you want to understand Her better, then read about and meditate upon Sri Sarada Devi, the Holy Mother. She has told us, *"Wherever you go, and whatever you have done, just say, 'I have a Mother.'"* On another occasion She said, *"Not even God can do anything to harm my children."*

QUESTION #3: "Are viveka and vairagya the main ways to stop the ego from identifying with objects and sensations?"

ANSWER: For the Vedantic spiritual aspirant, yes; these are the mainstays with which to destroy ignorance, the "go-to" moves for advanced sadhana. For many others, however, the case is different, and this depends on temperament. For the simple, "salt of the earth," types of souls, weaning them off attraction to unreal and unhealthy things and preoccupations is more a case of replacing them with the ideal of the Personal God. It is a matter of higher attraction removing the lower ones. Whatever the case, bliss must replace the longing for happiness on Earth. When it does, or begins to, all the undesirable elements of life that cause the soul to suffer will simply fade away. As Vivekananda used to say, when mankind sees the higher ideal, the lower ideal will disappear of itself. On another occasion he stated, *"I have a clear Light now, free of all hocus-pocus."*

But I can say more about this. *Viveka,* which was Swamiji's selected name, is what allows for this "clear Light" to manifest on Earth, and in the body. When one actually sees the Vedanta in action, applied by souls who are sincere and searching intensely for Reality, one cannot but be impressed and want to spread the method it uses, i.e., viveka-vairagya, everywhere and to everyone. I can put it in this way: if celebrating spiritual life is the point, then there are many ways and pathways that can facilitate this. But if removing the root ignorance that causes suffering is the issue, then there is nothing like the Vedanta. Notably, it is swift as well as effective. For how can one love *(bhakti),* serve *(karma),* and meditate *(raja/dhyana)* effectively if the thorn of ignorance still sticks in the mind? The thorn of knowledge must be utilized to remove it, and the prime qualities of knowledge are discrimination between the real and the unreal, and successful detachment from the unreal — *viveka* and *vairagya.* After this, then throw all thorns away and go and celebrate Divine Reality everywhere, and in everything.

QUESTION #4: "To what extent can Advaita Vedanta sadhana be summarized as first doing away with all vrittis except the one consisting of "I am Brahman" followed by nondual samadhi?"

ANSWER: This summary should only be proposed at a very high level, and not before. Otherwise the beginner may run the risk of compromising nonduality via the misunderstanding of it. To explain, doing away with "All" vrittis occurs only in a nondual state. Doing away with problematic vrittis occurs, or should occur, early on in one's sadhana, accomplished by paths such as Yoga, not Advaita. Yoga proposes that we do away with *klistha vrittis* using *aklistha vrittis,* as in *"watering the flowers and not the weeds" (pratipakshabhavanam).* Later on, with this accomplished, or even better, mastered, the adept can take up the Great Sayings *(Mahavakyas)* such as *"I am Brahman"* and not only benefit from a single utterance of them, but not run the triple risk of pretentiousness, compromise, and prevarication. Nondual samadhi, then, will be a matter of right timing and right perspective — and the Grace of Divine Mother.

QUESTION #5: "When we say 'from the relative standpoint' in Vedanta, Raja Yoga, or Sankhya, does this always refer to the standpoint of the dual, unoriginal mind?"

ANSWER: Most of the time, yes, but that is not to say that illumined minds cannot use the phrase to infer or communicate to others the negative effects of assuming such a mind. It is an invaluable asset in spiritual life and its practice to be able to hold awareness of two perspectives simultaneously. Certainly, when nondual samadhi takes over, there will only remain The Truth. But in the meantime — and both for helping others and assisting the mind in comprehending higher and higher truths — acknowledging, and even taking up the relative standpoint will be an aid, and for the luminary, neither a hindrance nor a crutch.

QUESTION #6: "In lesson 11, you wrote in response to question #1 from F.L.: 'And therefore, 'That' is Immovable and Unchanging. It stands at the center of all, including our individual existences, and directs us towards an inevitable union (Yoga). From the standpoint of Reality (the Self), this union is timeless; but from the standpoint of relativity (the mind), this union is timely (and from the standpoint of maya and ignorance, it is time-consuming!).' What do you mean by 'this union is timely?' Does it mean always at hand and transcendent of time?"

ANSWER: It was rather a quip, or turn of phrase — a play on words, if you will, the idea being that there is no time in Absolute Reality; time only comes into play in relativity, at the behest of the mind.

QUESTION #7: "Can Ishvara be defined as Brahman appearing to the jiva through the lens of Maya and manas?"

ANSWER: This is how it gets explained from a more nondual perspective, i.e., that all forms, even that of *Ishvara,* dissolve into the Brahman state. But there are two cautionary points to be marked here: first, the august station of Ishvara is a permanent channel through which souls pass into pure, conscious Awareness — *"....one gets to the Father through the Son."* Thus, it is not to be trifled with via mere words and concepts. Secondly, and related, is that Ishvara does not dissolve into Brahman in the way that other principles do. Sri Ramakrishna stated that all manifestations of God are like icebergs that form in the ocean of Consciousness due to the "cooling influence" of the bhakta's devotion. In the case of Ishvara, however, It is rather like an iceberg that has become so huge that the sun is never able to melt It, and in the process of melting, that iceberg turned to crystal and gave up Its "ice" form. Ishvara will even outlast dissolution, and souls in another cosmic cycle will recall It and take refuge There.

QUESTION #8: "Is Atmic sankapla basically any projection by a free soul where that soul maintains is identify with Brahman but only associates with form? Would this include when Ishvara projects the Mahat? Is this Atmic sankalpa essentially a contradiction since, by definition, sankalpa is based on desire and those who wield Atmic sankalpa are free of desire?"

ANSWER: Do not forget the distinction between Atmic sankalpa and Mayic sankalpa. Further depth around this subject, or query, comes when we consider that it is the collective mind that projected the "messy," pain and pleasure, karma-ridden levels of existence based upon domination over others. Lord Brahma's projection, at the cosmic level, well, let's just say that no being dwelling in the subtle body would want to leave it. It is based upon benign Lordship *(Aishvarya),* not power-hungry domination *(ishitva,* one of the eight occult powers). It is most sattvic. Heaven, or the life heavens, cannot compare to It. From there souls perceive Brahman as The Light of pure, conscious Awareness and cry out "Jai, Jai, Jai!"

QUESTION #9: "When we say that one imputes unreal things over the real Atman through avidya, we are referring to the ego-mind complex doing the imputing right?"

ANSWER: Yes. And the intellect that is influenced by the unripe ego and the dual mind is also involved. Thus, one develops clouded intelligence that begets limited and hampered vision, philosophically speaking, and the crossed-eyed delusion that results from it. All the stupid goings-on we see rampant in the world today is a result of this error. The *Antaraya* (impediment) called *Bhrantidarshana,* or false seeing, is evident here, though most beings have not yet even formulated a philosophy of life that is very deep. Further, this imputing that you bring up here is nothing other than *Mayic sankalpa's* helpmate. False decisions and incorrect conclusions are rife in the intellect that wanders away from its Source — what seers would call Mother Wisdom.

QUESTION #10: "Could one add restraint of the klishta vrittis via aklishta vrittis as a prerequisite for obtaining and practicing viveka in the Four Treasures and Six Jewels system of Vedanta?"

ANSWER: Yes, but maybe even as a prerequisite to a prerequisite. Why add anything to a system that is already authored, well-formulated, and confirmed by souls like Vedavyasa? Doing away with negative vibrations of the mind is hardly the area that warrants or requires the noble Vedanta. This would be somewhat like using advanced geometry to solve a simple problem in basic arithmetic, i.e., overkill.

Actually, destroying negative vibrations in the mind really needs to be accomplished early on, before beginning any spiritual practice. This should have been the job of morals and ethics, of religion properly taught, of proper parental upbringing, even of common sense, etc. Authentic spiritual practice should be utilized for matters pertaining to Enlightenment. It is this day and time, perhaps this entire age, that has made it otherwise.

And as for the noble Vedanta, it steps in much later, after the negative vrittis have long died away. One may refer to it to help transcend subtle things like attachment to good thoughts, pleasures, sattva, conventional thinking, but must finally get around to its real utility of effecting God-realization. The *Sadhanachatushtaya* system represents advanced tools for spiritual life that are pertinent to the mind's spiritual experiences in meditation, beyond the yogic limb called *dharana,* concentration. Ideally, it deals with subtle barriers relative to the internal Cosmos.

QUESTION #11: "When we speak of the ability of viveka-khyati to restrict the three gunas, does this really mean that the aspirant develops the ability to remain in sattva, or in other words, restrict raja and tamas? Would it be correct to say that this ability reaches a superlative or perhaps absolute state or culmination when the master yogi can dissolve the three gunas completely into the Self, and thus obtain ultimate restriction of the gunas?"

ANSWER: At this refined level of yogic mastery, remaining in sattva is not the ideal. A master yogi seeks and attains spiritual experiences that are beyond all things having to do with nature, with form. True, if there is a place of respite needed in all of this, a sort of default zone, then it would be sattva. But Shankara has explained nicely that beyond sattva there is "pure sattva."

Sri Ramakrishna has stated that *"No matter how high a bird might fly, it needs to come to rest on the branch of a tree at some time."* This is in reference to the illumined soul who, exploring the highest reaches of Awareness, returns at times to a relative position — say, like the branch of the tree of Yoga called *dhyana,* meditation. Or, they could rest in concentration, since they are always known for that.

QUESTION #12: "When the yoga commentators speak of restraining klishta vrittis via aklishta vrittis, can we really think of this as watering the flowers and not the weeds essentially where the flowers are higher thoughts of Truth alone and the weeds are basically every other thought?"

ANSWER: Yes, for as I said, the negative thoughts in the mind of a sincere practitioner are much different than the negative thoughts that fester in the mind of worldly and evil beings. The practitioner would not have obtained the desire to perform worship and study the scriptures, and to meditate, if base and gross thoughts were still exerting their influence in the mind. Put another way, there are no real "flowers" even present in the minds of those deluded by Maya. But despite the suggestion of old karmas that may still lurk in the practitioner's mind (as burnt ropes), he/she has good karmas and positive samskaras on the rise. These are *"aklistha,"* and have been there for some time, even lifetimes, in order that they influence the mind in a positive direction in the present life. This fact speaks volumes on behalf of the luminaries and their commentators, both.

QUESTION #13: "Does Patanjali ever say that jnana yoga is absolutely necessary for success in Raja Yoga? It seems rather difficult to be a yogi without being a jnani."

ANSWER: He does not need to say it. It is inferred in every sutra that graces his system. Seers of the past, like Lord Vasishtha, declared it, however, and also marked *Jnana Yoga* as a much more profound and beneficial pathway then anything related to hatha and pranayama alone. We should note how Patanjali went further, the entire distance, to bring all beings to meditation and samadhi. In other words, if we embody at all, we need to do so with a pure mind, with spiritual attainment already a confirmed fact. "Should a man be reborn?" they asked Swami Vivekananda when he arrived in the West and informed them about reincarnation. *"I certainly hope he will not,"* came his answer, *"not until he can do so in full Awareness.*

QUESTION #14: "Can vrittis to be a mixture of aklishta and klishta, like how karmas can be mixed? It would seem to me that most vrittis can be somewhat inscrutable when classified this way, especially for a person who does not seek God. For example, suppose a worldly professional person gets a promotion and becomes even more self-absorbed with works and gains wealth to the point that they forget God amidst their endless enjoyment of objects. Then we could say that their vrittis leading to the promotion were klishta because they took them even further from God, right? Now suppose that same person gets the promotion, then ends up hating their job due to seeing how power hungry upper management is, which then leads the person towards finding a spiritual path and dharmic work later. Then those same vrittis leading to the promotion would be aklishta since they were taking them closer to God, right? Please clarify."

ANSWER: The presence of karma of various kinds, the different gunas and their permutations, the insinuation of variegated thoughts, and the like, are all facets of Maya that cause the wise beings to get free of the entire sweep of cause and effect. Nature is as horrible as it is beautiful, suffering is unrelenting yet leading, and desire leads to pleasure as well as pain. Given all of this and more, the realm of thought and ego is not only a "mind-field," as Patanjali calls it, it is also a "mine field," ready to explode at the slightest provocation. You ask me to clarify this. Is that not funny? In a world where good and bad so easily trade places, and all devoid of any sense of conscience; and worse, where no clear delineation makes itself known, where admixtures confuse the matter all the more and cover the Truth deeper all the time, i.e., the eternal exacerbation going on, all that can be said is, save yourself all the interminable trouble and get free immediately.

And here is where I can offer a favorite quote of Vivekananda, speaking on the world of Maya in terms of false religion: *"I hate this world — this dream — this horrible nightmare — with its churches and chicaneries, its books and blackguardisms — its fair faces and false hearts — its howling righteousness on the surface and utter hollowness beneath and, above all, its sanctified shop-keeping."*

Perhaps this is why things that are of a mixed nature are eschewed by the wise — mixed acts, mixed thoughts, mixed pure and impure concepts, etc. Mixed often results in mixed up. The only real solution in the realm of the mind is gaining a pure mind, sometimes called "no mind." As Holy Mother, our superior guide in life, has said: *"From pure food one gets pure blood. From pure blood comes pure thoughts. From pure thoughts comes pure mind, and pure mind is God."*

Thus, keep it pure and generally avoid admixtures. Maya is stultifying wherever one finds it, and the only place it is not found manifest is in Brahman. So seek to realize That.

QUESTION #15: "Are sadhana and thoughts of the teachings of the dharma always an aklishta vritti when accompanied by sincerity and enthusiasm?"

ANSWER: Rising above the limitations of morals and ethics, one finds the dharma. Learning the dharma, one then finds that it must be realized, and that this realization will require sadhana — spiritual practice. If there be any such place left at all on Earth while in the body, this is the realm of authentic positivity, instanced by the fact that such things as depression, brooding, doubt, fear, and all their unsavory companions begin to wane, then go away altogether. Contentment, then peace, then bliss, arrive. There is no better testament to the presence and existence of full-fledged Divine Reality than this, further proven by the depth and grace we see and feel in our gurus. And yes, our sincerity and enthusiasm is what we give back to them in order that we escape ignorance and suffering for all time, or, cancel out our negativity forever.

QUESTION #16: "Can you please explain the difference between pratyahara and dama?"

ANSWER: Pratyahara, or control of the mind, and dama, self control, may look different in outer definition, but they amount to the same result after having been practiced and attained. The former is the fifth limb of Yoga, the latter is the second of the Six Jewels of Vedanta. So, no real difference, really. The best tact is to implement them into spiritual life and practice, each in their own setting, thus proving this fact to oneself and benefitting immensely in the interim.

QUESTION #17 "When the yoga student recognizes attachments or problematic dualities, is it generally good policy to practice some austerity that doesn't over tax the body to do away with such difficulties of the mind? For example, if one is attached to the comfort of a hot shower, and is averse to cold, would going and taking a cold shower be a good idea for helping the mind get over this?"

ANSWER: Such an experiment might conduce to some benefit, but it is unlikely that one will all of a sudden lose one's love of hot water and start to take cold showers instead. Such is the realm of preferences of the mind and personality. Besides, conditions play into the situation. If a hot shower lover visits Kolkata in the summer, for instance, he might suddenly begin to prefer and search out cold showers all of the time.

But these are small matters, at least to the practitioner of Yoga. The real issue here is whether or not the individual will take to austerities of any kind, at any time. It takes strength to recognize their benefit, and strength to undergo them. Most beings are weak. They would never even consider putting themselves through what they would consider to be hardship.

QUESTION #18: "Can being in holy company or the presence of the guru temporarily suspend worldly or negative samskaras for the sincere spiritual seeker?"

ANSWER: Yes, for certain, and both the key and the rub lies in the word, "temporary." Sri Ramakrishna used to tell this story: *"A man once sat on a park bench feeding the pigeons peas and grains, and watching them eat them all up. He was then satisfied that he had fed them well. Before leaving, however, he took one of the pigeons in his hands to examine it. As he felt its neck, he realized that all the delectables that the pigeon had eaten had only lodged in its craw, and had not gone to the stomach."* This story is meant to convey the unfortunate phenomena of students sitting in front of the guru and taking the teachings of the dharma. Later, when the guru observes his students, he realizes that the teachings he transmitted with such love and concern had only lodged in their surface mind, and had not gotten through to their heart-mind complex. This is how even gurus have to learn to give up expectations. What a disappointment!

So, temporary benefit is gotten by many of those who frequent the company of holy beings. It is good, overall, for they get some "breathing room" from their nagging karmas and insinuating samskaras. But they will have to do the real work sometime or other — the work of digesting the peas and grains of teachings and implementing them into their lives and their spiritual practices. What is only temporary will then transform into what is permanent. For, there is only one Verity that is Permanent, that being Brahman Itself.

Akshaya-Bhakti from New England writes:
COMMENTS: "When we began this Raja study, many of us were stunned to learn that we, too, had the capacity to experience samadhi as exemplified by Sri Ramakrishna, As we near the end of this momentous text, I have to admit that I am still stunned (!), especially since I have, regretfully, relied more on study than practice in this first go-around. Despite the intricate elucidations of the guru(s), I realize that the 8 limbs have been presented as such for teaching purposes, and for the most part, you can see how they flow into one another, especially Dharana into Dhyana (as the concentration in the former is merely extended in the latter). But I still have several questions about the nature of samadhi (reflecting only upon the meaning, no thought of form) and how it occurs. Deepest gratitude, dear teacher."
QUESTION: "As to Savitarka, the initial stage, it seems to me more like deep study because it is still so discursive. How does samadhi differ from contemplation? How does Dhyana (meditation) flow into samadhi? How does one fortify the memory so one does not have to rely upon textual 'instructions' as to what to reflect upon?"
ANSWER: Contemplation occurs early on to the introspective soul, while samadhi is usually (except for "glimpses") a much later stage, the latter utilizing a more focused force of Consciousness. This can be likened to the difference between first reading the scriptures, then later having the experiences described therein for oneself. Once concentration is mastered to any degree (hopefully to an extensive degree), meditation occurs. It happens differently in various aspirants. According to Holy Mother, one needs only to keep up the practice and wait for meditation to happen naturally. She states: *"Perform your sadhana by meditating upon the Lord. On that day on which you have the right mood, you will have meditation spontaneously."* At that time one will scarcely be aware of meditation flowing into samadhi, so natural will it be. One is just there, "of a sudden." All the practices — not just of one's day or week, but of one's entire spiritual life — will be forgotten, and the soul will simply be launched into the rare nondual condition, evenly poised for the "Grand View."

Consciousness is of three kinds, basically. There is consciousness of the world, extremely limited and courting suffering all the time. Then there is what is referred to as "Witness Consciousness." It oversees every happening going on in the world, as well as what occurs in the subtle and causal realms. Finally, there is Nondual Awareness. It has one view — the Grand View. It sees All, but only in the sense of what is Unchanging. The Three Worlds do not occur to It. Vast and conditionless, It is the Awareness that allows the Transcendent Overseer to see.

QUESTION #2: "Can the stages of the word shed any further light on samadhi?"
ANSWER: Of course they can, for as the aspirant approaches this "Unstruck Sound" in deepest meditation, he/she is getting very close to the Source and Essence of Reality. And even by the mere mention of your notes here, at all four levels of the Word, clues can be gotten and conclusions made regarding

deep experiences that are to be had at these inward stages. Whereas this dharma teaching is usually utilized for communicating the dynamics of manifestation coming from the Unmanifested, matching it up with the levels of samadhi provides much to consider — not the least of which is casting a bright light upon the mind's ability to both congeal and dissolve objects in space and time, which are both one of the impediments to and the facets of samadhi.

QUESTION #3: "When no effort is made to subdue the tamas and rajas gunas, they probably "roll over" at a fairly quick rate, kind of like biorhythms? Is it possible, though, that one's life can have periods of even longer 'cycles,' say, even a couple of years, which are dominated by one of the gunas, all the time struggling with tamas that affects one's very spiritual will itself? Is there any name for that?"

ANSWER: One name that is used for this is "a pain in the ass." Waves of good, bad, and mixed happenings go on in cycles throughout embodied existence. This is caused by the changing of the gunas, like the changing of the guard every night at the palace gates. At the same time, though good, bad, and mixed are in operation, an overall dominance of any of the three gunas is also occurring. Thus, pleasures, indifference, and pain, duly maintain their presence in life cycles. But if these three are experienced when sattva is predominant overall, then happiness is greater and suffering is less. The reverse is true when tamas is predominant over all. A man will say, "It has been a difficult year," or he may say "It has been a good year," or, "an okay year," but the pleasures, pains, and neutralities that he has experienced over all those months have really not changed that much; only his mind has changed.

And that is why the seers want to get beyond the influence of the gunas to that refined ether in the pure mind that suffers no change whatsoever, and is always constant. They will not stand for being dragged from birth to death and death back to birth by such ignominious and insentient forces as the three gunas. They will become *trigunatitananda* — immersed in the bliss of transcendence of all the forces of nature, even the most subtle ones.

**Pada IV, Sutra 17**
*tad uparaga apeksitvat chittasya vastu jnaya ajnatam (tad,* thereby; *uparaga,* conditioning; *apeksitvat,* replies; *chittasya,* thought process; *vasta,* real; *jnaya,* divided; *ajnatam,* not known).

"*The process of thinking relies upon the conditioning of the mind, which thereby divides knowing from not knowing regarding the objects and situations it encounters.*"

Mental conditioning is a powerful obstacle that must be neutralized before any appreciable progress can be made along the spiritual path. Few beings know how to get into the mind-stuff *(chitta)* and uncover the *samskaras* (mental complexes) that hinder and impede spiritual advancement. The question may be asked, how does a samskara actually get formed? It begins with attachment to/desire for the realms of name and form *(nama-rupa).* This is compounded further by experiences that are enjoyed and suffered there with the five senses *(shadayatana)*. This combination sets the stage for the three "thickeners" of mental conditioning called *sparsha, vedana,* and *trishna.* Sparsha contributes its influence via contact with the world and its peoples and the various relationships that arise therein. Vedana exacerbates the admixture through body-oriented pleasures that stimulate desire, and trishna is that very desire — the continual thirst for sense objects and the passing enjoyments that come from them. All of this, taken together and over time, leads to a new birth in the body — it oft-times forming before the soul has even left the present one. Of course, this new birth is taken under the limiting, often darksome presence, of these past conditionings, already figured into the equation.

Intensifying advanced spiritual practice once the early observances have been implemented and the lower limbs have been mastered, involves locating one's conditionings within the mind's inner confines and rooting them out. This ability suggests the presence of matured observances that have more to do with Witness Consciousness than with individual mind and will. As Sri Ramakrishna has explained by way of simple story, *"If thugs and dacoits are making themselves a nuisance on the banks of the public lake, merely putting a sign up saying "Cause no Nuisance" will not deter them. The authorities will have to send an official to the area, and his presence will put an end to the trouble."* This is stated to mean that when the higher authorities abiding in the illumined mind take over the lake of spiritual life, all the impediments that visit the shores of ordinary mind and human will can be destroyed. This relates perfectly to the forthcoming sutra and its confirming declaration.

## Pada IV, Sutra 18

*sada jnatah chitta vrittayah tat prabhu purushasya aparinamitvat (sada,* continually; *jnatah,* be known; *chitta,* thought; *vrittayah,* vibrations of the mind; *tat,* that; *prabhu,* the Lord; *purushasya,* pure awareness; *aparinamitvat,* immutable).

*"Thought vibrations of the mind can always be known due to the pure Awareness abiding there as the Lord of the mind."*

The winsome word, *"Prabhu,"* finds its welcome place here, late in the sweep of Patanjali's Yoga Sutras. As has already been mentioned, the father of this system scarcely mentions God in his entire set of sutras on Yoga. When he does, it is to say that God (in form) is a very special soul, *Ishvara,* who presides over and oversees all the workings of the Cosmos, inner and outer.

And this Prabhu, this Lord, resides in the mind. It is, as Patanjali states, *"The Lord of the Mind."* It could be said that He resides in the heart, but when wisdom has been gleaned and ignorance has been destroyed, heart and mind find their union in nondifference. The one who has befriended his mind is the happy individual, then, for all thoughts are known to such a one. There will be no problem with discernment from then onwards, for thoughts that are positive *(aklistha),* thoughts that are negative *(klistha),* and even the admixture of the two, can be duly known, thereby accepted or rejected easily.

And what to speak of mere thoughts, the realm of "no thought" awaits the yogic adept. "No vibrations" are far less troublesome than good, bad, and mixed vibrations. This realm of no vibration is where mind has first been controlled, then transcended, and finally shown the gateway to pure conscious Awareness — the *Purusha*. Vibrations cease there, and only bliss resides and prevails. Change is also not there. That conditionless condition is *aparinamitvat* — Immutable. Thus, this sutra holds many of the consummate yogi's favorite words and principles.

*(Repeated note: At present we are fairly deep into the fourth and final pada of Patanjali's Yoga Sutras. There are 33 sutras total in this fourth section. What to speak of looking ahead, however, a constant review of sutras past and studied is recommended, as this will bring a more ideal and consummate conclusion to the study of Patanjala overall.)*

## Lesson Ninety-eight 8/28/15
### Pada IV, Sutras 19, 20, & 21

As we head towards a rapt conclusion of the fourth and final pada of what is termed Patanjala, Raja Yoga, or Ashtanga Yoga, the intended route of purified mind expands with all its further ramifications. These are the real powers of Yoga, the occult package having been eschewed and abandoned by the consummate yogi and yogini long ago. As Patanjali states, and oft quoted by Vivekananda in more recent times, *"When the yogi rejects the occult powers, then he benefits by the raincloud of virtues,"* or Dharma-megha Samadhi. From here on in the mind is like a vast landscape of beneficial potential, whereas prior to this singular occurrence there were weeds and thorny bushes aplenty. Finally, avoiding such karmic foliage became too vexing, so the yogi got the fire of Yoga and burned it off, using the burnt remains as further nutrients for inward growth. As Sri Ramakrishna was wont to say: *"If a thorny bush outside one's door causes one pain, then it will not do to stand in front of it and merely yell, 'Burn bush, burn!' One has to collect fuel, procure fire, and set it ablaze, ridding oneself of it forever."* And this is precisely what students are attempting to do in the questioning process, some more of it illustrated below:

**Questions and Answers for Lesson 98**
Kanyakali from Hawaii writes:
QUESTION: "Sutra IV:18 contains one of my favorite commentaries by Swamiji because I love the logic of it. In finding a stationary reference against which one can perceive activity, he says, 'logic compels you to stop somewhere... behind this never-ending chain of motion is the Purusha, the changeless, the colorless, the ever-pure.' I also like how Witness Consciousness is described as a higher authority that oversees the mind's workings, like a peace officer keeping the trouble-makers in line. Sometimes I think I have a grasp of how we are defining Purusha, and other times I think I might have it confused with other realms. Is there a subtle difference between Prabhu and Purusha?

In this lesson we learned that Pure Awareness abides in the mind as Prabhu, the Lord of the Mind (residing in the mind), and also that the mind, once it is controlled and transcended, delivers one to Pure Awareness – Purusha. Hearing you differentiate the two might help me sort it out."

ANSWER: *Prabhu* means "The Lord." The word, *"Purusha,"* infers the "dweller in the city of nine gates" (i.e., the body and sense organs, etc.). When the Purusha gets realized by the jiva (embodied soul), then it is nothing short of the Lord. It is God dwelling in mankind. Otherwise, the Purusha gets covered over and the Lord vacates the premises quickly, not willing to be a party to the ignorance and suffering that ensues.

All this confusion happens to the mind, *manas,* not to Purusha or Prabhu. As Sri Ramakrishna has stated, *"The soul bound, is man; that same soul free, is God."* As students of Yoga we must learn to differentiate between what, where, when, why, etc., then allocate all that is dull and insentient to maya's realm, and recall and implement all that is noble and uplifting into the Lord. This is *"separating the wheat from the chaff,"* followed by *"Grant unto Caesar what is Caesar's, and take unto yourself what is the Lord's."* If one's "Witness Consciousness" is not called into the picture, then the mind is left to its own devices — the result being what we see all around us in the form of the restless and overactive world. Unfortunately for the denizens of this world, acts done in *rajas,* restlessness, cause karmas of like kind to occur. Perhaps this is why the seers tell us that God is not in this world. Prabhu, the Lord, only abides where Peace and Wisdom and Love and Bliss reside. Thus, the sensitive Purusha seeks Him there, in "The Abode of Peace."

Anurag from Oregon writes:
QUESTION: "We are really entering lofty atmospheres with these final sutras. The realm of 'no thought,' where from the position of Witness Consciousness both klishta and aklishta vrittis are transcended, is truly exhilarating to contemplate and recognize. You have referred to it in this recent commentary as the gateway to pure conscious awareness — the Purusha. In reply to my question in the last lesson regarding becoming free of the sankalpic projecting process, you made a curious mention of the real proof of the "purusha pudding" coming in the form of being in two states at once. I would appreciate it if you would expand a bit on this. I think I might know what you mean but am not exactly sure. Perhaps some elaboration will bring recognition, or at least help set us on the trailhead of such a subtle path to explore. Thank you!"
ANSWER: The rishi, Pippalada, states: *"The ignorant soul imagines that the three lower nadis are separate, and thus wanders in bondage. The aware soul, getting wisdom from the noble Vedanta, does not suffer this delusion in the three lower states, realizing the oneness of all four of them."*

What is basically being recounted here are the waking, dreaming, and deep sleep states of mankind, as well as what lies beyond them, i.e., Turiya, or "The Fourth." Further, and along these same lines, Gaudapada states: *"The "A" of AUM equates to the waking state. The "U" of AUM equates to the dreaming state. The "M" of AUM equates to the deep sleep state. When the adorable seer comes to know the three common and abiding qualities of these three states, that one, the great sage, is worthy of worship."* Going onwards, he states: *"Having known Omkara quarter by quarter, one should meditate on nothing else whatsoever."*

As for my comment, then, "being in two states at once" refers to that meditator who has linked up one state to another, thereby mastering his or her own awareness. As our recent study of the *Taittiriya Upanisad* showed us, connections are paramount in Vedanta. In Yoga, these same connections can be compared or equated to the internal art of *samyama,* or how the yogi comes to master the upper three limbs of Yoga and combine them into a singular force for illumination of mind. Knowing the qualities of the subdivisions mentioned by each of these two darshanas consists basically of waking up from the waking state, putting all dreams to an end, and plumbing the depths of the deep sleep state to find (and burn) the seeds *(bijas)* of all projecting power *(sankalpa).* Emerging from his sadhana within this cosmic process, the seer is free, and then has a choice to remain embodied or immerse into Brahman *(Yoga).* Then, two, three, or even four places, are no longer separate, and that Divine Oneness *(ekagra)* we so often hear about is realized and enjoyed fully. This is both bliss *(Ananda),* and, of course, the end of suffering.

Tadrupa from Wyoming writes:
QUESTION: "Of what utility are the 3 states of awareness, 3 bodies, and 5 koshas to the yogic practitioner? How do they enhance or augment the 24 cosmic principles as objects/supports of meditation?"
ANSWER: Here, one would have to simply change the questions into the answers, i.e., the 3 states of awareness, the 3 bodies, and the 5 koshas have great utility, and they all enhance the 24 cosmic principles. To see this, one only needs to lay them all out, side by side, next to one another, and see how they all connect, and how they all fit inside each other as well.
QUESTION #2: "Is the most important feature of Atmic sankalpa the fact that it is the use of the projecting power of mind in such a way that the wielder remains completely devoid of ignorance and its effects?"
ANSWER: No, I would not say so, for ignorance should never be a part of the sankalpic pattern to begin with. It is not found in the Trinity and its projecting power, where pure sattva only abides. It only insinuates itself at lower levels of mental projection, and can and does get denser and denser as it falls into the darkness of tamas. Atmic sankalpa has much better features to consider and utilize than all that.

Another student writes:
QUESTION: "As I understand classical Advaita, that which is nama rupa is unreal. What is nama rupa therefore only catches a reflection of the Real, but isn't Real itself. In other terms, every object consists of Sat, Chit, and Ananda and also nama and rupa; and only the Sat, Chit and Ananda in the object is Real,

not the nama and rupa. Thus a couch isn't Real in the deepest sense; only the essence of the couch, (or a car or a mountain or the world), is truly Brahman and therefore Real. So my question is this: when the Upanisadic seers thought of the world more as the temporary Brahman, (instead of that which is unreal), is it nama rupa that they were according temporary reality to? Or is that a misreading of Upanishadic doctrine??"

ANSWER: Yes, it was nama and rupa that was being accorded temporality, because Brahman is "the only Reality." They knew this, of course. It is a kindness to the world, and a concession for those not yet able to have the direct experience of Brahman, that the world is accorded any type of abidance at all. Yes, it appears real, since it seems solid, and that solidity persists over time. However, time is changing also, as is the mind that projected both, i.e., the world and time.

It is very likely, then, that the enlightened ones afford a sense of reality to the world so that we will use the mind in time to eventually disprove the so-called reality of the world. If the rug were merely yanked out from under us in perfunctory fashion, we might fail both the world (i.e., karma) and Brahman. Thus, regimens such as worship, service, sacrifice, and the like, are placed in the world so that beings can qualify themselves. Giving up the world prematurely has always been a problem — both for the monks and the householders. Therefore, there is a certain wisdom in considering the world to have a temporary reality — at least for as long as one abides in it. There is a path in India called *Dristisristivada* in Sanskrit that relates to this, meaning that the world is real as long as we perceive it, but not thereafter. Actually, there are some 35 or more other philosophical paths I have come upon, each a perspective worth considering, and covering so many levels of the deep thinking consciousness of India's sages.

Akshaya-Bhakti from New England writes:
QUESTION: "To what degree should we interrogate the specific samskaras that become visible to us? Would we have to ultimately know where they come from, (i.e., like drowning on the Titanic) in order to quell them, or is it just to continually reaffirm that they are not our true Self?"
ANSWER: Both of these ways of proceeding are right. Since some of these impressions of the past come to us in the form of memories, and therefore as samskaric residue, we have to deal with them as they appear; we do not always get to choose. Some samskaras are actually arising from upbringing in this life, while others are from past existences. Of course, they are both/all connected, but in the case of connections that cannot so easily be perceived, the method of refutation of the samskara's actual reality combined with affirmation of our true Self will be the best course.
QUESTION #2: "How we can best practice the involution of the alambanas remains a main focus of study for me. I still would like to know about how to incorporate the guru's gracious elucidations of explicit questions that we can apply at each stage of our inward journey to samadhi, such as their 'desirable

and undesirable qualities,' etc., and even the field of concentration in which to use them, such as the instrument of apprehension. In the last on-line classes of the Taittiriya Upanisad, you touched upon how lengthy and often overwhelming the process seems, but you reassured us that, yes, we do need to go through all of the steps and spend adequate time on every one. Could you please help me to better apply that knowledge? My mind still feels a little lost when I finish japa/mantra (which I assume is ending with Dhyana?) as to how to proceed. Some light was shed in Lesson 93 (in the answer to R. O.): 'As one commentator states, it is important to note that this concentration on the material principles is not on the objective word with its external forms, but relates to vrittis to be controlled which exist within the sentient personality. They are mastered within the mind.'"

ANSWER: If you have the mantra given by the spiritual preceptor, and instructions on how to use it in meditation, then you have the essentials. If, over years of practice with the mantra, there still seem to be blockages in your path to Enlightenment, then some specific contemplation on the alambanas might be very helpful. For instance, water has both desirable and undesirable qualities, i.e., it can be pure and it can become contaminated. It can save a man dying of thirst, but it can end the life of a drowning man. The cause of water here on earth is particularly edifying when contemplated. No, not the physical cause only, but the subtle cause. If water exists in one's dreams, does it do so because we experienced it here on earth first and then dreamed of it later, or is it that the subtle precedes the gross, and we solidify thought-water into liquid water as we emerge from subtler realms? Then, where does the thought water, or dream water come from?

    In this way we work our way inward, opening up channels in the mind that may have been closed down for lifetimes. Suddenly, through one of these opening channels, we catch a glimpse of "That." As the Great Master says about that experience, *"He then becomes mute, muttering to himself only, 'Oh! What is this? What is this?'"*

QUESTION #3: "Is the sentient personality referring to the make-up of samskaras? How to ensure that all this external knowledge is awakened internally? Could you please offer more reflections on this? How do I contemplate the visheshas without ego, as stated in the definition of samadhi?"

ANSWER: The ego will become transparent once you see its illusory nature. Then it will not get in the way of your inner vision anymore. All knowledge will become revealed to you. If the ego remains cloudy, and disruptive, then use it as an alambana. As the subject of meditation, how can it keep its individual identity anymore once you, yourself — your Self — has taken the position of witness? It will have to "fess up," will it not, and admit that all that knowledge that is within you was being hoarded by it all along, for lifetimes, when all the time it all belonged solely to the Wisdom Mother. Then, *"Let go thy hold, say Om Tat Sat Om...."*

QUESTION #4: "Since inquiry doesn't come easily to me, I really notice when my thoughts finally come together. Maybe that sense of 'knowing,' of going beyond the material into the meaning, is like what happens when the knowledge one brings to samadhi becomes experience, like a flash of insight. Are subtle thoughts defined as such only because they deal with subtle objects, or is there a different quality about them, such as being more related to feeling or awareness than actual words?"

ANSWER: Both objects and feelings are intertwined in life, and since the samskaras are formed using them both, therefore they will naturally have their connections within the mind. And knowing this will allow the deep meditator to pull apart such connections and then see that they are actually bonds. The desirable connections are different from these, and are listed in the scriptures (like in the Taittiriya Upanisad). They are not those that are associated with money, offspring, relationships, emotions, and the like. It is the unholy combination of this short list that forms binding karmas and samskaras; the dharma and its teachings, used properly, will break them apart. The problem is that 1) most beings do not know of the healthier connections, and 2) even if they did, or come to hear of them, they still prefer to wallow in the emotional states that result from them.

Self-inquiry does not come easy, as you say. Maya is strong. The desire for prana-based experience in the body, and in nature, is strong. The inward and outward pull of attraction from the ancestor realm is strong, as are the karmas and samskaras that make up such gravity. Avidya maya is stronger than vidya maya — at least and until that singular desire for freedom from the tyranny of all of the above suggests itself to the newly aspiring soul. Godspeed!

### Pada IV, Sutra 19
*na tat svabhasam drishyatvat (na,* is not; *tat,* that; *svabhasam,* self-illumined; *drishyatvat,* is known).

"*That mind is not illumined in and of itself; it is known by the Knower.*"

It is a mistake in philosophical understanding to think that the mind is the ultimate seer. There is a Witness of it and its workings, and that is the true Knower. As Ramprasad sings, "*Oh mind, you are the supreme sovereign in the land of awareness, but you have become a petty potentate by taking sole counsel of the five senses.*" So, whereas the mind may rule in the realm of senses and sense objects, it remains unawares of the higher climes of its own pure, conscious Awareness. In this regard it may help to think in terms of the distinction between ordinary mind, and Original Mind. Further elucidation of this point is given in the following sutra.

### Pada IV, Sutra 20
*eka-samaye cha ubhaye anavadharanam (eka-samaye,* simultaneously; *cha,* and; *ubhaye,* both; *anavadharanam,* unable to cognize).

"*(This is due to the fact that) the mind is unable to cognize two things at once.*"

To continue this line of reasoning from the previous sutra, the mind does not have its own light, as Lord Kapila revealed early on, due to it being dual by nature. And what to speak of "dual," it actually tends towards randomness, even scattered mind, if its movements are left uncontrolled, its abilities are left undisciplined, and its potential left untapped. More importantly for the seeker of Truth, the luminaries have concluded that there exists a witness of its various thoughts and processes. This, Witness Consciousness (sakshi bhutam) is worth striving to realize, for its controlling influence will put all troublesome tendencies on the run and deftly unify all dualities. Thus, the Upanisads state, *"We salute the Leader of our soul, through Whose grace our ignorance is dispelled. Who is beyond pleasure and pain, virtue and vice, life and death, and all other pairs of opposites. We recognize that One as the only Witness to the changing phenomena of this universe."*

This Seer of all seers, and of all that is seen, is the *"Inner Ruler Immortal seated in the Heart" — Antaryamin.* What all beings are calling everything from creation to miracles to intuition to God is this very Principle. The human mind is its matrix for expression. But if the many important connections that make up its all-penetrating network, both external and internal, get pulled apart, the Antaryami's divine energy cannot flow into its various vessels. It is much like Sri Ramakrishna's story about the two villages that were connected by a telegraph system. One was attempting to send the other an important message, but due to the shenanigans of some monkeys who had messed with the telegraph lines alongside of the road, nothing was getting through to the other village.

This simple story explains most all of the host of wayward human actions, and the ill results that spring from them. For most beings it is all a life of missed connections. Most of them, it is true, are very subtle. But it is also true that they are quite natural as well. Most any soil will accommodate growth. The yogic gardener simply knows what elements to add to the mixture of the mind, and which ones to alleviate.

And one of the counterproductive elements present in most minds is the presence of conflicting thoughts, these caused by the undisciplined mind listening to more than one source at a time, i.e., taking the counsel of a selfish ego *(ahamkara),* a skewed intellect *(buddhi),* or erratic thoughts *(chitta).* Contrary to what most living beings think of as a "well-informed mind," enlightened souls like Patanjali, Vedavyasa, and Vivekananda know it rather to be rapt and single-minded attention to that one Supreme Source called Atman, or Antaryami. It is the only trustworthy voice among them all. As Ramprasad sings, *"To hope for help from family, friends, and relatives, provides no profound solution. Don't you know that all are lost here? Everyone lives in pallid imitation of everyone else."* Selfishness, random acts, and scattered thought characterizes the minds of all worldly beings. What fool would want to imitate imitations? As Sri Ramakrishna has related, *"Wax fruit in a bowl on a table across the room makes one's mouth water, but when one approaches and tries to take a bite, disappointment is the outcome. Still, one is reminded of real fruits, and so heads for the marketplace to purchase some."*

Knowing pallid imitation to be part of the problem (in addition to the obvious lack of illumined minds in the worldly sector), the yogic practitioner does not seek counsel in the world, but swiftly follows the trail leading to Holy Company, called *Sadhu-satsanga* by Lord Vasishtha. A trusted source is the answer, then, for mind, matter, mentation, and masses of humanity cannot be relied upon. This wise removal of inferior sources is what the following sutra deals with.

**Pada IV, Sutra 21**
*chitta antara drishye buddhi-buddheh atiprasangah smriti sankarah cha (chitta,* mentation; *antara,* another; *drishye,* perceived; *buddhi-buddheh,* intelligent knower; *atiprasanghah,* proliferation; *smriti,* memory; *sankarah,* confusion; *cha,* as well as).

"*When the intelligent knower perceives another source than itself, and sees a proliferation of mentation thereby, confusion (about its knowledge) results.*"

With an entire train of cognizers in the internal field all vying for the position of chief knower (i.e., mind, ego, buddhi, ancestors, elementals, lower gods, etc.), the result brooks confusion. Ironically, that is also what is seen among friends and family, amidst the public, and even with professionals and intellectuals, i.e., always a conflict of opinions. And in the areas of religion and philosophy, this is where that strange statement, "You have your truth and I have my truth" comes up — when there is always and ever only one Supreme Truth.

In this regard, and in keeping with the tradition, the situation, and this sutra, Patanjali would advise the immediate transcendence of the three lower states of mind, i.e., *ksipta, mudha,* and *vikshipta* (see the chart in lesson #90 called "The Five States of Mind") and the swift attainment of *ekagra* — one-pointed mind. The fifth and final state of mind, or "no mind" *(nirodha),* can come later; ekagra must be attained and maintained first.

The only instance when the predicament cited in this sutra may not come up is in the case of the mature soul whose ongoing spiritual practice has downsized the ego. When the ahamkara is ripened, it ceases to fall into vexing and futile competition with other egos. Its intelligence, as well, does not bear the stamp of ownership, since it looks towards and relies upon the Wisdom Mother as its ultimate Source of knowledge. Further, the acts that it proposes to the body and senses via the mind are not hampered by the sense of agency. Raja Rajchandra composed a perfect bhajan to the Divine Mother around this free and easy condition with the fourfold mind, which was one of Sri Ramakrishna's favorites:

*O Mother, You cause all to happen by Thy own Sweet Will.*
*Truly, You are the Self-willed One and the savior of all living beings.*
*All work belongs to You, yet others call it their own.*
*You trap the powerful elephant in the mire*
*yet cause the lame man to scale the highest mountain.*
*On some You bestow the highest bliss; others You hurl into the world of suffering.*

> *O Mother, I am the machine and You are its operator.*
> *I am the house and You are the indweller.*
> *I am the chariot and You are the charioteer.*
> *I move, O Mother, as You move me.*

Work as worship, thought as Truth, labor as love, action in inaction — all of this is suggested ingeniously in the lines of this poem. When it is all realized then the human mind, called *antahkarana* — the inner cause — finds its true calling and intended purpose. It functions smoothly and mellifluously, and in accord with the Cosmic Mind *(Mahat)*. Its aims are peaceful, its ends are congenial, and its looks upon the other mental complexes around it as potential helpmates in the task of bringing all souls to realization of their innate divine Nature — Atman.

## Lesson Ninety-nine 9/29/15
### Pada IV, Sutras 22 & 23

Like a river flowing unto the ocean, the Raja Yoga sutras under examination, study, and implementation into our lives of dedicated practice, course on towards intimation of the highest secret of spiritual life. As Holy Mother said, *"We have to take the mind with us to Brahman, so we must keep it in fine and fettle shape."* And that is what Patanjali intends for the minds of the yogic aspirants as well. And nowhere is this fact more clearly underscored than in the sutras of this fourth and final pada. In this lesson a powerful review has been included, to help aid the mind in understanding its own territories. This is also what we strive to do through the process of in-depth questioning that clarifies dharma teachings for us — as is instanced by the queries of the group, below.

**Questions and Answers for Lesson 99**
R.O. from Hawaii writes:
QUESTION: "I recall from my readings that Sri Ramakrishna, when talking to a devotee, would sometimes find himself talking to God, and then there was nothing more to say. Could you comment on this?
ANSWER: For a being as inwardly sensitive as He, and with such openness to the power of spiritual suggestion that He exhibited, higher experiences happened to Him all the time, often without any warning. This is called samadhi, but it has different shades to it, i.e., there are different samadhis that happen (as described well in these Yoga sutras under study) at different levels of awareness according to situations that are brought about by special circumstances. For the Great Master, amazingly enough, and unlike any other luminary on historical record, samadhis of all kinds were everyday occurrences to Him. Some of the ones He experienced were not even recorded in the scriptures, so rarefied and rare were they! There were also bhavas that came to Him all the time, or spiritual moods. Samadhis often sent Him out of the realm of the senses and beyond the mind, while these bhavas put him in indrawn and abstracted moods.

Particular of your mention, however, speaking with human beings was an especially sensitive experience for Him. For since He was trained and prepared by Mother Kali Herself to perceive consciousness everywhere and in everything, and since this selfsame consciousness dwells most intensely in mankind more than in any other forms of nature, He could easily be transported into samadhi when He looked upon the devotees. Thus, He could disappear on you altogether in the middle of a conversation. Well, we are used to having people drop out on us due to distraction or boredom, or to seeing children lose their power of concentration due to daydreaming and the like, but the Great Master's vault into nondual Awareness was both obvious and unmistakable. Often He would be "away" for an hour or more. At night, He used to get so indrawn into God, Brahman, that Holy Mother felt She had to call the assistants to bring Him out, for fear He would not re-enter the body. He would revive when the Holy Names of God were whispered into His ear.

All of this is on record in our sacred tradition, and is not only a fine and inspiring read, it is an informative one as well — schooling us in the lost art of our own true nature as Samadhi.

QUESTION #2: "My second question is also about Sri Ramakrishna, and that is a statement by Him that, at times, the physical world seemed almost waxy or glowing, somewhat pliable. Could you comment on this also?"

ANSWER: It is said about the luminary who has completed the preliminary practices of spiritual life, that he or she develops subtle senses that can see through the appearance of name and form in time and space. The "third eye" mention, and the "inner ear" reference, are examples of this. We know that in the chapter of the Gita entitled, *Vishvarupa Darshanam,* that Sri Krishna touched Arjuna and transferred to him the subtle sight needed to see God's cosmic form. The world swiftly went away in this instance, leaving Arjuna shocked and unsettled — but also alerted to the fact of God dwelling in the especial form (Avatar) standing before him. The same thing occurred in more contemporary times with Swami Vivekananda, the young Narendra, when Sri Ramakrishna touched him on the head, and the young man saw the world recede and fall below, as it were, leaving him in a transcendent state of awareness.

In Sri Ramakrishna's direct experience, and when the samadhi bridged upon a particularly nondual type of spiritual elevation, that forms around him would recede to the background, leaving only a living Light shining through (obversely, we know from the Yoga Sutras that some samadhis are "seeded," or with form). When He was taken on a trip to the English wax museum, for instance, He stated that everything being made of wax reminded him of the way he saw all everything made of Consciousness in Samadhi. You see, the mind has in it the ability to perceive its Source, to involve back through all that it projected to arrive at that pure, conscious Awareness that is its true nature. Now, most beings need to meditate for a long period of time to have this extraordinary vision. For Sri Ramakrishna, Brahman being all that He cared for, it was a matter of minutes, even seconds, for this to happen to Him. And in fact, all the previous minutes and hours of His day were constantly striking at the veils of maya, and mounting up to culminate in samadhi every so often — again, often without warning — to Him as well as to others.

Questions like these — even though we are not given so easily and so often to samadhi as the Great Master was — nevertheless elevate the mind to a spiritual mood just by thinking on or writing about His samadhis. And this is one of the great examples of His life: to make us aware again of the truth of our inner, eternal Existence, and all the devotional wisdom experiences that It is attended with once It is realized.

QUESTION #3: "Is Soul One or is It Many? You speak of Soul reincarnating many times? But what is actually reincarnating? Also, in popular language we speak of Soul as 'my soul' or 'his/her soul,' or 'he/she is an old soul' But what actually is Soul? Is this the same self that we refer to as 'I', and if so, how does it differ, if at all, from Brahman; and if it doesn't differ, then how can it be separate from Brahman?"

ANSWER: A very good line of questioning, and of questions, here. I will try to take them in order of their appearance.

The Soul, as Atman, is one. The soul, as ego, is many (notice the upper case and lower case references) The human mind/ego complex is what moves from birth to death and death to rebirth, in a sort of dreamlike manner. It is having all its experiences in conjunction with Nature. The Atman is not in Nature. This answers the first two questions.

As far as what transmigrates, as said above, it is a complex. Calling it the ego/mind complex is an overall designation, but what the mind and ego contain is an amalgam of desires, attachments, unresolved issues, scattered thoughts, and karmas that pinion it to all manner of manifestation, say, for instance, the ancestors. Another example would be spouse, children, wealth, and family life. This is why the seers who prescribe and teach Enlightenment want beings to work out and fulfill their desires so they can move inward towards Freedom. For attachment to form is strong in the ego/mind complex. To conclude question 3, it is the stuff of the mind that incarnates, all under the ego's behest.

Question four asks, "what is the Soul." I see you capitalized it this time. Soul, as Atman, is pure, conscious Awareness. It consists, they say, of Existence, Knowledge, and Bliss — but all to the absolute degree.

Question five gets answered by stating that, in most beings, the real Soul is not what they are referring to when they use the word "self," or "I." They are usually referring to the ego-self in conjunction with the physical body. If they knew the ultimate Self, the little self would disappear.

Finally, the Self, Atman, does not differ at all from Brahman. That it appears to do so is by way of its association with body, energy, mind, intellect, and ego — what are called "The Five Sheaths" in Vedanta. But Atman only associates, never identifies — like the ego does. It might be added that Brahman never identifies or associates; It permeates.

Akshaya-Bhakti from New England writes:

COMMENTS: "Lately, as a way to connect my mind more to the eternal, I have been trying to link the joy I experience in this life to its source — to remind myself that all Bliss originates in Brahman. When I was younger my happiness often led to contrasting moments of feeling let down. While those contrasts are no longer as strong, however, even the happiness can be distracting, so this practice helps me to gain control of my mind. In various classes we have been talking about that need to make connections at all levels, so in Lesson 98 I especially appreciated how the guru tied the involution of the alambanas to mantra in response to one of my questions — that it (mantra) will clear the blockages that may exist even after many years of having that blessing, and that the revelation and resolution of these will be a very different experience for each of us. These facts will help me to ease my tendency towards rigidity in my application of teachings, and to understand how to make more connections of my own. Sometimes, my difficulty with terms comes from my inadvertent mixing of the various schools, mainly the Vedanta, Tantra, and Yoga. For instance, in your chart shown at classes, "The Higher Spandas of Shaivism," I don't see the term Prakriti."

QUESTION: "Where would Prakriti be understood in that chart as Maya, or at the top of the '24 Principles of Sankhya?' Does it depend on whether it is manifested or unmanifested? Also, in one of the early chapters of Raja Yoga, Swamiji talks about the two eternally-existing principles according to Lord Kapila, calling them Purusha and Akasha. Is the latter understood as Prakriti in this context?"

ANSWER: Prakriti, maya, pradhana, samsara, and other words are often used to express about the same thing. Various teachers and founders used them at different periods of India's history to shed light on all that is changing. In fact, words like changing, transitory, ephemeral, mutable, illusory — are they not close in meaning to one another? In the Spanda's chart, then, everything below Purusha *is* Prakriti, from unmanifested down to manifested. It is enough to know that the Purusha is Sentient, and that Prakriti (in its two forms) is insentient.

As far as Swamiji's mention of Purusha and Akasha (please cite the page number you read that from for me), the idea is that the sentient Soul will create space for itself to manifest in. That space is Akasha. In the West, and most everywhere in contemporary times (the Kali Yuga), the only space that exists and is accepted is "outer" space, i.e., physical space. What is inward in terms of space has been so much forgotten that it is outright denied by most beings today, even "intelligent" ones. Thus, beings do not seek it, or even "look within." If they did, with proper guidance and outright perseverance, they would see *"....the Kingdom of Heaven within,"* or catch a glimpse of some of the *"....chambers of my Father's Mansion."* Imagine, if you will, spending lifetime after lifetime in that Mansion, yet only knowing about the ground floor (and maybe the basement, called "hell"). Of course, most do not believe it belongs to God, for God is also denied. For most beings, the world belongs to their very own ego.

QUESTION #2: "Could you please help me understand more about the realm of ancestors as a resting point for subtle bodies?"

ANSWER: This follows well on the answer to your first question above. The Akashas are where beings move to when they depart this realm and the physical body. The ancestors move inward to the *Pranakasha,* the space of vital energy. They do not know of anywhere else, just as beings born here (in the *Bhutakasha*) do not know of any other worlds either. For the most part the humans and their ancestors do not know of one another, for dead is dead to the denizens of this planet. Only their memory keeps account of the departed.

But the seers know that if you stir up that memory *(smriti),* or better yet, keep it vibrant and alive with spiritual practices from lifetime to lifetime, knowledge of where beloved souls have moved to and the deeper wisdom of how they remain alive even after the body's death, comes to them. They can still have communion with them too, though unless both parties have this esoteric knowledge, and keep in intact from lifetime to lifetime, the connection is vague and, well, "dreamlike." In other words, they glimpse one another in the dream state occasionally.

And to further clarify your question here, the ancestor realm is not actually a "resting" point or "place." Customs and superstitions around death and burial rights, and going to a place called heaven somewhere in the sky, have distorted the understanding of most beings today. Expressions like, "He goes to his final rest," or to "Eternal Peace" — those are ridiculous if they are equated to what is called heaven in Christianity, or what is called the Pranakasha in Sanskrit. The Final Rest or Eternal Peace belong only to the luminaries who have merged with God, not with those who are still transmigrating in the dream worlds of the mind. No, heaven, or the pranakasha, where the ancestors are, is a place of restlessness just like here on earth. The only main difference is that there is less of pain there and more of it here. This is why earth is preferable to the ancestor realm, for here one can move to neutralize karma and thereby alleviate the pain that it causes. With this accomplishment the soul can transcend the realm of the ancestors and course through the celestial realm and the realms of the gods (Manakasha, Chitakasha). The Jnanakasha is the place of the wise. This is where the first authentic "rest" takes place, for the knowers of dharma abide here, and their knowledge of such has put ignorance to death for all time.

QUESTION #3: "On one of the earlier charts describing samadhi: The 'seeded' samadhis of Patanjali, savitarka and savichara, are listed, respectively, and also nirvitarka and nirvichara. As 'sa' has been defined as 'with' in Lesson 16, I thought that 'nir' might mean without, judging from some other words that start with that, like nirguna. But it wouldn't make sense to be with and without the same thing in each level, so could you please explain so as to clarify, then, just what nirvitarka and nirvichara mean in relation to these samadhis?"

ANSWER: Yes, it is true that "sa" and "nir" mean what you say. It is also true that they can occupy the same level, as you state. The real clarification comes when we introduce the words "external" and "internal," however, and with regards to objects and thoughts in meditation.

In brief, as these definitions can be found in the earlier lessons themselves, savitarka ("tarka" means gross thought) is concentration on thoughts of objects with regards to their outer names and forms. In the case of savichara, (chara means subtle thoughts) concentration shifts inward to focus on the subtle forms of objects that fill the mind.

In the case of nirvitarka and nirvichara, then, the mind is able to stop the presence of gross and subtle thoughts of objects from arising. So, simply put, there is savitarka and nirvitarka, then there savichara and nirvichara First the mind focuses on gross objects, then is able to transcend them inwardly. Next, the mind contemplates on subtle objects, then is able to do away with them inwardly. When these two seeded samadhis are well accomplished, then naturally, along comes the bliss (sananda samadhi) of being unencumbered with both objects and their insinuations in the mind. And in that state is found the source of individual bliss, the ego. But now it is ripened, having had its "hand slapped" due to always preoccupying itself with objects, inside and out. Thus sasmita samadhi and its trend towards meditating upon the true Self (Atman) has its time.

Tadrupa from Wyoming writes:
QUESTION: "Can you describe, in detail, the qualifications of one who is fit to become a yogi in six months to a year? What steps can be taken immediately for one such as myself toward getting closer to those qualifications?"
ANSWER: Swami Vivekananda once made that comment that a man should be able to become a yogi in six months. Such a being would need to:

• be well versed in Yoga from a past lifetime, that is, his samskaras would already be of yogic caliber when he took birth
• or have the grace of a great soul, i.e., guru, upon him
• or be relatively free of karmas from past births
• or possess intense commitment to the path, and great dedication to the Goal of Enlightenment.

One, several, or a combination of the above four might make this feat possible.

And unfortunately, most Westerners will not qualify for even one of these. And the few that we do see making substantial spiritual progress in contemplative life have bent their wills to the well-guided performance of sadhana, practicing:

• spiritual disciplines daily
• over a long period of time
• after having received the mantra from an authentic tradition
• after studying the scriptures and contemplating their meanings
• with guidance from a spiritual preceptor who is a teacher of the dharma

So, if you have, or are in the pursuit of any or all of these above criteria, then what to hope for a year, a single lifetime should be enough to establish you in all that is required to become an illumined soul in this very life.

Of course, several other subtler things may help as well, like assuming the position of qualification. If you think yourself to be a yogi, and are following that path, even as a lifestyle, you may be closer than you think to attainment of that. I am not talking about low pretense and posturing, the likes of which are seen in those who pretend to be spiritual but know next to nothing. I am speaking of combining serious self-effort with the proper state of mind to effect uncommon growth in the soul. Subtler still is the insight that all growth takes place in nature and in mind, not in the Atman — which is your Essence. So you will have to become your Self while already being the Self — a very tricky maneuver when working with the human ego.

**Pada IV, Sutra 22**
*chitteh apratisamkramayah tad akara apattau sva buddhi samvedanam* (*chitteh,* thoughts; *apratisamkramayah*, stationary; *tad,* that; *akara,* uncaused; *apattau,* assumes; *sva,* essence; *buddhi,* knower; *samvedanam,* cognizes)
  "*By assuming the uncaused essence of the ever-stationary knower, the mind becomes fully cognizant (of all its processes).*"
  Please allow me to write in here all the sutras of our recent study, from lesson 90 to the present, all having have to do with the mind. In this way we will not only be reminded of their wisdom, and gain the proper context of their order and explanation, but it will also be driven home to us how key the mind is to spiritual life and practice, thus Enlightenment. Also, reading them all in one flow like this is a powerful practice (forgive me for doing your homework for you):

*From the ego springs mind and its thought, which produce all projected things.*

*Though minds and their different activities are numerous, the one, Original Mind directs them all.*

*Among these diverse sets of minds, only that one that is born of meditation is free of conditionings from past lives.*

*Acts springing from the mind of the yogi are colorless, while nonyogis suffer the threefold results called good, bad, and mixed.*

*This triple designation forms subtle desires and impressions that will express themselves later in accordance with each one specifically.*

*Though differences may occur due to effects in time, space, and the march of species, there is a deep connection in them based upon memory and mental impressions of past lifetimes.*
*All these impressions are without origin, and unending, because of the strong desire for life in the body.*

*Impetus, desire for fruits, objects, and their foundations, all combined, cohese these impressions together, and they disappear when they are absent.*

*Regarding the past and the future, they exist in their own essence, but change with characteristics and circumstances along the way.*

*All these abiding attributes, whether apparent or subtle, are in their essence composed of the three gunas of Nature.*

*"Though objects appear to transform, their substance is based in unity, all coordinated by the gunas.*

*All existing things (such as objects) are identical to one another, but the mind's thought places them at variance, as if divided along multiple pathways.*

*All relative things, perceived or not by the mind previously, proceed from and become existent due to its thoughts.*

*The process of thinking relies upon the conditioning of the mind, which thereby divides knowing from not knowing regarding the objects and situations it encounters.*

*Thought vibrations of the mind can always be known due to the pure Awareness abiding there as the Lord of the mind.*

*That mind is not illumined in and of itself; it is known by the Knower. This is due to the fact that the mind is unable to cognize two things at once.*

*When the intelligent knower perceives another source than itself, and sees a proliferation of mentation thereby, confusion (about its knowledge) results.*

Here is a synopsis. Thankfully, there is a knower, or Lord, of the mind — an "Original" mind. This is especially helpful, since the mind's source is the ego. Also, rebirth, and what is getting reborn, is of the mind, i.e., the transmigrating soul *is* the ego/mind complex. The one who meditates from lifetime to lifetime purifies this complex and escapes rebirth in ignorance, but the rest accumulate residue via good, bad, and mixed karma in relation to the disposition of the cycles of gunas. Karma with gunas form subtle impressions in the mind that will eventually express themselves, one way or another.

Further, according to the implications here, memory of our past lifetimes should be current, but it is obvious in this day and age, and particularly in our culture, that this is not the case. Forgetfulness of God, Self, and self — et al — is the theme of the day. Desire for life in the body is the cause of this, what Sri Sarada Devi noticed, even among the Hindu culture, and called *"a piggish existence."*

Even further, karma, pleasure (with pain), and the conditionings they form in the mind create impressions that cohese together (as in my analogy of the bucket of nails that sits in the rain until conditions fuse them all into one lump of rusty iron). As if this is not enough, time gets into the picture and affords the march of objects that appear to be solid and constant, but are actually always undergoing change — all without the mind taking stock of the fact. Acting ignorantly, the mind divides these further and constructs thoughts and experiences around this false or mixed knowledge. To worsen the situation, the mind looks out and sees other minds that are most often is disagreement or at variance with it, and this causes doubt to thicken the mayic process.

Thus, just as early disciplines in religious and philosophical life try to convince the living being that he/she is not the body, just so, and in early spiritual life and practice, the more advanced teachings of the dharma try to explain that the mind is not the Self either. All this describes the deeper meaning of this sutra, and Patanjali's intention that the mind assume the position *(manasana)* of the Knower and get free from every veil, misconception, and masquerade that it can throw up in order to prevent realization of "That" which lies beyond it. This is what the mind needs to attain in order to transcend itself. As Swami Vivekananda states: *"....knowledge is not a quality of the Purusha. When the mind comes near the Purusha it is reflected, as it were, upon the mind, and the mind, for the time being, becomes knowing and seems as if it were itself the Purusha."*

## Pada IV, Sutra 23
*drastri drisya uparaktam chittam sarva artham* (*drastri,* the seer; *drisya,* what is seen; *uparaktam,* informed; *chittam,* mindstuff, *sarva,* all; *artham,* objects).

*"In this way, when the mindstuff is informed by the seer, it can see all objects (subtle and gross)."*

Just as the highest aim of the body is to gain strength and resilience in order to afford time for the indweller to realize God, so also is the highest aim of the mind to become the telescope and magnifying glass for the gross and subtle worlds. Not one facet of Brahman is to be overlooked; the entire puzzle of the mind's manifestation is to be put together piece by piece, with the soul remembering all the while that it was all a play, that it was done all in jest, as it were. Nature, in all its power and splendor was, all along, just the flexing of the muscles of projection possessed by the mind. And equally important was its ability to draw it all back into formlessness — nature returning to its unmanifested form, and living beings returning to conscious Awareness (in this context you can look at the very last sutra of these Yoga sutras, at the end of pada four). As Swamiji states in this context as well, *"On the one side the external world, the seen, is being reflected, and on the other, the seer, is being reflected; thus comes the power of all knowledge to the mind."*

# Lesson One-Hundred 11/13/15
## Pada IV, Sutras 24 & 25

On the advent of our 100th lesson together studying the Raja Yoga sutras of Patanjali, we find ourselves in the middle of his wonderful conclusion regarding the mind, its place in the cosmic scheme of things, and Who it serves when it is aware of higher Reality. All of this is key to higher understanding along the path of Enlightenment, and quells any subtle doubts about the mind's limitations — while still accounting for and appreciating its miraculous powers in the countless realms of name and form that it projects.

**Questions and Answers for Lesson 100**
Tadrupa from Wyoming writes:
QUESTION: "What is the essence of effortless meditation?"
ANSWER: It emerges when all outside distractions have been rendered null and void, i.e., bad habits, pleasure-seeking, nondharmic desires, and the like. Some inside habits will have to go next, such as unseen karmas based upon samskaras (mental impressions) created in past lifetimes, whose effects are cropping up in the present lifetime.

Before all this work (sadhana) the soul must even come to feel and develop a taste for peace, or as the Great Master has put it, "*....gain yearning for God.*" "God," here, can be the Ideal called Ishvara, or the highest form of God in mankind; or It can be the formless Reality. In both of these ways, meditation is both helpful and crucial for advancement of a higher and deeper kind. Those who meditate for health, for powers, or even to simply balance the mind (sattva) are really missing the boat. Profound and wondrous visions and realizations will seldom come to such as these; the experience of meditation is equal to the level of intensity and sincerity that one can muster.

And once contentment has replaced happiness, peace of mind has replaced pleasure-seeking mind, and love of God has replaced mere curiosity and prayer for satisfaction of desires, the aspirant is well on his/her way to the "essence" of meditation, as you put it here.

One of the best descriptions plus instructions I have seen about natural meditation is found in the Mahamudra teaching and its practice. There, the aim is to "*....focus without objective, stabilize without distraction, shift without grasping, and experience all manifestations as Reality as they rise in the mind. Then, when liberation comes, one must let it do so naturally.*" Of course, by the time this kind of mastery settles in, instructions are rather pointless. It is in the meantime that the aspirant must be on guard and use a Chosen Ideal. Those who attempt to jump to the top too early, i.e., strive for "attainment" of formless Reality, will either only fall over time, or get disoriented and remain in one limited space interminably. Along the way, the teachings of Patanjali are to be observed — in order to watch out for the four obstacles to meditation: sleepiness; restlessness; attachment and aversion; and the descent of superficial bliss.
QUESTION #2: "On retreat you had mentioned that meditation comes after

spiritual experience. Can you please clarify this?"

ANSWER: As is outlined above in your first question, when the criteria for stable and peaceful mind is achieved and implemented, and some time passes in which the mind gets used to the fresh and new level of consciousness that it is being introduced to, spiritual experiences will come naturally. These are unmistakable, and no worry should be undergone by the aspirant in this regard. In other words, a true spiritual experience — which is, as the saying goes, "as rare as hen's teeth," — is easily discernible from mental conjurings, hopeful dreams, blissful feelings, and the like. These pass, while authentic experiences remain and transform. Thus, such descent of sacredness is to be witnessed and observed in a calm and cool manner in order to examine its effects in its aftermath. If the experience is very intense, the same rule applies, i.e., that one must wait for the intensity to pass and look back on it through the lens of, well, what else — balanced and ongoing meditation.

Further through long periods of focused meditation, the nondual experiences of Yoga will begin to suggest themselves. Pertaining to the adept yogi, there are six doorways that are kept in mind, many of them having their locks intrinsically connected with time and space. Since the questions here are bridging on the "essence" in meditation, I place the chart on these doorways here. More will be said about these gateways at the end of the fourth pada.

QUESTION #3: "What is the essence of yogic living in light of modern conditions for householders in the West?"

ANSWER: The way your question is couched in consideration of modern times, particularly in materialistic America, opens wide the question of whether the Westerner is even anywhere near to being qualified for Yoga. In the light of this poignant and all-too-telling query, the present day facade or masquerade of so-called yogic living comes forward.

To the seers, whose emphasis is all and ever on the attainment of liberation from all bondages, today's complacent theme of yogic lifestyle is a caricature of the real article. Yoga is not a domestic lifestyle; it is a dharmic life stance. One does not "do Yoga"; one lives in Yoga. To be sure, placing a few spiritual pictures on the walls of a comfy home, pasting bumper stickers on the bumper of one's expensive car about saving this or that country or this or that species, eating organic foods free of contaminates, dancing about dressed in fashionable yogic clothes in mere pretentious show at local kirtans, stretching the body daily at hatha classes in town, and chanting Sanskrit chants devoid of any and all meaningful teachings from an enlightened teacher, does not a yogic aspirant make. Daily worship (puja), study of revealed scriptures under the guidance of an illumined preceptor, increasing devotion for God as the Chosen Ideal, and meditating upon Divine Reality beyond the worlds of name and form — in other words, participation in practice of the Four Yogas — count for a dharmic life. Nothing short of this, and all its beneficial concomitants, will grant Enlightenment

And if one can neutralize his/her karmas, and then and not until then, begin to serve God in living beings, selflessly, and without desire for reward or

# The Six Esoteric Yogic Gateways
## Yoga's Secret of Transcendence

 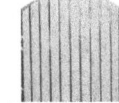

*"Each moment arises from Infinity. Each moment dissolves back into Infinity. The next moment also arises directly from Infinity. Concentration upon what is between the dissolution of the prior moment and the arising of the subsequent moment opens the gates of Infinity. These gateways, six in number, are the real powers of an illumined Yogi."* Patanjala Yoga Commentaries

- Perceiving internal movement of particles
- Seeing Time and Space to be apparent
- Comprehension of Eternity
- Observing moments forming the passage of time
- Knowing objects consist of particles
- Knowledge of creation as vibration

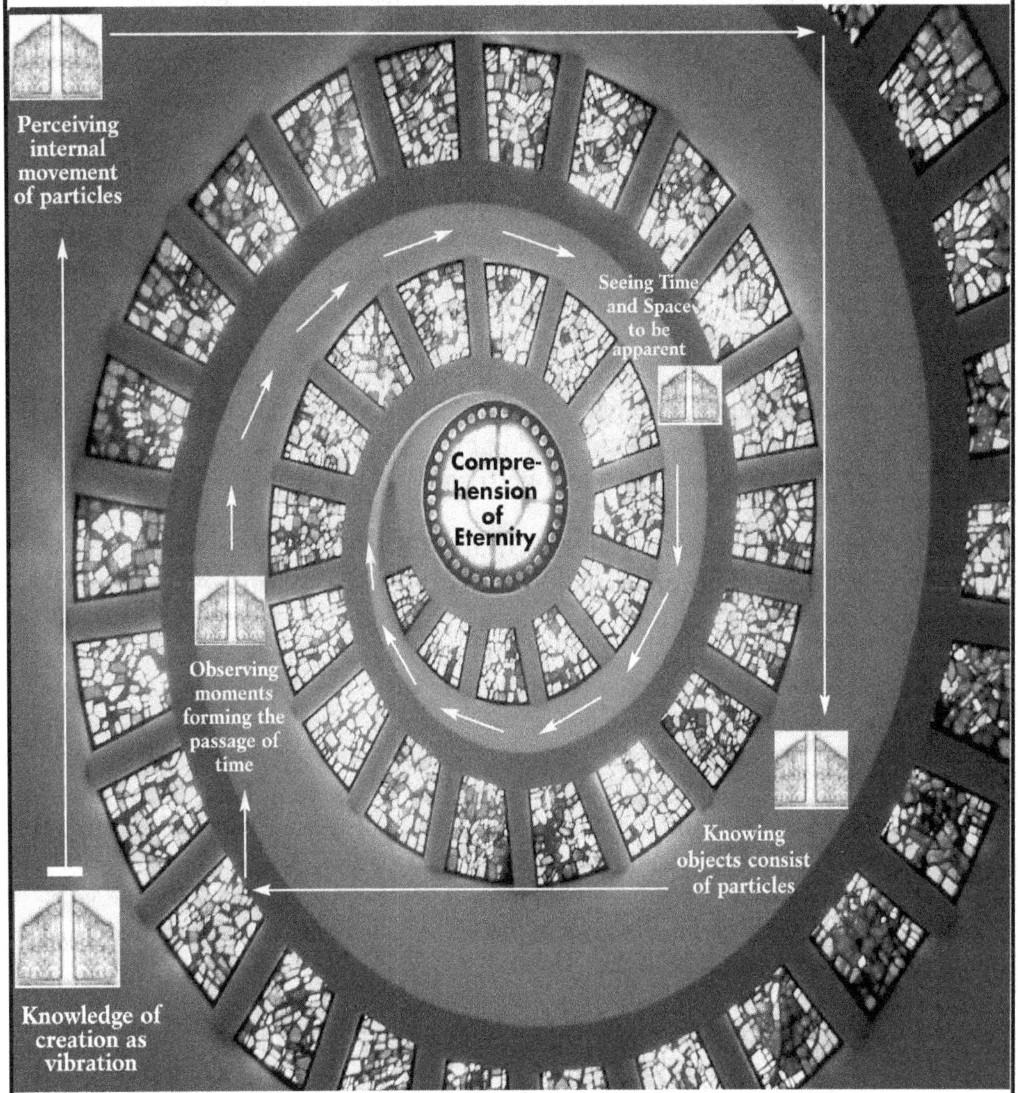

*"All of creation is made of vibrating particles. Each particle has an inner movement. Many particles together make up an object. Many moments following one upon another take up time. This cause and effect sequence in time and space is not literal – is only apparent. When this mental notion that time and space are real is transcended, Reality stands forth, revealed."* Patanjala Yoga Commentaries

recompense, the results will be what the seers might call a dharmic life. Resistance to and nonparticipation in any form of violence that causes harm to others — humans, animals, other cultures, etc. must also be enjoined. Ahimsa, Nonviolence, in all its forms, is required of the yogic aspirant. Non-coveting of the goods of other beings and countries based in truthfulness and generosity must also be in place. To be more specific, even, the five yamas and five niyamas of Yoga must be mastered first prior to engaging in the higher limbs of Yoga, and before other forms of activity, such as altruism, are attempted.

Importantly, and to conclude in brief, those householders who, having birthed children, educate them only in worldly subjects and engage them in the "eternal money-making," failing to school them in the dharma and its life-saving, true life-giving facets, are betraying the spiritual ideal of Yoga as they live and breathe. A superior society will be built on that eternal dharma, which is superior to all other modes of thought and action. Souls must be taught to give up personal gain sought within the illusory dream of a Utopian society and instead gain the strength to transcend the many ills of earthly life and attain Enlightenment — an Enlightenment that both a moral perspective (dualistic religion) and an intellectual frame of reference (materialistic science) alone will not be able to supply for them.

QUESTION #4: "How does the student of yoga discriminate between right discernment and sankalpa and vivarta? I am having a hard time telling when the mind is calling a spade a spade, or doing all sorts of false projections based upon unfulfilled egoistic desires, superficialities, and uncontrolled emotional insecurities."

ANSWER: If one has already identified such insinuations as "egoistic desires," "superficialities," and "emotional insecurities," the question is practically answered already. What one does through proper discernment, and what is enacted by the insecure ego in the realm, of desires — these two are distinct modes that foster widely variant feelings and cause completely opposite effects. Experiencing and seeing these effects for oneself is tantamount to making a final conclusion and thereby taking control of one's life. The real problem here is not so much perceiving the confusion and suffering that comes to the unbalanced and untrained mind caught in the world, but mustering up the strength and fortitude to take the right steps that will alleviate such wayward directions. This is why sadhana, spiritual practice, is the cutting edge that defines a spiritual life from the other half-hearted attempts at mastery that uninformed minds are turning to for solace and direction.

Kanyakali from Hawaii writes:
QUESTION: "In one of the very earliest Raja Yoga lessons I asked a question about my mind's tendency to splinter into more than one thought at a time. For example, I'm trying to meditate and mentally recite my mantra, but I'm also mentally hearing the refrain of a song, and random thoughts are also coming and going. I asked you if this was common and, if I am remembering right, you said yes, it is typical of our untrained minds to behave this way. The trans-

lation of Sutra IV:20 is, '...the mind is unable to cognize two things at once.' Now we seem to be going beyond merely thinking about two or more things at once, and actually distinguishing between the mind, which, at this point is an object being observed, and the witness of the object. Is this sutra saying that one cannot be aware of both an object such as the mind and the witness at the same time? It seems that once all objects are put aside, including the thinking instrument itself, there is only the direct experience of pure Consciousness remaining. This is the whole point, isn't it?"

ANSWER: Yes, and the forthcoming sutras of this lesson move on in that same vein of explanation as well. When we specify "the mind," we are really talking about *manas, chitta, ahamkara,* and *buddhi.* If we, in turn, specify any one of these four (together which make up the antahkarana), we find that even amidst, say, that one single aspect called *chitta,* that there are a multitude of thoughts always running along the multitudinous channels of the mind. How can we "know" them all? To "know our thoughts," in other words, is a very tall order, and what we are really saying by this term is that we have come to know their source. When we do know the source, then we naturally capture all the random thoughts and turn the negatives one's positive. It is like having a vast field of mongeese out back of one's home, but also knowing what food they prefer and owning a stock of it. All of these wild and unpredictable creatures will come to you sooner or later to be fed.

Therefore, as sutra 4:25 states, "*....when the unique nature of the seer as the Atman occurs to the mind, all false assumptions end and its erratic vibrations cease.*" Amazingly, you are that seer. We are Atman, all-abiding. We must therefore hand over the reigns of the body/mind mechanism to the Self and live freely from there on out, *"no matter what may be the mode of living."*

R.O. from Hawaii writes:
QUESTION: "In your poem, *We Are Atman All-Abiding,* verse 36, you write that Atman is formed from primal Essence. Is this the Turiya or primal Awareness that you write about on page 19? And if so, is Atman then secondary or created from That?"
ANSWER: Thanks for asking for clarification. When I use the word "formed" with regard to the Atman, it is not to suggest a beginning or a created state for the Atman. It is acreate. It is beyond form. It is more that the "essence" spoken of here is inherent in It — as they explain, *"like the green inherent in a tree rather than an ornament pinned on a tree."*

And with regard to Turiya, that is a simple word (meaning "the fourth") used to explain Consciousness in Its original state, beyond the three states of waking, dreaming, and deep sleep. That would describe the actual experience of the Atman that the meditator or seer is having. It would equate to words such as *moksha, mukti, kaivalya,* and *samadhi;* also *nirvana* and *satori,* etc.

Akshaya-Bhakti from New England writes:
COMMENTS: "Lesson 100!!! Surely, this must be auspicious! Thank you for

asking me to cite my comment that Swamiji referred to, the two eternally existing principles as Purusha and Akasha, for I discovered my huge mistake! When I went back to pages 33 & 34 in the Raja text, I realized it was not Purusha at all that was listed as the first principle, but Prana. And not only that, but I had misconstrued the context — that they are what comprise 'the whole universe,' not the Self. While I regret my carelessness, I appreciate the wisdom teachings it elicited in the reply, especially regarding inner space vs. outer. When I attempt to participate in the homework for this class, I can really feel my struggle to transcend the outer, to lift the veil, even intellectually."

RESPONSE: Thank you, in turn, for the frank explanation of your misconstrual, and also for your resultant insight into how the learning process takes place in svadhyaya. In several cases, when we read scriptures, the mind often makes conclusions prematurely based upon what one thought one understood. Come to find, that further study was needed to flush out the correct understanding and deeper meaning, both. Repetition is the spice of spiritual life.

QUESTION: "Sakshi (or detached witness) is listed along with Brahman as terms related to the Seer. But I thought that would rather be part of the unseen along with Ishvara, as I thought that Brahman would be beyond even the witness stage and that Ishvara is the level of seeing both the internal and the external "sides". Could you please explain this and discuss the concept of Sakshi once more so I can understand it better. Much gratitude."

ANSWER: It is a good point that you make, and it must be said that any discussion to be had concerning these terms for higher Awareness will be akin to "splitting hairs," as they say. The thing here, is that the Witness, though it may not be fully merged in the Absolute, is nevertheless awakened to Consciousness and full of Awareness. It is just that Sakshi is still aware of a subtle line of demarcation between itself and Indivisible Awareness. How to explain?

But it can be declared that it is closer to the Seer than to the Unseen, and part of the reason for this is that, when identifying with pure Consciousness it is less of a Cosmic Principle and more of a realized Presence. Ishvara, despite Its being supreme in all the realms, still holds a station for aspiring souls. Put in another way, these souls are searching, but the Seer, or Witness, is already Seeing.

Anurag from Oregon writes:
QUESTION: "In response to Tadrupa's question about qualification you summated with an exquisitely incisive thought: 'So, you will have to become your Self while already being the Self — a very tricky maneuver when working with the human ego.' This is similar to one of your quotes that has been an ongoing dharana for me: 'You are already That, but the psychophysical self is stubborn, resistant. You have to make yourself into Brahman. Destroy resistance via persistence.' So, until our delusion is gone, gone, utterly gone, how best to avoid getting caught in delusion of the ego while assuming the position that we are already That."

ANSWER: By making the assumption of that position you champion serious and real. A serious actor does not actually turn into a lawyer or a robber in a theatrical play, but he does convince the audience that he is one or the other. But it is not the onlooker who needs to be convinced of his authenticity/divinity; it is the player himself.

No one really sees the aspirant as he makes himself into Brahman; he simply emerges from the purificatory process as That which he truly is. He went in, perhaps, puzzled or uncertain, but came out divine. Others were not there to witness the stunning inner alchemy that transpired. Only the jewelers — only those who had managed that "self"same transformation themselves — can now truly assess the uncontestable worth of that freshly awakened diamond-cutter. The rest are still fooled into thinking him ordinary. As Sri Krishna states in the Gita: *"Fools declare Me as one clad in human form, not knowing My Divine Nature, unborn and supreme."*

## Pada IV, Sutra 24

*tad asankheya vasanabhih chittam api parartham samhatya karitvat* (*tad*, that; *asankheya*, multiple; *vasanabhih*, subtle impressions from past desires; *chittam*, thoughts; *api*, in addition; *parartham*, for the sake of another; *samhatya*, in tandem; *karitvat*, activity)

*"Thoughts are multiple; in addition, so too are the mind's desires. In tandem with one another, mental impressions form, but all this activity is for the sake of another."*

This one, singular and unique bit of information, easy to comprehend and natural to dharmic and divine life, is to be kept close and cherished by all beings who would split off from Brahman (apparently) and visit the realms of name and form in time and space, called relativity. As Jesus stated, these realms are worlds of *"....rest, sojourn, and activity."* But the *"bedrock of the Spirit"* is stable and immovable. In short, the mind conjures up form, locale, and activity, but the Soul remains ever-free from all these. It is *drashtir*, the Seer of all phenomena.

The mind, then, with millions upon millions of lives, forms, worlds, and activities of its own, must never deviate from knowledge of and connection to this Seer, or else there will come desire-ridden thoughts that will take it away from peace and balance, from right living. As one song of India puts it, as found in the Gospel of Sri Ramakrishna:

*High in the heaven of Mother's Feet, my mind was soaring like a kite,*
*When came a blast of sin's rough wind that drove it swiftly towards the earth.*
*Maya disturbed its even flight by bearing down on one side.*
*And I could make it rise no more.*
*Entangled in the twisting string of love for children and for wife,*
*Alas! my kite was rent in twain.*
*It lost its crest of wisdom soon and downward plunged as I let it go;*
*How could it hope to fly again, when all its top was shorn away?*
*Though fastened with devotion's cord, it came to grief while playing here;*
*Its six opponents worsted it.*

> *Now, Nareschandra rues this game of smiles and tears,*
> *and thinks it better never to have played at all......*

    Yet, most of this pain and pathos could be side-stepped, and life lived in the dharma become a success, if the mind was only "tethered" to the Soul rather than to the world. Patanjali states simply that the mind's immense and complex game only need be played for the sake of another, *"parartham."* This is Yoga. It is balance amidst the tossings and turnings of life's natural vagaries and vicissitudes. It is like trying to stay upright while standing on the deck of a double-masted sailing ship that is plying rough waters. The main question is not so much if we should attempt it, or even how to accomplish it, but more that it must be done.

    To put it all in perspective, we have on record Holy Mother's startling statement about the Three Great Boons, i.e., a human birth, a good teacher, and a desire for liberation. She admitted that She had met people who had gained or received all three of these boons, but that they did not necessarily gain Enlightenment even then. Why was that? Because they did not have the support or agreement of their own minds. Thus, She added on a fourth Great Boon to that traditional teaching — the friendship of one's own mind.

### Pada IV, Sutra 25

*vishesa darshinah atma bhava bhavana vinivrittih* (*vishesa,* uniqueness; *darshinah,* the seer; *atma,* indivisible Self; *bhava,* by nature, *bhavana,* assumptions; *vinivrittih,* end of erratic mental vibrations).

    *"Therefore, when the unique nature of the seer as the Atman occurs to the mind, all false assumptions end and its erratic vibrations cease."*

    Here is cause, effect, and solution at its cogent and lucid best. To know that the mind is 1) dual by nature, 2) responsible for all manifestation, 3) full of latent impressions, and 4) the veritable field of latent karmas formed over many lifetimes, explains the entire phenomena of cause and effect — of suffering and pleasure and the human being's attachment and aversion to them. Then, to perceive *"the unique nature of the seer as Atman,"* and have it *"occur to the mind"* via Self-Realization brought on via the practices of a well-guided sadhana, brings an end to all the many expressions — good, bad, and mixed — of an otherwise errant mind and erratic thought-process. Let us all turn our mind towards its Source then, the all-pervasive, inimitable Atman.

    At SRV Association's latest retreat on Divine Mother Reality, wherein we all took up in earnest the study of the powerful Devi Upanisad, the teachings of Mahamudra from the Tibetan Buddhist Tradition came to the fore one day. The three points called *the View, the Practice,* and *the Action* were contemplated and explained. Similar to these two particular Yoga sutras under study and their meaning, the View portion of Mahamudra declares that *"All manifestation, the Universe itself, is contained in the mind, and the true nature of mind is the realm of illumination, shining with radiance that can neither be conceived or touched."* The final result in tandem with realization of these teachings is

*"....freedom from intellection and conceptualization, freedom from false identities, and freedom from hopes and fears."* Even freedom from the thought of liberation and the agent of liberation occurs. High-minded teachings such as these grace the august halls of Indian dharmas, both untold and unnumbered over the ages.

With all this in mind, well contemplated daily until all false superimpositions dissolve in Consciousness, the luminary maintains Yoga, the aspirant attains Yoga, and the imbalanced soul regains Yoga. Without this unique stance of dharma in mind, the pretentious soul feigns Yoga, while the disinterested soul shames Yoga.

Whatever the case may be, Yoga — Union with Brahman — is both true and Truth. If it must be utilized as a practice, then the adversely affected and uneasy mind experiencing the ever-changing condition of the world has fallen into the need of deep and serious counsel. But left on its own, as innate and inseparable Unity, Yoga inspires beings at all levels of existence, revealing to them their own intrinsically perfect Nature that is beyond the reach of all that the adroit and dexterous mind can draw out and superinduce as hosts of clever coverings over Divine Reality.

## Lesson One-Hundred-one 12/13/15
### Pada IV, Sutras 26 & 27

More powerful questions arise as our Raja Yoga study group weaves its way along, not far from the closing sutras of Pada Four. The art of *"separating the wheat from the chaff,"* yogic style, is outlined, as the observant practitioner learns more about the subtleties of making the clear distinction between the ever-conscious Purusha and the insentient principle of internal and external Prakriti.

**Questions and Answers for Lesson 101**
Tadrupa from Wyoming writes:
QUESTION: "I have been studying Yoga Vasishtha lately, especially with regard to dealing with adharmic desires, and contemplating these teachings in light of Yoga, Vedanta, and other teachings mentioned. For example, you have mentioned how you witnessed Lex Hixon being too busy with sadhana to even have a restless mind, and thus never be tempted by adharmic desires or other ridiculous distractions. With all this said, I have come to the conclusion that one can simply abandon adharmic desires by replacing thoughts of them with those dedicated to sadhana, discrimination, and renunciation. Thus, it is not that adharmic desires are really a difficult problem, but rather that they can get put aside for higher things until the impressions that give rise to them exhaust themselves. Is this a good summary of these teachings with regard to what the great preceptors say about destroying adharmic desires and worldly addictions? Do the seers give us permission then to just be done with harmful desires here

and now and never look back?"

ANSWER: *"The unreal never exists; the Real never ceases to be,"* says Sri Krishna in the *Bhagavad Gita*. Anything and everything adharmic should not be allowed to intrude on life simply on the strength of this assertion alone. In the *Avadhuta Gita* it is stated similarly, that, *"Ignorance is unreal; then how can it cause any real doubt?"*

Two things have to be remembered, then, in this context: first, that adharma is unreal; and two, that maya, by its very nature, will insinuate itself into the picture if the seer becomes lackadaisical and allows it to do so. In other words, "permission" to do away with the unreal should not have to be given. If the practitioner finds that negative thoughts *(klishta vrittis)* have come into the mind, he simply gets rid of them with positive ones *(aklishta vrittis)*, just as you mentioned above in the case of Lex Hixon, our SRV Founder — though in his case he was long past having anything to do with negative thoughts. His mind was naturally geared towards Enlightenment.

As to your first reference above, yes, you have summated the process and practice fittingly. In Vedanta and Yoga, one "waters the flowers and not the weeds" *(pratipakshabhavanam)*. Soon, the weeds die away of themselves. There are other ways of dealing with detrimental desires, some swift and some needing more patience, but the end result ought to rid the mind of them forever so that no further sign of them will be seen or felt.

QUESTION #2: "Can you explain, psychologically speaking, the dynamics behind the qualified teacher's ability to read or sense karmas and samskaras of the student, and all those around them?"

ANSWER: When you ask about "....all those around them," a qualified teacher whose area of expertise includes the reading of samskaras, does so in a general way. It is not difficult, though most beings who have not been given the dharma teachings in their lives from aware parents will overlook the ability almost entirely. In other words, collective samskaras are not hard to perceive. They are harder to break than to see. For instance, though most beings are not aware of it, the entire human race holds a strong samskara around both the desire for vital energy, i.e., for physical incarnation, as well as around the fear of death. Any spiritually awake soul can see this twin tendency in mankind. Clinging to the stunted human condition is also a strong impression in them. It would be better if they developed a samskara for living free, which is what Yoga and its practice is all about.

As far as the individual is concerned, this is a more difficult proposition. And this is part and parcel of why the teacher wants the potential initiate to spend time with him/her, so that these hidden tendencies that block spiritual growth will emerge and can be seen and worked on. The guru must prescribe certain spiritual disciplines for the devotee, and they must be aimed at that area in the mind of the aspirant that is veiled, obstinate, or weak — as the case may be.

And "dynamics?" They are hardly describable, often being subject to the mercurial changes of the unstable mind. It is more a matter of time passing, and time well spent. If the aspirant is oriented towards yogic disciplines, then that is time well spent, and with the passing of time the samskaras will, of themselves, begin to weaken and dissipate. No one really sees them go; it is more a matter of signs revealing themselves over time. As Ramprasad would often sing, along the pathway of spiritual disciplines: *"One day I awoke, and my delusion was gone, gone, utterly gone!"*

QUESTION #3: "Can you please provide commentary upon the two paths of renunciation, dhyeya-tyaga and jneya-tyaga, as they pertain to control of the mind? It seems like in these paths, vrittis that are based in identification of the Self as nature are rooted out or simply abandoned. If this is the case, this general abandonment of certain thoughts seems to be practiced in other yogas as well — like abandoning the thoughts of differentiation between work and non work and sense of agency in Karma Yoga."

ANSWER: *Jneya-tyaga,* pertains to knowledge, and what is knowable, by the knower. It signifies the uprooting of all types of samskaras leading to liberation. *Dhyeya-tyaga* is commensurate with *Nirvikalpa* itself, because at this level of *tyaga* (renunciation) the high act of renunciation of all objects in meditation has been accomplished. *Vasishtha's Yoga*, the *Taittiriya Upanisad*, the *Bhagavad Gita,* and *Patanjali's Yoga Sutras,* all hold teachings on these two forms of renunciation.

QUESTION #4: "What is meant by the statement, 'To realize the Atman you must practice renunciation every moment of your life?'"

ANSWER: A good answer for this query came up in the live-streaming series on Yoga Vasishtha, recently. In that great scripture, one aspect of Uddalaka's discipline in the neti-neti practice was to *"render objects nonexistent."* This is just like Jesus's cautionary teaching of building one's house on sand instead of bedrock. Appreciable headway in spiritual life can be made only when one knows that this world and all the objects in it are all ultimately unfulfilling — or illusory, unreal, empty, nonactual, etc. Right comprehension of any one of these five words is sufficient to accomplish renunciation, but I would advise that all five of them be taken together to get the full picture, and to convince the otherwise stubborn and desire-prone mind to give them up and be free. As Sri Ramakrishna has put it, *"Repeated lives lived in ignorance soon convinces the deluded soul that this world is real."* At this late juncture of the game of embodiment it has lost its spiritual sensitivity.

And so, renounce this world with every passing moment, or with every breath. There is even an exercise for this. Breathe in and think, *"I am Brahman."* Hold the breath while thinking, *"I will always be Brahman."* Then let the breath out thinking, *"I am not the world."* There is also a set of stanzas of a poem that explain it:

> *Unseen fragrance from a flower*
> *Wood possessing fire's power*
> *Water present in the ice*
> *Whitish color in the rice*

> *Subtle like these bare depictions*
> *Futile to engage description*
> *Trying makes my tongue go dead*
> *Kali steps upon my head*
>
> *Even so, in sacred scripture*
> *Sages paint a glowing picture*
> *Seek the Atman, all declare*
> *Only world-renouncers dare....*

QUESTION #5: "What does it mean to control the mind by 'hook or by crook?'"

ANSWER: It is a mere expression, really. But a special spiritual significance can be attached to it. Two of the articles that are often seen in the Divine Mother's hands are the hook and the noose. These are important for the lover of Mother Reality, for with the first She will secure the soul and pinion it to Herself, while the other She will fasten around the "crook" of the neck and tether you to the Truth.

Kanyakali from Hawaii writes:

QUESTION: "How would you respond to a comment I heard recently that the reason there is so much violence in the world is because it is godless? On the one hand, the statement is true because God isn't in the world, the world is in God. Brahman can't be found in the world of maya. On the other hand, the statement is untrue because nothing exists but God, so how can the world be godless?"

ANSWER: Most important when manning these two perspectives is to acknowledge and understand that when the statement "Nothing exits but God" is uttered, that there is no world at that level. Nirvikalpa Samadhi, according to Shankara and Vivekananda, negates the existence of everything but God. This is why we must consider deep sleep while here in the body in this world, because it comes the closest to demonstrating what Brahman is really like for us, i.e., formless.

Take for instance Christ in meditation in the wilderness, and Lord Buddha sitting for so long under the Bo Tree. They were completely unaware of the world in the state they went into, i,e. — Beatific Vision, or Nirvana. The world did not exist for them. This was corroborated in present times by Sri Ramakrishna Paramahamsa as well, who stated *"The further you go towards God, the further away you go from the world."*

So be sure that when you have the thought of "God in Everything," that it does not suggest to you that "things" are God; or when you think that "God is everywhere," that you not conclude thereby that God is a "place" or "location." And importantly, that when you aver that "God is in Everyone," that you not play naive by thinking that people's ego, intellect, mind, senses, and body are God. Otherwise, before long, worldly, deluded, and evil people must be considered God. As Sri Krishna puts it in the *Bhagavad Gita*, "*I am in them, but they are not in Me. Behold, My Divine Maya...."*

As to the question of evil in the world, it works to indicate it that way. Because beings are not aware of Divine Reality, and do not seek It, that leaves the world in jeopardy of heavy karma — which it always has suffered. Of course, when we say "the world," we do not mean nature; nature is insentient. There is no fault in it. We mean the world of embodied souls. Few souls in any given cycle *(manvantara or mahayuga)* make it off the wheel of birth and death. If God were in their minds, never having been abandoned in the first place, they would see through the world in one lifetime and be free. May all be released from the world-bewitching maya.

R.O. from Hawaii writes:
QUESTION: "Does the concept of the 'Void' exist in Vedanta as in Buddhism? Could Shiva, the Destroyer, be performing the same function?"
ANSWER: The void exists in Vedanta, but in a slightly different way than in Buddhism. That is, if the void is equated with "emptiness," or what is called shunyata, there is much more to it than a sterile nothingness, like science or atheism might propose. Periods of voidness would be how the Vedanta would explain it, and that description would not be a philosophical venture, but a measure of time in cycles. That is termed *"pralaya."* There are many pralayas that pass over cycles, but there is a *Mahapralaya* where all form goes into deep abeyance for an indeterminate amount of time. Cosmologically speaking, yes, Lord Siva would be the great Soul who guides all into these periods of formlessness, and Lord Brahma would put the spin on each new cycle in due time.

So, to get a good grasp on all Indian views of voidness is to look at cycles of history, cycles of time beyond human reckoning, cosmology, anthropomorphism, and philosophy. A good contemplation of Timelessness would also be well-advised — though this will require the company of illumined souls to understand.

Akshaya-Bhakti from New England writes:
COMMENTS: "I have always enjoyed the intricacies of language, but lately, after the Divine Mother Retreat, I am trying to become more aware of how Consciousness permeates it (an aspect of Her I think that is called, the Vak Devi?). For instance, in the prayer Om Asato..., the original translation I learned was, ".....lead us from death to eternal life, but then I recently came across a newer translation that was rather, '....from death to internal life.' Whereas eternal life still seems abstract to me, that of inner life is something to which I can now better relate to after studying the process of involution on the 24 cosmic principles in our Raja lessons. In Lesson 100, in your reply to my question about how Sakshi fits into the Chart of *The Seer, the Seen, the Unseen, and the Obscene,* I appreciate the elucidation of how it is closer to Brahman as the Seer than to Ishvara as the Unseen, that aspiring souls are always searching while the Seer or Witness is already seeing, Sakshi is less of a Cosmic Principle and more a realized Presence. In your reply to Anurag, I was inspired by your

description of the "transformation" into the Self which we have always been, "that no one really sees the aspirant as he makes himself into Brahman; others were not there to witness the stunning "Inner Alchemy" that transpired — only the jewelers." I also liked the analogy of the actor that you gave to him, "....it is not the onlooker who needs to be convinced of his divinity, it is the player himself."

QUESTION: "Can ordinary human beings be considered as having a lila, or is that reserved for the Avatar? I think it might be freeing not only to think of our roles in this life in that way, but in our many lives that came before — that it might act as another tool in learning to isolate one's true Self from the body."

ANSWER: Yes, all beings have a "lila" with regard to them taking embodiment and playing here amidst the realms of name and form. This probably would not relate to beings who enact little else in their lives but suffering and delusion, however, for the word "lila" would not convey its original intent in those cases. In other words, Divine Play, or Divine Sport, is much different than superficial sport, mundane sport, meaningless sport, futile sport, fruitless sport, etc. The Mahalila of the Great Avatar is a grand statement, yes? It would not be fitting to place it alongside of lesser types of sport, even mere playfulness.

But you are right in saying that, as a healing or inspiring modality, the devotees and other worthy souls can apply it to their lives, say, as a sort of mental posture that will aid them in living a dharmic life or divine life. Dharmic Lila? I like it!

QUESTION #2: "While I am attracted to the teachings of the Mahamudra, especially since they enjoin us to '....meditate in a manner of non-doing, and non-effort,' which in and of itself brings a sense of Peace, I have a few questions about it. Could you please translate the title? I think a mudra is a hand position as a spiritual symbol, I am not sure how that fits in."

ANSWER: *Mahamudra* translates as "The Great Seal," as if to say that there is a deeply set seal of spirituality and Enlightenment impressed into all of existence. A hand gesture evinced in sacred worship, called "puja," is also termed a "mudra." It confers deep significance and blessings on certain portions of the ceremony.

QUESTION #3: "Could you please elucidate what it means to 'shift without grasping?'"

ANSWER: It is the mind that is being referred to here. Usually, the tendency of the mind, particularly with worldly people and beginning aspirants, is to seek the most comfortable position and hold on to it. In spiritual practice, new dimensions open up, quite often swiftly and without much warning, so the mind, stunned, wants to grasp at the first level it comes to. Sometimes this means to revert back to the old station, since it is fearful or not used to anything new at all. If forward progress is made in meditation, it is usually just one increment at a time, when much more is actually possible. So, to "shift without grasping" is to allow the mind to make substantial progress when the time is upon it, for such times do not come that often in periods of sadhana. What is being called for, then, is wide open willingness to expand the mind into higher experiences, and to develop a ready capaciousness in the interim. Once Brahman is glimpsed, or even sensed, the aspirant ought to make swift headway towards that Light, and not drag the feet by grasping onto to basic levels or passing experiences whatsoever.

QUESTION #4: "Also, could you explain what it means to 'experience all manifestations as reality as they arise in the mind?'"

ANSWER: This may not be possible for beginning aspirants, but those who have mastered the neti neti method to any degree can aspire for this. In earlier stages, the thoughts that arise in the mind are to be quelled or transcended, controlled or dissolved. But at later stages the soul begins to behold more beautiful and substantial expressions of the mind, coming from higher mind. These manifestations are closer to Divine Reality in proximity than earlier ones, Thus, the tight hold on the mind can be loosened, the reins made less taut, so as to allow for natural spontaneity in practice and progress. The soul sits back, as it were, and watches an inner panorama unfold, and all without the least effort. When this occurs, the aspirant will definitely want to "shift without grasping."

## Pada IV, Sutra 26

*tada viveka nimnam kaivalya pragbharam chittam* (*tada*, then; *viveka*, discernment; *nimnam*, tendency; *kaivalya*, isolation; *pragbharam*, inclination; *chittam*, thoughts)

*"As a result the mind and its thoughts gain discernment and become inclined towards isolation from bondage to nature."*

In Swami Vivekananda's own words, *"The veil drops from the eyes, and we see things as they are. We find that nature is a compound, and is showing its panorama for the Purusha, who is the witness; that nature is not the Lord, that the whole of these combinations of nature are simply for the sake of showing phenomena to the Purusha, the enthroned king within. When discrimination comes by long practice, fear ceases, and the mind attains isolation."*

These are words of wisdom if there ever were some, as well as being a clear and direct description of the dawning of Enlightenment in one of its final stages. This word, *kaivalya*, in Sanskrit, denotes penultimate samadhi, referring as it does to "isolation" of the Soul, or Purusha, from nature, or Prakriti. We know that the philosophical standpoint of Sankhya and Yoga has much to do with these two separate but interconnected principles, often thought of and explained as the Sentient and the Insentient.

For instance, in today's world it is so obvious that matter is all-important; beings will spend all their time and all their energy in acquiring it in its many forms. This has come to be called "materialism," and as a way of life it has many avowed followers who give not a thought to anything of a subtle nature. Patanjali saw this occurring even in his own time, and pointed out that *"the Seer (Purusha) has become attached to the seen (Prakriti)."* This creates a topsy-turvy world wherein the witness of nature becomes, as it were, nature itself, and due to such false identification, then begins to see itself as being created and destroyed — just like objects.

**Pada IV, Sutra 27**

*tachchhidresu pratyaya antarani samskarebhyah* (*tachchhidresu,* breaches of; *pratyaya,* quality of mind; *antarani,* various; *samskarebhyah,* unconscious impressions).

*"If breaches in this higher quality of mind occur, various subtle impressions arise from its subconscious level."*

In authentic Yoga and its exposition, great care is taken to ensure that the practitioner knows that subtle samskaras in the mind, if not stamped out completely, will return — even after certain samadhis have been experienced. As Vivekananda has spoken, *"The Purusha is happiness and blessedness by its own nature. But that knowledge is covered over by past impressions. These impressions have to work themselves out."*

If we look back to lesson #91, at the chart entitled "Some Obstacles and Solutions in Spiritual Life," we will find a description of these "breaks" that Patanjali has been referring to several times now. While it is true that all of the types of vrittis listed on that chart are a kind of break in the natural flow of consciousness, the last one listed, called *chanchala vritti,* fits the description to a tee. Defined as "Intermittent and inconsistent vibrations that cause gaps in awareness," the solution given is to make meditation constantly flowing so as to recognize that Awareness itself is one, unbroken continuity. This is ideal.

This is also the best way out of the potential labyrinth of latent impressions which lie in the mind's subconscious strata. Otherwise they may arise unbidden, at the most inopportune times, to spoil both weeks of preparation and their long sought after fruits. It is here that the real subtleties of spiritual practice, at the latter stages of growth, get ushered in for timely implementation or necessary adjustments, as the case may require. Patanjali's word to the wise about lurking samskaras is well-intentioned indeed, and if heeded, capable of saving the yogic aspirant on the road to realization much wasted effort and many unnecessary setbacks.

## Lesson One-Hundred-two 2/3/16
### Pada IV, Sutras 28 & 29

In this lesson, and in our long-ranging study of authentic Yoga — which is presently involved in taking up some of the closing sutras — we find the Father of Yoga wrapping up his teachings on the seventh and eighth limbs and drawing his final conclusions. Sutras 28 and 29 of the fourth pada are explained here. There are just 34 sutras in this pada, the final pada, so we have only some two to three lessons left to contemplate before we close the study. But do not brood or fret (since yogis and yoginis never do). We are planning to fashion this study into a book on Raja Yoga, replete with all the questions and answers that aspiring students have contributed over the several years of its duration. And some more of these fine queries appear below for your consideration.

## Questions and Answers for Lesson 102

Tadrupa from Wyoming writes:

QUESTION: "What does it mean to say that 'a ready and easy compliance with objects is not natural?'"

ANSWER: This is said in conjunction with the materialistic predicament of worldly people, as well as those aspirants who are still complacent in their practice of discrimination between the real and the unreal, between the eternal and the noneternal, between the essential and the nonessential. These two above-mentioned cross-sections of humanity should not entertain an "easy and natural compliance" with the objects of the senses. This is because both attachment and love of pleasure increase in these cases, spoiling any bid for freedom that the soul in Maya might have. Really, even advanced yogi and yogini practitioners are usually quite leery of courting objects, preferring instead the subtle bliss of renunciation and its unique fruits.

Only the adepts and masters need not worry about the world and its allurements, for they have gone beyond them and have ceased to be attracted to changing matter and constantly shifting events. Sri Krishna describes these special souls in the Bhagavad Gita by stating, *"Those who do not long for slothfulness, activity, and balance when they are absent, nor become attracted or averse to them when they are present, they are the free souls and are dear to Me."*

Overall, though, it is best to remain on vigil whenever the fivefold elements of Maya — name, form, time, space, and causality — are present. And further, seeking affinity with formless meditation and nondual samadhi is the overall cure and solution for any danger in this regard.

QUESTION #2: "In meditation, at times I will do japa and the mind will become calm, and it will feel natural to stop repetition of the mantra and meditate on the heart and attempt to be free of thoughts. How do I go deeper or get even more concentrated after this quietude is achieved? Is it not a matter of how, but just waiting in this state and continuing the practice until my awareness moves further inward spontaneously?"

ANSWER: Yes, that is correct. But again, no complacency can be allowed; no falling off from the inner vigil. A constant awareness and ongoing state of alertness is demanded at this stage, though effortlessness is also enjoined. It is a special admixture of subtle qualities that is needed here, and these eventually become the norm for one's internal practice. The advanced meditator can enter right into this unique state of alert awareness, and hold it until deeper experiences come, as if of their own accord. This is often termed "watching the emptiness." Of course, emptiness itself, though not the supreme goal, is difficult to attain for very long. This question goes well with this lesson's sutras, and in accordance with the seventh and eighth limbs of Yoga.

QUESTION #3: "How are strong emotional attachments eliminated? Is it necessary sometimes to investigate the origin of some attachments, while others can merely be transcended without such consideration?"

ANSWER: That is right. Humorously, "some scars (samskaras) run deeper than others." In the mind is where these impressions hide, lurk, or breed, as the case may be. One's daily practice, even minimal efforts, can remove surface impressions, for these are just "hangers-on" from daily life and events. It is those deeper samskaras that are most difficult to detect and extract, and that is because they do not always show themselves daily, or even weekly — sometimes possibly even yearly. A point could be made, in the case of worldly beings, that their hidden samskaras of bondage do not come up even in a lifetime! Even fundamentalist religionists go on all their life thinking that they are right and the rest of humanity is wrong, only to find out later (perhaps) that their narrow views and short-sighted conclusions were a type of bondage all along — that, "Jesus is not the only way," but that there are as many ways to God as there are souls on Earth. Deeper than that, even, is that all souls are God embodied in form. As Vivekananda has put it, *"Mankind is just God walking around on two legs."* Mankind only has to realize that fact.

But you also mention emotions. The Sanskrit word, *akshobha,* confers upon us moderns the insight that there were problems of this kind in olden days too, even though many more souls were aware of the higher consciousness in them back then. *Akshobasana* is that posture, or *asana,* that helps rid one of emotionalism. Emotionalism is a positive detriment to the attainment of peace of mind, thus equanimity of mind, thus any type of transcendent samadhi. It is also a huge problem in current times, where people will get entirely thrown off of their necessary mental balance by any little thing, what to speak of the major catastrophes that are always, and will always, threaten life and land. Since Indian spirituality proclaims adamantly that all phenomena occur in nature and not in the Soul, the wise always take pains to place their mind in an inviolable position at all times. This, again, is called *asparshasana,* meaning "I am impervious to all that happens outside of me." The mental postures, "I am actionless *(akarmasana)"* and "I am formless *(amurtasana)"* are also effective for destroying unwanted and unneeded emotions, for what harm can come to That which is essentially formless?

QUESTION #4: "Is contentment really about being devoid of the desire for the result of an action? It is not the absence of ambition, correct? How do we cultivate contentment?"

ANSWER: If one were free of the desires for fruits, then there would be no place for ambition in the mind, for it is based in desire for outcomes. Therefore, contentment dawns on the mind of the one whose wants have all been placated and put to rest, and who merely moves forward through life with simple faith in God and Truth.

And in terms of higher asanas (beyond the nearly useless twisting of the body into pretzel-like shapes), this could be termed *adidaivavidyasana,* meaning "I know all the cosmic laws." A well-informed mind that is peaceful to its core regulates prana, senses, body, and life naturally, which is really what we are seeing in those ever-balanced yogis and yoginis who live life to the fullest. It is hoped that more beings will discover *Manasana, the Art of Mental Postures,* and take advantage of what they offer for the aspiring soul. SRV

Associations has put out a new book on the subject for those interested in doing a purely mental sadhana leading to Enlightenment.

R.O. from Hawaii writes:
COMMENTS: "Many times you have spoken about reincarnation, but always in an abridged way, as though it occurs automatically. Such as: the person dies and then 'waa' — he/she wakes up in a baby's body with the old karma tacked on. Could you give us more details like –
QUESTION: "How long after death is the average incarnation time?"
ANSWER: This question can only be answered generally, and pertaining to categories. The basic reincarnation time for most beings is about a hundred years. This class of souls will rest or frequent subtle dream realms (heaven) and live a life that is much like it is here on earth (which is also a dream), but with less physical suffering due to the nature of the subtle body they are inhabiting. Souls with evil karmas will live a longer time in lower dream realms (*patalas*), and be reborn eventually to learn lessons on life and morals. Thus, heaven and hell (*lokas* and *patalas*) pertain to two types of souls, generally speaking.

There are realms, let's call them higher heavens, wherein the advanced soul neither goes to liberation nor falls back to reincarnate on earth. Time, here, hardly matters, nor is it noticed by souls. These lokas, or akashas, are quite blissful, and the soul enjoys much higher communion there. When barriers are encountered, a few exceptional souls (again, like here on earth) will take a master or guide and pierce through them to move towards Freedom (from all form).

Other than all these, there are souls, usually more conscious, that may come back to earth inside of a decade, or sooner. These either feel a strong need to perfect themselves, i.e., break the final karmic bounds that will allow them to go beyond all the above mentioned heavens, or they are souls who are already free of karma and want to help others accomplish the same feat.

Finally, for really masterful souls, your question does not apply, for they can appear in a body yet not actually be born at all. They are transcendent of time, always living in their Atman, or pure conscious Awareness. To understand them and their process, if they have any left, one must make a careful study of the Advaita Philosophy with a past master.
QUESTION #2: "Specifically where does the person, soul, or entity go while waiting to incarnate?"
ANSWER: In this regard, we hear mention of purgatory in Christianity, and *bardos* in Tibetan Buddhism. Much like your deep sleep state tonight in which you are unaware of any form or movement, and time and ego have expired, just so, there are periods of emptiness wherein the soul simply rests or remains clueless as to its condition. It is important, therefore, not to ask questions about time periods only, but also to understand that timelessness also exists. In this case, more aware souls would experience blissful, peaceful, timelessness, and less aware souls would simply turn off and shut down without a clue of what is transpiring. Rest can be good, then, but there is also a state of primordial ignorance that is very tamasic and dull. Practicing meditation in life and attaining

peace of mind in the body is thereby highly advised by the seers, so that all that takes place beyond earthly life will be advantageous for the soul.

QUESTION #3: "Is it normal or unusual for the person to change gender?"

ANSWER: Actually, it is normal for the soul to not change gender. Beings formulate characteristics based upon their lives as either male or female, and carry those forward in succeeding lifetimes as well. In other words, samskaras for being male or being female are formed and remain, and the tendency to change them, or change from them, is not all that common.

But there are two other tendencies that can prevail as well, namely: gender freedom; and gender confusion. Gender confusion can interrupt what is natural and set the soul on a different trajectory. For instance, if a living being fails in life again and again, or runs afoul of its normal course, it may be born as a member of the opposite sex in an attempt to change for the better, or to try to attain something that it feels is missing. This ought to be obvious given the fact that there are souls who supposedly change their gender even within the span of (their) one lifetime. This is based upon confusion and misorientation in the mind. This is also why we see very masculine looking women, and very feminine looking men in the world. Not only looks, but actions and affectations also follow this tendency.

With regard to gender freedom, this applies to two kinds of souls; one who utilizes the two sexes back and forth over lifetimes in order to help the world and its beings, along with the other who knows that the Soul ultimately has no gender, being beyond all dualities. They live in the body free of the restriction that there is any real difference whatsoever in people. In the case of the gods and goddesses, as well, they are often envisioned as a harmonious combination of the best of both male and female attributes

QUESTION #4: "Are there a lot of choices for a new body, considering the expanding world population, or are many new or old souls wanting to come into this modern era?"

ANSWER: Of course, we must first declare that there is no age to the Soul. But coming down from the nondual perspective a bit, one could say that there are souls who have been reborn many times, and then there are souls who have not even seen a body for some time. A person who seems very ethereal looking, for instance, may have spent a long time in heavenly realms, and seems out of place on the earth and in society. On the other hand, base humans have the world stamped upon their very features, looking very gross at times, and having no heavenly light coming off of them at all. These latter know only of birth, life, and rebirth with their hapless ancestors — all in ignorance. The Eternal Life that Jesus spoke about is more than a mystery to them; they do not think of God even by accident. If they worship anything it is the "three m's" — matter, money, and mammon — and a fourth "m," called Maya, is their unknown god.

Souls coming in and out of existence are rather like waves springing up on the surface of an ocean. The Ocean is the underlying Reality, while the waves are too numerous to keep track of, and too swift in their coming and going to be called constant. Therefore, what remains are two basic categories:

one set of beings that knows the Ocean, and the other that knows It not. If it be claimed that a third category exists, one that intuits the Ocean but does not yet know It, then the point can be made, like Lord Buddha confirmed, that this so-called third category knows the Ocean already, but is either pretending not to, or is in the process of realizing It. Whatever the case, and as Sri Ramakrishna put it: *"Does the Ocean belong to the waves, or do the waves belong to the Ocean?"*

QUESTION #5: "Are there spiritual beings that watch over the process of incarnation, and monitor and guard the gateways, so to speak."

ANSWER: Yes, these deities exist, though unseen and unknown by most of the denizens of earth. And they stand at many portals as well. Jesus's saying, *"My Father's Mansion has many chambers"* is a good way of explaining this. The most clear and comprehendible division of these levels of consciousness, or *"kingdom of heavens within,"* covers the earth-dwellers *(bhutakasha)*, the elementals and ancestors *(pranakasha)*, the celestials *(manakasha)*, the gods and goddesses *(chittakasha)*, and the luminaries, Trinity, etc., *(jnanakasha)*. The *Chidakasha* is Formless Reality. This telling changes a bit according to different scriptures and eras of Indian Religion and Philosophy. If the *jnanakasha* is subdivided to include the *vijnanakasha*, then we have the famous Seven Worlds, each presided over by their own Rishi, or seers of Truth. The main purpose of these beings is to assist souls in transitioning out of bodies and admit them into subtler worlds. The secondary purpose is to keep them from undeserved ascension, and send them back to lower worlds for further schooling if that is needed.

QUESTION #6: "What are these 'gateways,' and how does the person get from the 'waiting place' to the gateway?"

ANSWER: The transitioning being is no longer a "person" as we knew him/her, but is a soul complex that still has crystallizations, or thought patterns, inhibiting it. The passages you speak of can be envisioned as gateways, or at least that is what a devotee raised in Christianity would envision. If we consult the *Upanisads* and the *Puranas* together, an image of the above-mentioned Seven Worlds emerges, and these can be correlated with the seven *chakras* of the *Kundalini Yoga* system. Three great barriers exist among these realms. They are called *"granthis."* Two of these (*brahmagranthi* and *vishnugranthi*) restrict souls to lower worlds in accord with the three lower chakras, similar to hell, earth, and heaven. The third granthi (*rudragranthi*) is very subtle, and keeps souls abiding in the fourth, fifth, and sixth chakras. The seventh chakra is very hard to penetrate. This is a very basic description, of course.

As far as waiting, there is no need to do so. As I said, resting is natural to the soul, but restrictions are not. Attaining a conscious exit from the physical body, the soul can move inward immediately and take up stations as per its liking. The only weights on its freedom here are ones of unresolved karmas back on earth, and with the ancestors. Letting go of all karmic "baggage," as it were, and keeping relations with other souls clean and clear is the best way to move inward and accomplish such inward ascension. In other words, follow the way of transcendence rather than transgression, and all will be well. Put in yet another way, eschew attachments and favor Freedom, and help others to do the same.

QUESTION #7: "What is a 'desirable birth,' as the Buddhists would say?"

ANSWER: The one in which all auspicious markings, *linga* and *alinga,* attend upon the soul, as the Hindu's would say. Those markings are not the ones that society seeks and recognizes, like looks, fame, money, and power. The devotee may show all these as markings too, but in the other-worldly sense rather than in a bland or ugly sense. Moreover and above, he/she will have profound wisdom of the dharma in mind; the worldly will not have or have anything to do with this. Thus, they will go from the cradle to the grave in a confused state, and be ignorant and clueless in the bardos between births and deaths in the body.

Additionally, these special inner markings are impressed upon the subtle body, not just the physical body, and love of the Lord and Mother of the Universe will be in them. Also, an understanding of Nonduality and Universality, both, will mark them.

Importantly, and in the end, a "desirable" birth will not be needed or wanted anymore, and will be replaced by a desireless birth that ends the cycle for good. As the Lord Buddha Himself once said, *"I have gone beyond; beyond the beyond. Have no more hope for me forevermore. I am gone, and gone forever."*

QUESTION #8: "Anything else that you can add?"

ANSWER: Only that birth, life, and death are all a dream. The Atman, the Soul of mankind, perfect at all times, beyond time, does not suffer and enjoy, does not transform, does not come and go in and out of existence. It *is* Existence, in the absolute sense. It is unbound and Ever-Free. And, as Vivekananda has stated, *"Atman does not dream."* When it associates with the body, in play, Its main directive is to tear off all the veils that hide Its divinity, and do so in front of as many ready souls as possible so that they, too, can realize their inherent Freedom and Divine Nature. The Avatar does this very adeptly from age to age and liberates the most souls, but all of us must in some lifetime enact the final chapter of this play and, when ready, tear off the veils for the sake of families, friends, and loved ones. Enlightenment will then be recognized by them as the ultimate treasure of life, and many generations of ancestors, prior and ahead, will begin to perceive It alone as the only solution for illusory ignorance and unnecessary suffering, and the Supreme Goal.

Akshaya-Bhakti from New England writes:

COMMENTS: "Swami Vivekananda refers to the panorama of nature in Sutra 26 and how it is for the Purusha, but in the uplifting reply to my question about what it means to 'experience all manifestations as reality as they arise in the mind' you refer to an even more beautiful inner panorama toward which you have been guiding us all in these Raja lessons. However, I am reminded that the purpose of the show is not pleasure at all, but as a lesson to convince us of

our true Self, the Purusha, that is beyond even that and is 'happiness and blessedness by its own nature,' Hence the title of the chapter, 'Independence!'"
QUESTION: "The transitory nature of the external panorama makes it clear that we need to separate from it, but how will one aspire to 'isolation' from the inner display that seems so compelling?"
ANSWER: When one truly finds the inner terrain, while in the body or after one leaves it, and if he or she be sincere, the Light that illumines it will, by itself, lead one towards complete Independence. It is the boundless Light of Intelligence I speak of, not the alluring light of further dependence that leads to salvation alone. The Keepers of the Great Gate, like Buddha, Jesus, Vivekananda, etc., will usher the aspiring soul on through It if the soul should want that. If the soul wants to gather with others at "The Blessed Feet," then The Keepers will accommodate that as well. As the Lord told us in the 1800's, *"Some rare birds, even though thirsty, will only drink water that falls from the skies when the star Svati is in ascendancy, as rare as that is. Other birds will drink readily from earthly ponds, pools, and streams."* The soul who thirsts for the type of Isolation that you speak of here, what Lord Patanjali calls *Kaivalya*, is that rare winged creature who would rather die of thirst than to abandon its Goal of immersion into Divine Reality.

As to the "how?" of this greatest of all attainments, it will require patience, perseverance, and purity, as the Holy Mother, Sri Sarada Devi, has stated. It will also require more than your usual everyday bhakti perspective too, in that the soul will have to come to know itself as both the projector and purveyor of the two types of terrains, namely the inner and the outer. In short, knowledge that one is not the body, as rare as that is here on earth, will not be enough. One will have to come to know that one is not the mind either, and that the mind (antahkarana) is, as I just mentioned, responsible for all that one sees, internally and externally. Coming back and forth in and out of bodies in these two terrains — the first two of Three Worlds — is all accomplished, or caused, by the mind. Certainly, *prana* (energy) and *prakriti* (elements) have a part in it, but these two both emerge from the mind as well. Thus, some "esoteric knowledge" will be needed by the soul in order to gain isolation. It is really isolation from its own projections, you see, which of course smacks of the ego (also a part of the mind complex).

To explain further this important point, it is *jnanam,* uncompromising as it is, that removes the worlds of outer and inner nature from the quotient. Bhakti would have to be very intense, nay, ecstatic, to do that, as we know by looking at souls such as Chaitanya, Narada, and Thakur Sri Ramakrishna. But even a little of jnana will temper the world, at least enough so as to allow one a glimpse of the ego's insipid clinging to unreal things, as well as a strong intuition that there is such a thing as Formlessness, and that it is highly desirable of attainment. I offer then, that immature bhakti — the kind of which we see everywhere in the world today — is merely a dirt path. If developed by a spiritual guide it will lead to the paved highway of jnana, which in turn leads to the thoroughfare of *vijnana* — and that then leads to the wide open concourse of

Bhakti (*Prema*) combined with *Atmajnana*. Followed with dedication, this describes the "How?"

QUESTION #2: "When in the subtle state after the gross body is dropped, is that inner panorama still observed, as in a dream, once one has attained it (although they might still be in the wheel of karma, not yet liberated), or is it temporarily in abeyance?"

ANSWER: Please read my answers to R.O.'s questions earlier in this chapter for a partial answer to this query. What I will add here is that the inner terrain is not so much "attained" after the death of the body as it is encountered. It is there; you will not miss it! As told earlier in this lesson, souls who sleep in ignorance, or have built up a habit of abiding in tamas during their lifetimes, will be the ones who will not "see" with the inner eyes this light-filled terrain. Souls who rest after leaving the body will eventually awaken to it, just as we do to the light of the sun in the morning here on earth.

QUESTION #3: "In Sutra 27 as it appears in the text, we are referred back to Chapter 2, Sutra 10 to review how to dissolve the fine samskaras: 'When the chitta, which is an effect, is resolved into its cause, egoism. Then only the fine impressions will die along with it. Meditation cannot destroy these.' Wouldn't we need to be in meditation to ferret out these samskaras and to quell the chitta? What are the 'steps' to perform this resolution of the chitta into the ego?"

ANSWER: The steps vary according to the path one is following, but as I was stating above, recognition and acceptance of the connection between the ego/mind complex and its thoughts begins the process in earnest. For, what appreciable progress has anyone ever made in meditation, except learning how to do it? Stilling the thoughts and gaining control over their rise and fall, or having certain visions pertinent to one's practice — this is the nature and content of most being's meditations. In other words, it is not the meditation itself, but the awareness that is meditating that runs the show, and thus loosens all bonds in order to be free. That is why the path of nonduality is called "Self-realization." Put another way, yogically, this is the difference between the seventh and eighth limb, between meditation and samadhi.

Conclusively, meditation, knowledge, devotion, and the like — none of them destroy the subtle impressions lingering in the mind. You do that. The question is, when are you going to get around to it; when will the meditator, filled with knowledge and saturated with devotion, decide to bring an end to all this pretense and just be the Atman?

QUESTION #4 "And a related question, if the chitta can be defined as 'the mind's contents' (glossary of *Sri Ramakrishna's Stories* under Antahkarana), how is there still an 'ego' left if we have already emptied it of our memories and personality? I guess I am asking how the chitta is actually different from the ego."

ANSWER: Not different; connected. The antahkarana is one unit with four compartments, each managing its own field but mixing with the others. We must see their similarities and how they work together, or, if you prefer, get them to work together for a higher purpose — not one of personalized enjoyment and ownership based in individual knowledge, but one of cosmic bliss commingled with renunciation of the unreal based in nondual Truth. Memories and personality become divine under this principle of unification, and if we have to practice it for awhile, then so be it. Sempiternal mental postures will take us to the goal of Goals, and it will then feel as if we never left (since we never really did). As *We Are Atman All-Abiding* states: *"Atman never comes and goes; never thinks, but always Knows."*

QUESTION #5: "In the chart, *9 Obstacles to Spiritual Life,* could you please explain what are the Four Absorptions of the Mind?"

ANSWER: I think you are referring to my chart on the Four Noble Truths and Eightfold Path, wherein Stage Two mentions the Four Absorptions of Mind. It is a Buddhist teaching, of course, but it is quite Yogic as well. Patanjali admired Buddhism; what truly spiritual person does not? The Buddha lived probably some 700 years prior to his incarnation.

The first of the Four Absorptions is the relinquishing of all unwholesome roots and desires so as to be able to reach proper conceptualization and actual knowledge. Thus, *vitarka* and *vichara* are common to both Buddhism and Yoga. A healthy form of happiness, enthusiasm, and well-being are the results of this stage of absorption.

The second stage allows freedom from these very things, sort of like our Vedantic freedom from the sattva guna to gain deeper balance. A finer concentration, called one-pointedness, is the aim here, which cannot be gained through any form of happiness or joy, since they take the mind away from focus.

The third stage sees even one-pointed concentration lose its efficacy, to be replaced by pure and constant equanimity. Constant alertness is said to be the plateau here.

The fourth stage, well, what can be said through words? A subtler equanimity accompanied by an ever-awake state comes over the mind, which is now "Buddha Mind." Only those whose mind has ever gotten completely absorbed, even for a minute, will know what this is like. One song has it that, *"A man has come to me from a land that never sleeps. Now all my dreams have become radiant meditations."* Perhaps this describes in words, poetically, how the luminary feels upon arriving here, in final Absorption.

Avinashi from Pennsylvania writes:

QUESTION: "Recently, I've found myself considering the difference between the process of raja yoga and the path of jnana yoga as embodied in atma-vichara. In raja yoga, the technique is to return attention over and over to a single point, and this is of course often called meditation. But it seems that in atma-vichara, the process, as embodied in the practice of shravana, manana, and nididhysana, is less one of meditation in the raja yoga sense than it is a sustained use of deep, reflective intelligence until realization dawns. Doesn't even the third phase, nididhysana, involve the continued employment of focused reflection right to the end, though of course along the lines of a siddhanta? So although I often hear this process described as meditation, is it really? Or is the process of atma-vichara different in its character from meditation? It feels to me as if this query sheds a lot of clarity on what my path has so deeply become, and that is the path of self-inquiry; considering this question brings me a feeling of sure-footedness, like I was a llama on a mountain path. So will you shine more light on the subject?"

ANSWER: The word and act of meditation both contain several shades of meaning, and apply to different aspirants on multiple pathways at varying levels of practice. But what you are explaining here has already been touched on in my answers to the above questions of Akshaya-Bhakti concerning the difference between the practice of meditation and the one meditating. *Atma-vichara* is very effective for the latter, clearing up so many unseen and subtle blockages in its own inimitable way. That is why so many high-minded souls have taken to it, and with great success. Admittedly, *Raja Yoga* is practice-oriented, and we are glad that it is. If we only had access to systems of stark declaration and nondual siddhantas, we might be left in the lurch as to how to scale these highest heights, spiritually speaking. As well, there would be no way to explain or transmit to those whose minds are not so elevated yet the sublimities of Brahman and the stages leading up to Its realization.

One other thing can be said, and in partial answer to your question about *nididhyasana.* There is a fourth stage of the old *shravana, manana,* and *nididhyasana* triputi teaching that is usually not mentioned. It is called *Sakshatkara.* After hearing the truth (shravana) from an illumined preceptor (making sure to avoid questionable "teachings" coming from spurious teachers, which though they may sound reasonable, are nevertheless being transmitted through a flawed or skewed mind), the ardent aspirant can safely begin to contemplate these truths and axioms (manana), making sure, again, to always question the illumined preceptor in order to gain clarity, *khyati.* Intensifying one's sadhana is good, but to do so before clarifying the mind and its thinking process can be dangerous for spiritual life and its maturation. So listen carefully, then reason and contemplate over time. The third part of this triputi, called nididhyasana, will then happen spontaneously, and direct experience of what one seeks will begin to dawn. But again — and in *Atma Vichara's* inimitable style — experience is different from the Experiencer; the dream is not so important as the actual Dreamer. In other words, Nature, whether internal or external, is not nearly so amazing and beautiful as is the Divine Witness out of which both have emerged.

Thus is born Sakshatkara, or realization of the Witness of all that is done, Itself doing nothing! It is the revelation of the Inactive Agent, the Unmoved Mover, The Acreate Creator, the Inanimate Animator. August appelations like these explain, as far as words can tell, what the Atman is actually like.

**Pada IV, Sutra 28**
*hanam esam kleshavat uktam* (*hanam,* extraction; *esam,* those; *kleshavat,* past imperfections; *uktam,* explained previously)

*"The extraction of those past imperfections occur in the same way as explained previously."*

Whenever subtler impressions arise in the mind, distracting it from meditation and samadhi, we are to use the tools of Yoga already given to us. In other words, Patanjali refers us back to the methods explained earlier in the sutras in order to remove them — namely in Pada One, sutra 5; and in Pada Two, sutras 1, 3, 9, 10, 11, 12, and 25.

**Pada IV, Sutra 29**
*prasankhyane api akusidasya sarvatha viveka khyateh dharma-meghah samadhih* (*prasankhyane*, omniscience; *api*, as well; *akusidasya* disinterest; *sarvatha*, at all time; *viveka*, discrimination; *khyateh*, clarity; *dharma-meghah*, rain-cloud of virtues; *samadhih*, absorption of mind).

*"And when the yogi's constant discrimination has brought about complete disinterest in even powers such as omniscience, then the rain-cloud of virtues pours higher qualities upon him, effortlessly."*

The rain-cloud of virtues is a phrase used both in Buddhism and in Yoga. Noticing little facts like this assists the spiritual seeker in understanding the universal nature of all Indian *darshanas*, whether they be orthodox or "unorthodox." What to speak of telling hypocrisies, even tiny biases get removed from the mind when this type of harmonious concrescence gets pointed out by open-minded luminaries. Later, accepting and even integrating the teachings of other religious traditions can be effected successfully. There is no reason why Vedanta, Buddhism, and Yoga cannot only be accepted as familiars, but they also can be adhered to simultaneously so long as the proverbial "one deep well" is being dug as the seeker progresses towards higher religious perspectives. As Swami Vivekananda was wont to insist upon: *"Dualist, qualified monist, monist, shaiva, vaishnava, shakta, even the Buddhist and the Jain and others — whatever sects have arisen in India are all at one in this respect: that infinite power is latent in this jivatman (individualized soul); from the ant to the perfect man there is the same Atman in all, the difference being only in manifestation."*

The word "omniscience" is used by most commentators of the Yoga Sutras in English translations. This can a bit misleading. Despite the masquerades of phenomena such as seances and clairvoyance in the West, the word has positive connotations, being sometimes aligned with the Mind of God and so forth. This is actually also true in Indian Philosophy, but with a finer point put on it. That is, omniscience pertinent to the powers of God (*Astadhah Siddhih*), and omniscience related to the eight occult powers (*Asta-bala Siddhis*), are noted as two very different levels. The latter are estimated by both Sri Krishna and Sri Ramakrishna — the two major bookends of Indian's spiritual history — as being both dangerous and undesirable, being blockages along the spiritual pathway. The former have to do with transcending suffering via authentic means such as study of scripture, finding and dedicating oneself to a illumined guru, and making a spiritual sangha out of friends, family and other seekers.

With realization of God verily at stake, then, the sincere aspirant follows the tradition and makes steady headway, even through lifetimes, if necessary. We should note that Patanjali champions the teaching of constancy of discrimination (*sarvatha viveka*) as well, and once again, in order to gain clarity, *khyati*. The raincloud of virtues (*dharma megha samadhi*) may not pour forth its graces, or even gather, if continual alertness, like an "ever-awake state," is not secured by way of practice (*sadhana*). The human mind is far too volatile and mercurial, and filled with all manner of sidetracks — *karmas, samskaras,* psychological residues, attachments, desire for heavenly pleasures, impressions of death, subtle doubts and fear — to risk leaving it unattended, or to its own devices, even for a moment.

The yogi/yogini remains ever on vigil, then, until the undeniable descent of Divine Grace washes away, for all time, the clinging to ordinary mind and its wayward penchant for attachments and distractions. *"Pure Mind is God,"* said the Great Master, Sri Ramakrishna — the genuine and authentic Paramahamsa of this age. In Him we saw not only a "raincloud of virtues," but the holder of that raincloud itself. All of the facets that Patanjali so admirably lists and describes in his Eight-limbed Yoga, the Paramahamsa epitomized and manifested some seventeen or eighteen centuries later.

Glory be to Yoga, then, and to the Yogis and Yoginis who not only maintain its subtle power on Earth, but also live its unique and incomparable lifestyle in ready sight of all embodied beings.

## Lesson One-Hundred-three 4/1/16
### Pada IV, Sutras 30 & 31

Some of the Yoga darshana's most precious teachings fall in these late padas, ones that drive home to the mind the truth that all knowledge abides within the Soul. In any given lifetime, living beings find it, or not, but it is present, nevertheless. Adamant seekers will discover and keep track of this eternal wisdom, and learn to bring it with them in and out of embodiment. The questions of several of these striving souls attempting to do so are found just below, followed by two deeply profound sutras for our rapt study and contemplation.

**Questions and Answers for Lesson 103**
Tadrupa from Wyoming writes:
QUESTION: "In a recent dream I was told by a devotee that 'There is no desire in Siva.' Can you expound upon the meaning of this, especially in light of the jivanmukta's natural abidance in Chit-Shakti when associating with the body?"
ANSWER: Siva is named *Aptakama,* free of binding desires. The desire to dissolve ignorance might be his only desire. In anthropomorphical form, he has a family, children (like Ganesha), and a divine consort, but even then he frequents high elevations and mountain caves, representative and symbolic of peaceful locations and lofty states of Awareness.

As for the jivanmukti, the living liberated soul, that is a rare being. That state cannot be suddenly pretended; it does not come to one after only a few years of once a week study and a little unguided sadhana. So many pretend it here in the West. You are right that an authentic one of this caliber finds the Chit-Shakti, and She blesses him. He then acts to assist all beings and, in the interim, honors guru, dharma, and sangha with selfless service. There is none of the "bliss bunny" in him (like we see in many pretentious Westerners), but rather a healthy amount of fealty to the ideal, devotion to the guru, and humility in the face of growing realization. And the body? It becomes like a crystal that concentrates light. It will sit in meditation for hours at a time, housing the Atman and forgetting all other preoccupations.

QUESTION #2: "Are Shanti and desirelessness identical?"

ANSWER: No, but they abide together and complement one another. Desirelessness is mainly something to accomplish and move on, while Shanti, Peace, is a multi-faceted principle with far-reaching ramifications. It could be said that Peace will not come until desirelessness is attained, however — at least not constantly abiding Peace. But then again, the soul can become desireless for things of the earth but still hanker after heavenly bliss. Peace is three times — on earth, in heaven, and beyond heaven as well. One knows when one meets a being with three times worth of Peace. Desire does not play a part anymore. The *"Peace that passeth all understanding"* has moved in and taken over.

QUESTION #3: "Are the kleshas done away with in reverse order, meaning fear of death, raga, dvesha, asmita, and finally avidya? Or is it more of a mixture of all but centering on getting rid of the primal klesha, that being avidya?"

ANSWER: That is a well-thought question. Of course, the karmas of living beings are very different from soul to soul, so this would suggest that the impediments from seeker to seeker would need addressing via different orders. If I were to choose the more traditional way of proceeding, it would be that ignorance must go first, and fear of death will get dealt with later, maybe even towards the end of the path. Of course, asmita, or egoism, can be prevalent in many early on, but there again, its subtler elements will be eliminated towards the end of the practice phase, nearer to samadhi and after dharma-megha has settled in. Whatever the case, they all must go, and the seeker has to remain on vigil constantly to both check their advent, and eventually do away with their insinuations completely.

QUESTION #4: "Is Kriya Yoga enough to realize the Self? Why is this?"

ANSWER: If we are defining Kriya Yoga in the way Patanjali sees it, rather than any of the more shallow modern schools advising it, then it is a good start, but not enough for full Enlightenment. Its combination of study of scriptures *(svadhyaya)*, austerity *(tapas)*, and devotion to Ishvara *(ishvara-pranidhana)* will work wonders, to be sure, but are designed to take away impediments more than to reveal the Light. Again, it depends upon the quality of the consciousness of any given sadhaka, for in the more prepared, such a regimen may reveal the Atman for loving.

R.O. from Hawaii writes:

QUESTION: This question relates somewhat to last month's series regarding reincarnation, to which you gave a very detailed explanation. Is it correct to say that Ramakrishna did not reincarnate? Can you describe, then, the process Ramakrishna went through on his transition (physical death), and where he went? (Or perhaps there's no one there and therefore there's no place to go?). But my question revolves around the inner bodies. Do these have a lifespan of their own? Mainly I am referring to the astral and mental bodies. These apparently have a longer lifespan than the physical body, since people are living in these in the 'afterlife.' Do these also age and eventually go the way of the physical body forcing people to reincarnate? Do we know how long these bodies last? And if so, what happened to Ramakrishna's astral and mental bodies? Or did he still inhabit these bodies for some time after his physical death, perhaps teaching on 'the other side?' Regarding your answers last month, is it possible, then, that Ramakrishna is one of those masterful souls that can assume a physical body without incarnating. If so, has he appeared to anyone on earth?"

ANSWER: This series of questions inside of your main query can be taken all at once, even though there are aspects that must be focused on in the interim. The first of these aspects has to do with incarnating while remaining free. In other words, and as both the Advaitins and the Buddhists both ask, "What is it that incarnates, after all? Is there a personality that continues on? About that, and somewhat ironically, one could easily make a point that the personality continues on from life to life only so long as the soul remains bound to the reincarnation process, or the wheel of birth and death, but not after. It is here that all those teachings about karma and reincarnation apply; not otherwise. Even in the case of the gods and other higher deities, they are still embodied (though their bodies are causal and subtle), so they will necessarily be subject to a personality, or an ego — though in their case it will be a benign one (in some cases they will assume a wrathful one too). The main point, here, is that change and embodiment are still occurring, i.e., Maya is still in effect.

Coming to the case of the Avatar and other fully enlightened beings, the condition alters somewhat. They have transcended both the need to embody (*deha-vasana*) as seen in ordinary beings, as well as the desire to rule or oversee (*aishvarya* or *ishitva*, as the case may be) as in the case of presiding deities. Theirs is more of an overall transcendent compassion that only wants to see suffering lifted and illumination attained (*loka-sangraha*).

And so, in the context of your question, no, these great ones are really not in the body when they appear to us on earth, that is, the essential part of them (*Atman*) has overridden and outstripped all the non-essence (*anatman, maya, prakriti,* matter etc.). As far as the small self (*ahamkara*) is concerned — that individual complex that clings to the unreal — it is all but gone, and where any shred of it still persists, it is fully ripened and being used for the higher purposes mentioned above.

The difference here is clarity. To use an example, the ego of an ordinary being who believes that the world is real (and even that it is the only reality), and the great soul who knows the world to be unreal and Brahman to be the only Reality, is like the difference between a huge pane of glass that is covered with dust and dirt and a huge pane of glass that is crystal clear. It is the transparency of pure Consciousness that is present in the latter, along with the inner ability to keep mind and ego clean and clear. Ignorance, *avidya,* is the main cause of all problems in the world, and ignorance in India is defined as ignorance of one's true nature as Atman. Knowing oneself as Atman, and thereby one with Brahman, represents the end of all problems, impediments, sufferings — an end to embodiment in ignorance, you see. At that auspicious juncture these incomparable luminaries can take a body or not, and still remain the indivisible Self. Like in the case of Sri Ramakrishna, that is why Mahatma Gandhi said of Him that *"When we look at Sri Ramakrishna we are seeing God face to face."*

Focusing upon that part of your question next, the "Great Master," as He is endearingly called now, is as present now as He was when he assumed a form in 1836. Physical bodies, mental bodies, etc., are assumptions for souls such as He. However, this does not make them unimportant. Via His causal body Sri Ramakrishna is reaching all planes of existence with healing, insights, and boons for all beings, and by invoking His subtle body, various aspirants, devotees, and luminaries are reaching Him as well — like in their deepest contemplations and fondest meditations. So really, just like His Essence that goes nowhere, as you infer here, so too do all His bodies go nowhere, i.e., remain in place for Him to inhabit and for others to have communion with — or as we say in Vedanta, have *darshan* with. With well over five million souls meditating upon Him at the present time, and millions of others having meditated on Him over lifetimes in His prior forms (like as Rama and Krishna), a huge amount of subtle power has stored up and is being stored up. This is a power for the highest good, so different than the negativities and evils that mankind is conjuring up and unleashing upon one another.

And specific to inner bodies again, when you ask about His transitions after death, or better put, His apparent movements after He transcended death, it is much like movements here on earth. Just as one can now step on an airliner in America and step off a few hours later in Japan, much like that, an illumined soul who has mastered the dynamics of conscious birth, life, death, and rebirth, shifts planes of awareness at will and, as he/she does so, takes on bodies of subtler or grosser nature as each shift requires. To put a finer point on it, Consciousness does not shift or move at all; it does not need to, since It is everywhere (all-pervasive, vyapi); but it does appear to do so for those who do not yet know the nature of transcendent Reality, or possess the ability to move at will among the various realms (akashas) that are projected by their own minds.

A last few final details here. Just as with their physical forms, these exceptional beings can also remove their temporarily-assumed subtle bodies from existence. It was even stated by the Great Master while he was on earth that He would keep a subtle body for some 300 years in order to be available for souls who were willing and desirous of getting off of the wheel of birth and death (*kalachakra*) for good. Therefore, they are not only unattached to their physical forms, but are even unattached to their subtle forms — to any form that they may decide to assume or withdraw for the higher good of all embodied beings in all the lokas.

Finally, yes, many beings have seen Sri Ramakrishna since He passed out of the body in 1886. People living at the same time as He, who never met Him, had visions of Him when He was still in the body. Then, after He passed, they saw Him in dreams, in visions, in meditation, etc. Some, much like Paul seeing Christ on the road to Damascus, saw the Great Master (whom many of us see as the same Soul as Christ) actually appear to them on the physical plane. Holy Mother was one of these, recounting Her clear vision of the Master shortly after His passing. In deep sorrow She was taking off her few items of jewelry and putting on a white cloth, as Hindu widows are wont to do, and He appeared before Her and said: "Why are you doing that? I have not died; I have simply moved from one room into another."

Akshaya-Bhakti from New England writes:
COMMENTS: "In Lesson 102, it was beautiful to hear the guru's assurance that, after death, the inner terrain is 'not so much attained as encountered,' describing this as '....souls who rest after leaving the body will eventually awaken to it, just as we do to the light of sun in the morning here on earth,' and how dedication to sadhana will be advantageous when we go beyond earthly life so that we will be able to visit inner realms (as we would in meditation), maybe even not to come back into the body, ever! I loved the other incredible insights into the nature of the afterlife too."
QUESTION: "It was mentioned that life after passing from this body is similar to life on earth, but I am wondering how far this could extend? Emotions and relationships might still exist, but would you imagine a routine, a sequence of events, and continuity that would distinguish that existence from living dreams, where this is usually not the case? Could you offer a little bit more about this?"
ANSWER: Actually, I was using life on earth in accord with heavenly existence as an analogy. They are similar in that they are both dreamlike, but the soul will focus in on only one at a time, leaving the other aside for that duration. Similar to waking up in and falling asleep to the dreams that come to us at night, in this way do we awaken and sleep to the waking state as well. Due to this occurrence, or predicament, if you will, the state of deep sleep is to be considered, and even encountered consciously. To do that, meditation is the aid. Daily forays into the formless realm are to be taken up. Just as waking will predicate dreams, and dreaming may color the waking state, similarly will formless meditation reveal some of what is in the deep sleep state. It is in this very subtle way that the subtle phenomena of formlessness can be approached.

As for relationships and such, they will cease in deepest communion. Waking and dreaming, earth and heaven, all have them (relationships); deep sleep does not. Deepest meditation requires that relationships cease as well —

all except that singular relationship one develops with God with form, Ishvara. Taking up this more enlightened perspective defeats desire for rebirth in the physical body, and attendance upon heaven in a subtle form as well. It thus prepares the soul for seeing the One, the Atman, alone. And if and when the soul does come back down *"the amber stairs of birth and death,"* say, to do some of Divine Mother's works, it will do so in possession of the rare wisdom that the Atman is in everyone, and in everything. This is Divine Life, as contrasted to earthly and heavenly life.

QUESTION #2: "We have talked about how there are mind-born children of advanced Yogis, but it seems another step to say that they themselves could appear in bodies without being 'born.' Could you please explain this more?"

ANSWER: Yes. It is rather the point that one must attain the realization of being born of the mind first, and taking up a physical body later, especially seeing how the "mind-only" schools perceive the order of things, and how the cosmic principles flow from causal, to subtle, to gross in their outward trajectory before reversal takes place. In the case of this involution (that science and evolution theorists do not account for), the projected soul simply returns to its source of origin. This emanation and return are not accomplished from beginning to end, but from inside to outside and back again — with no end. It is not a case of a so-called beginning of time leading to a presumed end, but rather an endless flow of consciousness emanating from deep inside the Original Mind, outward to the body/brain complex, and back again. Thus, we do not have to go to the zoo to see our ancestors, but instead move inside, beyond the physical realm in time, to a more timeless realm where dynasties of Solar beings, filled with light reside in worlds of Light, begetting mind-born beings.

So here is yet another perspective on the "mind-born" children. We, ourselves, are that, but many of us are getting fooled by maya's outward show, by her adept prestidigitation, her slight of hand. Bodies and brains are only the most outward phenomena, all projected by subtle bodies and creative minds. When we see an amazingly intelligent person, we say, "What a great mind!" We never say, "What a great brain" That is because focused intelligence is of the mind, while random thoughts are of the brain.

QUESTION #3: "I appreciate the discussion of the mental postures in this lesson as presented in your new book, *Manasana,* as a way to eliminate the subtle samskaras. I am gradually becoming acquainted with these asanas of the mind and their organization into three levels. How do I keep the amplitude of these positive 'statements' in the forefront of my existence? By using their power as one would an affirmation? Please help me to implement the art of 'manasana' to its full advantage."

ANSWER: Similar to the five *bhavas* of Vaishnava practice, i.e., servant of the Lord, friend of the Lord, etc., one should take up one mental asana and practice it for a time. It is good to contemplate on one's self to see where the most work is needed, then select a mental posture that will help heal, uplift, or transcend, as the case may be. If one is not able to do this, then the guru can be consulted and the regimen outlined.

As far as maintaining the energy and awareness of any given mental position, that is a matter of personal discipline. Let's say one has a disease, and the doctor prescribes the perfect medicine for the cure; all you need to do is take it daily per his instructions. Does it take discipline to do this? Not really, for it may be a life-saving, suffering-alleviating, measure. It is important to you, so you "just do it." In the same way, sadhana and its practices are spiritual life-saving measures. If Eternal Life is important to you, you will do them. At this juncture, discipline is synonymous with necessity.

So many people let spiritual life go, and thus lose hold of any inner life. The mental postures represent a way to bring back memory of what it must have been like to live free of confusion and attachment to frenetic activity. From this return of memory, and with a little practice, will come fresh determination to stay seated in spiritual postures forever more, and to never give ignorance and suffering a chance to enter again. Then life will become an inspiring song again, and the soul the contented singer. Vivekananda describes this well in his own song: *"Where rolled the stream of knowledge, truth, and bliss that follows both. Sing high that note....."*

**Pada IV, Sutra 30**
*tatah klesha karma nivrittih* (*tatah,* thereafter; *klesha,* conditionings; *karma,* impression-based actions; *nivrittih,* get dissolved)

*"Thereafter (dharma-megha samadhi), all impressions and conditionings get dissolved."*

Dissolution of the mind stream — a rather well-known and positive spiritual phenomena among informed yogic aspirants — has been described well, yogic style, over the past few sutras, and generally in and throughout this fourth pada. The way that Patanjali expresses this, in his own inimitable style, accounts for the emergence of admirable qualities called a "raincloud of virtues" from out of the interior of the advanced practitioner's mind. These qualities are available to all, but the ones who acquire and bring them out using spiritual practice and austerity turn out to be the ones with the highest and noblest character. Thus, the Christian saying, *"If you bring out what is within you, what you bring out will save you."* This saying is two part, and goes on (and it must be admitted, in a more yogic than Christian style) *"....if you do not bring out what is within you, what you do not bring out may destroy you."* In brief, bringing out the good in the mind (*aklishta vrittis*) is the surefire way to progress, eventually to freedom. Please see the chart on page 71 for teachings on the *Chitta Vrittis* — *klistha* and *aklistha vrittis.*

However, bringing out the negativities in the mind (*klishta vrittis*) must also be accomplished, for if they are allowed to fester within, all manner of karmas will certainly manifest themselves in time. This fact is seen the world over in countless suffering and pleasure-loving souls who are constantly being accosted by rising karmas, usually unknown and unseen until they appear. Of course, that wise saying does not intend one to express the negativity within, but infers that by bringing it to the surface of the mind, and becoming aware of its existence, the sincere aspirant can then deal with it and be free of it. This is also a part of the process of the dissolution of the mind stream practice (you can review the chart on Dissolution of the Mind Stream in Yoga on page 310, in volume 1 of this work). By inspecting the contents of the mind in *alambanic* fashion, as Patanjali teaches, hidden clinging bits of mental debris can be loosed from the subtle walls of the subconscious mind and disintegrated. The happy practitioner can hardly believe it when, suddenly, he or she is free from these impositions. *"I woke up one day,"* as the song from India expresses, *"and my delusion was gone, gone — utterly gone."* For alambanic meditation of this nature, look back and review the chart in lesson #80, page 269).

## Pada IV, Sutra 31

*tada sarva avarana mala apetasya jnanasya anantyat jneyam alpam* (*tada,* thus; *sarva,* all; *avarana,* overlays; *mala,* imperfections; *apetasya,* taken away; *jnanasya,* knowledge; *anantyat,* infinite; *jneyam,* to be known; *alpam,* little).

"*Thus, when all imperfections and overlays are taken away in this manner, then infinite knowledge dawns and little remains to be known.*"

Many sayings found in the wisdom scriptures of the world, all springing from the mouths of sages and seers, come to mind when this sutra is contemplated. From the Upanisads comes the famous advice, *"Seek That, by which knowing, nothing here remains to be known."* From the mind of the Buddha, whose name infers infinite intelligence, came this utterance: *"Verily, from yoga arises wisdom; from lack of yoga springs the loss of wisdom. Having become aware of this twofold path leading either to progress or decline, let the seeker place himself in such a way that his wisdom increases."* Regarding conditionings and the disapearance of imperfections, one Christian sage describes: *"And I turned within to behold wisdom, as well as madness and folly. Then I saw that Wisdom excels folly as far as light outstrips darkness. So I invested myself with Her as a raiment of glory and placed her on my head as a crown of joy."* As Swami Vivekananda has stated it, *"If you have known Atman as the one Existence and that nothing else exists, for whom, for what desire do you trouble yourself? Through maya all this doing good, etc., came into my brain — now they are leaving me. Now I get more and more convinced that there is no other object in work except the purification of the soul — to make it fit for knowledge."*

A related outlook is taken by the swami in his commentary on this very sutra: *"One of the Buddhistic scriptures sums up what is meant by the Buddha (which is the name of a state). It defines it as infinite knowledge, infinite as the sky. Jesus attained to that state and became the Christ. All of you will attain to that state, and knowledge becoming infinite, the knowable becomes small. This whole universe, with all its knowables, becomes as nothing before the Purusa. The ordinary man thinks himself very small, because to him the knowable seems to be so infinite."*

All of the Vedantic wisdom points to this supreme Goal, *Paragatam.* But Yoga adeptly indicates where the trip wires along the way are concealed.

Ironically, many of these are only coverings, as is instanced in the Sanskrit word, *"avarana"* in this sutra. They can and should be torn away. Uncovering, or unveiling, is the art here — what Vedanta infers by the word *"vivarta."* Born into form is the grossest veiling, and it comes with five coverings, or sheaths *(koshas)*. But inside these sheaths are other coverings, such as karmas from past lifetimes and samskaras formed from repetitive, unconscious actions. Most beings do not know of them, for society, parents, upbringing in lower knowledge, fundamentalist religion, to name a few — all of them ending up as producers of more coverings to sort through — are never informed by dharma and spiritual life. Among those rare ones who hear of them, few go forth to find a teacher who can explain them and help implement special regimens (sadhana) to see through them. Therefore, Divine Reality — God, Allah, Yaweh, Atman, Brahman — remain hidden behind a thick set of veils. Thus, the Upanisads state: *"Few there are who hear of the Great Self within. Those who hear of It, fail to comprehend it. Fortunate is the one who hears of It. Wonderful is the one who speaks of It. But extremely blessed is that one who, having heard of It from the lips of an illumined teacher, is able to realize it here and now, in this very lifetime."*

## Lesson One-Hundred-four 4/21/16
### Pada IV, Sutras 32, 33, & 34

We, as a group of Westerners who are looking deeply into the Indian darshana of Raja Yoga, or Patanjala, or Ashtanga Yoga, have reached the end of our ten year on-line (and "snail mail") study of this supreme system of spiritual practice. The final three sutras of the fourth pada are herein contained, and all that is to follow will be your responses to them, equating to the final lesson. Of course, we have met for retreats in the company of guru and sangha several times over the years around this darshana, which has enriched both our knowledge of it, as well as our questions regarding it. Just below, then, are your penultimate queries and my answers from lesson #103. Many students are following these lessons, but only a small percentage of them actually send in questions regularly. My gratitude is tendered to those of you that have extended yourself (and exalted yourself) in this manner, helping the entire study to proceed along the famous premise of Atmic Inquiry — deep inspection of the nature of Divine Reality.

**Questions and Answers for Lesson 104**
Tadrupa from Wyoming writes:
QUESTION: "What is the difference between 'thoughts not arising' and 'empty mind.'"
ANSWER: This question proceeds from our recent study on Zen Buddhism, but it definitely applies to the mutual intentions of the Yoga darshana as well. "Thoughts not arising" is a phrase that refers to a later stage of practice wherein

it is not an effort to keep the mind from vibrating anymore, like it was in earlier stages of practice. One can rise from one's seat, then sit again, in somewhat the same state of mind or level of consciousness, free of the deviations of erratic or unsettled mind — that which Patanjali calls the *vikshipta* state of mind. Please look back to lesson #90 to find the helpful chart on The Five States of the Mindfield in Yoga. The fourth and fifth are what the practitioner seeks, and it is at the fourth state, called *ekagra,* that the welcome and coveted condition of "thoughts not arising" takes place.

Zen refers to this as *Hakushi*, or "white paper," referring to the empty and ideal state of mind to meditate with. The Christian mystic, Meister Eckhart, also realized this, and said, *"....leer und ledig aller dinge — it is empty and devoid of all things."* Sri Ramakrishna used the "white paper" analogy as well, stating that, like white paper seen from a distance, there seems to be no blemish, meaning that if one looks at the mind casually, one will see that everything seems fine. But taking a deeper look brings to the discriminating devotee's attention the many indiscrepancies and imperfections of the mind, much like holding that piece of white paper in front of a light and noticing it's dark specks.

At a deeper level still, these many problems in the mind, if not resolved via spiritual practice, will condition the mind further and drive grooves *(samskaras)* into it and its thinking process, affecting the balance of one's life and, importantly, all future lives as well. If you have ever questioned why people are the way they are in life, and why they think and act the way they do, then you will one day have to gravitate to the conclusion that they have rendered themselves this way by previous habits and acts, and in previous lifetimes as well. The entire law of retributional karma (*"You reap what you sow."*), undeniable and inscrutable, is based upon and proceeds along these dimly lit avenues of casual and careless thinking. And since *"The mind is everything, my child,"* then one's entire existence gets colored, or conditioned, in this way.

QUESTION #2: "Is the statement, *'Emptiness is form, and form is emptiness,'* analogous to saying, *'Brahman and Shakti are one Reality?'* Also, can you comment on how the first statement aligns with the sloka from the Gita which states: *'The unreal has no existence, the Real never ceases to be. The truth about both has been realized by the seers?'"*

ANSWER: Yes, some very good connections are being drawn here, and whereas I would say that each of these three teachings are corollaries, they each have their own areas of operation as well. The first, about emptiness and form, applies at a very high and advanced level of comprehension for the individual and advanced practitioner. Around Brahman and Shakti, yes, there is the principle of form and formlessness present as well, but this is a much vaster level of understanding, prevailing at the cosmological level rather than just the individual. Finally, the "real and the unreal" teaching by Sri Krishna pertains more to the purification of the mind and its thinking process, where maya, and delusion, are concerned. Again, and though it has ramifications on the nondual level, it is extended more for the individual in order to remove the last vestiges of ignorance from the (Arjuna's) mind.

Sri Ramakrishna once sat and held a coin with one hand and a clod of earth in the other, muttering something to the effect that *"earth is gold, and gold is earth."* Then he threw both into the river. This practice He engaged in was to show us that we need not assign any more or special significance to one element than another, thereby becoming attached to one (metal) and adverse to another (dirt). This same type of discrimination, only on a more lofty level, will have to be undertaken by the adept who, seeking nonduality, must rid the mind of the subtle duality of form and formlessness. When only Brahman exists, and It is ever whole and complete, all else that tends to (attempt to) divide It must go, being purged from the mind for good. *"Only renunciation is fearless."*

QUESTION #3: "Can you please explain why learning concentration will destroy mayic influences on the aspirant?"

ANSWER: Simply put, where the mind is perfectly concentrated, maya does not exist. In short, maya only really exists where one-pointed mind is lost.

Directly put, loss of concentration is illness, pure and simple. Mankind, who has been given a mind — that animals, insects, and plants do not have — should not then sacrifice it and become thoughtless like animals, scattered like insects, and insentient and brooding dully like nature. This is not only a waste, it is "unthinkable."

R.O. from Hawaii writes:

QUESTION: "I appreciate your in-depth reply re: Ramakrishna's transcendence of the physical body in RY #102. Also, this is the first time, I think, that you mention those '....masterful souls that dwell in the Atman (or are they Atman Itself?) and who can project a physical body.' Is this a real flesh and blood body that can function in this world — working, eating, and sleeping? Can you elaborate more on this?"

ANSWER: There are really three bodies we all have access to. In this world, and for most beings, they inhabit only two of these, i.e., the physical and the subtle (mental). And of those who inhabit these two, most of them do not consciously know of or account for the second, the subtle body. To these it is but a brain. The mind, with its powers and territories, remains unknown to them. Of course, and as an aside, the causal body is known by even fewer. It is like a deep sleep body wherein no thoughts, worlds, or objects exist — except in seed form.

So, given this philosophical explanation, and as regards the Avatar or Divine Incarnation, they can project and hold bodies at several levels, simultaneously. For instance, we say that God is manifesting in Jesus, Buddha, Ramakrishna, etc. What we are really saying is that God is holding a station called Jesus, Buddha, etc., and will give up that physical station after a time while simultaneously holding the subtle form of Jesus, Buddha, and the like, within. All the while the potential for these subtle and gross forms are being held is their causal forms as well, which is where formlessness begins to enter the picture. Besides facilitating the death of the notion of death, this knowledge helps us reorient ourselves to our own subtle and causal bodies. All of us have them, but most have sacrificed two of them and live only in the outer one, appropriately named the "gross" body.

The main point, in the context of your question here, is that bodies are projected by mind, and the more facile and conscious the mind is, the more powerful and useful the bodies will become. And yes, the more conscious minds among us are in knowledge that they *are* Atman, all-abiding. The less conscious see themselves as mental complexes, while the unconscious souls see practically nothing at all, perceiving themselves only as bodies, as matter.

To be certain, flesh and blood bodies are also projected by the mind. Consciousness (soul) will get into the fetus while this projection process is underway — mentally, before inception, and physically, afterwards. The whole concern really is, will the transmigrating soul insert itself into matter consciously and be a seer, or will it merely appear there, unawares, as in the case of so many souls here on earth. For a yogic look at how to master awareness to be among the few who know what they are doing in life and after death, please refer to the chart in volume 1, page 324, titled: The Seven Methods for Mastering Awareness.

The Great Master has Himself said that He will be here among us in the subtle body for some two to three hundred years after His passing. He will help beings move under the net of maya while He holds it up for a time. Lord Buddha has kept His causal body for 2500 years, and Christ for 2000. Thus, God is among us, alive and well, eternally. The voice inside our "head" is always telling us, "I will always be with you," and the Divine Mother of the Universe, in all Her mercy, will make certain of that.

QUESTION #2: "Can you point out and identify any who might have lived in the past, or are living today? Where would such souls live and work, or do they only appear briefly?"

ANSWER: Yes, some, only briefly. Many others are here, but remain unnoticed by the masses. They all know this is not their home. *"Birds have nests, and foxes have holes, but the son of man hath no place to rest his head here."* The problem with actually seeing this divinity in others, even in the Great Ones, is a matter of doubt versus faith. With those who have eyes to see, God is not only in the great souls, but in everything, and everywhere. There is no need to wait hundreds, or even thousands of years for the return of an Avatar; this "strand of hope" method is mainly for lost souls, and the fallen and lowly ones.

Put in another way, when the Avatar abandons the physical form *(stula sharira)*, He/She swiftly returns to His/Her subtle form *(sukshma sharira)*. When they are disembodied, then, we must take access to Them in meditation, using our own subtle bodies. This is what has been termed an inner life, though few present on earth today actually have one. The contemporary expression, "Get a life," is best put into effect by acquiring one of these — as soon as possible.

As far as souls of this type on earth are concerned, yes, there are — as Sri Ramakrishna has stated — some yogis and yoginis among the householders. These are rarely present in the West today, so many of us have frequented monastic communities in the East to find these spiritual emanations. The problem here is that few among the monastic calling are teachers. They also prefer to live lives of solitude, so are not available to us. The guru must be accessible. Thus the need for illumined souls to return to the householder path, so that seeking souls and, particularly, children and youth, can have access to the Wisdom of the Ages, the *Dharma.*

QUESTION #3: "You say to understand this process one must study Advaita under a past master? Which past master, and how is this done? Is this a master no longer in the physical body? So the contact must be made in the inner realms? Would this be a reason you mention in RY #103 that Ramakrishna keeps his subtle body available? Is this the body between the physical and astral bodies?"

ANSWER: No, it is a body beyond the physical, and the "astral" body is an imagination. And since this queer expression has come up, the "astral body" is a mere projection, with little use or merit at all. Being a projection of the unclear brain rather than the thinking mind, it is even further externalized than the physical body. Thus, the wise do not hold it, along with all its foggy projections. People having drug experiences, for instance, inhabit it solely, and by doing so they weaken their brains and close off any access to their real mind and its capacities. Pseudo gurus, with famous books ("autobiographies") that are laden with preoccupation with occult powers, speak of astral bodies. So do immature souls, with their fantasies.

As to the balance of your questions, the answer to them is "both;" we must have access to these souls both externally, while they are in the body, and afterwards as well, while they are still close, in the subtle body. Swami Vivekananda would be an excellent example of a superlative soul who is maintaining a subtle body close to the earth and its collection of souls. He himself has stated that, though he is presently in a transcendent state, he will not quit working as long as he can free even one being from bondage. He has said that he will take a thousand births, even, to facilitate this. So he is a masterful soul to meditate upon, and to draw wisdom from — even when he is "disembodied."

QUESTION #4: "Does the 'masterful soul' have individuality when it projects a physical body. What happens to this individuality when it returns to the Atman. Would this personality or individuality, exist in the Atman? To draw upon your answer to Akshaya-Bhakti re: the projected body you talk of is the soul constantly moving to its origin, and then back to the physical. Does this imply individuality? You then speak of a stream of consciousness continually moving back and forth from the origin to the physical. How does this soul and consciousness differ from Atman?"

ANSWER: A masterful soul has abilities that extend to all levels and elements of the psycho-physical being. The ego, or *ahamkara,* is one of the twenty-four cosmic principles *(tattvas),* and it represents a very early appearance within the strange phenomena of individualization. The soul, or *Purusha,* uses this vehicle to separate itself from homogenous Awareness (apparently) and take on a limited form. Advanced beings accomplish this mock separation for high-minded reasons, but others simply wander mindlessly into individual existence out of ignorance. By way of analogy, you can imagine a flock of sheep wherein the wisest stay close to the center where there is less danger from wolves, while others on the periphery wonder off and get lost. Or think of a host of iron filings, some that have a natural charge and are always attracted to a central magnet, while others lose their charge and get easily scattered, far from the source.

Sri Ramakrishna used to warn about the ego complex, saying that so long as one requires it, one must keep it a "ripe" ego, i.e., surrendered to God. If the "unripe" ego takes control of life, then all manner of unwise actions and painful repercussions will be the result. Millions of unripe egos result in the manifestation called *"....the fields of the Lord,"* or the fields of karma — *karmashaya,* as Patanjali calls it.

So yes, the adept soul can deftly project and withdraw this ego, this sense of individuality. If it is kept ripe while it sports in these life-fields, then it is easily absorbed back into the Atman at the time of the body's passing.

QUESTION #5: "Anything else you can add?"

ANSWER: Everything I have related to you on the subject of reincarnation over the past few lessons is all relative. The ultimate truth is that all movement — from the mind's thoughts, to the flow of prana, and on down to the body's birth and its actions — is all nonactual. What better word can be used? It is projection, conception; it is all ephemeral, illusory, or dreamlike in nature. Only Nondual Reality exists, and it is Formless. Still, it must be admitted that, within Divine Reality, there is the possibility for individual forms to congeal and dream — much like icebergs form in cold water, or clouds form in a clear sky. What I mean to say, then, and using another analogy, is that dreamless sleep is best. That is Peace absolute. If one chooses to dream, however, it is best to dream close to the Source where there is always Light to awaken with. Dreaming far from the Source is not advised, then, where nightmares rise and form in dense darkness — all seeming to be actual.

Akshaya-Bhakti from New England writes:

COMMENTS: "For a long time now, especially throughout these years of Raja Yoga (with its exquisite teachings on meditation and its practice), I have been grappling with how to maintain a more consistent sadhana. I have often repeated to myself, and even to others, that this was the priority of my life, thinking this would shame me into following through. But it was all to no avail, and I have often pondered why. Then Eureka!!! Several threads of Lesson 103 tied together and I realized that I have been missing the point entirely. The insight first came when the guru said that we should 'make sadhana a priority, because eternal life is a priority' and that 'discipline means necessity.' Also, that 'meditation requires that relationships cease, all except that one with Ishvara that prepares the Soul for seeing The One.' And further, how we must practice conscious dreaming (while we are in the body) 'by taking daily forage into the formless realm that reveals to us some of what is in deep sleep.' Thus, I have finally accepted that sadhana is only the vehicle, and not my ultimate priority after all. In regards to choosing my first stance from your book, *Manasana*, I also realized that while it might appear that I should start with the Salubrious or physical category, it is the Spiritual, and ultimately, the transcendent or Sempiternal, that I need. For instance, if I can begin to truly accept that I am birthless and deathless, the goal of eternal life will shine forth immediately, which will make following through on sadhana very sweet indeed! In your reply to Tadrupa's question we are told that 'Kriya Yoga is not enough to realize Self,' but rather that 'it is designed to take away impediments more than to reveal light.'"

QUESTION: "Once all impediments are gone, are we just receiving reflected light? How do we receive the true Light itself? Is it through the teachings of the Atmajnan scriptures (somehow this comes back to me from many lessons ago) and are those the ones that deal with the mind only as have been referred to in this lesson?"

ANSWER: The Atmajnan scriptures deal mainly with Atman first, the mind after. We do get the highest perspective from them, but this will still be reflected light revealing itself in the Buddhi. You put it well here, that we are "receiving" Light. But when we have direct spiritual experience, we do not receive Light anymore; we *are* Light. Until this ultimate Light occurs to us we must be satisfied with reflected light. We will not risk the danger of becoming content with reflected light if we know that it *is* reflected, called Chidabhasa. Only those who do not attempt the final push, or plunge, will settle for second best in this case. But for the time being, and until Divine Mother and our sadhana (do not give this up as a priority yet) prepares us for the final inward ascension, the peace that comes from knowing of the presence of the Atman will suffice. This represents a huge advantage over others who are still lost in doubt around this. That is why, in his Vivekachudamani, Shankara states: *"Hearing about Brahman is good. Taking teachings on Brahman is better. Better still is direct meditation upon Brahman, but best of all is that meditation wherein all doubt about the nature of Reality dies away forever."*

QUESTION #2: "Going back to Lesson 102 for a moment, I was quite surprised to hear that when reincarnating, we usually choose the same gender as before. Even though I understand how our samskaras and karmas would lead us to do so, I suddenly felt the impact of what it would be like to have been a woman throughout a sequence of generations. So, are we taking on not only a personal, but a collective karma, when making a gender choice, as well as we would with a particular, shared, historical event? Could you please explain what collective karma is, for reference?"

ANSWER: Yes, beings usually follow habit in all matters. They are basically creatures of comfort and followers of convention. The wise push away the creature comforts and break the bonds of mundane human convention. Thereby they get free — whether they be male or female!

Regarding collective karma, you ask for the impossible when you request an explanation. Still, the basic brunt of it revolves around the loop of reincarnation concerning ancestors and human beings. The karma there is "collective" and not just individual. And since there are still so many animalistic beings caught in this loop, then one could make a case in point about including animals into this mix. In short, human beings should recognize animalistic tendencies in themselves and be rid of them quickly, tendencies like primal savagery (of the wolf and tiger), outright attachment to food (of the cow and horse), gluttony and jealousy (of the dog and chicken), etc. To rise out of karma is to transcend both the animal and human condition. We have a divine nature. Human nature — what has that ever done for us by way of freedom? And the mixture of animal and human breeds only suffering.

So if freedom be our main concern, as it is for the seers and sages, we must snap the chains of birth and death, along with the links of karma that form them. As Vivekananda puts it, *"This thirst for life, forever quench; it drags from birth to death, and death to birth, the soul. He conquers all who conquers self. Know this and never yield...."*

As far as Patanjali is concerned, and if sadhana be the modus operandi that leads to freedom, there are two sets of fives that must be encountered and mastered if collective karma is to be neutralized. Please look back on the chart entitled, "The Insinuation of the Five Kleshas on Spiritual Life," in volume 1, page 143. Further, the chart entitled "Controlling the Five Senses in Yoga," can be reviewed, on page 95, of this very volume. Obstacles that imbalance and corrupt the otherwise pure, though limited, senses, threaten yogic equipoise.

QUESTION #3: "It struck me deeply that if my main identity has always been a woman, then Sri Ramakrishna's dramatic statement that he sometimes looked upon women as 'she-monsters' (which I recently came across in my rereading of the Gospel, p.593) becomes much more personal to me — more than if women (and gold) are just a general symbol for distraction. Could you help me to understand more about why that might have been said, in its particular context, so I will be able to see my gender choice as less of a burden? (I also feel so limited that I would not have been able to be in His inner circle if I had lived at that time, unless I had made a particular choice to come back as a man at that time!)"

ANSWER: Very assuredly, worldly women are nothing other than "she-monsters" on earth, just as worldly men are the equivalent in masculine form. But why should this apply to you who are a long-time devotee of the Great Master? You are Atman, beyond gender; He sees you that way. We must remember that He had several women around Him that He Himself pointed out to be manifestations and partial manifestations of the Goddess. Then there was Holy Mother at His side! No, references such as these were not aimed at gender differences, but rather at differences in levels of conscious Awareness. It is the old *"Grant unto Caesar what is Caesar's, and take unto thyself what is the Lord's"* type of teaching. Why, just read in Vivekananda's Complete Works and such to find many instances of the great admiration and esteem he held Western women in. In this way, that old expression of "women and gold" in the Gospel of Ramakrishna will cease to rankle the fairer sex, and instead point out the real culprits among them.

QUESTION #4: "In following a reference back to Lesson 80, I came across Milarepa's beautiful poem about the many branches of spiritual guidance. In particular, this line caught my eye: 'The protectors, the three Precious Ones, are the guides with no faults or mistakes.' Could you please explain who these are?"

ANSWER: In Buddhism they are also termed *Triratna,* or the Triple Gem. Namely, they are Buddha, Dharma, and Sangha, and are considered the "Three Great Refuges" as well. If one takes refuge in them, the stage of "stream-entry" *(shrota-apanna)* opens to him/her, and spiritual life gets well launched. Each of these three are considered perfect in and of themselves, thus are to be venerated. The first, "Buddha," means Shakyamuni Himself. The second, "Dharma," is the wide and catholic body of teachings. The third, "Sangha," comprises the group of fully dedicated and committed followers who live under the Buddha and in His dharma teachings.

Kanyakali from Hawaii writes:
QUESTION: "We have been studying Raja Yoga together for a long, long time! As I contemplate the ending of this long series of classes, I am humbled when I reflect upon this journey and consider where it has taken me. I feel compelled to look back at the condition of my ego when we began, who I hoped I would become after the process, and what has actually developed in me as a result. Spiritual progress is difficult to gauge, and we are often warned about declaring any definite results so as to avoid getting egotistical about it. But if we could use an objective approach and ask ourselves, scientifically, 'what benefits did we derive out of 10 years of Raja Yoga study?' the answers would be so illuminating. In my case, I did not make the giant leaps I expected to make. But I have managed to garner the subtle shifts in my character that were so necessary: I have built a solid foundation of patience, steadiness, non-brooding, fearlessness, and detachment. This slow process brings to mind the old adage of the wearing away of the hardest stone by the constant dripping of water. We don't really notice that the transformation is happening, but when we stop and look back we suddenly realize what has taken place. Over the last decade, I took initiation, went on two pilgrimages to India, lost a good job, found a good job three years later, survived a serious illness, and experienced the death of my mother. In other words, life happened. I'm sure everyone else has similar lists. Throughout everything, you were here for us, expounding upon the profound importance of controlling the mind. There are times when I feel inadequate in both effort and aptitude, but what I love about these teachings is that they constantly challenge us to use our God-given intelligence for gaining higher wisdom. I feel that the striving to bring myself up to the worthiness of these incomparable teachings helps keep my mind focused where it should be. I am feeling tremendous gratitude to you for continuing to plumb the depths of this gold mine of teachings for so many years, and for so patiently answering each and every one of our many questions. I just have one final question: Will I ever become a yogini?"

ANSWER: Yogis and Yoginis! From the standpoint of the Atman, all of us are That. It is just that from the standpoint of the body/mind mechanism it is much harder to make such an assignment for ourselves. And as you wrote, we cannot readily gauge spiritual progress.

But the challenge you speak of also figures into the overall quotient. That is, if increase in character based upon the gaining of *"patience, steadiness, non-brooding, fearlessness, and detachment,"* is any barometer, then stand up and walk forth as a yogini right away. The entire matter and its worthy undertaking reminds me of Swamiji's wonderful poem on the subject, called "Angels Unawares:"

> *One bending low with load — of life,*
> *That meant no joy, but suffering harsh and hard —*
> *And wending on his way through dark and dismal paths,*
> *Without a flash of light from brain or heart*
> *To give a moment's cheer — till the line*
> *That marks out pain from pleasure, death from life*
> *And good from what is evil, was well-nigh wiped from sight —*
> *Saw, one blessed night, a faint but beautiful ray of Light*
> *Descend to him.*
> *He knew not what or wherefrom,*
> *But called it God and worshiped.*
> *Hope, an utter stranger, came to him,*
> *And spread through all parts,*
> *And life to him meant more than he could ever dream,*
> *And covered all he knew,*
> *Nay, peeped beyond his world.*
> *The Sages winked and smiled, and called it 'superstition.'*
> *But he did feel its power and peace*
> *And gently answered back —*
> *'O Blessed Superstition!'*

## Pada IV, Sutra 32

*tatah krita arthanam parinama krama samaptih gunanam* (*tatah,* moreover; *krita,* consummated; *arthanam,* function; *parinama,* transformation; *krama,* gradual; *samaptih,* finalize; *gunanam,* modes of nature).

*"Moreover, after dharma-megha samadhi, the three gunas gradually cease to work their transformations, and their functions are consummated and get finalized."*

Timeless, deathless Awareness, or pure, conscious Awareness, lies ever-peaceful and undisturbed beyond the three gunas of nature. When a mere thought-ripple concerning name and form and their manifestation passes across these serene Waters of Existence, the equilibrium of these three get broken and cycles of time and space initiate. It will be an exceedingly long time before an initiated series of these cycles comes to a close, just as it takes a long time for a wave created in the middle of a lake to reach its shores. Then the complete dissolution of all things conceptual enters into and ends in Mahapralaya.

Meanwhile, along these great and extended roadways of time, and during their continuous fluctuations, certain special souls master the mind and go beyond the three gunas — even in the midst of such cycles, and many times, as well. To do this they must necessarily see beyond the many appearances of all these seeming transformations and pierce through the laws and functions that support and surround them. At first all is veiled, as the soul learns to detach from the outer senses and man the inner senses. Then, with the practice of intense and ongoing yoga, all barriers fall away. Finally, the statement *"Thou shalt know the Truth, and the Truth shall set you free,"* itself, comes true.

As preceding sutras have evinced, the advent of *dharma-megha samadhi* proves to be a great boon upon the striving soul, and compels it onwards towards *Kaivalya* — the welcome separation of the sentient Soul from insentient Nature. This final "isolation," as it has been called, has been described in the *Upanisads* by the phrase *"The flight of the Alone, to the Alone."* The Sanskrit statement, *Kevala Asti* — which is almost a *Mahavakya* in and of itself — brings home the deeper meaning as well, for the soul is now lodged deeply in and solely with its own Essence. And time, itself, *kala,* with its many sections, *ksana,* begins to fade and retreat from the gradually evaporating mind, as the next sutra explains.

**Pada IV, Sutra 33**
*ksana pratiyogi parinama aparanta nigrahyah kramah* (*ksana,* increments of time; *pratiyogi,* flowing sequence; *parinama,* transformation; *aparanta,* conclusion; *nigrahyah,* intelligible; *kramah,* gradual process).

*"The sequence of time in increments then becomes intelligible (to the yogi), and the gradual flow of its process reaches its conclusion."*

Few beings actually see time. This is true incrementally, but is even more true conceptually. As our great contemporary commentator, Swami Vivekananda, states in his own inimitable way: *"....perception of time is always in the memory. This is called succession, but for the mind that has realized omnipresence all these have finished. Everything has become present for it; the present alone exists, the past and future are lost. This stands controlled, and all knowledge is there in one second. Everything is known like a flash."* This knowing everything in an instant is what we call the Eternal Moment in today's more elevated and informed spiritual circles. It places the yogi/yogini beyond the three phases of time, like Siva Mahadev, who is *Trikaladarshi* — the Seer of Time.

For the inward moving yogi, *urdhvaretoyogi,* this process proceeds in a much different way than the ordinary soul, being starkly truncated in its duration. The secret teaching in Patanjala Yoga, and in all higher Yogas overall, gets referred to as "The Six Gateways of Yoga" (look back at the chart on page 501). First comes the esoteric knowledge that all of creation (projection by the mind) takes place under the principle of vibration. As even the second of Patanjali's sutras stresses, way back in the beginning of our study, to get into union (Yoga) with Divine Reality is to quell the vibrations of the mind. This great secret of vibration was also what Jesus wanted His disciples to learn about, so He told them that *"In the beginning was The Word, and The Word was with God, and The Word was God."* The following sutra will intimate what, or better put, "Who," initiates the earliest of all vibrations, in order to urge all principles into manifestation and all beings into expression.

But back to the Six Gateways, after the yogi comes to know the secret of vibration in all things, the second gateway becomes accessible and, entering there, he becomes aware of the existence of particles and their unimaginably swift movements. In contemporary scientific terms, this would amount to atomic particles and subatomic particles changing (i.e., vibrating) at a rate of a billionth of a second. But the yogi is not interested in matter. It is not his field of endeavor for one thing, but he has also seen it to be 1) empty of substance and 2) empty of any possibility of fulfilling him so he gave it up long ago. Now he is engaged in realms where much finer particles (like tanmatras and jnanamatras) are calling his attentions.

But there is one observation that got noted when he detached from matter and perceived that all objects are made of particles. Rather than capturing and preoccupying his mind, like this discovery has done to so many scientists and intellectuals, this fact freed his mind by revealing to him that all objects really come from the mind. That is, they are not there to be blithely observed after the brain develops senses to merely experience them; they are present because the mind projected them. What is more, before their manifestation on the physical plane, the seeds for all of them existed always as thought vibrations. This entire set of realization ushers him through the third gateway and on to the fourth.

The fourth gate reveals the connection of objects and worlds with the principle of time. The "increments" of time, which are part and parcel of the sutra under study here, get duly noted by him, and also get wisely associated with the mind and its abilities. This is not just a remarkable scene to view within, or like the discovery of particles earlier, another outer phenomena to entangle the mind with. For the yogi who is seeking release, or the *"The Peace that Passeth all Understanding,"* it is a key for turning off the cosmic clock and getting off of interminable cycles of birth and death for good — or as Ramprasad Sen sings in his wisdom song, *"to practice meditation and cut down time."* This is noteworthy as well, for it is at these very subtle junctures that beings like Patanjali and Vedavyasa indicate the presence of *prakriti-layas*, who are beings that falter along the path to liberation just because they become privy to these inner secrets of mental projection. They want to grab ahold of them and use them for producing worlds that are peopled with beings of their own design. Thus, they can hold power and lord over them. The expression, "Cloud castles in the sky" comes to mind here, as well as the saying "He became a legend (but only) in his own mind."

And much more to the point of Yoga, and the sentient Soul, *Atman/Purusha*, the fifth gate tells the real story and gives the final key to liberation. The fresh luminary perceives that all of space and time, along with the projecting powers of the mind, are apparent only. They are ultimately nonactual. There is such amazing and alluring attracting power, then, in the *maya* that fashioned it all with the mind's own participation. Seeing the attraction that the mind can develop for things fantastic, then, he moves to shut it down. He will "kill the mind," thus rendering it inoperable, and unable to engage in such fanciful legerdemain ever again. He will not create a simulacrum, or likeness, of Brahman, outside, ever again. He will not project a separate locus, or location, away from Brahman, ever again. There will be no more experimentation with a melange of mental ingredients for him, ever again. Instead there will remain only the Absolute, and he will pass through it as the sixth gate, i.e., full comprehension of Eternity and Infinity. As Lord Buddha said, endowed with this level of realization *(nirvana)*, "*I am gone, and gone forever.*" He also stated, and worth repeating: "*O architect of these many worlds, I have seen thee. Now I will not build any more homes — not of earth, or stone, or flesh and bone, or wise conception....*"

For those students who want to spend more time in meditation and study on the Six Gateways, using them to dive deeper into this particular sutra, kindly look back at lesson #82 and inspect the chart entitled "Stages of Dissolution of the Mind in Yoga."

**Pada IV, Sutra 34**
*purusha artha shunyanam gunanam pratiprasavah kaivalyam svarupa pratistha va chiti shaktih iti* (*purusha,* sentient soul; *artha,* intention; *shunyanam,* bereft; *gunanam,* modes of nature; *pratiprasavah,* involve; *kaivalyam,* liberation/freedom from nature; *svarupa,* essence; *pratistha,* stabilized; *va,* or; *chiti,* consciousness; *shaktih,* primal force; *iti,* concludes).

"*The primal force responsible for involving consciousness back to its essence, and rendering nature bereft of form, stabilizes and neutralizes both, and the sentient soul gains final liberation.*"

In the final sutra of this fourth pada, and of the entire illumined system of Patanjala, we find gracious and welcome mention of the *"chiti-shakti,"* or dynamic Divine Mother power. Much like in Buddhism, Divine Mother is seen as and equated to the highest intelligence, essentially nondual in nature, but capable of producing all the worlds of name and form in time and space, and managing all of their manifestations and expressions as well. Regarding the outer signs of Her great inner spiritual force, Swami Vivekananda has placed in his own commentary on this sutra, "*Nature's task is done, this unselfish task which our sweet nurse Nature had imposed upon herself. As it were, she gently took the self-forgetting soul by the hand, and showed him all the experiences in the universe, all manifestations, bringing him higher and higher through various bodies, till his glory came back, and he remembered his own nature. Then, the kind mother went back the way she came, for others who had also lost their way in the trackless desert of life.*"

A sutra like this one makes a strong case for the existence of an embodied soul, and its process of involution after its play and process in the external world is over. The wise thinker, after deep and apt study of the salient facts of nature and its manifestation, can simply let evolution take place, either actually or seemingly, and allow it to take its course as well. Accounting for the involution of all things, material and spiritual, is the province of the seer; it is also the responsibility of the seeker after Truth to come to know it. As Lord Kapila has stated in this regard: *"Sancharah prati sancharah,"* meaning, *"There is a chain of transition from unmanifest or nonevolved prakriti and its evolutes, ending in the grossest evolute, earth. There is also a reverse transition of evolutes ending in dissolution into unmanifested prakriti."* This explains what happens to all manifested things.

But as far as the sentient Soul is concerned, It takes another trajectory altogether (if it decides to move at all). It courts and finally attains, or regains, its essential freedom. Patanjali calls this *Kaivalya*. It is isolation from all produced things. As our astute commentator and beloved Swamiji explains, *"The resolution in the inverse order of the qualities, bereft of any motive of action for the Purusha, is Kaivalya, or it is the establishment of the power of knowledge in its own nature."* To repeat Patanjali's final sutra of the entire Yoga darshana, shown above: *"The primal force responsible for involving consciousness back to its essence, and rendering nature bereft of form, stabilizes and neutralizes both, and the sentient soul gains final liberation."*

To end our deep study of authentic Yoga with another reference to the *Chiti-shakti* and Her inscrutable power, Swami Vivekananda offers a fitting prayer on the behalf of all yogis and yoginis, and for all of her precious spiritual children — saluting the Father of Yoga as he does so:

*And thus she is working, without beginning and without end.*
*And thus through pleasure and pain, through good and evil,*
*the infinite river of souls is flowing into the ocean of perfection,*
*of Self-realization.*
*Glory unto those who have realized their own nature!*
*May their blessings be upon us all!*

Shanti, Shanti, Shantih — Om Peace, Peace, Peace.

## Here ends Volume Two, Padas 3 & 4, of Atmic Testament on Yoga

# Patanjali's Raja Yoga Sutras
## English Translation (Repeat from Volume 1)
### (by Babaji Bob Kindler)

**Pada I**

1 "Now, concentration is explained."
2 "Yoga is restraining the mind-stuff (chitta) from taking various forms (vrttis)."
3 "Then the seer remains steady in his own true nature."
4 "Otherwise, the seer may identify with ever-changing mental fluctuations."
5 "The thoughts of the mind fall into two categories — pure and impure — and are of five types."
6 "The five types of vrittis are: direct proof, false thinking, deluded perceptions, sleep, and memory."
7 "Immediate cognition, inference, and revealed scriptures are the three proofs of Truth."
8 "Distorted perception is false knowledge that is contrary to and has no basis in true nature."
9 "Reliant on sounds that are devoid of wisdom and based in imagination, such is verbal delusion."
10 "The vrtti of sleep is founded on the sense of absence or voidness."
11 "Objects and experiences which remain as impressions in the mind are called memory."
12 "Control (of those vrttis) is achieved by constant effort combined with renunciation."
13 "Combining spiritual practice with mature detachment, steadiness leading to proper exertion ensues."
14 "Yogic practice, in any case, is only set upon a firm foundation when it is avidly sought after with dedicated reverence, and for an extended and uninterrupted period of time."
15 "That masterful attainment of clear seeing, which results after the seeker gains experience and finally loses all desire for phenomenal experience, and which is supported by the scriptures of religious tradition, is designated as true detachment."
16 "That discernment which proceeds from the sentient Self that has left off with desires, and has successfully detached from the modes of nature, is said to be of the superior type."
17 "The state of subtle wisdom, called samprajnata, ensues, in attendance with a combination of base cognition, subtle cognition, the sense of individuality, and its experience of bliss."
18 "Asamprajnata Samadhi is the alternative state attainable by the discipline of awareness, in which all mental impressions are arrested and remain only in a residual form."
19 "Certain videhas who are disembodied, and those who have merged their

*awareness in prakrti, duly enter and re-enter a samadhi of the causal condition."*
20 *"Faith, intelligence, memory, and the power to discriminate afford others the awakening of wisdom, leading to samadhi."*
21 *"Progress in Yoga is imminent for those whose efforts are intense."*
22 *"Variegations exist among these advanced beings as well, who are divided into meek, moderate, and intense levels of practitioner."*
23 *"Or it (samadhi) may occur via the yogi's practice of awareness of God."*
24 *"God (Ishvara) is a unique Soul who is never tainted by activity and its development as various potentialities."*
25 *"That, and its seed of all-knowingness, is unlimited."*
26 *"Even though He is not restricted by time, He nevertheless appears in time as the ancient firstborn teacher of all other teachers."*
27 *"His Word of Power is Om."*
28 *"Repetition of that Name while understanding its meaning constitutes the true pathway."*
29 *"His subtlemost awareness gets illumined and revealed by utilizing That (Presence of Ishvara), which renders neutral all impedances."*
30 *"Impediments to Yoga are listed as disease, stodginess, indeterminancy, carelessness, torpor, indiscrimination, false conception, backsliding, and instability. These are dire impediments."*
31 *"Further distraction and its resultant outcome arrives in the form of overall suffering, mental depression, trembling of limbs, and unevenness of the breathing process."*
32 *"To affect success one must focus upon a singular principle with concerted effort, and thereby restrict these impediments and their correlating distractions."*
33 *"By inculcating into the thought process qualities such as friendliness, empathy, joyfulness, and equanimity with respect to beings who are meritorious, sinful, happy, and sad, the mind is rendered pure and clear."*
34 *"Or by the practice of exhaling and restraining the breathing process, the mind is made stable."*
35 *"When the cognizance of the subtle senses and their properties gets manifested, in accordance with their objects, then the mind becomes stable, its knowledge secure."*
36 *"Or meditate on that radiant Light in which sorrow is utterly absent...."*
37 *"....or, the yogi's mind becomes steady while meditating in the heart, after attachment to pleasure via the sense-objects is absent...."*
38 *"....or, when objects in the dreaming and deep sleep states are cognized as Self-wisdom by the seer...."*
39 *"....or when meditating in whatever favored way he selects."*
40 *"The yogi applies superior and skillful inner means over what is both miniscule and what is great."*
41 *"When the mental vibrations have become pure, the perceiver, the per-*

ceived, and the process of perceiving all merge and appear like reflections in a crystal, and thus comes perfection."
42 "When, through root cognition coupled with imagination, knowledge, the word, its meaning, and the object are all associated, the result is vitarka level samadhi."
43 "When the mind is pure and memory is retentive, and where the form remains only in its own essence and gets revealed, then appears the samadhi of subtle cognition."
44 "The two samadhis, one characterized by subtle mentation having finer concepts as a foundation, and one completely free of conceptualization, are now explained in similar fashion."
45 "The presence of subtle objects ends with the nonmanifest state, which is devoid of all characteristics."
46 "All of these (aforementioned) are called seeded samadhis."
47 "In the state of purity and stability which is enabled by complete mastery over the thought process, perfect spiritual clarity is attained."
48 "The fullness of wisdom is imminently borne within the highest truth."
49 "Areas and divisions of knowledge gleaned from religious study and analysis are at variance with fuller wisdom, which has unique purpose."
50 "Mental impressions which manifest from spiritual wisdom neutralize other impressions present in the mind."
51 "Upon dissolution of even that samskara (samskara of wisdom), the dissolution of everything occurs and the condition of pure Awareness is experienced."

## Pada II
1 "The yoga of conscious action is performed via austerities and study of scriptures — all performed in an atmosphere of devotion to God."
2 "(Kriya Yoga practice) engenders spiritual experience which dissolves all impediments to yoga, leading to samadhi."
3 "Ignorance, egotism, attachment, aversion, and clinging to life/fear of death are the five main impediments to being in Yoga, Union with Reality."
4 "Ignorance is the main field upon which rest all the subsequent kleshas and their modifications, classified as: potential, modified, overcome, or operational."
5 "Ignorance consists of a false reckoning that accepts all that is ephemeral, impure, and pain-bearing in place of what is eternal, pure, and beneficial."
6 "When the barrier of I-consciousness causes a distinction between the seer and its power of seeing, ignorance is the result."
7 "Attachment is the result of seeking happiness by courting pleasure."
8 "Aversion is the result of pain due to thwarted pleasure, and leads to suffering."
9 "Even knowledgeable beings, what to speak of others, cling to life and fear death, which naturally occurs due to its own nature."
10 "These kleshas are to be given up promptly via the process of mental dissolution."

*11 "Meditation is the way to attenuate the impeding vibrations of the kleshas rising from the mind."*
*12 "Karmas, perceived or not, spring from the field of repercussive action as results of lives already lived, and yet to come."*
*13 "When foundational causes from acts based upon pleasure and pain become imminent, their effects duly mature in one's series of lifetimes."*
*14 "Due to the causes of beneficial and detrimental fruits, the effects of pleasure and pain manifest themselves in life after life."*
*15 "The discriminating being sees pain and suffering everywhere, in the modes of nature, in the oppressive heat of ongoing transformation, and all due to constant conflict residing in the mind full of unresolved mental impressions."*
*16 "All this pain is to be avoided, so that none will be manifested in the future."*
*17 "By unifying the seen in its source, which is the seer, the cause of future karma-based pain is annulled."*
*18 "The presence or experience of pain/suffering lies with the body and senses composed of matter, and has as its cause the gunas of nature, and is for the purpose of experience leading to liberation."*
*19 "These states, or gunas, are portionized ingredients of defined nature, undefined nature, subtle intelligence, and matter in potential."*
*20 "The seer, only, possesses the innate ability to see, and being pure, allows for the cognition of all that the intellect perceives."*
*21 "All things exist only on account of the presence of that one Self, who alone, sees."*
*22 "Though all things perceived have gone into final dissolution for the one whose goal has been attained, they are still present for others who hold them in common."*
*23 "Through union of the two principles, nature and soul, comes the observation of their difference resulting in realization of one's true essence."*
*24 "Ignorance is the result of this union."*
*25 "With the loosing of ignorance in the mind comes its end, and being dispossessed of it, the seer realizes his complete independence."*
*26 "Discrimination leading to right knowledge free of turmoil epitomizes the process of wise abrogation."*
*27 "The absolute stage of wisdom reached by the great ones is divided sevenfold."*
*28 "Via scrutiny of Yoga and its limbs of practice, which dispatches all impurities, a gradual awakening of foundational spiritual knowledge takes place resulting in the revelation of highest wisdom."*
*29 "Spiritual observances and practices, bodily positions, regulation of the breathing process, control of the senses, concentration, meditation, and samadhi — these are the eight limbs of Yoga enumerated."*
*30 "They who follow yoga practice nonviolence, truthfulness, nonstealing, moderation, and nonpossessiveness."*

31 *"These yamas are to be undertaken as great vows, regardless of time, location, circumstance, race, or culture."*
32 *"The niyamas, restraints and practices, cover observance of purity, being content, undertaking of austerities, spiritual studies, and performing devotions to God."*
33 *"Distractions and deviations in the mind are to be overcome by their opposite qualities and the positive spiritual impressions they create."*
34 *"Violent or harmful thoughts and acts involving greed, anger, and delusion, whether self-actuated, instigated in tandem with others, or consented to, bring about sorrow and suffering and therefore are to be subjected to contemplation upon opposing positive qualities."*
35 *"The presence of nonviolence in the yogi engenders a natural renunciation of antagonism in other beings."*
36 *"The presence of truthfulness in the yogi makes him the happy recipient of the fruits of all his actions."*
37 *"Grounded in the practice of noncovetousness, all treasures come easily to the yogi."*
38 *"Being well grounded in the strict observance of abstinence and moderation, great strength accrues to the yogi."*
39 *"Becoming free from receiving and grasping, the yogi perceives the reasons for his incarnations over cycles of time."*
40 *"Practicing purity naturally causes one to refrain from undue contact with one's body, and those of others."*
41 *"By practicing mental purification, control over the senses, mental focus, and clarity are attained, making one fit for Yoga."*
42 *"With the attainment of self-settledness comes an incomparable sense of fulfillment."*
43 *"Austerities bring an end to impurities, resulting in perfect control over body and senses."*
44 *"Through study of scriptures in conjunction with meditation on one's chosen ideal comes yogic communion."*
45 *"Abidance in the nondual state is accomplished through complete self-surrender to God."*
46 *"A position which is firm & settled brings satisfaction to the meditator."*
47 *"By integrating meditation on the illimitable one with practice, restlessness goes away and posture becomes stable."*
48 *"Thus, and as well, the pairs of opposites no longer cause suffering to the aspirant."*
49 *"Based upon sure posture, the lack of balance in the in-breath and out-breath is dispelled and the prana is controlled."*
50 *"That is pranayama which is divided into three phases — the inner, outer, and suspended — and then rendered drawn out and subtle by patient practice over time, and in specific locations."*
51 *"Another pranayam, a fourth, transcends the other breathing exercises which take place in the inner and outer modes."*

52 "In this way the darkness of obscuration disappears and the radiance of light emerges."
53 "It (practice of pranayam) also aids the ability of concentration in the mind."
54 Noninvolvement of the senses with their objects returns them to the mental realm as products of the mind's own nature, and this brings about natural restraint."
55 "This is how pratyahara allows for the attainment of ultimate sense-control."

## Pada III
1 "Concentration (the sixth limb of yoga) consists of directing the mind's thoughts to one area, locale, or ideal."
2 "Within that blissful space of focused thoughts occurs the single-minded state of meditation."
3 "When all places and objects become empty or equal, as it were, and deep meditation only on the essence occurs, radiating forth meaning, then the mind gets absorbed in samadhi."
4 "The final three limbs, integrated together as one, are known as samyama."
5 "By gaining victory over that, living intelligence appears within the adept yogi."
6 "The application of this should proceed via succeeding levels."
7 "The three limbs (of concentration, meditation, and samadhi) are more subtle than all those previous."
8 "Yet, even these three lack subtlety compared to seedless samadhi."
9 "Where there is the practice of neutralization of the emerging mental thoughts in relation to their expiration, the mastery of cessation occurs in spontaneous fashion."
10 "That quiescence of mind and its natural flow itself forms a samskara."
11 "When single-pointed aspiration unifies the mind-field so that the tendency towards multiplicity is overcome, then mind itself transforms into samadhi."
12 "Thus, as the thoughts of the mind-field rise and fall repeatedly in similar fashion, the transformation of one-pointedness prevails."
13 "The ongoing transformation of form, time, and various stages are thus understood in relation to objects, elements, and the mind and senses."
14 "The underlying and all-abiding state is acted upon by the appearance of form and objects in constant flux."
15 "This series of changes, in shifting cycles, is responsible for all the transformations of nature."
16 "By focusing comprehensive awareness on these changes, wisdom regarding the three phases of time is gleaned."
17 "The admixture present in the mind's reckoning of word, meanings, concepts, and physical objects as superimpositions gets clarified via samyama on the differences inherent in them, with the result being wisdom regarding all utterances pertaining to the realm of sound."

18 *"Along with this (aforementioned, previous sutra), and in addition to the ability to witness samskaras, comes the direct perception of previous existences."*
19 *"When the yogi focuses his mental processes (performs samyama) on the appearance of another, the general makeup of that person becomes known."*
20 *"But not the deeper contents of it, which remain imperceptible, requiring a different foundation."*
21 *"When the yogi performs samyama on his own physical sheath, the power of transparency gets revealed, and what is otherwise perceptible to the eyes of others becomes withdrawn."*
22 *"This power of transparency (gained via samyama) also clarifies why sounds and other sensual instruments become useful to the yogi."*
23 *"Results of action come either swiftly or slowly. By studying these types of karmas via samyama, the yogi can foretell the time of his passing from the body."*
24 *"Performing samyama on friendship brings forth hidden powers."*
25 *"For imbibing strength, the yogi performs samyama on the force of an elephant."*
26 *"Samyama assists the yogi in gaining awareness of all wisdom that is subtle, obscured, and far away (deep within)."*
27 *"By performing samyama on the sun as a symbol for inner wisdom, subtle atmospheres become accessible."*
28 *"By performing samyama on the moon as a symbol, an internal map for the subtle regions can be gained."*
29 *"Utilizing samyama on the pivitol star allows for knowledge of the movement of the inner cosmos."*
30 *"Utilizing samyama on the navel provides knowledge of the entire body."*
31 *"Samyama focused at the base of the throat of the yogi brings cessation to hunger and thirst."*
32 *"Simulating the steadiness of the tortoise, the yogi meditates on the kurma passageway adjacent to the throat, in undisturbed fashion."*
33 *"When concentration gets centered at the crown of the head, the yogi sees the spiritual light and has darshan with the illumined souls abiding there."*
34 *"Or by the flow of spontaneous knowledge, everything may become known."*
35 *"By meditating in the heart, the entire mental complex, and other minds, become known."*
36 *"Enjoyment springing from mental balance proceeds due to the self-interest of another (the ego), but samyama on the Soul (Purusha) uncovers knowledge of the real Self."*
37 *"When this higher knowledge, called pratibha, dawns, the five senses of perception get purified and behold their inner powers."*
38 *"The effects of this attainment (called pratibha samadhi) are both an attainment and an impediment to higher realization, depending on the resultant externalized thoughts."*

39 *"Letting go of the causes of bondage, the yogi acquires wisdom of all types of forms, and can then deeply associate with the bodies and minds of other beings."*
40 *"Gaining victory over the prana of ascension, the yogi can transcend all contact with earth, water, fire, and the sharp thorns of other pain-bearing elements."*
41 *"Gaining victory over the digestive prana that grants comprehensive abilities, an atmosphere of radiance surrounds the yogi."*
42 *"The yogi applies samyama on the interrelation between the element of ether and the power of hearing and attains the realm of divine sound."*
43 *"Like air passing through cotton cloth, the yogi's samyama on the interrelation between his purified body and the element of ether produces swift penetration of all atmospheres and ultimate Union."*
44 *"All gross obscurations of the external world and body get obliterated when the thought vibrations of the mind combine with that light of inner intelligence that produces a transcendent Seer."*
45 *"Implementing samyama with regards to the five elements, the yogi perceives their real meaning — like their essence as solidity, all-pervasiveness, etc. — and attains to victory through knowledge of the connection between mind and matter."*
46 *"Through such realization the yogi can gain mastery over subtle powers like invisibility and more, and express them in right accordance, free of impedance."*
47 *"This well-rounded body possesses beauty, strength, firmness in thought and activity, and is able to forbear all troubles that may afflict it."*
48 *"Mastery over the senses is gained by making samyama on refined components such as the power of mental comprehension, natural permeation, the refined sense of I-ness, and one's own pure Essence."*
49 *"Mastery over the mental organ brings about cognition of the inconceivable speed of the mind and its higher thoughts, as well as perception of the primal cause out of which all manifestation arises."*
50 *"All-knowingness, and the mastery of all states of Awarenesss, occurs when the distinction between a merely balanced mind and the Eternal Soul becomes clear, resulting in omniscience."*
51 *"The yogi attains absolute freedom from form upon developing the quality of detachment from seed desires, as well as rejection of powers such as omniscience."*
52 *"The yogi should avoid the company of lesser deities whose prideful accomplishments are used to attract others, resulting in binding and unwanted connections with them again and again, through lifetimes."*
53 *"By concentrating, meditating, and having samadhi upon phases of time, the right wisdom is born via proper discrimination."*
54 *"Anything that is indistinguishable with regard to species, markings, space, time, etc., can be rightly known through this process of samyama."*
55 *"This higher knowing, brought about by discriminative wisdom, is the

means and end of all means and ends, and transcends conventional sequence and order, naturally."

56 "Revelation of the equality between the balanced state and the conscious indweller brings about separation from form, and final freedom."

**Pada IV**

1 "The five ways the yogis use to attempt perfection are: utilizing abilities from previous births, ingesting herbs and elixers, practice of the mantra, performing austerities, and gaining samadhi."

2 "In order to complete all processes and realize their true nature, they move from one form to another."

3 "Good acts do not remove the subtle causes found in nature, but do help overcome them — much like a farmer breaks down barriers to allow water into his field."

4 "From the ego springs mind and its thought, which produce all projected things."

5 "Though minds and their different activities are numerous, the one, Original Mind directs them all."

6 "Among these diverse sets of minds, only that one that is born of meditation is free of conditionings from past lives."

7 "Acts springing from the mind of the yogi are colorless, while nonyogis suffer the threefold results called good, bad, and mixed."

8 "This triple designation forms subtle desires and impressions that will express themselves later in accordance with each one specifically."

9 "Though differences may occur due to effects in time, space, and the march of species, there is a deep connection in them based upon memory and mental impressions of past lifetimes."

10 "All these impressions are without origin, and unending, because of the strong desire for life in the body."

11 "Impetus, desire for fruits, objects, and their foundations, all combined, cohese these impressions together (4:10), and they disappear when they are absent."

12 "Regarding the past and the future, they exist in their own essence, but change with characteristics and circumstances along the way."

13 "All these abiding attributes, whether apparent or subtle, are in their essence composed of the three gunas of Nature."

14 "Though objects appear to transform, their substance is based in unity, all coordinated by the gunas."

15 "All existing things (such as objects) are identical to one another, but the mind's thought places them at variance, as if divided along multiple pathways."

16 "All relative things, perceived or not by the mind previously, proceed from and become existent due to its thoughts."

17 "The process of thinking relies upon the conditioning of the mind, which thereby divides knowing from not knowing regarding the objects and situa-

tions it encounters."

18 "Thought vibrations of the mind can always be known due to the pure Awareness abiding there as the Lord of the mind."

19 "That mind is not illumined in and of itself; it is known by the Knower."

20 "(This is due to the fact that) the mind is unable to cognize two things at once."

21 "When the intelligent knower perceives another source than itself, and sees a proliferation of mentation thereby, confusion (about its knowledge) results."

22 "By assuming the uncaused essence of the ever-stationary knower, the mind becomes fully cognizant (of all its processes)."

23 "In this way, when the mindstuff is informed by the seer, it can see all objects (subtle and gross)."

24 "Thoughts are multiple; in addition, so too are the mind's desires. In tandem with one another, mental impressions form, but all this activity is for the sake of another."

25 "Therefore, when the unique nature of the seer as the Atman occurs to the mind, all false assumptions end and its erratic vibrations cease."

26 "As a result the mind and its thoughts gain discernment and become inclined towards isolation from bondage to nature."

27 "If breaches in this higher quality of mind occur, various subtle impressions arise from its subconscious level."

28 "The extraction of those past imperfections occur in the same way as explained previously."

29 "And when the yogi's constant discrimination has brought about complete disinterest in even powers such as omniscience, then the rain cloud of virtues pours higher qualities upon him, effortlessly."

30 "Thereafter (dharma-megha samadhi), all impressions and conditionings get dissolved."

31 "Thus, when all imperfections and overlays are taken away in this manner, then infinite knowledge dawns and little remains to be known."

32 "Moreover, after dharma-megha samadhi, the three gunas gradually cease to work their transformations, and their functions are consummated and get finalized."

33 "The sequence of time in increments then becomes intelligible (to the yogi), and the gradual flow of its process reaches its conclusion."

34 "The primal force responsible for involving consciousness back to its essence, and rendering nature bereft of form, stabilizes and neutralizes both, and the sentient soul gains final liberation."

# Yoga Vedanta Tantra Sanskrit Glossary

**Abhasa** — Appearance; reflection, as in God/Brahman appearing in the Universe.

**Abhava** — Devoid of moods; negation; absence, nothingness other than Self.

**Abavapadarthas** — Examples of things that cannot exist, utilized in Vedanta to explain what is inexplicable – like maya – by way of inference, such as the horn of a hare, or a snake in a rope, etc.

**Abhava Yoga** — The highest state of Yoga reached by the knowers of nondual Reality.

**Abhaya** — Fearlessness.

**Abhidya** — Desire, in Buddhism, being one of the Five Hindrances (nivarana) of mind in its quest to attain meditational stages of absorption.

**Abhijnas** — In Buddhism, the powers of an illumined Buddha.

**Abhinivesha** — Fear of death/clinging to life, which is one of the five kleshas in Yoga. It is considered the lowest type of hell to fall into, since the Soul of mankind is birthless and deathless, i.e., Eternal.

**Abhyasa Yoga** — The path of constant and dedicated practice, well-defined by Lord Krishna in the Bhagavad Gita.

**Acharyas** — Teachers; preceptors who guide one in the study of the scriptures and spiritual life in general.

**Achina** — A mythical tree which none have been able to see, which is used as a metaphor for Ultimate Reality which cannot be perceived with the senses.

**Adhibautika** — One of the Threefold Miseries; dangers or sufferings arising from external forces proceeding from the presence of other living beings.

**Adhidaivika** — One of the Threefold Miseries; dangers or sufferings arising from cosmic forces or celestial beings.

**Adhikara Vichara** — The highest qualification granting spiritual life and practice.

**Adhimatra** — The ninth of the Twelve Levels of Detachment wherein dispassion becomes so intense that enjoyment of the world actually becomes a source of pain.

**Adhyaropa** — A mode of discrimination used by the jnanis which aids in the detection and removal of false superimposition and mental delusion.

**Adhyasa** — A superimposition or covering of one thing over another, philosophically speaking, like form over formlessness, or ignorance over knowledge.

**Adhyatma-prasad** — One of the Four Kinds of Clarities, relating to purity of heart and soul/spirit.

**Adhyatma-vidya** — The constant pursuit of the highest wisdom, leading to Truth.

**Adhyatmika** — One of the Threefold Miseries; dangers and sufferings arising within the individual in the twin modes of mental and physical imbalances.

**Adishakti** — A name for the Mother of the Universe as the first and foremost of all benign spiritual powers.

**Adishankaracharya** — An honorific name for Sri Shankaracharya, the great Advaitan.

**Advaita** — The Nondual Philosophy espoused by the ancient rishis of India, and more recently propounded by Gaudapada and Shankara, that is the foundation of all Hindu Scriptures; monism; direct perception of Brahman.

**Advaitic** — Referring to the supreme path or philosophy of Nonduality, Advaita Vedanta.

**Advaitavada** — The path of the Nondualists who comprehend the truth of non-origination, or non-evolution.

**Advaitist** — One who follows the way of Advaita Vedanta.

**Advesta** — Nonhating.

**Agastya** — A revered ancient rishi who caused the Vindhya mountains to fall and who taught the Dravidian tribes in South India; husband of the woman rishi, Lopamudra; a name for Shiva.

**Agrayana** — An adept practitioner of the nondual system of Asparsha Yoga, who renounces all that is unfit to be taken (agrahya) in life.

**Ahaituka** — Free of all motive power.

**Aham Brahmasmi** — "I am Brahman." One of the Four Mahavakyas or sacred declarations of the Upanisads.

**Ahamkara** — Egoism, or sense of individual I; one of the fourfold aspects of mind, the antahkarana.

**Ahimsa** — Nonviolence, or refraining from harming living things; one of the Ten Yamas and Niyamas of the Patanjala Yoga system.

**Aishvarya** — A rare type of spiritual wealth; riches on earth.

**Ajanatah** — Insensitivity, being one of the Three Stupefactions that rob one of both inherent spirituality, and the impetus to practice and realize it.

**Ajati** — Having no birth, applied to those rare souls who come into the body in full realization that they are really Atman, or Awareness.

**Ajativada** — The path or way of those who have come to know the birthless, deathless nature of all beings, all things.

**Ajna chakra** — The subtle spiritual vortex located at the third eye region, symbolically located in the middle of the forehead between the eyes.

**Ajnana** — Ignorance of one's true nature as pure, conscious Awareness; the antithesis of knowledge.

**Ajanabhumikas** — The Seven Lowers Stages of Knowledge/Worlds.

**Ajnani** — One who is ignorant of one's true nature.

**Akama** — Freedom from desire.

**Akamahata** — One of the Four Qualifications of the Illumined Guru, namely freedom from any and all desires for the disciple other than he/she attain liberation.

**Akarma** — One of the three grades of karma based upon the subtle art of nonaccrual of karma, or what has been called "inaction" by the seers. It is attained via practice and gaining of the virtue of selflessness.

**Akartrtvama** — Moderation in all things in order to attain balance for spiritual practice.

**Akasha** — Subtle space, in any of its modes, such as consciousness space, intelligence space, thought space, energy space, material space (chidakasha, jnanakasha, chitakasha, pranakasha, bhutakasha); ether, one of the five elements of nature.

**Akhanda Satchitananda** — An incomparable Name for Divine Reality, meaning Indivisible Existence, Knowledge, and Bliss.

**Aklista vrittis** — Non pain-bearing thoughts of the mind that are beneficial, and which are meant to replace klista-vrittis in yoga practice.

**Akshara Brahman** — A name for Brahman, denoting Its indestructible nature.

**Akshobha** — Nonemotionalism, or emotional calm and balance.

**Alabdhabhumikatva** — Lack of assurance and the inability to muster any forward momentum in religious practice, being the eighth of The Nine Distractions in Spiritual Life cited by Patanjali in His Yoga Sutras.

**Alambanas** — The Twenty-four Tattvas, or cosmic principles of Sankhya, taken for stations of meditation rather than just philosophical study.

**Alasya** — Laziness, idleness, or mental inertia, often due to physical obesity, which is the fifth of Nine Distractions in Spiritual Life cited by Patanjali in his Yoga Sutras.

**Amsa-Avatar** — A partial incarnation.

**Anadi** — Without beginning; a term applied to the scriptures of Vedic Sanatana Dharma, which are of divine origin and not ascribable to human authorship.

**Anahata chakra** — The spiritual center, vortex, or "lotus," symbolically located at the heart region.

**Anahata Dhvani** — The subtle sound of AUM heard by the yogis in deep meditation.

**Anandamayakosha** — The sheath of bliss, or conceptual ego structure, the subtlest of The Five Sheaths of human existence as explained in the Adhara System of Vedanta.

**Ananya-bhakti** — The devotion of nonseparation espoused by Sri Krishna in the Bhagavad Gita, wherein devotion and wisdom are correctly conjoined; one-pointed concentration on any one of the various forms of God.

**Anasakti** — The sixth of Twelve Levels of Detachment that signals arrival at a foundational level of dispassion which is moderate and conducive towards higher attainment.

**Anatma** — The nonself, or what is insentient — like matter and ego.

**Anava** — The power of primal bondage; one of the Three Pasas, malas or limitations according to Tantra which bind in order to save. Anava represents connate impurity which deludes the soul and makes it a victim of samsara. Along with karmika and mayiya, anava binds certain kinds of evolving souls and veils from them their inherent nature as Shiva. Gaining initiation from a guru and attaining jnana, they can manage to get free.

**Anavasthitatvani** — Stagnation, instability, and the inability in spiritual life to attain higher levels of awareness, being the last of Nine Distractions in Spiritual Life cited by Patanjali in His Yoga Sutras.

**Angamejayatva** — Unsteadiness or shakiness of the body and limbs in meditation, which, according to Patanjala Yoga, is one of the Four Main Causes of Distraction.

**Anima** — One of the Eight Siddhis or Eight Occult Powers which enables the seeker of lower ideals to reduce physical matter to nothingness or to attain weightlessness.

**Anishtam** — Scattered results occurring due to actions done with an inattentive mind.

**Anitya** — Mutable; non-eternal; in Buddhism, transitoriness, being one of the Three Marks (trilakshana) wherein everything existing is assigned as impermanent.

**Annamayakosha** — The gross, physical, or apparent sheath of human existence, the body, as a part of the Adhara system explained by Vedanta science.

**Annaprasada** — Sacred food offering; one of the Four Clarities of Food; a Hindu rite celebrating the auspicious occasion of childbirth.

**Annapurna** — The Divine Mother of the universe who feeds and thus sustains all living beings.

**Anoraniyan** — The subtlest of the subtle, which is a descriptive word for Brahman.

**Antah-jnana** — Recognition of the fact that all knowledge lies within the Soul.

**Antahkarana** — The internal organ or fourfold mind. It consists of manas, the basic mind which considers; chitta, the mind's contents; buddhi, the intellect that determines; and ahamkara, the ego or sense of individuality.

**Antaranga** — The noble membership of the inner circle of devotees who gather around an Avatar, or true world teacher; also a name for the mind, or inner organ.

**Antarayas** — Obstacles; impediments; the chitta-vikshepas, sometimes called the Nine Distraction to Spiritual Life in Yoga.

**Antaryami** — The "Inner Ruler Immortal" seated in the heart, i.e., Atman.

**Anubhava** — True Being; the direct perception of Divinity which is the result of self-effort and Grace; after shruti, hearing the Truth, and yukti, contemplating the Truth, it is the third in this triputi of Vedantic practices which allows for the direct perception of Reality.

**Anugraha** — Grace.

**Anya-samskara-pratibandhin** — The willingness of the aspirant to dive deep into the mind in meditation to find what is obstructing its purification leading to Enlightenment.

**Anupalabdhi** — Nonapprehension, used as a proof of Reality in that the absence of a thing, being, or principle proves that it was once present and accounted for.

**Ap, or Apah** — The fourth element, water.

**Apakvahamkara** — The human ego, ahamkara, that has not yet become refined or matured, i.e., surrendered unto God, and is thus apakva — unripe.

**Apana** — Downwards/outwards moving prana.

**Aparavidya** — Lower or secondary knowledge, usually pertaining to secular or worldly subjects but sometimes even associated with mere scriptural knowledge as compared to the direct experience of Reality.

**Aparigraha** — One of the Five Yamas of Yoga, which tempers both the giving and receiving of goods and wealth based upon the danger of forgetting one's past lifetimes due to immediately engaging with all manner of material commerce at an early age.

**Aparinama** — The principle of nontransformation that, when seen as the truth of existence, reveals all worlds of name and form in time and space nonactual due to their constantly changing nature.

**Aparokshanubhuti** — Direct spiritual experience of the Truth gained by contact with holy company and studying the revealed scriptures under a competent guru.

**Apaurasheya** — Not of human authorship, used often in reference to the sacred scriptures of the Sanatana Dharma of India.

**Apavada** — A discriminatory power that, in conjunction with its partner, adhyaropa, recognizes and destroys delusions of the mind and false superimpositions over Reality.

**Aradhana** — Deep reverence.

**Archa** — Forms; objects of worship and their names; offerings made at the time of worship.

**Archanam** — Ritualistic worship; one of the Eight Devotional Aids, being adoration of the Lord, which is duly cited by Devarshi Narada in his Bhakti Sutras.

**Arjuna** — One of the five Pandava brothers who was a great devotee of Lord Krishna and who received the great Avatar's discourse and message of the Bhagavad Gita on the battlefield at Kurukshetra.

**Arthavatta** — Eulogy and explanation; scriptural texts wherein convincing passages are given to induce the seeker to reject worldliness and commit to a path and go forward in spiritual life.

**Arupaloka** — In Zen, the realm of blessings and formless meditation.

**Arya-Satya** — The Four Noble Truths of Buddhism, i.e., there is suffering, a cause for suffering, a possible end to suffering, and a means to bring about an end to suffering (astangika-marga — the Eightfold Path).

**Asamprajnata Samadhi** — Described by Patanjali in Yoga Philosophy as a superconscious state of pure Awareness wherein all cognitive traces of the relative universe and the individual self are obliterated completely. It is generally synonymous with the Nirvikalpa Samadhi of the Vedanta school.

**Asamvedana** — A fully matured condition of mind that allows the luminary complete detachment from desires and impediments, which is really a special kind of nonreceptivity to them.

**Asana** — A physical seat used for formal meditation; third limb of Yoga concerned with basic and singular posture, recommended by Patanjali in his Raja Yoga system to facilitate a strong and steady foundation for the body so that it will remain stationary and still, allowing the mind to concentrate on Reality.

**Ashani** — Lord Siva in his all-powerful aspect.

**Ashrama** — One of the four divisions of living beings, according to their station in life; a physical location where the student meets with the guru to study dharma and meditate.

**Asrsti** — That which is beyond creation, or can never be subject to beginnings or inception, i.e., Consciousness/Brahman.

**Ashtavakra** — An enigmatic holy man, great sage, and rishi of the Vedic period, who was born deformed due to a curse from his father while in the womb, but who later saved his father's life and thus had the curse reversed. He is the author of the famed Ashtavakra Samhita.

**Ashtavakra Samhita** — A Sanskrit text concentrating on Nondual Wisdom that is one of the finest scriptures of Advaita Vedanta.

**Ashuddha** — What is impure.

**Asparsha Yoga** — The "Nontouch" Yoga transmitted by the great nondualist, Gaudapada, to his qualified students.

**Asaucha** — Impurity, as opposed to saucha which is one of the Niyamas or daily practices of Yoga; ritualistic observance of a period of purification due to the death of a relative or loved one.

**Asta Siddhas** — The Eight Occult Powers, proclaimed by enlightened beings to be detrimental sidetracks along the path of spiritual realization.

**Ashtanga Yoga** — The Eight-limbed Yoga of Patanjali, also called Patanjala and Raja Yoga, it focuses upon meditation and samadhi as the goal of life but also treats preliminary exercises and disciplines leading up it.

**Asmita** — Egoism, which is one of the Five Kleshas of Yoga.

**Astabala Siddhis** — The eight occult powers, which act as impediments on the road to Enlightenment.

**Astamurti** — The eight invisible forms of Lord Siva.

**Astangika Marga** — The Eightfold Path of Buddhism, one of Thirty-seven Limbs of Enlightenment, consisting of clear view, firm resolve, ennobling speech, dharmic conduct, right livelihood, pure aspiration, mindfulness, and perfect concentration.

**Asteya** — One of the Yamas of Yoga's first limb, which requires noncoveting of the goods and belongings of other beings and countries.

**Asti** — Growth, which is another of the false transformations over the immutable Soul, Atman.

**Astika** — Orthodox, referring to the traditional darshanas of India.

**Astikya** — Reliance upon the words of the illumined souls in spiritual life.

**Ashuddha** — Impure, referring to tattvas such as the five elements and active senses, called such not due to things vile and evil, but due to their being far away from their source, i.e., Brahman.

**Asukham** — Devoid of abiding happiness, referring to the physical world.
**Asuras** — Powerful beings and demonic forces who vie with the gods for supremacy; negative forces or demons.
**Asuric** — Having to do with the influences of the asuras,
**Asvattha** — The banyan tree.
**Atma Bodha** — Self-knowledge; a sacred advaitic scripture of Sri Shankara dealing with the principles of Atman, Brahman, Maya, and Vedantic Philosophy in general.
**Atma jnana or Atmajnan** — Absolute Knowledge of the Immortal Self, the highest knowledge knowable to the human mind, actually beyond its scope, and by knowing which the soul will be led to spiritual realization.
**Atman** — The eternal Soul residing within every being and permeating creation, though indivisible and nonmaterial in nature, which is birthless, deathless, pure, and perfect.
**Atmarama** — A name for Siva in his all-pervasive form, as the Atman in all beings.
**Atma tripti** — The three requisites for receiving the highest wisdom, namely sankalpa-vinashana, upekshanam, and brahmakaravritti.
**Atma-vichara** — The classic way of proceeding in advanced spiritual life by inquiring into the nature of Reality by analysing the self/Self. The question "Who am I" is pertinent here, but it must be accompanied by inspecting all that the Soul/Self is not, i.e., matter, nature, tattvas, etc.
**Audasinya** — An intense degree of detachment; the tenth plateau of the Twelve Levels of Dispassion wherein there is complete indifference to the objects and concerns of relativity.
**Aum or Om** — The primal vibration which is the sound symbol for Brahman, Ultimate Reality, and which is an essential element in all systems of Hindu Philosophy. From this primal sound come all aspects of the creation, yet being beyond the manifest universe it is the bija or sacred symbol for formless Reality Itself.
**Autsuka-puraka** — Possessing a ready store of inspiration for spiritual life, and for attaining Enlightenment.
**Avadhut** — A wandering ascetic belonging to the class of Avadhuts who represent a high state of sannyasi.
**Avadhuta Gita** — A sacred scripture focusing on Nondual Wisdom which, besides addressing the nature of Reality, also describes the condition and philosophy of the Avadhut, a wandering ascetic.
**Avarana Shakti** — A power of Shakti which seems to veil Reality; one of the two obscuring forces of Maya, the other being vikshepa, which appears to distort Reality.
**Avasthas** — States, stages, or levels of spiritual growth.
**Avataravada** — The sacred pathway of those who focus upon and involve themselves with the Divine Incarnation as He takes birth in the world of name and form throughout the span of human evolution.
**Avatar** — One who descends; the appearance of Divinity in human form; an incarnation of God.
**Avidhi** — Rites and rituals performed for inferior reasons.

**Avirati** — Non-abstention, as opposed to uparati, wherein the seeker fails to subordinate worldly life to the spiritual path; over-indulgence in sensual appetites, being the sixth of Nine Distractions in Spiritual Life, called antarayas or vikshepas according to Yoga.

**Avisheshas** — Aspects of the human being, finer than the visheshas, such as the tanmatras and the ego.

**Avrijina** — One of four necessary qualifications of the authentic guru which shows him/her to be one who lives a simple and unostentatious life, attended by qualities of detachment and equanimity.

**Avyaktam** — Unmanifest; invisible, like the three gunas prior to breaking into differentiation.

**Ayamatma Brahma** — "This self is Brahman." One of the four great declarations (Mahavakyas), or nondualistic mantras.

**Ayodhya** — The city of King Dasaratha where the young Prince Ram had his childhood, youth and homelife.

**Bahirmukhavritti** — The outward-going vibrations of the mind that bind the soul to external phenomena and its consequences.

**Bahutva Marga** — The path of religious convention that beings who only dabble in religion follow from lifetime to lifetime.

**Bandha** — Bondage, which in Vedic philosophy is mainly associated with nature, livelihood, and family/ancestors.

**Bhagavad Gita** — The quintessential sacred scripture of the Hindus containing the comprehensive message of Lord Krishna.

**Bhagavan** — An especially sacred name for God which implies the Supreme Being who is endowed with the Six Treasures of the Godhead: power, virtue, fame, glory, detachment and freedom.

**Bhagavati** — A sacred name for the Divine Mother of the Universe; the Supreme Being in feminine form.

**Bhairavi** — A female ascetic, usually strong, independent, and fiercesome in character; a worshiper of Shiva and a Tantric aspirant or adept.

**Bhajanam** — Heartfelt devotions to and worship of the Lord; one of the Eight Devotional Aids according to Devarshi Narada.

**Bhakta** — A devotee of the God, of the Lord and Mother of the Universe; a follower of the path of bhakti.

**Bhakti** — Love and devotion for God.

**Bhati** — That which shines; Consciousness.

**Bhavas** — Devotional moods or spiritual feelings associated with the awakening of God-Consciousness.

**Bhaya** — Fear.

**Bhedabheda** — Difference in nondifference, indicating a philosophical perspective that interprets the soul as being both independent of and one with Supreme Reality.

**Bhogamarga** — The path of superficial enjoyment that worldly societies and living beings fall into, life after life, into dalliance with material objects and wealth alone.

**Bhrantidarshana** — False perception, or distorted perspective, being the seventh of Nine Distractions in Spiritual Life (antarayas) cited by Patanajli in His Yoga Sutras.

**Bhumikatva** — Stages or steps.

**Bhumis/Bhumikas** — Lands or grounds; in Buddhism, one of ten higher ascending lands that a bodhisattva passes through in order to attain full buddhahood.

**Bhur Loka** — The earth plane.

**Bhuvarloka** — The intermediary plane just above (further within the mind)) earth.

**Bhushandhi** — A crow mentioned in stories in the Vedic Itihasa or mythology.

**Bhutas** — Beings occupying the physical plane, along with its astral planes.

**Bhutakasha** — The earthly plane; the gross, physical atmosphere where bodies and forms exist.

**Bhuvanas** — Planes of existence within the Great Mind.

**Bibhishana or Vibhishana** — The brother of Ravana who, having gained Brahma's boon of never committing an unrighteous act, betrayed Ravana and, upon Shiva's advice, allied himself with Sri Ram.

**Bijams** — Subtle seed words of power which are the impetus for all of creation/projection, and which are found in slokas, sutras, and mantrams for the purification and enlightenment of the mind.

**Bindu** — The point of the Light of Consciousness from which all comes into manifestation, connected deeply with The Word.

**Boddhamanah** — Transformation of ordinary mind by the illumined intellect.

**Bodhisattva** — In Buddhism, an illumined soul who has attained freedom from ignorance, and who returns to the embodied condition for purposes of helping to free others.

**Brahmacharya** — Practice of celibacy in the young aspirant, it is one of the five yamas of Yoga.

**Brahm'advitiye** — One without a second, being a word describing Brahman.

**Brahmagranthi** — According to Vedanta and Tantra, a knot or barrier at the lowest of the seven chakras that keeps embodied beings from rising to higher centers of Awareness.

**Brahma-nistha** — One-pointed devotion to God; one of the Seven Qualifications of a Tantric Aspirant.

**Brahmapadesha** — Receiving the Feet of Brahman, i.e., taking mantra-diksha, or initiation.

**Brahma-parayana** — Taking full refuge in God; one of the Seven Qualifications of a Tantric Aspirant.

**Brahmaikya-upadesha-vakya** — Statements in the scriptures which concern themselves only with the knowledge of Brahman, especially through the vakyas, or great declarations.

**Brahmajnana** — The knowledge of Brahman, used in the sense of that which is to be known about Ultimate Reality, through direct experience.

**Brahmakaravrittidhyan** — The subtlemost act of dissolving all the vibrations of the mind into Brahman.

**Brahmaloka** — The highest of the seven realms lying in Consciousness, also called Satyaloka.

**Brahman** — The Absolute; the Ultimate Reality; formless Essence; pure Consciousness.

**Brahmanas** — The first of four sections of the Vedas; a sage of higher Wisdom; a word for Brahmin priests; one of the four castes of the Hindu social order.

**Brahman satya, jagad mithya** — One of the famous sayings in Vedanta meaning, Brahma is real, the world is unreal.

**Brahmapada** — How Brahman, Absolute Reality, disports Itself in the realms of name and form, usually described as appearing in the waking, dreaming, and deep sleep states of humanity.

**Brahmasvarupa-nirupana-vakya** — Statements on the nature of Brahman, direct and indirect, which indicate both the characteristics and inherent properties of Reality.

**Brahmavadi** — The path to Brahman alone; one of the Seven Qualifications of a Tantric Aspirant.

**Brahmavid** — A knower of God; the fourth qualification of the authentic spiritual teacher according to Shankaracharya; the first in a class of the Four Divisions of Knowers of Brahman who has attained mastery over the first four of the Seven Stages of Higher Wisdom.

**Brahmavidvan** — See Brahmavid.

**Brahmavidvara** — The second in a class of the Four Divisions of Knowers of Brahman who has attained mastery over the first five of the Seven Stages of Higher Wisdom.

**Brahmavidvarishtha** — The fourth in a class of the Four Divisions of Knowers of Brahman, who has attained mastery over all of the Seven Stages of Higher Wisdom.

**Brahmavidvariya** — The third in a class of the Four Divisions of Knowers of Brahman, who has attained mastery over the first six of the Seven Stages of Higher Wisdom.

**Brahmetara-nirakarana** — Statements in the scriptures of the neti-neti perspective which differentiate Brahman from everything that is not Brahman.

**Brhadaranyaka Upanisad** — Literally, "Great Scripture from the forest"; a lengthy and profound Upanisad from the White Yajur Veda containing many teachings of the rishi, Yajnavalkya, on Brahman and Atman.

**Buddha** — An enlightened being, considered to be an Avatar by the Hindus, and the founder of the religion that bears His name.

**Buddhehparatah** — The ability in the spiritual aspirant to transcend the relative plane of reference and gain intuitive wisdom of what lies within Consciousness at higher levels.

**Buddhi** — Intelligence; one of the four parts of Antahkarana, the mental sheath or thinking mind according to Samkhya and Vedanta.

**Chaitanya** — Consciousness fully aware of Itself; a great God-man of 14th-century Bengal, considered by some to be a divine incarnation of Radha and Krishna conjoined.

**Chakra** — A subtle center or vortex of spiritual energy, sometimes referred to as a lotus, through which Kundalini Shakti flows on its ascent to the crown of the head. There are said to be seven such lotuses from the base of the spine to the crown of the head and twelve more in the brain.

**Chandala** — An outcaste; a member of the untouchable caste.

**Chandhi** — One of the two great Mother scriptures of India, also known as Sri Durga Saptasati.

**Chatak Bird** — A mystical bird often characterized in the scriptures and stories of India to explain certain teachings and their inner meanings.

**Chetana Samadhi** — A class of samadhi, rare and special, which leaves the experiencer in a state of remembrance of all that occurred to it in that state, even after returning to the embodied condition.

**Chidabhasa** — The reflected Consciousness or Intelligence of the Supreme Brahman into the worlds of name and form in time and space, which when understood as just a reflection, assists the seeker of Truth in both separating Reality from nonreality ("wheat from the chaff" "God from Mammon"), and further to arrive safely and correctly at the Great Statement, "All Is Brahman."

**Chidakasha** — The boundless space of pure Spirit which is a realmless realm occupied by nothing other than pure Conscious Awareness, timeless, deathless and unlimited.

**Chinmatra** — Intelligence particles of Consciousness; Consciousness Itself.

**Chitta** — The "stuff" of the mind, such as thought, conception, ideation, etc.; one of the four conditions of the antahkarana

**Chitta-bhati** — The thoughts of the mind that remain illumined, always contemplating divine reality.

**Chitta-chinta** — The thoughts of the mind which tend towards heaviness, causing the mind to form habits of unnecessary brooding.

**Chitta-lochana** — The thoughts of the mind that tend towards aspiration and higher thinking.

**Chitta-nirodha** — The destruction of thought waves in the mind, leading to formless samadhi.

**Chittaprasad** — Purity or purification of the mind's thoughts, which is one of the Four Clarities.

**Chit-shuddhi** — Purity of mind; the third of the Three Kinds of Purity, which is hardest of attainment, the other two being Dravya Shuddhi and Kriya Shuddhi, purity of atmosphere and purity of action.

**Chittakasha** — The subtlest space of mind containing the infinite potential for thoughts, ideas, concepts, etc.

**Chittavrttis** — The vibrations or waves of the mind, i.e., the thoughts.

**Chowrie** — A fan used for ritualistic worship, usually made out of a yak's tail.

**Daiva** — Divine; the god who controls the destiny of living beings; one of three classifications of a seeker in Tantra, after pasu (animalistic) and virya (heroic), signifying a being who has reached the stage of identification with the inner Self.

**Daivi-maya** — The divine maya of the Universal Mother, as opposed to ordinary or deluding maya.

**Daksha** — Intelligent; able; one of the Seven Qualifications of a Tantric Aspirant.

**Dakshinabandha** — The bondage to conventional life, thereby stripped of dharma and higher attainments.

**Dakshineswar** — The temple where Sri Ramakrishna Paramahamsa served as priest in His youth, and where He performed His twelve-year world-transforming sadhana and gained the vision of Mother Kali.

**Dama** — Self-control, one of the Six Jewels, Shatsampatti, which bestows upon an aspirant the ability to control the mind and senses easily and naturally.

**Danam** — Charity and giving of alms in the right state of mind.

**Dhammapada** — The original scripture of Buddhism, being a compilation of all of Lord Buddha's sayings that were remembered by His students (Arhats) after he had passed from this world.

**Dharmi** — One who lives life in observance and practice of the dharma.

**Darpa** — Pride; pride of good conduct, which is one of the Eight Fetters.

**Darshan** — Literally, to see clearly; referring to the Six Darshanas, which when studied under an authentic teacher, enable the aspirant to be free from bondage and limitation and behold inherent divinity; direct association with a divine being.

**Darshanas** — The six orthodox systems of Vedic Philosophy, namely, Samhkya, Patanjala (or Yoga), Uttara Mimamsa (or Vedanta), Purva Mimamsa, Nyaya, and Vaisheshika — whose main proponents were Kapila, Patanjali, Vedavyasa, Jaimini, Gautama, and Kanada, respectively.

**Dasabalas** — The ten powers of a Buddha.

**Dasabhumikas** — In Buddhism, the Ten Pure Lands of Bodhisatvahood.

**Dasya Bhava** — Servant; one of the Five Divine Moods for Worshipping God found in Vaishnavism.

**Dehadhyasahamkara** — The primal mistake of the ego in superimposing the body over the Soul

**Deh'anuvartanam** — One of the three great desires of living beings, which is to inhabit bodies in order to enjoy the worlds of name and form.

**Devavak** — A name given to the Sanskrit language, meaning "divine speech."

**Devayana** — The Path of the Gods, beyond the ancestor regions, but short of Absolute Reality.

**Dharmashrama** — The system of the four orders of dharmic living, namely the renunciate, the forest dweller, the householder, and the celibate student.

**Dhatus** — Various elements of the physical body

**Daurmanasya** — Sorrow; despair; one of the Four Causes of Distraction according to Yoga.

**Daya** — Compassion, especially associated with the removal of suffering and specifically the ignorance which causes it.

**Deha** — The physical body.

**Dehadhyasahamkara** — One of the Three Types of Ego; the lowest and basest type of egotism which reflects in the mind as the actual belief that one is one's body.

**Deha-samatva** — Stationary position of the body in meditation, free from the desire to shift about — either out of discomfort, or due to the desire for hatha-yoga asanas.

**Desha** — Physical space; subtle space; locale.

**Devabhasya** — "The language of the Gods," a title assigned to the Sanskrit language, through which a cross section of an entire race (India) gained final liberation (moksha) from bondage to maya/nature.

**Devas** — The gods, like Indra and his pantheon, who oversee the affairs of celestials, ancestors, and mortals.

**Devi** — A name for the Goddess, often used as a suffix to Her many names.

**Dhairya** — Patience that serves one along the spiritual path, in anticipation of reaching the highest goal.

**Dhananjaya** — The master of wealth, which is a name for Arjuna in the Bhagavad Gita.

**Dharana** — Concentration; the sixth limb in the eight-limbed system of Patanjali's Yoga, which when mastered allows the aspirant to access deeper states of meditation.

**Dharma** — Proper and balanced living and thinking according to the scriptures; righteousness; virtue; one of the Four Fruits of Life (Purusharthas) granted by the Divine Mother of the Universe.

**Dharmakaya** — One of the three bodies of the Buddha, being the transcendental body.

**Dharma-megha-samadhi** — The "raincloud of virtues" state of mind, wherein all qualities come out of the mind and manifest themselves in the awakened human being.

**Dharmic** — Having to do with or pertaining to righteous thought and action.

**Dhriti** — Patience.

**Dhyana** — Meditation; the seventh limb in the eight-limbed system of Patanjali's Yoga which leads to Samadhi.

**Diksha** — Spiritual initiation, the conferring of mantra-diksha upon the ready aspirant.

**Dik shakti** — The Divine Mother's power of illusion or projection, especially in accordance with Her ability to produce space or atmospheres.

**Dirgha-pranava** — Uttering AUM once, with one long breath.

**Dirghasvapna** — An extensive dream, usually referring to life and the march of terrestrial and human evolution over millions of years.

**Doshadristhi** — Fault-finding; the inability to see perfection while always focusing on apparent imperfections.

**Dravya** — Substance, as in the five elements or other materials of creation.

**Dravya Shakti** — An aspect of the Divine Mother Shakti who aids in the creation of the phenomenal universe; the producer of substances.

**Dravya Shuddhi** — Purity, or purification of place and object.

**Driti** — Firmness, steadiness, like resolve to realize the highest Goal.

**Duhka or Duhkha** — Suffering; pain, misery; one of the Four Causes of Distraction in Yoga.

**Durga** — The Divine Mother of the Universe; the ten-armed Goddess who is the essence of all gods and goddesses; the first and foremost of Five Main Aspects of the Universal Mother (Prakriti Panchaka) according to the Srimad Devi Bhagavatam.

**Dvaita** — One of the three levels of philosophy in India, along with Visishtadvaita and Advaita.

**Dvaitahina** — An adherent of the nondual path; one of the Seven Qualifications of the Tantric Aspirant.

**Dvaitist** — Followers of dualism, which centers upon worship of God with form.

**Dvandva-mohena** — Delusion arising from the incorrect view which accepts multiplicity and diversity to be real and which fails to perceive Unity in everything; the infinite sets of pairs of opposites in relativity.

**Dvapara Yuga** — The third of four divisions of time, coming after the Satya and Treta Yugas, wherein living beings are in possession of one third of their inherent spiritual knowledge. In the present age, the fourth, called Kali Yuga, most living beings have lost touch with all spiritual sensibilities.

**Dvesha** — Aversion; hatred, dislike; one of the Five Obstacles to Yoga; one of the Eight Fetters according to Vedanta.

**Ekam** — One.

**Ekam sat viprah bahudha vadanti** — "Truth is One, seers refer to it in multiple divine ways," which is the oldest testament in writing as to the true nature of Existence, found in the Rig Veda.

**Ekangi** — One of Four Types of Love mentioned in Vaishnava scripture, called "one-sided," wherein there is no reciprocation forthcoming from the one who is loved.

**Ekarnava** The boundless ocean of etheric waters upon which rests the deities at the time of pralaya.

**Ekasana** — The single-pointed position of the body that allows for meditation, representing the best of all asanas and their transcendence as well.

**Eshanatrayam** — The triple bondage of spouse, children, and wealth according to Tantra and Vedanta, which becomes a frightful bond when human life is not utilized for gaining spirituality and is instead given to the search for pleasure, superficial pursuits, and amassing fortune; one of the Sixteen Evolutes of Maya.

**Ganapati** — The elephant-headed god who grants success and good fortune.

**Ganapatya** — The path or sect of those who worship Ganapati, or Ganesha.

**Ganesha** — Another name for Ganapati, the elephant-headed god of the Hindu pantheon.

**Gangasagar** — A holy location where the sacred river Ganga meets with the waters of the ocean.

**Gaudapada** — An illumined rishi who was a major exponent of the Advaita Vedanta. He is said to have been the guru of Shankara or possibly the guru of Shankara's guru.

**Gauna-bhakti** — Fundamental devotional practice, sometimes called Vaidhi-bhakti, which is followed by Raga bhakti and Prema bhakti as the devotee matures.

**Gauri** — Fair; brilliant; beautiful; the Divine Mother of the Universe, consort of Shiva, and manifestation of Parvati; another name for the earth.

**Gautama Buddha** — An honorific name for Lord Buddha.

**Ghanta** — The sacred bell used for worship in puja and at temples

**Ghat** — Any of a series of landings along a lake or a river where boats put in and people bathe.

**Giridhara** — Holder of the mountain; a name for Sri Krishna associated with the tale of His lifting of Mt. Govardhan to use it as an umbrella of protection for the village of Vrindaban during a deluge caused by Indra's wrath.

**Golakdham** — A game.

**Gopala** — Protector of cows; a name for the baby Krishna.

**Gopaniyata** — Secretiveness; one of the Eight Fetters.

**Gopi** — Any one of the young cow-herd maidens who loved Sri Krishna.

**Gotra** — Pride of lineage; one of the Eight Fetters.

**Govardhan** — A mountain lifted by Sri Krishna to protect Vrindaban from a deluge of rain.

**Govinda** — Master of the mountain; knower of creation, referring to Sri Krishna as the master of the earth and the senses.

**Granthi** — Knot, or knots, or blockages in body, life-force, mind, and thought, that impede progress along the natural course of both earthly and divine life.

**Grihastha** — The second stage of life, wherein the individual marries, rears children, makes a living — all ideally while practicing dharma in spiritual life.

**Guna** — A trait or traits, attributes of nature; qualities born of nature of which there are three, sattva, rajas and tamas, balance, frenetic activity, and inertia.

**Guru** — Satchitananda or Ultimate Reality appearing as the Atman or true nature of every living being; the revered spiritual preceptor who is the provisional guru.

**Guru-anushasana** — The requirement of an illumined preceptor in spiritual life and practice, to be combined with Vidya-shastra and Aparokshanubhuti — deep study of the revealed scriptures and gaining one's own direct experience of Enlightenment. The three together are know as The Three Pillars of Advaita Vedanta, and/or the Three Great Sources.

**Guru Nanak** — The Founder of Sikhism and the first of its standing line of ten gurus.

**Guru Parampara** — The succession of a line of gurus and disciples through which the transmission of precious spiritual teachings passes from generation to generation.

**Guru-Shishya Dashangika** — The system of the Ten Conditions of the Guru/Disciple relationship.

**Guruyoga** — The path of union with God through following the illumined preceptor and his instructions with one-pointed devotion.

**Hardwar** — A holy city in India.

**Hari** — A special name for God associated with Lord Vishnu.

**Harsha** — Joy, bliss, exhilaration.

**Hatha Yoga** — A stage of Kundalini Yoga associated with natural and spontaneous expression of asana, mudra, pranayam, and kriyas; a system of body postures undergone for health of the body, longevity, and the attainment of occult powers, the practice of which is often detrimental to spirituality.

**Himalayas** — The wondrous mountain range which runs through Northern India and which is considered sacred to the Hindus.

**Himsa** — Violence, the opposite of ahimsa.

**Hiranyagarbha** — Literally, a "mass of Light," containing all the worlds, gross subtle, and causal, that lay inside of it like the contents of a "Cosmic Egg." It is often associated or likened to Cosmic Intelligence itself as it appears as The Trinity, The Word, and other profound principles.

**Hiranyaksha** — The demon who was slayed by Vishnu in His incarnation as a boar.

**Homa** — A ritualistic ceremony wherein offerings are made into the sacred fire, accompanied with recitation of slokas and mudras.

**Homa Bird** — A mythological bird who lays her eggs miles high in the sky so that they hatch in midair before touching the earth. It is used as a metaphor for the illumined being who is not really born of matter and only briefly sojourns on earth with the purpose of helping others realize their divine nature.

**Hrdaya** — The heart, specifically the heart center, also called anahata chakra.

**Hrdayaguha** — The secret subtle chamber of the heart where the yogis and spiritual practitioners meditate.

**Hri** — Modesty; one of the Twenty Yamas and Niyamas of Tantra listed in the Srimad Devi Bhagavatam; when defined as shame, it is one of the Eight Fetters.

**Hrilleka Mantra** — The mantra for Sri Durga, containing Her power bijam, Hrim.

**Hrim** — A powerful bija or seed syllable representing the power of purification, transformation, beauty, and Grace.

**Iccha** — Will; desire; one of the four main shakti powers of Divine Mother.

**Iccha Shakti** — The power of indomitable will inherent in the Divine Mother by which She accomplishes all manifestation, all action and all conceptualization; Dravya, Kriya and Jnana Shakti; Divine Will.

**Indra** — The Lord of all the Gods.

**Indraloka** — The inner world where Indra presides.

**Indriyas** — The ten senses, five active and five cognitive.

**Isha** — A word meaning Lord; a name that the Hindus have given to Jesus.

**Ishana** — Siva appearing as the Sovereign Lord.

**Ishitva** — One of the Eight Occult Powers by which those attracted to lower ideals attain domination over beings and situations.

**Ishtam** — One's chosen Ideal.

**Ishta-nistha** — One-pointed devotion to a single ideal.

**Ishvara** — The supreme and most comprehensive aspect of Divinity presiding over the three worlds who oversees its various lesser powers and their functions; God with form; Saguna Brahman.

**Ishvarakoti** — A class of illumined beings who are perfected in spiritual life, and who usually attend on a Divine Incarnation when such a being embodies.

**Ishvara-pranidhana** — One of the five niyamas of Yoga which encourages the worship of God with form as an aid towards self-realization.

**Ishvari** — The Divine Mother as Ishvara; the supreme power of the universe manifesting through a feminine aspect.

**Ishvariya** — One of the Four Points of View as to the Origin of the Scriptures, this one being that they were created by Ishvara.

**Itihasa** — Spiritual history and mythology of India, especially reflected in the Mahabharata, Ramayana, and other famous texts.

**Iti-iti** — "All this, all this," which is the conclusion that the mature practitioner comes to after practicing the discipline of neti-neti, "not this, not this."

**Jagannath** — The Lord of the Worlds; the deity worshiped primarily in Bengal, whose famous temple, visited by thousands of pilgrims, lies in Puri in the state of Orissa.

**Jagat** — The world; universe.

**Jagrat** — The waking state of the human being.

**Jai** — Victory.

**Jayati** — Birth, listed as one of the false transformations over the unborn Soul, Atman.

**Jal** — The Bengali word for water.

**Janaka** — A famous king, the father of Sita, who attained both lordship and enlightenment. The famous rishi, Yajnavalkya, was his court priest and guru.

**Janaloka** — The fifth of seven worlds within Consciousness, lying below Taparloka and Satyaloka.

**Japa** — The efficacious practice of silently reciting the sacred mantra or names of God while turning the holy beads (mala).

**Japam** — The same as japa.

**Jara** — Old Age, which is among the six transformations belonging to the body, not the Soul, Atman.

**Jitendriya** — Controller of the senses; one of the Seven Qualifications of a Tantric Aspirant.

**Jivanmukta** — An illumined being who is liberated while living, enlightened while still residing in the body.

**Jivanmukti** — The state of liberation attained by fully illumined beings.

**Jivas** — Embodied beings of the earth plane.

**Jivatman** — The Atman dwelling inside the embodied soul, unbeknownst to it.

**Jnana** — Special knowledge, more like wisdom, that centers around philosophy and spirituality and which, when acquired, easily takes the soul out of bondage and towards Freedom.

**Jnanabhumikas** — The seven higher stages of knowledge/worlds.

**Jnana-chakshu** — The "Third Eye," being the sixth and penultimate center (ajna) of the Kundalini system.

**Jnanamatras** — Particles of intelligence, extremely close to Consciousness and aligned with The Word.

**Jnana Shakti** — A power of the Divine Mother used for sustaining knowledge and wisdom; force of intelligence.

**Jnana-vakyas** — One of three groups or classifications of knowledge having to do with statements in the scriptures pertaining to the nature of Brahman.

**Jnanakasha** — The subtle space which supports intelligence and wisdom, and where illumined souls keep their subtle bodies in order to help the outer worlds.

**Jnanamarga** — The path of wisdom that leads the soul out of bondage via higher knowledge, as contrasted to the bhogamarga that embroils one into attachment to pleasure and its resultant suffering.

**Jnanendriyas** — The five cognitive senses, namely smelling, tasting, seeing, touching, and hearing.

**Jnanis** — Practitioners of the path of Jnana Yoga; one who has spiritual knowledge.

**Jnano-daya Yoga** — The rare path of giving out the noble dharmic teachings with the aim of compassionately removing the suffering of living beings. This yoga has seen a re-emergence in present times due to Sri Sarada Devi's presence on the world scene.

**Kailas** — The Holy Mountain sacred to Lord Shiva, said to be His abode.

**Kaivalya** — Spiritual emancipation; absolute independence or transcendence synonymous with the terms moksha or mukti, used particularly by Patanjali in his Yoga system.

**Kaivalya-prag-bhara** — Liberation stream; one of the Two Directions of the Mind-Stream after death mentioned by Patanjali and Vedavyasa. One stream of souls moves towards liberation, and the others towards bondage and rebirth in ignorance (samsara-prag-bhara).

**Kala Shakti** — Power of time; the shakti of Lord Shiva.

**Kala** — Time; a name for Yama, the god of death; a name for Shiva.

**Kalachakra** — The wheel of birth and death into which unawakened beings are born, experiencing various dualities such as good and bad, pleasure and pain, etc., according to their karmas until enlightenment dawns.

**Kalas** — Phases of time; one of the twelve higher tattvas in Shaivism.

**Kali** — The Divine Mother of the Universe in Her four-armed form, worshiped by Sri Ramakrishna Paramahamsa; the consort of Lord Shiva from the Tantric viewpoint.

**Kalmi creeper** — A plant which grows in water and covers the surface.

**Kalpa** — A phase of time consisting of many yugas.

**Kalpanika** — Imagings of the mind in time which, like seeds, will produce life and its dream-like experiences.

**Kama** — One of the Four Fruits of Life (Purusharthas) granted by the Divine Mother wherein one gets fulfillment of all legitimate desires; desire.

**Kamadhatu** — In Zen, one of the three worlds, being the world of desires, or earth.

## 576 Sanskrit Glossary

**Kama-vasayita** — One of the Eight Occult Powers which allow those who seek lower ideals to thoroughly enjoy all desires which come to mind.

**Kamarpukur** — The small village in Bengal where Sri Ramakrishna took His birth in this incarnation, which has now become a scared pilgrimage place.

**Kamakala** — In Tantra, a designation that denotes Siva and Shakti in deepest Union.

**Kanchukas** — Limiting adjuncts; sheaths that constrict or seemingly modify Consciousness, causing It to think in terms of a finite being.

**Kapila** — Revered rishi who was the main proponent of the Sankhya System of Philosophy.

**Kapilavastu** — The birthplace of Lord Kapila, which several millennia later was also the birthplace of Lord Buddha.

**Karanas** — Causes of the external worlds and their objects, i.e., the senses connected to the mind.

**Karana Sharira** — Of the human being's three bodies, it is the causal body consisting of powerful seeds held in abeyance. Both the subtle and gross bodies, as well as the worlds, are drawn from these seeds.

**Karanavairagya** — The fourth of the Twelve Levels of Dispassion which comes about due to outer circumstances like the death of a loved one, but which does not last and gives way eventually to further attachment to the world.

**Karika** — A commentary on a scripture.

**Karma Shakti** — That power of the Divine Mother of the Universe Who oversees all action and compels beings to action.

**Karmendriyas** — The five active senses, as in speaking, handling, moving, procreating, and excreting.

**Karmika** — Limiting cognitive power; one of the three pasas, malas or limitations according to Tantra which bind in order to save. Karmika blinds beings to subtle truths by fastening their minds upon the accrual of merit and demerit. Along with mayiya and anava, karmika binds certain kinds of evolving souls and veils from them their inherent nature as Shiva. Gaining initiation from a guru and attaining jnana, they can manage to get free.

**Kartikeya** — One of the sons of Lord Shiva, often called Skanda or Subrahmanya.

**Kartritva-abhimana** — The mistaken notion the Brahman/Atman is somehow the agent of actions, when it is really the ego-mind complex.

**Karya Maya** — One of the twelve cosmic principles of Shaivism citing the overall power of the Mahashakti to provide all and everything for the benefit of the entire creation.

**Katha Upanisad** — An Upanisad sacred to the Vedic tradition in which Nachiketas, a young man, journeys to the realm of Yama, the god of death, to uncover what lies beyond death and learn what is the essence of life.

**Kavirajis** — Members of a sect in India.

**Kauravas** — The greedy clan of brothers who strove to take away the kingdom of the Pandavas by deceit and war, as described in the Mahabharata, setting the stage for the acts/yogas of the Bhagavad Gita.

**Kenopanisad** — A short but powerful scripture that concentrates upon the transcendent and all-pervasive Atman and which includes a story about the gods and their encounter with the Absolute Brahman. In this Upanisad, the Divine Mother of the Universe also makes a rare appearance.

**Keshava** — A name for Lord Krishna meaning "long-haired; slayer of Keshi."

**Khyati** — Clarity of mind, most highly valued by all the luminaries.

**Kileshas** — Same as kleshas in Yoga, which in Buddhism are the various impediments to Nirvana.

**King Janaka** — A famous king of old India who gained both all that the world had to offer, plus spiritual Enlightenment.

**Kirtan** — Dancing and singing in adoration of the Lord.

**Kirtanam** — Singing and dancing in devotion to the Lord; one of the Eight Devotional Aids according to Devarshi Narada.

**Kleshas** — The five impediments to freedom in Yoga, namely ignorance, egoism, attachment, aversion, and clinging to life/fear of death; kileshas in Buddhism.

**Klistha-vrttis** — Pain-bearing thoughts in the mind that bring about havoc in life.

**Kosha** — Sheath or covering. The term is used in Vedanta to indicate those aspects of creation — namely body, life-force, mind, intelligence, and ego — which obscure or apparently condition pure Consciousness called Brahman; a small metal container used for water offerings in sacred puja.

**Krama Mukti** — The gradual way or path to Enlightenment taken by awakening devotees who proceed from birth in the lower realms to those in higher realms, and finally into Brahman.

**Kriya** — To act; in Tantra, spontaneous divinely-oriented action; the internal rising of Kundalini Shakti which produces certain external effects on the body and mind; practice aimed at higher understanding with regards to spirituality.

**Kriyamani** — As in kriyamani karma, which is unexpected karma arising inscrutibly that surfaces in life while the aspiring jiva is attempting to work out other karmas and attain a balanced existence.

**Kriya Shakti** — That power of the Divine Mother which infuses beings with the energy to act and think, and pours life-force into the gross and subtle creations, permeating all worlds and realms with vitalizing power. Not only is She responsible for the activating force, She also acts in and through that which She animates.

**Kriya Shuddhi** — Purity of action.

**Kriyayoga** — According to Vedavyasa, that revitalizing aspect of Yoga which powerfully combines austerity (tapas), study of scripture (svadhyaya), and devotion to God (Ishvara-pranidhana), the three essential niyamas of Yoga, into a consummate method for realization.

**Krodha** — Anger; one of the Six Passions.

**Kshama** — Forgiveness; graciousness.

**Kshara** — Decay, one of the six transformations falsely imputed over the imperishable Soul, Atman.

**Kshipta** — Disturbed state of mind; the first and most difficult of the Five States of the Mind Field in Yoga, which makes the unfortunate sufferer unfit for both terrestrial and spiritual life.

**Kubir or Kabir** — A famous poet/songwriter of the Fifteenth Century who, as a boy, was adopted by poor Muslim and Hindu parents of a low caste, and whose collection of songs, called Bijak, are sung to this day by Hindus and Muslims alike.

**Kumbhaka** — The breathless state of suspended animation; retention and suspension of breath.

**Kundalini** — Coiled-up spiritual force; the powerful yet subtle spiritual power, that when awakened, brings illumination to all levels of one's being.

**Kundalini Shakti** — The wielder of the primal power of Kundalini.

**Kurukshetra** — A famous location in India where the great war spoken of in the Mahabharata took place, and upon whose field Sri Krishna gave His inspirational discourse on Yoga to a confused and dejected Arjuna.

**Kutastha** — Eternal underlying substratum which is changeless, as in pure, conscious Awareness.

**Kutichakas** — A class of roaming ascetics who are spiritual adepts that are steadily fixed in their realization.

**Laghima** — One of the Eight Occult Powers by which those who seek lesser attainments become weightless and are said to defy gravity.

**Lakshmana** — Literally, "bearing auspicious marks"; the devoted and illumined half-brother of Sri Ramachandra and husband of Sita's sister.

**Lama** — A teacher and guide in Tibetan Buddhism.

**Laya** — Dissolution; immersion.

**Loka** — Literally, world or realm; world of names and forms.

**Lok'anuvartanam** — One of the three primary desires of living beings, which is the desire to visit and abide in the various worlds of name and form in time and space..

**Lokayatika Marga** — The path of following the gross material world only.

**Lopamudra** — Literally, "of extremely subtle form." The illustrious wife of the renowned sage and rishi, Agastya, she was the authoress of a portion of the Rig Veda.

**Mada** — Vanity; one of the Six Passions; one of the Seven Malas of Maya.

**Madhava** — The Sweet One, being a name for the Lord, Sri Krishna.

**Madhura Bhava** — The love of the lover for the Beloved; one of the Five Divine Moods for Worshiping God, in Vaishnavism.

**Madhyama** — The third phase of the manifestation of pure knowledge from the primal sound vibration wherein thought and meaning are formed and fused; subtle sound.

**Madhyavairagya** — A mild and moderate level of detachment; the third of Twelve Levels of Dispassion noted in Vedanta Philosophy.

**Mahabhutas** — Great principles, tattvas; the Five Element: ether, air, fire, water, and earth.

**Mahadeva** — Literally, "Great God," which is a name for Lord Shiva.

**Mahalila** — The great play or sport of Consciousness; the cosmic theater with all beings as actors and actresses and the Divine Being as the writer, producer, and director; the divine sport of an Avatar.

**Mahamaya** — The grand illusion; the superimposition of the universe and its constituents over Brahman; the One who conjures up the grand illusion, the Divine Mother, the Mahashakti.

**Mahamudra** — In Tibetan Buddhism, one of the foremost of all practices, termed "The Great Seal" since it recognizes that all things bear the steadfast seal of spontaneous emptiness and luminosity.

**Mahanarayana Upanisad** — A fine Upanisad dealing with the religious life of Vedic culture in general, said to be transmitted by the revered rishi, Yajnatma Narayan.

**Mahaprakriti** — A name for the Divine Mother of the Universe, under whose auspice and control all of prakriti, nature, operates.

**Mahapralaya** — The withdrawal of all worlds of name, form, and concept back into their primal Essence at the time of universal dissolution.

**Maharloka** — The fourth of seven worlds within Consciousness, finer than svarloka but short of janaloka.

**Mahasamadhi** — An explanatory abd distinctive term utilized to describe the merging of an illumined soul into Brahman after its passing from the body and the physical realm.

**Mahasamhitas** — Great cosmic connections which are primal in their inception, they are eternally present in the Mind of God.

**Mahashakti** — The Supreme power inherent in Ultimate Reality which causes the powers of creation, preservation, and dissolution to formulate and activate the worlds of name and form.

**Mahat** — Cosmic Intelligence; the first principle of creation according to the Sankhya Philosophy of Kapila.

**Mahatattva** — Great principle, like the Bindu.

**Mahat-seva** — Service of the great ones, like the sages, seers, rishis, and the guru.

**Mahavakyas** — The four divine declarations of nondual experience; Tat Tvamasi, Aham Brahmasmi, Prajnanam Brahma, and Ayamatma Brahma.

**Mahayoga** — The fullest expression of Yoga, including all paths and philosophies within it.

**Mahayuga** — The collection of all four yugas, satya, treta, dvapara, and kali, as a very long phase of cyclical time.

**Maheshvara** — A powerful name for Divine Reality appearing as Lord Siva.

**Mahima** — Greatness, glory; one of the Eight Occult Powers which bestow upon those who seek lower pursuits the ability to become radiant, impressive or suffused with light.

**Mahut** — Elephant driver.

**Maitrah** — Friendliness.

**Malas** — Limitations; imperfections; negative tendencies in the mind which, according to Tantra, are ripened and transcended via spiritual practice. (These are not to be confused with a mala, which is a set of holy beads, like a rosary, used for mantra practice.)

**Malaya breeze** — The mythical, mystical wind blowing from the direction of Malaysia that was supposed to transform all trees into Sandalwood, an analogy used to illustrate the fact that when the wind of God's grace is blowing, all worthy beings realize their inherent divinity.

**Mallika** — A fragrant flower prized for its use in worshiping God in puja.

**Mamakara** — Strong sense of ownership; possessiveness; one of the Sixteen Evolutes of Maya.

**Mamatva** — The sense of I, me, and mine.

**Manahpranasambandha** — Literally, connecting oneself to the luminous mind via the purified prana, the idea being that most beings have not found and awakened their prana, so their subtle body (mind) remains unreachable to them. Thus, their consciousness remains only in the brain, or physical body.

**Manasa-japa** — Reciting the mantra silently, in the mind.

**Manasana** — The art of mental postures which, when assumed, heal, spiritualize, and perfect the mind.

**Manasika** — Having to do with the mental faculty.

**Mandukyopanisad** — A major upanisad made all the more important by Gaudapada's karika or commentary on it. Its teachings explain the four quarters of the sacred bija Aum and transmit the essence of nonduality called Advaita Vedanta.

**Manipura** — The chakra, "lotus," or spiritual center, third in succession, located at the navel.

**Mano-buddhi Yoga** — The rare yoga of focusing on the mind with purificatory disciplines designed to remove limitations and sufferings at their source. This yoga has seen a re-emergence in this day and time due to the influence of Sri Sarada Devi's presence on earth.

**Manojavittvam** — Acquiring mastery of the speed of the mind's thoughts, which is one of the victories of the Tantra tradition.

**Manomayakosha** — The sheath of the mind; the mental body as a covering over Reality.

**Mantra** — A powerful formula consisting of seed syllables and Holy Names that the initiate uses to purify the mind and invoke the presence of God.

**Mantra Diksha** — Initiation by a spiritual teacher into religious life.

**Mantreshvaras** — In Shaivism, a cross section of beings who still have a trace of desire left for the worlds of name and form, but whose minds vibrate with a subtler intelligence than most embodied beings.

**Mantri Guru** — That aspect or type of guru that facilitates and confers initiation into spiritual life.

**Manus yatvam** — A human birth, which is one of the three great boons needed in order to gain enlightenment.

**Manvantara** — An extended period of time consisting of 71 celestial yugas, and over which Manu rules.

**Mara** — In Buddhism, an enemy or demon; passion; desire; destroyer; a name for Siva.

**Matras** — Particles, or units, often used in the sense of the three sections/letters (matras) of The Word, AUM.

**Matrika** — Alphabets, words, letters, all in conjunction with their innate power to formulate worlds of name and form in time and space.

**Matrika-shakti** — The power of the Divine Mother inherent in all words, statements.

**Matsarya** — Jealousy; one of the Six Passions.

**Mauna** — Silence; a vow of silence taken by those who are striving for spirituality.

**Maya** — The deluding power that posits form over Formless Essence, and that consists mainly of name, form, time, space, and causality — all assumed to be real due to its stultifying influence.

**Mayahamkara** — Worship of the ego in maya by worldly and ignorant beings.

**Mayic** — Having to do with maya and its ever-changing effects.

**Mayika** — Projecting, deluding power; one of the three pasas, malas or limitations according to Tantra which bind in order to save. Mayika provides beings with the psycho/physical being and the many worlds and embroils them in enjoyment of the objects of pleasure. Along with karmika and anava, mayika binds certain kinds of evolving souls and veils from them their inherent nature as Shiva. Gaining initiation from a guru and attaining jnana, they can manage to get free.

**Medhakendra** — The knowledge of the heart.

**Milarepa** — A luminary of the Mahasiddha lineage of Tibet who was a fine songwriter and an uncommon and unique teacher. He was a student of Marpa who brought the yoga-based teachings of the Mahasiddhas to Tibet from India. His songs communicate the essence of enlightenment and are a living transmission even today.

**Mirabai** — North Indian princess of the Fifteenth century whose passionate collections of devotional songs of surrender to Lord Krishna, called Padavali, are popular all over India and abroad.

**Mishtram** — Mixed results, borne via works done with half-hearted attention.

**Mithya** — False, illusory.

**Mithyajnan** — Knowledge thought to be true, which is actually false.

**Mithyajnan Marga** — The path of delusion that ignorant beings fall into, life after life.

**Moha** — Delusion; false identification; infatuation; one of the Seven Malas of Maya; one of the Six Passions listed in Vedanta.

**Mrduvairagya** — Meek or exceedingly mild detachment, which has little or no lasting or beneficial effect on life; the second of the Twelve Levels of Dispassion of Vedanta Philosophy.

**Mudha** — Foolish; slothful; the second of the Five States of Mind in Yoga which conduces only to laziness and inadvertence and makes the aspirant unfit for spiritual realization.

**Mudhavastha** — One of Five States of Mind wherein one is completely forgetful of one's true nature; one of the Sixteen Evolutes of Maya.

**Mudita** — Unbridled joy, felt by the devotee upon communion with the Lord.

**Mukhya Prana** — The prana gotten from eating pure food, that must be transformed into refined energy for doing sadhana.

**Mula** — Root, as in the basis of a thing — like root ignorance, or mulashrama.

**Muladhara Chakra** — The root chakra located at the base of the spine where Kundalini Shakti lies coiled up until it is awakened by spiritual disciplines.

**Mula-trikona** — The "Primal Triangle," involved intricately with the conception of the first form.

**Mulavidya** — Root ignorance or primal ignorance. It is the same as mulajnana in that all potentialities, positive and negative, spring from it.

**Mumukshutvam** — A strong desire or longing for liberation; the fourth of the Four Jewels of Vedanta sadhana and spiritual attainment.

**Mundakopanisad** — Literally, the "cutting edge of a razor," this Upanisad gives teachings designed to cut away ignorance from the mind. Its profound authority comes from the fact that its wisdom, a direct transmission from the god Brahma, is given by the great rishi Angiras to the famed disciple Saunaka.

**Muni** — A wise person or sage, often one that observes mauna, silence.

**Murti** — Form; an idol to be worshipped.

**Mussalman** — An adherent and follower of the Muslim religion.

**Nadis** — Subtle channels, similar to the nervous system in the physical body, but permeating the subtle body and beyond. It is through these subtle nerves that prana, psychic prana, and shakti power course in the awakened aspirant and adept.

**Nagas** — A class of beings that inhabit the intermediate regions between earth and lower heaven, often seen in reptile form.

**Namarupa** — A cover-all term for name and form, applying to the world of created things that are transitory and impermanent.

**Nandi** — The sacred bull who acts as Shiva's mount and companion.

**Narada** — A luminary who wrote the Narada Bhakti Sutras which are definitive texts of Bhakti Yoga. Sage Narada appears throughout the many scriptures of Hinduism where he is privileged to have the darshan of Lord Vishnu and many other gods and goddesses. Sri Ramakrishna mentions him as a holy man of the highest order.

**Narayan** — A name for God; God manifest in mankind.

**Nastika** — Unorthodox, in reference to those darshanas or systems of philosophy that do not base their authority on the Vedas (i.e,. Buddhism, Jainism, etc.), as compared to Astika (i.e., Yoga, Vedanta, Sankhya, etc.), which do.

**Nataraj** — A name for Siva as the purifier of all impurities, and remover of limitations.

**Natmandir** — A music or lecture hall adjoining the temple precincts, usually used for devotional song and dance.

**Neti-neti** — "Not this, not this." A Vedantic practice of the Jnana Yoga school which proceeds by negating all phenomenal things until the Ultimate Reality stands revealed. The practice culminates in iti-iti, "all this, all this," which declares that all is indeed Brahman.

**Nidanas** — In Buddhism, the twelve links that bind the body into the cycle of rebirth by conditioning the mind into forms of bondage over several lifetimes.

**Nididhyasana** — Realizing the Truth after completing the steps of shravana and manana.

**Nidra** — Deep sleep; a type of samadhi wherein everything merges into formlessness.

**Nimitta** — Causality; one of the five aspects of maya, as in name, form, time, space, and causation.

**Nirguna** — Having no gunas, or qualities, thus formless and free of all conditionings.

**Nilkantha** — The blue-throated one, which is a name for Lord Siva.

**Nirmamo** — Freedom from egotism.

**Nirmanakaya** — One of the three bodies of the Buddha, being the body of transformation.

**Nirodha** — The end of all the mind's activities, culminating in nirvana or samadhi.

**Nirvana** — Literally, "Free of desire," it is the direct experience of freedom uninhibited by any condition or limitation; spiritual emancipation.

**Nirvashana** — The extinction of desires.

**Nirvikalpa Samadhi** — Direct nondual experience of the impersonal or egoless type; the highest Samadhi; immersion into formless essence.

**Nischaya-dardhyam** — The full inward resolve that "Existence Is."

**Nistha** — Firmly established; one-pointedness, as in Ishta-nistha, devotion to a single ideal; or Atma-nistha, dedication to Realization of the Atman; or Brahma-nistha.

**Niskama karma** — Work or actions performed without any desire for personal gain or recompense. It is the kind of activity, transcendent of any karmic residue, that enlightened beings engage in.

**Nishtam** — One-pointedness, like in works done for the Lord dwelling in living beings.

**Nitai** — An affectionate nickname for Chaitanya's beloved disciple, Nityananda.

**Nitya** — The Eternal, referring to Brahman, or pure, conscious Awareness.

**Nityanitya-vastu-viveka** — Exacting and noncompromising discrimination between the Real and the unreal, the changing and the Unchanging, which is an indispensable mainstay and often overlooked requisite for spiritual life and its aim of Self-realization.

**Nitya-shuddha-bodha-rupa** — The very nature of eternal purity and supreme intelligence.

**Nityasiddha** — A class of ever-free beings who are always aware of their inherent perfection.

**Nivrittijnana** — Higher knowledge that is based upon renunciation of the world, as contrasted to pravritti which follows the path of the world.

**Nivrittimarga** — The path of higher knowledge leading to the renunciation of the world.

**Niyamas** — Five practices in Yoga which constitute the second limb of Patanjala which, along with the five yamas, prepare the practitioner for encountering the six higher limbs in order.

**Niyati** — The principle of cosmic laws, which is one of the twelve higher tattvas in Shavism.

**Ojas** — Subtle internal power gathered from spiritual practices involving the ingestion of pure food, control of prana, striving for scriptural knowledge, etc., — all sublimated and brought inwards for purposes of purification leading to Enlightenment.

**Omkaravrittidhyan** — The dissolution of all the mind's thought-waves into The Word, AUM.

**Pada** — The formulation of letters and words into profound statements that illumine awareness; a principle that is taught and maintained, as in the Four Padas of Lord Siva.

**Padartha Bhavana** — The sixth of seven states of Higher Knowledge, a level of Consciousness that is penultimate to the highest realization, i.e., Turiya.

**Pakvahamkara** — The human ego, ahamkara, that through spiritual disciplines and self-surrender, has become refined or matured, i.e., surrendered unto God, and is thus pakva, ripe.

**Panchakarana** — The original ancient wisdom of the fivefold cause, which lists and traces the origin of all forms and worlds based upon the sets of fives, i.e., five elements, five senses, five pranas, etc.

**Panchakosha** — The classical five sheaths of Vedanta, listed as coverings over Reality, namely body, energy, mind, intellect, and ego.

**Panchamahabhutas** — The great five elements, namely earth, water, fire, air, and ether.

**Pancha-yajna** — The five sacrifices performed by dharmic beings, namely, to the rishis, the deities, the ancestors, the sub-species, and mankind.

**Pandavas** — The righteous clan of Arjuna and his brothers and family who fought for justice against the evil Kaurava clan in the sacred scripture of the Bhagavad Gita, contained in the Mahabharata.

**Pani** — Water.

**Para** — Supreme; the first stage of manifestation of highest knowledge through the primal sound vibration. It is an undifferentiated state where no concepts, thoughts, meanings or words are yet manifest.

**Parabrahma** — The Ultimate Reality or Supreme Being as formless essence or Pure Consciousness.

**Paragatam** — The supreme Goal; Nirvana.

**Parama-drk** — Clear grasp of the Supreme View.

**Paramahamkara** — One of the Three Kinds of Ego referred to in Vedanta scriptures, two positive and one negative, mainly Paramahamkara, Sakshahamkara, and Dehadhyasahmakara. The first is the most refined, subtle, and allows for the advent of spiritual Consciousness into the body/mind mechanism.

**Paramahamsa** — Literally, "Great Swan." A title referring to the highest class of sanyasins, as in the authentic Paramahamsa of this day and time, Sri Ramakrishna Paramahamsa.

**Paramasiva** — The Transcendental Siva, or Siva in His whole Essence as Formless Reality.
**Paramatman** — The Supreme Soul.
**Paramukti** — Absolute liberation.
**Paraprakasha** — The supreme space of nondual Awareness.
**Parashakti** — The highest aspect of shakti.
**Parasparadhyasa** — A stolid delusion in the human mind that perceives and enforces the idea of the physical body as the indwelling Self, and the indwelling Self as the body; one of the Sixteen Evolutes of Maya.
**Paravairagya** — Supreme detachment, being the highest station of dispassion possible; the final stage of the Twelve Levels of Dispassion.
**Paravidya** — Supreme knowledge associated with the direct experience of Brahman; sometimes used to indicate the distinction between knowledge of the truths of the scriptures as opposed to secular knowledge.
**Parigraha** — The habitual exchanging of gifts and wealth among the peoples of the world, which takes attention away from the Goal of Life — to realize God.
**Parigraha Shaktis** — Lord Siva's two auspicious dynamic powers, through which he accomplishes the work of His four padas.
**Parikarmas** — Four types of beneficial attitudes to adopt in spiritual life in accordance with different kinds of beings one meets, namely friendliness, compassion, reverence, and indifference.
**Parinama** — The illusory phenomena of change; the appearance of transformation when there can be none — since all is unoriginated.
**Partha** — A name for Arjuna, the son of Priti.
**Pasas** — In Tantra, limitations or temporary imperfections that bind embodied souls to the sense of karma, relativity, and duality.
**Pasyanti** — The second stage of manifested knowledge through the primal sound vibration where undifferentiated Wisdom begins to condense and form in order to manifest as conceptualized thought on the cosmic level.
**Pashupati** — A name for Lord Siva, which is one of the most ancient appelations given to him.
**Pasu** — Animalistic, referring to the Three Designations of Aspirants in Tantra Philosophy, divine, heroic, and animalistic. The aspirant at the pasu level is still attached to the body and the senses and has gained little detachment from the world and its pleasures/sufferings as a result.
**Patala** — Nether region; the seventh and lowest of the hell realms.
**Patanjala Yoga** — Called Raja Yoga and Ashtanga Yoga, it is the classic yogic pathway with eight progressive but interconnected practices, namely: yamas, niyamas, asana, pranayama, pratyahara, dharana, dhyana, and samadhi. It bears little resemblance to, nor should it be mistaken for what passes for Yoga in present times, which is often just Hatha Yoga, a series of body postures practiced merely for gaining health, longevity and the occult powers, which are potentially detrimental to the attainment of true spirituality.
**Patanjali** — The founder of the Patanjala Yoga system and author of the Yoga Sutras.

**Paurusheya** — Of human authorship, used often in reference to the sacred scriptures of the Sanatana Dharma of India.

**Phalaharini Devi** — An aspect of the Divine Mother of the Universe in Her capacity of granting the fruits of actions, positive, negative, and mixed, to living beings.

**Phalgu** — An river in North India which over the course of time went underground and flows under a bed of sand.

**Pitriyana** — The Path of the Fathers, or the ancestors, wherein beings return to earth after heaven.

**Pradhana Jaya** — One of the seven victories of the Tantric aspirant wherein he/she gains control over the initial creative principle, i.e., Prakriti.

**Prahlada** — A sage written of in the Puranas, who though born of a demon King, and tortured as a boy for his purity, nevertheless became a great devotee of Vishnu.

**Prajnanam Brahma** — "Brahman is Pure Consciousness"; one of the four Mahavakyas or divine declarations of Advaita Vedanta.

**Prajnaparam** — A powerful Name for Brahman, declaring It as Supreme Intelligence.

**Prajnaparamita** — The Mother of the Buddhas; a set of sutras of great import in Mahayana Buddhism.

**Prakamya** — One of the 8 Occult Powers which allows those who pursue lower ideals to become free willed with regards to fulfilling any desire.

**Prakarana** — A section or a chapter of a scripture or commentary.

**Prakasha Shakti** — The Divine Mother's power of revelation.

**Prakriti** — Nature; causal matter; the universe of name and form and those ingredients which comprise it; the pradhana of Samkhya which corresponds to the Maya of Vedanta with these main distinctions; it exists independent of Spirit, Purusha, and it is considered real.

**Pralaya** — The dissolution of all worlds and forms at the end of a cosmic cycle, to be followed by another cosmic projection of worlds thereafter.

**Pralaya-kalas** — In Shaivism, a cross section of subtle beings who are still bound by maya, but who gain liberation at the time of pralaya.

**Pramachadika** — One of the five cosmic bondages, being attachment to nature, or gross form.

**Pramada** — Inattentiveness; negligence; one of the Nine Distractions to Spiritual Life listed in the Yoga Sutras by Patanjali.

**Pramoda** — Actual enjoyment of an object, used in conjunction with the Three States of Enjoyment of Objects: priya, joy of seeing the object; moda, approaching and gaining the object; and pramoda, the actual enjoyment of said object. The "object" in question here can be material in nature, but refers also to the joy of darshan with Ishvara, or realization of Brahman as well.

**Pramuchadaka-prakriti-bandha** — Attachment to insentient matter as if it were the only Reality.

**Prana** — The life-force running through all of nature, and all bodies, which though unseen, both animates and helps connect all of existence back to its Source.

**Pranakasha** — The space of subtle energy, prana, wherein the ancestors dwell; lower heaven.

**Pranam** — The act of bowing down in reverence before a divine image or an illumined soul.

**Pranamayakosha** — The vital sheath; life-force as a covering over Reality.

**Pranas** — The five types of the singular prana that operate to facilitate flow and health on the physical plane. These five have a fivefold counterpart on the subtle plane, or dream-state, which assume a psychic nature in order to move thoughts through different levels of consciousness.

**Pranava** — Another name for the sacred Word, AUM.

**Pranayam** — Breathing exercises designed to awaken subtle energy in both body and mind, it occupies the position of the fourth limb of Yoga's Eight-limbed system (ashtanga).

**Pranic** — Having to do with the prana.

**Prarabdha** — As in prarabdha karma, which is karma from previous existences that is taken up in the present lifetime for working out.

**Prasad** — Clarity, often connected to purification of food prior to its ingestion.

**Prastanatraya** — The three great landmarks is scriptural history, namely The Brahma Sutras, the Bhagavad Gita, and the Upanisads.

**Pratibha** — The flint-like intelligence that cuts through maya and its various overlays.

**Pratibhandaka** — The presence of obstructions and impediments potential in everything.

**Pratibhandakabhava** — The underlying power of subtle intelligence lying in every mind, every situation that, when accessed, provides thorough solutions for life's problems.

**Pratibhasikasatta** — The overall dream projection by the mind in its three phases, cosmic, collective, and individual.

**Pratika** — An object of sacred atmosphere utilized in early meditation to aid the mind's concentration.

**Pratima** — Similar to pratika, usually made of a physical substance like wood, metal, etc.

**Pratipakshabhavana** — The helpful mood or attitude wherein the aspirant causes the mind to raise an opposite wave in order to do away with negative or habitual thoughts.

**Pratistha** — Steadiness.

**Prati-tantra siddhanta** — The way of arriving at a philosophical conclusion based upon contrasting one path, way, or religion, against another.

**Pratitya Samutpada** — "Conditioned Arising," enumerating the Twelve Nidanas, or links that bind the soul to the reincarnation process.

**Pravrittijnana** — Lower knowledge that focuses upon action to assist earthly existence.

**Pravrittimarga** — The path of lower knowledge that beings who desire the world of objects and pleasures walk, life to life.

**Pratyagatman** — A word pertaining to the supreme Self, or Atman as Brahman.

**Pratyahara** — Freeing the mind from attachment to senses objects, which is the fifth limb of Yoga falling after control of the prana, and before actual concentration.

**Prema** — Ecstatic Love for God; one of the Four Perfections of the Heart.

**Prema-bhakti** — The highest kind of devotion, beyond Vaidya and Raga Bhakti, which involve ritualistic devotion and the various devotional moods. To paraphrase Sri Ramakrishna, Prema Bhakti is that purest of Love which makes one forget all personal considerations, even the body that is usually so dear to human beings.

**Pretas** — A cross section of lost beings who are bound to lower realms, or patalas.

**Priya moda pramoda** — With regards to the Lord, the bhakta loves to see, approach, and enjoy bliss.

**Puja** — Ceremonial worship attended by offerings, mudras, mantras, and devotional music.

**Pujari** — The officiating priest at a puja ceremony.

**Puraka** — The indrawn breath, in conjunction with suspended breath, kumbhaka, and the exhaled breath, rechaka.

**Purna** — Fullness; completeness.

**Purna Brahma** — A name for Divine Mother in Her role as the identity of Brahman.

**Purnahanta** — The real "I," in fullness.

**Purusha** — The Sentient Soul, different from prakriti, matter; The Supreme Soul, as in Paramapurusha.

**Purushanyathatakhyati** — Knowing the Divine Self to be completely unique and different from all created things; the highest or deepest of the Seven Victories of Involution in Tantra Philosophy.

**Purusharthas** — The Four Fruits/Ideals of life as granted by the Divine Mother of the Universe, namely dharma, artha, karma, and moksha.

**Purva** — View, or perspective.

**Purva Mimamsa** — One of the six orthodox philosophies, or darshanas, of India.

**Puryastaka** — The eight-fold body, deha, consisting of the five senses and a three-fold mind.

**Pushkar Dvipa** — The subtlest of all realms, often correlated with Brahmaloka.

**Rabindranath Tagore** — A great poet and philosopher of modern India.

**Radhakrishna** — The conjoining of Radha and Krishna.

**Raga** — Attachment, which is one of the seven malas of maya; a higher tattva in Shaivism which is the attracting power present in all of creation.

**Raga bhakti** — The second stage of bhakti's development wherein what was worshipped externally (in the vaidhi bhakti stage) begins to show up as devotion in the heart, internally.

**Ragadveshau** — The troublesome combination of two of the five kleshas in Patanjali's Yoga teachings, namely attachment and aversion.

**Rahasya** — Secret, as in Sristhi Rahasya, wherein the secret of all things is traced back to The Word.

**Rajas** — Rajo guna, the mode of Prakriti that, on a cosmic level, places all things in motion, and on an individual level, induces beings into all manner of activity, usually of a frenetic variety.

**Rajasic** — Influenced by the guna of rajas.

**Ram** — The Divine Incarnation of the Treta Yuga whose heroic actions and superior teachings appear in the *Adhyatma Ramayana* and other scriptures.

**Ramachandra** — The full name of Sri Ram, the Avatar of the treta yuga.

**Ramakrishna** — The great God-intoxicated holy man of nineteenth-century Bengal who was the guru of Swami Vivekananda and the husband of Sri Sarada Devi. Accepted by many as the Kali Avatar, the Divine Incarnation of this age, He came with a host of Ishvarakotis and illumined followers who founded the Order named after Him and whose followers sustain it in the present day. His advent has been responsible for the reemergence of the Divine Mother path and other beneficial blessings.

**Ramana Maharshi** — A fully realized seer of India who lived recently, in contemporary times, and who, among other things, brought the ancient nondual wisdom of Atma Vichara to practitioners of this era.

**Ramanuja** — The father and representative of qualified nondualism, contrasted to Madhva as the representative of dualism, and Shankara as the representative of nondualism.

**Ramprasad** — The well-loved poet/saint of eighteenth-century Bengal whose wisdom songs to Mother Kali, the Divine Mother of the Universe, inspired a nation and are still inspiring the world today.

**Rasas** — Fluid essences of the physical body.

**Ravana** — A powerful and arrogant rakshasa who abducted Sita and was finally destroyed by Sri Ramachandra.

**Rechaka** — The expelled breath.

**Rishis** — Illumined beings from ancient Vedic times who practiced extreme austerities in order to receive the truths contained in the Vedas and Upanishads. Most were married, of both sexes, and passed their wisdom to their children.

**Roshi** — A revered teacher in Zen Buddhism.

**Rudra** — Lord Siva in his wrathful or purificatory form.

**Rudragranthi** — A subtle knot or barrier at very high levels of Awareness, that nevertheless keeps souls from reaching the highest Formless Reality.

**Rudraksha** — A seed that is used to creat a special mala, considered extra auspicious for recitation of the mantra.

**Rupaloka** — In Zen, the realm of desireless form, being one of the three worlds.

**Sadakhya** — One of the twelve cosmic principles in Shaivism; an incredible teaching system that employs six higher principles in order to explain the appearance of all the worlds of name and form in time and space.

**Sadasat** — Being both real and unreal, simultaneously, which is a description of the world-bewitching maya.

**Sadasiva** — One of the twelve higher spandas of Shaivism; a name for the highest aspect of Lord Siva.

**Sadguru** — A rare world teacher of outstanding realization.

**Sadhana** — Spiritual disciplines undertaken to realize God.

**Sadhanachatushtaya** — The Four Treasures and the Six Jewels of Vedanta, the third treasure containing the six jewels. If there is any type of "practice" present in the Vedanta — it being all a statement of Truth — it is this system, which is really a stance of higher mind maintaining itself in nonduality amidst the vagaries of the world and maya. Thus it can be named Advaita Vedanta Sadhana, well-deserved.

**Sadharani** — An ordinary love that seeks its own good and ends first, regardless of the good of the beloved; one of the Four Categories of Love.

**Sadhika** — One who practices sadhana, or spiritual disciplines.

**Sadurmi** — The six waves, or transformations, in Vedanta, namely grief, delusion, hunger, thirst, decay, and death.

**Sagara** — Ocean, primarily used to describe the ocean of suffering (samsara sagara) and the ocean of bliss (bhava sagara).

**Saguna** — Invested with gunas and qualities, thus having to operate under their influence.

**Saguna Brahman** — God with attributes; Reality with name, form, and qualities.

**Sahaja-tantra siddhanta** — The way of arriving at a religious or philosophical conclusion based upon knowing the natural synthesis of all religions and pathways, all of them sourced and centered in Divine Reality.

**Saham** — "I am She," a nondualistic statement of the Divine Mother worshipper.

**Sahasa** — Courage, not just of the physical kind, but rather the courage to maintain spiritual life in the face of obstacles.

**Sahashrara chakra** — The highest center of awareness, called the crown chakra, located at the top of the head.

**Sakalas** — In Shaivism, a cross section of subtle beings who, though they have Siva's grace, are still bound by several malas of maya.

**Sakama** — With desire, as in actions done in selfishness.

**Sakhya Bhava** — A mood or attitude assumed by a devotee which looks upon God as friend or companion; one of the Five Divine Moods for Worshiping God.

**Sakshi** — A word referring to Witness Consciousness, which oversees all phenomena without getting involved in it or affected by it.

**Sakshahamkara** — One of the Three Kinds of Ego referred to in Vedanta scriptures, two of them positive and one negative, mainly Paramahamkara, Sakshahamkara, and Dehadhyasahamakara. It is the kind of ego that is the detached witness (sakshi) of all phenomena.

**Salokya** — Abiding in the same plane, realm, or world with the Lord.

**Sama** — Inner peace, one of the Six Jewels, Shatsampatti, being a state of calm and silent mental balance requisite to attaining deeper spiritual qualities of spiritual life and enlightenment.

**Samadhana** — One of the Six Jewels, Shatsampatti, which is a special type of concentration which naturally restricts the mind from falling back from higher states of meditation.

**Samadarshitvam** — Same-sightedness, looking upon all equally.
**Samadhi** — Literally, "to make immovable," steady and impervious to external conditions. Any of the various kinds of spiritual moods or states of Consciousness brought about by meditation upon Reality, either with form or without form.
**Samana** — The digestive, distributive prana.
**Samanjasa** — Love that seeks the good of the beloved, but whose motive is based upon its own good as well; one of the Four Categories of Love.
**Samanya** — Common, or ordinary; the second category of causes of diseases that are purely physical.
**Samapati** — Abiding equanimity of mind, which is one of the three treasures of Yoga.
**Samartha** — The highest type of love which seeks only to fulfill the needs of the beloved; one of the Four Categories of Love.
**Samasti** — The collective whole rather than the individual, the macrocosm as compared to the microcosm.
**Samatva** — Abiding calm and steadiness, throughout.
**Sambhogakaya** — One of the three bodies of the Buddha, being the blissful enlightenment body.
**Samhitas** — One of the primary sections of the Vedas containing hymns and sacred formulas.
**Samipya** — Exceedingly dear to the Lord while enjoying God's direct presence.
**Samittis** — In Jainism, the six types of conduct that ensure nonviolent action and lifestyle.
**Sampradaya** — A sect or religious organization.
**Samprajnata Samadhi** — A high state of Awareness mentioned by Patanjali in the Yoga Sutras which is still accompanied by traces of individualized consciousness. In it, an awareness of the triad of meditator, meditation and that which is meditated upon still remains. It is generally synonymous with Savikalpa Samadhi in the Vedanta school.
**Samprasad** — One of the four prasads or clarities, wherein the peaceful mood is attained and maintained.
**Samsara** — The wheel of birth and death in suffering caused by ignorance.
**Samsaric** — Referring to what involves samsara.
**Samsaris** — Beings caught in samsara.
**Samsara-prag-bhara** — Bondage stream; one of the Two Directions of the Mind-Stream after death mentioned by Patanjali and Vedavyasa. One stream of souls moves towards liberation (kaivalya-prag-bhara), and the other towards bondage and rebirth in ignorance.
**Samshaya** — Doubt; one of the Nine Distractions to Spiritual Life according to Yoga Philosophy.
**Samskaras** — Positive and negative latent impressions in the subconscious and unconscious mind that shape human character and which are caused by repetitious actions through many lifetimes.
**Samskaraskandhas** — Collections of samskaras that form subtle and impeding complexes in the mind.

**Samvit** — A word for Absolute Reality, nondual Awareness.

**Samyama** — The combination of dharana, dhyana, and samadhi, the final three stages of Patanjala Yoga, which enables the yogi to attain anything desired.

**Sananda Samadhi** — One of the four seeded samadhi's of Patanjala Yoga.

**Sanatana Dharma** —The Eternal Religion of the ancient Vedic culture; which is Eternal Truth, which is transcendent of conception by the human mind, and is ever-existent. All of the many pathways, religions, and darshanas of India make up this Eternal Truth. Sri Ramakrishna has stated that "...the Sanatana Dharma of India has always existed, and will always exist."

**Sanchita** — As in sanchita karma, it is the collected karma of many past lifetimes, a portion of which is taken up to be worked on each new lifetime.

**Sandhya** — Daily ritual of purification for the devout Hindu consisting of ablutions and prayer.

**Sandilya-vidya** — Proper orientation in spiritual life, which aids with right view.

**Sangha** — Literally, "in good company," the term is used to denote holy company, particularly with regards to the spiritual family of seekers with which the devotee associates.

**Sankalpa** — Mental projection, usually done out of desire for forms, worlds, wealth, and objects, it, along with its desire, are responsible for the appearance of the worlds of name and form in time and space.

**Sankhya** — One of six orthodox systems of philosophy in Vedic culture which astutely outlines the various principles that comprise the universe. Its widespread acceptance is noted in both Yoga and Vedanta.

**Sanyasin** — One who takes a vow of renunciation of the world and enters spiritual life, following the fourth and final station of the dharmashrama.

**Santosha** — One of the five niyamas of Yoga that is a blissful contentment.

**Sarada Devi** — The Divine Mother in human form manifesting in this age, also known as the Holy Mother, the spiritual consort of Sri Ramakrishna Paramahamsa. She lived from 1853 to 1920 and was the inspiration and spiritual leader of the Ramakrishna Order after the Great Master's Mahasamadhi, initiating hundreds of devotees into spiritual life.

**Sarasvati** — The Goddess of art and learning who is listed as one of the Five Main Aspects of the Universal Mother (Prakriti Panchaka) in the *Srimad Devi Bhagavatam*.

**Sarupya** — Being of the same form as God

**Sarva-tantra siddhanta** — The way of arriving at a religious or philosophical conclusion based upon accepting the beliefs of all paths, ways, and religions.

**Sarvahimsa Vinirmukta** — Complete nonviolence towards all beings; one of the Seven Qualifications of a Tantric Aspirant.

**Sarvamukti** — The totally emancipated state wherein all and everything is liberated.

**Sarvam Khalvidam Brahman** — "All This Is Brahman."

**Sarva vyakatva shakti** — The all-pervasive power of Divine Mother.
**Sasmita Samadhi** — One of the four "seeded" samadhis of Yoga, wherein the ripe ego enjoys subtle bliss.
**Satatam** — Steady in meditation.
**Satchitananda** — Pure Being, pure Consciousness, pure Bliss Absolute; a name for the formless Brahman.
**Sati** — The ancient practice of offering the body into fire as sacrifice
**Satguru** — A world teacher such as Krishna, Christ, Buddha, Mohammed or Sri Ramakrishna and other founders of the world's great religious traditions.
**Satsang** — Gathering in holy company to hear about, reflect, and question about the Truth.
**Satta-samanya** — Homogenous Existence, Absolute.
**Sattva** — Sattva guna. The mode of Prakriti that, on a cosmic level, fills the universe with peace and unity and, on an individual level, induces balance and equilibrium in human action and behavior.
**Sattva Purusha Anyatakhyati** — The ultimate Victory of the seven Tantric victories wherein the now illumined soul espies the Atman as the only Reality, and sees It existing on its own, in its own, self-effulgent Light.
**Sattvic** — Being in a balanced and positive condition where sattva guna is predominant.
**Satyaloka** — Same as Brahmaloka.
**Satyam** — Truth; truthfulness in thought, word, and deed. It is one of the ten yamas and niyamas of Patanjala Yoga and a mainstay of spiritual life in general.
**Saucha** — Purity; one of the five niyamas of Yoga's second limb.
**Savichara** — Deliberate inquiry; in Patanjala, a type of seeded samadhi.
**Savikalpa Samadhi** — A very high state of Consciousness wherein Brahman with attributes is experienced through the refined mechanism of the detached and ripened ego/mind complex.
**Savitarka** — Explanation utilizing logic and argumentation; in Patanjala, a type of seeded samadhi.
**Sayujya** — Attaining oneness with Divine Reality; one of the Four Kinds of Liberations in form.
**Seva** — Selfless service rendered unto the guru, the ashrama, and the devotees.
**Sevanam** — Serving all beings as God; one of the Eight Devotional Aids according to Devarshi Narada.
**Siddhantavakyashravana** — Coming to the right conclusion about the nature of Divine Reality via counsel of the preceptor and study of the scriptures.
**Shabda** — The sound Brahman; God as subtle vibration.
**Shaiva Agamas** — Tantric Scriptures having to do with the worship of Shiva and His Shakti.
**Shaivite** — A worshipper of Lord Siva, follower of Shaivism.
**Shaktadvaitavada** — A superlative path that combines nonduality with Divine Mother worship.

**Shakti** — The creative force of the universe that is the active principle of Brahman yet identical with It. Shakti is different and more subtle than prana, which is a force that it uses to create. As the Mahashakti or Universal Mother, It is also the wielder of the forces of Maya and Prakriti.

**Shakti Agamas** — Tantric scriptures having to do with the worship of the Divine Mother of the Universe in Her many forms.

**Shaktiman** — The wielder of Shakti; Divine Mother.

**Shamata** — The "calm-abiding" practice, path, and meditation.

**Shankara** — The great exponent of Advaita Vedanta who brought it into prominence and spread it broadcast throughout India and the world. He authored such important texts as the Vivekachudamani and Atma Bodha among others; a name for Lord Shiva.

**Shankaracharya** — Shankara's name reflecting his guru status.

**Shanta Bhava** — One of the five devotional moods adopted by the bhakta, being the peaceful mood.

**Shanti** — Peace, particularly of mind.

**Sharanagata** — Taking refuge in God and spiritual life.

**Sharanam** — Taking whole-hearted refuge in the Lord; one of the Eight Devotional Aids according to Devarshi Narada.

**Sharira** — A sheath, or covering over Reality, like the body and mind.

**Shastr'anuvartanam** — One of the three great desires of living beings, which is to perform various rites and rituals — not to extract knowledge or higher purpose from them, but simply to be engaged in action and its ordinary fruits.

**Shastras** — The sacred scriptures.

**Shatavadana** — Doing a thousand things at once; one of the Sixteen Evolutes of Maya.

**Shatsampatti** — The third of the Four Treasures of Vedanta, consisting of six jewels, namely, inner peace, self-control, forbearance, contentment, concentration, and faith.

**Shishya** — An initiated disciple of a guru.

**Shoka** — Grief; one of the Eight Fetters.

**Shraddha** — Faith, one of the Six Jewels, Shatsampatti, signaling a firm and unshakable realization of the existence of Divine Reality.

**Shravana** — Hearing the Truth from an illumined preceptor, which along with its two concomitants, Manana and Nididhasana — contemplating and realizing the Truth — comprise the Three Great Practices of Advaita Vedanta.

**Srimad Devi Bhagavatam** — One of two Divine Mother scriptures in the world, very important to our day and time, wherein the Goddess teaches all beings in various ways through over 1000 pages of Wisdom.

**Shravanam** — Hearing the scriptures; listening to God's glories daily; one of the Eight Devotional Aids according to Narada along with smaranam, archanam, kirtanam, vandanam, sevanam, bhajanam and sharanam – remembering the Lord, adoring Him, singing His glories, worshipping Him, serving Him and His devotees, fostering devotion to Him and taking complete refuge in Him.

**Shrotriya** — One of the four classic qualifications of the guru wherein he/she possesses the ability to transmit the essence of the teachings unto the disciple.
**Shruti** — Hearing the Truth, to be followed by contemplating (manana) and realizing It ((nididhyasana).
**Shuchi** — Pure, untainted; one of the Seven Qualifications of a Tantric Aspirant.
**Shuddha** — Pure and untainted.
**Shuddhabuddhamukta** — Ever pure, ever aware, ever free, which is an assignment befitting the true Self, or Atman/Purusha, of mankind.
**Shuddha Vidya** — One of the twelve higher spandas of Shaivism, revealing the purest of wisdom.
**Shuddhashuddha** — A mixture of the pure and the impure, as in the middle grade tattvas like mind, and ego.
**Shvasaprashvasah** — Unevenness of breathing; one of the Four Causes of Distraction to Meditation and Spiritual Life in Yoga according to Patanjali.
**Shunya or Shunyata** — Emptiness, referring to the insubstantial nature of all things.
**Siddhanta** — An established tenet or philosophy; definitive conclusion around a philosophical perspective.
**Siddhas** — A class of perfected beings; a class of beings attracted to the attainment of limited occult powers.
**Sita** — The Divine Mother of the Universe in Her aspect of immaculate Purity who manifested in the Treta Yuga as the divine consort of Sri Ramchandra.
**Sivakala** — A name for Lord Siva in his role as the overseer of all phases of time.
**Skandha** — A collection of subtle residues in the mind that form into samskaras, mental impressions, and which, in turn, can form a collection of samskaras as well.
**Slokas** — Verses found in scriptures, written there by the seers, which are studied, memorized, and recited by the sincere spiritual aspirant.
**Smaranam** — Continual remembrance of God; one of the Eight Devotional Aids according to Devarshi Narada.
**Smritihetu** — Original memory, or the source of all memory, which is stored in the mind throughout its cycles of transmigrations. Accessing it brings knowledge of one's past incarnations to the fore.
**Smriti-shuddha** — Purity of mind and memory.
**Spandas** — Vibrating spheres of consciousness within the Great Mind, as in Akashas, Lokas, Fields of the Lord, or Kingdoms of Heaven within.
**Sphota** — The primal manifester, i.e., The Word, which bursts forth spontaneously.
**Sri Aurobindo** — A seer and luminary of contemporary India, and the author of numerous books on Vedic and Yogic Paths.
**Sristi** — Creation, which in Indian philosophy is used to explain the apparent beginning of things and cycles of time, all of which are really unoriginated, thus eternal.

**Sristi Rahasya** — The Secret of Creation.

**Srotriya** — One of the four qualifications of the illumined guru, meaning that he can transmit the essence of the scriptures to the disciple.

**Sthiti** — Preservation, or sustenance, existing as the middle stage between sristhi and laya.

**Sthiti Prajnasya** — An elevated state of steady wisdom, covered by the luminaries.

**Stula Sharira** — Of the human being's three bodies, it is the gross body consisting of five elements, the five active senses, and the body.

**Sthulavairagya** — Immature detachment; a rudimentary to moderate type of detachment; the seventh stage of the Twelve Levels of Dispassion cited in Vedanta Philosophy.

**Sthiramatih** — Steady-mindedness.

**Stotram** — A classic Vedic hymn consisting of Sanskrit slokas set in musical form.

**Styana** — Incapacity; one of the Nine Distractions in Spiritual Life cited in Yoga Philosophy by Patanjali, wherein the aspirant can muster little or no ability to remain focused on the path and the practice.

**Sukadev** — A great rishi, son of Vedavyasa.

**Sukshma Sarira** — Of the human being's three bodies, it is the subtle body consisting of the prana, the five senses of knowledge, the five subtle elements, the fourfold mind, and kama and karma.

**Shukracharya** — Illumined guru of the invincible asura, Bali.

**Suresha** — Lord of the gods; another name for Shiva.

**Surya** — The God of the Sun, used as an epithet in both a physical and a cosmic sense.

**Sushumna** — The subtle spiritual canal which carries the Kundalini Shakti through the ascending lotuses to the Sahashrara Chakra in the crown of pure mind. Indicated as the central nadi, Kundalini power rises when She is awakened by yogic practices. This "lotus" and all lotuses lie within Consciousness, and the physical spine is an external facsimile of it.

**Sushupti** — Deep sleep, which is one of the three states of Consciousness in living beings. It is represented by the "M" of The Word, AUM, and is where all the seeds to manifestation are contained in potential prior to the dreaming and waking states to follow.

**Sutra** — A Sanskrit phrase, sentence or verse with profound meaning.

**Sutratman** — The Self within, which intrinsically connects to everything else due to its subtle and threadlike essence; the cosmic Self, or Hiranyagarbha; the sum total of all selves in existence.

**Svadharma** — One's highest path or way, the ultimate dharma of one's lifetimes.

**Svadhisthana** — The second chakra, located symbolically at the organs of sex and voiding.

**Svadhyaya** — The act of engrossing oneself in an in-depth study of the scriptures, particularly the Srutis, with a view towards comprehending Truth. If this prerequisite, one of the ten niyamas of Patanjala, is not satisfied, no appreciable success in yoga is possible.

**Svajatiyavrittipravaha** — The concentration of the mind on one's Divine Nature, only.

**Svapna** — The dreaming state of the human being.

**Svapnamayasvarupa** — The entire gamut or body of imagined or illusory phenomena perceived as real as in a dream.

**Svara** — The segment of the written word, AUM, not connected to the rest of the word, and that represents transcendental Awareness, or Turiya.

**Svarupa** — Essence, used in relation to the Essence of Consciousness or the highest aspect of pure Spirit.

**Svarupanyathabhava** — The condition of being either totally unaware of or completely in denial of one's true inner nature as pure conscious Awareness; one of the Sixteen Evolutes of Maya of Neo-Vedanta.

**Svarupapratistha** — The state of being fully ensconced and established in the Atman, one's true nature.

**Svatantriya** — Unbounded, spontaneous freedom.

**Svati** — The star Arcturus, used in Hindu Itihasa and story to represent an auspicious period.

**Svayamjyoti** — Literally, shining by its own light; a name used to describe the Atman.

**Svetasvataropanisad** — One of the less ancient of the Upanisads which gives salient teachings ranging from dualism to Advaita. It is found as a portion of the Black Yajur Veda.

**Swami Aseshananda** — The last living direct monastic disciple of Holy Mother, Sri Sarada Devi, until his passing into Mahasamadhi in 1996.

**Swami Vivekananda** — The foremost disciple of Sri Ramakrishna Paramahamsa, he lived from 1863 to 1902. Considered to be an emanation of Lord Shiva, he was also the first to bring the spiritual teachings of Vedanta and establish them in the West. He is also credited, along with the monastic order He helped found, with giving lucid contemporary interpretations to many ancient scriptures. His auspicious appearance and august presence at the Parliament of Religions in Chicago in 1893 is a major spiritual event in the history of the Western hemisphere, holding profound significance.

**Swami Brahmananda** — One of Sri Ramakrishna's 16 direct disciples, often called His "spiritual son," who was considered a world teacher (jagad-guru) and who was the first President of the Ramakrishna Order and was a close brother monk of Swami Vivekananda.

**Taijasa** — A name for the individual as he abides in the dreaming state, the "U" of AUM.

**Tamas** — Tamo guna; the mode of Prakriti that induces slothfulness and inertia.

**Tamasic** — Being of the condition of tamas, slothful and dull.

**Tandava** — The cosmic dance of Siva Nataraj which sends all into a formless state.

**Tanmatras** — The elements in a rudimentary state, prior to the quintuplication process.

**Tanmishra** — Darkness, as in deep ignorance.

**Tantra** — Scriptures concentrating upon living a divine life in the world through the balancing of the Shiva and Shakti energies within the human being. Though they are considered by the orthodoxy as secondary scriptures, there is reason to believe that they are as old and as important as the Vedas since many of the Rishis were Tantric practitioners. Also, the worship of Shiva and Divine Mother Shakti probably predates the Vedas which suggests that the Tantric stream is extremely ancient.

**Tantracist** — One who practices Tantra.

**Tantric** — Having to do with Tantra, the ancient philosophy which stresses direct experience of spirituality while living in the world.

**Tapana** — To heat, the word usually being used in correlation with the word tapas, spiritual austerities, that heat up and purify the body/mind mechanism in yogic practice.

**Taparloka** — The sixth of seven inner realms lying in Consciousness, the realm of the mature ascetics.

**Tapasvin** — A yogic practitioner who uses intense austerities to purify all elements of life.

**Tapatraya** — The three types of sufferings as noted in the Vedanta philosophy and other darshanas.

**Tara** — A name for the Divine Mother of the Universe in Her compassionate aspect.

**Tarkika-buddhi** — The tendency of the mind and intellect towards argumentation, which later on becomes a huge problem when higher wisdom comes through the guru and the student merely argues it.

**Tat tvam asi** — Literally, "That thou art" in reference to the individual soul and its connection to the Supreme Soul.

**Tatastha-lakshana** — One of three groups of knowledge classification noted by Advaita Vedanta concerned with indirect statements that point to characteristics of Brahman, which are, nevertheless, not necessarily Its intrinsic qualities.

**Tathagatagarbha** — True inner being; the transcendent conscious Awareness that is the true nature of all things, all beings.

**Tattva Samasa Sutras** — One, if not the only, of a rare few scriptures from the time of Lord Kapila and his ingenious Sankhya Yoga system.

**Tattva Shuddha** — Purification of principles, referring to the crucial mental practices which, when accomplished, render the mind free of misconceptions as to the nature of relativity and the essence of Reality.

**Tattvajnana** — Knowledge principle, or knowledge of Reality, similar to Brahmajnana.

**Tattvas** — Cosmic principles; in Sankhya Philosophy, a term for twenty-four constituents of Prakriti which make up the universe of name and form.

**Tattvavichara** — A state of being fully qualified in knowledge of cosmic principles.

**Tavaivaham** — A devotional saying, mantra, and Tantric Vakya among the Tantric adepts meaning, "I am Thine alone," stated in regard to the devotee's self-surrender and immersion in the Divine Mother of the Universe.

**Tejas** — The light of fully sublimated ojas that luminaries utilize for transmitting wisdom and Truth to devotess and aspirants.

**Tirodhana** — Self-limitation; one of the Pancha-krityas of the Tattva Prakasha School of Tantra, which form the Five Essential Functions of Shiva with regard to His appearance aspect as opposed to His Consciousness aspect. They are: Sristhi (creation), Sthiti (sustenance), Samhara (dissolution), Tirodhana (self-limitation), and Anugraha (expression-grace).

**Tirthankaras** — In Jainism, the twenty-four illumined souls who have held and have taught the precious teachings of Jainism over the ages, the most recent being the great soul, Mahavir.

**Tiryanmarga** — The path of living beings who constantly take lower births from life to life.

**Titiksha** — Forbearance, one of the Six Jewels, Shatsampatti, allowing the aspirant to patiently endure and eventually transcend the various dualities such as heat and cold, pleasure and pain.

**Tivyavairagya** — The penultimate stage of detachment which is said to be of a very intense nature, and only just short of Paravairagya, Supreme Detachment; the eleventh of the Twelve Levels of Dispassion cited in Vedanta Philosophy.

**Treta Yuga** — The second of four phases of time within a Mahayuga, where living beings are said to lose one third of their remembrance of their divine nature.

**Trigunatita** — The state of being transcendent of the three gunas of tamas, rajas, and sattva.

**Triloka** — An expression citing the Three Worlds of Bhur, Bhuvah, & Svar, or sometimes designating the three partitions of worlds in general, as in gross, subtle, and causal, or imminent, transcendent, and absolute.

**Trimargabhedam** — The threefold pathways taken by the three types of beings, the divinities, the human beings, and the demonic.

**Triputis** — Any of a set of three principles which have an intrinsic connection and profound meaning such as the seer, what is seen, and the ability to see, or the knower, what is known, and the act of knowing.

**Tulku** — A teacher and guide in Tibetan Buddhism.

**Tulsi** — A sacred leaf used in the worship of Sri Krishna; a name for the Goddess; a short name for the poet-sage, Tulsidas.

**Tulsidas** — A famous devotional poet/saint of India who was a great devotee of Sri Ram and wrote many divine songs.

**Turiya** — Literally, "the fourth," referring to the fourth and highest state of Consciousness beyond waking, dreaming and deep sleep.

**Tushti** — Contentment.

**Tyaga** — Renunciation of the world for the sake of Enlightenment.

**Udana** — The upward moving prana.

**Uddhava** — Literally, "one who uplifts"; a member of the Yadava clan who was a great devotee of Sri Krishna.

**Uddhava Gita** — The Song of Uddhava, being a portion of a scripture excerpted from the Bhagavata Purana, the eleventh chapter, which constitutes Sri Krishna's final teachings to His disciple, Uddhava.

**Ugra** — Siva appearing as the undefeatable one.
**Unmana Samadhi** — A samadhi that takes one beyond the mind, manas.
**Upadhis** — Limiting adjuncts; body; vehicle; a subtle veil that obscures the true nature of a thing.
**Upaguru** — A preliminary teacher, through whose aid the aspirant is often brought in contact with the Guru.
**Upalabdhi** — Inner perception combined with spiritual attainment.
**Upanisads** — The Brahmakanda portion of the Vedas dealing with the knowledge that confirms the Truth of Brahman and reveals the Atman.
**Uparamavairagya** — The fifth of the Twelve Levels of Detachment which comes about due to satiety with the things of the world and experiences of earthly life. It signals the beginning of true detachment.
**Uparati** — Self-settledness or contentment, one of the Six Treasures (Shatsampatti) of Vedanta practice (sama, dama, uparati, titiksha, samadhana, and shraddha) which keeps the mind from drifting back to old habits and actions.
**Upasana** — Contemplation of God with form in meditation.
**Upeksha** — Equanimity; detachment; indifference.
**Upeksha-ananyata** — Absolute equanimity, even in the face of hard trials.
**Urdhvaretoyogi** — The luminary in whom the sexual energy has been controlled, refined, and sublimated and is flowing upwards to the crown of the head, emanating an abundance of qualities and boons upon life and living beings as a natural matter of course along the way.
**Utpatti** — The study of origins, based on inward examination to find the source for all that is external.
**Utpaya Pratyaya** — A helpful aid gained by the sincere practitioner which allows him/her to always move towards the highest Goal, and not settle for lower attainments.
**Utsaha** — Enthusiasm, as found in the most intrepid and forward moving devotees and aspirants of the Lord.
**Vachaka** — The pervading presence.
**Vachya** — The thing or object pervaded; that which can be denoted by speech.
**Vahudakas** — A class of roaming ascetics who are still seeking Self-realization and peace of mind.
**Vaichitra** — Varieties; one of the Seven Malas of Maya that distract the mind by spreading its attention over a wide range of considerations.
**Vaidhi bhakti** — Rudimentary devotion utilizing the practice of rites and rituals before the shrine and altar.
**Vaikhari** — The external form of sound, worlds, bodies, and objects as a gross vibrational level of manifestation; one of the Four Manifestations of the Word, after Para, Pashyanti, and Madhyama.
**Vaikuntha** — The celestial city which is the subtle abode of Lord Vishnu.
**Vandhyaputra** — "Son of a barren woman," which is an example of an abhavapadartha.
**Vairagya Shatakam** — The Six Verses on Detachment composed by Shankara.

**Vairagya** — Detachment. Also defined as dispassion, it is one of the Four Jewels of Vedanta practice. After discrimination is applied revealing what is Real and what is unreal, detachment supplies the necessary power to withdraw from what is unreal.

**Vaishikara** — An intense level of detachment called "the lower level of the highest dispassion"; the eighth stage of the Twelve Levels of Dispassion cited in Vedanta Philosophy.

**Vaishnavas** — Followers of Vishnu; devotees of Krishna and Ram; those who follow Vaishnavism.

**Vaishvanara** — A name for the individual while he abides in the waking state, the "A" of AUM.

**Vaishya** — One of the four castes of Hindu society, or the merchant caste.

**Vajrayana** — The "Diamond Vehicle," referring to Tibetan Buddhism.

**Vak** — The Word, speech, language.

**Vakdevi** — Goddess of the Word; a name for Sarasvati, the Goddess of knowledge and learning. It is She who connects the thought, the sound, the word, and its meaning together, and it is She who is inherent in all four as the very power of comprehension.

**Vaichika** — The method of reciting the mantra out loud, as compared to muttering it or repeating it inaudibly.

**Vaishesika** — One of the six orthodox philosophies, or darshanas, of India.

**Vaitrsnyamukti** — The force of complete detachment which insures liberation from all manifest things.

**Valmiki** — Best known as the author of the Ramayana, he is also credited with writing the Yoga Vasishtha. Venerated as a sage, he was not always so. It was he, in his life as a thief, who attempted to rob Narada, but Narada reasoned with him and Valmiki repented. Entering spiritual life, Valmiki is said to have remained so long in meditation that an anthill (valmiki) rose up around him — thus, his name.

**Vanaprastin** — The third stage of dharmic living, wherein the husband and wife retire to the forest, away from society, to practice austerities, study, and meditate.

**Vandanam** — Devout worship of the Lord; one of the Eight Devotional Aids according to Devarshi Narada.

**Vardhate** — Disease, which is one in a list of six transformations superimposed over the ever-healthy Atman.

**Varna** — Caste; a form of the word; one of the six ways (sadakhya) in which to realize Brahman.

**Vasanas** — Desires, which when obsessed with and repeated, form subtle complexes in the mind and lead to rebirth in ignorance.

**Vashitva** — One of the Eight Occult Powers which allows those in pursuit of lower ideals to draw others to them.

**Vasishtha** — The great rishi, one of the seven great original Rishis according to Manu, who is said to be the author of the Rig Veda. The Yoga Vasishtha of Valmiki consists of instructions given to Rama by this great sage, for he was also the family priest of Ram's father, King Dasaratha.

**Vastu** — The difference between one substance or object and another.

**Vatsalya Bhava** — The relationship of parent and child; one of the Five Divine Moods for Worshiping God according to Vaishnavism.

**Vedanta** — One of the six orthodox darshanas, or paths of clear seeing, among India's host of high-minded philosophies.

**Vedanta Dindima** — The apt and final conclusion of the Vedanta, i.e., that "All is Brahman."

**Vedavyasa** — A name for Vyasa, the sage who gathered the Vedas into a collection, thereby preserving them for our times.

**Vibhu** — The all-pervading.

**Vibhuti** — Divine glory in manifestation; a special expression of God who reflects mastery over one power or area of spirituality.

**Vichara** — Inquiry into the nature of any aspect of Reality, such as the Atman, or a Mahavakya.

**Vichikirsa** — The indomitable Will of the Divine Being.

**Vichikitsa** — Perplexing; variegated; in Buddhism, the tendency towards skepticism that impedes the acceptance of spiritual truths.

**Videhamukti** — Freedom from all bodies, or ever taking birth in a body again out of ignorance.

**Vidvan** — A knower of Reality, applied specifically to those who are conscious of their inner divine nature.

**Vidyadharas** — A class of high-minded beings who are holders of the Eternal Wisdom, Dharma.

**Vidyeshvaras/Vidyas** — In Shaivism, two classes of higher beings who, though they still maintain a slight sense of separation from Siva, nevertheless have accomplished transcendence of maya's ill effects.

**Vijnana** — Highest knowledge denoting supreme intelligence, its acquisition is based on Self-realization.

**Vijnana-kalas** — In Shaivism, a cross section of subtle beings who possess wisdom during their lives and gain liberation at the time of pralaya.

**Vijnanamayakosha** — The sheath of the intellect; the intellectual body as a covering over Reality.

**Vijnani** — One who has gone beyond the duality of knowledge and ignorance. To paraphrase Sri Ramakrishna, in a spiritual context, an ajnani is ignorant that there is fire potential in wood; a jnani knows that there is fire potential in wood; but a vijnani knows how to kindle that fire in wood and can therefore cook his meal and receive nourishment. This demonstrates the difference between a worldly person, a wisdom seeker and an enlightened being.

**Vikalpas** — Creative imaginings; projections of the vibrating mind, usually based in desire, but used in the cosmic sense to reflect the initial power of the original creative urge.

**Vikara** — Modification, change, or transformation.

**Vikarma** — One of the three grades of karma arising from evil or ill-considered actions

**Vikarana Bhava** — One of the seven victories of the Tantric aspirant wherein he/she comes to know with certainty of the existence of Consciousness/God beyond the embodied condition.

**Vikshepa** — A power of Shakti that seemingly distorts Reality; one of the two obscuring forces of Maya, the other being avarana, which appears to veil Reality.

**Vikshepas** — Another name for the nine antarayas, the "despoilers," in Yoga.

**Vikshipta** — Distracted; not collected; one of the Five States of the Mind Field according to Yoga wherein the mind continually vacillates from calm to erratic in turns.

**Vilva** — A sacred leaf used in worship, especially auspicious for Lord Shiva.

**Vimoha** — Freedom from delusion.

**Vina** — A very ancient Indian stringed instrument associated with Sarasvati, the Goddess of art and learning.

**Vinasha** — Destruction.

**Vinashini** — An epithet for the Divine Mother in Her capacity for destroying ignorance in the minds of the devotees.

**Viparita-bhavana** — A particularly deluding evolute of maya which causes even intelligent beings to suppose that the physical world is the only reality, or that, obversely, nothing else exists but it.

**Viseshas** — Aspects of the human being that have special qualifications, such as the mind and the senses.

**Viratrupa** — The Lord in His form as the manifested universe.

**Virochana** — A king of the asuras who was the son of Prahlada.

**Virya** — Heroic; one of the Three Designations of Aspirants in Tantra Philosophy.

**Visamvada-bhrama** — Maya's power that causes beings to mistake one thing for another, like Consciousness for matter, etc.

**Vishada** — Depression; sorrow; listed as one of the Four Deadly Traps in Vedanta and one of the Seven Malas of Maya in Tantra Philosophy.

**Vishalakshi** — A name for a deadly whirlpool in a river in India; a name for the Divine Mother of the Universe.

**Vishaya** — An object of attraction.

**Vishayashakti** — One of the sixteen evolutes of maya that attracts the mind of the worldly person to enjoyment of the five senses only.

**Visheshas** — Attributes, like senses and elements of special quality.

**Vishnu** — The second deity in the Hindu Trinity; the God of preservation and the one from whom the Avatars emerge.

**Vishnu Agamas** — Tantric scripture having to do with the worship of Vishnu.

**Vishuddha chakra** — The spiritual vortex or chakra which is the fifth center of Kundalini Yoga Science, described as the "throat" chakra.

**Vishnugranthi** — A knot or barrier above the three lower chakras that must be penetrated before the soul can arrive at the heart chakra, thus go beyond rebirth in the lower worlds.

**Vivarta** — False superimposition; a term Vedanta teachers use to indicate the often unexplainable phenomena of the appearance of the unreal over the real, the apparent over the actual, of falsehood over Truth.

**Visvamitra** — An illumined Indian rishi.

**Vishvarupa** — The Cosmic Form; a being having all forms, like Lord Vishnu.

**Viveka** — Discrimination, of the type that allows one to see through all personal and collective delusions and penetrate the coverings over Reality.

**Vivekachudamani** — Crest Jewel of Discrimination; a profound text by Shankaracharya citing the value of spiritual life and containing deep philosophical teachings.

**Vivekajnan** — Special wisdom gained from the maturation of discrimination in the mind.

**Vivekananda** — See Swami Vivekananda.

**Viveka-khyati** — A special type of discrimination in Yoga that reveals to the aspirant the distinction between the buddhi, intelligence, and the Purusha.

**Vrata** — Vow

**Vrindavan** — The holy city in India associated with the life of Lord Krishna.

**Vrittijnan** — The subtle power of maya which causes beings to think that knowledge gotten from the world, from the senses, and from the ordinary mind is absolute knowledge.

**Vrittis** — Mental vibrations or thought forms.

**Vyadhi** — Disease of the body; one of the Nine Distractions to Spiritual Life according to Yoga Philosophy.

**Vyahrtis** — Bhur, Bhuvah, and Svah, eternal words for the Three Worlds.

**Vyana** — The all-pervading prana.

**Vyapi** — The all-pervading one.

**Vyapti** — One of the Eight Occult Powers which allow those who are attracted to lower ideals to increase in size and weight or appear bigger.

**Vyasti** — The individual rather than the whole, the microcosm rather than the macrocosm.

**Vyavaharika** — life and activity lived only in the phenomenal world, devoid of dharmic knowledge and spiritual realization.

**Vyutthana-chitta** — The worldly mind; worldliness; one of the Three Stupefactions of Neo-Vedanta.

**Yahweh** — A name for God in the Jewish religion.

**Yajnavalkya** — An ancient rishi of great repute who authored portions of the Upanisads, and who was the founder of the school of the White Yajur Veda. His discourse to Maitreyi, one of his two wives, forms an important part of the Brhadaranyaka Upanisad.

**Yama** — The Lord of Death.

**Yamas** — Five exercises in Yoga which constitute the first limb of eight in Patanjala, and which the practitioner should practice and accomplish before moving on to the successive seven limbs.

**Yashodara** — The wife of Lord Buddha

**Yatamana** — Control of mind based upon self-effort; one of the Four Steps to Fundamental Detachment.

**Yogi** — A practitioner and master of the path of Yoga.

**Yogini** — A woman who succeeds in the path of Yoga.

**Yugas** — One of four ages or divisions of time, called Satya, Treta, Dvapara, and Kali, each consisting of thousands of years, which together make up a Mahayuga or Chaturyuga.

**Yukti** — Reasoning about the Truth, to be utilized in connection with first hearing It, Shruti, and thereafter gaining personal experience of It, Anubhava.

Other Books by Babaji Bob Kindler

- Twenty-Four Aspects of Mother Kali *
  (Kindle edition e-book available)
- The Ten Divine Articles of Sri Durga *
  (Kindle edition e-book available)
- The Avadhut and His Twenty-Four Teachers in Nature
- Sri Sarada Vijnanagita
- An Extensive Anthology of Sri Ramakrishna's Stories
- Swami Vivekananda Vijnanagita
- A Quintessential Yoga Vasishtha
- Reclaiming Kundalini Yoga *

- Dissolving the Mindstream *
- Jnana Matra – The Wisdom Particle *
- Manasana – The Superlative Art of Mental Posture
- Cosmic Quintuplications – The Secret of Panchakarana
- Footfalls of the Indian Rishis

Planned Future Releases

- Teachings of the Matri Avatar
- The Nine Limbs of Bhakti of Sri Ram
- Guru Yoga in Contemporary Times
- White Crane, White Swan: The Commonality of Zen and Advaita Vedanta

*Further inquiries at:*
SRV Associations
P.O. Box 1364
Honoka'a, Hawaii 96727
website: www.srv.org
email: srvinfo@srv.org

To purchase full-size charts appearing in this and other works of Babaji Bob Kindler, visit:

www.ingramcontent.com/pod-product-compliance
Lightning Source LLC
Chambersburg PA
CBHW080036100526
44584CB00023BA/3195